THE ENCYCLOPEDIA OF
NORTH AMERICAN WILDLIFE

THE ENCYCLOPEDIA OF
NORTH AMERICAN
WILDLIFE

STANLEY KLEIN

cop 1

Facts on File, Inc

460 Park Avenue South
New York, NY 10016
A Bison Book

CONTENTS

MAMMALS
PAGE 8

Above: The Coyote (*Canis latrans*) hunts in small packs or pairs and is dependent on its keen sense of smell to track prey. It is an exceptional runner and a strong swimmer.

BIRDS
PAGE 100

Above: The Brown Thrasher (*Toxostoma rufum*) is the only thrasher found east of the Rockies and central Texas, where it dwells in brushy or wooded areas. It is a perching bird and loud singer.

REPTILES
PAGE 232

Above: The Black Rat Snake (*Elaphe obsoleta obsoleta*) is a powerful constrictor and a capable climber that will seek out birds and eggs in trees. It also feeds on small mammals and lizards.

First published in the USA by

Facts on File, Inc.
460 Park Avenue South
New York, NY 10016

Produced by
Bison Books
17 Sherwood Place
Greenwich, CT 06830

Klein, Stanley
   The encyclopedia of North American wildlife.

   1. Zoology—North America—Dictionaries. I. title.
QL151.K58   596.097   82-5183

ISBN 0-87196-758-8   AACR2

Designer and Picture Editor:
Bill Yenne
Editor: Tom Aylesworth

10 9 8 7 6 5 4 3 2 1

Printed in Hong Kong

AMPHIBIANS
PAGE 278

Above: **A Pine Barrens Treefrog (*Hyla andersoni*) in Florida lives in swamps, streams and bogs but is usually only seen when breeding. Its numbers are threatened due to a diminishing habitat.**

FISH
PAGE 298

Above: **A Chinook Salmon (*Oncorhynchus tschawytscha*). The largest of Pacific salmon, it stops feeding when it leaves the ocean and uses stored energy for months of traveling up streams.**

APPENDIXES
PAGE 316

Page 1: Bighorn Sheep (*Ovis canadensis*) near Swiftcurrent Lake, Glacier National Park in Montana. They live in herds near rocky cliffs, well isolated from human populations.

Page 2-3: The Moose (*Alces americana*) is the largest deer in the world. An adult male may weigh as much as 1400 pounds.

Natural Features of North America
Showing Major Mountains and Larger Canadian and American National Parks and Monuments

INTRODUCTION

The North American continent is endowed with an abundance and variety of wildlife. The United States alone is home to more than 2000 species of vertebrates – mammals, birds, reptiles, amphibians, and fish – in addition to the tens of thousands of invertebrate species. This rich bounty of North American wildlife essentially is the result of evolutionary, geological and climatic processes.

All animals fall into one of two categories – invertebrates or vertebrates. The invertebrates are a far more numerous, heterogeneous group of animals without backbones, some of which are distinctly related and others exhibiting no known relationships. The vertebrates, on the other hand, demonstrate a clear progression up the evolutionary ladder. When vertebrates first appeared on earth more than 600 million years ago, they were all aquatic. Since then, a progressive series of classes have emerged, representing successive evolutionary steps. First there were only the fish, then fish and amphibian-like creatures, later fish, amphibian and reptiles. Eventually, all the classes we know of today emerged.

The step from fishes to amphibians was primarily a move from a water habitat to a land habitat for the adult stage of the life cycle. The step from amphibians to reptiles represented growing proficiency and adaptation to a terrestial habitat at all stages of the life cycle. The final emergence of birds and mammals demonstrated further adaptations; one adaptation to an aboreal and then an aerial environment; the other, as evidence of adapting to a relatively even (and higher) body temperature.

These evolutionary changes kept pace with the changing conditions of the physical world. At different times in the geological history of North America, there have been different patterns of climate with wide variations of temperature that had significant effect on animal distribution. For example, during the Pleistocene Ice Age, the earth was covered with more ice and less water, revealing landmasses normally covered by the seas. One such landmass stretched through the Bering Strait, bridging the North American continent with Eurasia. This provided access for vertebrates to pass in both directions and resulted in today's sharing of many species among North America, Asia and Europe. Similarly, the existing Central America bridge has provided for an interchange between North and South America.

Today, the distribution of animals in North America is divided between two regions; the Boreal, or Canadian; and the Sonoran. The Boreal region roughly encompasses the northern half of the continent, including Alaska, Canada and large tracts of the northern United States which share similar climatic conditions with northern Europe and Asia. The Sonoran region includes most of the remainder of the continent. The vertebrates of the Boreal region contain few amphibians or reptiles because of the relatively cold temperatures. The vertebrates of the Sonoran region, which include most of the amphibians and reptiles, are typically subdivided into two additional groups; one adapted to the relatively moderate deciduous forest vegetation of the United States, and the other to the relatively arid grasslands and deserts of the central and southern regions.

Obviously the geological and climatic history of North America helped to determine the wide variety and distribution of species on the continent. Indeed, the wildlife population is plentiful and diverse. Yet, not too long ago, the bounty was richer.

It has been estimated that since the Pilgrims arrived in the 'new world' in 1620, more than 500 different species and subspecies of both plants and animals have become extinct. (Compare the figure with the estimate that no more than 90 species of birds and mammals became extinct during the entire 3000 years of the Ice Age.) It appears that man can cause more destruction in a few hundred years than nature can cause in several thousand.

Originally, animals were an essential part of the early economy, frequently providing for the food, clothing and shelter of early settlers. A balance was maintained because the weapons of the early hunter were crude and the number of hunters few. Later, weapons became more sophisticated and lethal, and natural animal habitats were destroyed as settlement increased. Industry and technology contributed pesticides and other pollutants into the land, water and air.

The United States government lists more than 200 species as endangered or threatened by extinction. The problem is neither national nor regional. It is global. Scientists calculate that there are more than 2,000,000 species of plants and animals worldwide and that about 10 percent may now need protection.

Efforts are being made. There are hundreds of private and government agencies educating the public about the plight of wildlife, engaging in research, promoting legislation and establishing wildlife preserves. If we are to continue to enjoy the richness and variety of existing wildlife, we owe them our support.

MAMMALS

A mammal is a warm-blooded, air-breathing animal with hair and a backbone. Almost all mammals give birth to live young, as opposed to animals such as birds, most reptiles and fish, which lay eggs. Only two kinds of mammals, the Duck-billed Platypus and the Spiny Anteater – both natives of Australia – lay eggs.

With only about 5000 species, mammals are not the most numerous animals. They are, however, the most dominant animals on this planet. Man, the most dominant animal, is a mammal. The first mammals are believed to have evolved about 140 million years ago. However, for more than 100 million years, mammals were eclipsed by reptiles, particularly the large dinosaurs. Some 70 million years ago, the dinosaurs became extinct. The mammals had the adaptations that allowed them to survive in the conditions that caused the demise of the dinosaurs and to become the dominant life forms. Today, mammals are found in every habitat and climate from polar regions to tropics. Mammals live in every environment – oceans, bodies of fresh water, mountains, plains, forests, deserts and more. There are mammals that swim, fly and burrow in the ground.

Mammals, like birds, are able to maintain a relatively consistent body temperature regardless of the outside temperature. Unlike reptiles which become inactive in cold conditions, most mammals can remain active in a wide range of temperatures. The minimum temperature at which the animal can survive varies from one species to another, and some mammals survive cold winter conditions by going into a state of suspended activity called hibernation.

Extremely important to the success of the mammals is the way they bear their young and take care of

Below: **A young Gray Fox (*Urocyon cinereoargenteus*). The Gray Fox is an adept climber and uses its skill on occasion to seek food and safety in tree branches. Hollow trees are one of its favorite locations for a den.**

Above: The Caribou (*Rangifer tarandus*), common to Alaska and northern Canada, is one of the most migratory mammals and is usually seen in a large herd. It is a good short-distance runner and a competent swimmer because it is very buoyant in water.

them. Mammals develop inside the female in a specialized structure called the uterus. The developing young are less likely to be consumed by predators than are eggs. A pregnant mammal has a chance to get away from a predator and, if she does, she saves not only herself but also her unborn offspring. A bird or reptile cannot carry eggs away from a predator. It can only try to fight off the predator or hide the eggs when they are laid. Mammals produce milk for their young in special glands. The ability to produce milk is a singular characteristic of mammals. The word mammal comes from the Latin *mamma* which means breast. Not all mammals have breasts, but almost all have teats or nipples on which the young suck to obtain milk in the early stages of life.

Mammals have more highly developed brains than either birds or reptiles. Some mammals are capable of highly sophisticated activities such as coordinating the hunting of prey. Lions and wolves, for example, hunt in groups and exercise what seems to be highly developed strategy. Some animals such as chimpanzees and dolphins may be able to reason and solve problems.

Mammals take more care of their young than other forms of animal life. (Birds also care for their young, but practically all avian parental behavior is mechanical action triggered by instincts.) Much mammalian parental behavior is also instinctive, but many mammals plan their actions, exercise choices and teach their young survival skills at a higher level.

The time mammals take care of their young varies from a few days in some rodents to decades in humans. The care given by mammals makes up for their relatively slow rates of reproduction. A mouse that has five or six litters of 10 to 15 young a year is considered to be a prodigious producer. Most mammals have much longer gestation periods and have only a few young at a time. A single fish can lay hundreds of thousands of eggs at a time. However, only a very small fraction of the fish eggs will survive to become adult fish. Young mammals, on the other hand, have a much better chance for survival because of parental care.

In general, the larger the mammal, the longer the gestation period and the smaller the number of offspring. The gestation period of the elephant, for example, is almost two years, and one baby elephant is the usual result. Mice have gestation periods measured in weeks and produce litters containing many offspring.

In addition to warm-bloodedness and the production of milk, mammals have:
- bodies with hair or fur
- four-chambered hearts
- lungs used for breathing
- seven cervical (neck) vertebrae (some exceptions)
- highly developed nervous systems
- young which are born alive (except monotremes)

Mammals can be divided into three groups on the basis of how they reproduce. The monotremes are those mammals that lay eggs, such as the Platypus. The marsupials are the pouched mammals. They give birth to very immature young that must find their way to the pouch where their development is completed. The only North American marsupial is the opossom. Other familiar marsupials are Kangaroos and other Australian mammals such as Koalas and Wombats. Most mammals are placental. Placental mammals develop in the uterus and receive their nourishment through a structure called the placenta. Although the young are born helpless, they are in a much higher state of development than is the case with marsupials.

Humankind has had a long relationship with mammals. Since prehistoric times, they have provided food, transportation and other needs. Hunted in the early stages of human history, mammals such as cattle, sheep and pigs were later domesticated to provide food and fiber. Although no longer essential, horses are still used for transportation. Other mammals, particularly dogs and cats, are kept as pets. Dogs, who have had a long relationship with humankind, are also used as working animals.

MAMMALS

ANTELOPE, AMERICAN:
see Antelope, Pronghorn

ANTELOPE, PRONGHORN:
(*Antilocarpa americanus*)

The Pronghorn lives in open grasslands and bunch-grass and sage-brush areas of the western United States. Its range includes Wyoming, Colorado, Utah, Arizona, New Mexico, Nevada, western Texas, eastern Montana, southeastern Oregon and small areas in Washington and northern California. It is also found in southern California and the extreme southern portion of Idaho, northern Mexico along the Texas border and Baja California.

A medium-sized deer, the Pronghorn is about 3 to 3.5 feet (.9 to 1 m) high at the shoulder, and from 4 to 4¾ feet (1.2 to 1.4 m) long. Males weigh from 80 to 160 pounds (36 to 170 kg) and females weigh from 70 to 110 pounds (32 to 50 kg). The upper and outer parts of the body are pale tan to reddish-tan, while the underside, rump patch, cheeks and lower jaw are white. Two white blazes run across the throat. The bucks have a distinctive broad, black band that runs from the eyes, down the snout to the nose, and a black crescent across the neck and black antlers. One foot to 1⅔ feet (.3 to .5 m) long at maturity, the antlers curve back and slightly inward. On each side there is a broad, short prong that juts forward and slightly upward. Does have short antlers no more than 3 or 4 inches (7.6 to 10 cm) long that usually lack a prong.

The Pronghorn is well adapted for its life in open grasslands. It can run at speeds of 70 mph (112 kph) for bursts of three or four minutes, a pace that makes it the fastest animal in North America and one of the fastest in the world. It moves along easily at speeds of 30 mph (48 kph), and sustained runs at 45 mph (77 kph) are not unusual. Its large eyes have a wide field of vision, and it detects motion at distances of four miles (6 km) or more. It is also a strong swimmer. When it is alarmed, the rump hairs become erect, forming

Above: **A Pronghorn or American Antelope buck, the fastest mammal in North America.**

a 'flash' that can be seen for great distances and probably serves as a danger signal.

The summer graze includes a variety of grasses and cacti. In winter it browses mostly on sagebrush, but will take other plants if no sagebrush is available.

The sexes form separate, small herds in the summer. Does and fawns herd separately from groups of bucks, yearlings and two-year-old males. During the breeding season, which begins in the autumn, older males compete to form harems of about 20 does which are maintained in territories. Bucks defend their territories with snorts, chases, postures and occasional fights. The young are born in May or June. A doe's first breeding usually results in one fawn; subsequent births are usually twins and sometimes triplets. If the doe has more than one fawn, she delivers them at spots several hundred yards apart. The doe hides the fawns in high grass or brush, and grazes away from them to distract predators.

In the 1920s the Pronghorn almost became extinct, mainly because of fencing put up by ranchers which re-stricted their movements. Cattlemen also killed large numbers of them in the belief they reduced graze for cattle. Management programs, including transporting animals to new areas, have increased their number to almost 500,000.

Pronghorn are similar to the White-tailed Deer (*Odocoileus virginianus*), which do not have the prong on their antlers.

ARMADILLO, NINE-BANDED
(*Dasypus novemcinctus*)

The Nine-banded Armadillo's range includes Texas, Oklahoma, Arkansas, Louisiana, Mississippi, southern Alabama, southern Georgia and Florida. The armadillo was named by early Spanish explorers of the Americas who called it 'little armored thing' because of the bony plates in its upper body skin. Unlike its prehistoric forebears, which could be as large as a small elephant, the armadillo today is about 2 feet (61 cm) long, including its tail, and weighs about 15 pounds (7 kg).

BADGER
(Taxidea taxus)

The badger is found in the United States in all states west of the Mississippi River except Alaska, Louisiana, Arkansas and parts of Missouri, Texas, California, Oregon and Washington. The range extends southward into Mexico. East of the Mississippi River, its range includes Wisconsin, Illinois, Indiana, Michigan and most of Ohio. In Canada it is found in eastern British Columbia, most of Alberta, southern Saskatchewan and Manitoba and in extreme southern Ontario.

The badger is from 1.7 to 2.9 feet (.5 to .9 m) long and weighs from 8 to 25 pounds (3.5 to 11 kg). Its flat body is wider than it is high, and it has short legs that bow outward. A lightly upturned snout gives it somewhat of an inquisitive appearance. Its shaggy fur is a grizzled gray to brown, and it has a white stripe running between the shoulders. The fur on the short bushy tail is yellowish.

The badger is mostly nocturnal in areas near human populations, but it can sometimes be seen in the daytime in open plains, farmlands and the edges of woodlands, moving in a shuffling, rocking-from-side-to-side gait. It can move at a fair, but clumsy, trot, but it does not depend on speed to get its food or to escape from potential predators. Feeding primarily on ground squirrels, gophers, rats and mice, it takes these animals by digging out their burrows. The intended prey sometimes escapes by scampering out another exit, a tactic the badger may attempt to circumvent by burrowing into an empty burrow and waiting for the tenant to return. Badgers sometimes lose potential catches to coyotes who wait at an exit hole for the prey to be chased out of the burrow by the badger.

Badgers also take food on the surface, including birds, various invertebrates and rattlesnakes, which appear to be a particular favorite. The badger was long believed to be immune to the rattlesnake's venom, unless it was bitten on the nose but in fact, its thick fur

Above: The Badger is known for the white badge-like marking on its forehead.

The Nine-banded Armadillo, common to the United States and South America, is so called because the hinges of its shell consist of nine narrow bands of armor which move upon one another to give the animal some flexibility.

Armadillos have long, narrow tongues which they use to lick up insects, earthworms and land snails, their principal food. They are also known to eat small snakes and toads.

Above: A Nine-banded Armadillo.

Their powerful claws enable them to dig rapidly and they resort to tunnels and burrows for protection. Their teeth are small and rootless, set well back in the mouth, and thus ill-adapted to self-defense.

The Nine-banded Armadillo generally sleeps during the day and comes out at night to feed, moving quickly on land and swimming strongly when necessary. Its mating season is in July and August, followed by a comparatively long gestation period of nine months. There are usually four young to a litter, and they are invariably of the same sex and bear identical sets of genes. This fact has made them valuable to scientific researchers, a value augmented in 1971 when they were discovered to be one of the few creatures besides man known to contract leprosy. The Nine-banded Armadillo is well-developed and mobile at birth, but its skin is soft and hardens only gradually into the protective carapace.

Armadillo meat is considered a delicacy by the Indians of Mexico; in the United States it is eaten most frequently in Texas, where the animal is both popular and plentiful.

prevents the snake's fangs from penetrating its skin anywhere else. It also eats carrion, and caches excess kills by burying them. The badger is an excellent swimmer, but it seems to take to the water more for comfort than in pursuit of prey. On particularly hot days, it may lie down in shallow water.

The badger is a fastidiously clean animal. It buries its droppings, and when it is at rest, cleans and grooms itself almost constantly with its tongue, swallowing the loose hair. It digs out a den or burrow with an elliptical entrance that accommodates the animal's shape. During very cold weather the badger holes up in a chamber deep inside the burrow and goes into a deep sleep, but does not hibernate.

Mating takes place in late summer. Litters of two to five young are born, after delayed implantation, in March and April. The young leave to go out on their own when the mother is ready to mate again.

The badger is seldom the prey of other meat-eaters. Thick fur, heavy neck muscles, and a loose, tough hide enable it to withstand biting and clawing attacks. It fights back with tooth, claw and a foul-smelling musky secretion, but it prefers to retreat if possible by backing into a burrow, holding off the adversary for only as long as it takes to plug up the burrow. If there is no burrow around, it may start digging one at a remarkable rate of speed, throwing dirt in the face of its enemy.

Badger hair is still considered to be superior to synthetic fibers for producing the best quality paint brushes. The coarse hairs were once used to make shaving brushes, a use that has declined with the advent of aerosol shaving cream cans. Badgers seldom take a domestic animal, but they are considered to be a nuisance by cattlemen, because cattle, horses and sometimes the cattlemen themselves fall into their burrows and break legs. Farmers, however, consider them to be beneficial animals because of the large numbers of rodents they destroy. Badger hunting was once a popular sport, and a breed of dog, the low-

Above both: A Common Brown Bat (*Eptesicus fuscus bernardinus*) male.

slung, short-legged Dachshund – which means 'badger hound' in German – was developed for the purpose of going into burrows after the badger. The word 'to badger,' which means to torment or harass, stems from badger hunting.

There is no other North American mammal quite like the badger. The face of the Coati (*Nasua nasua*) has a vague resemblance to that of the badger, but is not really similar.

BAT, BIG BROWN
(*Eptesicus fuscus*)

The Big Brown Bat is found in all of the United States except the southern tip of Florida and south central Texas. It is found in southern Canada from coast to coast.

Somewhat larger than the Myotis Bats, the Big Brown Bat is from 4⅛ to 5 inches (10.5 to 13 cm) long and weighs about ⅝ ounce (18 g). Those that live in desert areas have light brown coloration, while those in forests tend to be a glossy brown. The undersides are a pale tan color, and the interfemoral membrane is black.

The Big Brown Bat roosts in small groups of five or six in a variety of sheltered spots including buildings,

caves, mines, storm sewers and hollow trees.

The Big Brown Bat feeds mostly on large beetles, but it also takes flies, moths, wasps, leafhoppers and other kinds of insects. Thought to be the fastest flyer among the bats, it has been clocked at 40 mph (64 kph).

One or two young are born in May or June. Over the winter they hibernate, making use of body fat stores.

The Evening Bat (*Nycticeius humeralis*) is a similar species.

BAT, BIG FREE-TAILED
see Bat, Brazilian Free-tailed

BAT, BRAZILIAN FREE-TAILED; MEXICAN FREE-TAILED BAT
(*Tadarida brasiliensis*)

The most common bat in the southwestern United States, the Brazilian Free-tailed Bat is found in the southwestern area of the country from Texas northward to southern Nebraska and westward to the California Pacific coast. It is also found in Louisiana, Mississippi, Alabama, Georgia, South Carolina, Florida, eastern Kentucky and Tennessee, and west central Ohio. Its range extends southward into Mexico, Central and South America. With a population estimated to be in excess of 100 million, it is probably one of the most numerous mammals in North America.

The smallest of the free-tailed bats, the Brazilian Free-tailed Bat is from 3½ to 4⅜ inches (9-11 cm) long and weighs from ⅜ to ½ ounce (11-14 g). The fur is dark brown above and somewhat whitish below. Like all free-tailed bats, it has a naked tail that extends behind the interfemoral membrane, the membrane that stretches between the hindlegs.

Like all bats, the Brazilian Free-tailed Bat is nocturnal and feeds mainly on insects which it finds through echolocation. To echolocate, it emits high-pitched ultrasonic sounds, well beyond the upper limit of human hearing. The sound waves bounce off objects, are picked up by the bat's large ears, and interpreted to give information on size, shape, and motion. Echolocation also enables the poorly sighted bats to find their way in dark areas without bumping into anything.

The Brazilian Free-tailed Bat lives in huge colonies, generally in caves. A colony of about 1 million exists in Frio Cave, Texas. The emergence of bats from this and other large colonies, as in the Carlsbad Caverns in New Mexico, is a tourist attraction. At sunset the bats begin to leave the cave, emerging in groups in a counterclockwise spiral. After a few preliminary 'bursts' of bats, the entire colony emerges in a continuous stream that makes a loud, roaring noise and a huge dark cloud that is visible for miles

A Brazilian Free-tailed Bat can eat up to one-third of its own weight in insects during one night of hunting. They catch the insects while flying, taking them with their mouths or scooping them up with wings or the interfemoral membrane. At sunrise they return to the cave and sleep, hanging upside-down from the roof.

Some hibernate in the winter, but most of them in the United States fly south to Mexico, leaving toward the end of October and returning in

March. Mating takes place in March, and the young, usually one and occasionally twins, are born in June.

Because of their numbers, Brazilian Free-tailed Bats are important in the control of harmful insects. It is estimated that half a million of these bats can consume a ton of insects in one night. Guano, the droppings of the Brazilian Free-tailed Bat, was once a widely-used fertilizer. Also once used as a source of nitrate for gunpowder, the guano was mined from the floor of caves where deposits more than 50 feet (15 m) thick were not uncommon. The Carlsbad Caverns were a major guano mining area. Although the Brazilian Free-tailed Bat is known to be a carrier of rabies, these bats are not a danger to man or domestic animals as they go about their nightly activities. Entering the caves can be dangerous, however, either because of bites from disturbed bats or from airborne rabies virus.

Similar species are other free-tailed bats, such as the Pocketed Free-tailed Bat (*Tadarida femorosacca*), the Eastern Free-tailed Bat and the Big Free-tailed Bat (*Tadarida macrotis*).

BAT, CALIFORNIA LEAF-NOSED; LEAF-NOSED BAT (*Macrotus californicus*)

In the United States, the California Leaf-nosed Bat is limited to southern Arizona, southern California and the extreme southern tip of Nevada. It is the only leaf-nosed bat found in the United States.

The California Leaf-nosed Bat has grayish to dark brown fur above and white or nearly-white fur below. It is from 3⅜ to 3⅝ inches (8.5-9 cm) and weighs from ⅜ to ½ ounces (9-14 g). Like all leaf-nosed bats, it has an erect flap of tissue on its nose that is thought to function in the emission of ultrasonic sounds for echolocation.

The California Leaf-nosed Bat rests by day in colonies of about 100 individuals. Frequently used daytime roosting areas are abandoned mine tunnels, close to the entrances. It emerges at night, hunts for about an hour until its stomach is full, and then retires to a

night roost in some sheltered area where it stays until it returns to the daytime roost.

The California Leaf-nosed Bat eats flying and ground insects. It is often seen to hover over the ground and then swoop down to pick up an insect it has detected through echolocation.

The sexes generally stay apart, except at mating time. Young are born in May or June.

Similar North American species include the Hognosed Bat which has its flap over a rather long, slender nose, and the Longnosed Bat which, as its name suggests, has an even longer nose than that of the Hognosed Bat.

BAT, HAIRY-LEGGED VAMPIRE; VAMPIRE BAT (*Diphylla ecaudata*)

The Vampire Bat's normal range is from Mexico south through Central America and South America. Rarely found in the United States, the very few documented sightings have been in Texas. All species of Vampire Bats are found only in the western hemisphere.

The Hairy-legged Vampire Bat is from 2⅝ to 3⅜ inches (6.6 to 8.6 cm) long. Its fur is reddish-brown to dark brown above and lighter below. The middle upper incisor teeth are modified into large, sharp piercing tools. Since this bat lacks a tail, the interfemoral membrane has more fur on it than that of most other bats.

The Hairy-legged Vampire Bat's diet is limited to the blood of other warm-blooded animals. By day it roosts in caves, mines and other secluded areas in small groups, usually of no more than three, sometimes a dozen or so. At night it seeks out animals such as chickens, turkeys, ducks, geese, cattle, horses and pigs. Unlike most bats, the Hairy-legged Vampire Bat has large eyes and well-developed vision, and a rather poor echolocation sense.

One of the few bats that can use its wings for walking, it lands near its prey and walks over to it in a scuttling motion, using its wings. If the prey is small, such as a chicken, it will climb up the leg. It might jump onto a larger animal such as a cow. It is light enough ⌐o that it seldom alerts the animal as it moves about on its surface. With its specialized incisor teeth, it makes a wound that is usually too superficial for the victim to notice. The bat then laps up the blood that flows freely from the wound because of an anticoagulant in the bat's saliva. The amount of blood the bat takes is of no consequence unless the host animal is very small. Any problems that may result from the bat's taking of blood usually occur afterwards. The open wound may be subject to infection or maggot infestation, and may continue to bleed due to the anticoagulant. Also, the bite of the Vampire Bat has the potential for spreading rabies. The Hairy-legged Vampire Bat and other Vampire Bats are a problem for cattle ranchers, poultrymen and other animal breeders in Mexico, Central America and other parts of the animal's range.

Vampire Bats groom each other's fur by licking, a habit that has made possible a degree of control. The bats are caught in nets, poison is spread on the fur, and they are released. When they return to the roost, other bats are exposed to the poison during grooming.

Other bats in the United States that are similar to the Hairy-legged Bat are the Leaf-nosed Bats. However, these bats do not have specialized incisors and do not take blood meals.

BAT, EASTERN FREE-TAILED:
see Bat, Brazilian Free-tailed

BAT, EVENING:
see Bat, Big Brown

BAT, HOARY: see Bat, Red

BAT, HOGNOSED:
see Bat, California Leaf-nosed

BAT, LEAF-NOSED:
see Bat, California Leaf-nosed; Bat, Hairy-legged

Above: Both Red Bat males and females can be distinguished by their color.

BAT, LITTLE BROWN:
see Myotis, Little Brown

BAT, LONGNOSED:
see Bat, California Leaf-nosed

BAT, MEXICAN FREE-TAILED:
see Bat, Brazilian Free-tailed

BAT, POCKETED FREE-TAILED:
see Bat, Brazilian Free-tailed

BAT, RED
(*Lasiurus borealis*)

The Red Bat is found in all of the United States except southern Florida and the Rocky Mountain areas. It is also found in most of Canada except the northern and Pacific Coast regions.

A richly colored bat, the Red Bat is one of the few in which there is a difference in coloration between the sexes. The fur of the male is a bright red or orange-red, while that of the female is a dull red. The fur of both sexes is a frosty white on the back and underside. The Red Bat is from 3¾ to 5 inches (9.5 to 13 cm) long and weighs about ½ ounce (14 g).

The Red Bat roosts in dense foliage rather than in caves or other sheltered areas, usually hanging from 4 to 10 feet (1.2 to 3 m) above the ground. The roosting sites are chosen carefully to provide shade from above and the sides and an opening for a take-off below.

In the evening they leave their roosts to hunt for insects. Fast, steady flyers, they take a variety of insects, including ants and beetles as well as flying insects such as moths and flies. Red Bats appear to have definite hunting routes which they work over repeatedly. Those in the northern parts of the range migrate south in winter.

The females bear two to four young in June. Females with young roost some 10 to 20 feet (3 to 6 m) from the ground. The young cling to the mother until they become so heavy that they prevent the mother from taking off.

Similar species include the Yellow Bat, Hoary Bat (*Lasiurus cinereus*), and Seminole Bat (*Lasiurus seminolus*).

BAT, VAMPIRE:
see Bat, Hairy-legged Vampire

BAT, SEMINOLE: see Bat, Red

BAT, YELLOW: see Bat, Red

BEAR, ALASKAN BROWN:
see Bear, Grizzly

BEAR, BLACK
(Ursus americanus)

Bears are among the chief attractions at national parks such as Yellowstone; but it has become more difficult to observe them under recent park policies aimed at visitor safety. Although the bear most likely to be seen by the tourists visiting the park is the Black Bear, chances are that the color of the bears they see is more of a brown than black. The Black Bear, also called the Cinnamon Bear, exists in several color phases. In eastern North America, the animals are black with a brownish tinge; in the west they are cinnamon or brown in color, with a white blaze on the chest. A 'blue' or 'glacier' phase is found around Yukatat Bay in southwestern Alaska, and those found on Gribble Island in Alaska are almost white. The face is brown in all the color phases.

The smallest of the North American bears, when on all fours, the Black Bear is from 5 feet 6 inches long (1.5-1.8 m), some 2 feet 3 inches high (.6-.9 m) at the shoulders and weighs from 200-600 pounds (90-270 kg).

The Black Bear is found in most of Canada and Alaska. In the eastern United States it is found in northern New England, eastern New York, central Pennsylvania and in the Allegheny Mountains, northern Minnesota, Michigan and Wisconsin. It also occurs in Florida, Louisiana, Arkansas, southern Missouri and Illinois. In the west it is found in the Rocky Mountain States, western Washington and Oregon, extreme northern California and in the Sierra Nevada mountain range. Its range extends into the Mexican state of Chihuahua. Although it is quite abundant in mountainous territory, it is seldom seen at heights higher than around 3000 feet (900 m).

The Black Bear is usually nocturnal, but it can often be seen at midday, especially in areas where they have learned to expect handouts from

Above: **The Black Bear has a clumsy walk but is able to run at great speed.**

people. Although classified as a meat-eater, bears will eat almost anything. Their diet includes berries and other fruit, roots, insects and their grubs, nuts, eggs, small animals and carrion. In the spring, they peel the bark off trees to get at the green, growing area under the bark. They tear apart rotting logs to get at insect grubs, beetles and other insects. They also rip open bee trees to get at the comb, honey and bee larvae. In areas near human habitation, they are commonly seen in garbage dumps. Good fishermen, they often wade into streams and rivers to catch fish with their paws.

Bears are excellent swimmers and tree climbers. Usually, their method of moving is a clumsy-looking shuffle. They are, however, capable of running as fast as 30 mph (48 kph). They retire to a sheltered den during the winter. Although they spend much of the

winter sleeping, their winter retirement is not a true hibernation. They wake up from time to time, while a hibernating animal will not revive even if it is handled.

Black Bears are usually solitary animals except at mating time, which occurs in June and July. Females usually bear a litter every other year. The cubs are born in the winter in January and February. Most often two cubs are born; triplets are born occasionally. A first-time mother usually gives birth to one cub which weighs about ½ pound (.2 kg) when it is born. Emerging from the den with its mother, it will stay with her for about a year. Females are ready to breed when they are about three years old.

Black Bears tend to keep to themselves and are usually not a danger to people. Females with cubs, however, have a strong protective instinct and

MAMMALS

Above: **A Grizzly Bear and her cubs.**
Right: **Grizzly or Brown Bears.**

can be quite dangerous. Bears that live in areas around human habitation lose their fear of humans and can be dangerous. Attacks have occurred around garbage dumps and in national parks when people try to feed the Black Bears. They sometimes raid campgrounds, looking for food. Occasionally, people are killed or seriously injured. Bear hunting is a popular sport in some areas. The meat is considered to be excellent, although it must be thoroughly cooked to avoid getting a parasitic infection. The hides are used for rugs and ornamental fur pieces.

BEAR, BROWN:
see Bear, Grizzly

BEAR, CINNAMON:
see Bear, Black

BEAR, GRIZZLY; KODIAK BEAR, BROWN BEAR
(Ursus arctos)

American folklore is filled with stories and songs of heroic characters like Davy Crockett who wrestled and killed ferocious, 20-foot-tall Grizzly Bears with a hunting knife. While the Grizzly Bear is indeed the largest of American bears and can be dangerous,

the stories and legends about the size and ferocity of this animal tend to be exaggerated.

When Europeans first came to North America, the range of the Grizzly Bear included the entire western half of the United States and Canada. Today, this bear is limited to wilderness areas in Alaska and in Canada: in British Columbia, the Yukon Territory, western Alberta and the Northwest Territories. Rare in the United States today, the Grizzly Bear is limited to high mountain areas in northern Idaho, eastern Montana and the higher ranges of the Rocky Mountains in Wyoming and Colorado. Most of them are in national parks such as Yellowstone and Glacier. The Alaskan Brown and Kodiak varieties are found on the Alaskan coast and on islands along the coast. The name of the Kodiak Bear comes from Kodiak Island, Alaska.

Grizzly Bears, while on all fours, are from 6 to 7 feet (1.8-2.1 m) long, about 4¼ to 4½ feet (1.2-1.3 m) high at the shoulders, and weigh from 300 to 1500 lbs (136-680 kg). The claws on the front paws are an impressive 4 inches (10 cm) long. The Kodiak Bear (Brown variety), or Alaskan Bear, reaches lengths of around eight feet (2.4 m) and weighs as much as 1700 lbs

(770 kg). These bears are the largest of the terrestrial carnivores. Grizzly Bears are yellowish-brown to black. Often, the tips of the hairs are white, giving the bear its characteristic grizzled appearance. The profile of the face is somewhat concave and there is a definite hump above the shoulders. The Grizzly Bear walks in a low, clumsy stance, swinging its head back and forth as it moves. It can, however, move at speeds of 15-20 miles an hour (24-32 kph). The cubs can climb trees, but this ability is lost in adulthood.

Grizzly Bears are active day or night, roaming by themselves or in small family groups. Although classified as carnivores, they will eat almost anything they can get, including plants, large and small mammals and carrion. They dig out small rodents from their burrows. If a Grizzly Bear finds carrion, it will store the carcass in a hiding place, returning to it from time to time to eat. Grizzlies are also quite adept at catching fish. They gather along rivers to catch salmon as these fish swim upstream to spawn. They snap the fish out of the water with their jaws or pin them under the water with their forepaws. The Bears engage

Kodiak and Brown are the same or separate species. Some biologists say there are as many as 70 separate species of 'Grizzly' Bears while others say there is only one. Still other biologists put the number of species at some number between one and seventy. All of these bears, however, are closely enough related in appearance and habits to be considered together.

BEAR, KODIAK:
see Bear, Grizzly

POLAR BEAR
(Ursus maritimus)

The Polar Bear, king of the North, may weigh 1000 pounds and measure eight feet from nose to tail. The large individual is five feet high at the shoulders and may tower 12 feet above the ground when erect on its broad hind feet. These magnificent animals are unbelievably powerful and unpredictable, a combination that makes them dangerous, especially when they are caught by surprise or when a female with cubs is approached. Furthermore, the polar bear may show little fear of people where protected from shooting. In Churchill, Manitoba, which lies on a polar bear migration route, the bears become accustomed to roaming through the center of town, poking their snouts into open doors and feeding at the dumps.

Through most of their wide range, however, the Polar Bears belong to the wilderness. They live in the Arctic regions of five countries: Canada, the United States, the USSR, Denmark (Greenland), and Norway. Problems for the Polar Bear intensified when men with guns began invading the Arctic. Today those five nations have an agreement to help protect the bears; joint commissions study the bears and cooperate in setting regulations. Even with this protection, Polar Bear numbers total probably fewer than 20,000.

These sea-going bears are seal

in vicious fights to establish claims to the best fishing spots.

In the winter they hole up in a den. Their winter sleep, which is not a true hibernation, is characterized by frequent awakenings and they sometimes actually leave the den during the winter months. They tend to return to the same den every year.

Grizzly Bears mate in June and July and the cubs are born in January. Females are ready to mate when they are three years old, and they generally have a litter every other year. The litters range from one to four cubs; the usual number is two. The cubs, which weigh about a pound (.45 kg) when

they are born, stay with their mother for a little more than a year.

Although the Grizzly Bear has a reputation for ferocity, it usually minds its own business and avoids contact with humans. However, its behavior is unpredictable, and it should be considered dangerous if ever encountered. Many of these bears were killed by ranchers and farmers who believed they destroyed livestock. Today, few of these animals are in areas where they are a threat to domestic animals. The Grizzly is considered to be a species threatened with extinction.

Biologists disagree on whether all the bears commonly called Grizzly,

MAMMALS

Above and right: The Polar Bear is active throughout the year, unlike other bears.

hunters and their major prey is the ringed seal, which weighs, when grown, 100 pounds or more. The polar bear has two basic hunting techniques. One is to lie in ambush beside the seal's breathing hole. As the seal surfaces to breathe, which it must do frequently, a giant paw flashes out and crushes the seal's skull. The other method for hunting is to slip up on sleeping seals. When a seal rests on the ice, it must be constantly alert, sleeping only a few minutes at a time, then lifting its head to survey the scene. While the seal is looking, the stalking bear freezes in place and waits for the seal's head to drop again. The bear advances cautiously, taking advantage of ice ridges to help hide its movements. The perfectly camouflaged bear often, but not always, gets close enough to rush the seal before it can escape to the water.

Polar Bears spend large parts of their lives drifting on ice floes. Traveling with the currents, they may cover several hundred miles a year. Meanwhile, the female about to bear young is snugly hidden in a den. She has moved inland and chosen a steep bank where the snow will drift and cover her well. She hollows out a room, keeping a breathing hole open.

In the dead of winter she gives birth usually to twins, each weighing about a pound and a half. The tiny cubs are blind and helpless, but by the end of winter they are big enough to leave the den with their mother. For two and a half years they stay with her, learning to capture food. The female gives birth only every second year, which leaves sufficient time to care for her cubs until they can survive alone.

The giant bear is well outfitted for life in the Arctic. It wears a thick coat of long, white hair which covers even the soles of its feet. Beneath the skin lies a layer of fat, sometimes four inches thick, that serves as both insulation and a source of energy. The bear can lumber along at speeds of 35 miles an hour. It is also at home in the water, where it can swim at six miles an hour and may travel for a hundred miles or more.

The Polar Bear possesses a sense of smell so keen that Eskimos insist the bear smells odors from miles away.

In recent times, biologists have made extensive field studies of Polar Bears to learn more about the bears'

needs and how to protect them from modern hazards. By using small transmitters which emit signals that can be followed by airborne biologists, scientists have brought us new information on how the bears live and where their travels take them.

BEAVER
(Castor canadensis)

When Europeans came to North America, the Beaver's range extended over most of what is today the United States and Canada, including Alaska. Excessive trapping soon diminished its range considerably. However, in recent years, as the result of reduced trapping, it has returned to much of its original range. Today it is found in all of the United States and Canada, except most of Florida and parts of Utah, Arizona, Nevada and California, and the extreme northern parts of Canada and Alaska. In Mexico, it is limited to the northern areas along the Rio Grande.

One of the larger rodents, the Beaver is dark brown except for its horizontally flattened, paddle-like tail which is black and scaly. It is from about 3 feet to 3.8 feet (.9-1.2 m) long, and generally weighs from 45 to 60 pounds (20-27 kg). Some specimens as heavy as 100 pounds (45 kg) are on record. The Beaver has large incisor teeth that continue to grow throughout the animal's lifetime; otherwise they would be worn away by the Beaver's constant gnawing on wood. The tail makes a loud slapping noise when it hits the water. Loud enough to be heard at considerable distances, it is thought to be an alarm signal.

The Beaver is well adapted for life in the water. It has webbed hind feet that enable it to swim with great efficiency. The tail is used as a rudder, freeing the paws to hold objects. The Beaver, which spends a great deal of time underwater, can remain submerged for as long as 15 minutes at a time. The Beaver is protected underwater by valves that close off the ears and nostrils and by skin flaps that seal the mouth, except for the incisor teeth which are used for carrying branches. The eyes are protected by clear membranes. The Beaver waterproofs its fur with secretions from its anal glands applied to the fur with its hind feet which are equipped with nails that serve as a comb. Additional protection is provided by a layer of fat.

The Beaver remains active throughout the entire year. Mostly nocturnal, it is seldom observed in daylight hours. Beavers live near or in bodies of fresh water such as rivers, ponds and streams. Those that live around large rivers dig burrows along the riverbank, with entrances below the water level. Those that live in smaller streams, ponds and lakes build much more elaborate homes.

The Beaver's home-building activity, which involves the construction of dams and lodges with underwater entrances, is one of the most fascinating animal behaviors. The dams are built to raise the water level in the stream or pond so that the lodge entrance will be under water. Both dam and lodge are built of wood, generally with branches of poplar, aspen, willow, birch or maple. The building materials are also the Beaver's food.

Beavers fell trees by gnawing around the trunk, biting out deep chunks. Trees with trunk diameters from two inches to six inches are usually selected, although Beavers are capable of gnawing down much larger trees. Trees with trunk diameters of 30 inches or more are known to have been felled by Beavers. The Beaver can cut down a tree at speeds a lumberjack would envy. A tree four feet in diameter can be felled in five minutes.

Tree branches, stones and mud are the main construction material for the dams and lodges. The Beaver eats the bark and then uses the stripped branches for building the dam. The lodge, also built of branches, has a floor of wood chips, and is generally 3 to 5 feet (.9-1.5 m) wide with a ventilation hole at the top. Additional branches are stored by sticking them into the bottom mud at some point near the lodge. Thus the Beaver has a ready food supply in winter when the pond is frozen over. Beavers are constantly repairing their dams and adjusting them for changing conditions. For example, in flood conditions they construct temporary spillways along the sides of the dams.

Thought to form lifetime pairs, Beavers mate in late January and early February. The kits are born in late spring to early summer. Litters vary from one to eight kits with four or five being the usual number. The kits, which weigh about a pound (0.5 kg) at birth, are adept swimmers by the time they are a week old. In the water the kits are sometimes ferried on the mother's back. On land they may be carried on the mother's tail. The upper chamber of the lodge serves as living quarters, with the ventilation hole concealed by sticks, and the lower chamber, beneath the water level, is a food storage area. Since the underwater tunnels provide the only access to the lodge, the beaver is safe from almost every predator.

Around the middle of the 19th century, practically every gentleman in America and Europe was expected to own a tall 'stovepipe' hat. Almost all

MAMMALS

of these hats were made of beaver fur, a circumstance that almost led to the extinction of these remarkable rodents.

The Beaver reached the peak of its economic importance in the early to middle 19th century. The pelts were much in demand for coats and ornamental trim as well as for hats. Great fortunes were made from Beaver trapping. The Beaver has made a remarkable comeback and is considered to be a pest in some areas by farmers. Their dams sometimes flood cropland and roads, and prevent salmon swimming upstream to spawn. However, the dams retard erosion and provide a feeding and drinking area for other life forms.

Similar rodent species are the Muskrat (*Ondatra zibethica*) and the Nutria (*Myocastor coypus*), both of which are smaller than the beaver. The River Otter (*Lutra canadensis*) is similar in that it lives in water.

BISON, AMERICAN BUFFALO
(Bison bison)

Although the Bison or American Buffalo never received serious consideration as the official animal symbol of the United States, it has come to be regarded as the unofficial symbol of the country. To many people, the Bison evokes America much as the Kangaroo is evocative of Australia. It is estimated that, in the century before Europeans came to North America, some 60 million Bison roamed the continent. By 1900 there were fewer than 1000. Today there are about 30,000 Bison in the United States.

The Bison once ranged over most of North America from the Atlantic almost to the Pacific, and from Mexico north into Canada. Today, free-roaming herds are found only in Yellowstone National Park in the United States and in Wood Buffalo National Park in Northwest Territories, Canada. Custer State Park in South Dakota has the largest fenced herd.

The Bison is the largest terrestrial animal in North America. The males

Above and right: Bison or American Buffalo.
Top: Bison in Yellowstone National Park.

are up to 6 feet (1.8 m) high at the shoulder, from 10 to 12.5 feet (3-3.8 m) long and weigh from 900 to 2000 pounds (400-900 kg). Females are about 5 feet (1.5 m) at the shoulders, 7 to 8 feet (21-24 m) long and weigh from about 800 to 1000 pounds (360-450 kg). The head is massive and broad, topped by short, curving, pointed horns in both sexes. The Bison has dark brown shaggy fur over the head, neck, shoulders and forelegs. The fur on the rest of the body is shorter and sometimes lighter brown in color. Its tail is long with a tuft of fur at the tip.

Bison move in herds, but the sexes stay in separate groups except at mating time. From time to time, smaller groups gather into larger herds. When they were at their peak population, Buffalo herds sometimes stretched as far as the eye could see across the plains. They will stampede if startled, a characteristic the Indians used to advantage by forcing them over cliffs. They are excellent swimmers and they can run at speeds between 30 to 35 miles per hour. When they were abundant, they would go on annual migrations of 200 miles or

ground nests, young rabbits and carrion. The largest animals they are known to eat are fawns.

Usually foraging in family groups of sow and young, families sometimes come together in groups of 50 or so animals. Males forage alone or in small groups, joining the females and young during the mating season.

Mating usually takes place in December. After a gestation period of 16 weeks, a litter is born in a nest that is a depression in the ground dug by the sow and lined with grass and branches. The usual number of young in a litter is four or five, but litters as large as 14 or 15 have been observed. The piglets, which are about 6 to 8 inches (15-20 cm) long at birth, stay with the mother until the following spring. Wild Boars are sexually mature at age 1½, usually reach their maximum growth at about age five or six years, and have a life span of from 15 to 25 years.

Hunting Wild Boars, both pure-blooded and hybrid, is a popular sport in many parts of the United States. Some states maintain hunting seasons and limits on the number that may be killed. In some areas, hybrids and feral pigs are considered to be agricultural pests, and there are no restrictions on hunting them. The meat of older animals tends to be tough, while that of younger acorn-fed animals is just as tender as domestic pork. Because of the effectiveness of their tusks as a fighting tool, adult Wild Boars are seldom taken by predators other than man.

A similar species is the Peccary, found in Texas, southern Arizona and northern Mexico. The Peccary is much smaller than the Wild Boar, has upper tusks that point downward, and has more uniformly colored fur.

BOBCAT
(Felis rufus)

The most common wildcat in North America, the Bobcat's range extends in scattered populations over most of the United States and southern Canada. It is believed to be most

abundant in the far West, and it is probably almost absent in most of the central and lower midwest and the San Joaquin Valley of California.

A tawny tan in the summer and somewhat gray in the winter, the Bobcat is some 2⅓ to 4 feet (.7-1.2 m) long and weighs from about 14 to 70 pounds (6.3-32 kg). The males are larger than the females. The legs have black horizontal bars, and the face has thin black lines that fan out into a broad cheek ruff. The short tail has a black tip above and is white on the underside.

A daytime hunter, the Bobcat hunts

Above: **Bobcats live only in North America.**

by hiding in a thicket, rock cleft or other concealed place where it waits for prey. A good climber, it also waits in trees, but less often than the Lynx. Usually well camouflaged by its spotted fur, it pounces on prey as they pass by. Tending to use the same hunting pathways repeatedly, it preys on snowshoe hares, rabbits, small rodents, porcupines and cave bats, but it very seldom eats carrion.

Although females can breed any time of the year, most come into heat in February or March. Litters, generally born in April or May, may contain one to seven kittens, but two or three is the usual number.

Bobcats may sometimes prey on domestic animals, particularly poultry if they can get into the poultry farm. Bobcats are hunted with hounds in some areas, and they are still killed for their fur, which is used for trim, although this practice is becoming more rare. The population appears to be stable or increasing in most areas.

The Bobcat is similar to the Lynx (*Felis lynx*) which has no spots and is a bit more gray. The Lynx generally ranges farther north.

BUFFALO: see Bison

BUFFALO, AMERICAN: see Bison

CACOMISTLE: see Ringtail

CAT, CIVET: see Ringtail

CAT, MINER'S: see Ringtail

CATAMOUNT: see Mountain Lion

CHAMOIS: see Goat, Mountain

CHICKAREE: see Squirrel, Red

CHIPMUNK, EASTERN; TAMIAS (Tamias striatus)

The range of the Eastern Chipmunk extends from southeastern Canada to all states of the continental United States east of the Mississippi except Florida, southern Mississippi, southwestern Alabama, southeastern Georgia, eastern North Carolina and most of South Carolina. West of the Mississippi it is found from northern Louisiana to Minnesota, and in the extreme eastern sections of Oklahoma, Kansas, Nebraska, South Dakota and North Dakota.

The Eastern Chipmunk is from 8½ to 19½ inches (21 to 30 cm) long and

weighs from about 2¼ to 5 ounces (66 to 142 gm). It has reddish-brown fur on the upper parts and white fur below. White stripes, bordered by black, run down the sides. A wide dark band runs down the back and there are faint stripes on the face. Rounded ears top the pointed face.

The Eastern Chipmunk usually looks for food on the ground, but it can and will climb large trees such as oak and hickory to get acorns and nuts. It also feeds on seeds, fruits, insects, snails and other invertebrates, eggs, and meat of small vertebrates when it can get it. It often fills its cheek pouches with seeds and nuts. The Eastern Chipmunk stores food in storage burrows, constantly making trips between food-gathering sites and the burrow. It is often seen in the daytime scurrying about forest edges, brushy areas, stone walls and around houses. It chatters constantly with rapid trills and slow 'chuck-chuck' sounds. They are also noisy eaters, making snap-like sounds when they bite into nuts.

Chipmunks are true hibernators, holing up in underground burrows or tree limbs. They often wake up in midwinter and feed on their hoard of food. They also make use of the hoard when they awaken in the spring.

Eastern Chipmunks mate in early spring, and litters of three to five young are born in May. First-year females may have their first litters in July or August.

Above: A Least Chipmunk.
Right: The Bobcat or Wildcat.

The Eastern Chipmunk may occasionally do some damage to flower gardens, but most of its activities are harmless. A fascinating, amusing animal to watch, it is sometimes kept as a pet. Many are taken by weasels, foxes, hawks and bobcats and some are killed by domestic cats and dogs.

Similar species are the Least Chipmunk (*Eutamias minimus*) and the Thirteen-lined Ground Squirrel (*Spermophilus tridecemlineatus*).

CHIPMUNK, LEAST (Eutamias minimus)

This small chipmunk is found from the southern Yukon and northeastern British Columbia, southeastward through southern Canada to northern Ontario and northern Minnesota, Wisconsin and Michigan's upper peninsula. In the eastern United States the range extends southward from central Montana to northern Arizona and westward to central Washington and Oregon and western California.

One of the smallest of the chipmunks, the Least Chipmunk is about 4 to 6 inches (10 to 15 cm) long and weighs from 1 to 2½ ounces (28 to 70 g). Color of fur varies with the region in which it is found, from a pale, yellowish-gray with tan dark stripes in dry areas to brownish-gray with black

MAMMALS

side strips in wetter areas. The fur on the sides is orange-brown and the underside is grayish-white. The rather long tail is light brown above and yellowish below.

Adapted to live in a variety of habitats, the Least Chipmunk lives in sagebrush deserts, in coniferous forests and on rocky cliffs. The Least Chipmunk feeds on seeds, acorns, soft fruits such as berries, grasses, fungi, insects and other invertebrates. It may eat a small vertebrate such as a mouse. It readily climbs trees for acorns and nuts. Like most chipmunks, it stores food and hibernates in a burrow built under a stump log or rock. Its distinctive call is a series of high-pitched chirping notes.

Litters of two to six young are born in May.

The Least Chipmunk does no damage to crops or gardens, and is often seen in national park campgrounds.

Similar species include the Eastern Chipmunk (*Tamias striatus*), Townshend's Chipmunk (*Eutamias townsendii*), and the Redtail Chipmunk (*Eutamias ruficaudus*).

CHIPMUNK, REDTAIL: see Chipmunk, Least

CHIPMUNK, TOWNSHEND'S: see Chipmunk, Least

COATI (*Nasua nasua*)

The Coati is found in Mexico northward to the southwestern United States including southern Texas, southwestern New Mexico and southeastern Arizona. It is particularly abundant in the Huachuca Mountains of Arizona.

The Coati is from 3⅓ to 4⅜ feet (1 to 1.3 m) long and weights from 15 to 30 pounds (7 to 14 kg). The males are considerably larger than the females. It has grayish-brown fur on its body and indistinct bands of coloration on the long, thin tail. The snout is long and pointed and tipped with white fur. White rings circle the eyes.

Above: **The Coati spends its day searching for food, including lizards in the ground.**

The Coati walks with its tail high in the air and curled at the tip. The Coati is more gregarious and does more daytime hunting than other raccoon-like animals. They are often seen in noisy groups of five to twenty-five individuals, made up of females with young. The young play constantly, noisily chasing each other up and down trees. Coatis of all ages vocalize with grunts, screams, chatters, and whines.

The omnivorous animal eats a variety of foods including insects, spiders and other invertebrates, snakes, lizards, birds' eggs, fruits and nuts. Since it lives in a warm climate, it does not retire to a den, but usually spends the night in trees. During the hottest part of the day it generally naps in a shady spot. It is a good swimmer and a nimble tree climber, using its prehensile tail for balance and for wrapping around branches and vines for support and slowing of descent.

The mating season is from January to March. Litters of four to six young are born in July in a maternity den set up in a shelter such as a rocky crevice.

Coatis are believed to occasionally kill a chicken or a dog. They are sometimes hunted with dogs and treed, similar to the way raccoons are hunted. However, they may descend from the tree and attack the dogs. Some people have tried to keep Coatis as pets, but this is discouraged by wildlife experts.

The Raccoon (*Procyon lotor*) and Ringtail (*Bassariscus astutus*) are among similar species.

CONY: see Pika

COTTONTAIL, DESERT: see Cottontail, Eastern

COTTONTAIL, EASTERN (*Sylvilagus floridanus*)

One of the most frequently seen rabbits in North America, the Eastern Cottontail is found in all of the United States east of the Mississippi except northern New England and northern New York. The range extends westward to the tier of states from Texas to North Dakota, eastern New Mexico, eastern Colorado and central Arizona, and southward into Mexico. In Canada it is limited to southern Ontario and small areas in southern Manitoba and Saskatchewan.

The Eastern Cottontail is from 1.2 to 1.5 feet (.35 to .45 m) long and weighs from 2 to 4 pounds (.9 to 1.8 kg). As is the case with most rabbits and hares, the does are larger than the bucks. The fur is grayish-brown and flecked with a little black on the upper regions and white below. The nape of the neck has a distinctive rust-colored patch.

Active from evening to late morning, Cottontails are often seen grazing in back yards in the early morning. They adapt to a range of habitats including open fields, woods, cultivated fields, gardens, thickets and brush piles. Strictly herbivorous, cottontails eat a variety of green vegetation in the summer and twigs and bark in the winter. Like other rabbits and hares, they eat quickly and return to a hiding place where they defecate soft green pellets of undigested food. These are later eaten and digested. During the day Eastern Cottontails hide in a burrow beneath a brush pile or in a slight cavity or depression in the ground. In the winter, they may make a network of runs under the snow when there is sufficient brush to support the snow. In very cold weather, they might hole up in an abandoned burrow of another animal. They sometimes play in

Right: **An Eastern Cottontail.**

MAMMALS

groups on crusted snow.

The Cottontails usually move by hopping; however, they can move quickly in leaps of ten to fifteen feet (3 to 4.6 m). When pursued by a predator, they circle, often jumping sideways to break the scent trail. Sometimes they 'freeze' when threatened. When alarmed, they may thump the ground with their hindlegs, setting up vibrations that can be detected by other rabbits. If necessary, they will take to water, although they prefer not to get wet. Normally silent, they can give a piercing scream-like distress call. Does may grunt or purr while nursing, and the young squeak softly.

The breeding season runs from February to September. Males fight with each other and attempt to attract the attention of does with elaborate

Below: **A Nuttall's or Mountain Cottontail (*Sylvilagus nuttallii*) in Canada.**

courtship rituals. A doe can produce three or four litters a year that can contain as few as one or as many as nine young. However, four to five young is the usual litter size. The doe makes a nest in tangled brush, high grass or other concealed areas. She digs out a depression in the ground and lines it with downy fur she bites off from her underside, mixed with dead grass and leaves. The biting off of fur also serves to expose the nipples, facilitating nursing. The doe hides the blind furless young under a layer of nest lining while she is away foraging, returning to them at dawn and dusk for nursing. The young rabbits are nursed for about two weeks, after which they may leave the nest. A doe is ready to mate again hours after giving birth. Without a high predation rate, cottontail rabbits would soon overpopulate their feeding areas, as indeed they do occasionally in isolated areas free of

predators. The Eastern Cottontail is widely hunted and frequently consumed. The meat is considered to be excellent, but should be well cooked to avoid parasitic worm infestation, especially in warmer climates. These rabbits may also carry tularemia, a serious febrile disease. When dressing a rabbit it is sensible to wear gloves as a precaution against tularemia. Pelts, which are not particularly durable, are sometimes used for trim.

Similar species include the New England Cottontail (*Sylvilagus transitionalis*), the smaller Desert Cottontail (*Sylvilagus audubonii*), Swamp Rabbits (*Sylvilagus aquaticus*) and Marsh Rabbits (*Sylvilagus palustris*) and the larger Snowshoe Hare (*Lepus americanus*).

COTTONTAIL, NEW ENGLAND
see Cottontail, Eastern

COUGAR: see Lion, Mountain

COYOTE
(Canis latrans)

The range of the Coyote is known to extend over western Canada and all of the United States including eastern Alaska, and southward into practically all of Mexico. It is also found in southern Ontario and extreme southern Quebec. Although commonly associated with the West, Coyotes appear in Wisconsin, Michigan, Indiana, Ohio, Pennsylvania, Vermont and western Massachusetts.

Smaller than wolves, Coyotes are from 2 to 2.2 feet (.6 to .7 m) high at the shoulder, 3.5 to 4.3 feet (1.1 to 1.3 m) long, and weigh from 20 to 50 pounds (9 to 23 kg). The fur is a grizzled or reddish gray above, and somewhat buff below. The legs have a rusty-yellowish fur interrupted by a vertical line of black on the foreleg. The tail is bushy with a black tip.

Coyotes hunt at anytime of day, but are more likely to be active at dusk and night. They eat whatever they can catch, including rabbits, rodents, gophers, birds, snakes, lizards, frogs and insects. They have been known to take larger prey, such as deer and pronghorn, although the cooperative efforts of two or more coyotes are usually needed to bring down larger animals. If they cannot find animal prey they will eat fruit and carrion. They frequently hunt in pairs or groups of three or four, and one might chase the prey toward another coyote waiting in ambush. They also steal the prey of other carnivores through such tactics as waiting at one end of a burrow to pounce on an animal as it emerges after being flushed out by a predator such as a badger.

Well adapted to a variety of habitats, they can move for extended periods at speeds of 25-30 mph (40-48 kph) and as fast as 40 mph (65 kph) for short bursts. Experiments with tagged coyotes have shown they can travel distances of 400 miles (654 km) or more. They are strong swimmers and will readily go after prey in water.

Above: **The Coyote or 'barking dog.'**

The vocalizations of Coyotes are familiar night sounds in many parts of the United States, particularly the western states, and have passed into legend as the epitome of mournfulness and solitude in the great open spaces. This vocalization is a series of yelps and barks followed by a sustained howl that often terminates with a few short yaps. When one Coyote starts to vocalize, others usually join in, creating the cacophany of howls and barks that is a familiar night chorus in the West. The howling is believed to be a way of keeping members of a hunting band in communication.

Many Coyotes are believed to stay with the same partner for life. Coyotes mate from February to April. Litters consisting of one to twenty pups are born in April through May. The young are born in a nesting chamber which is typically part of a den located at the end of a five to thirty foot long tunnel. Dens may be abandoned badger or fox burrows enlarged by the female. If dens are not available, the female will have her pups in a variety of protected spots such as logs, culverts or caves.

The Coyote population continues to increase despite poisoning, trapping and the loss of their habitat to human settlement. They are trapped for their fur and killed by sheep ranchers and poultry growers who regard them as threats. Ecologists point out that while a Coyote will, indeed, take a domestic animal if it can, it is of greater benefit through killing rodents that prey on chicks and other young livestock. Suburban housing developments have encroached on the coyote's habitat on the fringes of cities such as Los Angeles and Phoenix. There has been considerable interbreeding with domestic dogs in these areas, producing what are called 'coydogs.'

The Gray Wolf (*Canis lupus*) is similar to the Coyote, which is often called the prairie wolf, but considerably larger. The Gray Wolf is very much like the Coyote. Coydogs, especially shepherd mixtures, are usually larger than coyotes.

COYPU: see Nutria

DEER, BLACK-TAILED: see Deer, Mule

DEER, COUE'S: see Deer, White-tailed

DEER, FALLOW
(Cevus dama)

Originally a native of Asia Minor and the Mediterranean region, the Fallow Deer was first introduced to North America on James Island, British Columbia. A later group was brought to a recreational area in Kentucky. Today, the Fallow Deer also occurs on Saint Simon and Jekyll Islands off the coast of Georgia and in small groups in Maryland, Alabama, California, Oklahoma and Texas.

One of the smaller deer species, the Fallow Deer is a little more than 3 feet (1 m) high at the shoulder, about 4.6 to 6 feet (1.4-1.8 m) long, and weighs from some 85 to 175 pounds (39-80 kg). They are variable in color, and brown with white spots is the usual summer coloration; grayish-brown without spots is a prevalent winter color pattern. The Fallow Deer can also be white, pale yellow, black, cream, silver-gray and spotted (piebald). All, however, are white on the underside. The tail is longer than those of most other deer, and has a black stripe. It has a short neck with a distinctive, prominent larynx. The hind legs are a bit longer than the forelegs, and the animal stands with its rump held high. They run in a bouncing, stiff-legged gait. The bucks have

MAMMALS

Above: **Fallow Deer (*Cevus dama*).**
Right: **A Mule Deer doe.**
Far right: **A Mule Deer buck.**

branched antlers with flattened palms at the ends. A pair of prong-like horns is located on the forward central part of the head.

Among the more gregarious of the deer, the Fallow Deer gathers in herds of 150-175 or more individuals of all ages and both sexes. They graze in the summer on grasses and herbaceous plants. In the winter they eat woody plants.

During the mating season in November, bucks engage in fights. Mating is polygamous, and a single spotted fawn is born after a gestation period of six to seven months.

Fallow Deer are semi-domesticated in 'deer parks' in many parts of the world. The North American species which they most resemble is the White-tailed Deer (*Odocoileus virginianus*).

DEER, KEY:
see Deer, White-tailed

DEER, MULE
(*Odocoileus hemionus*)

The most abundant deer in the west, the Mule Deer is found in the west coast states, all the Rocky Mountain states, North Dakota, South Dakota, Nebraska, Kansas, Oklahoma, Texas, Minnesota and Iowa, and in Canada from western Manitoba to the Pacific, and north to the Yukon and Northwest Territories. In Mexico it occurs in Baja California and in the north central states.

The Mule Deer is about 3 to 3.5 feet (.9-1.1 m) high at the shoulder and some 4 to 6.6 feet long (1.2-2.0 m). Bucks, which are larger than the does, weigh about 120 to 450 pounds (55-205 kg), while does weigh from about 80 to 150 pounds (36-68 kg). The upper and outer hair is reddish to yellowish-brown in summer and somewhat grayish in winter. A cream to tan color persists in all seasons on the undersides, throat patch, rump patch and inside of the ears. Bucks have equally-branching antlers with a spread of about 4 feet (1.2 m). The antlers are shed in February. The distinctive feature that gives the animal its name is the large, long ears. About 4.5 to 6 inches (11.5-15 cm) long, each ear can be moved independently. Mule Deer have a stocky body and sturdy-looking legs. Back and front legs move together, giving them a stiff, bounding gait.

In the summer, Mule Deer are active mostly in the mornings, even-ings, and on moonlit nights. In the winter they are more likely to browse at midday in addition to morning and evening. They have a varied diet that includes both herbaceous and woody plants. Herbaceous plants are the more frequent summer fare, while woody plants comprise the winter browse. They also eat acorns and apples. Mule Deer that live in mountainous areas avoid heavy snow by migrating down the slopes in winter.

The Mule Deer usually moves in small groups, seldom gathering in large herds. A doe forms a small group consisting of fawns and yearlings. Doe groups tend to keep to themselves in areas spaced out from other groups. If does meet, they are likely to fight. These fights serve to maintain the feeding areas of each group. Bucks are generally solitary, but small groups may form just before and after the rutting season. Herding, when it does occur, tends to be limited to the winter.

During the mating season, which begins in November, the bucks establish small harems of does through fights and display threats. Fights are infrequent, consisting of crashing of antlers, with each buck trying to bring the other's head down. Serious injuries are rare, and the major hazard is

the possibility of the antlers becoming locked, in which case both bucks will probably starve to death.

Fawns are born after a gestation period of six to seven months. Newly-bred does give birth to one fawn, while older does usually deliver twins. Fawns are concealed by the mother for the first month, after which the fawns follow the doe. Fawns may stay with the mother for two years, at which time they are sexually mature. The fawns seem to recognize the mother by sniffing at secretions of a gland that is located on each of the hind feet. Also present on the bucks, hairs around the glands stand erect when the bucks engage in aggressive behavior.

The Mule Deer, a popular game animal in the western states, is prized for its meat and as a trophy. In some areas, they damage crops and young timber. They are prey for coyotes, cougars and wolves. Bears and bobcats may take fawns or an occasional adult.

The Mule Deer and White-tailed Deer (*Odocoileus virginianus*) are in the same genus and have many similarities. The White-tailed Deer does not have the long ears of the Mule Deer. Also, the Mule Deer's nose is considerably broader than the White-tailed Deer's, and it has a shorter, blunter face. The Black-tailed Deer is considered to be a subspecies of the Mule Deer by most biologists. It differs from the Mule Deer primarily in the brownish to blackish color of the tail.

DEER, VIRGINIA: see Deer, Fallow; Deer, White-tailed

DEER, WHITE-TAILED; VIRGINIA DEER; WHITETAIL; KEY DEER (*Odocoileus virginianus*)

The most familiar and abundant of the American deer, the White-tailed Deer ranges over almost all of the United States with the exception of most of California and sections of Arizona, Colorado, New Mexico and Nevada. It is also found across southern Canada and in extreme northern Mexico.

The White-tailed Deer is about 3 to 3.5 feet (.9-1 m) at the shoulder and some 4.5 to 7 feet (1.4-2.1 m) long. The bucks weigh from 200-300 pounds (90-136 kg) and the does weigh from about 150-250 pounds (68-115 kg). Tan to reddish brown in summer, and a darker grayish-brown in winter, the White-tailed Deer gets its name from its tail which is brown but is edged with white above and is all white below. When alarmed, the animal 'flags' its tail, exhibiting the white underside. The bucks have antlers with a forward main beam and several unbranched tines. Does do not usually have antlers. Antlers are shed shortly after the mating season.

Although it is primarily nocturnal, the White-tailed Deer can be active at

MAMMALS

Left and above: White-tailed or Virginia Deer (*Odocoileus virginianus*).

any time of day, looking for food in woods, brushy areas, and land that has been cleared for farming. It eats a wide variety of plant foods, including nuts, aquatic plants and corn. In the winter its diet is mainly woody plants such as twigs and buds of trees. When food is scarce, it may strip trees of bark. Good runners and strong swimmers, they can move at speeds of 35 mph (56 kph) in short bursts. They usually take to cover when alarmed, rather than run great distances. Their vocalizations are limited to snorts when they are nervous and agitated.

Bucks and does move in separate herds through most of the year. In winter they gather in small herds of a male, a few does, and young. These herds may coalesce into groups of 25 or more individuals.

The White-tailed Deer breeds from late September to November. Fawns are born after a gestation period of seven months. First-time mothers usually give birth to one fawn, while subsequent births are usually twins, and triplets may occur if food is abundant. The doe hides the spotted newborn fawns in thickets for the first four or five weeks following birth, after which the young follow the mother. The white-tail 'flag' helps the young to follow the doe in flight.

The White-tailed Deer was near extinction in some deforested areas of the northwest and midwest. However, the decline in predators such as mountain lions and bobcats, and restrictions on hunting have resulted in an increase in deer population in these areas. In some areas, particularly the east, the populations tend to exceed food supplies, and they become agricultural pests, raiding orchards and vegetable crops. Hunting is limited to specified

seasons in most areas of the United States, although extended seasons and increased kill allotments are instituted from time to time in areas where there are overpopulation problems. Today the most abundant game animal in eastern North America, they are hunted for their meat (venison), which is considered to be excellent, and as trophies. Many are struck by automobiles and killed.

Two smaller subspecies are the Key Deer (*O.v. clavium*) of the Big Pine Key area of Florida and Coue's Deer (*O.v. covesi*) of the Arizona and New Mexico desert. These 'toy' deer seldom exceed 50 pounds (23 kg) in weight. An endangered species, the Key Deer was protected by the National Key Deer Refuge set up in 1961, and is making a comeback.

Similar species include the Mule Deer (*Odocoileus hemionus*), which tend to be heavier than White-tailed Deer, and which have rather long ears.

MAMMALS

DOLPHIN, ATLANTIC BOTTLE-NOSED; PORPOISE; DOLPHIN
(Tursiops truncatus)

The most commonly seen dolphin in the waters off North America, the range of the Atlantic Bottle-nosed Dolphin extends from Cape Cod southward into Central and South American waters.

The Atlantic Bottle-nosed Dolphin attains a length of about 12 feet (3.6 m) and weighs from 300 to 400 pounds (135 to 180 kg). The overall body color is gray, and is somewhat lighter on the underside than on the upper parts of the body. A pointed, swept-back dorsal fin is located about midway between the head and tail. The fish-like body ends in a horizontal tail or fluke.

The Atlantic Bottle-nosed Dolphin tends to swim in groups of 50 to 60 individuals. Capable of swimming at speeds as fast as 20 mph (12.5 kph), they are often seen swimming in the wake of ships, frequently leaping out of the water with the body in a graceful arch, in a maneuver called 'porpoising.' Feeding almost exclusively on

fish, dolphins locate prey and find their way around in the underwater darkness by means of echolocation or 'sonar.' They emit high-pitched clicks and squeaks which bounce back to the dolphin as echoes, and are interpreted to give information on the size, speed, shape and location of everything in its environment.

Capable of remaining submerged for an hour or more, the dolphin must come to the surface to breathe. The animal breathes through the blowhole located on top of the head. Also used to produce vocalizations such as a high-pitched squeal, the blowhole is closed while the dolphin is submerged.

Breeding in spring and summer, dolphins seem to engage in almost constant sexual play. After a gestation period of about 12 months, a single young is born underwater. Immediately pushed to the surface, the young can submerge for less than a minute when first born, but slowly increases the amount of time it can remain underwater. Nursing underwater, the nursing periods are, of necessity, short and frequent at first, but increase in duration and become less frequent as the young dolphin grows. Young

Above: **A female Dolphin with her young.**

dolphins remain with the mother and nurse for as long as two years, although they are able to eat fish by the time they are about three months old.

The trained dolphin of the seaquarium shows that the Atlantic Bottle-nosed Dolphin has a high degree of intelligence and they are thought to be able to communicate with each other in a highly developed language. It does well in captivity, learns quickly and seems to enjoy the company and attention of humans.

Classified as a toothed whale, there are more than 30 species of dolphins in the world, of which about ten are commonly seen in North American waters. These include the Pacific Bottle-nosed Dolphin, the Atlantic and Pacific White-sided Dolphin, the Common Dolphin, the Spotted Dolphin, and the Striped Dolphin. Large numbers of dolphins in the Pacific drown in nets of tuna fishermen when they become trapped going after the tuna. New net designs and techniques have reduced the numbers of dolphins lost in nets, enabling fishermen to usually keep within kill limits set by regulation.

**DOLPHIN, ATLANTIC
WHITE-SIDED:**
see Dolphin, Atlantic
Bottle-nosed

DOLPHIN, COMMON:
see Dolphin, Atlantic
Bottle-nosed

**DOLPHIN: PACIFIC BOTTLE-
NOSED**
see Dolphin, Atlantic
Bottle-nosed

**DOLPHIN, PACIFIC
WHITE-SIDED:**
see Dolphin, Atlantic Bottle-
nosed

DOLPHIN, SPOTTED:
see Dolphin, Atlantic
Bottle-nosed

DOLPHIN, STRIPED:
see Dolphin, Atlantic
Bottle-nosed

ELK, WAPITI
(Cervus e. canadensis)

Before European settlers came to North America, the range of the Elk extended over most of what is today the United States and southern Canada. Now, the Elk is primarily a western species. It is found in Colorado, Utah, Wyoming, Montana, Idaho, western Washington and Oregon, northwestern California, extreme northern Arizona and New Mexico, Vancouver Island, southwestern Alberta, eastern British Columbia, central Saskatchewan and southern Manitoba. Isolated groups are found in central Arkansas, south central California, Nevada, Oklahoma, South Dakota and Michigan. Isolated remnants of the once large eastern population are seen in a few eastern states, particularly Pennsylvania and Virginia.

One of the largest of the deer, the bull Elk is from 4½ to 5 feet (1.4-1.5 m) high at the shoulder, some 6.5 to 10 feet (2-3 m) long, and weighs from 600 to 800 pounds (270-362 kg).

The cow Elk weighs about 300 pounds less (136-226 kg) and is proportionately smaller. The fur is brown, lighter on top and darker on the underside. The tail and rump hair are a lighter yellowish-brown. Males have dark brown hair on the throat. The most notable feature on the bulls is the large antlers. When mature, these antlers, which are shed every spring, have six tines or branches and have a beam length of 5 feet (1.5 m) or more.

Elk are active mostly in the night hours, particularly at dusk and dawn. Although they are primarily grazers, they will feed on practically any kind of plant. They are strong animals capable of running speeds of 35 to 40 miles per hour (56-64 kph) and swimming in strong currents, but they can move through the forest almost silently in a graceful, pacing trot. In the winter they graze at lower altitudes, often in thick forest. In the summer, they move to higher, open pastures. They mark their territories by stripping bark off seedling trees. Cows strip the bark with their teeth, and bulls use the base of their antlers, chin and muzzle.

Elk make a variety of vocalizations. The adults constantly make snorting

Above: A herd of Elk or Wapiti.

and grunting noises, and the calves squeal. Cows call their calves with a sound similar to a horse's neigh. During the rutting season bulls, which are the most vocal of American deer, make their 'bugle' or 'whistle' call. It begins as a low bellow, changing almost immediately to a loud, high-pitched noise that can be described as a whistle or scream. The 'bugle' is both a challenge to other bulls and a signal of domination over cows. Cows also whistle, but their vocalizations are not as loud as those of the bull.

Cows and young move in separate herds until the mating season, when they are joined by bulls. Running from August to November, the rutting or mating season reaches its peak in October and November. During the mating season, the males vocalize frequently, particularly with the bugle call. They also roll in mud puddles to coat themselves with mud and urinate on piles of verdure which they then pitch onto their backs with their antlers. Bulls engage in mating fights which consist of banging their antlers together. Although serious injuries

MAMMALS

Above: A six-point bull Elk.

are rare, some do occur, and a few are fatal when antlers lock. Bull Elks assemble harems that usually number six to eight cows. However, harems as large as 60 cows have been observed.

The cows leave the herd after a gestation period of 255-275 days to find a place to give birth. An Elk usually gives birth to one calf weighing from 25 to 40 pounds (11-18 kg). However, twins are not uncommon. The cow and calf rejoin the herd about a week after the birth, and the calf suckles for about nine months. As the young bulls grow older, they spend less and less time with the cow-dominated herd, and eventually leave to join herds of bulls. Cows stay with the female herds and are ready to breed at about age 2½. Elk have a lifespan of about 14 years.

The Elk was once more of a plains animal than it is today. They were, however, killed in large numbers by cattle ranchers who considered them to be pests that reduced cattle grazing areas. They were also hunted for their meat and antlers. Many were killed to satisfy a market for 'elks' teeth,' the upper incisor teeth, which were used as watch-fob charms.

The Elk is similar to other American deer, but is much larger than other North American deer species, with the exception of the Moose (*Alces americana*). The Moose has a large overhanging snout, and large, flattened antlers which give it an appearance quite distinctive from that of the Elk.

ERMINE, SHORT-TAILED WEASEL
(*Mustela erminea*)

The Ermine is found in all of Alaska and Canada except extreme southern Manitoba and a small area of eastern Alberta, and its range extends southward in the east to New England, New York and Pennsylvania, centrally to Minnesota, Wisconsin, northern Iowa and eastern North Dakota, and into much of the northwestern United States, including western Montana, most of Idaho, northern California and Nevada, western Colorado, most of Utah and a small area in northern New Mexico.

The male Ermine or Short-Tailed Weasel is from ½ to ¾ of a foot (.15 to .2 m) long and weighs from 2½ to 6 ounces (71 to 170 gm), while the smaller female is from ⅓ to ⅖ feet (.1 to 12 m) long and weighs from 1 to 3 ounces (28 to 85 g). In the summer months, the fur is dark brown above and whitish below. The fur of those in the northern part of the range becomes white in the winter, except for a black tip on the tail. In the summer, the white winter coloring on the underside persists as white lines running down the hind legs.

An excellent runner and climber, the Ermine hunts prey on the ground and in trees. It does not hesitate to go into water. The Ermine takes its prey by pouncing on it with all four feet and delivering a fatal bite through the neck near the base of the skull. It feeds on mice and other rodents, baby rabbits, shrews and birds. It builds a den with several entrances beneath a log, stump, stone wall or brushpile.

Mating takes place in July, and litters of four to nine young are born the following spring. The male takes part in caring for the young.

The winter white coat of the Ermine is one of the most highly prized of furs.

Similar species include the smaller Least Weasel (*Mustela nivalis*) and the Long-tailed Weasel (*Mustela frenata*) which is considerably larger.

FERRET, BLACK FOOTED:
see Weasel, Least; Weasel, Long-tailed

FISHER
(*Martes pennanti*)

The Fisher is found in most of Canada except the northern regions, northern New England, northern Minnesota, western Montana, northern Idaho, western areas of Washington and Oregon and northern California.

The weasel-like body, thinner than that of other weasel-like animals, is from 2.6 to 3.4 feet (.8 to 1 m) long, and it weighs from 3 to 18 pounds (1.3 to 8 kg). Males tend to be larger than females. The fur is dark brown over most of the body and a somewhat grayish color on the head. White-tipped hairs over most of the body fur give it a frosted appearance.

The Fisher's name is somewhat of a misnomer. Although fish are sometimes included in its varied diet, they are not its major food. Animals most often eaten by the fisher are porcupines and snowshoe hares. It is one of the few animals to successfully prey on porcupines. It takes porcupines by flipping them over and ripping open the abdomen. In spite of their adeptness at capturing porcupines, Fishers are occasionally pierced, sometimes fatally, by the quills. The Fisher also eats squirrels, chipmunks and other rodents, fruits and other plant food. The Fisher is a strong runner and swimmer and an efficient tree climber, often moving from tree to tree in pur-

Above: **An Arctic Fox in winter colors.**   *Below:* **An Ermine in its winter coat.**

suit of squirrels. It dens in a variety of sites including rocky crevices, hollow trees, brush, or a hole dug in the snow.

Mating takes place in March and April. After delayed implantation and a gestation period of almost a year, litters of one to five young are born in the following spring.

Heavily trapped for its valuable fur, its populations have been seriously reduced in many areas.

Similar species are the Marten (*Martes americana*) and Mink (*Mustela vison*).

FOX, ARCTIC
(*Alopex lagopus*)

The Artic Fox is found in northern and western Alaska, northern Canada including the Arctic Ocean Islands, southward through the northern and eastern parts of the Northwest Territories, northeast Alberta, northern Manitoba, northern Quebec around Hudson Bay and northern Labrador.

The Arctic Fox is about a foot (.3 m) high at the shoulder, 2½ to 3 feet (.8 to .9 m) long, and weighs from 10 to 12 pounds (4 to 5 kg). Variable fur color is one of the many adaptations of the Arctic Fox to life in the Arctic regions. In the summer the fur is gray or bluish-brown, and white on the undersides. In the winter the coat thickens and the new hair that grows in is white. There

is also a rare blue phase, which is a pale blue-gray in the winter and a darker blue-gray in the summer. Short legs and ears cut down on heat loss, and fur on the foot pads provides traction on ice and insulates against cold.

The Arctic Fox's varied diet includes rabbits and hares, rodents, birds, birds' eggs, carrion, fish and berries. Occasionally they may be able to take a young seal or sea lion. They sometimes follow polar bears, eating the remains of their kills. In the summer, the Arctic Fox hunts and eats enormous amounts of food even when it is not hungry. In the winter, surplus food is stored by freezing it in holes dug in the ground or by hiding it under

rocks. When food becomes scarce in the northern parts of its range, it may migrate southward.

Litters that can contain as many as 25 kits, but usually number six, are born in April and June. Cared for by both parents, the young go out on their own around August.

Many Arctic Foxes, particularly the blue phase, are trapped for their pelts. The Arctic Fox is raised commercially for fur on islands off Alaska.

The Arctic Fox is similar to other foxes such as the Gray Fox (*Urocyon cinereoargenteus*) and Red Fox (*Vulpes vulpes*), but has shorter ears and legs as well as distinctive color phases depending on the season.

MAMMALS

FOX, GRAY
(Urocyon cinereoargenteus)

The Gray Fox is found in the eastern United States westward through most of Texas, Oklahoma, the Dakotas, Kansas, Nebraska, New Mexico, Arizona, Colorado, southern Utah and Nevada, western Oregon and most of California.

The Gray Fox is some 1⅛ to 1¼ feet (.3 to .4 m) high at the shoulder, from 2⅝ to 3⅓ feet (.8 to 1.1 m) long, and weighs from 7 to 13 pounds (1.8 to

Above and below: **Juvenile Gray Foxes.**
Opposite page: **Adult Red Fox and kits.**

6 kg). It has grizzled gray on most of the upper parts of its body, reddish fur on the underside and the top of the head. The tail is black fur along the top and the throat has a patch of white.

The Gray Fox does most of its hunting at night; however, it is often seen in the daytime. Its varied diet includes rabbits, rodents and other small mammals and insects. An excellent climbing ability enables it to include birds in its diet. Plant foods include apples, persimmons, grapes, cherries, pokeweed berries and grasses.

In the winter it may hole up in a den. Dens are usually small caves, hollow logs, trees and rock piles. However, if necessary, it will dig a den, either from scratch or by enlarging an abandoned woodchuck burrow.

Mating takes place in February, and litters that usually consist of two to four kits, but may contain as many as seven, are born in March or April. The male sometimes helps to feed the young, but he does not go into the den with them. The young Gray Foxes are ready to hunt on their own when they are four months old.

Related species include the Insular Gray Fox (*Urocyon littoralis*), the Red Fox (*Vulpes vulpes*), and the Kit Fox (*Vulpes macrotis*).

FOX, INSULAR GRAY: see Fox, Gray

FOX, KIT: see Fox, Gray

FOX, RED
(Vulpes vulpes)

The Red Fox is found in Alaska, practically all of Canada except for an area in Alberta and Saskatchewan and in most of the United States, except Florida, the coastal regions of North and South Carolina and Georgia, the western portions of Texas, Kansas, Nebraska and South Dakota, the eastern parts of Montana, Wyoming and Colorado, Arizona, coastal and southern California, eastern and western New Mexico (the range extends into central New Mexico). The Red Fox was originally a European species brought here to provide a hardier breed than the native gray fox for fox hunting. Present populations are a mixture of the Red Fox and the native gray fox which has expanded its range over the past 200 years.

The Red Fox is from 1¼ to 1⅓ feet (.4 to .5 m) high at the shoulder, from 3 to 3¼ feet long (.9 to 3.7 m) long and weighs from 7.5 to 15 pounds (3.4 to 7 kg). The hair is a rusty-red color

above and white on the underside. The long bushy tail has a white tip, and the backs of the ears, lower legs and feet are black.

A shy, nervous animal, the Red Fox hunts mostly at night. It eats whatever it can find or catch, including both animal and plant foods. Prey includes small mammals, such as rabbits and rodents, insects and crayfish. It consumes a wide variety of plant foods including apples, cherries, corn, various berries, acorns and grasses. It caches surplus food in snow in the winter and in leaves or dirt in the summer.

The Red Fox mates from January to March. Shortly after mating, the pair sets up a den, usually in an area of sparse ground cover on a slight rise that provides a view of the surrounding area. The Red Fox den is commonly an enlarged abandoned burrow of a woodchuck or badger. Spare dens are built to which the kits are moved if the vixen perceives a danger. Litters are born from March to May, and may contain as many as 10 kits, but 4 to 8 is the usual number. For the first few days after birth, the male brings food to the maternity den; both share in this duty later. Kits emerge from the den at about age one month, and play at the den entrance. At first, the kits eat partially digested meat regurgitated by the parents, advancing later to live prey brought by the mother. At age four months, the kits can take care of themselves and leave the den. The vixen and the male split up around August, and remain solitary until the next early winter when they find new mates.

Red Foxes do not usually retire to dens in the winter, nor do they migrate. On a cold, windy day, a fox might curl up in the snow, protecting its nose and foot pads with its tail.

Red Foxes are both bred and trapped for their pelts, which are among the most widely used in the fur industry. In many areas, particularly where poultry growing was a big industry, there was a bounty on foxes. Today, most have been abolished.

Red Foxes take few chickens today, mainly because it is impossible to break into a modern poultry farm.

Similar species are the Coyote (*Canis latrans*), Gray Fox (*Urocyon cinereoargenteus*), and the Arctic Fox (*Alopex lagopus*), all of which lack the white tip at the end of the tail.

Left: Adult Mountain Goat.
Above: A Mountain Goat kid.

GLUTTON: see Wolverine

GOAT, MOUNTAIN
(Oreamnos americanus)

The Mountain Goat is found in mountainous regions of northwestern Montana, Idaho and Washington, much of British Columbia, southwestern Alberta and southeastern Alaska. The Mountain Goat lives in rocky mountainous regions above the timber line.

Mountain Goats are from 3 to 3.5 feet (.9 to 1.1 m) high at the shoulder, are from 4 to about 6 feet (1.2 to 1.8 m) long, and weigh from about 100 to 300 pounds (45 to 135 kg). The males tend to be somewhat larger than the females. The Mountain Goat is a compact, chunky, short-legged animal with yellowish-white fur that is long and shaggy in the winter and shorter in the summer. Both sexes have a 'beard' that is about five inches (13 cm) long, and sharply tipped backward-curving black horns. The beard grows from the neck rather than the chin, as it does in true goats. The horns are about a foot (.3 m) long in the male and some 9 inches (23 cm) in the females.

Throughout the year the Mountain Goat moves up and down the mountains with the season, migrating to lower altitudes in the winter. The hooves have a hard outer rim surrounding a rubbery inner surface, providing excellent traction.

Most of the mountain goats' feeding activity is in the morning and evening or on bright moonlit nights. On a warm day, they may bed down during the late morning and afternoon. Their feeding follows a seasonal pattern. In the summer, they eat grasses, sedges, and other warm-weather plants and in the winter, moss, lichens and year-round woody plants.

Mountain Goats form small herds of separate sexes until the mating season which extends from November to January. Males do not usually engage in fights over females. The skull bones and horns are fragile compared to those of other hoofed mountain animals such as bighorn sheep. Butting battles would likely result in injury. They do adopt threatening postures. Males sometimes mark or 'claim' a female by rubbing it with a musky oil that is secreted from a gland at the base of the horns. Kids are born in May and June. The usual number is one, but twins and triplets can occur. The kids stay with the mother until she gives birth again.

Mountain Goats trot with apparent

Above: **A Mountain Goat foraging.**

ease across ledges, rocky outcrops, cliffs and ledges. Although they are remarkably sure-footed and able to move in areas that many predators could not negotiate, they do sometimes fall to their death. Many are killed by avalanches and rock slides. The major predators are mountain lions at lower altitudes and golden eagles in the peaks. Predators usually go after kids, in deference to the sharp horns and hooves of the adults.

While referred to as a goat, the Mountain Goat is not classified as a true goat by biologists. Mountain goats belong to the group called the goat antelopes. They are more closely related to the chamois, a deer-like animal of Europe, than to goats.

GOPHER, NORTHERN POCKET
(Thomomys talpoides)

A western species, the Northern Pocket Gopher is found in southwestern Canada, southward into North Dakota, South Dakota, the Rocky Mountain states as far south as northern Arizona and New Mexico, eastern Washington and Oregon, and northern Nevada.

The Northern Pocket Gopher is from 6 to 9 inches (15 to 23 cm) and weighs from 2¾ to 4¾ ounces (78 to 135 g). Varying in color from brown to yellowish-brown to gray, the fur color often approximates the color of the soil in which it lives. Built for a life of burrowing in the soil, this and other pocket gophers have thick bodies, relatively short, almost naked, tails, short necks and short fur that can lie forward or backward to facilitate movement in burrows. Large, yellow incisor teeth are always exposed in the front of the mouth, even when the mouth is closed. The lips remain closed when the gopher is gnawing or digging to keep dirt and debris out of the mouth. Pocket gophers get their name from large fur-lined external cheek pouches that extend from the cheek to the shoulder. The reversible pouches open on either side of the mouth.

Like all pocket gophers, the Northern Pocket Gopher digs burrows. They dig burrows close to the surface for gathering food, and deeper ones for storing food. The major cutting tools are the long incisors. These large teeth grow throughout the life of the animal; if not, they would soon be worn down to nubs. The forefeet are used like shovels, and the hindfeet push the dirt behind the body.

The Northern Pocket Gopher moves through the surface burrows, foraging for roots, tubers and stems which it cuts and pulls down into the burrow. Able to obtain all its water needs from the food it eats, it does not have to go to the surface to drink. The Northern Pocket Gopher eats some food immediately and stores some in its pouch. From time to time, it goes down to the deeper tunnels and stores plant material in food chambers. The Northern Pocket Gopher empties the pouches by squeezing them forward with its forepaws, turning them inside out and cleaning them and then pulling them back into place.

It is a solitary animal, and a fight usually occurs if two Northern Pocket Gophers meet. While they do not hibernate, they retreat to deeper burrows and sleep during very cold weather. In the spring, males start to seek females, and male-female meetings during mating season are almost the only time when encounters of these gophers do not result in fights. One to two litters a year of one to two young are born. Young gophers start to dig burrows while they are still being cared for by the mother. When they are about two months old they disperse.

Pocket Gophers damage crops, particularly alfalfa and root crops. Their burrow mounds interfere with harvesting, but they also aerate the soil and bring subsoil to the surface.

The Northern Pocket Gopher is similar to most other pocket gophers including the Plains Pocket Gopher (*Geomys bursarius*) and the Western Pocket Gopher (*Thomomys mazama*).

GOPHER, PLAINS POCKET
(Geomys bursarius)

The Plains Pocket Gopher is found in the prairie areas of the midsection of the United States from northeastern Texas northward through Oklahoma, Kansas, Nebraska, southern and eastern South Dakota, eastern North Dakota, western Louisiana, western Arkansas, northeastern Missouri, Iowa, most of Minnesota, western Wisconsin, central Illinois, southeastern Wyoming, northeastern Colorado, south central New Mexico and a small area in northern Indiana.

MAMMALS

Above: A Snowshoe or Varying Hare, in its winter coat.

The Plains Pocket Gopher is from 7¼ to 14 inches (18 to 35 cm) long and weighs from 4 to 12½ ounces (113 to 355 g). Those that live in the northern part of the range are larger than those in the southern parts. The fur color varies from light brown to black depending on the color of the soil. Most of the black gophers are in Illinois.

Like all pocket gophers, the Plains Pocket Gopher digs burrows. The burrows of this pocket gopher are in sandy loam, loam soils, grasslands and sometimes along railroad tracks. In the summer, the burrows are only about an inch from the surface; in the winter, they are dug considerably deeper. Food is gathered in the upper burrows and stored in chambers, usually at lower levels. Food is stored temporarily and transported in the gopher's long cheek pouches or 'pockets' which are emptied by the gopher pushing its forepaws against them.

Mating begins in early spring. After a gestation period of 18 to 19 days, litters of one to eight young are born. The nests are in deeper underground tunnels in the north and may be in large surface mounds in the south. Those that live in the south may have two litters or more a year.

Plains Pocket Gophers can be quite destructive to crops and lawns.

Similar species include the Northern Pocket Gopher (*Thomomys talpoides*) and the Valley Pocket Gopher.

GOPHER, STRIPED:
see Squirrel, Thirteen-lined Ground

GOPHER, VALLEY POCKET:
see Gopher, Plains Pocket

GOPHER, WESTERN POCKET:
see Gopher, Northern Pocket

GROUNDHOG:
see Woodchuck

HARE, PIPING: see Pika

HARE, SNOWSHOE; VARYING HARE (*Lepus americanus*)

The Snowshoe Hare is found in almost all of Alaska except the extreme north and the extreme southeastern areas, southward into almost all of Canada except extreme southern Ontario, the extreme north and the Arctic Ocean Islands, southward to New England except Connecticut and eastern Massachusetts, New York, Pennsylvania and the Appalachian area in the east, centrally to northern areas of Michigan, Wisconsin, Minnesota and North Dakota, and in the west southward from Canada to Washington, most of Oregon, northern Idaho, western Montana, western Wyoming, the central areas of Utah and Colorado, northeastern California and north central Arizona.

One of the smaller hares, the Snowshoe Hare is from 1¼ to 1¾ feet (.4 to .5 m) long and weighs from 2 to 4 pounds (.9 to 1.8 kg). The name of the Snowshoe Hare stems from the large hindfeet that are from 3¾ to 6 inches long (9.5 to 15 cm) and have fur-covered soles. The fairly long ears are from 2½ to 3¼ inches (4.6 to 8 cm) long. In the summer months, the fur is a dark brown and the tail is grayish-brown with a white underside. In most parts of the range the fur turns white in winter. Those in Washington and Oregon stay brown all winter, and a small group in the Adirondack Mountains of New York are black. The changing of fur color is caused by the periodic increase and decrease of the hours of daylight as the seasons change. Although the white fur provides protective coloration in winter snow, there are times when the changing and molting of fur does not synchronize with snowfall and melt. The first snow may come before the Snowshoe Hare's change to white is complete, and the animal will be exposed to predators. The Snowshoe Hare seems to know that it is vulnerable at these times and spends more time hidden in protective cover.

Active mostly at night, the Snowshoe Hare spends the day resting in a protected place such as a hollow log, abandoned woodchuck burrow or a form. It feeds on grasses, berries and green vegetation in the summer and browses on bark and conifer buds in the winter. It is one of the few rabbits and hares that will eat meat if it is available, and it often steals bait from traps. It often takes a dust bath, frequently in the dusting wallows of grouse. If forced to flee from a predator, it will run in a wide circle of several acres in leaps of twelve feet (3.6 m) or more, often leaping sideways to confound its pursuer. If it can, it will take protective cover rather than run. A good swimmer, if necessary it will go into water to escape a predator, although it does not like to get wet.

Two to three litters of one to six young are born a year. Like most hares, the young are capable of running about within hours of birth. The population of Snowshoe Hares appears to peak at nine to ten year intervals and then drop and slowly increase to another peak. The population fluc-

tuations may be related to those of predators, particularly the lynx, whose population peaks and valleys follow the Snowshoe Hare's by a year. Another factor that may contribute to the fluctuation is overcrowding that produces stress which interferes with reproductive activity.

The Snowshoe Hare is a major food of a number of predators, including, the lynx, fox, weasel, mink, wolverine, hawks and owls. An important game animal, it has been known to damage gardens and newly-planted timber conifers.

Similar species include the Arctic (*Lepus arcticus*) and Tundra Hares.

HARE, TUNDRA:
see Hare, Snowshoe

HARE, VARYING:
see Hare, Snowshoe

HARE, WHISTLING: see Pika

JACK RABBIT, BLACK-TAILED
(*Lepus californicus*)

The most abundant and widespread of the jack rabbits, the Black-tailed Jack Rabbit is found in much of the southwestern United States from Texas, northward to Nebraska and westward to Oregon. It is also found in western parts of Arkansas and Missouri, southern South Dakota, southeastern Wyoming, and south central Washington. It is also found in much of Mexico including Baja California.

The Black-tailed Jack Rabbit is from 1½ to 2 feet (.45 to .6 m) long and weighs from 4 to 8 pounds (1.8 to 3.6 kg). The fur on the upper parts of the body is sandy to buff gray and speckled with black. The fur on the underside is white, and the tail has a black stripe on the top that extends forward to the rump. This hare has very large ears that range from 5 to

Above: **The Black-tailed Jack Rabbit is a hare, not a rabbit.**

MAMMALS

6 inches (13 to 15 cm) or more and large hindfeet that are from 4¼ to 5¾ inches (11 to 14.5 cm).

A hare rather than a rabbit, since it bears its young above ground rather than in the underground burrow used by the rabbit, the Black-tailed Jack Rabbit is the most commonly encountered of the large jack rabbits in the barren prairies and meadows of the southwestern United States. Active mainly at night, its summer fare includes a variety of plant foods, particularly alfalfa which seems to be a favorite. In the winter, it eats dried woody vegetation. More gregarious than most hares and rabbits, it feeds in loosely associated groups.

The large ears of the Black-tailed Jack Rabbit help it to pick up sounds from some distance away. It can often be seen standing still, moving its ears to catch sounds. It usually moves by hopping, rather than walking. Hops of five to ten feet (1.5 to 3 m) are a normal pace; if fleeing from a predator, the Black-tailed Jack Rabbit is capable of twenty foot (6 m) leaps and speeds of 45 mph (72 kph) for short bursts.

Below: **A White-tailed Jack Rabbit in the Grasslands National Park, Canada.**

At moderate hopping speeds, every fourth or fifth leap is unusually high, apparently to give it a better view of the surroundings. It 'flashes' the underside of its tail when pursued, apparently to alert other jack rabbits of the danger.

If necessary, it will take to water to avoid a predator, swimming in a dog-paddle with all four feet. Black-tailed Jack Rabbits are preyed on by foxes, coyotes, snakes, owls and hawks.

Mating occurs at any time of year, but is more frequent in warmer weather. One to four litters of one to eight young are born a year. As is the case with all hares, the young are born fully furred and with eyes open. The mother deposits her young in scattered forms to reduce the chances of all being lost to a predator. She stays away by day, but returns at night to nurse. The young can take care of themselves at age one month.

The Black-tailed Jack Rabbit is considered to be a nuisance by cattle ranchers because it eats vegetation that can be used as cattle graze. The meat is considered to be fair.

The White-tailed Jack Rabbit (*Lepus townsendii*) is similar, lacking the black stripe on the tail.

JACK RABBIT, WHITE-TAILED
(*Lepus townsendii*)

The White-tailed Jack Rabbit is found from southern Alberta, Saskatchewan and Manitoba, southward into the United States from Wisconsin westward to central Washington, southward to the Sierra Nevada mountain region and westward to Kansas and Iowa.

The White-tailed Jack Rabbit is from 1⅞ to 2⅜ feet (.6 to .7 m) long and weighs from 5½ to 10 pounds (2.5 to 4.5 kg). The fur is buffy gray above, and the underside, tail, and the black ears have white edges. The large ears are 3¾ to 5 inches (9.5 to 13 cm) long. In most parts of the range, except for the southern areas, the fur turns white or pale gray in the winter.

Active mainly at night, the White-tailed Jack Rabbit feeds on clover, grasses and other green vegetation in the summer and browses on twigs, buds and other dried plant material in the winter.

Rather than walking or running, the White-tailed Jack Rabbit normally hops in twelve to twenty foot leaps (3 to 6 m). It can move at a sustained speed of about 35 mph (56 kph) and can attain short bursts of 45 mph (72 kph). If necessary, it will go into water and swim in a strong dog paddle.

Mating takes place in late April and May. Bucks fight viciously for does, kicking furiously with their hind feet and biting. Litters of one to six young are born after a gestation period of 30 days in loose vegetation rather than prepared nests. Growing rapidly, the young White-tails are independent at age three or four weeks.

The White-tailed Jack Rabbit is considered to be a fine game animal with meat that is more tender than that of other hares.

JAGUAR
(*Felis onca*)

Although the Jaguar's range is thought to extend into the southern parts of Texas, New Mexico and Cali-

Above: **The Jaguar is the biggest and strongest cat found in North America.**

fornia, there has been only one documented sighting of a Jaguar in the United States since the 1940s. However, it seems to be increasing in the parts of its range that extend southward through Mexico, Central America and South America to Brazil and Argentina.

A large cat and the only one in the western hemisphere that roars, the Jaguar is from 5 to 8 feet (1.5-2.1 m) long and weighs from 110 to 300 pounds (50-136 kg). Its fur is yellowish-tawny and spotted with horizontal rows of open black rosettes with one or two spots inside. The spots on the tail, leg, and head are smaller and solid.

A versatile hunter, the Jaguar can take prey on the ground and by pouncing from trees. It has a varied diet that includes rabbits, deer, peccaries, fish, frogs, birds and sea turtle eggs. The Jaguar is unlike most cats in that it seems to like going into water both for food such as fish and other aquatic life and for apparent enjoyment.

The Jaguar is usually solitary except at mating time. Some pairs stay together for life, but most pairings last only a year. Litters of one to four kittens are born in April or May. The male takes some part in bringing food both to the young and to the nursing mother a few days to weeks after the kittens are born.

Worshiped as a god by some pre-Columbian peoples in Mexico and Central America, the Jaguar is a frequent killer of livestock in some areas.

The Mountain Lion (*Felis concolor*) is similar in size, but is unspotted. The Ocelot (*Felis pardalis*) is much smaller.

JAGUARUNDI:
see Mountain Lion

LEMMING, BLACK-FOOTED:
see Lemming, Brown

LEMMING, BROWN; COMMON LEMMING; BLACK-FOOTED LEMMING (Lemmus sibiricus)

The Brown Lemming is found in almost all of Alaska, the Yukon, southward to northern British Columbia and eastward to the Northwest Territories and the southern Arctic Ocean Islands.

The Brown Lemming is from 4¾ to 6¾ inches (12 to 17 cm) long and weighs from 1¾ to 4 ounces (50 to 113 g). The body fur is a rich chestnut-brown above and buff-gray below, and the head fur is gray.

Living on western tundra and alpine meadows, the Brown Lemming feeds on a wide variety of vegetation, including grasses, sedges and leafy plants in the summer, and bark and twigs in the winter. Brown Lemmings build nests in chambers off underground runways and tunnels. They also build spherical nests made of grass on the surface.

The Brown Lemming is related to the Scandinavian Lemming which is well known for its often suicidal mass migrations. The Brown Lemming exhibits a migratory behavior in response to dwindling food supplies, but does not go on mass migration like its Scandinavian cousin. The population of Brown Lemmings reaches peaks every three or four years, usually in the summer. When overcrowding and lack of food become critical, the lemmings become hyperactive and begin to disperse in swarms moving in different directions. Many drown attempting to swim across water barriers, and in their weakened condition, they become easy prey for a number of predators, including grizzly bears, foxes, weasels and owls. When the swarms are reduced to a few individuals, normal reproductive behavior resumes and the cycle begins again. Brown Lemmings mate from June to August, and two or more litters of two to ten young are born each year.

Brown Lemmings are a major food of foxes, and their decline in numbers influences fox population size.

Similar North American species include the Northern Bog Lemming (*Synaptomys borealis*), the Collared Lemming (*Dicrostonyx torquatus*), and Voles.

LEMMING, COLLARED:
see Lemming, Brown

LEMMING, COMMON:
see Lemming, Brown

LEMMING, NORTHERN BOG:
see Lemming, Brown;
Lemming, Southern Bog

**LEMMING, SCANDINAVIAN:
see Lemming, Brown**

**LEMMING, SOUTHERN BOG
(Synaptomys cooperi)**

The only lemming with an extensive range in the continental United States, the Southern Bog Lemming is found in the Maritime Provinces, southern Quebec and Ontario, southward into the United States from New England to Virginia, eastern Kentucky, the Blue Ridge areas of Tennessee and North Carolina, westward to Kansas and northward to Minnesota.

The Southern Bog Lemming is from 4½ to 6 inches (11 to 15 cm) long and weighs from ¾ to 1¾ ounces (21 to 50 g). The fur is brown above and silvery gray below.

It spends much of its time in runways and burrows about 6 inches (15 cm) below the ground. Spherical grass nests are built in underground chambers and on the surface. More likely to be found in meadows and forests than in bogs, the major components of this lemming's diet are clover and grass, supplemented with algae and fungi.

In the southern part of the range, the Southern Bog Lemming breeds throughout the year, while in the northern range, breeding is more likely to be limited to the summer months. Three or more litters of two to six young a year may be produced. The Southern Bog Lemming has wide fluctuations in population. Similar species include Voles and the Northern Bog Lemming (*Synaptomys borealis*).

**LION, MOUNTAIN;
CATAMOUNT; COUGAR;
PUMA
(Felis concolor)**

Although the number of Mountain Lions in North America today is only a fraction of what it was a hundred years ago, it is still the most widely distributed cat on the continent. The Mountain Lion is mainly a western cat with a range that extends from British

Above and below: **A Mountain Lion or Cougar, the most widely found North American cat.**

Columbia and southern Alberta south through the Rocky Mountain states and west coast areas and western Texas. Isolated populations are also found in the eastern United States in Louisiana, Alabama, Tennessee, Arkansas and Florida.

One of the larger cats in the western hemisphere, the Mountain Lion is from 6 to 7 feet (1.8-2.1 m) long and weighs from 70 to 280 pounds (32-128 kg). Its fur is a tawny yellow above and white with a buff overlay below. The long tail is tipped with black,

and the rather small head is tipped with rounded, small ears. Vocalizations include hisses, grunts and a hair-raising mating call that sounds like a woman screaming in pain. They apparently vocalize only when excited, alarmed or agitated.

Except at mating time, Mountain Lions are solitary. They stalk prey in a variety of habitats, including mountains, forested hills, swamps, semi-arid, subtropical and tropical areas. While most cats are mainly nocturnal, the Mountain Lion, although it prefers to hunt at night, is active at any time of day. They are excellent climbers and can jump more than twenty feet and can run as fast as a deer for short distances. It may travel miles in a single night in search of game. Its preferred prey are larger mammals such as deer. It will, however, take whatever is available including beaver, porcupines and other rodents, rabbits, raccoons, birds and insects. Mountain Lions usually take prey by advancing on it slowly to a distance from which they can pounce or run it down. They will also lie in wait for other animals in tree branches and usually leap on the victim's back, biting into the neck.

Females come into heat at any time of the year. Pairs form when a female is in heat, and during the breeding period of about two weeks the pair will hunt and sleep together, mating frequently. After a gestation period of

about 90 days, the female seeks out a protected place such as a cave, thicket or crevice where she gives birth to one to six kittens. Young lions may stay with the adults for as long as two years before they become independent.

Designated as an endangered species, many were killed by ranchers and farmers who considered them a threat to livestock. In some areas there was a bounty on them. Although a Mountain Lion will take a domestic animal, such as a sheep or cow, if it can, such kills seldom result in serious economic loss. On rare occasions, however, a single Mountain Lion might, for unknown reasons, kill an entire herd of sheep in one night. Older lions generally prey on old and diseased deer. Mountain Lions are rarely dangerous to man. Latin-American legend holds that their nature is playful and friendly and that a child may sleep safely out of doors when they are nearby.

The jaguar (*Felis onca*) is similar to the Mountain Lion, but is extremely rare in the United States. The Jaguarundi (*Felis yagouaroundi*) is a similar, but much smaller, species.

LYNX
(*Felis lynx*)

The Lynx is found in deep forested areas in Alaska and most of Canada. Its range also includes areas of Washington, Oregon, Idaho, Montana, Wyoming and Colorado. Small populations exist in extreme northern New England, northern New York, Michigan and Wisconsin.

A stocky cat with short legs, the Lynx is about 2½ to 3½ feet (.8-1.1 m) long and weighs from 10 to 40 pounds (4.5-18 kg). Males are somewhat larger than females. It has a buff or tawny coat sprinkled with black hairs and the underside is a darker cinnamon-brown color. The cheeks have a paler cast than other parts of the body and the ears have long, black tufts. Whitish hairs hanging from the throat form a forked beard. The large feet are covered with fur.

The Lynx hunts mostly at night. A frequently-used hunting tactic is to wait in a tree and pounce on prey passing below. The wide, furred feet enable the Lynx to move swiftly and silently through snow. Its favorite food

Above: **The Lynx is a strong swimmer.**

appears to be the snowshoe hare, one of the few animals that can move through the snow with greater speed than the Lynx. The population of the Lynx and snowshoe hare fluctuate and peak every nine to ten years in a cycle that is a classic ecological study. The Lynx also eats small rodents, birds, an occasional weakened deer or other hoofed mammal, and carrion. It rarely takes a domestic animal. The Lynx is prey for wolves mountain lions, and hunters, who kill them for their fur.

Mating takes place in March and April. Kittens, usually in litters of two, are born between May and July. The kittens remain with the mother until the following spring. A similar species is the Bobcat (*Felis rufus*), which is more tannish and has a longer tail.

MANATEE
(*Trichechus manatus*)

The Manatee is found in shallow coastal waters, bays, rivers and lakes along the Gulf and Atlantic Coast,

Above: **A Manatee and her calf.**

north to North Carolina. The largest populations are found in Florida.

Massive, torpedo-shaped animals, Manatees grow to about 15 feet (4.5 m) in length and to a weight of about 2000 pounds (908 kg). The grayish body appears to be black when wet, and is almost completely without hair. The body tapers from front to back, ending in a broad, horizontally flattened, paddle-shaped tail. The massive head has a deep upper lip cleft, and bears a number of stiff, bristle-like hairs.

Although not herding animals, Manatees tend to move to warm waters in groups in the winter months, where they feed and play. When Manatees meet, they embrace, cavort and may even press their lips together in what could be considered to be a 'kiss.' Mainly nocturnal, the completely vegetarian Manatee browses on aquatic vegetation including grasses and water hyacinths, consuming 60 to 100 pounds of food a day.

Spending all their lives in water, Manatees are accomplished swimmers capable of remaining submerged for 15 minutes or more. They propel themselves through the water by undulating the hind end of the body, using fore flippers and tail primarily for steering and maintaining stability. They rest by hanging downward in the water, some-times using aquatic plants for partial support. Highly vocal, Manatees make a variety of sounds including chirps, squeaks and a high-pitched scream which is both a distress call and a mother's call for her young.

Not too much is known about the breeding habits of the Manatee. Females are believed to have a calf every two or three years. The Manatee delivers the calf underwater, and immediately brings it to the surface on her back, where it remains for about 45 minutes before being slowly reimmersed. The calf stays with the mother, nursing underwater for one to two years.

Requiring water no colder than 46°F (8°C) to survive, the Manatee moves upriver to warmer lakes in the winter. Often, it is attracted to the warm water discharge of power plants, areas which usually do not have enough browse to satisfy the Manatee's enormous daily food need. Human habitation and activity have greatly encroached on the Manatee's habitat. Boat propellers are a major danger and have killed and injured many of them. Laws forbidding power boats or regulating their speed are in effect in some areas where Manatees are prevalent. These animals provide a useful service in consuming great quantities of the water hyacinth, a plant that can clog waterways if not controlled. Manatee meat is considered to be excellent, a circum-stance that almost led to their extinction. Designated as an endangered species, the Manatee is fully protected.

No other North American animal is similar to the Manatee. Similar species are found in India, Africa and South America.

MARMOT: see Woodchuck

MARMOT, MOUNTAIN: see Marmot, Yellow-bellied

MARMOT, YELLOW-BELLIED; MOUNTAIN MARMOT; ROCKCHUCK; YELLOW-FOOTED MARMOT (Marmota flaviventris)

Found mostly in higher elevations up to 11,000 feet (3,350 m) of the northwestern United States, the range of the Yellow-bellied Marmot includes central British Columbia, southward to Idaho, most of Washington and Oregon, most of Nevada, eastern California, western Montana, most of Wyoming, central Utah and north central New Mexico. The range also includes a small area of southwestern South Dakota.

The Yellow-bellied Marmot is from 1½ to 2⅓ feet (.45-.7 m) long and weighs from 5 to 10 pounds (2.2 to 4.5 kg). The fur on the upper parts of the body is yellowish-brown, while that on the underside is yellow. The fur on the neck is light, and seems to separate the body fur from the darker fur on the face.

The Yellow-bellied Marmot feeds on a variety of vegetation such as grasses, herbs and alfalfa found in the rocky slopes, valleys and foothills that comprise its habitat. It constructs a den under a rockpile, crevice or other sheltered place. Not usually venturing very far from its den, the Yellow-bellied Marmot dashes into it when alarmed, and emits several chirps and whistles once it is safely inside.

A true hibernator, the Yellow-bellied Marmot puts on a layer of fat in preparation for the winter period of

Above: A Yellow-bellied Marmot.

inactivity. It remains in hibernation from around August to February or March. In the mountains of New Mexico, it may start hibernating in August. Some may also estivate in the summer.

Litters of three to six young are born from March to April. They emerge from the den when they are about a month old.

The Yellow-bellied Marmot can do serious damage to crops of alfalfa. Abundant in Yellowstone and other National Parks, they are interesting animals to observe.

MARMOT, YELLOW-FOOTED:
see Marmot, Yellow-bellied

MARTEN, PINE MARTEN; AMERICAN SABLE
(Martes americana)

The Marten is found in most of Canada and Alaska, northern New England, northern New York, northern Idaho, western parts of Montana, Wyoming and Colorado, northern Utah, western areas of Washington and Oregon and northern California.

With a low-slung, weasel-like body, the Marten is from 1⅔ to 2¼ feet (.5 to .7 m) long and weighs from 1 to 3½ pounds (.45 to 1.5 kg). The males are slightly larger than the females. The fur is blondish to brown above, and a pale buff on the underside and head.

The short legs are somewhat darker than the rest of the body and there is a distinctive orange-buff patch of fur on the throat.

Spending much of the time in trees, Martens are active in the early morning, late afternoon, and on overcast days. The red squirrel appears to be its favorite food, which it often takes in trees. The Marten's varied diet also includes other rodents, rabbits, birds, eggs, carrion, seeds and honey.

The Marten hunts alone and, in most instances, if two meet they will bare their teeth and snarl at each other until one backs off. Mating takes place in midsummer. Due to delayed implantation, the young are not born until the following April in dens in fallen trees or holes in trees. The usual litter size is two to four young.

Hunted for their fur in the past, the range and number of Martens were drastically reduced. Lumbering reduced their numbers in other areas. In many localities Martens are protected, and the populations are increasing.

Similar species include weasel-like animals such as the Fisher (*Martes pennanti*) and Mink (*Mustela vison*).

MARTEN, PINE: see Marten

MINK
(Mustela vison)

The Mink's range extends through all of Alaska, most of Canada except the extreme northern area and the Arctic Ocean Islands, southward to include most of the continental United States except the southwestern part of the country from western Texas westward to southern New Mexico, Ari-

Below: The Mink is prized for its fur.

zona, most of Utah and Nevada, and southern California.

The Mink is 1.1 to 1.4 feet (.3 to .4 m) long and weighs 1½ to 3 pounds (.7 to 1.3 kg), and the females are 1 to 1.2 feet (.3 to .36 m) long and weigh from 1¼ to 2⅓ pounds (.6 to 1.1 kg). Minks that live in the wild have fur that ranges from brown to black with spots of white on the chin and throat.

The Mink spends much of its time near rivers, lakes, marshes, ponds and other bodies of water, preying mostly on muskrats but also including rabbits, mice, chipmunks, fish, snakes, birds, turtles and an occasional chicken stolen from a poultry farm in its diet. They also den near water, frequently in the abandoned burrow of a muskrat. Minks run down their prey, pouncing on them and biting them in the neck. Kills are usually eaten on the spot, but surplus is often cached in the den. Like many weasel-like animals, they give off a foul-smelling musk from their anal glands. It marks its hunting territory with the musk, and generally fights any other mink that violates it.

Minks mate in January and February, and litters of three to six young are born in the spring. Males fight viciously during the mating season, mate with several females, but eventually stay with one female for the duration of the breeding season.

The lustrous fur of the Mink is among the most valuable in the fur industry. Very few Mink, however, are trapped today compared to the past. Most fur comes from mink raised on ranches where mink are bred to produce a fairly wide range of colors.

Similar species are the Marten (*Martes americana*) and the Black-footed Ferret (*Mustela nigripes*).

MOLE, COMMON:
see Mole, Eastern

MOLE, EASTERN;
COMMON MOLE
(Scalopus aquaticus)

The Eastern Mole is found in southern New England, southern New York, eastern Pennsylvania and all

other states east of the Mississippi River with the exception of most of West Virginia and part of Wisconsin. West of the Mississippi, it is found from Louisiana and most of Texas to Nebraska, Iowa and southern Minnesota.

The Eastern Mole is from 3½ to 8½ inches (9-22 cm) long and weighs from 3 to 5 ounces (85-142 g). It has broad paddle-shaped forefeet that have turned-out palms. The tail is very short and the toes are slightly webbed.

Like all moles, the Eastern Mole is a burrower. Its progress through the soil is aided by a body that is almost without a neck indentation. The velvety fur has no grain, an adaptation that allows it to move backwards with as much facility as it moves forward. A narrow pelvis enables it to change direction quickly in the narrow confines of its tunnel, sometimes by somersaulting.

Most active at dawn or dusk, the Eastern Mole spends practically all the time underground. It burrows or 'swims' through the soil, shoving aside the earth with alternate sweeps of its forefeet and packing the dirt behind it with its hindfeet. Its main food is earthworms, but it also feeds on insect grubs, insects and vegetable matter.

Moles are solitary except at mating time when males go into tunnels other

Opposite: A Star-nosed Mole.
Above: A common or Eastern Mole burrows for earthworms, its favorite food.

than their own to seek a female. The males might even come to the surface in their search for a mate. Mating takes place in March and litters of four to five young are born some six weeks later in a maternal nest chamber lined with dried plant matter. The young are sexually mature at age ten months.

Moles make deep tunnels and sub-surface tunnels. It is the latter which are often marked by ridges and by six to eight foot high (1.8-2.7 m) molehills that mar the appearance of lawns and gardens. Sometimes the burrow damage can be repaired by simply walking over the ridges. Thousands of moles are killed every year with poison and traps, but moles may more than make up for the damage they cause by eating Japanese beetle grubs.

The Eastern Mole is not particularly liked by many homeowners who are concerned about the appearance of their lawns. The burrowing activities of these animals do, indeed, damage lawns and golf courses but they also help to control harmful insects.

Similar species include the Hairy-tailed (*Parascalops breweri*) and Star-nosed Mole (*Candylura cristata*).

MOLE, HARY-TAILED:
see Mole, Eastern; Mole, Star-nosed

MOLE, STAR-NOSED
(Candylura cristata)

The Star-nosed Mole is found in the Allegheny Mountain area, coastal Virginia, and North Carolina, and north to Quebec, Labrador and west to most of Ontario, Michigan, northern Minnesota and northern Wisconsin. It is also found in a small area of coastal Georgia and the extreme southern coast of South Carolina. It occupies a range of habitats, including swamps, wet woods, lawns, and dry areas. In addition to burrowing in the soil, it is a good diver and swimmer. It takes to water in search of food when the ground is frozen too hard for burrowing.

The most outstanding physical feature of this mole is the collection of 22 pink, fleshy projections on its nose, the characteristic that gives the animal its name. The Star-nosed Mole is from 5 to 8 inches (13-20 cm) long and weighs from about 1 to 2¾ ounces (28-78 g). It has black fur and a rather long tail that is covered with fur. The nose projections are apparently used to find its way through the burrow and to find food. The projections are constantly in motion, rapidly tapping the top, bottom and sides of the tunnel as the mole burrows through the soil. The animal's preferred food is earthworms, but it also eats insect grubs and fish.

The Star-nosed Mole is active both day and night. It is more likely to be found in groups than is the common mole. Mating takes place in February or March. In the South, the young are born in March; in the North they are born in May. The average size of the litter is 4 to 5, and they are ready to breed when they are about a year old.

Star-nosed Moles are much less destructive of lawns than the common mole. They do burrow in lawns from time to time, which aerates the soil. They also eat harmful insects.

Similar species include the Eastern Mole (*Scalopus aquaticus*) and Hairy-tailed Mole (*Parascalops breweri*).

Below: The Shrew Mole (*Neurotrichus gibbsii*), uniquely capable of climbing low bushes, is the smallest North American mole.

MAMMALS

MOOSE
(Alces americana)

The largest deer in the world, the Moose is found in most of Canada and Alaska. In the rest of the United States, it is limited to Maine, extreme northern Minnesota, the northern fringe of Michigan's Upper Peninsula, and the continental divide area of the Rocky Mountains in Idaho, Montana, Colorado, Utah and Wyoming.

The Moose is about 6½ to 7 feet (2-2.3 m) high at the shoulder, and from 7 feet to 9 feet (2.1-2.9 m) long. Males weigh from 900 to 1400 pounds (408-635 kg) and females weigh from 700 to 1100 pounds (318-500 kg). The Moose has dark brown hair and grayish brownish fur over its long legs. The shoulders have a high humped appearance and the face has a pendulous, curved muzzle and a large, rather long, dewlap hangs under the chin. The most distinctive characteristic of the male is the large, flattened antlers.

Above and below: **Moose gather to feed in summer in Glacier National Park, Montana.**

The antlers, which have small prongs at the edges, have a usual spread of 4 to 5 feet (1.2 to 1.5 m), but spreads of 6¾ feet (2.05 m) have been observed. The antlers are shed between December and February.

Moose are most active at night, but can be seen at any time of the day. Generally solitary in the summer, they come together in small groups during the winter. However, groups of several individuals gathered near streams and lakes to feed on water plants and willow trees are common summer sights. In addition to water plants, Moose eat twigs, buds, and the bark of balsam, aspen, birch, maple and other trees. The Moose spends a great deal of time in or near water. Some of their favored foods are water plants such as water lilies, and they commonly submerge to escape from swarms of black flies. Wallowing in mud puddles to acquire a protective coating of mud is another method of protection from those flies. Moose are drawn to salt licks and will eat salty earth near their mud wallows.

They can move quietly at speeds up to 35 mph (56 kph). Strong swimmers, they can swim up to two hours at a stretch. During the rutting season, males are quite vocal, frequently emitting a loud roaring bellow that can be heard for some distance. The cow's call is softer, ending in a cough-like sound. Hunters often try to lure the Moose within shooting range by imitating the mating calls of both cow and bull through cupped hands or a horn.

The seasonal migration of Moose consists of moving up and down mountain slopes. The winter herds pack down the snow, which makes it easier for them to move and find food. During the mating season, which runs from about mid-September to late October, a bull will tend to stay with one cow for about a week before going on to another. Mating battles between the bulls are rare; a threatening posture will usually cause one Moose to retreat.

Calves are born in May after a gestation period of about 245 days. Only one calf is usually born, but twins are fairly frequent. Calves are able to walk and swim along with their mothers when they are two weeks old. The young stay with the mother until just before she delivers again.

The Moose is highly prized as a

Above: Moose are usually seen near water.
Below: A juvenile Moose.

game animal, both for its meat and as a trophy. It was almost exterminated by hunters in the eastern United States before it was protected by law. Although they usually avoid contact with humans, they can be dangerous. Cows with a calf are extremely protective. Bulls in rut are unpredictable and will charge almost anything for no apparent reason.

Similar species are elk (*Cervus canadensis*) and other deer. Elk and caribou most closely resemble the Moose in size and structure, but both lack an overhanging snout and flat antlers.

MAMMALS

MOUSE, COTTON
(Peromyscus gossypinus)

The Cotton Mouse is found in the south central United States from eastern Texas to all of Louisiana, southern Arkansas, western Tennessee, southwestern Kentucky, all of Mississippi, Alabama and Florida, southern Georgia, and northward along the Atlantic coast to Maryland.

The Cotton Mouse is from 6¼ to 7¾ inches (16 to 20 cm) long and weighs from ¾ to 1¾ ounces (21 to 50 g).

At home in a variety of habitats, including wooded areas, brushy areas, rocky areas, swamps and beaches, the Cotton Mouse is an excellent tree climber and swimmer. Omnivorous and noctural, it feeds on seeds, nuts, fruits, insects and other invertebrates.

The female has one or more litters of one to seven young a year.

Similar species include the smaller White-footed Mouse (*Peromyscus leucopus*) and Deer Mouse (*Peromyscus maniculatus*), the Oldfield Mouse (*Peromyscus polionotus*) and Golden Mouse (*Ochrotomys nuttalli*).

MOUSE, DEER
(Peromyscus maniculatus)

One of the most widely distributed of the mice, the Deer Mouse is found from central Alaska southeastward to the Yukon, the southwestern Northwest Territories and all of the rest of Canada except northern Quebec and the Arctic Ocean Islands. In the United States it is found in all states west of the Mississippi except Louisiana, eastern and southern Texas and southern Arkansas. It is found in all states east of the Mississippi River except the deep South, southern Tennessee, eastern North Carolina and Virginia, southeastern Pennsylvania, Delaware, eastern Maryland, Connecticut, Rhode Island and eastern Massachusetts.

The Deer Mouse is from 4¾ to 8¾ inches (12-22 cm) long and weighs from ⅜ to 1⅛ ounces (11-32 g). It is

Above: **A Deer Mouse, one of a variable species.**

grayish to reddish brown above and white below.

Occurring in many varieties the deer mouse exists in two main forms – the Prairie and the Woodland. The prairie form is the smaller of the two and is found mostly in the Midwest. The woodland form is found mostly in the North, although there is considerable overlapping of the populations.

This Mouse has a varied diet that includes seeds and nuts, berries and other small fruits, insects, centipedes and ground fungi. The Deer Mouse may store seeds and small nuts in logs and other protected areas. The prairie form commonly nests in cultivated areas, eating wheat and corn seeds and caterpillars.

The Woodland Mouse digs small burrows in the ground and is likely to

Above: **The Woodland Deer Mouse feeds on nuts and fruits.**

build nests in hollow logs.

The mating season varies with the latitude, but generally occurs from February to November. Two to four litters of one to eight young are born a year. Females are ready to breed at age five to six weeks.

Deer Mice, even those that live in cultivated fields, seldom eat enough to cause a discernible loss. They may be of some benefit by eating caterpillars.

Similar species are the White-footed Mouse (*Peromyscus leucopus*) and the Cotton Mouse (*Peromyscus gossypinus*).

MOUSE, FIELD:
see Vole, Meadow

MOUSE, GOLDEN
(Ochrotomys nuttalli)

The Golden Mouse is found throughout the southeastern United States and its range extends from east Texas eastward to Georgia and the northern half of Florida northward to southern Virginia and westward to Kentucky, southern Illinois, southeastern Missouri and Arkansas.

The Golden Mouse is from 6 to 7½ inches (15 to 19 cm) long and weighs from 2¼ to 3¼ ounces (64 to 92 g). One of the more strikingly colored mice in North America, the Golden Mouse has golden-cinnamon fur above and white fur below.

This adaptable mouse is at home in

Above: **A Western Harvest Mouse (*Reithrodontomys megalotis*). Harvest Mice have smaller ears than House Mice.**

hedgerows, swamps, thickets and trees. An excellent climber, the Golden Mouse is more gregarious than most other mice. Groups of them climb high trees and run through the high branches using their tails for balance and support. They feed on acorns and a variety of seeds, including those of greenbrier, wild berry, sumac and poison ivy, insects and other invertebrates.

The Golden Mouse builds spherical nests of leaves, Spanish moss, pine needles and other vegetation. Varying in diameter from 3 to 12 inches (7-30 cm), they are built both on the ground in tangled vegetation and in trees.

Not harmful in any way, the Golden Mouse may be of benefit in controlling poison ivy by consuming its seeds.

MOUSE, HARVEST:
see Mouse, House

MOUSE, HOUSE
(*Mus musculus*)

Originally an Asian species, the House Mouse came to North America with Spanish explorers and *conquistadores* who landed in Florida in the early 1500s. It was also brought to northern North America in English and French ships. Today, the House Mouse is found throughout the continental United States, southern Canada and in Mexico.

The House Mouse is a grayish-brown above and, unlike most other mice, it does not have white fur on its underside. While the fur on the underside is somewhat lighter than that on the upper side, a difference in color is not particularly noticeable. It is from about 2½ to 4 inches (6 to 10 cm) long and weighs from ⅝ to ¾ ounces (18 to 21 g).

The House Mouse has become well adapted to areas of human habitation, including houses and other buildings, and in cultivated fields. Almost com-pletely omnivorous, the House Mouse will eat practically anything, but it seems to be more selective in its food when it lives in cultivated fields and other outdoor areas. It is more likely to eat weed seeds, caterpillars and insects than crop plants in fields, where it can actually be of benefit to farmers. However, when it gets into buildings such as houses, barns and storage houses it becomes very destructive, eating whatever it can get and contaminating what it doesn't eat with urine and droppings. The droppings may contain eggs of parasitic worms that can infest humans. These mice chew on almost anything, damaging furniture, walls, floors and sometimes starting fires when they gnaw on electrical wires. Millions of dollars worth of stored grains are destroyed or contaminated by the House Mouse.

In the wild they build individual nests, but live in groups in a way that is neat and ordered compared to their ways inside houses. The nests have separate areas for eating and waste

MAMMALS

Above: **The Western Harvest Mouse.**

elimination. They groom each other constantly, particularly on the head and back.

Much of the reproductive and other behavior of the House Mouse is governed by fluctuations in population. Breeding throughout the year, the House Mouse has an enormous reproductive potential. The gestation period is only about three weeks and a female can produce several litters a year. If the population becomes too dense in a particular area, many females become sterile. If they are in areas of abundant food, such as a cultivated field, the rate of reproduction increases. When the crop is harvested, the mice disperse, often going into buildings.

In 1926-1927, there was a massive population explosion of the House Mouse in the central valley of California, believed to have been caused by excessive sport killing of snakes and birds of prey, the major predators of the House Mouse. The normally retiring mice swarmed into towns, biting people and crowding into houses and other buildings.

The House Mouse has been selectively bred to produce albino strains, the 'white mice' that are used in research laboratories and sold as pets.

Similar species include the White-footed Mouse (*Peromyscus leucopus*) and the Harvest Mouse.

MOUSE, MEADOW JUMPING (*Zapus hudsonius*)

The range of the Meadow Jumping Mouse extends from southern Alaska and most of British Columbia eastward through the central western provinces, almost all of Manitoba, Ontario, most of Quebec and Labrador. In the continental United States, it is found from New England south to northern Georgia and South Carolina west to eastern Kansas, most of Nebraska, North Dakota, South Dakota, and eastern Montana and Wyoming.

The Meadow Jumping Mouse measures from 7¼ to 10 inches long (10 to 25 cm) with the tail making up as much as 6 inches (15 cm) of the total length. The fur is yellowish on the upper parts of the body with black speckles on the back and white on the underside. The hind feet are large for the size of the body, from 1⅛ to 1⅜ inches (.3 to .35 cm). The incisor teeth are orange and deeply grooved.

Mostly nocturnal, the Meadow Jumping Mouse feeds on grass seeds and other plant food, caterpillars, beetles and other insects. In the spring, insects make up more than half of its diet. In late summer and fall it eats a great deal of the fungus *Endogone*. Unlike many other mice, it does not store food.

Meadow Jumping Mice inhabit brushy country, moist fields, thick woods, stands of touch-me not and other areas that provide cover. When startled in a hiding place, they will initially jump in leaps of three to four feet (.9 to 1.2 m), and then in shorter

Above: A Plains Pocket Mouse.

hops. It then remains motionless in a hiding place. It uses the tail to help maintain balance during the jump.

The Meadow Jumping Mouse hibernates for a long period of time. Starting their hibernation in October, they put on several grams of fat in late September to last them through the hibernation period, since if they do not put on sufficient fat they will not survive hibernation. Hibernation nests are made of shredded grass in protected places such as hollow logs, clumps of grass and underneath logs and boards.

They emerge from their nests in late April or May after six to eight months of hibernation. Mating takes place one to two weeks after the end of hibernation. With a gestation period of 19 days, two litters a year of two to nine young each, in June and August, respectively, are produced.

The meadow mice have no impact on economic activities.

Similar species include other species of jumping mice such as the Woodland Jumping Mouse (*Napaeozapus insignis*).

MOUSE, MERRIAM'S POCKET:
see Mouse, Plains Pocket

MOUSE, OLDFIELD:
see Mouse, Cotton

MOUSE, PLAINS POCKET:
(Perognathus flavescens)

Limited in range to the western United States, the Plains Pocket Mouse is found from southern Minnesota, southeastern North Dakota and most of Iowa, southwestward to Nebraska, most of Kansas, eastern Colorado, western Oklahoma, the Texas panhandle and extreme southeastern New Mexico.

The Plains Pocket Mouse is from 4½ to 5 inches (11.4 to 13 cm) long and weighs from ¼ to ⅜ ounces (7 to 11 g). The soft fur is yellowish-buff sprinkled with black. External cheek patches are adapted for carrying food.

Inhabiting sandy, sparsely vegetated plains, the nocturnal Plains Pocket Mouse forages on seeds and leafy plants, eating some on the spot and storing some. Obtaining its water needs from the seeds it eats, it does not need to drink water. These small rodents dig systems of tunnels with separate chambers for food storage, sleeping and nesting. During the day it plugs up the main entrance to the nest but leaves smaller entrances open.

Several litters a year (more in the southern range) of one to eight young are born in burrow nests. Similar species are the Silky Pocket Mouse (*Perognathus flavus*) and Merriam's Pocket Mouse (*Peromyscus merriami*).

MOUSE, PRAIRIE:
See Mouse, Deer

MOUSE, SILKY POCKET:
see Mouse, Plains Pocket

MOUSE, WHITE:
see Mouse, House

MOUSE, WHITE-FOOTED; WOOD MOUSE
(Peromyscus leucopus)

The range of the White-footed Mouse includes all states east of the Mississippi River except the southeast, and extends west of the Mississippi to the Rocky Mountains.

The White-footed Mouse is from 6 to 8 inches (15 to 20 cm) long and weighs from ⅜ to 1½ ounces (11 to 42 g). The upper body fur of the White-footed Mouse is gray to a dull orange-brown and the underside is white. The feet are covered with white fur, and the rounded ears, at ½ inch

Above: A White-footed Mouse or Wood Mouse.

(14 mm), are rather large for the size of the face. The tail is about half the length of the body.

This omnivorous mouse eats a variety of foods, including seeds, nuts, fruits, insects and larvae. The centers of black cherry pits and jewel weed seeds are particularly favored.

Nests are constructed in almost any concealed location, including birds' nests and abandoned burrows of other animals and nooks and crannies in buildings. In the autumn, caches of nuts and seeds are stored near the nest. Most White-footed Mice are active throughout the year. While they may sleep through particularly cold days, only a few actually hibernate. If a White-footed Mouse becomes alarmed, it will rapidly drum its forefeet.

During the breeding season, the female may exhibit territorial behavior. Mating takes place in March-June and September through November in the North. In the South it is thought to occur throughout the year. As many as four litters of two to six young are born each year.

Similar species include the Deer Mouse (*Peromyscus maniculatus*), Cotton Mouse (*Peromyscus gossypinus*) and Golden Mouse (*Ochrotomys nuttalli*).

MOUSE, WOOD:
see Mouse, White-footed

MOUSE, WOODLAND:
see Mouse, Deer

MOUSE, WOODLAND JUMPING
see Mouse, Meadow Jumping

MUSK OX
(Ovibos moschatus)

Musk Oxen have roamed the North American arctic region in great numbers, but they are now comparatively rare and their range is limited to Alaska, Greenland and some islands of the Arctic Ocean. Overhunting was a major factor in their decline. Although their appearance is that of a true ox, they are more closely related to goats and sheep.

The bull Musk Ox stands 4 to 5 feet (1.2-1.5 m) tall and is usually 7 to 8 feet (2.1-2.4 m) long. Bulls weigh between 700 and 900 pounds (317-707 kg), but as with most of the ruminants, cows are smaller. The Musk Ox has short, stocky legs and a proportionately heavy body which looks even heavier because of the animal's humped shoulders and thick hair. Its shaggy dark-brown coat is curly and matted over the shoulders and straight on the rest of the body, not unlike that of the bison. The bull bears hollow horns joined at the base of the forehead and curving down, outward and up to a sharp point. The Musk Ox takes its name from the pungent odor it emits when excited.

Musk Oxen feed on grass, willows, lichens and other small plants of the tundra. They will fight courageously and powerfully if attacked by wolves or bears, their chief natural enemies. Bulls are especially aggressive during the mating season in September.

The female Musk Ox is ready to breed at the age of two years, and calves are born in late May or early

Above: Musk oxen forage for woody plants in the winter.

June, sometimes relatively few of them to a herd. Observed populations at Spitsbergen in the Arctic Ocean appear to reproduce themselves very slowly.

Efforts to keep and breed Musk Oxen in American zoos have had very limited success due to their nonresistance to indigenous sheep and cattle diseases.

MUSKRAT
(Ondatra zibethicus)

The extensive range of the Muskrat includes all of Canada and northern Alaska except the extreme northern regions, and all of Florida, most of

California, southern Arizona and New Mexico, central Texas, southern Alabama, and Georgia, extreme southeastern North Carolina, and a small area in west central Utah.

A fairly large rodent, the Muskrat is from 1⅓ to 2 feet (.4 to .6 m) or more in length and it weighs from 1 to 4 pounds (.45 to 1.8 kg). The roundish, somewhat vole-shaped body is covered with dense, glossy fur that is a rich, dark brown above and somewhat lighter on the sides, becoming paler on the undersides and almost white on the throat. The tail is from 7 to 12 inches (18 to 30 cm) long, scaled, and is flattened vertically, tapering to a point. The partially webbed hind feet are larger than the forefeet.

This aquatic rodent spends most of its time in and around bodies of fresh water such as rivers, lakes, ponds, canals and fresh, brackish or saltwater marshes. Excellent swimmers, they propel themselves forward and backward with their partially webbed hindfeet, using the vertically flat tail as a rudder. Able to remain submerged for several minutes at a time, the mouths close behind the incisor teeth, allowing them to chew underwater without swallowing water.

Muskrats build houses of aquatic plants, particularly cattails, in marshy areas and along riverbanks. In marshes they may be built on supports such as piles of roots. The houses are as much as 8 feet (2.4 m) in diameter and some 5 feet (1.5 m) high. The houses constructed in marshes usually contain only one nesting chamber, while those made along river banks may have several chambers and many underwater entrances. Those that live along rivers also construct burrows in the river banks. Feeding platforms, made of cut vegetation, are also built in water or on ice. The Muskrat keeps the houses and feeding platforms scrupulously clean, and constantly repairs them and makes additions. Houses usually contain only one individual or family, although two or more nonrelated individuals may occupy the same house more or less amicably except at breeding time when they become aggressive.

The Muskrat's varied diet includes aquatic vegetation, some terrestrial plants, crayfish, frogs, fish and freshwater clams in areas where they can be found. Food is usually dragged to the feeding platforms for consumption.

The mating season begins in September. Female Muskrats can produce one to five litters of one to eleven young a year. At age two weeks, the young muskrats have fur and can swim and dive. They are driven away by the mother when they are a month old.

Muskrats do not hibernate, although they may spend more time in their houses during particularly cold weather. When living conditions are made unfavorable by conditions such as overcrowding, droughts, flooding or food scarcity, they may migrate.

One of the most important fur animals in North America, more than ten million Muskrats are trapped every year. The fur is extremely lustrous, durable and water-resistant, qualities that add to its value in the fur industry. Muskrat meat, called 'marsh rabbit' in some areas, is still consumed, but much less so than in years past. The Muskrat sometimes damages dikes and dams, and occasionally crops.

Similar species include voles, the Nutria (*Myocastor coypus*), and Beaver (*Castor canadensis*).

MYOTIS, CAVE:
see Myotis, Little Brown

MYOTIS, GRAY:
see Myotis, Indiana

MYOTIS, INDIANA; SOCIAL MYOTIS
(Myotis sodalis)

One of the more commonly seen bats in the Midwest, the range of the Indiana Myotis extends from New England eastward through New York,

Below: **Muskrats rest near water.**

Above: The Little Brown Myotis or Little Brown Bat is the most common American bat.

and Pennsylvania to Missouri, northward to the shores of Lakes Michigan and Erie and southward to northern Virginia, Tennessee, Arkansas and the northern parts of Alabama, Mississippi and Georgia.

The Indiana Myotis is from 2¾ to 3⅝ inches (7 to 9 cm) long and weighs about ¼ ounce (7 g). It has a distinctive pinkish brown color.

The name of this bat alludes to the way they sleep or hibernate in neat, tightly packed rows. The bats hang from the roof of a cave or other den in tightly packed clusters, usually one row deep. The noses and lips of the bats appear to be a continuous line of pink in rows of bats formed with almost military precision.

Mating takes place shortly after the hibernating groups form in October. They emerge from hibernation in the spring, and the young are born in June. Some groups break up during the summer months.

Similar species include the Little Brown Myotis (*Myotis lucifugus*), the Mississippi Myotis and the Gray Myotis (*Myotis grisescens*).

MYOTIS, LITTLE BROWN; LITTLE BROWN BAT (*Myotis lucifugus*)

The Little Brown Myotis, one of the most commonly seen bats in the United States, is found in southeastern Alaska, most of Canada except the northern regions, and southward through almost all of the United States except most of Texas, southeastern New Mexico, the southern fringes of Georgia, Alabama, Mississippi and the southern parts of Nevada and California.

The Little Brown Myotis is from 3⅛ to 3¾ inches long (8 to 9 cm) and weighs no more than ⅛ to 1½ ounces (3.5 to 14 g). It is a glossy brown above and somewhat buff in color on the undersides.

In the summer, the Little Brown Bat lives in nursery colonies in secluded parts of buildings. In the winter those that live in the East hibernate in caves and mines. Others migrate hundreds of miles.

The Little Brown Bat leaves its roost at dusk to hunt insects which it captures on the wing, with the aid of a well-developed echolocation sense. Swarms of bats can sometimes be seen at dusk around cave or mine entrances.

The nursery colonies begin to form in April or May. The young, which are born anytime from May to July, are nursed constantly for the first two to three days after birth, except when the mother is out hunting. A Little Brown Bat might carry its offspring in flight if it is disturbed. The young bat holds on

Below: A front view of a Little Brown Bat.

to a teat with its mouth, and tucks its hindlegs under the opposite armpit of its mother. The young bats are independent when they are a month old.

The guano, or droppings, of the Little Brown Bat was once a valuable fertilizer. Although many people have a revulsion toward this often seen bat, the Little Brown Bat is completely harmless and it helps to control insect pests.

Similar species include the Indiana or Social Myotis (*Myotis sodalis*), the Cave Myotis (*Myotis velifer*) and the Mississippi Myotis.

MYOTIS, MISSISSIPPI: see Myotis, Indiana

MYOTIS, SOCIAL: see Myotis, Indiana

NUTRIA; COYPU (*Myocastor coypus*)

The Nutria is a South American rodent that was introduced into the United States in Louisiana in the hope of raising it as a fur-bearing animal. Today, it is found in widely scattered populations, both wild and in captivity. A fairly large wild population of this aquatic rodent exists in marshes in Louisiana and Washington. Much of the Louisiana population is descended from animals that escaped from captivity during floodings from hurricanes in the 1940s.

A large rodent, the Nutria is from about 2¼ to 4½ feet (.7-1.4 m) long, and weighs from 5 to 25 pounds (2.3 to 11.4 kg). The fur is brown in the upper regions, and somewhat lighter below. The hair on the muzzle and chin is whitish, and the long rounded tail is scaled and has only a few hairs.

Seldom venturing far from a stream, pond, marsh, or other body of fresh water, the nocturnal Nutria looks for food both on land and in water. It will eat practically any green plant, terrestrial or aquatic, often dipping its food in water before eating.

If disturbed on land, the Nutria will jump into the water with a loud splash.

Above: Little Brown Bats hibernate in caves.   *Below:* The Indiana or Social Myotis.

MAMMALS

Capable of remaining submerged for several minutes it often floats semi-submerged with only its eyes and nose above the water. It often takes food to feeding platforms where it can feed or rest in relative safety from predators.

The Nutria may dig a burrow with an above-water entrance in a riverbank in which it builds a nest of plant material. Nests may also be built on land or in shallow water or in burrows of other animals or beaver lodges.

Females may produce as many as four litters a year of one to eleven young, but four to six is the usual number. The young are born fully furred and with eyes open. They can swim with the mother when they are 24 hours old.

Nutria fur has value, but most commercial grade pelts are from domestically raised animals. In the wild they compete with muskrat, an important fur animal, for food. The Nutria sometimes raids rice crops, and its burrowing may undermine stream banks

The smaller Muskrat (*Ondatra zibethicus*) and the larger Beaver (*Castor canadensis*) are similar.

OCELOT
(Felis pardalis)

In the United States, the range of the Ocelot is limited to most of Texas, extreme southern Oklahoma, extreme

western Louisiana and a small area of southeastern Arizona. It is far more common in the part of its range that extends southward from Mexico into Paraguay.

A medium-sized cat, the Ocelot is from 3 to 4.5 feet (.9 to 1.4 m) long and weighs from 20 to 40 pounds (10-20 kg). The Ocelot is heavily spotted with black-banded brown spots that tend to form lines. The fur is gray, gold, or tawny.

Hunting in dense chaparral, forested or brushy areas, often in pairs, Ocelots take a variety of prey including small rodents, rabbits, snakes and

Above: The Ocelot is a protected species.

lizards. Good climbing and swimming ability help them to include birds and fish in their diet. The pairs, which communicate with domestic cat-like meows, are probably mates. Kittens (usually two) are born in the autumn.

Like many wild cats, Ocelots have been killed in large numbers in attempts to protect livestock, and for their pelts. The selling of Ocelot kittens for pets also reduced their numbers, since it is usually necessary to kill the mother to capture them. While Ocelot kittens make amusing pets, many were killed as they aged and became unpredictably dangerous. In the United States today, the importation of pelts and the selling of Ocelots for pets is forbidden by law.

Similar species include the Bobcat (*Felis rufus*) and Lynx (*Felis lynx*).

OPOSSUM, VIRGINIA
(Didelphis marsupialis)

One of the better-known behaviors of the opossum has become part of our language. 'Playing possum,' which has come to mean pretending inaction in order to deceive an adversary, alludes to the opossum's rolling over and ap-

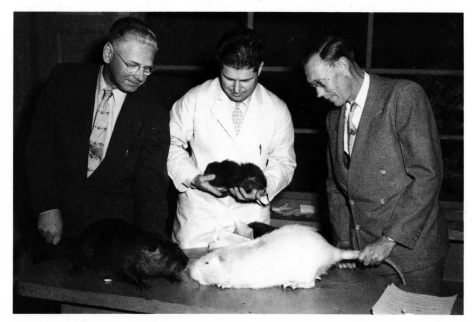

Left: The familiar brown and rare white Nutria.

Right: A juvenile Virginia Opossum.

pearing to be dead when confronted by a predator. This is probably not a voluntary act, but a catatonic involuntary reaction to stress. Often the predator is confused enough to leave the opossum alone. 'Playing possum' is but one of the many adaptations that have helped this rather primitive mammal to survive in today's world. The Opossum, the only marsupial in North America, is not only thriving, but seems to be increasing in some areas of its range.

The Opossum is found throughout the eastern United States except Maine, west to Colorado and Texas, north to Minnesota, and south into Mexico. It is also found in Pacific coastal areas and in some parts of Arizona and New Mexico.

The Opossum is from 25 to 40 inches (80-100 cm) long, and weighs from about 4 to 15 pounds (1.9-6.8 kg). In the north, the Opossum tends to be a grizzled white along its back with white hairs covering black-tipped fur along its belly. In the south they are brownish to blackish. The head, throat and cheeks are whitish, and the black ears have white to pinkish tips. It has short legs with an opposable thumb-like first toe on the hind feet. The Opossum's prehensile tail is long and naked. A good tree climber, it uses both its feet and tail for climbing.

Mostly nocturnal, the Opossum feeds on insects, frogs, birds, eggs, snakes, earthworms and small mammals. It also eats plant food, particularly apples, corn and persimmons when they are in season. It also eats carrion. Many are killed by automobiles when they are attracted to highways by the remains of other animal highway casualties.

Active throughout most of the year, the Opossum does not hibernate. However, it does hole up in a den in extreme winter conditions. The den can be a hollow tree, log, or an abandoned burrow of another animal. Although it generally 'plays possum' when cornered, it will fight or at least threaten in some instances. The

Opossum has 50 teeth, more than any other North American land mammal.

A female Opossum might have as many as three litters a year. When she is ready to deliver, she builds a nest of leaves in the den. After a gestation period of only 12-13 days, the one to fifteen (average about ten) tiny offspring, which have been described as 'living embryos,' are born. A typical litter of newborn Opossums can fit comfortably into a teaspoon. Only about ½ inch (1.3 cm) long, and weighing only some 1/15 of an ounce (2 g), they climb through the mother's hair and enter the brood pouch through a vertical slit. Eleven to 13 milk nipples are inside the pouch. Each of the young takes a nipple in its mouth – which it is then unable to release for some weeks – and continues its development. Sometimes there are not enough nipples for all the young opossums, and those who do not obtain a nipple do not survive. The size of the young increases some 1000 percent in a week. They continue to take milk for about nine weeks, and at age four weeks they stick their heads out of the pouch; by age five weeks they leave the pouch for short periods of time. When they are eight weeks old they can take care of themselves. They are ready to breed at age one year and they live for about seven years.

Opossums are believed to be in-

creasing in number, especially in the north. Although they live mostly in wooded areas, they are commonly seen in suburban backyards, and have even been seen in streets of large cities. They are considered to be a pest by farmers and poultry growers, mainly because of their fondness for eggs. However, they destroy large numbers of mice and insects. The fur is used for ornamental trim, and the meat is considered to be very tasty, but a bit oily.

ORCA: see Whale, Killer

OTTER, RIVER
(*Lutra canadensis*)

The River Otter is found in Alaska, all of Canada except the extreme northern regions, and is unevenly distributed through all of the continental United States except southern Texas, the extreme southern areas of Arizona and New Mexico, eastern Utah, southern California and most of Nevada.

The River Otter's elongated body is from 3 to 4 feet (.9-1.2 m) long and it ranges in weight from 10 to 30 pounds (4.5-13.6 kg). The males are larger than the females. It has dark brown fur that appears to be a shiny black when wet. The underside is a lighter brown, the throat region of many individuals is silvery-gray, and prominent, and there

MAMMALS

Above: **A River Otter (*Lutra canadensis*).**

are white whiskers on the face. It has webbed feet and a long tail that is very thick at the base and gradually tapers to a point.

As its name suggests, the River Otter spends most of its time in and around bodies of fresh water such as rivers, lakes and ponds. It does, however, wander away from the water from time to time. Although its main food is fish, crayfish and other aquatic animals, it also eats small terrestrial mammals such as mice. When catching fish alone, it snaps them up quickly. Often, pairs of Otters work together to drive fish into a blind inlet. Fish are eaten both on land and in the water while the Otter floats on its back. It hunts primarily by day in areas away from human habitation, and it tends to be more nocturnal in populated areas.

Its many adaptations for life in the water include a lithe, streamlined body, webbed feet, a tail that acts like a rudder and ears and nostrils that can be closed off to keep out water. A strong, graceful swimmer, the Otter can move at high speeds both submerged and on the surface, and can remain submerged for minutes at a time. It can swim backwards almost as rapidly as it can swim forward and it also moves well on land.

Very playful animals, Otters slide down mud banks into the water and toboggan on their bellies down snow banks in the winter. They body surf on swift currents, and frolic with each other in the water. Tending to stay together and play in family groups, they often communicate with whistles, chuckles, chirps, grunts and growls.

The Otter builds permanent dens along riverbanks. The dens, built with above water and underwater entrances, contain nests built of grass, sticks, reeds and other plant materials. The Otter may also use beaver lodges for a den.

Otters mate in early spring just after the birth of a litter. Litters of one to four young are born after a gestation period of nine to ten months. Delayed implantation enables the births to take place in the spring rather than the winter months. The male is kept out of the den by the female when the young are small, but takes part in their care when they are about four months old. Young Otters disperse and take care of themselves at age eight months.

In the past, Otters were trapped for their pelts, a practice that reduced their numbers greatly in many areas. In more recent years, pollution of rivers has had an impact on the Otter population. Similar species include the Sea Otter (*Enhydra lutra*) and the Mink (*Mustela vison*).

Below: **Sea Otters are playful animals.**

OTTER, SEA
(*Enhydra lutra*)

The Sea Otter is found in Pacific coastal waters, no more than a mile from shore, in rocky shallows and kelp beds from California to Alaska.

The Sea Otter is from 4 to 5 feet (1.2-1.5 m) long and weighs from 30 to 80 pounds (13.5-36 kg). Males are larger than females. The body fur is dark brown and that of the head and back of the neck is yellowish to grayish, Whiskers grow on the face. All feet are webbed, and the hind feet are constructed like flippers.

The Sea Otter stays in the water most of its life, going ashore only when there are severe storms. An excellent, strong swimmer, the Sea Otter uses its feet, body and tail for propulsion. The Sea Otter dives for much of its food, and can stay submerged for 4 to 5 minutes.

The Sea Otter feeds on fish, abalone, sea urchins, crabs, clams, mussels and other sea life, which it eats while floating on its back. Often, when it comes to the surface with a shelled

Left: Sea Otters are larger than the River Otter and spend more time in the water.
Above: A Pika, Cony or Whistling Hare.

sea animal such as a clam or abalone, it also brings a rock, places the rock on its chest and smashes the shell against it.

Sea Otters appear to be fun-loving creatures, and will often interrupt a meal to play and frolic with other Sea Otters. It also plays with other animals such as seals and sea lions. From time to time, it will stand in the water, shade its eyes with its paws and look out over the sea for predators. It sleeps in the water, wrapping a piece of kelp around its body as a tether. The Sea Otter has no insulating blubber to protect it from cold, depending instead on air trapped in its fur. If the fur is slicked down by oil from a spill, the animal could die from exposure.

Sea Otters mate in the water, and the young are born at sea in May or in June. The female usually has one kit and twins occur rarely. The mother floats on her back while the young nurses, naps and plays on her belly. If alarmed, the mother will tuck the kit under her arm and submerge.

The Sea Otter was hunted extensively for its fur almost to the point of extinction until the trade was stopped by an international treaty in 1911. It made a slow comeback, but was thought to be extinct in California until 1938, when a herd was discovered near Carmel. The population in that area is thought to be about 1000 today, while much larger populations exist off the southern coast of Alaska and in the Aleutian Islands.

Abalone fishermen in California complain that the Sea Otter is depleting the California coastal area of this valuable shell fish. However, ecologists maintain that the Sea Otter does not take enough abalone to be an economic threat to the industry.

The River Otter (*Lutra canadensis*) is similar, but smaller, and it does not have flipper-like rear feet.

PECCARY: see Boar, Wild

PIKA; CONY; WHISTLING HARE; PIPING HARE (*Ochotona princeps*)

The Pika is found in scattered populations from southern British Columbia southward to central Washington and Oregon, northeastern California, and southward from the Montana-Idaho border to central Utah and Colorado, central Nevada and northern Arizona. It lives in steep boulder-covered hillsides, rock slides and other rocky areas in mountains at elevations from 8000 to 13,500 feet (2440 to 4115 m).

The Pika is from 6¼ to 8½ inches (16 to 22 cm) long and weighs from 3½ to 4¼ ounces (9 to 11 g). The fur is brownish over the entire body. Shaped somewhat like a small guinea pig, the Pika has small rounded ears and no visible tail.

Unlike most of the related rabbits and hares, the Pika is a gregarious, very social animal that lives in large, constantly vocalizing colonies. They communicate with chattering sounds and shrill nasal bleats. When it makes a sound, it jerks its body forward.

Active by day, the Pika consumes a wide variety of green plants, eating some as it is found, while some is stored. In the late summer, the Pika scurries back and forth from feeding sites to boulders near its den where it spreads vegetation in 'haystacks' to dry. Some stacks may contain a bushel or more of vegetation. The stacks consist mostly of grasses and sedges, but they also include thistle, sweetgrass, stonecrop and fireweed. Stacks are constantly tended to enhance drying and to protect them from rain. When the vegetation is well dried, it is stored in the Pika's den, which is usually under a rock. Each Pika seems to maintain its own food stack territory.

The Pika remains active throughout the harsh winter of its high altitude habitat. Well protected by its long thick fur, it feeds on lichens and its hoard of dried vegetation.

Two litters a year of two to five young are born in May or June and July or August.

Often seen in national parks in the mountain states, Pikas do not live in built-up areas, and do not eat crop plants or compete with cattle for graze. The Collared Pika (*Ochotona collaris*) is similar and considered the same species by some biologists.

PIKA, COLLARED: see Pika

MAMMALS

PORCUPINE
(Erethizon dorsatus)

The range of the Porcupine includes most of Alaska and Canada and extends southward from Canada into New England, New York, most of Pennsylvania, and small areas of Virginia and West Virginia, from central Canada southward into northern Michigan, Wisconsin and Minnesota, and from western Canada into Washington, Oregon, most of California, the Rocky Mountain states, almost all of Arizona and New Mexico, western portions of North Dakota, South Dakota, Nebraska, and Kansas, southwestern Texas and the north Texas panhandle.

One of the larger rodents, the Porcupine is 2 to 3 feet (.6 to .9 m) long and weighs from 7 to 40 pounds (3.2 to 18 kg). Its name is derived from the French for 'spiny pig.' The large, chunky body has a high-arching back and the legs are short. The body is covered with long hairs in the front, and sharp quills are on the rump and tail. Hair color varies from black or brown in the eastern part of the range to a yellowish color in the West. There are small fleshy knobs on the soles of the feet, which have long curved claws.

Active mainly at night in wooded areas, the strictly vegetarian Porcupine forages alone for a variety of plant foods including leaves, twigs, and leafy green plants such as skunk cabbage and clover. Its major winter food is the tender inner bark (cambium) of trees, which it gets to by chewing off the outer bark. It has a particular liking for salt, which it often satisfies by eating salt spread by road crews and by eating sweat-soaked wooden tool handles. The Porcupine does not hibernate, although in particularly cold weather it may hole up in a burrow or rocky bluff, sometimes with other Porcupines. During the day, it may rest in a number of sheltered places such as burrows, hollow logs or hollow trees, but it is more likely to be at the top of a tree, which it reaches in a slow but steady climb.

Not a fast mover, the Porcupine

Above and opposite: **The Porcupine.**

moves in a slow waddling walk. For protection against enemies it uses its quills, if it cannot take the preferred action of retreat or climbing a tree. A Porcupine has 30,000 quills on its body. Modified hairs, the quills are solid at the base and at the sharp tip and hollow through much of the shaft. The quills are loosely attached to a layer of muscle that lies just beneath the skin. Contrary to a rather venerable myth, a Porcupine cannot throw its quills. However, its method of delivering quills to an enemy is more than effective. The Porcupine erects the quills, lowers its head, and strikes the enemy with its tail, embedding the quills in the enemy's body. When the Porcupine retracts its tail, the loosely attached quills come free from the Porcupine and remain in the enemy. The victim's body heat causes small barbs in the quills to expand, embedding them firmly in its flesh.

How much damage the quills do to the vicim is determined by their location. If they are in the mouth the victim may not be able to eat. They may enter the eyes and blind the victim. In almost all instances, the quill wounds become infected and fester. A few predators, notably the fisher and other weasel-like animals, bobcat, and coyote are adept at flipping the Porcupine over so that the unquilled underside can be attacked. However, even these animals often receive serious, sometimes fatal, quill injuries.

Mating takes place in October and November, at which time the Porcupines become very vocal, emitting groans, squeaks and grunts. One young Porcupine is born in May or

June after a gestation period of seven months, which is rather long for a rodent. The young have quills when they are born. However, since the quills are soft and the young are in placental sacs and are born head first, the mother Porcupine is not injured during the birth.

Porcupines may occasionally kill trees by stripping away the bark, and they sometimes gnaw furniture, structural wood or tool handles, but the Porcupine does not damage crops. The meat is edible, and Indians made jewelry and other decorative items from the quills.

PORPOISE:
see Dolphin, Atlantic Bottle-nosed

PRAIRIE DOG, BLACK-TAILED
(Cynomys ludovicianus)

The range of the Black-tailed Prairie Dog extends southward from extreme southern Alberta and Saskatchewan through eastern Montana to northeastern Texas and includes the eastern portions of Wyoming, Colorado and New Mexico, and the western parts of North Dakota, South Dakota, Nebraska, Kansas and Oklahoma. The range also includes a small area of southeastern Arizona and extreme northern Sonora and Chihuahua in Mexico.

One of the larger ground squirrels, the Black-tailed Prairie Dog is from 1⅛ to 1¼ feet (.3 to .4 m) long and weighs from about 2 to 3 pounds (.9 to 1.4 kg). The fur is a pink-brown above and buff-white below. The thin, almost hairless tail has a black tip, a unique feature, which gives the animal its name.

One of the most gregarious of mammals, the Black-tailed Prairie Dog constructs extensive elaborate networks of tunnels, burrows and underground chambers in its short-grass prairie habitat. Seldom, if ever, going very far from the burrow entrances, the Black-tailed Prairie Dogs live in 'towns' extending over 100 or more

MAMMALS

acres, populated by several thousand individuals. Two hundred years ago, one town in the Texas Panhandle measured 250 miles long and 100 miles wide. Conical mounds of earth around the exits and entrance holes serve to keep out flood water and to provide 'observation posts' at which the animals sit on their haunches and scan the area for danger. 'Towns' are divided into smaller territories called 'wards' which are made up of family groups called 'coteries,' consisting of a male, one to four females and young up to age two years. Ward members recognize each other by touching noses and giving each other a side-wise 'kiss.' This is actually a contact of the incisor teeth for identification purposes. There is also a great deal of mutual grooming.

From the entrance the Prairie Dog digs the burrow extending down to a depth of about four or five feet (1.2-1.5 m) and then constructs lateral tunnels that serve as turn-arounds and listening posts. The entrance shaft is extended to depths of as much as 14 to 15 feet (4.25 to 4.5 m) from which a long horizontal 'hallway' tunnel is built. Several nests and excrement chambers are built along the 'hallway.' The Prairie Dog covers its excrement with dirt and when the chamber is filled, it is closed off and the prairie dog digs a new one. Nesting chambers are lined with dry grass and the entrance and exit mounds, built at different heights, set up ventilating air currents in the burrows. Prairie Dogs cooperate in the building of burrows, and there is considerable interlinking of burrows. Prairie dogs go through recognition rituals when they meet in burrows, sometimes engaging in brief scuffles.

The activity of the Prairie Dog is related to weather conditions. On very hot days, the Prairie Dog may stay in its burrow during the hot midday hours, coming up to forage in the early morning and evening. On cool or overcast days, it may be active throughout the day, but during severe rainstorms it retires to its burrow. The Black-tailed Prairie Dog does not hibernate but may sleep in its burrow during extremely cold weather or severe snowstorms. A layer of fat is deposited to help it through the food-scarce winter months.

The Black-tailed Prairie Dog feeds on various prairie grasses including bluegrass, gramgrass, burro grass and purple needle grass. It also eats grasshoppers and other insects and may occasionally eat meat. The habit of

Below: **A Black-tailed Prairie Dog.**

Right: **A female White-tailed Prairie Dog.**

eating all the vegetation around the entrance mound serves to deprive potential predators of cover.

Black-tailed Prairie Dogs are very vocal. It is believed that the animal has nine separate calls, each of which has its own meaning. Calls include the shrill dog-like bark which gives the animal its name, squirrel-like chirps, chatters and snarls. The alarm call is a chirp, followed by a wheeze, to the accompaniment of a tail flick. Other Prairie Dogs pick it up and then dive into their burrows. The jump-yip is an interesting display consisting of the prairie dog giving a wheezy whistling 'yip' as it jumps up with its head thrown back and forelegs raised. It is thought to be an 'all-clear' signal.

The mating season runs from February to March. After a gestation period of about a month, one litter of four to five young a year is delivered in a nesting chamber. When they are about six weeks old, the young emerge from the burrow with the mother. They leave to take care of themselves at about age ten weeks, and are fully grown at age ten months.

The Prairie Dog population increased sharply after the bison was almost eliminated and larger tracts of western prairie were used for farming and raising cattle. Since Prairie Dogs were formidable competitors of cattle for prairie grasses, cattle raisers embarked on extensive extermination campaigns, primarily with poisons. In arid regions, valuable irrigation water can be lost to drain-off into burrows. However, studies have indicated that balanced populations of Prairie Dogs can actually improve rangeland and many ranchers make efforts to preserve some Prairie Dog towns on their acreage.

The major predators of the Prairie Dog are the coyote, badger, bobcat, fox, eagle, hawk and snake. Prairie Dog meat was once a food staple of the Indians and early settlers. However, it is seldom eaten today. Lewis and Clark sent a 'wild dog of the Prairy' to Thomas Jefferson in 1805 from the

newly acquired Louisiana Purchase.

Similar species include the White-tailed Prairie Dog (*Cynomys leucurus*) and the Rock Squirrel (*Spermophilus variegatus*).

PRAIRIE DOG, GUNNISON'S: see Prairie Dog, White-tailed

PRAIRIE DOG, UTAH: see Prairie Dog, White-tailed

PRAIRIE DOG, WHITE-TAILED (*Cynomys leucurus*)

Restricted to a small range in the western United States, the White-tailed Prairie Dog is found at high elevations in western Wyoming, northwestern Colorado and east central Utah.

A stockily-built squirrel, the White-tailed Prairie Dog is from 1⅛ to 1¼ feet (.3 to .4 m) long and weighs from 1½ to 2½ pounds (.7 to 1.1 kg). The fur is pinkish-brown, sprinkled with white above, and is a somewhat lighter brown below. The nose is yellowish, and there are dark patches above and below the eye. The short tail is tipped with white fur.

Like the related Black-tailed Prairie Dog, this prairie dog digs burrows, but with fewer interconnecting burrows. The White-tail is much less social than

the Black-tail, and engages in very little touching and 'kissing' compared to the Black-tail. Their vocalizations, including alarm calls, are similar to those of the Black-tail.

The White-tailed Prairie Dog feeds on grasses and herbs that grow on the high sagebrush plains that comprise its habitat. White-tailed Prairie Dogs gain weight rapidly over the summer months in preparation for winter. True hibernators, they retire to their burrows around October and emerge in March. During the hibernation period they may awaken at times to feed on roots and in-ground seeds. They may also estivate for short times during the hottest parts of the summer.

Mating begins in March, and litters of four to five are born after a gestation period of about a month. The young hibernate with the parents the first year and disperse on emerging in the spring. Predators include badgers, bobcats, coyotes, snakes and birds of prey, which are particularly feared.

In addition to the Black-tailed Prairie Dog (*Cynomys ludovicianus*), other similar species are Gunnison's Prairie Dog (*Cynomys gunnisoni*) and the Utah Prairie Dog (*Cynomys parvidens*), which are considered to be the same species as the White-tail by some biologists.

PUMA: see Lion, Mountain

MAMMALS

RACCOON
(Procyon lotor)

The Raccoon, one of the most frequently seen mammals in North America, is found in almost all of the United States, southern Canada and northern Mexico. Portions of the Rocky Mountain states are the only areas of the United States not included in the Raccoon's range.

The Raccoon is from 2 to 3⅛ feet (.6 to .9 m) long and weighs from about 10-50 pounds (4.5 to 23 kg). The fur is reddish-brown tinged with black above and is somewhat grayish on the underside. The long, bushy tail has alternating black and brownish-gray rings. A patch of black fur, lined in white, forms a black mask.

The nocturnal Raccoon eats almost anything, including small mammals such as mice and voles, insects, and a wide variety of plant foods. It climbs trees, both to escape from predators and to get birds' eggs and nestlings, acorns and fruit. The Raccoon regularly hunts along stream banks and swims in the stream in pursuit of crayfish, fish, worms, frogs, insect nymphs, turtles and turtle eggs. The Raccoon commonly dips food in water, if near a stream or pond, not to wash it, but to soften it so that it can tear the food, discarding what it regards as unsuitable to eat. The Raccoon does well in areas of human population, regularly knocking over garbage cans and raiding food stores with its almost monkey-like hands. It can readily pry the tops off garbage cans, open cabinet and refrigerator doors and turn on water faucets. It does not hibernate but may sleep in its den during cold spells.

Raccoons are solitary except at breeding time which starts in December in the south and in February in the north. Typically, a male spends about a week denned up with a female and then leaves to find another one. Females build nests of leaves in dens that are usually hollow trees but can be in almost any protected place. Litters, born from April to May, usually number four or five, but can be as large as seven kits. When the kits are very

Left and above: Raccoons prowl by night.

young, the mother Raccoon carries them cat-fashion by the nape of the neck. When they are about four weeks old, they begin to follow the mother. Very protective, Raccoon mothers hiss at intruders, send the young up trees and fight viciously if cornered.

Although a Raccoon may occasionally raid a henhouse or take some corn or other produce from a farmer's field, it is not generally considered to be a serious agricultural pest. 'Coon' hunting is a popular sport, particularly in the South. Dogs are used to trail a Raccoon and drive it into a tree. The meat is considered to be excellent, with a taste somewhat like lamb. In colonial times coonskin caps and sleigh robes were common. Raccoons are still hunted for pelts, although much less so than in the 1920s when coonskin coats were popular. Kits make amusing pets, but become cranky and dangerous as they age.

Similar species include the Coati (*Nasua nasua*) and Ringtail (*Bassariscus astutus*).

RABBIT, BRUSH: see Rabbit, Marsh

RABBIT, COTTONTAIL: see Cottontail

RABBIT, JACK: see Black- or White-tailed Jack Rabbit

RABBIT, EUROPEAN; DOMESTIC RABBIT
(Oryctolagus cuniculus)

The European Rabbit was introduced to North America first on Farallon Islands, California; San Juan Islands, Washington; and Middelm Islands, Alaska. Other groups were released in Pennsylvania, Illinois, Indiana, New Jersey, Maryland and Wisconsin. Today, the European Rabbit is found throughout North America, particularly in rural and suburban areas.

The European Rabbit is from 1½ to 2 feet (.45 to .6 m) long and weighs from 3 to 5¼ pounds (1.3 to 1.6 kg). Variable in color, most European Rabbits are from brownish to grayish with white fur on the underside of the tail. However, some are almost white, while others are black.

Introduced in an effort to provide a game animal larger than the cottontails, the European Rabbit has thrived in North America. Active mostly at night, they are not as successfully hunted by man as are the Cottontails, which can be found in the open at dawn and dusk. They eat a wide variety of plant foods, including garden and crop plants, a circumstance that makes them a serious agricultural pest in many areas.

The burrowing activities of these rabbits also damage agricultural land. The European Rabbit digs extensive networks of burrows called warrens. On one island off the coast of Washington, their burrowing caused pieces of cliffside at the shore to fall into the sea.

The expression 'breed like a rabbit' comes from the enormous reproductive potential of the European Rabbit. Breeding throughout the year, a doe can have six or more litters of four to twelve young annually. The doe delivers the young in a grass-lined nest in a burrow enlarged to serve as a nesting chamber.

The Cottontail Rabbit is a similar but smaller species.

RABBIT, MARSH
(Sylvilagus palustris)

The range of the Marsh Rabbit extends from Florida northward to extreme southern Alabama, southeastern Georgia and the eastern areas of South Carolina, North Carolina and the southeastern tip of Virginia.

The Marsh Rabbit measures from 1.2 to 1.5 feet (.36 to .45 m) long and weighs from 2½ to 3½ pounds (1.1 to 1.6 kg). The fur is dark brown above, white below. The nape of the neck is a dark cinnamon color, and there is reddish-brown fur on the feet. The ears are short compared to those of most other rabbits.

The Marsh Rabbit is somewhat unusual among rabbits in that it readily takes to water when threatened. Once in the water, it floats with only the eyes and nose exposed. With short legs, it cannot move as quickly on land as can most other rabbits.

The food of the Marsh Rabbit in-

Above: **The Marsh Rabbit lives near water.**

cludes a great deal of marsh vegetation such as cane, rushes and other grasses of its bottomland, swamp and coastal waterways habitat. It also eats bulbs, leaves and twigs. Rushes are also used to provide protective cover.

The mating season begins in February, and several litters of four to five young are born every year in large, covered nests made of grass, leaves and rushes. The Marsh Rabbit, a widely hunted game animal, seldom invades human food-growing areas.

Similar species are the Swamp Rabbit (*Sylvilagus aquaticus*) and the Brush Rabbit (*Sylvilagus bachmani*).

RABBIT, SAN JUAN:
see Rabbit, European

RABBIT, SWAMP:
see Rabbit, Marsh

RAT, BLACK; SHIP RAT; ROOF RAT; WHARF RAT
(Rattus rattus)

Originating in central Asia, the Black Rat spread through Europe long before Columbus made his first voyage. It was well established in Europe by the time Europeans began to explore and colonize the New World. The Black Rat was first introduced into the western hemisphere in Central and South America by Spanish explorers, and the first Black Rats in North America came ashore from the ships that brought English colonists to

Jamestown in 1607. Today, the Black Rat is found all along the Atlantic, Gulf and Pacific Coasts. Inland, it is most abundant in the South and the southwestern United States. Its range was once much more extensive, but it has been pushed out of much of its former range by the more aggressive Norway Rat.

The Black Rat is from 1 to 1½ feet (.3 to .45 m) long and weighs from 4 to 12 ounces (113 to 342 g). The fur is brown to black above and a light gray below. The scantily-haired, scaly tail is longer than half the total body length.

Found primarily in and around seaports and city buildings, the Black Rat is also found in fields and woods, but much less so than the Norway Rat. The Black Rat is totally omnivorous, but has a particular liking for grain. Contaminating what it does not eat with its droppings, it is a particular problem around docks and warehouses. Although it is not as aggressive as the Norway Rat, it is much more agile. It climbs the sides of buildings and crosses from one building to another on telephone and electric wires. It is commonly found in the roofs of buildings in the South, and it also nests in trees. Breeding thoughout the year, a female can produce several litters of two to eight young.

The Black Rat carries a number of diseases including bubonic plague and typhus. Eating rat-contaminated food can possibly result in a parasitic worm infestation. Its chief predators are snakes, owls, domestic dogs and cats.

RAT, BROWN: see Rat, Norway

RAT, CHISEL-TOOTHED KANGAROO:
see Rat, Ord's Kangaroo

RAT, COUE'S RICE:
see Rat, Marsh Rice

RAT, GIANT KANGAROO
(Dipodomys ingens)

Limited in range to the western San Joaquin Valley of California, this

Kangaroo Rat is distinguished by being the largest of the kangaroo rats. The Giant Kangaroo Rat is from 1 to 1⅛ feet (.3 to .35 m) in length, of which some 6 to 7¾ inches (15 to 20 cm) is tail. It weighs from 4½ to 6¼ ounces (127 to 177 gm).

Like most kangaroo rats, the Giant Kangaroo Rat eats seeds, but it also eats the green parts of plants. Seeds are eaten on the spot and carried in cheek pouches to burrows for storage. When disturbed, the Giant Kangaroo Rat can make leaps of nine feet (2.7 m) or more. The feet are also used to drum the ground as a danger signal. Tapping a burrow sometimes induces the kangaroo rats inside to drum in response. Breeding takes place from January to May. One or two litters of three to five young are born each year.

Similar species include the Heerman (*Dipodomys heermanni*), Pacific and Santa Cruz Kangaroo Rats.

RAT, HEERMAN'S KANGAROO: see Rat, Giant Kangaroo

RAT, KANGAROO: see Rat, Giant Kangaroo

RAT: KEY RICE see Rat, Marsh Rice

RAT, MARSH RICE; RICE RAT (*Oryzomys palustris*)

The only rice rat with an extensive range in the United States, the Marsh Rice Rat is found primarily in the southeastern United States from eastern Texas and Oklahoma, eastward to the Carolina coast, including Florida, northward along the Atlantic coast to eastern Maryland, Delaware, southeastern Pennsylvania and southern New Jersey. It is also found in Kentucky, southern Indiana and Illinois, southeastern Missouri and a small area of southwestern Missouri.

The Marsh Rice Rat is adapted for life around marshes and grassy or sedge-filled areas. A strong swimmer, both on the surface and under water, this rice rat has a varied diet including tender parts of aquatic plants, crabs, snails, insects, berries and other fruits. It also eats the underground fungus *Endogone*.

Mainly nocturnal, the Marsh Rice Rat constructs runways on land and builds nests in debris above the high water mark. Breeding throughout the year, a female has three to four litters of one to seven young annually. Females are sexually mature at about age four weeks.

Above: **The Norway Rat invades homes.**

Although it may occasionally cause minor damage in a rice field, it seldom causes serious losses.

The Key Rice Rat is similar, so much so that many biologists do not consider it a separate species. Coue's Rice Rat (*Oryzomys couesi*), which is found in the United States in only two counties of Texas, is also similar.

RAT, MOUNTAIN PACK see Woodrat, Bushy-tailed

RAT, NORWAY; BROWN RAT; WATER RAT; SEWER RAT (*Rattus norvegicus*)

Originating in central Asia, the Norway Rat spread across Europe in the 16th, 17th and 18th centuries. It is believed to have been introduced into North America in grain shipments sent for the Hessian troops hired by the British to fight in the American Revolution. Reintroduced again and again on ships from all parts of Europe, the Norway Rat is found today in all parts of the United States and in southern Canada. The name Norway Rat is a misnomer, stemming from the once-held belief that the animal was intro-

MAMMALS

***Above:** An Ord's Kangaroo Rat.*

duced into North America from a Norwegian ship.

The Norway Rat is from 1 to 1½ feet (.3 to .45 m) long and weighs from 6 to 17 ounces (170-482 g). Often heard reports of Norway Rats as large as house cats or medium-sized dogs are exaggerations. The fur is brownish-gray above and gray below. The long snaked tail is scaly, and comprises somewhat less than half the total body length.

The totally omnivorous Norway Rat will eat practically anything, including material generally not thought of as food. It seems to have a particular liking for stored grains, which it will consume in great quantities if it can get into storage areas, and it contaminates what it does not eat with its droppings. It is also fond of chicken eggs and young chicks. In houses and buildings they gnaw wallboard, woods, plaster, furniture and electric wires, sometimes causing fires.

The Norway Rat digs interconnecting tunnels, usually about 1½ feet (.45 m) deep and 6 feet (1.8 m) long, with chambers for nesting and feeding. It digs with teeth and forefeet. Able to adapt to a variety of habitats, the Nor-

way Rat lives in fields, farms, all kinds of buildings and on ships. They can gnaw through brick walls to get into a building.

Breeding at any time of the year, the Norway Rat has an enormous reproductive potential. Females, which sometimes mate again only hours after delivering a litter, are capable of bearing as many as 12 litters a year. Many factors, however, such as food supply, usually keep the total far below that number. However, the usual production of 5 litters of seven to ten young still exceeds the rate of most other rodents. The young, born blind and without fur, open their eyes at two weeks and are weaned at three weeks. Females are ready to breed at age three months.

Mass migrations may occur if local food supplies become unusually scarce. These mass migrations are possibly the basis of the Pied Piper legend.

In addition to destroying food and property, these rats occasionally bite and severely injure sleeping people, particularly children and infants. They also carry diseases such as typhus, bubonic plague and tularemia. Albino strains of Norway Rats are widely used as laboratory animals. The Black Rat (*Rattus rattus*) is a similar species.

RAT, ORD'S KANGAROO
(*Dipodomys ordii*)

The range of Ord's Kangaroo Rat extends from northern Mexico to the southern tip of Texas, northwestern Texas, northward through the Rocky Mountain states including all of New Mexico, Colorado and Utah, most of Nevada, Arizona and Wyoming, eastern Montana, southern Idaho, eastern Oregon, a small area of south central Washington and the northeastern fringe of California. It is also found in the western parts of the tier of states from Oklahoma to South Dakota, and in southwestern Saskatchewan and southeastern Alberta.

More closely related to ground squirrels and pocket gophers than to rats, Ord's Kangaroo Rat is from 8⅛ to 11 inches (21 to 28 cm) long, of which 3¾ to 6⅜ inches (9.5 to 16 cm) is the tail. Its weight ranges from 1¾ to 3⅝ ounces (50 to 102 g). The fur is buff above and white below, and there may be white spots at the base of the ears. The hind feet are large in comparison to the rest of the body.

Found in arid, sandy areas, Ord's Kangaroo Rat forages on the ground for seeds, mostly those of sunflower, mesquite, tumbleweed, Russian thistle and sandbur. A nocturnal burrowing animal, it is active throughout the year in Texas. In the northern parts of the range it spends most of the winter months in its burrows, subsisting on stored food. The burrows contain chambers for nesting, food storage and waste disposal.

Normally, Ord's Kangaroo Rat moves about on the ground in a rapid scurry. However, if it is disturbed, it can make hops of from 6 to 8 feet (1.8 to 2.4 m). The large, spring-like hind feet, which give the animal its name, are also used to kick sand in the face of a predator and to thump the ground as a danger signal to other kangaroo rats. During the leap, the tail helps to maintain balance.

This and other kangaroo rats eat some food on the spot and carry some in their cheek pouches for transport to the burrow for storage. They obtain their water needs from the seeds they eat, an adaptation for their dry habitat. Ord's Kangaroo Rat also takes advantage of its environment by taking sandbaths to keep its fur from getting matted.

One or two litters of two to five young are born a year. Litters are usually born in May and June.

Ord's Kangaroo Rat has little if any impact on the economic activity of man. They are major food for carnivores, snakes and birds of prey including badgers, skunks, foxes, weasels, coyotes, rattlesnakes and owls.

Similar species include other kangaroo rats, particularly the Panamint Kangaroo Rat (*Dipodomys panamintinus*) and the Chisel-toothed Kangaroo Rat (*Dipodomys microps*).

RAT: PACIFIC KANGAROO: see Rat, Giant Kangaroo

RAT, PACK: see Woodrat, Bushy-tailed

RAT, PANAMINT KANGAROO: see Rat, Ord's Kangaroo

RAT, RICE: see Rat, Marsh Rice

RAT, ROOF: see Rat, Black

RAT, SANTA CRUZ KANGAROO: see Rat, Giant Kangaroo

RAT, SEWER: see Rat, Norway

RAT, SHIP: see Rat, Black

RAT, WATER: see Rat, Norway

RAT, WHARF: see Rat, Black

RINGTAIL; MINER'S CAT; CIVET CAT; CACOMISTLE (*Bassariscus astutus*)

The range of the Ringtail extends

Above: **A Ringtail, Miner's or Civet Cat.**

northward from Mexico into Arizona, New Mexico, western Oklahoma, southern Kansas, most of Texas, western Colorado, the southern two-thirds of Utah, southern Nevada, all of California except the central valley, and southwestern Oregon.

The Ringtail resembles the raccoon, to which it is related. It is some 2 to 2⅔ feet (.6 to .8 m) long and weighs from 2 to 2½ pounds (.9 to 1.1 kg). It has fur that is yellowish-gray above and whitish below. Its body is low and catlike, and the small face is topped by rather large ears. The very long, bushy tail has 14 to 16 black and white bands; the white bands completely encircle the tail while the black bands do not, except for the one at the tip of the tail.

The nocturnal Ringtail is omnivorous, feeding on insects, spiders and other invertebrates, small mammals such as rabbits and rodents, lizards, frogs, fruits and nuts. The Ringtail typically waits in ambush for prey such as small mammals, pouncing on it, forcing it down with a forepaw and killing it with a bite on the neck. The name 'Miner's Cat' stems from the practice of placing Ringtails in mines to control rats and other rodents.

If attacked or threatened, the Ringtail emits a foul-smelling fluid from its anal glands, a behavior that added 'civet cat' to its many names. Civet, a musky substance emitted by an African carnivore, is used as a perfume base. However, attempts to put the

secretions of the Ringtail to a similar use have not been successful.

Mating is believed to take place in early April in the United States part of the Ringtail's range. Litters of two to four kits are born in May and early June. When the young are three to four weeks old, the males start to help in their feeding. Young Ringtails are ready to hunt independently at about age four months.

Not hunted for either food or fur, its chief predators are the bobcat and the great horned owl.

Similar species are the Coati (*Nasua nasua*) and Raccoon (*Procyon lotor*).

ROCKCHUCK see Marmot, Yellow-bellied; Woodchuck

SABLE, AMERICAN: see Marten

SEA LION, CALIFORNIA (*Zalophus californianus*)

The range of the California Sea Lion extends from Vancouver, along the Pacific Coast southward to Baja California, and into the Gulf of California.

The males, much larger than the females, are from 6½ to 8¼ feet (2 to 2.5 m) long and weigh from 400 to 650 pounds (182 to 295 kg). The females

MAMMALS

Above: California Sea Lions at rest.

are from 5 to 6½ feet (1.5 to 2 m) in length and weigh from 100 to 225 pounds (45 to 102 kg). The fur varies from buff to brown, but appears to be a shiny black when the animal is wet. The males have a distinctive high forehead.

The California Sea Lion is the trained seal of circuses, aquariums and animal shows. As playful in the wild as it is in captivity, the California Sea Lion frequently throws objects, catching them on its nose, and cavorts with other sea lions. Highly gregarious, these sea lions hunt and play in separate male and female groups, coming together only in the breeding season.

The California Sea Lion spends much of the day sleeping on shore. It hunts at night, and its diet includes octopus and abalone, in addition to the fish which are its main food. The fastest of the sea-going carnivores, it can swim gracefully at speeds in excess of 25 mph (40 kph). Capable of remaining submerged for as long as 20 minutes, it locates prey and finds it with a 'sonar' method of emitting sounds and interpreting the echoes. Like other eared seals, the California Sea Lion can move fairly well on land using its folded flippers as 'feet.'

The breeding season begins in June, when males and females come ashore on California's Channel Islands, and ends in July. The males establish terri-tories which they defend to the accompaniment of loud, honk-like barks. Unlike the Northern Fur Seal, the male California Sea Lion defends territories, not harems, and mates with any female in his territory. A male does not mate until it is large enough to defend a territory.

Females give birth to single, blue-eyed pups weighing about 36 pounds (16 kg) at birth, and mate shortly afterwards. Females vocalize with an undulating wail that is a call for the pup, and with growls and barks of annoyance directed at other females. Pups recognize the mother's vocalizations and respond with lamb-like bleats. The pup stays with the mother for about a year, nursing, eating fish and learning to swim.

Once hunted for its blubber and meat, which was used for dog food, the California Sea Lion is today fully protected by law. Many are taken by killer whales and several species of sharks.

Similar species include the Northern Fur Seal (*Callorhinus ursinus*) and the Northern Sea Lion (*Eumetopias jubatus*).

SEA LION, NORTHERN: see Sea Lion, California; Seal, Northern Fur

SEA WOLF: see Whale, Killer

SEAL, ALASKA FUR: see Seal, Northern Fur

SEAL, GRAY; see Seal, Northern Elephant

SEAL, HAIR: see Seal, Harbor

SEAL, HARBOR; LEOPARD SEAL; HAIR SEAL (Phoca vitulina)

The Harbor Seal is found on the Arctic Ocean coast, south into Hudson Bay and in the freshwater Seal Lakes, south along the Atlantic Coast to the Carolinas, along the entire coast of Alaska, the Pacific coast of Canada, and south along the coast into California.

Unlike most other seals and sea lions, male and female Harbor Seals are about the same size. The Harbor Seal ranges in length from about 4 to 5½ feet (1.2 to 1.7 m) and weighs from about 250 to 300 pounds (113-136 kg). Harbor Seals are quite variable in color, ranging from cream to dark brown above and a creamy white with spots below. However, yellowish-gray or brownish fur above with spots is the most prevalent coloration.

The Harbor Seal is an example of an earless seal. Often called 'true seals,' these seals have stiff fur as adults and no external ears. While the hind flippers are highly efficient swimming tools, they are permanently turned backward and cannot be folded for movement on land. Consequently, the Harbor Seal and other earless seals cannot move well on land, and are propelled only by muscular contraction of the entire body. Whenever possible, they take advantage of inclines for rolling or sliding down the ice.

Highly gregarious, Harbor Seals can often be seen in groups of 500 or more individuals resting on beaches and rocky shores. Very strong, graceful swimmers, they can dive as deep as 300 feet (97 m) and stay underwater for almost 30 minutes.

The Harbor Seal's diet is mostly fish such as herring, cod, mackerel, flounder and salmon, supplemented by squid, clam, octopus, shrimp, crabs and crayfish. The feeding activity is often keyed to the tide. As the tide comes in, they go up the river with the tide, going ashore to sleep when the tide is low and taking to the river again at the next high tide. In the spring they may follow the movements of fish several hundred miles upstream, and return to the sea in the fall.

Pups are born from March to August. Although males usually mate with several females, they do not form harems or maintain mating territories as do many other seals and sea lions. Pups usually enter the water for the first time when they are a few days old.

Harbor Seals sometimes tear up the nets of commercial fishermen to get at the fish inside. The flesh of the Harbor Seal is used as food in some parts of its range, but the fur has little, if any, commercial value.

The Spotted Seal (*Phoca largha*) is a closely related species and the Ribbon Seal (*Phoca fasciata*) is similar.

SEAL, HOODED:
see Seal, Northern Elephant

SEAL, LEOPARD:
see Seal, Harbor

SEAL, NORTHERN ELEPHANT
(Mirounga angustirostris)

The Northern Elephant Seal is found along the Pacific coast from the Gulf of Alaska to Baja California.

The largest of the sea-going carnivores, the female Northern Elephant Seal is from 9¾ to 11½ feet (2.9 to 3.5 m) long and weighs up to about 2000 pounds (908 kg) and the male is from 14¾ to 21⅓ feet (4.5 to 6.5 m) long and weighs up to 7800 pounds (35 kg). The fur is brown or gray in the upper regions and a bit lighter below. The male has a large snout that droops over the muzzle and is inflated during the mating season. Like all earless or true seals, the flippers of the Northern Elephant Seal are not well adapted for movement on land.

From August to December, the Northern Elephant Seal stays out at sea, feeding on fish such as ratfish, hagfish, small sharks and other deepwater

Above: **Harbor, Leopard or Hair Seal.**

marine life such as squid. A strong swimmer, the Northern Elephant Seal can dive to depths of 200 feet (61 m) and remain submerged for as long as 40 minutes.

Starting in December, the seals start to return to islands off the California coast for breeding. Bulls arrive first, and immediately begin to fight for harem territories. The fighting starts when the bulls threaten each other by inflating their huge snouts and bellowing and roaring at each other. The inflated snouts act as resonating chambers which make their vocalizations audible for more than a mile. Northern Elephant Seals fight by slamming into each other with their massive necks and biting whenever they can. The ter-

ritorial disputes are generally settled by the time the females arrive, and the bulls concentrate on building their harems.

Females begin to come ashore in late December and early January. Soon after arrival, the female delivers a single, black-furred, 65 pound (29.5 kg) pup. After a month of nursing on the mother's rich, 54.5% fat-content milk, the pup grows to a weight of about 400 pounds (182 kg). When the pup is weaned, the mother abandons it and again becomes available for mating. Mating takes place from January to March, and during that time many pups are crushed by bulls lumbering over them to get at females. During the mating seasons, the bulls do not eat, but females continue to take feeding swims. Females

Above: **A sleeping male Northern Elephant Seal, the largest North American seal.**

begin to molt in late May, and bulls begin their molt in July and August. Shortly after the molt is complete, the seals return to the sea. The weaned pups live on accumulated fat and teach themselves how to swim until May when they, too, take to the sea.

Widely hunted in the 19th century by whalers for their blubber, the Northern Elephant Seal was believed to be extinct or near extinction when a small colony was found on Guadalupe Island off Baja California in 1892. The animals were placed under protection, and today they number about 65,000. The increase in population has forced some elephant seals off the islands onto mainland beaches. There is a rookery near Santa Cruz, California.

Similar species include the Hooded Seal (*Cystophora cristata*) and the Gray Seal (*Halichoerus grypus*).

SEAL, NORTHERN FUR; ALASKA FUR SEAL (*Callorhinus ursinus*)

Like most seals and sea lions, the Northern Fur Seal spends most of its life at sea, coming ashore to mate, give birth and rest. They come ashore at points on the Pacific Coast and Arctic Ocean coast ranging from Point Barrow, Alaska southward to San Diego, California, depending on the season.

As is the case with most of these ocean-going carnivores, the bulls are considerably larger than the females. Bulls are from 6¼ to 7¼ feet (1.9 to 2.2 m) long and weigh from about 235 to 600 pounds (147 to 272 kg). The fur of the bull is black on the upper parts of the body, except for a grayish cast over the massive shoulders, and red-

Above: **A female Northern Elephant Seal and her young.**

dish below. Bulls have enlarged, bulging necks. Females are from 3⅔ to 4⅔ feet (1.1 to 1.4 m) long and weigh from about 85 to 120 pounds (38 to 54 kg). The fur of the females is gray over all regions of the upper body, and somewhat reddish below.

Belonging to the eared seal group of ocean-going carnivores, the Northern Fur Seal has small but observable external ears. Although highly adapted to life in the oceans, the eared seals can move on land with greater facility than can the earless seals. The hind flippers rotate under the body, and the fore flippers turn out at the wrist to provide somewhat crude but serviceable 'feet' with which they can walk or move more rapidly in a lumpy gallop. When swimming, the fore limbs are used for propulsion and the rear flippers are held together to work as a rudder.

The Northern Fur Seal probably spends more time and travels greater distances in the ocean than do other seals and sea lions. Returning to land only for breeding, the Northern Fur Seal spends most of the year far out at sea, hunting for its major foods of fish and sea birds. It rests in the ocean by floating on its back, bending the hind flippers over the belly and holding them there with a fore flipper. The seal does most of its feeding at night when fish come closer to the surface. It is capable of diving as deep as 450 feet (137 m) and staying submerged for several minutes at a time. It swallows smaller fish while submerged, and comes to the surface to bite larger prey into smaller pieces.

Northern Fur Seals begin to arrive in the spring on land at rookeries to give birth and mate. The largest and most extensive rookery is on the Pribilof Islands in the Bering Sea. Other rookeries are on San Miguel Island off the California coast and two small islands – Commander and Robben – near the USSR. In most years, more than a million seals gather in the 30 square mile Pribilof Islands. The first arrivals are older bulls who come ashore around May and early June. They immediately fight viciously to establish reign over the best spots, those near the water where the females come ashore. The females start to arrive around the middle of June and continue to come in until around mid-July. As the females arrive, the bulls gather them into harems that can number from a few, to as many as 100 or so, depending on the size of the bull and his ability to outbluff and outfight other bulls. In general, the larger the bull, the larger the harem is likely to be. During the two-month breeding season, the bulls do not eat. They spend all their time mating and defending their harems.

The females give birth to a single, glossy black, 10 to 12 pound (4.5 to 5.4 kg) pup, the result of the previous year's mating, a few days after coming ashore. Females mate three days to a week after giving birth, usually with

the bull who reigns over the territory in which she gave birth, unless she has been 'stolen' by another bull in the meantime. Implantation of the fertilized egg is delayed so that birth will coincide with the next year's breeding season.

The female remains with the pup for about a week, and then goes out to feed, returning at intervals to nurse the pup with her very rich milk that is about 50% fat. Cow's milk, in comparison, is about 3.5% fat. Pups stay with the mother and those that survive the crowded, hectic conditions of the rookery, leave when the seals depart for winter feeding areas.

The final phase of the breeding season occurs in August, when females who have not yet bred come ashore. These females usually mate with bulls too young and small to maintain harems and territories. The seals begin to leave the rookery, shortly after the arrival of the young females, to migrate to winter feeding areas. The bulls, thin, weak and battle-scarred, leave in August to spend the winter south of the Aleutian Islands, the Gulf of Alaska or areas off the Pacific Coast of the USSR.

Females and juveniles remain on the rookery until November, when they

Above: **The Elephant Seal pup lacks the distinctive snout that is particularly characteristic of the adult male.**

start to make their separate ways to winter areas. Females and juveniles migrate much greater distances than do bulls. Some swim more than 6000 miles to southern California.

One of the most important commercially hunted animals in the world, Northern Fur Seals are killed for their fur and their blubber, which is rendered into oil. The flesh is sold for meat, primarily mink food, and the bones are ground up into a meal. Overhunting had brought the Northern Fur Seal near extinction by the mid-19th century. Since then international treaties have afforded some protection. Hunting quotas are set, and the populations are carefully managed. Killing of females is forbidden; allowable kills are limited to males in bachelor herds. Similar species include the Northern Sea Lion (*Eumetopias jubatus*) and the California Sea Lion (*Zalophus californianus*).

**SEAL, RIBBON:
see Seal, Harbor**

**SEAL, SPOTTED:
see Seal, Harbor**

MAMMALS

SHEEP, BIGHORN; MOUTAIN SHEEP; ROCKY MOUNTAIN BIGHORN SHEEP
(Ovis canadensis)

In many parts of the Rocky Mountains, the Bighorn Sheep is more often heard than seen. Generally found in areas away from human habitation, they are rarely seen by the casual passerby. However, when they engage in their horn-butting battles, the resounding crack that is made as they crash together can be heard for a mile or more, depending on conditions.

The range of the Bighorn Sheep is from Mexico north through western California (the Sierra Nevada), Nevada and the Rocky Mountain states to British Columbia and Alberta. They spend much of their time in meadows and foothills close to rocky cliffs. They

Left and below: **Bighorn Rams high in the Rocky Mountains of Banff National Park.**

are also found in desert regions such as Death Valley.

One of the larger of the sheeps, the Bighorn Ram is 3-3½ feet (.9-1.05 m) high at the shoulder, 5 to 6 feet (1.5-1.9 m) long, and weighs from 125 to 320 pounds (57-145 kg). The smaller female is 2½ to 3 feet (.75-1.0 m) at the shoulder, 4 to 5 feet long (1.2-1.5 m) and weighs from 75 to 200 pounds (34-90 kg).

The most notable physical feature is the pair of massive curved horns on the ram. The horns curve backwards, downward and then forward past the cheeks, forming a huge C. Horns that measure more than 4 feet (1.2 m) along the length of the curve have been observed. The full C shape of the horn is called a 'curl.' Some older animals, ages 7 to 8 and older, have curls that curve around until the tips are level with the base of the horns. Ewes have short, slender horns that curve slightly. The hooves of the Bighorn are hard along the outer rims and spongy in the

center, giving the animal good traction. In addition to being a good climber and jumper, it is also a strong swimmer.

The color varies from a pale tan to dark brown. The darker color is more likely to be seen in the northern mountainous part of its range, and the lighter color is more prevalent in the desert regions.

Bighorn Sheep eat grasses, sedges and woody plants. In the summer they migrate to higher slopes, and return to the valleys in the winter. Active through most of the daylight hours, they feed in the morning, afternoon and early evening. When they are not feeding they lie down and chew their cuds. A Bighorn Sheep tends to use the same spot for bedding down at night, returning to it every night for years and years.

Bighorn Sheep live in small herds of about ten animals that include ewes, lambs, yearlings and two-year-olds. In winter, the size of the herds grows to

Left: **A Dall Ram (*Ovis dalli*).**
Above: **A Bighorn Ram (*Ovis canadensis*).**

times take the lambs. The meat of Bighorn Sheep is considered to be excellent, and they are also hunted for their horns which are prized as trophies.

Similar species include the Dall Sheep (*Ovis dalli*) and the Mountain Goat (*Oreamnos americanus*).

SHEEP, DALL:
see Sheep, Bighorn

SHEEP, MOUNTAIN:
see Sheep, Bighorn

SHEEP, ROCKY MOUNTAIN BIGHORN
see Sheep, Bighorn

SHREW, CINEROUS:
see Shrew, Masked

SHREW, COMMON:
see Shrew, Masked

SHREW, DUSKY:
see Shrew, Vagrant

SHREW, MASKED; COMMON SHREW; CINEROUS SHREW
(*Sorex cinereus*)

This shrew is found in almost all of Canada, southward into the northern United States and extreme northern Kentucky, south central Utah, north central New Mexico and the Appalachian mountains.

A very small animal, the masked shrew is 2¾ to 4½ inches (7 to

about 100, when the rams rejoin the group. The herd leader is usually an old ewe. The rams leave the herd in the spring, moving to the summer range higher in the mountains. Many Bighorns have been killed by trophy hunters and their numbers further depleted by stock-grazing and disease.

The start of the mating season is heralded by the rams' butting fights and the mating season runs from August to early January, depending on the latitude. As the mating period approaches a peak, the butting fights become almost continuous. The rams stand about 20 feet apart, lower their heads and charge, coming together with a loud crack. In spite of the intensity of the contests, the animals are seldom injured. Status is determined by horn size and fights almost always

occur between males with similarly-sized horns. Males will follow the nearest ewe in heat, and fights occur whenever two or more rams follow the same ewe. Mating can occur any time during the August to January mating season.

Well-developed, wooly lambs are born after a gestation period of 180 days. Births are usually single; twins occur occasionally. Ewes hide the lambs for a week, after which the lambs follow their mother. Ewes are sexually mature at about two-and-a-half years of age. Rams stay with the small ewe-lamb until they are two, when they join groups of rams.

Bighorn Sheep have a life span of about 15 years. They are preyed on by wolves, coyotes and cats such as bobcats and mountain lions. Eagles some-

Above: **A Short-tailed Shrew, the largest North American Shrew.**

11.5 cm) long and weighs from ⅛ to ⅜ ounces (3.5 to 11 g). It has brown fur above, silvery-grayish fur below, and a long tail. The snout, more reddish-brown than the rest of the body, gives it a masked appearance.

This shrew is seldom seen, even though it is one of the most widely distributed mammals in North America. A nocturnal hunter, it is noted for its appetite which is particularly voracious even when compared to that of other shrews. Frequently consuming more than its own weight every day, the masked shrew feeds on insect larvae, slugs, snails and spiders.

Several litters a year may be produced, born in nests of leaves or grass built in or under a stump.

Similar species are the Mt Lyell Shrew (*Sorex lyelli*) of California and Preble's Shrew (*Sorex preblei*).

SHREW, MT LYELL:
SHREW, PACIFIC:

SHREW, NORTHERN WATER:
see Shrew, Water

SHREW, PACIFIC:
see Shrew, Vagrant

SHREW, PACIFIC WATER:
see Shrew, Water

SHREW, PREBLE'S:
see Shrew, Masked

SHREW, SHORT-TAILED
(*Blarina brevicauda*)

One of the most abundant mammals in North America, the Short-tailed Shrew ranges from southeastern Canada, south to the northeastern United States, westward to Minnesota, Iowa, the Dakotas, and Nebraska, and southward into Virginia, West Virginia, Kentucky, and along the Allegheny Mountains into Georgia and Alabama.

Like all shrews, the Short-tailed Shrew is small compared to other mammals, but is the largest shrew in North America. It is from 3¾ to 5 inches (9.5-13 cm) long and weighs from ½ to 1 ounce (15 to 30 g). It is brownish, and, as its name suggests, it has a short tail that measures from ¾ to 1 inch (2-2.5 cm) in length. The tails of most other shrews are four to six times longer.

The Short-tailed Shrew uses its snout and forefeet to dig underground runways in a search for prey. When it bites its prey, it paralyzes it with a poison in its saliva, and the prey is dragged to the shrew's underground nest to be eaten. Eating more than its body weight in a day, feeding frequently to satisfy the needs of a very high rate of metabolism, the Short-tailed Shrew's diet includes earthworms, insects, snails, centipedes, small mice and other shrews, plus underground fungi. They are preyed on by owls, snakes and other mammals, but many are killed and not eaten, apparently because of an odor that is repellant to some predators.

The Short-tailed Shrew will usually fight viciously any animal it perceives to be an intruder, particularly other Short-tailed Shrews. Fights between Short-tailed Shrews are fierce and intense, but usually end without serious injury when one lies on its back in a submissive position. Males mark off territories in their burrows with secretions from glands on the belly and hip. During the mating season, these markings prevent female-hunting males from entering the burrows of other males. Complex courtship rituals usu-

Below: **The Common or Masked Shrew has an exceptional appetite.**

MAMMALS

ally prevent fights between sexes.

Litters of five to six young are born in the spring or summer in above-ground nests of leaves or grass built under stump or log. When the family group is alarmed, each young takes the base of the tail of a litter mate in its mouth, while one takes the tail of the mother in its mouth. The resulting chain of shrews can then be dragged to safety by the mother. Almost all species of shrews exhibit this behavior.

Closely related species are the Swamp Short-tailed Shrew (*Blarina telmalestes*) and the Southern Short-tailed Shrew (*Blarina carolinensis*).

SHREW, SOUTHERN SHORT-TAILED:
see Shrew, Short-tailed

SHREW, SWAMP SHORT-TAILED:
see Shrew, Short-tailed

SHREW, VAGRANT; WANDERING SHREW
(Sorex vagrans)

A western species, the Vagrant Shrew is found in the Rocky Mountain states, northern Nevada and California, Oregon, Washington and southern British Columbia.

Brown to gray above and tinged with brown or red below, the Vagrant Shrew is from 3¾ to 4⅞ inches (9.5 to 12 cm) long and weighs from ⅛ to ⅜ ounces (3 to 8.5 g). It moves about in the runways of voles, looking for insect larvae, slugs, snails, spiders and other invertebrates. It also eats fungi.

After a gestation period of about 3 weeks, a litter of two to nine young is born. The young are weaned in about 2 days. Known to have at least two breeding periods, one from January through May and another in late autumn, a female probably produces more than one litter a year.

The Pacific Shrew (*Sorex pacificus*) and Dusky Shrew (*Sorex monticolus*) are similar but have shorter tails.

SHREW, WANDERING:
see Shrew, Vagrant

SHREW, WATER; NORTHERN WATER SHREW
(Sorex palustris)

This shrew is found in most of Canada except Newfoundland and the northern areas, and southern Saskatchewan and Alberta. The range extends southward into New England, New York, Pennsylvania, West Virginia, the mountainous area where Kentucky, Tennessee, and Virginia meet, northern Michigan, Minnesota and Wisconsin. It is also found in Washington, Idaho, eastern Montana, Wyoming, and Colorado, most of Utah, eastern Nevada, north central New Mexico, north central California and a small area in Arizona.

The Water Shrew is from about 4 to 6½ inches (10-16.5 cm) long and weighs about ⅜ to ⅝ ounces (11-18 g). Well adapted to life in and around water, the Water Shrew has dark brown, velvety, water-resistant fur. The hind feet have fringes of stiff hair which increase its buoyancy and improve its swimming ability.

The Water Shrew swims and dives into small streams, searching for a variety of aquatic organisms such as the immature nymphal forms of mayflys and stoneflys. It also eats terrestrial insects and other invertebrates. It

Above: **Eastern Spotted Skunks are carnivores.**

commonly dives to the bottom, and when it stops its swimming motions, air trapped in its fur pops it to the surface. The fringe on the hind feet increases the surface area to the point where the Water Shrew can actually run on the surface of the water in short, quick bursts. In the water, it is preyed on by bass, pickerels, pike and large trout. When the Water Shrew goes ashore after swimming, it dries itself with the stiff hind leg hairs that act as a comb. On land, Water Shrews are often eaten by weasels.

Litters of four to eight young are born from February through June. It is thought that females, which are ready to breed at age three months, have more than one litter a year.

SKUNK, COMMON:
see Skunk, Striped

SKUNK, EASTERN SPOTTED; SPOTTED SKUNK
(Spilogale putorius)

The range of the Spotted Skunk extends from Mexico northward to include most of the United States except Montana, western Washington and northern North Dakota, New Eng-

Above: **The Striped Skunk is an omnivore.**

land, the Middle Atlantic states, the Midwestern states east of the Mississippi and the coastal areas of Virginia, North Carolina, South Carolina and Georgia.

Smaller than other skunks, the Spotted Skunk is from about 1.1 to 1.8 feet (.3 to .52 m) long and weighs from 1.7 to 2¼ pounds (.7 to 1 kg). It is black with horizontal white stripes on its neck and shoulder and it has irregular stripes and elongated white spots on the sides.

The Spotted Skunk moves with greater speed, agility and grace than other skunks. It is a good climber, often taking to trees to avoid predators and to look for food. More carnivorous than other skunks, the Spotted Skunk's diet consists mostly of small mammals, particularly mice, but it will also eat insects, insect grubs and a variety of plant foods including grapes and corn.

The Spotted Skunk's distinctive coloration advertises its ability to spray a foul-smelling musk from its anal glands. Once a potential predator has received a burst of the pungent spray, it is unlikely to try to take a Spotted Skunk again. If the predator continues to press its attack, the Spotted Skunk turns its back to the preda-

tor. Then, standing on its forefeet, it raises its tail, spreads the hind feet out, and sprays over its head. The spray can carry for a distance of 12 feet (3.6 m) or more. Most predators who have learned by experience will back off when they see the Spotted Skunk go into the preliminaries to spraying.

The Spotted Skunk dens in rockpiles, burrows and under buildings. While other skunks den alone, the Spotted Skunk often dens up in groups, particularly in the winter. The winter inactivity of the Spotted Skunk is not a true hibernation.

Mating takes place in late winter. Litters of four to five are born the following spring. By summer they have adult coloration and follow the mother. The Great Horned Owl sometimes takes young Spotted Skunks by striking from the air before the mother skunk can spray.

The Spotted Skunk is trapped in some areas for its silky fur, which has moderate value in the fur industry. Skunk fur was called 'black marten' or 'Alaska sable' before fur-labeling laws required that all fur be sold under the name of the animal from which it came. Although they may take an occasional hen, their presence around a farm serves to control destructive rats and mice, which they take in much greater numbers than does the Striped

Skunk. They are suspected of being carriers of rabies.

Similar species include the Striped Skunk (*Mephitis mephitis*) and the Western Spotted Skunk (*Spilogale gracilis*) which is considered to be the same species by some biologists. Skunks, members of the weasel family, are found only in North and South America.

SKUNK, HOGNOSED:
see Skunk, Striped

SKUNK, SPOTTED:
see Skunk, Eastern Spotted;
Skunk, Striped

SKUNK, STRIPED; COMMON SKUNK
(Mephitis mephitis)

One of the more widely distributed mammals in North America, the Striped Skunk is found in the southern half of Canada southward through all the continental United States except the extreme southern tip of Florida and into northern Mexico. Members of the weasel family, both the Striped and Spotted Skunk are found only in North and South America.

The Striped Skunk is from 1.7 to 2.6 feet (.5 to .8 m) long and weighs from 6 to 14 pounds (2.7 to 6.3 kg). Most are black with two broad white stripes running down the back to the middle of the forehead. There is a broad patch of white fur on the back of the neck. The bushy black tail is usually tipped with white. Some individuals are grayish to almost white.

The omnivorous skunk has a varied diet that includes insects, small mammals, birds' eggs, amphibians and various plant foods. Primarily nocturnal, they walk in a shuffling, waddling, bouncy gait, stopping often to dig for insect grubs and other food.

The best-known adaptation of the striped and other skunks is its ability to spray a strong-smelling oil from its anal glands. Other animals soon learn to recognize the rather conspicuously colored skunk and to avoid it if possible. Only the great horned owl, which

Above: **Like adults, young Striped or Common Skunks waddle or shuffle when they walk.**

can swoop and pick up a young skunk before the mother can spray, is a serious predator. A skunk will often spray in the direction of what it perceives as a threat. A mother skunk with young is quite likely to spray if disturbed. The skunk goes through a behavior that serves to warn the intruder of the intention to spray. First it snarls, then it stamps its feet, raises its hind legs, clicks its teeth, arches its tail over its back and then turns its rump toward the intruder and sprays. One jet or burst of the anal gland oil – about a fifth of a tablespoon –, spreads out some ten to fifteen feet, and the visible mist can diffuse some 50 feet. The smell can carry for a mile or more, although the mist cannot be seen at that distance. If the fluid gets into the eyes, intense pain results. Contrary to a widely repeated myth, a skunk can spray if held by the tail.

Striped Skunks mate in late winter. Litters of four to seven young are born in May. By late June or early July they are weaned and follow the mother in single file on hunting walks. They can spray when they are six to seven weeks old.

Skunks eat constantly in the fall to store fat for the winter. In very cold weather they may hole up in a den, usually an abandoned burrow of another animal, and become dormant. However, their winter sleep is not a true hibernation. If necessary, a Striped Skunk will dig its own den, or it may den up in a hollow log or under a house or building. Striped Skunks denning in crawl spaces of houses are a frequently encountered problem.

Striped Skunks live in a variety of habitats including woods, plains and suburban areas. Although seldom seen in the daytime, the smell of skunks' spray is quite common in many populated areas in the evening or early morning. Many are killed on roads and highways, and the death of a skunk is often broadcast for miles as it gives off spray in its death agony. Dogs, particularly puppies and young dogs who have not learned to avoid skunks, are frequent spraying victims.

A Striped Skunk may, on very rare occasions, take a chick or an egg from a poultry house. However, it eats large numbers of harmful rodents and insects. Pelts, although not very valuable, are used to make fur products.

Descented Striped Skunks are sometimes kept as pets. It is the chief carrier of rabies in the United States.

Similar species are the Hog-nosed Skunk (*Concepatus mesoleucus*) and Spotted Skunk (*Spilogale putoris*).

SQUIRREL, DOUGLAS'S
see Squirrel, Red

SQUIRREL, EASTERN FOX:
see Squirrel, Fox; Squirrel, Gray

SQUIRREL, EASTERN GRAY:
see Squirrel, Fox; Squirrel, Gray

SQUIRREL, EASTERN RED:
see Squirrel, Fox

SQUIRREL, FOX; EASTERN FOX SQUIRREL
(Sciurus niger)

The Fox Squirrel is found in all the United States east of the Mississippi River except New England, New York, New Jersey, northeastern Pennsylvania and extreme northern Wisconsin. West of the Mississippi it is found in the tier of states from Louisiana to Minnesota, and in almost all of the tier of states from Texas to North Dakota. It is also found in northern New Mexico along the east Texas border.

The largest of the tree squirrels, the Fox Squirrel is from about 1½ to 2⅓ feet long (.45 to .7 m) and weighs from 18 to 38 ounces (510 to 1075 gm). Three color phases are known to exist. In the Northeast, the fur is gray above and yellowish below; in the South, the fox squirrel is black but may have a white blaze on the tail and face; in the West, this tree squirrel is a rusty color. Like all tree squirrels it has a large, bushy tail.

The Fox Squirrel is most likely to be seen in and around nut trees in the early morning and late afternoon. Its major foods are hickory nuts and acorns, but it also eats other nuts, seeds, fruits, berries and corn. It spends much of its time sitting in trees,

Right: **The Fox Squirrel eats mainly acorns.**

eating or sunbathing. It also spends some time on the ground burying seeds. Like other tree squirrels, it does not remember where it buries a nut, but it can find them with a keen sense of smell even through several inches of snow.

In the summer, the Fox Squirrel may build a nest of leaves in a tree. Although it does not hibernate, it spends much of the winter in a tree hole, usually in a family group of several squirrels.

The winter mating season is heralded by males chasing females before the latter come into heat. Litters of two to four young are born after a gestation period of 44 days. Litters are usually born in February or March, but some are also produced in June or July and occasionally in late August or early September. From the age of two years onward, females usually have two litters a year.

The Fox Squirrel causes some damage to crops, particularly corn. It is a game animal in some rural areas, and is an attractive and interesting animal to watch in city parks. It has been introduced into some west-coast cities, notably San Francisco and Seattle.

Similar species include the Red Squirrel (*Tamiasciurus hudsonicus*), Eastern Gray Squirrel (*Sciurus carolinensis*, and Eastern Red Squirrel.

SQUIRREL, GRAY; EASTERN GRAY SQUIRREL (*Sciurus carolinensis*)

In all probability, the most frequently seen wild mammal in the eastern United States is the Gray Squirrel. It is found in all states east of the Mississippi River except extreme northern Maine and a small area in western Florida. It is also found in the tier of states from Louisiana to Minnesota, westward to the eastern areas of the tier of states from Texas to North Dakota. In Canada it is found in the southern Maritime Provinces, southern Ontario, Quebec, Manitoba and Saskatchewan. The Gray Squirrel

thrives in a variety of deciduous tree habitats from forests to suburban areas to city parks and streets.

The Gray Squirrel is from 1⅜ to 1⅔ feet (.4 to .5 m) long and weighs from 15 to 25 ounces (425 to 710 g). The fur is a dark gray color above and a paler gray on the underside. The flattened tail is covered with bushy gray silver-tipped fur. Black and albino phases exist in some parts of the range

Moving adeptly both on the ground and in trees, the Gray Squirrel is most active in the morning and early evening. Most of its diet consists of nuts, such as walnuts, acorns, beechnuts, hickory nuts and chestnuts, as well as various soft fruits, maple tree seeds and other seeds and corn. Sometimes it eats nuts where it finds them, but it usually buries the nut at a spot other than where it found it. Each nut is buried individually in a hole the squirrel digs with its forefeet, and is tamped down with fore and hind feet

and nose. It does not remember where the nuts are buried, but can sniff them out, even under a foot or so of snow. The nut-burying activity of the Gray Squirrel serves to plant trees and spread them to new areas.

While the Gray Squirrel does not hibernate, it does hole up in a den in particularly cold weather. Dens and nests are established by both sexes, usually in trees, either in cavities such as woodpecker holes or in leaf nests in thick-limbed older trees, living or dead. Winter nests are much sturdier and tighter than summer nests. The summer nests are not necessarily in the same location as the winter nest. Loosely-constructed temporary nests are sometimes constructed near corn fields.

The Gray Squirrel moves smoothly through the trees by leaping from branch to branch. The bushy tail provides some lift during the leap, slowing descent in case of a fall. The tail also

MAMMALS

Above: The Gray or Eastern Gray Squirrel.
Below: Red or Pine Squirrel.

serves as an umbrella in the rain, a rudder for swimming and an effective blanket in the winter. They vocalize in a chattering bark.

Gray Squirrels mate in mid-winter. Litters of two to three young are born in the spring in leaf nests or tree-hole dens; there may be a second litter in the summer. Females often move their young between dens and leaf nests.

The Gray Squirrel is a widely hunted game animal. The meat, considered to be excellent, is a diet staple for people in some parts of the country. The Gray Squirrel occasionally causes crop damage, particularly to corn, and it may nest in the eaves of houses, causing some structural damage.

Similar species include the Eastern Fox Squirrel (*Sciurus niger*) and Red Squirrel (*Tamiasciurus hudsonicus*).

SQUIRREL, NORTHERN FLYING:
see Squirrel, Southern Flying

SQUIRREL, PINE:
see Squirrel, Red

SQUIRREL, RED; PINE SQUIRREL; SPRUCE SQUIRREL; CHICKAREE (*Tamiasciurus hudsonicus*)

The Red Squirrel's range extends from most of Alaska, southward to include almost all of Canada except the Arctic regions, southern Alberta and Saskatchewan and Newfoundland. From British Columbia the range extends southward into the Rocky Mountains area, to Arizona and New Mexico. In the east the range includes New England, southward to Virginia and the Blue Ridge Mountain area, westward from New York and Pennsylvania north of the Ohio River to Minnesota and eastern North Dakota. Populations of Red Squirrel are also found in a small area of western Kentucky.

One of the smaller tree squirrels, and the smallest in its range, the Red Squirrel is from 10 to 15 inches (25 to 38 cm) long and weighs from about 5 to 9 ounces (142 to 255 g). The fur is a rusty red to grayish-red color and white to grayish-white below. The brightest red fur is on the sides. The bushy tail is similar in color to the back fur but has a broad black band outlined in white. During the summer months, the coat color dulls and a line of black fur separates the red upper fur from the white fur on the underside.

In coniferous forests, it feeds mainly on pine seeds, so much so that a forest floor littered with remains of pine cones is a sign of the presence of the Red Squirrel. Also included in the Red Squirrel's diet are acorns and other nuts, various tree seeds, birds' eggs, nestlings and fungi. In fall, the Red Squirrel buries large quantities of green pine cones and other foods.

Nests are made of shredded bark in hollow or fallen trees. Although it does not hibernate, it may stay in its nest during particularly bad winter weather. In the winter, it tunnels through the snow in a search for food.

Mating takes place in the winter, preceded by frenzied chases through trees. Litters of three to seven young are born in March or April, and there may be a second litter in August or September. The Red Squirrel is interesting to watch in its natural habitat, but too small to interest hunters. It sometimes gets into woodland vacation cabins, causing minor damage.

Similar species are the Gray Squirrel (*Sciurus carolinensis*), Fox Squirrel (*Sciurus niger*) and Douglas's Squirrel (*Tamiasciurus douglasii*).

SQUIRREL, ROCK:
see Prairie Dog, Black-tailed

SQUIRREL, SOUTHERN FLYING (*Glaucomys volans*)

The Southern Flying Squirrel is found in all of the United States east of the Mississippi River except Maine, northern Wisconsin, and Southern Florida. West of the Mississippi, it is found in the tier of states from Louisiana to Minnesota, and in the eastern parts of Texas, Oklahoma, Kansas, and Nebraska, and extreme eastern North and South Dakota.

The smallest of the tree squirrels, the Southern Flying Squirrel is from 8 to 10 inches long (20 to 25 cm) and weighs some 1¾ to 3½ ounces (50 to 100 g). The silky fur is grayish-brown above and white below. The tail is flattened and covered with gray-brown fur and there is a loose fold of skin between the front and hind legs.

The nocturnal Southern Flying Squirrel eats acorns and other nuts, berries, insects and bird's eggs. It is much more likely to prey on other small rodents than are other squirrels.

Above: A Western Flying Squirrel.

SQUIRREL, SPRUCE: see Squirrel, Red

THIRTEEN-LINED GROUND SQUIRREL; STRIPED GOPHER (*Spermophilus tridecemlineatus*)

The Thirteen-lined Ground Squirrel range extends from southeastern Alberta and southern Manitoba southward through the central continental United States to Texas, east to Ohio and west to Montana.

This ground squirrel is from about 6¾ to 12 inches (17 to 30 cm) long and weighs from 3¾ to 10 ounces (106 to 283 g). The fur is brown, and there are thirteen alternating brown and white lines running lengthwise on the back and sides. The lines may be broken into spots.

Solitary and active by day in yards, cemeteries, and golf courses, the Thirteen-lined Ground Squirrel feeds on seeds and insect larvae, occasionally taking a bird, shrew or mouse.

This ground squirrel builds burrows from 15 to 20 feet long, sometimes longer. The burrows have several side passages, and at least one deeper chamber for hibernating. The Thirteen-lined Ground Squirrel starts to put on a layer of fat and to store seeds in the hibernation burrow in late summer. In the fall it enters the burrow and goes into a fairly deep hibernation rolled in a tight ball. Respiration drops from about 100 to 200 breaths a minute to less than five. If picked up in the deepest phases of the hibernation, it

Active throughout the year, the Southern Flying Squirrel builds nests of leaves, bark and twigs in woodpecker holes and other protected places, usually in trees. It does not hibernate, but in severely cold weather it may hole up in a nest with several other flying squirrels.

The Southern Flying Squirrel does not actually fly, but it glides an impressive distance of 240 feet (73 m) or more with the help of the loose fold of skin between its legs. It leaps, spreads out its legs, stretching out the fold of skin so that it acts somewhat like a combination between an airfoil and a parachute. During the glide, it can change direction and rate of descent. It cannot, however, gain altitude. As it lands, it drops the tail and begins to retract the outstretched fold of skin, an action that makes an airbrake out of the fold. It lands lightly on a tree trunk with all four feet, immediately scurrying around to the other side of the tree.

Mating takes place in early spring, and litters of two to six young are born after a gestation period of 40 days. There is sometimes a second litter in the late summer. Sometimes kept as a pet, the Southern Flying Squirrel has no economic impact on human activity other than occasionally nesting in attics and causing minor damage.

The Northern Flying Squirrel (*Glaucomys sabrinus*), which is found in Canada and parts of the northern United States, is a bit larger and grayer in color than the Southern Flying Squirrel. The two species are similar in all other respects, including habits.

SQUIRREL, SPOTTED GROUND see Squirrel, Thirteen-lined Ground

Above: A Thirteen-lined Ground Squirrel.

will not awaken. They sometimes hibernate in small groups.

Mating activity begins soon after the Thirteen-lined Ground Squirrel emerges from the burrow in late March or early April. Litters of eight to ten young are born in May. There is sometimes a second litter in the summer.

Preferring well-mowed and tended lawns and golf courses, the Thirteen-lined Ground Squirrel has adapted well in areas of human population. Although it does eat some crop plants, and sometimes damages lawns with its burrows, it also eats weed seeds and harmful insects. In populated areas large numbers are killed by cars.

Similar species include Chipmunks and the Spotted Ground Squirrel (*Spermophilus spilosoma*).

Below: **A Columbian Ground Squirrel (*Spermofilus columbianus*) at Grand Canyon National Park.**

TAMIAS:
see Chipmunk, Eastern

VOLE: see Lemming, Brown

VOLE, LONG-TAILED:
see Vole, Meadow

VOLE, MEADOW; FIELD MOUSE
(*Microtus pennsylvanicus*)

The Meadow Vole is found in most of Alaska and Canada except the extreme northern regions, southward into the continental United States including all the northeastern states, the Atlantic Coast states southward to northeastern Georgia, all the states bordering the Great Lakes, West Virginia, eastern Kentucky and Tennessee, Iowa, eastern Nebraska, northern Missouri, North and South Dakota, Montana, most of Idaho and Wyoming, central Colorado, northwestern New Mexico, north central Utah and northeast Washington.

The Meadow Vole is 5½ to 7¾ inches (14 to 20 cm) long and weighs about ¾ to 2½ ounces (21 to 71 g). The tail is from 1¼ to 2½ inches (3 to 6.3 cm) long. The body fur is variable, ranging from yellowish to reddish-brown peppered with black to blackish-brown in the upper regions. The fur on the underside is buffy, silvery or dark gray, and the feet are usually darker than the rest of the body. The overall body shape is somewhat ovoid.

The Meadow Vole is most likely to be found in grassy fields, but this adaptable rodent can also be seen in mountainous areas and in woodland glades. A good swimmer, it also adapts to conditions around marshes. The Meadow Vole constructs a system of burrows, often used for nesting purposes, particularly in the summer. It

may also nest on the surface in a slight depression covered by vegetation. In the winter when there is snow cover, the Meadow Vole may construct a spherical grass nest under the snow.

Active throughout the day, the Meadow Vole's varied diet includes tubers, green plants, clover, plantain, seeds, grain, bark and insects. They eat almost constantly and are believed to consume almost their own weight daily. An alarmed vole will stamp its hind feet.

The Meadow Vole breeds throughout the year and is believed to have several litters annually of one to nine young.

The Meadow Vole and other voles can damage fruit trees by removing bark from roots and girdling the trunks. They have been seen to damage stored hay and grain. Voles are the major prey of a number of fur-bearing animals, including mink and ermine, and hawks and owls.

Similar species include the Mountain Vole (*Microtus montanus*), Prairie Vole (*Microtus ochrogaster*), and the Longtail Vole (*Microtus longicaudus*).

VOLE, MOUNTAIN:
see Vole, Meadow; Vole, Water

VOLE, PINE:
see Vole, Woodland

VOLE, PRAIRIE:
see Vole, Meadow; Vole, Woodland

VOLE, RICHARDSON'S:
see Vole, Water

VOLE, WATER;
RICHARDSON'S VOLE
(*Arvicola richardsoni*)

The Water Vole is found in mountainous areas around the border of British Columbia and Alberta, southward into northern Idaho, western Montana, northwestern Wyoming, northeastern Oregon, and southwestern Washington. There is also a population extending from south central British Columbia into central Washington and Oregon.

The largest vole in its range, the Water Vole is from 7¾ to 10¼ inches (20 to 26 cm) long and weighs from 2½ to 3½ ounces (71 to 99 g). The body fur is long, grayish to reddish-brown above and grayish with a white or silvery cast below. The tail is 2¾ to 3⅝ inches (7 to 9 cm) long.

An excellent swimmer, the Water Vole often jumps into water to escape from predators. Spending much of its time around mountain streams and lakes, the Water Vole builds burrows between sedges and under willow and alder trees. It moves away from water in the winter and builds nests of grass in runways under the snow. It eats a variety of leafy plants, including valerian, lousewort and lupine, and willow buds and twigs.

It is not known whether the Water Vole has a breeding season or breeds throughout the year. The usual litter size is believed to be three to five young. Water Vole populations are seldom near areas of extensive human habitation. They are prey for bobcats, other carnivores and birds of prey.

Similar species include the Mountain Vole (*Microtus montanus*) and Meadow Vole (*Microtus pennsylvanicus*).

VOLE, WOODLAND;
PINE VOLE
(*Microtus pinetorum*)

The Woodland Vole is an eastern species and its range extends through all the United States east of the Mississippi River except Maine, parts of Florida and New Hampshire, and northern Wisconsin. West of the Mississippi it is found in Louisiana, Arkansas, Missouri, eastern areas of Iowa, Kansas and Oklahoma, and eastern Texas, excluding the Gulf Coast area.

The Woodland Vole is 4 to 5¾ inches (10 to 15 cm) long and weighs from about ¾ to 1⅜ ounces (21 to 39g). It has reddish brown fur in the upper regions and buff fur below. The tail is about ¾ to 1 inch (2 to 2.5 cm) long and is covered with reddish fur.

Inhabiting deciduous woodlands that have thick growths of herbaceous ground cover or a thick covering of leaf mold, the Woodland Vole constructs systems of tunnels several inches below the layer of leaf mold. The vole is sometimes colonial, but colonies often break up. Active through the day, the Woodland Vole eats a variety

Below: A Meadow Vole or Field Mouse.

of plant foods, but mainly roots and tubers. This vole stores large amounts of food in its burrows.

In the southern part of the range, the Woodland Vole breeds throughout the year, while in the North, breeding takes place between January and October. Three to four litters of two to seven young are born each year.

Woodland Voles sometimes damage trees in orchards. They are prey for a variety of carnivores, birds of prey and snakes.

Similar species are the Prairie Vole (*Microtus ochrogaster*) and the Meadow Vole (*Microtus pennsylvanicus*).

WALRUS
(Odobenus rosmarus)

The Walrus exists in two distinct populations or races, the Atlantic and the Pacific. The Atlantic race is found from Greenland south to Hudson Bay. Pacific Walruses are found in the Chukchi Sea off the coast of northeastern Siberia in the summer and the Bering Sea off southwest Alaska in the winter.

One of the larger of the sea-going carnivores, Walruses vary in size according to sex and race. The Pacific Walruses tend to be larger than the Atlantic Walruses and the males of both races are larger than the females. Atlantic males are from 8¼ to 11½ feet (2.5 to 3.5 m) long, and have an average weight of about 1600 pounds (726 kg). The Atlantic females range from 7½ to 9½ feet (2.2 to 2.9 m) in length and average some 250 pounds (568 kg) in weight. The larger Pacific males are as long as 12 feet (3.6 m) and can weigh as much as 3000 pounds (1362 kg). Female Pacific Walruses are only slightly larger than their Atlantic counterparts, and average about 1400 pounds (636 kg).

All walruses have hairless bodies yellowish to reddish brown in color that become pale after a long dive, when the blood goes from the surface capillaries to internal organs. The hair is limited to the muzzle 'beard' composed of about 400 one-inch (2.5 cm)

bristles. The most distinctive features are the tusks, which are enlarged upper canine teeth. Tusks up to 40 inches (101 cm) long have been observed on Pacific bulls, while those of Atlantic bulls are usually around 16 inches (41 cm) long. Females also have tusks, but they are shorter, narrower and more curved in the middle than those of the bull.

Highly sociable animals, Walruses gather in herds of 2000 or more, bulls, females and juveniles separating by sex only during the breeding season. Herding Walruses defend each other against attacks by predators, and help those who are injured. The Walrus spends more time on land sunbathing and resting on beaches and ice than other sea-going carnivores. It also rests and sleeps at sea, hanging vertically in the water, using air sacs in the neck to stay afloat.

Although they appear to be ungainly, clumsy animals on shore, they are excellent graceful swimmers. Capable of easily swimming at speeds of 15 mph (24 kph), they can dive to depths of 300 feet (91 m) or more and remain submerged for as long as 30 minutes. Walruses often forage along sandy sea bottoms using their tusks and feeling out the sand with their sensitive muzzle bristles for clams and other mollusks and crustaceans which are

their major food. In the autumn months they may feed in shallow, ice-covered waters, keeping air holes in the ice open by butting through with their heads. Walruses eat clams much like people at a clam bar, sucking the meat off the shell with their dome-shaped mouths. An adult Walrus may eat 100 pounds (45 kg) or more of food a day, but in good weather it can go for a week or so without eating.

The tusks are used for defense, mating fights, hunting and other purposes such as providing a pulling anchor for sliding on ice and snow. Walruses occasionally take a seal by stabbing it with a tusk. The major predators, polar bears and man, soon learn to respect the deadly potential of the Walrus's tusks. The size of tusks establishes a bull's dominance.

Above: This Walrus bull (center) has a broken tusk. *Below:* A rookery of Walruses.

Mating and courtship behavior begin at sea in April and May. Bulls may engage in courtship fights during which the tusks may be broken. At mating time, males become very vocal, emitting pealing bell-like sounds in addition to the usual bellows and grunts. A single pup, weighing from 100 to 150 pounds (45 to 68 kg) is born about a year later. Female Walruses mate every other year, not immediately after delivering a pup, as do many of the seals and sea lions. The pup remains with the mother for about two years, often hanging on to the mother's neck as she swims and feeds. Fiercely protective, a mother Walrus will charge anything, including polar bears, that she regards as a threat to her pup. When the tusks begin to grow out of the mouth, the young Walrus goes out on its own.

The Pacific Walrus migrates from the Chukchi Sea to the Aleutian Islands in the winter. Migrating Walrus often make use of an ice flow in their migration, quickly disembarking if the floe starts to drift in the wrong direction. Pacific Walrus mate during the migration back to the Chuckchi Sea.

The Walrus has traditionally been the most important animal in the life of Eskimoes. Although many Eskimoes no longer follow all the traditional ways, many, including those who work at regular jobs, still hunt Walrus, using rifle and power boat, rather than the considerably more dangerous harpoon and kayak method of their ancestors. Walrus flesh supplies meat, the hides are used for boat covers and clothing, and the blubber is rendered into an oil used for fuel. Tusks, no longer used for tools and sled runners, are now made into scrimshaw, an important source of revenue. The Marine Mammal Protection Act of 1972 forbids commercial hunting of walrus, allowing hunting only by Eskimoes for personal use.

WALRUS, ATLANTIC:
see Walrus

WALRUS, PACIFIC:
see Walrus

WAPITI: see Elk

WEASEL, LEAST
(Mustela nivalis)

The Least Weasel is found in Alaska, in almost all of Canada west of the St Lawrence River except the extreme north and the Arctic Ocean Islands and the Pacific Coast area, southward into the midwestern United States from northern Montana eastward to Pennsylvania, south to Nebraska and in the Allegheny mountains in West Virginia, Virginia, Tennessee, North Carolina and Kentucky.

The smallest carnivore in North America, the Least Weasel measures from 6¾ to 8⅛ inches (17 to 21 cm) long and weighs from 1¼ to 1¾ ounces (35 to 50 g). The fur of the Least Weasel is brown above and white below; the feet are white. Those that live in the northern part of the range turn white in winter.

What the Least Weasel lacks in size it more than makes up for in ferocity. Usually nocturnal, it is an intense hunter of Meadow Mice which are its primary diet, pouncing on them and delivering a fatal bite at the base of the skull. If Meadow Mice are not avail-

Below: **A Long-tailed Weasel in summer.**

able, it will take a shrew or a mole for its food.

The Least Weasel mates at any time of the year. As many as three litters a year of three to six young are produced. The female delivers the young in an abandoned den of another animal such as a gopher, ground squirrel or mouse.

The Least Weasel is preyed upon by owls, foxes and an occasional house cat. Similar species are the Ermine (*Mustela erminea*) and Black-footed Ferret (*Mustela nigripes*).

WEASEL, LONG-TAILED
(Mustela frenata)

The range of the Long-tailed Weasel extends from New Brunswick westward through southern Quebec, Ontario and the southern parts of the western Canadian provinces almost to the Pacific, and southward to include almost all of the continental United States and Mexico except portions of New Mexico, Arizona, Nevada, California, Baja California and western Sonora.

The males are from ¾ to ⅞ feet (.22 to .26 m) long and weigh from 7 to 12 ounces (198-340 g), while the smaller females are from ⅔ to ¾ feet (.2 to .22 m) long and weigh from 3 to 7 ounces (85 to 200 g). The fur is brown

MAMMALS

on the upper part of the body and white on the underside. In the southwestern parts of the range, many have white fur on the face. In the northern part of the range, the Long-tailed Weasel turns white in the winter except for a black tip on the tail.

Weasels are ferocious hunters, and they will go after prey many times their own size. They are one of the few animals known to kill apparently just for the sake of killing. They will kill their own litter mates if they are injured. The Long-tailed Weasel preys on mice and other rodents, shrews and birds. It will readily take chickens and other poultry if it can get into the poultry farm. Weasels move in sinuous, almost fluid ways that enable them to get into small burrows and slip through narrow cracks and crannies, an ability that increases their chances of getting into a modern poultry farm. Kills are often cached in dens established in the abandoned burrows of other mammals, particularly chipmunks, but they also make their own dens and nests.

The Long-tailed Weasel is one of the more vocal of the weasel-like animals, making a variety of noises including hisses, squeaks, purrs and chatters. The females make a sound similar to a bird's chirp during mating season.

The weasel mates in midsummer. When weasels are sexually excited, their anal glands secrete a foul-smelling musk. The musk is also sometimes produced when the animal is frightened or aggressive toward another Long-tailed Weasel. Often, the weasel drags its rump along the ground, leaving a trail of musk that identifies it as a male or female. Litters of four to nine young are born in May. When they go on their own at age seven to eight weeks, the male young are already larger than their mother. Long-tailed Weasels are sometimes trapped for their pelts, but the fur is not valuable. Others are killed by poultry keepers.

Similar species include the Ermine (*Mustela erminea*) and the Black-footed Ferret (*Mustela nigripes*).

WEASEL, SHORT-TAILED: see Ermine

Below: A Killer Whale in captivity.

WHALE, FINBACK: see Whale, Gray

WHALE, GRAY (*Eschrichtius gibbosus*)

A Pacific Ocean species, the Gray Whale migrates from the Arctic Ocean along the west coast of North America to the Gulf of California.

A medium-sized baleen (toothless) whale, the Gray Whale measures up to 45 feet (14 m) in length and weighs from 34,000 to 74,000 pounds (15,000 to 33,000 kg). The body color is a mottled splotchy grayish-black. With a more slender looking body than most other baleen whales, the Gray Whale's spouts are low on the body and it has distinctive longitudinal folds on the throat. Instead of teeth, there are strips of baleen or whalebone hanging from the roof of the mouth. The baleen strips, fringed at the inner side, serve to strain the tiny marine organisms that are the whale's food out of

Above: **A Gray Whale spouts and dives off the California coast.**

the water. The organisms stick to the baleen and the whale licks them off with its massive tongue and swallows them.

The Gray Whale goes on the longest yearly migration of any mammal. Starting in late December, Gray Whales leave the Bering Sea and start to move southward to the coast of Baja, California, where they deliver their young and mate. They move back to the Bering Sea in March and April, covering a total of 16,000 miles (25,600 km).

The migration of the Gray Whale has become a tourist attraction. Every year, boats from the West Coast carry tourists to view the whales on their annual migration. Tourists also travel to the shallow water off Baja, California, to observe the Gray Whales' courting behavior that includes leaping out of the water.

The Gray Whale was once one of the more widely hunted whales. From time to time, kills were restricted or banned by the International Whaling Commission, but these were often ignored by the major whaling nations. The total population was estimated to be between 100,000 to 200,000 in the mid 1970s.

Similar species include the Right Whale (*Eubalaena australis*), the Finback Whale (*Balaenoptera physalus*) and the Humpback Whale (*Megaptera novaeangliae*).

WHALE, HUMPBACK:
see Whale, Gray

WHALE, KILLER; SEA WOLF
(*Orcinus orca*)

The Killer Whale (also called Orca, Grampus and Sea Wolf) is found in warm and cold oceans, close to the coast. It frequents bays, inlets and coves, particularly on the Pacific northwest coast of North America.

The largest of the dolphins, the Killer Whale can be as long as 30 feet (9.1 m). Females are several feet shorter than the males. Killer males have a distinctive pointed dorsal fin that can be as high as 6 feet (1.8 m) in the male and is usually about 3 feet (.9 m) high in an adult female. The fin points straight up on the male, and is somewhat hooked on the female. Like all the toothed whales, the Killer Whale has a single blowhole rather than the two blowholes seen in the baleen whales. The Killer Whale is dark black on the upper body regions and a true white on the sides and underside. A white spot is present under each eye. The snout is rounded, and an open mouth reveals rows of 10 to 15 sharp teeth, on each side of the upper and lower jaws.

The Killer Whale is the only whale known to regularly eat sea mammals including seals, sea lions and other whales, particularly baleen whales. In fact, whales have no other natural enemies besides man. It may also take water birds such as penguins. Capable of speeds of 24 mph (38 kph) it can outpace most prey. It also eats fish such as tuna. Killer Whales often hunt cooperatively, herding fish and other prey into blind inlets. They travel in family groups, called pods, of ten to

fifty individuals, and often play and cavort with each other. They are sometimes seen to hold their bodies upright in the water, with the head above the surface in an attitude referred to as 'spying.' Often done by several killer whales in a neat row, spying is believed to be a way of scanning the water for prey. In general, however, whales depend more on their keen sense of hearing than on their sight.

Believed to mate for life, Killer Whales frequently engage in sexual play. After a gestation period of at least 12 months, the female delivers a single young, born under water. They call to each other with distinctive wailing cries which are believed to have specific meanings. Observers of these whales soon learn to recognize individuals by their vocalizations.

Although seafarers' folklore is filled with tales of Killer Whales attacking and eating humans, there are very few documented cases of such attacks, and these are primarily attacks by wounded animals. While the Killer Whale can be quite ferocious when attacking prey in the wild, it is docile and friendly in captivity. Intelligent, trainable animals, their use in seaquarium shows has increased in recent years. It was never an important species in the whaling industry, except in Japan and Norway, so the Killer Whale population is believed to be holding steady.

WHALE, RIGHT:
see Whale, Gray

WHITETAIL:
see Deer, White-tailed

MAMMALS

WOLF; GRAY WOLF; TIMBER WOLF
(Canis lupus)

The range of the Gray Wolf once extended over almost all of North America. Today, the Gray Wolf is found in Alaska, almost all of Canada, including the Arctic Ocean Islands, with the exception of Quebec east of the St Lawrence River, the Maritime Provinces and Newfoundland. It is also found in coastal Greenland. In the United States, the Gray Wolf is limited to Michigan's Upper Peninsula, extreme northern Minnesota and Wisconsin, and scattered populations in Wyoming, Colorado, Utah, Montana, Idaho, Washington, Texas, Arizona and New Mexico. A well-studied population exists in Isle Royal National Park in Lake Superior.

The Gray Wolf is 2 to 3 feet (.6 to .9 m) high at the shoulder, 3.3 to 6¾ feet (1 to 2 m) long, and weighs about 60 to 130 pounds (27 to 59 kg). Males are larger than the females. Fur varies from almost white to black, but a grizzled gray is the usual color.

The Gray Wolf lives and hunts in tundra and forest in groups or packs of two to 15 individuals. Usually composed of family groups, the packs are generally led by the strongest male. Packs hunt in territories of approximately 100 to 250 square miles (259-648 sq km) that generally overlap with those of other packs. Usually hunting at night, the pack uses cooperative tactics to bring down prey which are usually large herbivores such as deer, moose and caribou. However, they will also eat a variety of other foods including smaller mammals, birds, fish, insects and even berries and other fruit. Since healthy large mammals such as deer can usually outrun Wolves, they seldom run after prey for long distances, preferring to surround the victim and drive it back to other wolves waiting in ambush. Wolves can usually capture a healthy adult moose, deer or other large animal if the prey becomes mired in deep crusted snow. Wolves will generally be supported by the crust while the larger, heavier animals may fall through and flounder. Wolves usually take young, slower-moving animals or older ones that are sick or injured.

One of the most distinctive features of the Gray Wolf is its howling. Often heard at night, the howling may be a preliminary to the hunt. As soon as one Wolf starts to howl, the others in the pack join in. Often they gather in a circle, and stragglers bound in, apparently eager to join the howl. They have been observed to change the pitch of the howls, in what could be interpreted as an attempt to harmonize. In addition to howling, Wolves bark, yap, whine and growl. Wolves separated from the pack signal their location with the 'lonesome call,' a short howl that rises in pitch and then fades.

Mating takes place in February and March. In some packs, only the dominant male mates. Litters of five to 14 pups are born in April and June. The black-furred pups come out of the den to play at about age one month. All members of the pack take part in caring for the young. When pack members returning from the hunt are nipped on the snout by the pups, the hunters regurgitate undigested meat for them. Folklore abounds in stories of 'wolf children' like Romulus and Remus who had wolf foster parents.

As farming, sheep-herding and cattle-raising appeared in the Wolf's habitat, bounties were offered for killing them, and their population was drastically reduced. They were also considered to be competitors for game animals such as deer and moose. Although they may take an occasional domestic animal, Wolves are not a serious threat to livestock in any part of their range. Their hunting patterns more or less ensure that only sick, diseased or old game animals will be taken, a circumstance that is actually beneficial to the species. Although wolves are much feared animals in many parts of the world, documented attacks on people are extremely rare. Some scientific observers have been able to befriend them in the wild. However, attempts to keep wolves as pets are not usually successful.

The Coyote (*Canis latrans*) is similar to the Wolf, but smaller. The Red Wolf (*Canis rufus*) of Texas, Louisiana and Arkansas is smaller than the Gray Wolf and has reddish fur.

WOLF, GRAY:
see Coyote, Wolf

WOLF, RED: see Wolf

WOLF, TIMBER: see Wolf

Below: **The Gray or Timber Wolf will often live and hunt in a pack.**

WOLVERINE; GLUTTON
(Gulo luscus)

The Wolverine's range includes almost all of Alaska, the northern half of Canada from Yukon to Labrador, almost all of British Columbia and scattered populations in Colorado, California and possibly other Rocky Mountain states.

Looking somewhat like a small, chunky bear, the Wolverine (a member of the weasel family) is from 2.6 to 3.6 feet (.8 to 1.1 m) long and weighs from about 18 to 45 pounds (8 to 20 kg). Males are larger than females. The fur is dark brown and broad yellowish bands run from the shoulders to the rump and meet at the base of the tail. There are light patches of fur over the ears. The feet are rather large for the size of its body.

Although it is a determined, ferocious and skilled killer, it prefers carrion to fresh kills. However, when carrion is not available it will go after any animal it can find and kill, including moose, elk, caribou, deer, beaver, porcupines and rodents, birds and eggs. It also eats plant foods such as roots and berries. It often eats trapped animals and other animals' food caches. The name 'glutton' stems from a voracious appetite, which is probably an adaptation for survival over periods of food scarcity. It carelessly caches food it cannot immediately eat, often marking it with a foul-smelling anal gland musk, urine and feces.

The Wolverine covers a wide area of 1600 square miles (4144 sq km) or more in its search for food. Typically, a hunting territory of that size serves a male and two or three females, and overlaps with those of other Wolverines. The Wolverine moves in a slow lope, but can cover great distances in intense three to four hour periods of activity, alternating with rest periods. It is a good swimmer and an efficient tree climber, often pouncing on prey from trees. It builds dens in protected places such as crevices and under uprooted trees, but does not hibernate.

Above: The Wolverine is the mascot of the University of Michigan. Michigan is also known as the Wolverine State.

Wolverines have a long mating season, extending from April to September. This long season increases the possibility of widely dispersed Wolverines meeting at a time when the female is receptive. Litters of two to three are born from February to April. Females are believed to have a litter every two or three years. The young remain with the mother for at least two years before leaving to establish their own territories.

Wolverines have been known to raid cabins and campers' tents, eat their fill and render what they don't eat useless by marking it with musk, urine and feces. Wolverine fur has oils in it that make it frost resistant, a quality that encourages its use as a lining for parkas.

A lone Wolverine can successfully drive off large predators, including bears and mountain lions, from its kills.

MAMMALS

WOODCHUCK; GROUNDHOG; MARMOT
(Marmota monax)

The range of the Woodchuck extends from east central Alaska southeastward to include most of southern Canada. The range extends southward from Canada to include the northeastern states of the United States including the Middle Atlantic states, all of the states bordering the Great Lakes, Iowa, Missouri, Arkansas, Kentucky, West Virginia, Virginia, most of Tennessee, western North Carolina and northern Georgia and Alabama. It is also found in northeastern North Dakota and the extreme northern 'leg' of Idaho.

One of the larger rodents, the Woodchuck is from 1⅓ to 2½ feet (.4 to .75 m) long, and weighs from about 4½ to 14 pounds (2 to 6.3 kg). The fur varies from grizzled brown to reddish to blackish. The fur on the belly is often paler than that of the upper parts of the body. The Woodchuck has a stocky body and short, powerful legs well adapted for digging.

The diurnal Woodchuck is particularly active on sunny days, usually in the morning and later afternoon. Feeding primarily on vegetation, including grasses, clover, plantain and alfalfa, it will also feed on garden and crop plants.

An efficient digger, the Woodchuck digs burrows as much as 5 feet (1.5 m) deep and 30 feet (9.1 m) long. The burrow may have several tunnels, each of which may end in an enlarged nesting chamber. Woodchuck nesting chambers are frequently used by other mammals, including raccoons, skunks, rabbits, foxes and others who may use the burrow as the Woodchuck made it, or enlarge it to suit their own needs.

It is a good swimmer and will nimbly climb a tree to escape a predator, but it prefers to stay near its den. It has a variety of vocalizations including a shrill whistle, hisses, growls and teeth chattering. The latter is a sign of anger.

A true hibernator, the Woodchuck begins to put on a layer of fat in late summer and early fall. As the winter

Above: **A Bushy-tailed Woodrat or Pack Rat.**

approaches, it retires to its burrow, curls up in a tight ball on a mat of grass, and falls into hibernation. During hibernation, the body temperature falls from the normal range of 97°F (36°C) to 40°F (4.4°C), and the heartbeat drops from about 100 to 4 beats per minute. The emergence of the Woodchuck from its hibernation burrow in early spring is the basis of the 'Groundhog Day' observance of February 2. The actual day of emergence varies with conditions and latitude; in the northern parts of the range, it usually emerges in March.

The mating season starts as soon as the Woodchuck emerges from hibernation. A male seeks out a receptive female in its burrow, remaining with her a short time. Litters of four to five young are born in April or early May. Although they do not open their eyes and crawl until they are one month old, they are ready to go out on their own when they are only two months old.

Woodchucks are among the more widely hunted of 'varmints,' and large numbers are killed by automobiles. Woodchucks can damage crops and gardens; however, their digging and excrement serve to aerate and fertilize the soil.

Similar species include other marmots such as the Yellow-bellied Marmot (*Marmota flaviventris*).

WOODRAT, BUSHY-TAILED; PACK RAT; MOUNTAIN PACK RAT
(Neotoma cinerea)

The Bushy-tailed Woodrat is found from British Columbia, extreme southwest Yukon and extreme western and southern Alberta, southward into the northwestern continental United States from Washington south to northern California, eastward to include most of Nevada, all of Utah, western Colorado, extreme northern Arizona and New Mexico, and northward to include Wyoming, Montana, Idaho and western North and South Dakota.

The Bushy-tailed Woodrat is 11 to 18 inches (28-46 cm) long and weighs from 5 to 16 ounces (142-454 g). The bushy, but somewhat flattened tail of 4½ to 9 inches (11-23 cm) long can be as much as half the total body length. Variable in color, most are pale-grayish to blackish above and whitish below. Some have brown fur sprinkled with black.

Like all woodrats, the Bushy-tailed Woodrat stores and 'trades' a variety of objects, which it stores in houses built of sticks in concealed spots in rocky crevices. It may also build its house fairly high in trees in its rocky coniferous forest habitat, but the tree house nests are used only for storing dried vegetation. With a strong preference for shiny objects, it will drop whatever it is carrying and 'trade' it for something shiny such as a coin or other piece of metal.

The Bushy-tailed Woodrat eats a variety of vegetation including leaves, stems, nuts, seeds and mushrooms, and may occasionally eat the flesh of the small mammals. Excellent climbers, they use their bushy tails for balance. They thump their hind feet on the ground, particularly when alarmed, but will also thump at other times.

Not found in areas of dense human population the Bushy-tailed Woodrat has no impact on human activities. They are a major food of bobcats and owls.

Similar species include the White-tailed Woodrat and the Desert Woodrat (*Neotoma lepida*).

WOODRAT, DESERT:
see Woodrat, Bushy-tailed

WOODRAT, WHITE-TAILED:
see Woodrat, Bushy-tailed

Above: The Woodchuck or Groundhog often falls victim to hunters and cars as well as predators like the Red Fox.

BIRDS

Above: Clark's Nutcrackers (*Nucifraga columbiana*) are commonly found in conifers near the timberline in the western states.

A bird is a feathered, warm-blooded, egg-laying animal of the biological class Aves. More than 100 species of birds nest in North America. Some are year-round residents of southern areas, while those birds that nest in northern territories are usually only part-time dwellers. When the duties of raising the next generation are completed, most northern birds move southward in migratory journeys that bring them to hospitable winter feeding grounds. In springtime, flight directions are reversed and these winter sojourners fly north again to nest.

All birds have feathers, from 900 to 25,000, depending upon the species, although not all birds can fly. Some fluffy, some stiff, lightweight feathers provide insulation, retaining body heat and keeping the bird's body dry. Feathers originated as reptilian scales, which eventually thinned and frayed. Shed at least once a year and a new set grown, the molt is controlled by small muscles at each feather's base, which also enables a bird to fluff, raise or spread them.

Usually, the feathers of male birds are more brightly pigmented than those of females, the brilliant plumage used as a visual message to repel rivals and to attract mates. Drab coloration of female birds helps conceal them from attackers as they quietly incubate their eggs for the necessary length of time.

Originally evolving from a reptilian form, birds have a body plan efficiently designed for flight. Approximately 65 million years ago, birds appeared resembling those that live today: heavy, toothed jaws replaced by a lightweight beak; tails dispensed with and legs instead acting as a counterbalance; some bones eliminated, others fused, hollowed or reinforced for strength.

A system of air sacs acting as bellows supplements lungs and supplies the bird's warm blood, approximately 105°F (41°C), with the huge supply of oxygen it requires. The air sacs are also a means of heat dispersal. A stepped-up metabolism is fueled with abundant quantities of high energy foods such as insects, seeds and nuts.

Acute hearing enables a bird to zero in on prey, and keen eyesight can recognize an enemy at a distance or a meal close up. Weighty muscles to move a bird's large eyeballs have been eliminated; instead, a bird's eyes are in a fixed position but placed well back on the side of the head to command a nearly full field of vision.

A bird's body has adapted to its way of living. Birds that have short, rounded wings as Grouse or Quail cannot fly far, but are capable of rapid bursts of speed. The medium length, pointed wings of Plovers and Falcons, allow for fast smooth flight. The broad wingspan of the Vulture holds the bird aloft for hours, supported by warm currents of ascending air.

Those birds that tear their food have hooked beaks like the Golden Eagle, those that spear fish have long, thin bills like the Bittern and those that strain plants from water have serrated bills like the Red-breasted Merganser. Long legs are built for wading, free and mobile toes are meant for perching and webbed feet are designed for paddling.

In response to increased length of springtime daylight in Northern climates, a bird's hormones trigger reproductive behavior. At this time, many male birds perform age-old mating rituals such as plumage displays, feather fluttering, strutting, bobbing, singing, food offering or aerial acrobatics, all meant to exhibit special charms and to attract the amorous attentions of a mate. An area – perhaps a single branch, a few square yards of sandy beach, or an acre of woodland – in which to raise a family is chosen and defended by the male from intrusions of male rivals of his species whose similar breeding and feeding requirements would represent undesired competition. Among the songbirds, vigorous and repeated recitals of particular vocalizations warn off interlopers and serenade the female bird, reinforcing the pair bond, which can last for a season or for life, depending upon the species.

Nest construction varies greatly from species to species. Many birds make no nest at all and simply place their eggs on the ground or in a slight depression, some build simple stick assemblages, some lay their eggs in a natural cavity and others weave elabo-

Above: The Long-billed Curlew (*Numenius americanus*) is distinguished by its cinnamon underwing lining.

Above: Abundant on the Great Plains, the Ferruginous Hawk (*Buteo regalis*) consumes a diet of rodents.

rate structures, using a variety of materials, including saliva. Hummingbirds build the smallest known nest of .8 inches (2 cm) across and about the same in height, while the nest of the Osprey may be approximately a yard (.9 m) in diameter and two yards (1.8 m) high.

The building of the nest and the incubation of eggs is often performed largely by the female, although in many species these duties are equally shared. Warmed by the heat of the parent bird, the length of time for the infant to develop in the egg can be from 10 to 80 days, determined by the size of the bird or egg, the length of the bird's life or the stage of the chick's development at hatching.

The young of birds such as ducks, geese, many shore birds and domestic fowl are born open-eyed, down-covered, and can leave the nest by the first day or two to follow parents, and find their own food. These chicks are known as precocial birds. The hatch-lings of songbirds or perching birds are called altricial, and have closed eyes, little or no down, are unable to leave the nest until feathered out and are fed by their parents.

Since the 1600s, 80 kinds of birds have become extinct, due to overhunting or to destruction of their habitats. In the early 1900s, laws gradually were enacted designed to protect birds from slaughter within the United States borders. Prohibiting all hunting of songbirds that migrate across North American borders, in 1916 the United States and Canada and in 1936 the United States and Mexico signed Migratory Bird Treaties. These agreements also regulate the hunting of migratory game birds and prevent the sale of their nests, eggs, and feathers. Both the United States and the Canadian governments maintain hundreds of wildlife refuges covering millions of acres of land where thousands of wildfowl can breed and feed unmolested.

Above: The Willet (*Catoptrophorus semipalmatus*) is found near fresh and salt water. *Center:* The American Avocet (*Recurvirostra americana*), also a wader, lives near fresh water. *Right:* Wilson's Phalarope (*Steganopus tricolor*) prefers land.

BIRDS

ANHINGA:
see Pelican, Brown; Turkey, Water

AUK, LITTLE: see Dovekie

BALDPATE
(Mareca americana)

Also known as American Widgeon, the Baldpate is a duck that breeds from northwest Alaska to northeastern California and east to northern Indiana and Hudson Bay. Although breeding occurs mostly in the northwestern part of its range, the Baldpate can be found in winter from Massachusetts to Vancouver Island and southern Alaska to Panama, along both coasts of the United States.

With a length of 22 inches (55.88 cm) and a wingspread of 35 inches (88.9 cm), the male Baldpate is slightly larger than the female. The Baldpate gets its name from the conspicuous white crown of feathers centered atop the drake's head. The female's head is pale gray. The male is colored mostly pinkish-brown, with white patches under the tail and on the forewings. The female is a duller brown but also has a white wing patch. Both sexes are colored white beneath. A flock of flying Baldpates is easily distinguishable because of the large, white areas along the foreparts of their wings. This white section is duller in immature birds.

The Baldpate is a wary water bird, quick to take wing when frightened. It is surface feeder, but it is especially fond of wild celery and other aquatic plants that grow deeper in the water than the bird is capable of digging up. To obtain the food it prefers, the Baldpate lives near ducks that dive deep for their food, such as the Canvasback, *Aythya valisineria*; The Redhead, *Aythya americana*; and the Scaup, *Aythya affinis*. When a diving duck surfaces with food in its bill, it is often accosted by a Baldpate poacher, which snatches the juicy green from the beak of the diver. The thief swims off to relish its stolen morsel, then quickly returns to pilfer the next course.

Above: The male Baldpate has a white crown.

As if to compensate for its piracy, the Baldpate warns the divers of trouble by its quick departure from the scene of potential danger. This nervous forewarning signals the slow-rising diving ducks to also beat as hasty a retreat as is possible for them. Surface feeding ducks like Baldpates bound almost vertically into the air on takeoff from the water, while diving ducks must run along the surface to power their rise, thus delaying their getaway.

Warning signals also serve while Baldpates fly. The migratory flight is either in a line nearly abreast or in a group. If any one of the group is alarmed, it emits a loud whistle, warning the others to climb higher in the air. During their journeys, many Baldpates are shot by hunters in the northeastern states while the birds fly to feed from pond to pond. As the ducks proceed across country, they become more wary, and by the time they reach the Atlantic coast, they have heeded so many whistled warnings that they fly too high to be shot.

During courtship, the male swims with neck extended and wings raised, giving whistling notes of whee-whee-whew to vie for the attention of a fe-

male. Once mated, Baldpates return to their breeding grounds as a temporarily committed pair. On dry ground, often far from water, nests are neat, well-built structures for a duck, lined with abundant down, which the female pulls from her breast and which provides a blanket of insulation. Nine to eleven creamy colored, unblotched eggs are laid in the soft down layer. Eggs are unmarked with the streaked and speckled protective coloration of many other birds, as they are well concealed beneath the brooding mother, or covered over with the down when she leaves the nest for a short time to feed and drink.

The young hatch out fully feathered in their natal down, and fully capable of walking, swimming, finding food and heeding the quacked signals of the mother duck, warning them to hide or dive. Birds hatched in such an advanced stage of development are known as precocial birds, as opposed to songbirds, which hatch completely naked and helpless. Because the labor of the mother duck is much less strenuous than is the work of mother songbird in the care and nurturing of the young, larger duck broods are produced than the broods of the birds with dependent young. Unlike male songbirds which often assist greatly in the

Above: A Bittern in the Everglades.

task of infant feeding, drakes have left the domestic scene completely to the competent attention of the female duck. Baby ducks, though, swimming about in a group but essentially on their own, are more vulnerable to predation than the hidden, fussed-over nestlings of songbirds.

Late in August, the young Baldpates have grown their flight feathers and are mature enough to join others to comprise a flock, journeying to their winter grounds along the coasts of the United States.

BITTERN, AMERICAN
(Botaurus lentiginosus)

The Bittern is a marsh bird that is not abundant, but is widely distributed throughout North America. It breeds from British Columbia to southern Newfoundland to southern California, Kansas and southern New Jersey. In winter, it can be found from California, Arizona, southern Texas, the Ohio valley and Virginia, south to Cuba and Guatemala.

With a length of 24-34 inches (60.96-86.36 cm), the Bittern has a slender body, stretched out neck, a lengthy, sharply pointed bill with fine serrations near the tip and long rounded wings. Mixed tawny, brown, black, and white streaked plumage coloration matches the marsh reeds among which it lives.

The adornment and the habits of the Bittern make the bird a master of concealment; Thoreau said that it is the genius of the bog. Walking slowly and deliberately through the marshy ooze, the Bittern's weight is distributed over long slender toes, especially adapted to prevent the bird from sinking in the mud. The slightest cause for alarm will freeze the Bittern into a unique posture of disguise in which the neck and bill become completely rigid, pointing skyward and the feathers are tightly compressed, so that the entire body appears elongated. Its striped underside now revealed blends into a background of reedy plants and its lengthened form mimics the shape of the slender stems. It moves with drawn-out slowness so as to remain inconspicuous while keeping an eye on the source of danger. In further imitation of a reed, the Bittern waves its body in rhythm with the swaying windblown motion of the plants.

The Bittern's diet is greatly varied, consisting of any small animal that frequents the marsh and meadows, the preferred morsels being fish or frogs. As the masked bird stands in wait or moves with quietness and stealth so as not to alarm its potential dinner, food is swiftly speared with the sharp, dagger-like beak.

In the spring, as part of a nuptial performance, sometimes in the summer, and rarely in the fall, the male produces noises with peculiar acoustic properties. One unmusical rendition resembles the sound of an old fashioned wooden pump and the other note sounds like a stake being driven into the soft ground. Like a ventriloquist who throws his voice, the Bittern emits its pumping and banging thumps so that their distance and location are difficult to gauge. These puzzling vocalizations account for some picturesque popular names for the Bittern: Stake Driver, Thunder Pumper, Butter-pump, Mire Drum, and Bog Bull.

In courtship, Bittern couples perform a mutual and showy display, exposing large white patches of feathers on either side of their body. They rise a few feet and fly toward one another, then clinch with feet and bills and rise another six to eight feet (1.8-2.4 m) while whirling around and around, and finally descend to the ground.

Nests are hidden among the dense marsh plants and the tall dead stems of the previous year's growth that are also used to build the platform. A foot or more in diameter, the nest is raised only a few inches above surrounding water. The Bittern lays four to six eggs, their buff colors matching the nest material, and incubates them for 28 days.

Parents feed the young in the nest for about two weeks by regurgitation, the babies grabbing at the adult's beak and swallowing the food as it passes from the parent's throat to its mouth.

At the newly hatched, helpless stage, the awkward young are often eaten by minks, muskrats, water snakes, hawks, eagles and owls. To protect the hatchlings, the watchful mother fluffs up her feathers to twice their volume, appearing menacing to a possible enemy, and defends her offspring with well-aimed thrusts of her powerful beak. So as not to attract predators to the little Bitterns, the mother never flies directly to or from the nest. Instead, she follows a pathway, about 20 feet (6 m) long through the vegetation which leads up to the nest. Landing at the end of the path, she proceeds along its course so cautiously that it could take her as long as 15 minutes to traverse the little safety route.

Leading a solitary existence, the Bittern is no more in evidence in its winter home in the southern states that in its nesting territory in more northerly areas.

The smaller Least Bittern, *Ixobrychus exilis*, measuring 14 inches (35.56 cm) in length, is also widely distributed throughout temperate North America.

BITTERN, LEAST: see Bittern

BLACKBIRD, BREWER'S: see Blackbird, Red-winged

BLACKBIRD, RED-WINGED (*Agelaius phoeniceus*)

Ranging from coast to coast throughout North America from Alaska and northern Canada, south to Florida and central Mexico, the Red-winged Blackbird is commonly found in marshes, stream borders, and pastures. Those individuals inhabiting the northern portions of the wide Redwing range migrate in autumn to winter grounds in the more congenial southern states and return again by March.

A medium-sized 8½ inches (21.59 cm) in length, the Red-winged Blackbird has a long rounded tail and a sharply pointed bill. The male is coal black in color, but its shoulders are adorned with bright crimson, yellow-bordered patches, also known as epaulets. These brilliant flashes of color become visible signals when he lowers his wings to reveal their splendor. The female bird is dressed in entirely different array; she is a dull gray-brown, heavily streaked in sooty black above and below. Young Red-wings resemble females in coloration, but

red epaulets distinguish the immature males.

In early spring the male returns to breeding grounds among the cattails and marsh reeds or in a fallow field, and stakes out a place to call his own. Although as few as two or as many as several hundred nesting sites may exist in one area, the male chooses several square yards as his domain and vigorously defends them against intruders. Perched on a willowy plant stem, he churns out his strident song, *ok-a-lee*, *kong-ka-ree*, to human ears a harbinger of spring, but to other male Redwings, a serious proclamation of territory ownership and defense, a guardianship that lasts throughout the family rearing season.

When the female arrives about two weeks later, the male is at the peak of his performance, accompanying his bravado nasal notes with a visual display to call attention to his handsome form and colors. Wings and tail are fanned out, feathers on the neck and back are fluffed up, and large areas of showy bright crimson and yellow shoulder patches are flashed. The male's song and display serve at once the dual and opposing purposes of repulsion and attraction, keeping out the competition and drawing in a mate.

Above: **A Red-winged Blackbird.**
Right: **A Yellow-headed Blackbird.**

The female Red-wing finds the male's exhibition irresistible, and in crowded colonies polyandry and polygamy may occur. Despite the number of her matings, the female builds the nest alone, which she usually places suspended among reed stalks about a foot above the marsh, sometimes in small trees or bushes and occasionally on dry ground. The nest is woven of long strips of reeds and cattail leaves, which are tied around supporting stalks among which the nest is positioned. Open spaces are chinked with moss and mud and the inside bowl is cushioned with soft grass.

Alone again, she incubates the three to five eggs for the necessary 11 days, but in feeding the hungry young, she is assisted by the male bird. The young are in the nest for about ten days and the diet of the little birds consists entirely of insects, mostly mayflies and caterpillars. Insects also comprise the summer food of the adults, but the old birds' menu is augmented by seeds and grain.

As fall approaches, Red-winged Blackbirds gather in communal feeding and roosting groups that range the

Above: **The Eastern Bluebird is the only bluebird found east of the Great Plains.**

countryside by day and retire to resting places at night. By winter, populations in these flocks reach enormous numbers, sometimes in the thousands, even millions, especially in the southern states where big gatherings of Grackles and Starlings join the Redwings. In the west, Brewer's Blackbirds, *Euphagus cyanocephalus*, become part of the foraging assemblies of blackbirds.

The Yellow-headed Blackbird, *Xanthocephalus xanthocephalus*, inhabits open regions of western and central North America, and the Tricolored Red-wing, *Agelaius tricolor*, lives along the coast of northern California and Oregon.

BLACKBIRD, YELLOW-HEADED:
see Blackbird, Red-winged

BLUE-BILL, LITTLE:
see Scaup, Lesser

BLUEBIRD, EASTERN
(*Sialia sialis*)

The well-loved Bluebird and its subspecies range widely in North America from southern Canada to El Salvador and Honduras. In winter, the Bluebird

moves from the northern portions of its breeding range to more hospitable southern grounds. In southern areas, these birds are present all through the year, although not the same individuals, the local breeders having migrated southward and replaced by others coming down from the north.

Sometimes known as the Blue Robin, the Bluebird is 7 inches (17.78 cm) in length. It has brilliant azure blue upper parts, a rusty-red breast and a white abdomen. The female resembles the male, but her blue feathers are duller in color and her cinnamon breast is paler in tone.

A gentle and trusting species, the Bluebird has adapted readily to the presence of human civilization. Its early spring arrival in northern breeding grounds, along with the Robin and the Red-winged Blackbird, announces for winter-weary humans the welcome coming of warmer days.

The Bluebird's original habitat was among scattered clumps of trees in open areas where nests were built in natural tree cavities or abandoned woodpecker holes. When orchards were planted, openings in apple trees became sought after nesting sites. Unhappily for Bluebirds but good for apples, these desired breeding loca-

tions have been largely eliminated, as old apple trees are trimmed of dead branches, removed entirely, or replaced by young trees that are regularly sprayed and pruned. To encourage the Bluebird to continue nesting in its habitual haunts where it consumes enormous quantities of insects, birdlovers and food growers have put up nesting boxes in which the cavity-inhabiting birds have readily set up housekeeping.

Competition for nesting sites has always been one of the Bluebird's greatest problems, vying with native species like the House Wren and the Tree Swallow for available openings, but taking possession often enough to maintain its numbers. However, since the introduction of the Starling and the House Sparrow, also hole-nesting species, the Bluebird has been driven away from many of its former locations. Pushed out by the more aggressive alien interlopers, today the Bluebird has declined in population, especially in the more crowded sections of the northeast. Making the entrance hole in a nesting box less than 1½ inches (3.81 cm) in diameter keeps

BIRDS

Above: The Bob-white is abundant in fields.

the larger Starling from entering, and placing the box close to the ground attached to a fence post discourages the House Sparrow, with its preference for higher locations, from moving in.

When searching for prey, the Bluebird is often seen on a low perch, as most of its insect food such as grasshoppers, crickets and beetles is found on or near the ground. From its lookout, the bird swoops down, seizes its morsel, and returns to its station to continue its vigil. Amidst the foliage, the Bluebird darts in chase of low-flying insects or picks other insects from leaves and twigs where fruits and berries are also plucked.

Arriving at its breeding grounds a few days in advance of the female, the male Bluebird selects a territory and defends it with low sweet warbling tones that warn off intrusions from males of the same species. His endearing notes also attract a female which he woos with caresses and gentle feedings preparatory to leading her to the nesting cavity he has chosen. Both partners loosely line the chamber with dried grass and weed stems, a firm structure not required in the snug opening. The five or six bluish-white unmarked eggs are incubated for about 12 days almost entirely by the female, while the attentive male occasionally feeds her and guards against unwelcomed visitors.

After 15 days of being well cared for in the nest by both adults, the young take wing, but the male parent continues to bring them food and teaches them to feed themselves. The female raises a second family, and perhaps a

third, the fully grown first brood assisting in the care of the younger batch. The family group remains in the general vicinity of their nesting area until the first crisp cold of October signals flocks of from 12 to 70 birds to start their southward drift to wintering grounds.

BOBOLINK:
see Meadowlark, Western

BOB-WHITE
(*Colinus virginianus*)

A year-round resident, the Bob-white, including four subspecies, the Eastern, Florida, Key West, and Texas Bob-whites, inhabits a range that covers most of the United States. Bob-whites can be found from South Dakota, southern Minnesota, southern Ontario and southwestern Maine south to northern Texas, the Gulf coast and northern Florida, and west to eastern Colorado.

With a length of up to 10 inches (25.4 cm), the Bob-white has a tawny mix of plumage above of chestnut, black and ashy colors, while below it is shaded with marks of brown and black. A white line over the eye extends to the back of the head; the chin and throat are also white, but in the female they are buff. The reddish tints of the male are less intense in the female, fading out to a dull pinkish hue.

The Bob-white is a quail, a member of a group called Gallinaceous birds, which are ground dwellers, fowl-like in appearance, with short stout bills, small heads, heavy bodies, chunky moderately long legs and short rounded wings. Gallinaceous birds obtain their food almost entirely from the ground, and to gather it they frequently scratch the earth. This scratching behavior results in well developed thigh muscles, richly supplied with blood vessels, which makes the thigh the dark meat of the tasty bird when it is brought to table.

It lives mostly in association with cultivated fields, and man's agriculture provides abundant food for the Bob-white. A destroyer of pernicious

weeds and injurious insects, the Bob-white consumes seeds in winter and grasshoppers, potato beetles, chinch bugs and squash bugs during summer. Thus, farmer and bird perform mutually beneficial services, man creating conditions which feed the quail and the quail reducing the harmful results of man's cultivation.

The Bob-white travels in a small flock of family members called a bevy or a covey. When individuals in the feathered group are scattered for reasons of defense, the repeated two-syllabled call of *bob-white, bob-white* signals respective positions and helps reunite the flock. The bevy settles down on the ground in a tight circle, tails toward the center, heads facing outward. If an attacker approaches, the birds spring swiftly out and up, the group scattering in all directions with each member disappearing in the brush. The multiple displacements leave a potential enemy totally confused over which target to follow or where it is concealed. An escaping quail will often flatten itelf on open ground, and by virtue of its matching coloration seems invisible. As further protection, a Bob-white can withhold its scent by tightly compressing its feathers.

Bob-whites huddle together in winter in their circular coveys where the warmth of close-packed feathered bodies under piles of insulating snow enables the birds to survive the cold. Severe conditions sometimes cause their deaths as ice packs them in and encases them in a frozen tomb.

Nests of dry grasses are built on the ground, sheltered by thick plant growth. Twelve to eighteen pure white eggs are laid, ends pointed downward, all skillfully packed in to economize space. Incubation is alternated by the hen and cock, a monogamous pair, for 24 days. The obliging quail will lay another clutch of eggs in a season if the original is destroyed, and will adopt chicks from other pairs, if needed. The young are ready to leave the nest as soon as their natal down has dried, following the parent like baby chicks in the constant hunt for food. The hatchlings heed the mother's warning to hide in grass, under her feathers, or to flatten out their fluffy bodies on the ground and blend into their backgrounds, concealed from a fox, a hawk or man.

The Bob-white Quail is the state bird of both Oklahoma and Rhode Island. Other quails within our range, but confined to the western United States are the California Quail, *Lophortyx californicus*; Gambel's Quail, *Lophortyx gambelii* and the Mountain Quail, *Oreotyx pictus*.

BOB-WHITE, EASTERN: see Bob-white

BOB-WHITE, FLORIDA: see Bob-white

BOB-WHITE, KEY WEST: see Bob-white

BOB-WHITE, TEXAS: see Bob-white

BOG BULL: see Bittern

BRANT
(Branta bernicla)

The Brant is a goose that is seen in the United States only during the winter. Its breeding grounds in spring and summer are on Arctic islands within the shadow of the frozen north. It winters on the Atlantic coast from Massachusetts south to North Carolina and rarely to Florida. Some interior sightings have been recorded. On the Pacific coast, it can be found from British Columbia south to Mexico.

The Brant is the smallest of our wild geese, measuring 24 inches (60.96 cm) in length. Its color is brownish-gray above and ashy-gray and white beneath. It has a long slender neck and, like other geese, the sexes are colored alike.

Geese are members of the family *Anatidae*, which means 'Goose-like swimmers' and includes ducks and swans as well. There are about 40 species of geese throughout the world,

ten or twelve of which can be found in the United States, mostly as winter residents or migratory visitors. Among those occurring in North America are Snow Goose, *Chen hyperboreus*; Blue Goose, *Chen caerulescens*; White-fronted Goose, *Anser albifrons* and Canada Goose, *Branta canadensis*.

Similar to the Brant is the Black Brant, *Branta nigricans*, which has black feathers on the head and breast that extend over most of its underparts. The Black Brant is found on the Pacific coast of North America. The name Brant comes from the sound the bird makes, which is a rolling call.

In their winter feeding grounds of intertidal zones on the southern Atlantic coast, Brants gather in large companies to gorge on a plant which is almost their exclusive food – eelgrass, *Zostera marina*. Growing in the shallow water of the shoals, eelgrass appears as long stringy seaweed, but unlike seaweed, it is a rooted plant. Clumps of eelgrass when washed up on beaches look like dried masses of blackened shoelaces. Between the years 1930 and 1940, a disease attacked the eelgrass on both sides of the Atlantic, almost decimating the plant and in turn threatening the continued existence of the Brant for which the eelgrass is the principal food. As mysteriously as the plant disease appeared, so did it eventually depart, allowing the eelgrass to reestablish itself in the coastal waters. In direct relation to its rebound, the Brant population regained its strength. The

Above: **Atlantic Brants once faced extinction.**

eelgrass-Brant relationship illustrates the extreme dependency of animals on the plant world, and the danger to animals which are specific feeders if their food supply is threatened.

In the Middle Ages, a strange belief existed regarding the Brant Goose, particularly in Ireland. It was thought this goose hatched from barnacles and was therefore a fish rather than a fowl; it was thus allowed as food on meatless Fridays.

Brants have been clocked at flying speeds of 62 miles (99.2 kph), compared with 40 miles (64 kph) for Canada Geese. Rarely straying far from salt water, flocks almost skim the wave tops when facing a strong headwind, but even without the wind, the birds do not fly high. At an average flying height of approximately 300 feet (90 m), Brant flocks, consisting of about 50 birds, fly in long undulating lines, unlike large geese which fly in highly organized formations.

Breeding in colonies of about 150 lifelong mated pairs per square mile, the female constructs a bowl-shaped grassy hollow, lined with down, in lowland coastal tundra, usually just above the high tide line. The nesting grounds are highly susceptible to flooding by storm tides. An egg a day is laid until they number three or four, and when the full complement is deposited, the female starts her incubation period which lasts for 25-28 days. Even though the eggs are laid a day apart, all

BIRDS

goslings hatch together because they were all incubated for the same length of time, the warming period starting simultaneously for all.

Sitting on her eggs in the rounded bowl, the female flattens her body and extends her neck low so she is barely visible above ground level. The gander stays nearby to forage and to keep watch, chasing gulls and jaegers from the vicinity of the nest. Although the goslings hatch out covered with thick down feathers and are able to walk, run, swim and find their food immediately, fully half of the young die before reaching winter grounds, victims of predation and disease.

BRANT, BLACK: see Brant

BROAD-BILL:
see Scaup, Lesser

BUFFALO BIRD: see Cowbird

BUFFLEHEAD:
see Canvasback; Oldsquaw

BUNTING, INDIGO
(*Passerina cyanea*)

The Indigo Bunting can be found as a summer resident throughout the United States and southern Canada from the great plains to the Black Hills east, except in southern Florida and southern Texas. In winter it migrates southward to Mexico and Central America.

Approximately 5 inches (12.7 cm) in length, the Indigo Bunting has the short, stout, conical bill of other members of its Finch family. The adult male is colored a bright cerulean blue, but at certain angles, because of the refraction of light through the outer feather cells, the bird can appear greenish-blue or, from a distance, black. A fall molt of feathers replaces the blue with brown, but blue continues to appear on the wings and tail. The female bird is shaded in subdued olive-brown above and dull white below.

In such dimly hued colors compared to the electric tinges of the male's plumage, the female Indigo Bunting

seems to have been short-changed by nature; however, her lack-luster raiment serves a practical function. Vivid tones for the female would attract the undesired attentions of potential predators as she incubates her eggs, but instead her dingy brown stripings blend into her background and provide necessary concealing protection.

Unlike the female's cryptic colors designed to hide, the male's gaudy coat is meant to attract, to call attention to his charms as he struts his glossy finery before his modest mate in breeding season. The male Indigo Bunting is one of the most showy birds, and despite his tempting brilliance, makes no attempt to keep himself from view. The male sings persistently while exhibiting himself on a bare twig, roof, chimney top, telephone wire, fence or other exposed perch. Undaunted by the heat of summer when other birds have quieted for a noonday respite or have ceased singing entirely, the Indigo Bunting holds forth in loud sweet melody, sometimes described as canary-like. He is one of the few birds in North

Above: A female Indigo Bunting nesting.

America whose volume and intensity of performance increases as the season wanes, his recitals continuing until he molts his feathers in late August.

What has this flashy, resonant bird have in common with its dingy sparrow cousins who delight in dust baths that leave their dull brown feathers only a little dimmer than they normally are? The Indigo Bunting shares many traits with sparrows, such as feeding on the ground, eating mostly grass and herb seeds with a few insects for variety, flying in short labored movements, and building grassy nests in low bushes.

The Indigo Bunting's preferred locations for nest construction are woodland borders, roadside thickets, shrubby fields and even garden shrubbery. Because such habitats are more abundant today than they were during the early settlement of North America, the numbers of this species have increased.

Nests are built about 5 feet (1.5 m) from the ground in an open brushy

Above: The male Snow Bunting (*Plectrophenax nivalis*) has large white wing patches.

Above: The male Canvasback has a red head.

place, cleverly concealed in undergrowth or thicket. Made of twigs, grasses and weed stalks, the nest is lined with fine grass, hair and feathers, and after necessary repairs, may be occupied repeatedly for many years by the same couple. The female alone incubates the four plain pale blue eggs, while, as is true of most brightly colored birds, the male remains at a distance so as not to reveal the hiding place of the nesting brood. An alarm note, though, from the female brings him down in agitated concern to protect his family-to-be.

In South American winter feeding grounds, Indigo Buntings remain together in small flocks, the same individuals comprising a group from one year to the next and returning annually to the same jungle clearing.

In the midwest, where the range of the Lazuli Bunting, *Passerina amoena*, and the Indigo Bunting overlaps, these two species interbreed and produce fertile offspring, leading some ornithologists to believe that these birds should be considered as one species.

The Painted Bunting, *Passerina ciris*, is a southern bird of such a quiet manner that it is not very well known. Because it is a favorite cage bird in Mexico, Americans along the border call it the Mexican Canary.

BUNTING, LAZULI: see Bunting, Indigo

BUNTING, PAINTED: see Bunting, Indigo

BUSHWACKER: see Hawk, Sharp-shinned

BUTTERPUMP: see Bittern

BUZZARD, TURKEY: see Vulture, Turkey

CALICO-JACKET: see Turnstone, Ruddy

CANARY, MEXICAN: see Bunting, Indigo

CANARY, WILD: see Goldfinch, American

CANVASBACK (*Aythya valisineria*)

A diving duck, the Canvasback is a strictly North American species. It breeds from central Alaska to Wisconsin, south to New Mexico. In winter, it can be found from southern British Columbia to New York, south to central New Mexico and Florida.

The Canvasback measures 24 inches (60.96 cm) in length, the drake slightly larger than the duck. The head and neck of the male are a rich chestnut-brown, the breast blackish and the rest of the body mostly white, with the exception of a black rump. The colors of

the female are a somber brown and gray, her subdued markings camouflaging her presence as she incubates her eggs. In both sexes the bill is three times as long as it is wide, and because no clear indentation between the head and neck exists, the profile of the bird is long and sloping.

The Canvasback is a member of a family of diving ducks that submerge themselves completely underwater for their food. From a position on the surface of the water, they dive underneath, instead of tipping only the front part of their bodies forward as do the surface feeders. Twenty species of divers are found in North America, among them the Redhead, *Aythya americana*; the Ring-necked Duck, *Aythya collaris*; the Greater Scaup, *Aythya marila*; the Lesser Scaup, *Aythya affinis*; the Common Goldeneye, *Bucephala clangula*; the Bufflehead, *Bucephala albeola*; Oldsquaw, *Clangula hyemalis*; the White-winged Scoter, *Melanitta deglandi* and the Common Eider, *Somateria mollissima*. Diving ducks waddle clumsily on land because their legs are placed toward the rear part of the body. Unable to spring readily into the air on takeoff from water as can dabbling ducks, divers must patter along the surface to get a long running start before they become airborne. Once aloft, the Canvasback is the fastest flying diving duck in North America, moving like an arrow at a speed often in excess of 70 mph (112 kph).

Each fall large concentrations of Canvasbacks once converged in the Chesapeake Bay area, which was the gourmet resort destination of the southern migratory flight. There, in keeping with its scientific name, *Aythya valisneria*, the Canvasback gorged on a favorite tender plant, the wild celery, *Vallisneria spiralis*. Various other water plants also comprise its preferred diet, and because the Canvasback is primarily a vegetarian, as opposed to other diving ducks which eat animal matter, its flesh tastes flavorful and delicious instead of rank and fishy. Due to the drainage of feeding areas, to destruction of breeding habitats and mostly to overhunting because of its marvelous flavor, Canvasback numbers have greatly dwindled. Market hunters shot the tasty sporting bird by the thousands when hunting laws were not enforced.

Today, Canvasbacks and Redheads, too, are protected in their flyways, but no longer do they converge in countless numbers along the south Atlantic coast of the United States. Adapting to the pressures of hunting, the birds have become shy and wary. In some areas they sleep far out in the bays during the day and return to the shore to feed under the safe covering of night.

Very early in the spring, flocks of Canvasbacks in V formation travel northward from their winter quarters to their breeding grounds in the broad prairie regions of western Canada. Following its age-old migration route, known as a flyway, the Canvasback's early season journey is often slowed by frozen ponds and wetlands along the way.

Near marshes and sloughs in the interior northwest, nests like wicker baskets are woven of dead plant stems and lined with soft, gray down. The bulky structure is a semi-floating mass, usually housed in a clump of reeds or rushes growing at least knee-deep in water.

Above: The male Cardinal, like the female, has a pointed crest and thick red beak.

The female lays six to ten pale olive-gray eggs, frequently with the eggs of other ducks mixed in among them. Areas in the northwest are common breeding grounds for a great many wild ducks who often lay their eggs in each other's nests. The Redhead and the Ruddy Duck sometimes exchange incubation chores, and sometimes they charge the accommodating mother Canvasback with some of their brooding and rearing duties. After 23 days of the necessary, patient sitting, the fluffy, yellow Canvasback ducklings emerge, together with any other babies that were incubated, all covered with their natal down. In 10 weeks, feathers grow and by October the young Canvasbacks have developed the strong muscles and the flight feathers that enable the juveniles to join the southward flying flocks.

CARDINAL
(*Richmondena cardinalis*)

Originally a bird of the southern states, the Cardinal is becoming more and more common as a year-round resident as far north as Ontario, Connecticut and Ohio, and west to the edge of the Great Plains.

The Cardinal is approximately 9 inches (22.85 cm) in length, a little smaller than a Robin. The male is adorned in brilliant orange-red and even its strong, stout beak is colored rich vermillion. It wears a high cap of peaked plumage, making it North America's only red bird that has a crest. In sharp contrast to its brazen hue, its chin and a band around its bill are somber black. The female Cardinal has more muted coloration, the red subdued with browns and buffs, her overall appearance a faded version of the male except for her brightly colored bill.

The male Cardinal can be seen as a short-lived streak of fire as it flies amidst low dense clusters of verdant foliage, often in the company of his toned-down mate. The Cardinal's favorite habitats are in thickets and tangles of moist upland forests, but it also enjoys hedgerows, parks and orchards where it forages, nests and roosts. To perch or roost, like other members of the order Passeriformes, or perching birds, the Cardinal clamps its toes around a branch and special muscles lock the grasp in place, thus supporting the bird by preventing it from losing its grip.

The fat and powerful conical beak reveals the Cardinal as a seed-eater; three-quarters of its diet is comprised of seeds, wild fruits and grains, while the remainder of its menu is made up of pesty insects, such as the Rocky Mountain locust, Colorado potato beetle, boll weevil and cotton cutworm. In winter Cardinals may be seen searching barnyards for corn and visiting feeding stations, especially looking for sunflower seeds.

In its reproductive season, the male Cardinal marks out a breeding territory and diligently defends the area with musical warnings meant to keep away potential rivals of the same sex and species. With tuneful deterrents effective, nesting areas are apportioned among Cardinals, thus relieving them of competing among themselves for the same food and living space, especially at the time that nestlings require abundant nourishment.

The Cardinal sends out a wide variety of loud clear whistles, one of the most common songs a rich rounded sound rendered as *cue-cue-cue. Cheer-cheer-cheer* is also often vocalized, sometimes at dawn, sometimes at night, and unlike most species, songs are delivered throughout the year. Unusual in birds, the female also sings, but her outpouring is softer than the male's and is sounded from a less exposed perch. Singing as an invitation to mating and sometimes crooning even from the nest, her season of recital is shorter than the male's.

In the southern portion of the Cardinal's range, nesting may start as early as February, and nestlings from a later brood may be found as late as October. The nest is a loosely constructed deep cup of twigs, leaves, weed stems, shredded bark and grasses, lined with hair and grass. It is placed in the bush, thicket, briar tangle or brush pile of the female's choice. She alone builds the structure, and she alone incubates the two to four variously marked eggs for the necessary 12 days.

As is often true in brightly colored species, the male Cardinal stays away from the nesting site, so his flashy chroma does not lure an enemy to the hidden brood. He does, though, feed the female during the incubation period, but for safety's sake he attends her only when she is away from the nest. He also takes complete and careful charge of the young for three weeks after they leave the nest, while the female embarks upon the entire reproduction operation again, and perhaps

for a third time in any breeding year. The pair bond is maintained for successive broods throughout the season, and has been known to persist for as long as three years.

CHEWINK: see Towhee

CHICKADEE:
see Chickadee, Black-capped

CHICKADEE, ACADIAN:
see Chickadee, Black-capped

CHICKADEE, BLACK-CAPPED
(Parus atricapillus)

Found throughout northern North America from the Atlantic to the Pacific coasts, the Black-capped Chickadee is a permanent resident in most of its wide range. In winter a general southward movement takes place among more northerly Chickadee populations, and individuals seen in winter are not necessarily the same birds as the summer inhabitants.

Only 5 inches (12.7 cm) in length, the plump, big-headed Black-capped Chickadee has a short straight bill and soft, puffy plumage with a fur-like appearance. For warmth in cold tem-

Above: A Mountain Chickadee.

peratures, the small round bird grows a winter coat of a greatly increased number of feathers, and the entire downy covering can be fluffed up, trapped air spaces providing additional insulation and making the Chickadee look like a furry tennis ball.

In keeping with its name, the Black-capped Chickadee wears a hat of black plumage and under its chin has a bib patch of feathers that are also colored black. Gray upper parts and white underparts complete its attire.

The Black-capped Chickadee is in constant communication with others of its kind. Its song in spring is a familiar, sweet, two-note whistled *fee-bee*, the first note higher and the second sometimes delivered with a quaver. Both male and female sing out their sharp melody in a conversational mode, one bird responding to the other's completed phrasing.

A cavity nesting bird that is unable to completely peck out its own nest hole, the Black-capped Chickadee's favored sites are abandoned woodpecker excavations or natural niches found in deciduous trees or fence posts, anywhere from 2-50 feet (0.6-15 m) above the ground. Despite the

BIRDS

strength of the Chickadee bill, it is not strong enough to penetrate sound wood, so the bird must enlarge an opening already begun or chip out a nursery in soft, decaying wood. Once entrance through the hard outer wood coating is gained, both male and female work diligently to fashion a chamber to suit their needs, each taking its turn at digging out a mouthful of wood chips and scattering the tell-tale signs of habitation a distance from the nesting cavity. Generally, holes are carefully concealed and entranceways are large enough to admit only the little bird and not a larger predator. The bottom of the incubation room is lined by the female with a variety of fluffy, soft materials, collected from furry, fuzzy plants and animals and used as a bed and warm covering blanket for the eggs.

The entire nest construction operation requires about two weeks to accomplish, the six to eight eggs need 12 days of incubation by the female before they hatch, and the young are fed for 16 days in the nest until they fledge and fly away. The male feeds his mate while she warms the eggs and both parents deliver food to their hungry growing offspring.

Once the responsibility of rearing a family is fulfilled, Chickadees leave their brood chamber and collect in small, high-spirited flocks, composed of fewer than a dozen other Chickadees, not necessarily parents and siblings. The ebullient group remains loosely together throughout the winter, roving the cold woodland and communicating among themselves with their *chick-a-dee-dee-dee* call. A definite friend of man, the Chickadee's winter food is comprised primarily of the eggs of injurious moths, plant lice and scale insect eggs, which the bird searches out, often in an upsidedown position, by minute examination of tree bark crevices and crannies. About 5000 eggs a day are destroyed by a single bird.

Wild fruits supply the bulk of the Chickadee's vegetable food, the favorite being the wax-covered berries of bayberry and poison ivy. Only the fleshy portions of the berries are consumed, while the indigestible kernels are passed through the digestive system, thus spreading the noxious poison ivy where the seeds are dropped. The proliferation of this rash-producing plant is a small price to pay for the large insect egg devouring service the Chickadee performs.

The winter Chickadee feeding group returns each night to the same roosting area in the coniferous forest and scatters itself amidst the dense foliage, settling quietly down to sleep among the branches of the trees.

Closely resembling the Black-capped Chickadee is the Mountain Chickadee, *Penthestes gambeli*, a bird of slightly different coloration than its eastern cousin and an inhabitant of the mountains of the western United States. The Chestnut-backed Chickadee, *Penthestes rufescens*, lives in the Pacific coast area, while the Acadian Chickadee, *Penthestes hudsonicus*, is a bird of the southeastern Canadian Provinces and the extreme northeastern United States.

CHICKADEE, CHESTNUT-BACKED:
see Chickadee, Black-capped

CHICKADEE, MOUNTAIN:
see Chickadee, Black-capped

CHUCK-WILL'S WIDOW:
see Whip-poor-will

COMMON WAVY:
see Goose, Snow

CONDOR, CALIFORNIA
(Gymnogyps californianus)

The largest land bird on the North American continent, the California Condor is in grave danger of extinction. The relative handful known to survive lives in Los Padres National Forest in southern California, and members of this group can sometimes be observed over Ventura County soaring in search of food.

The California Condor, a member of the vulture family, reaches a length of 45 to 55 inches (1.1-1.4 m) and weighs between 20 and 25 pounds (7.4-9 kg). Its wingspread extends to 11 feet (2.8 m). The body is black-feathered except for a strip of white under the front of each wing, and a ruff of black feathers circles the neck. The Condor's head is bald and may be either orange or yellow on top, and it has the hooked beak characteristic of birds of prey.

Primarily a carrion eater, the Condor has exceptionally keen eyesight that enables it to spot wounded or dead animals from miles away. It can readily kill a disabled young goat or sheep, as well as smaller prey, by tearing at it with its powerful beak. It is not known to attack man.

The California Condor's preferred nesting site or aerie is a cave high in a

cliffside, and it lives in pairs during the mating season (November to March) and while rearing its young. The female condor lays only one egg per year, plain white with a greenish or bluish tint and large enough to hold half a pint of fluid. It takes a full year for the young condor to reach maturity, and the parents feed and care for it throughout that period. The young Condor is not yet full grown when most fledgling birds of prey are leaving the nest at the age of about three months. This slow rate of reproduction, with other factors including loss of habitat, added to the near demise of the California Condor as a species.

The California Condor population has been dwindling over the last several decades and by the 1980s the species total reached 20. In that time bird conservationists have been struggling to increase that population. In 1982 they were closely watching the progress of an egg laid in the wild only to see it be destroyed accidentally when the Condor parents were arguing. In 1983 a scientific breakthrough was reached when the first Condor to be born in captivity was hatched in the San Diego Wild Animal Park in California and survived.

The chicks each weighed under 8 ounces (229 g) when they were born, but within days their weight had more than doubled. In order to encourage the Condor chicks to accept food, they were fed by means of a hand puppet, a

device which was used to replace the parent Condor. The initial diet consisted of a daily feeding of minced young mice mixed with fresh vulture vomit, a balanced diet for Condors that supplied the bacteria essential to their development. As the chicks grew stronger and increased in strength they were fed grown mice and then baby chickens.

CORMORANT:
see Pelican, Brown; Cormorant, Double-crested

CORMORANT, DOUBLE-CRESTED
(Phalacrocorax auritus)

A dark-colored diver, the Double-crested Cormorant is North America's most widely distributed Cormorant. It breeds from Newfoundland to central Alberta, south to Nebraska and Maine. It winters from North Carolina to the Gulf coast, congregating in great numbers on pilings near harbors, looking for an easily caught fish dinner.

The Double-crested Cormorant measures about 30 inches (76.2 cm) from tip to tip. Its long, stiff, rounded tail, composed of 12-14 feathers, is used to assist the bird in walking and climbing. Aside from a yellow-orange throat pouch, this Cormorant is a solid, iridescent, greenish-black color. A crest of feathers appears on each side of the head in both sexes during courtship. These plumes fall out soon after nesting begins.

Fossil evidence shows the ancestors of Cormorants date back 50 million years. Unlike other diving birds of ancient lineage like Loons and Grebes, Cormorants do not have waterproof plumage. After diving, the Cormorant must return to a sunny perch where it sits with wings half spread and hung out to dry. It has a comb-like growth on the claw of its middle toe which it uses to preen its feathers.

When making long-distance flights, the Cormorant is capable of flying high in the air, but ordinarily it does not rise far above the water. Diving readily for fish, always from a low perch and

never from the air, it captures prey with a powerful hooked bill, well adapted for catching and holding. Feet and wings are used in swimming. After a successful catch, the Cormorant returns to the surface of the water and juggles the fish into a head-down position, readying it for swallowing.

The Cormorant can lower or raise its body in the water as it swims along. This elevator-like operation is done by flattening the feathers against the body and forcing out the trapped air. Buoyancy can also be controlled by enlarging or contracting air sacs in the body.

The birds gather in colonies on rocky coasts and the nests are built on cliffs overlooking the sea. Nests are also built on the ground and in rushes or trees of interior swamps and islands. Crudely arranged, they are constructed of sticks and weeds, with two to four pale, blue-white eggs deposited within.

The young hatch out in about 30 days, at first naked, black and so shiny as to appear greasy. Within a few days after hatching the babies grow black down feathers. The little chicks feed by thrusting their heads down the throats of the parents and consuming the partly digested fish captured for that purpose.

The Cormorant is called by some a Shag. Although fishermen often complain that Cormorants are depriving them of fish, the fish caught by the birds are of no commercial value. Relatives of the Double-crested Cormorant were used by the Chinese as fishing helpers. A string was tied around the bird's throat to prevent a fish from being swallowed after it was captured by the bird. The fisherman could then retrieve the fish.

COWBIRD
(Molothrus ater)

In farms, meadows and open woodlands, except in portions of the Pacific coast, the Cowbird makes its home throughout most of the United States, southern Canada and northern Mexico. Partially migratory, Cowbirds in the more northerly sections of the

Left: **The California Condor is nearly extinct.**
Above: **A Double-crested Cormorant.**

BIRDS

Above: A Bronzed Cowbird (Tangavius aeneus).

range move southward in autumn, although small groups remain in colder regions throughout the winter if ample food is available. Winter grounds are from Maryland, the Ohio Valley and central California, southward.

Eight inches (20.32 cm) in length, the Cowbird has a thick cone-shaped bill and broad rounded wings. It is unassuming in appearance, the male dressed in greenish-black with a brown head, the female colored a plain dull gray.

It is best the Cowbird does not call attention to itself with flamboyant coloration as it seeks a place to enact its peculiar behavior. Having no instinct for constructing its own incubation quarters or rearing its own young, the parasitic Cowbird lays its eggs in the nests of other species. It leaves the thankless and energy-consuming task of child raising to others while it remains unencumbered to devote itself to the serious pursuit of insects.

After mating, the female Cowbird hunts out the nest of a smaller bird, containing one or more freshly deposited eggs, and when the luckless victim is inattentive, the Cowbird simply slips in and lays her own large egg. Four to six eggs are thus pawned off in as many days, each usually in a different nest. Over 150 species have been listed in whose nests Cowbird eggs have been found.

In most cases the deceived parent uncomplainingly assumes the burden of incubating the Cowbird egg, often at the expense of its own young, but Robins and Catbirds resent the

blotched intruder and push it out. The Yellow Warbler, *Dendroica aestiva*, does not eject the foreign object, but builds instead a covering over it to serve as a new nest for its own eggs, but that, too, can become a depository for another Cowbird egg. Some four or five Yellow Warbler nest levels have been found, each layer covering a big, parasitic egg.

Because the Cowbird egg is usually larger than the others in the nest, it receives more warmth from the accepting sitters, and because it usually requires less time for incubation, it hatches earlier. The young Cowbird monopolizes the food delivered by the host birds, while the smaller, weaker, legitimate heirs perish from lack of proper nourishment or from being pushed out by the larger interloper. The foster parents nurture the young Cowbird as if it were their own, despite the size disparity between the big baby and the little parent dupes.

When great herds of American Bison roamed the western plains, the Cowbird, then called Buffalo Bird, lived in close association with the huge beasts, picking off ticks from their backs, and gorging on stirred-up insects on the ground. The demise of the bison, the domestication of cattle, and the clearing of eastern forests transferred the Cowbird's loyalty from buffalo to cows and greatly extended its range. The Cowbird continues to live more commonly in the west than in the east, where it benefits from the large assortment of bugs and insects that live with and near cattle, including many harmful species such as grasshoppers, boll weevils and army worms.

In winter, roving flocks of Cowbirds comb the countryside in search of food, often accompanied by groups of other species, such as Starlings, Red-winged Blackbirds and Grackles. Due to the scarcity of insects in winter, the adaptable bird changes its cold weather diet to seeds.

CRANE, BLUE:
see Heron, Great Blue

CROW: see Crow, Common

CROW, COMMON
(*Corvus brachyrhynchos*)

The big, black Common Crow, including all five subspecies, is widely distributed throughout the greatest part of the North American continent. The Eastern race breeds from southwestern Mackenzie Territory to Newfoundland, south to Maryland and northern Texas. It winters between the northern and southern boundaries of the United States.

The Crow reaches a length of 21 inches (53.34 cm) and is charcoal black in color. Although the Common Crow is probably the best known bird in America, it is often mistaken for the smaller Fish Crow, *Corvus ossifragus*, which measures 14 inches (35.56 cm) in length and is also glossy black. The much larger Raven, *Corvus corax*, 27 inches (68.58 cm) long, also covered with all black plumage, is a bird of Oregon, Montana and South Dakota, east to Missouri, Illinois and Indiana.

Not only is the Common Crow one of the most abundant birds in North America, it is also one of the most adaptable and intelligent. It is felt by ornithologists that Crows represent the peak of development in avian evolution, evidenced by the bird's high mentality and complex social organization. Although the Crow has been persecuted by farmers and gunners for centuries because it relishes newly planted corn, more Crows have thrived nourished by the easily available increased food supply than have been massacred for taking advantage of the table that man has spread before them. The crow population today is greater than it was at the time of America's early settlement by the Europeans.

The Common Crow does not dine exclusively where it is unwelcome; it also eats many insect pests and carrion, thus serving a valuable role in the ecological process of ridding the environment of harmful species and of decomposing matter. Primarily a bird of fields and the edges of the woods, it makes itself at home in a large assortment of habitats, except deserts, deep thickets and mountaintops, where it indulges its omnivorous appetite for toads, salamanders, turtles, snails, grain, wild fruits, small birds, eggs, mice and large quantities of destructive insects. At the seashore, a Crow, like a Gull, will drop a clam or mussel from a height to crack open the shells on the rocks below, then swoop down to devour the meat contained within. A full grown crow eats its own weight in food every day, the total consumption divided among eight to ten full meals.

Crows usually gather in small groups of three to eight birds, but during the winter they often assemble from miles around in great nocturnal roosts made up of many thousands of birds. From such mob scenes, they fly out during the day to scour the countryside for 50 miles around in search of food. All gather together at a prearranged meeting place before retreating to the roost at night.

The familiar discordant *caw-caw-caw* call of the Crow contains a great variety of subtle variations, each ex-

pressing a particular state of mind, such as warning, threatening, taunting, or cheer. A seldom heard utterance is delivered while the bird is hidden among the foliage and is an uncharacteristic sweet musical warble known as a whisper-song. Pet Crows can be taught to articulate an assortment of words because they possess a complete set of vocal muscles.

Both sexes take part in building a nest, often placed as high as 75 feet

Below: **The well-known Common Crow.**

BIRDS

(22.5 m) in conifers or other trees, but if trees are lacking in the breeding territory, the adaptable bird nests on the ground. A bulky but well built structure 12 inches (30.48 cm) in diameter of coarse twigs, grasses and tree bark, the nest is lined with soft inner bark which imparts a warm yellow-brown hue to the inside bowl.

Partners share in the incubation of the four to six eggs and both participate in the care of the young. After 18 days of warming, the blind, flesh colored hatchlings emerge, at five days of age the eyes open, and when five weeks old, the fledglings make their initial flight.

CROW, FISH:
see Crow, Common

CUCKOO, BLACK-BILLED:
see Cuckoo, Yellow-billed

CUCKOO, GROUND:
see Cuckoo, Yellow-billed

CUCKOO, YELLOW-BILLED
(Coccyzus americanus)

The caterpillar consuming Yellow-billed Cuckoo, with its western subspecies, is distributed throughout almost all of the United States and some of southern Canada. It is much more commonly seen in the southern states than in the northern portions of its range; in the northeast it is outnumbered by a bird of similar habits and behavior, the Black-billed Cuckoo, Coccyzus erythropthalmus.

The Yellow-billed Cuckoo is a slender bird, longer than a robin, measuring approximately 12 inches (30.48 cm) in length, its tail alone 6 inches (15.24 cm) long. It is colored olive-brown above and white below and only at close range can the yellow of its lower beak be seen. In flight, black and white markings on the lengthy tail are visible.

The cuckoo's graceful easy flight is attributed to its ultra-streamlined shape, its long tail-rudder steering it soundlessly through the branches of the trees. For long periods, it retreats to a hidden shady perch to conduct a patient vigil or moves quietly about in search of prey.

Few birds share the Yellow-billed Cuckoo's peculiar appetite, a taste that makes this bird and the Black-billed Cuckoo, too, of invaluable service to man – it eats hairy caterpillars that are injurious to trees. Most bird species avoid the bristly crawlers, but cuckoos seem to relish them. One was seen to consume 41 gypsy moth caterpillars in 15 minutes, another to eat 47 tent caterpillars in six minutes. An observer reported that in one-half day every tent caterpillar in a badly infested area was devoured by cuckoos and the caterpillar nests were also destroyed.

When the cuckoo's stomach becomes so packed with caterpillar spines and tussocks that digestion is obstructed, the bird simply sheds its entire stomach lining and grows a new one. The bill of fare is not confined to fuzzy larvae; other insects are also consumed, including armyworms, beetles, ants and wasps. Grapes and berries are also eaten.

The vocal ability of the Yellow-billed Cuckoo does not resemble the timely musical renditions of cuckoo-clock birds, but is merely an unmelodious series of gutteral *kuks* and *chucks*.

Although the European relatives of the Yellow and Black-billed Cuckoos often indulge in a parasitic practice of laying their eggs in other birds' nests, the cuckoos in America usually build their own nests and rear their own broods. Occasionally, though, the two American kinds interchange mothering chores, one depositing its eggs in the other one's nest, thus sponging off only a close relative and not a perfect stranger.

No showplace, the Yellow-billed Cuckoo's nest is a ramshackle assemblage of twigs, grass, leaves, and catkins, placed 25 feet (7.5 m) high in the crotch of a tree, so shallow that it seems unable to contain the three to four pale green eggs that are deposited in it. The young hatch out at various intervals, as the eggs are laid at different times, and babies of diverse ages are found in the nest. An unattractive, naked, black hatchling emerges, greasy in appearance and helpless in demeanor, but able to call a low *cuk-cuk-curr-r-r* as a signal to the parents to be fed.

Another American cuckoo is the Road Runner, *Geococcyx californianus*, of the southwest. Slim and long-tailed, also known as Ground Cuckoo, it races with remarkable swiftness to catch its fast moving lizard prey.

CURLEW, PINK:
see Spoonbill, Roseate

CUTWATER:
see Skimmer, Black

DARTER, AMERICAN:
see Turkey, Water

DEVIL-DIVER:
see Grebe, Pied-billed

DEVIL DOWNHEAD:
see Nuthatch, White-breasted

DOVE, MOURNING
(Zendaidura macroura)

The sad-sounding Mourning Dove is a familiar bird throughout North America. It breeds from New Brunswick to British Columbia and south through interior United States, Mexico and the Bahamas. It winters from Iowa and Massachusetts, west and south to Panama.

The Mourning Dove is 11 inches (27.94 cm) in length, with a pointed, white-bordered tail that accounts for 6 inches (15.24 cm) of that measurement. The tail is longer than the wing. The prevailing color of this pigeon is grayish-blue above, and below it is reddish-fawn in hue, the female similar in appearance to the adult male, but duller in tone.

The song of this bird is distinctive and serves well to identify it and to give it the well-deserved common name of Mourning Dove. The slow mellow five-syllable notes evoke profound melancholy, or perhaps tender affec-

Above: Fledgling Doves.
Right: Four-week old Mourning Doves.

tion. Shrill, whistling sounds could be construed as a part of its singing repertoire, but these whirrings are made by the swift flapping of its wings in flight. In mating season, in exuberant display, the male rises from its perch with energetic wingbeats and ascends to a height of 100 feet (30 m) or more, then returns in a glide.

The Mourning Dove, a migratory bird, is a common summer resident within the northern part of its range where its long breeding period lasts from May to September. During that length of time, this pigeon may raise three or even four broods. The female wastes no time in nest construction, as she builds only a scanty structure made of a few sticks, lacking a rim or lining, placed on the ground or low in a bush.

BIRDS

The two eggs are incubated for about two weeks, both sexes alternating warming periods.

When the young hatch out, they are without feathers and completely helpless as they wait in the nest to be fed by both parents. Nourished on pigeon's milk, a milky soup of predigested food, the young drink from the crop of the adult. The parent's food is composed primarily of seeds, but to feed the young, the adults consume insects and caterpillars, which are processed into the liquid baby food.

Mourning Doves are shy birds, couples tenderly devoted to each other and caring nothing for the society of others of their kind. In its solitary ways, the Mourning Dove is unlike its now extinct and highly gregarious, larger, more brightly colored cousin, the Passenger Pigeon, *Ectopistes migratorius*. The Mourning Dove is often mistaken for the Passenger Pigeon, but the latter was totally exterminated after a long period of relentless exploitation. Extremely companionable, nesting and migrating in enormous flocks of millions, the Passenger Pigeon was highly vulnerable to human predation. To conserve shot, often these birds were netted and clubbed to death for food.

In 1913 the Federal Migratory Bird Law classed the Mourning Dove as a migratory species and it came under the law's protection, no longer to be shot for game, but the law was enacted far too late to save the Passenger Pigeon. In 1914, the last Passenger Pigeon died, a victim of its delicious flesh and its intense sociability. The Mourning Dove is now hunted legally in many states without depleting the species.

The Band-tailed Pigeon or Wild Pigeon, *Columba fasciata*, of western forests, was also hunted almost to extinction, but today, thanks to protection, flocks are making a comeback.

DOVE, SEA: see Dovekie

DOVEKIE
(Alle alle)

The Dovekie is a sea-going bird that breeds along the coasts of Greenland and other islands of the north Atlantic. In winter, it moves to somewhat warmer coastal waters that are less locked in by ice, and can be found as far south as New Jersey.

With a length of 8 inches (20.32 cm), the Dovekie is shiny black above and pure white below. In summer, the white of its underparts extends to its bill and to the sides of its head and neck. The small round head, short neck and short thick bill give the bird the appearance of a Quail.

Other names for the Dovekie are Little Auk and Sea Dove. Gregarious in nature, it swims in small flocks in the open sea. Diving with agility, it pursues its food of fish and crustaceans underwater, using its wings and feet to propel it. Like others of its relatives, the Auks, the Murres and the Puffins, the Dovekie drops like a stone beneath the surface of the water to escape from danger.

The Dovekie leaves the water only to breed. Gathering in huge colonies on deserted, rocky islands of the north Atlantic waters, the Dovekie deposits a single pale blue egg, usually unmarked. The crevices created by the loose rubble hide the egg from predators. For 24 days, parents alternate the job of incubating the egg, while the unoccupied partner goes off to feed. The downy young hatch out in poor imitation of the adult coloration, sooty above and lighter gray beneath. The babies are fed crustaceans carried to them in their parents' gullets.

The habit of the little Dovekie of communal nesting that brings crowds of them together, and their seeming lack of fear of people makes their capture convenient and easy during breeding season. The Eskimos kill many of these birds and use their densely feathered skins for making shirts that insulate from the frigid cold. Eskimos also eat the birds and their eggs.

Although the Dovekie spends all its non-breeding time in an oceanic habitat, it occasionally is found far inland. It seems to have a peculiar facility for becoming battered or disoriented by winter storms and sometimes is blown on to land. Stranded in a snow bank or in a field, the helpless bird tries to find the water, as only from its surface can the Dovekie alight. Unless the bird can be returned to the sea, it will die.

DUCK, BLACK
(Anas rubripes)

The Black Duck is a common wild bird, especially prevalent in the eastern half of North America. It breeds from Manitoba to Labrador and south to North Carolina and Colorado. It spends the winter along the Atlantic coast of the United States, south to Florida and west to Colorado.

The Black Duck is 24 inches (60.96 cm) in length. Both male and female greatly resemble the female Mallard, *Anas platyrhynchos*, so much so that a popular name for the Black Duck is Black Mallard. Not black in color, both male and female Black Ducks are a dusky-brown and both have a purple-blue wing patch like the female Mallard. The drake's bill is yellowish, its legs orange, while the female Black Duck has an olive bill with feet not as brightly colored as the male's. In flight, this duck can be distinguished from other ducks by the white linings of its underwings.

Although the Black Duck and the Mallard are alike in appearance, they differ markedly in temperament. The wild Mallard is shy and timid, but it loses its self-protective ways in captivity. The Black Duck is persistent in its wildness and when reared in captivity it retains its apprehensiveness.

In winter the Black Duck can be found in both salt marshes and freshwater swamps. Coastal dwellers feed on shrimp, periwinkles and small mussels, while freshwater inhabitants eat pondweed, wild celery and grasses. Crayfish, fish and insects are also eaten, but most of its food is plant material. As a surface-feeding duck, its diet of chiefly vegetable matter is plants that grow near the surface of the water. To reach its food, it dabbles, meaning it tips its body forward submerging its front half and up-ending its rear. Dabbling ducks also waddle onto land occasionally to raid a corn or grain field.

Like most other ducks, the Black Duck has a broad, flat bill with tooth-like edges on the upper and lower parts. This kind of beak is called a lamellate bill and permits the duck to grasp a piece of food while the water drains from its mouth.

Because the Black Duck is the most widely hunted wildfowl for food and game in the eastern United States, it has good reason to have developed secretive and wary behavior. In keeping with its timid ways, it lives close to thickly vegetated waters where it finds its food and hiding places. It flies and feeds mostly under cover of the night and in the faded light of dawn and

dusk. When alarmed, the Black Duck, like other dabbling ducks, can make a quick escape by springing directly into the air from water without the need to patter a running take-off.

During breeding season the drakes perform communal displays, a showing-off to gain the attention of a mate. The males court by executing short flights and by bobbing their heads. Not monagomous, a male can mate with several females and after copulation the female is left to her own devices to incubate and rear the young.

On the ground, she constructs a nest of reeds, sedges and grasses found in the vicinity of her brooding site, and lines the deep-cupped structure with down feathers, which she pulls from her breast. The softness of the down cradles the eggs, helps keep them warm and hides them when the mother duck must infrequently and temporarily leave the nest to feed and drink.

The fluffy yellow ducklings peck out in 26-28 days, immediately capable of following their mother to the water, there to paddle themselves around and find their food, always within protective sight and hearing of the adult bird. At this time in their lives, unable to fly, the young are in most danger of becoming prey to hawks, gulls, crows, raccoons, skunks, snapping turtles and even large game fish. At a loud warning quack from mother duck, the babies quickly hide in plants or go underwater, yet first year deaths among wild ducks may average 50 percent or higher. Despite the dangers of predation, disease, parasites, habitat destruction and shotguns, some individuals reach a remarkable old age. A banded wild Black Duck killed in Pennsylvania was 20 years of age.

Other longevity records of wild ducks include a Green-winged Teal, *Anas carolinensis*, 20 years; Canvasback, *Aythya valisineria*, 20 years; Common Goldeneye, *Bucephala clangula*, 17 years; Pintail, *Anas acuta*, 17 years; and Gadwall, *Anas strepera*, 16 years.

DUCK, LONG-TAIL:
see Oldsquaw

DUCK, PINTAIL:
see Duck, Black

DUCK, REDHEAD:
see Canvasback

DUCK, RING-NECKED:
see Canvasback

DUCK, SWALLOW-TAIL:
see Oldsquaw

DUCK, WOOD
(*Aix sponsa*)

The gorgeously colored Wood Duck is well deserving of its scientific name, *Aix sponsa*, which means 'a water bird in bridal dress.' It breeds in most of the United States and in the southern provinces of Canada, rarely farther north. It winters along wooded streams and inland lakes from southern British Columbia to southern Virginia and south to central Mexico.

The Wood Duck measures about 20 inches (50.8 cm) in length, the female smaller than the drake. The drake is clad in dazzling raiment all year round, except for a short time in the summer when he molts and regrows feathers. During this molt his feathers are dull and blotchy in appearance and he is dressed in what is known as eclipse plumage. Having temporarily lost his flight feathers, he is unable to fly; therefore he becomes very wary and protective in his eclipse period.

For the remainder of the year, he appears as if arrayed in precious gems. His head is iridescent in shades of green, bronze, blue and black, strikingly adorned with a conspicuous crest. His upper body parts are of dark, shiny green and black feathers, contrasting with light tan, fine lined sides. The deep chestnut-colored chest is flecked with little triangles of white. The underparts are white, the feet a dull yellow, and the bill a unique pattern of white, red and black, most brilliant during the breeding season.

Compared with the male Wood Duck, the female seems drab, but next to hens of other species, she sparkles like a jewel. She has a crest, although it is smaller than the male's, and overall she is brownish, much less brilliant and iridescent than he.

The Wood Duck belongs to a group of pond or dabbling ducks, which includes the Mallard, *Anas platyrhynchos*, the Gadwall, *Anas strepera*, and the Shoveler, *Spatula clyplata*, all of which spring almost vertically into the air from water during takeoff. Diving ducks, such as the Redhead, *Aythya americana*, the Canvasback, *Aythya valisineria*, and others, require a long running start to build up the momentum enabling them to ascend. Once airborne, the Wood Duck's flight is swift and direct, but it is also capable of agile maneuvering when weaving through wooded areas. The flight speed is about 47 miles (75.2 km) per hour, and the bird can be recognized in the air by the crested head held high, the bill angled downward, the short neck and the contrasting white underparts.

As its name implies, the Wood Duck is associated with wooded places,

Below: **The Wood Duck is the only duck to have a long slicked-back crest. The female has white-ringed eyes and this colorful male has a long square tail.**

swamplands, freshwater marshes and rivers bordered by forest lands. Keen eyed and alert to danger, it avoids large expanses of open water, flushing quickly when approached. If danger is extreme, the Wood Duck will dive and swim underwater, emerging among the protective plants of water's edge. On land, it walks with greater ease and speed than other ducks, a distinct advantage as it searches for seeds, fruits and nuts on the forest floor. Its relatively short and narrow bill is better suited for picking up seeds than for straining food out of water as is the broad bill of other ducks. A strange behavior for a duck is the Wood Duck's habit of perching in trees.

Courtship and pairing takes place on the wintering grounds. During courtship, the male and female swim side by side, the drake caressing his partner's head lightly with his bill. They return to their nesting grounds as mated pairs, the female leading the way to reinhabit a former nesting site or to find a suitable tree cavity in which to lay the eggs. The most desirable nesting holes are 20-40 feet (6-12 m) high in trees along woodland streams, but some may be a mile or more from water. Besides natural cavities, the

Wood Duck will use a man-made nesting box.

Inside the hole, the hen lays an egg each day until her clutch of 10 to 15 eggs is completed, and she covers them with an insulating blanket of down tugged from her breast. For 30 days, the hen alone sits on the eggs inside the cavity, meeting the drake for short times during the day when she leaves to feed and drink. By the time the ducklings hatch out, the drake is no longer near the domestic scene.

A day after the ducklings hatch the mother Wood Duck entices her babies to jump from the cavity and follow her to water. At a soft, clucking communication from her, each round, downy baby flings itself from the nest into the water or on to the ground, depending on the nest's distance from a stream. Like light, fluffy parachutes, the fearless ducklings land with a splash or with a bounce, aided by outstretched, webbed feet and outspread fluffy wings. Instinctively, they follow the mother in close formation to the water, there swimming behind her in a tight cluster, a survival measure against predators more apt to attack stragglers separated from the little brood.

EAGLE, BALD
(Haliaëtus leucocephalus)

The Bald Eagle, the national symbol of theUnitedStates, lives exclusively in North America, widely but unevenly distributed throughout the continent. It breeds in various areas throughout its extensive range.

The length of the male Bald Eagle can reach 35 inches (88.9 cm), while the length of the larger female can be 43 inches (109.22 cm). Both sexes are similar in coloration, and when they are three years old, Bald Eagles develop white feathers on the entire head and neck. Until this adult plumage is complete, juvenile birds have dark heads and tails. The Bald Eagle is named after its whitened head covering, not after a bald pate.

A distinguishing feature of the Bald Eagle as compared to the other eagle of North America, the Golden Eagle, *Aquila chrysaetos*, aside from its mature white head, is the feathers on the legs. The Bald Eagle's leg feathers reach only to an inch above the toes, whereas the Golden Eagle has legs entirely feathered, covered down to the toes.

The Bald Eagle possesses the highly developed hunting adaptation of a bird of prey, such as keen eyesight, powerful wings, superb strength, swift flight, large, hooked beak and strong, curved talons. Despite its specialized features, and in behavior unbecoming to a national emblem, the Bald Eagle's hunting style is one of piracy and plunder. Near the sea and other large bodies of water, the big bird perches on a cliff or tree limb overviewing the panorama and watches fishing birds, especially the Osprey or Fish Hawk, *Pandion haliaëtus*, as they search out fish. On witnessing a successful catch, the Bald Eagle chases and torments the Osprey in the air until the fish is released from the Osprey's talons and the eagle dexterously catches it before it hits the water.

The Eagle will also resort to eating dead fish cast up on shore or floating on the water's surface, and occasionally it joins the Crows and Ravens in

Above: **The Bald Eagle eats mainly fish, while the Golden Eagle eats mostly rodents.**

picking clean various dead, decaying animals. Not living exclusively on dead or stolen food, the Bald Eagle will capture fish, birds and mammals. A powerful bird, it can lift an object its own weight, approximately 12 pounds (5.4 kg), but there is no truth to the persistent legend that eagles carry small children away to their nests.

A huge, bulky nest called an aerie is built near water on an inaccessible cliff ledge or high in a large tree. A voluminous accumulation of sticks, sod, weeds, roots, plant stems and other coarse material is added to annually by the life-long mated pair, until the entire structure can reach a size of 4-5 feet (1.2-1.5 m) across and more than that in height. The ample nursery holds two ivory-white eggs which require approximately 35 days to hatch under the alternating incubating attentions of both the male and the female eagles.

The eaglets spend their first ten weeks of life in the security of the nest, their food delivered to them by the industrious parents. For the remainder of the year the massive construction serves as meeting place, look-out point and dining room for the adults, the fattened young ones having been driven off.

For the first three years of their lives, the immature Bald Eagles are so different in plumage coloration from the adults that Audubon thought them a distinct species and named them Birds of Washington.

Although both the Golden and Bald Eagles are protected by Federal laws and the Endangered Species Act, these birds continue to be shot by vandals. Other threats to the continued existence of these large members of the hawk family are electrocution from high power lines when the birds are flying and loss of their wild nesting habitat. The Bald Eagle, because it is a fish eater, has been adversely affected by the use of DDT, a long-lived insecticide stored in the tissues of fish. When large amounts of DDT were ingested by the Bald Eagle, the accumulated poison interfered with the bird's calcium production, which caused eggshells to be so thin that they cracked when the eagle attempted incubation. In 1972 DDT was outlawed, and from a low point of 1000 or fewer Bald Eagles in the United States, wildlife biologists in 1982 estimated a total population of

BIRDS

25-30,000 birds in North America, with about 4000 to 5000 dwelling in the lower 48 United States.

As a national symbol, the Bald Eagle has a unique place in American history. Western native Americans prized its wing and tail feathers for their war bonnets before the covered wagons crossed the plains. As early as 1776 the first eagle on a United States coin appeared on a Massachusetts penny. In 1782, under the Congress of the Confederation, the United States took as its emblem the Bald Eagle with outspread wings, bearing a shield on its breast, with an olive branch in one claw and a sheaf of arrows in the others.

EAGLE, GOLDEN
(Aquila chrysaëtos)

The Golden Eagle, a big hunting bird, breeds from northern Alaska south to lower California and east through the Rocky Mountains. Its breeding area formerly included the New England states, but it is now found primarily in the mountainous areas of the west. Throughout its range, except in the most northerly parts, the Golden Eagle is a permanent resident, leaving the snow-covered north only for more hospitable winter hunting grounds in Florida and Texas.

The total length of the female Golden Eagle can measure up to 41 inches (104.14 cm) with a wingspread of 92 inches (233.68 cm) and a tail 16 inches (40.64 cm) in length. As is true of all raptors or birds of prey, the male is several inches smaller than the female. The Golden Eagle's average weight is between 7 and 12 pounds (2.6-4.5 kg).

The dominant color of the bird is dark brown, but the feathers on the back of its head, nape and sides of the neck, an area called the hackles, are colored a deep golden hue, the tone that gives this eagle its name. Its legs are covered with brown feathers completely down to the toes, the fluffy leg warmers allowing the Golden Eagle to inhabit cold localities.

A powerful bird, the Golden Eagle can carry off a victim weighing up to its own weight and can drag a heavier weight a short distance. With strong hooked talons, the eagle immobilizes and kills its prey of small mammals, primarily rabbits, fawns, ground squirrels, woodchucks and prairie dogs. Its food preferences help keep the numbers of little nuisance animals in check, which is of benefit to man. For its occasional habit, when wild food is scarce, of carrying off a lamb, piglet, kid or chicken, the large feathered hunter has been shot or poisoned to the point of its becoming an endangered species. The killing of this eagle is now outlawed.

Its hunting fashion is straightforward, swift and dashing, and when falconry flourished in England, the Golden Eagle was flown only by kings. A close relative of the Bald Eagle, *Haliaëtus leucocephalus*, the national emblem of the United States, the Golden Eagle's nobler habits would seem better to equip it for such a lofty honor, but the Golden Eagle is not exclusively a North American bird as is the Bald Eagle. The Bald Eagle's hunting style is one of piracy and plunder, compared to the Golden Eagle's speedy, clean, unassisted attack on live prey, sometimes even taking on animals larger than itself.

Left: Mature Bald Eagles have white heads. *Right:* The Golden Eagle's large nest is an accumulation of several years of building.

Throughout the breeding season, the life-long mated Golden Eagles indulge in mutual aerial maneuvers of spiral glidings in ever-rising circles, sometimes almost touching, and downward, arrow-swift nosedives.

A large bulky nest called an aerie is built on an inaccessible cliff located in a commanding position where the birds can look out over a wide expanse of open country. Always in keen search for prey, especially to feed the hungry eaglets, Golden Eagles must have a broad view of the ground. Firmly woven of thick sticks and lined with softer materials, the aerie is returned to every year by the pair. Each year, new sticks are added until the structure becomes a voluminous 5-6 feet (1.5-1.8 m) in diameter and almost the same measurement in-height, large and strong enough to hold a 6 foot (1.8 m) man.

For approximately 35 days, the female alone incubates the two white eggs that are strikingly marbled with shades of chestnut and purple, and are prized additions to an egg collector's store. The male attends the sitting mother by bringing her food. Parent eagles do not defend their eggs or young if an intruder threatens. The frightened female flies quietly away and disappears, or she may remain at a distance, but despite her ability to do so successfully, she will not fight off an enemy as do many other kinds of birds.

Stripped of fur and feathers, the food of the eaglets is brought to the aerie by the male, and tidbits are picked out by the female to give to the young. When the youngsters are strong enough to tear up their own food with their special beaks, the game is left whole and placed beyond their reach, so that the little ones are encouraged to exercise their legs and wings in learning to feed themselves.

The full power of flight is not achieved by the young eagles until they are three months old, and four years must pass before the birds develop the

complete adult plumage.

Western Indians preferred Golden Eagle feathers to all others for their war bonnets. This led to its being called the War Eagle in the West.

EAGLE, WAR:
see Eagle, Golden

EGRET:
see Egret, American; Egret, Snowy

EGRET, AMERICAN
(*Casmerodias albus egretta*)

A tall white heron, the American Egret is a bird of temperate and tropical America. It breeds in Oregon and California and from North Carolina, Florida, the Gulf coast and Mexico south. In winter, it lives from the Gulf of Mexico southward.

Among the longest, most slender and most majestic of birds, the American Egret measures to a length of 41 inches (104.14 cm). Both male and female have plumage that is entirely white and have yellow bills and black feet. During the breeding season, both sexes develop a train of long, magnificent white plumes, growing from the back and extending a foot or more beyond the tail feathers.

As desirable as these gorgeous feathers may appear as articles for human adornment, the Egrets have developed productive and natural uses for their full dress decoration. During courtship, the male Egret struts around the female emitting gurgling noises and raises his snowy plume-train almost erect to display his magnificent attire. Plumes are also raised and displayed for mutual admiration during the ceremony of nest relief when egg incubation positions are switched between the mother and the father. The female erects her beautiful plumes above her back before she feeds her young, perhaps a physical indication of the strong instinctive need to nurture her offspring.

Before the turn of the century, fashionable women wore hats decorated with bird feathers, sometimes

even with entire stuffed birds. What more graceful luxurious adornment to surmount one's head than with the flowing breeding plumage of the Egret? The beauty of the bird almost caused its extinction, as plume hunters shot them by the tens of thousands in response to the heavy market demand. In 1903 hunters received $32 per ounce for Egret plumes, which made these feathers worth twice their weight in gold.

For the hunters to acquire the feathers, the Egrets had to be shot in their nesting colonies while nurturing the young. If the slaughter began before the eggs had hatched, the adults might have deserted their nests and eggs, but once the babies emerged and demanded to be fed, the adults could not deny the strong parental instinct.

At the cost of their lives, the adults stayed to care for their young, and once the parent birds were killed, the helpless babies also died. Driven from its former haunts, the Egret population became dangerously near extinction.

In the early 1900s, legislation was enacted which outlawed the killing of wild birds for their plumage. Plucked from the brink of annihilation by the pressures and the protection of the National Audubon Society, the Egret is now the symbol of that organization.

Forced to occupy the most remote and inaccessible nesting locations, the Egret builds its nest in steamy swamplands. Congregations of birds construct loosely made nests of sticks and twigs, placed in bushes or higher in tree limbs. When the three or four

Left: **The American Egret is one of the largest of the white herons.**
Above: **Snowy Egrets in California.**

young hatch out in about 24 days, those in lower nests wander around their immediate vicinity, but those in higher quarters remain until they can fly.

The food of the adult bird consists of small fish, frogs, lizards, snakes, fiddler crabs, mice, moles, insects and some vegetable matter. Standing in marshes, or moving at a slow, deliberate pace, the big white bird strikes with unerring swiftness at a moving, edible target with its rapier-like bill. Unlike most other herons, the American Egret does not feed at night, but flies off at dusk to a favorite protected roosting place where numbers often congregate.

Through protection, and by virtue of its own natural wariness, the American Egret has miraculously survived the wholesale slaughter. Although its numbers have been greatly reduced, fewer American Egrets were killed than were their smaller relative, the Snowy Egret, *Egretta candidissima.*

EGRET, SNOWY
(Egretta candidissima)

A white-plumed wading bird, the Snowy Egret lives in temperate and tropical America. The Snowy Egret formerly bred from New Jersey to Nebraska and south to Chile and Argentina; now its breeding area has been confined to the southern part of the United States, along the coast from North Carolina to Texas. It winters from Florida and Mexico south.

The Snowy Egret is 24 inches (60.96 cm) in length, smaller than its close relative, the American Egret, *Casmerodias albus egretta*, which measures 41 inches (104.14 cm) in length. The Snowy Egret is pure white in color and during breeding season it is adorned with about 50 delicate plume feathers that are curved at the tip and are growing down the bird's back like a filmy bridal train. Its legs and bill are black, but appearing as if wearing colored shoes, its feet are yellow, while the larger American Egret has feet and legs that are all black.

Both the Snowy Egret and the American Egret were slaughtered to the brink of extinction at the turn of the century because of their filmy plumage, greatly prized as an adornment on the hat of the human female. Millions of Egrets were shot by hunters while the birds were performing their parental nurturing duties in their large breeding communities, their airy feathers pulled out of their dead bodies to decorate women's hats, and the helpless young left to starve to death.

The Snowy Egret was killed in greater numbers than was the larger bird because it was originally much more numerous and more widely distributed, because it was less shy and more accessible and because its shorter delicate plumes were in higher demand than the longer stiffer plumes of the American Egret. To the plume hunters, the smaller bird was known as Little Snowy or Short White and the bigger species was called Long White. Close to being totally wiped out, the Snowy Egret and the American Egret became a concentrated cause of preservation by the National Audubon Society whose efforts resulted in the protection of these birds.

Snowy Egrets nest in crowded colonies; the rookeries might have consisted of many scores of pairs. Flat nests with shallow depressions are built near isolated boggy marshes, some close to the ground and some five or six feet high in a bush, loosely constructed of sticks and dead plant stems.

Eggs are deposited every other day until they number five or six, with incubation starting when the first egg is laid. Many birds do not start to sit until the entire clutch of eggs has been produced, but because Snowy Egrets breed in warm climates, eggs could cook if left unattended for a long period of time. The first egg laid is the first to hatch, each egg taking 18 days to develop. With little ones hatching out every other day, there is a disparity in the size and strength of each bird in the nest, although all are small and helpless when very young. Under drooping wings that act as parasols, one or the other of the parents shields the young birds from the sun.

Both sexes alternate incubation tasks and both adults share the job of

BIRDS

feeding the hungry young. When one parent is off the nest the other guards the babies, and when the absent mate returns the couple caresses and coos as if separated for weeks, a devoted pair. The downy white young are fed on a kind of fish chowder, which is passed from the parent's bill to the youngsters', accompanied by convulsions of the adult's neck as the food is regurgitated from gullet to mouth.

In about a year and a half, the young Egrets attain full adult feathered finery. Adult birds molt their feathers in summer when the beautiful, but now worn, plumes are shed and replaced by shorter, straighter feathers of their winter garb. The following winter produces the filmy reappearance of the breeding plumes.

EIDER: see Eider, Common

EIDER, COMMON
(Somateria mollissima)

A sea duck of the far north, the Eider breeds on rocky coastal islands of Labrador, Newfoundland, eastern Quebec, Nova Scotia and Maine. Winters are spent from Newfoundland and the Gulf of St Lawrence to Massachusetts and even as far south as Virginia. Flocks of Eiders frequently congregate in huge rafts offshore near Chatham, Massachusetts.

Below: The Common Eider eats mollusks.

The Eider duck reaches a length of 26 inches (66.04 cm), the male somewhat smaller than the female. The drake has a white throat, upper breast and back, with a gray head and black underparts. The female is brown, the body evenly streaked with a darker brown.

Eiders are sluggish fliers, moving low over salt water and remaining close to rocky, coastal land. In migration, they fly in long, wavy lines, alternating stroking and gliding in the air. They are generally silent birds, but the female may emit a guttural quack if startled on her nest and the male sometimes utters a quiet croak during breeding season.

The food of the Eider is essentially mussels, which are captured by rather shallow dives. With its beak, the bird tugs the mussels from their rocky attachments and swallows them whole, crushing the hard mollusk shells in its powerful gizzard. The grinding action of the gizzard is assisted by a small amount of gravel which the duck swallows and retains for crushing purposes. The gravel acts as teeth, which are lacking in birds so as not to contribute extra weight. The Eider's food preference of animal matter gives its flesh a decided fishy taste, making the bird unpalatable.

Swimming in the frigid northern waters, the Eider is protected from the extreme cold by its fluffy layer of down feathers. Air is trapped in the fluff and provides warm insulation, enabling the bird to withstand the Arctic sea temperature. Compact feathers also keep the duck's body dry. To maintain the efficiency of the plumage, the Eider, like other birds, must preen its feathers by conditioning them with oil. The oil is secreted from a gland at the base of the tail, called the uropygeal gland, and is spread throughout the feathers with the beak. The oil-treated feathers cause water simply to bead up and roll off, like water off a duck's back, preventing the plumage from becoming saturated.

On rocky seashores, nests are built in a community, placed in a crevice on the ground and fashioned from moss, seaweed and lichen. To provide a warming layer for the six to ten dull greenish-colored eggs deposited within, the female tugs from her breast her eiderdown and lines the nest with an insulating softness. More than an ounce of down mats the nest and extends up the sides to provide a flap or blanket over the eggs when the duck must occasionally waddle off to feed and drink. During the month of incubation, more down is added to the pile, and if the eggs and fluffy heap are removed from the nest, the female will obligingly lay and tug an additional supply.

In the 18th century, the Eiders were clubbed to death for their feathers and nests were robbed of down during their communal breeding season when the birds were grouped together. Since that time, eggers, fishermen, and settlers have continued to threaten Eider duck populations until their numbers have greatly dwindled. The lucrative industry that has grown up around the lightweight eiderdown is now supplied by duck farms where Eiders can nest unmolested, their fluffy feathers used for making clothing, quilts and sleeping bags.

Other species of Eiders also have down feathers in high demand. The Spectacled Eider, *Lampronetta fischeri*, the Northern Eider, *Somateria dresseri* and the King Eider, *Somateria spectabilis*, live mostly in the northern part of the Northern Hemisphere.

EIDER, KING:
see Eider, Common.

EIDER, NORTHERN:
see Eider, Common

EIDER, SPECTACLED:
see Eider, Common

FALCON, PEREGRINE:
see Kestrel, American

FINCH, CASSIN'S:
see Finch, Purple

FINCH, HOUSE:
see Finch, Purple

FINCH, PURPLE
(Carpodacus purpureus)

In open evergreen woodlands, the Purple Finch is a common summer resident primarily of the Midwest and the New England states. It also occurs in western coastal ranges from British Columbia to northern Baja California, breeding in a strip of mixed coniferous and deciduous forest. It winters south to the Gulf coast, while birds of the western mountains simply move to a lower elevation rather than undertake a strenuous southern journey.

Approximately 6 inches (15.24 cm) in length, the male Purple Finch is colored in rich raspberry-red and brown, its pigment more pinkish than purple. The female, not as attractively adorned, is washed in dull olive-gray above and white below with all-over conspicuous streaking. Males that are fully plumed in their raspberry-rose feathers are hard to find, as it takes several years and several molts before their adult coloration is attained. The young male birds resemble females in the color of their coats.

The rounded, stout cone-shaped bill of the Purple Finch, and of other Finches as well, makes the bird unmistakable as a seed eater, although the generic name, *Carpodacus*, means fruit-eating. Observations of the bird while it is feeding in orchards shows it poking into pears and cherries as if to eat the fruit, but examinations of the

Above: **This Purple Finch is a woodland bird.**

stomach reveal that its major food is seeds. The Finch would not come equipped with a powerful, nutcracking beak for soft pulpy food.

The song of the Purple Finch is delivered from a topmost perch of a balsam or a spruce tree. His notes are a rapid tumble of flowing musical twitters that could be confused with the song of the Warbling Vireo, *Vireo sylvagilva*, but the Finch's style is more variable. Singing reaches sweet-voiced richness when, during breeding season, the male performs his arias to call a female's attention to his charms and to announce to other male Purple Finches his territorial rights. Melodies emanate from the bird's syrinx, the simpler functional equivalent of the human's larynx or voice box.

Well hidden in concealing branches of dense conifers, the Purple Finch's nest is a deep, frail cup of openwork made of grass, rootlets and strips of bark, padded with softer material. The female alone constructs the nest, and she alone incubates the four or five eggs for 13 days, while the male supplies her food. Although the Purple Finch is primarily a seed eater, its young are fed large quantities of insects, including plant lice, caterpillars and cutworms.

The closely related species of Carpodacus occupy completely separate breeding areas, thus avoiding unnecessary competition. The House Finch, *Carpodacus mexicanus*, breeds in the dry, open country of the west, and Cassin's Finch, *Carpodacus cassini*, the evergreen woodlands high in western mountains.

FLAMINGO
(Phoenicopterus ruber)

The Flamingo was once a regular visitor to the isolated tropical swamps and shores of Florida, but now it has disappeared from the wild. Adapting well to captivity, the big pink bird can be seen in many tropical parks. Flamingos nested in the West Indies and in South America where colonies of as many as 7000 had been seen. Today it has disappeared from much of the area where it once bred in large numbers.

With a length measuring to 48 inches (121.92 cm) including a 5 inch (12.7 cm) bill, the Flamingo has an abnormally long slender neck and stick-like extruded legs, both neck and legs of about equal length. The plumage of this striking bird is sometimes a startling pink color and sometimes a pale pink hue, with scarlet and vermillion on the black-tipped wings. The legs are red.

The unusually long legs and neck of the Flamingo aid the bird in feeding in shallow water, the legs raising the body up, and the neck enabling the beak to reach the bottom. The head is hidden underwater as food of small mollusks and algae is scooped up from the mud with the highly specialized beak. The bill bends sharply down at the middle, and when the bird lowers its head to feed, the beak turns upside down with the upper mandible then serving as the lower one. In shovel motions, the turned-over bill dredges up the mud, and through straining structures that line the edges of the horny mouth, mud and water are drained away, pumped out by rapid motions of the tongue. When all the mud is washed away, the bird lifts its head and swallows its food whole; the shells are ground up in the stomach, the walls of which are thick and muscular.

Although its legs are stilt-like and ungainly, the Flamingo is capable of resting on one leg for long periods and running swiftly. Its flight is slow, steady, and labored, powered with quick wing beats, legs and neck fully outstretched. When asleep, the long

BIRDS

hose-like neck is coiled and curved, the head tucked snugly beneath the feathers of the back. Resting in flocks, should one bird honk an alarm note, all necks will shoot up like a wiggling jumble of scarlet snakes.

In great colonies on remote and inaccessible tropical islands, Flamingos once built their numerous nests, often only 2 feet (.6 m) apart. Constructed

Below: **The female Flamingo lays one egg at a time and both parents care for it.**
Right: **Adult American Flamingos in southern Florida, where they live on mudflats.**

almost entirely of mud, sometimes with twigs, roots or leaves, nests are conical in shape from 5-13 inches (12.7-33.02 cm) in height. The mud is scooped up with the bill and patted into a cone-shaped structure with bill and feet. A single egg is laid, warmed for the necessary 30 days by both sexes, which alternately sit atop the little crater with gangly legs folded under them, changing daytime incubation duties with nighttime feeding.

The young Flamingo when newly hatched is thickly covered with white

down and is sufficiently developed to swim and run. Its bill is straight, but in about two weeks the peculiar bent shape begins to form. The food of the young is the partially digested food of the adult, a blackish liquid regurgitated by the parent and delivered a drop at a time in response to the baby's open-mouthed appeal.

Also called American Flamingo, Greater Flamingo, and Scarlet Flamingo, the birds are relatively long-lived. One captive bird lived 18 years. The Flamingo has been a symbol of

miraculous regeneration since ancient Egyptian times when it stood for the sun god Ra. Early Christian literature equated it with resurrection and immortality.

FLAMINGO, AMERICAN:
see Flamingo

FLAMINGO, GREATER:
see Flamingo

FLAMINGO, SCARLET:
see Flamingo

FLICKER
(Colaptes auratus)

The Flicker, a brightly colored woodpecker, also known as the Yellow-shafted Flicker, has a wide range in eastern North America from the northern tree limit south to the Gulf coast. A close relative, which lives west of the Mississippi and is similar in behavior, is the Red-shafted Flicker, *Colaptes cafer*.

The 11 inch (27.94 cm) long Flicker is colored a rich grayish-brown, barred

with black above, and its underparts are lilac-brown, black, and yellowish in tone. Seen from below, the underside of the tail and wing are a brilliant yellow. Although the male and female Flickers share similar coloration, the male's distinguishing feature is an elongated patch of black on its cheek, appearing as a mustache, while the female lacks this adornment.

The long list of common names given to the Flicker is indicative of its numerous outstanding physical and behavioral features. Yellow-shafted Flicker or Yellowhammer describes its golden hued underwing and undertail feathers. Because of the Flicker's habit of chiseling out a nest hole high in trees, it is called High-hole or High Holder. One of its calls, as it flies about in search of its meal of insects, sounds like *yarrup-yarrup*, so it is affectionately termed by that utterance, Yarrup, and another of its many vocalizations gives it the name, Flicker. A treatise on the bird written in 1900 lists 132 popular names, titles varying according to locality.

The Flicker feeds primarily on the ground, a food-gathering method seldom shared by other members of its family like the Red-cockaded Woodpecker, *Picoides borealis*; Three-toed Woodpecker, *Picoides americanus*; Red-Headed Woodpecker, *Melanerpes erythrocephalus*; Lewis's Woodpecker, *Picoides borealis*; Three-toed Woodpecker, *Centurus uropygialis*, which often drill into trees in search of grubs and insects. The Flicker's bill is less powerful than that of other woodpeckers, and its eating habits do not include the wood-boring techniques of the better equipped species.

Not a bird of the deep thickets, the Flicker prefers open country or sparsely wooded regions where it scrutinizes the ground for its favorite food, a taste which helps keep in check the number of destructive insects. To uncover ant nests, it scratches among the leaves, then probes into the milling colony with its long bill, causing a general scurrying about. With a mucus coated, sticky tongue, the Flicker captures the escaping ants, then pokes

the lengthy, gluey probe deep into the nest to catch the eggs and young. Other insects and a variety of seeds and berries also comprise the Flicker's diet.

Although some Flickers remain all year in the northern parts of their range, in the spring there is a large northward migration of those birds that spent the winter in the south. Often traveling in loose, scattered flocks, its arrival at the breeding area is noisily announced by the male with a loud *wicker-wicker-wicker* from a treetop height, which proclaims territorial guardianship and calls out for a prospective mate. A long continuous drumming repeated frequently during early morning hours on a hollow limb is another land ownership announcement and an attention-getting device

Below: **Red Shafted Flickers (*Colaptes cafer*).**

for attracting a female Flicker. At other times of year, the bird performs his ratatat for what seems sheer amusement, as the staccato sound resonates on a garbage can lid or on the side of a house at an unwelcome five o'clock in the morning.

The newly mated pair work together to refurbish a formerly used cavity or to excavate a new one in which to house the six to eight lustrous white eggs. The nesting hollow, placed in a dead or dying tree or stump, may be as deep as 20 inches (50.8 cm) and take from one to two weeks of diligent labor to complete. The birds gather wood chips with which to make a bed for the eggs. Sometimes nesting boxes will be used by Flickers, and sometimes the birds will raise their brood inside a crevice of a building.

For about 14 days, both birds share the task of incubation, changing the

egg warming positions approximately every two hours. In their very early lives, the naked, helpless vermillion-colored infants are fed by regurgitation, the parent bird poking its bill well down the baby's throat. Later, when the little Flickers come out of their nursery chamber, they pick their food out from under a piece of bark where ants have been placed by the parents to teach the young ones to eat on their own.

By the time the fledglings leave the nest, their plumage resembles that of the adult male. Whatever the sex of the adolescent Flickers, they all have black mustaches.

FLICKER, RED-SHAFTED: see Flicker

FLICKER, YELLOW-SHAFTED: see Flicker

FLINTHEAD: see Ibis, Wood

FLYCATCHER, CRESTED:
see Flycatcher, Scissor-tailed

FLYCATCHER,
OLIVE-SIDED:
see Flycatcher, Scissor-tailed

FLYCATCHER, SCISSOR-
TAILED
(Muscivora forficata)

A bird of the southern United States, the Scissor-tailed Flycatcher breeds from southern Texas to southern Kansas, although individuals have wandered widely beyond this range, north to Hudson Bay, east to Massachusetts and Florida and west to Colorado. Winters are spent from Mexico to Panama.

Of the Scissor-tailed Flycatcher's overall 14 inch (35.56 cm) length, approximately 8 inches (20.32 cm) of that measurement is the male bird's long forked tail; the female's tail is somewhat shorter. Dull in tone, both sexes have similarly colored pale gray heads and bodies, pinkish backs and blackish wings with white markings. The bill of this Flycatcher, like others in its family, is broad and flattened and bends downward near the tip, which tapers to a sharp point. Its feet are small and weak.

Flycatchers belong to an order called Passeres, or perching birds, which is comprised of birds of high development and the ability to grasp a branch or perch with four toes designed for that purpose. Flycatchers are also classified among the Clamatores, or songless perching birds, indicating their vocal organs are not as highly developed as those of other perching birds, the songbirds.

The Scissor-tailed Flycatcher is one of the most graceful American birds, its picturesque flight accentuated by the exaggerated length of its tail. Like a pair of scissors, the two long tail feathers are often opened and closed, the tail movements indicative of excitement or high spirits.

In a bizarre aerial performance, the Scissor-tail abruptly interrupts straightforward flight with a swift series of upward darts and downward dives, accompanied by the scissor motions of the tail and wild shrieking screams. Its seemingly addled exhibition caused Mexican peasants to believe derisively that its food is the brains of other birds.

Actually, as its name reveals, the food of the Scissor-tailed Flycatcher is insects, which the agile bird often collects while both it and dinner are on the wing. It is a bird of open country; the few trees that dot its preferred area are no obstruction to the view of the surrounding scene. Perched upon a branch or post, sighted prey is snatched with a quick dart outward and a decided snap of the bill.

The nest of the Scissor-tail is placed on a horizontal tree limb in a wide variety of locations, such as a quiet city street or the edge of the woods. The crossbars of a telephone pole or the framework of a bridge also provide attractive nursery quarters. Roughly built, the nest is comprised of plant stems, weeds, thistledown, cotton and wool and lined with rootlets, horsehair or cotton. Incubation of the four to six eggs lasts for twelve days and is accomplished by the female alone, while the male acts as guardian, repelling all suspicious intruders who appear nearby. Both parents feed the young a diet that consists entirely of insects. Nourished by their high protein food, the fledglings leave the nest in about two weeks.

In late summer, Scissor-tailed Flycatchers congregate in huge groups to feed in the cotton fields and open prairies in preparation for their southward migratory flight.

The Crested Flycatcher, *Myiarchus crinitus*, is a close relative of the Scissor-tail that lives in the eastern United States and southern Canada and is known for its unexplained habit of using a shed snake skin among the materials with which it builds a nest. The Olive-sided Flycatcher, *Nuttallornis borealis*, a bird of very wide distribution, exhibits the uncommon Flycatcher behavior of perching high in a tree instead of in a location closer to the ground. Traill's Flycatcher, *Empidonax trailli*, ranging throughout the United States, except the southeast, has the typical Flycatcher habit of frequently flicking its tail.

FLYCATCHER, TRAILL'S:
see Flycatcher, Scissor-tailed

GADWALL:
see Duck, Black; Duck, Wood

GANNET
(Morus bassanus)

The Gannet is the largest marine bird on the Atlantic coast. In North America, it breeds on islands in the Gulf of St Lawrence and winters from the coast of North Carolina south to the Gulf of Mexico.

The Gannet achieves a length of 40 inches (101.6 cm) and a wingspread of 72 inches (182.88 cm). Adult sexes are alike in appearance with the body being mostly white and the head and neck a pale amber-yellow. A dark blue area of skin shows on the throat. The tapering bill is grayish-blue and the feet and wingtips are black. Shaped like a goose, the head is large and the neck is rather long and muscular. The name Gannet comes from the Old English *gan*, meaning gander or goose-like.

Gannets are birds strictly of the ocean, preferring the coastal waters and, except when migrating, never venturing far out to sea. Slender, pointed wings move the birds quickly through the air, vigorous wing beats alternating with gliding on thermal updrafts.

A great variety of fish is the Gannet's food, including herring, mackerel, cod, smelt and anchovy. Flying usually at a height of from 60 to 100 feet (18-30 m), the Gannet plunges downward with nearly closed-up wings and disappears like an arrow, completely underwater long enough to snatch its prey. Even though the bird plummets from great heights, the depth of its dive is surprisingly shallow. The impact on the water sends a spray 10 feet (3 m) into the air.

Prey is not speared, as the long pointed bill and the plunging action might indicate; rather, the bird gets under the fish and grasps it with the beak, while coming to the surface. Large fish can be gulped down whole, as the Gannet has a throat that can be greatly distended.

On the surface, the bird swallows its meal, then rises again in search of other morsels. A stiff breeze is required to power its launch from water and from dry land, only a very strong wind will lift the Gannet off the ground. Living and nesting on high sea cliffs gives the added momentum of the downward glide over the edge.

Abiding by the adage that there is safety in numbers, Gannets nest in such densely populated colonies that it seems they all share the same space. Each pair, though, occupies its own fiercely defended territory which has a diameter of six to eight feet (1.8-2.4 m). Lined up in evenly spaced rows on high, sheer cliffs overlooking the sea, simple nests are constructed of seaweed. Peace reigns among the crowded families as long as each remains within its own little area, but if a trespass should occur, the intruder is resoundingly attacked with open, hammering bills.

For 38 to 42 days, the single blue-white egg is incubated by both sexes in a most unusual fashion: the egg is held between the parents' webbed feet. The newly hatched chick is naked and helpless, colored almost black. The fluffy down feathers that appear in a few days are yellowish in hue. Parents feed the young for two months by regurgitating fish into the nest, the meal being eagerly snatched up by the hungry baby. Before the young are able to descend to the sea to search out their own food, the parents stop feeding their fattened offspring. At this point, the immature birds have been so stuffed they are bigger than the adults. Waiting for additional hand-outs that are not forthcoming, the abandoned youngsters live off their accumulated fat reserves for about ten days until, lean and hungry, they are forced to fly and hunt.

GOARDHEAD: see Ibis, Wood

GOATSUCKER: see Nuthatch, White-breasted

GOLDENEYE, COMMON: see Duck, Black; Canvasback

GOLDFINCH: see Goldfinch, American

GOLDFINCH, AMERICAN (Spinus tristis)

Often known as the Wild Canary, the Goldfinch and subspecies breed from coast to coast throughout North America from central British Columbia and central Quebec south to northern California and the Gulf coast. Although individuals occupy any part of the breeding range throughout the year, in winter a general southward population shift occurs, therefore summer and winter residents may not be the same birds.

The length of the Goldfinch is 5 inches (12.7 cm). It has a small, cone-shaped pointed bill that is typical of finches, long pointed wings, a short forked tail and rather short legs. In summer, the male calls attention to himself with his bright lemon-yellow plumage and sharply contrasting black tail and wings. The male in winter and the female all year have subdued tones of olive-brown above and grayish-white below with blackish wings and tail.

One of the most endearing characteristics of the Goldfinch is its fearlessness of humans while it is feeding. Some insect food is eaten by the Goldfinch, but its heavy, seed-cracking beak points up its culinary preference. Large quantities of thistle, goldenrod, milkweed, sunflower and other weed seeds are consumed, and in winter, when the seed supply is depleted or snow-covered, catkins of birch or alder, or seeds of hemlock, spruce and larch provide abundant cold weather fare.

A late breeder, the Goldfinch song is often heard when other voices have quieted down during the spring season of nesting and rearing young. Proceeding through the air in undulating flight as if riding ocean waves, the male Goldfinch performs his sweet *per-chic-o-ree*, *per-chic-o-ree*, a loud flowing of sharp trilled whistles.

Nesting activities do not begin until July or August with the blooming of

Left: Gannets nesting in typical colonies.
Right: A male Goldfinch and its young.

Left: Canada Geese, the most common wild geese.

the wild thistle plant. The thistle provides not only the seeds that are the bird's favorite food, but also the fluffy down attached to the seeds that is used by the Goldfinch as a nest lining. Although the soft materials from the seed-pods of cattails or milkweeds are sometimes used for cushioning the nest, only in areas where there is an abundant thistle growth will the Goldfinch breed.

In close proximity to other Goldfinches, pairs nest in the same area of open, brushy terrain with a scattering of tall trees. Because its weed seed sustainance is produced in great profusion, groups of birds can share a feeding territory without feeling the press of competition that would occur if food supply were limited. Nests are built in forks of a bush or a sapling 5-30 feet (1.5-9 m) high, constructed of plant down, mosses, grasses, leaves and other soft contributions collected from the nests of other species that have completed their rearing tasks for the season.

In the fall the males molt their sunny yellow feathers and grow a covering of dull olive. The young and old alike gather into foraging flocks that scour fields and marshlands in search of seed cuisine, some groups drifting southward. During the winter, Goldfinches often join with other small finches of similar food habits and preferences, especially the Redpoll, *Acanthis linaria*, and the Pine Siskin, *Spinus pinus*. All of these species exhibit the flight pattern of undulating wavy motion, giving a moving flock an imprecise internal progress that identifies an assembly of finches even from a distance.

GOOSE, BLUE: see Brant

GOOSE, CANADA
(*Branta canadensis*)

The black-necked Canada Goose, a large migratory bird, nests in the immense stretches of the Canadian marshes that extend almost to the Arctic coast. It also breeds in many localities in the northwestern United States. In winter, this big bird can be found from southern British Columbia to southern New England and Nova Scotia south to southern California.

There are eleven subspecies or geographical races of *Branta canadensis*, but they all have the well-known long black neck, and black head with white cheek patches joined under the throat. The body is brownish gray with pale belly and black tail. The Todd's Canada is probably the most numerous and popular race of the large family.

The main difference among the subspecies is size, varying from the 22 inch (55.9 cm) Cackling Canada Goose to the large 48 inch (121.9 cm) Giant Canada Goose. Voice also differentiates the various races, the smaller birds chatter in high-pitched tones, while the larger ones, known as Honkers, utter nasal calls of much lower sounds. To the Cree Indians of Hudson Bay, the cry of the geese sounded like barking; they called the big geese the Hounds of Heaven.

The strong instinct for migration brings great waves of Canada Geese, some 3,000,000 strong, over four age-old routes known as flyways. During the journeys south in the fall and north in the spring, the Atlantic, the Mississippi, the Central and the Pacific flyways are as traveled as interstate highways. Well spaced along the routes are huge areas that offer safety and food in the lakes and marshlands of National Wildlife Refuges.

An internal biological clock signals the Canada Goose to move towards its ancient breeding grounds, accompanying the leading edge of melting ice in springtime. With too few answers to the many questions regarding bird migration, scientists think that Canada Geese migrate by the use of an inborn star chart, the position of the sun, wind direction, the pull of earth's magnetic field, landmarks and the honks and calls of other geese which help them stay on course.

Flying in family groupings of mothers, fathers, children, brothers, sisters, in-laws and grandparents in the familiar tight V formation, Canada Geese are often up 3000 feet (900 m) in the air, but sometimes as high as 9000 feet (2700 m). The lead bird forms the point like an arrow tip, and makes flying easier for the other birds by breaking up the air ahead and creating updrafts with its wings. The air to the side of a flying bird is less turbulent than the air behind it. The birds following take advantage of these updrafts by flying just outside and behind the bird in front. If they flew directly in back of the forward bird, it would be as difficult to proceed through the air as it would be to swim behind a churning motor.

The bird out front of the skein of flying Canada Geese is not always a seasoned gander, familiar with the migratory route – it may be a female goose – nor does the leader make the entire journey in that position. Forward birds change often, as the job of breaking the airwaves is more difficult than simply flying forward.

Feeding in the water, tipped up in the manner of dabbling ducks with head immersed and tail in the air, the Canada Goose yanks aquatic plants from the bottom of a pond or lake. The serrated edges of its sensitive bill act as a strainer through which water drains from the mouth, and the front of the beak is a cutter that can strip kernels from ears of corn and clip grasses and other plants when the goose walks on land. A natural lawnmower, the versatile bill nips the grass and a quick backward pull of the head shears the plant close to the earth. Feet placed near the center of the body give the goose balance and make it an adept walker as it waddles on dry ground to feed on grass and grain.

In winter feeding grounds, mates who will remain lifetime partners are chosen, or a new partner is chosen by a gander whose goose might have died.

Below: **The Canada Goose breeds on lake shores and coastal marshes.**

Mates are fiercely loyal to each other and to their relatives and intermingle only with members of their family group.

In Arctic breeding grounds, a nest site is chosen by the couple in a location that must have a solid foundation, isolation, good visibility, plant protection and a nearby browsing area. In addition, the 5 inch (12.7 cm) deep nest, which is built of grass and twigs and lined with down, must be near open water.

In early June, four or five eggs are laid and incubated for 28-30 days by the female under the male's vigilant guard. The young of small subspecies can fly in about 42 days; the juveniles of the larger races fly in about 60 days, but all goslings are able to leave the nest and follow their parents to the water just 24 hours after hatching.

GOOSE, CACKLING CANADA: see Goose, Canada

GOOSE, GIANT CANADA: see Goose, Canada

GOOSE, GREATER SNOW: see Goose, Snow

GOOSE, SNOW (*Chen hyperborea*)

The Snow Goose is a western bird that breeds in the subarctic regions of the Northwest and winters from southern British Columbia and southern Illinois, south to lower California, central Mexico and Louisiana.

Reaching a length of 25 inches (63.5 cm), the Snow Goose is a small white bird with gray-based primary feathers that are black at the tip. Its short bill is pale red in color with a white tip and a black cutting edge. Both male and female adult birds are similarly colored and the young are covered with plumage that is entirely gray.

A subspecies, the Greater Snow Goose, *Chen hyperborea vivalis*, looks like the Snow Goose but it is larger in size. The Greater Snow Goose also breeds in the far north, the full breeding range unknown. In winter it is found from southern Illinois, Chesapeake Bay and Massachusetts, south to Louisiana, Florida and the West Indies. Early writers told of enormous flocks of the large white birds on the Atlantic coast, but Greater Snow Goose populations have been greatly

BIRDS

Above: Mature Snow Geese of both sexes are pure white with black-tipped wings.

reduced because of the conspicuousness of the bird and the tastiness of its flesh.

The Snow Goose is a close relative of swans and ducks, all belonging to the family, *Anatidae*, meaning goose-like swimmers. Although the colors of male and female ducks often differ widely, the goose and gander appear alike. The bills of geese are high at the base and taper toward the end, while the bills of ducks are broad and flat.

Feeding habits are also somewhat different between ducks and geese. Often wandering into fields far away from water, geese walk less awkwardly on land because their feet are set further forward on their bodies than are the feet of ducks. The food of the Snow Goose, and of other geese as well, is usually vegetable matter. In the water, it searches beneath the surface for seeds and roots of aquatic plants with its long neck and head immersed, the front portion of the body tilted forward and the rear end pointed straight up in the air in the manner of a dabbling duck.

During long migratory flights, the Snow Goose stops to feed on land, gorging in spring on newly sprouting grain and in the fall on the stubble residue of corn, wheat and barley. Resting on the western fields in former days when their numbers were abundant, the great profusion of these birds looked like banks of Snow.

Snow Geese fly in wide ranks, somewhat V-shaped, but not as sharply angled as a skein of Canada Geese, *Branta canadensis*, in flight. The flight formation is in a wavering line and looks like a beaded necklace, loosely strung. Describing the pattern of the line, one of the popular names of the Snow Goose is Common Wavy.

Mated for life in the habit of geese, pairs of Snow Geese arrive at their nesting territory in early spring. On a small plot of land near a northern lake, the female settles herself among the high protective grasses and, rolling her body from side to side, hollows out a depression. She lines the hollow well with a dense coverlet of soft down feathers plucked from her breast. Four to six creamy white eggs are laid, the female alone providing the incubation task, while the faithful gander guards her in the performance of her duty. When she leaves the nest to feed, she buries the eggs under the downy blanket, always under the watchful eyes of the gander.

Snow Goose eggs made welcome additions to the diets of Eskimos who lived near the breeding grounds. Gulls, jaegers, foxes and ravens also find the eggs to their liking. In the 1800s, so many Snow Geese nested in crowded colonies that the adult birds were easily clubbed to death for food by natives on horseback.

The habit of the migrating Snow Goose to lay bare newly planted grain fields did not endear them to the planters of the fields. Many thousands of birds became victims of an irate farmer's shotgun.

The past uncounted millions of Snow Geese are gone, but due to protective legislation enacted in 1917, their numbers are not completely decimated. The white birds are still abundant in migration in the far western part of North America, and are numerous in winter along the Pacific coast of the United States.

GOOSE, TODD'S CANADA:
see Goose, Canada

GOOSE, WHITE-FRONTED:
see Brant

GOSHAWK:
see Hawk, Sharp-shinned

GRACKLE:
see Grackle, Common

GRACKLE, BRONZED:
see Grackle, Common

GRACKLE, COMMON
(Quiscalis quiscula)

Found throughout eastern and central North America from southern Mackenzie Territory and Newfoundland to southeastern Texas, the Common Grackle and its subspecies, the Purple Grackle and the Bronzed Grackle, are partially migratory. In October and November most leave the northern portions of their range and move to the southern states, returning in early March to breed. Scattered individuals overwinter in the north mostly in coastal areas, occasionally visiting feeding stations set out around human habitation.

A 12-inch (30.48 cm) long bird, the Common Grackle has a long, pointed bill and a lengthy tail with a rounded tip that bears a longitudinal crease. The plumage of the male is black, but bright sunlight creates a metallic gloss of glittering purple, teal and bronze, an iridescent kaleidoscope of colors. On dull days, the color-shine is subdued, as it comes not from pigmentation, but from the light reflected off the scale-like feather surface. The female Grackle is browner and duller than the male, with fewer metallic glistenings, and she has indistinct streakings.

Many species of birds are so specific in their food and breeding requirements that if their livelihood is threatened, they cannot effect required changes in order to survive. The Grackle, though, is generalized in its needs for living, and with its varied menu and its assorted satisfactory nesting sites, it has flourished even near human settlements.

The long and powerful bill of the Grackle is a suitable tool to serve a wide variety of functions, such as probing, seed-cracking, snatching and spearing. It feeds on the ground and insects comprise the Common Grackle's early summer food, its taste for Japanese Beetle grubs being of benefit to man. Minnows, salamanders, snails, small fish, tadpoles, mice and even an occasional bird egg or nestling are snapped up by the voracious bird. It wades and spears aquatic food like a heron, plunges into water like a kingfisher, or scavenges from rubbish cans like a crow. Piracy is also an effective food-gathering technique employed by the aggressive Grackle, as it can relieve a Robin of a newly dug up worm. In the fall, acorns are easily cracked open by direct pressure of a bill that can perform as a nutcracker.

A large variety of nesting site locations are attractive to the adaptable Grackle, and often the same place satisfies many pairs as they settle in near one another. A grove of evergreens, a cattail marsh, a swampy thicket, an apple tree, a natural tree cavity, an abandoned woodpecker hole or even under the eaves of a hay barn are all serviceable nursery quarters. One of the most unusual nesting situations chosen by the Grackle is among the openings and fis-

Right: **Grackles are abundant on farmlands.**

sures of the bulky nest of sticks of the Osprey, *Pandion haliaetus*. These huge, clumsy constructions offer enough crannies and crevices to accommodate several pairs of Grackles. The fish-eating Osprey presents no food competition to the breeding tenants, nor do the Grackles interfere with the fishing bird.

Three to five strongly blotched eggs, varying greatly in size, color and markings, are laid in a large, rough nest of sticks, grass, bark strips and roots. Although the female alone carries out the incubation task, the male guards the developing family against potential enemies, warding off intrusion with the collective aid of other male Grackles who are summoned by an alarm note call.

Both parents feed the nestlings with lavish quantities of worms and insects until after approximately three weeks time, the youngsters join the Grackle flocks at a common nighttime roost. Daytime descent of these foraging assemblies upon stands of ripening corn does little to endear the birds to the owners of the fields.

GRACKLE, PURPLE:
see Grackle, Common

GREBE, PIED-BILLED
(*Podilymbus podiceps*)

A diving bird of rare aquatic talents, the Pied-billed Grebe is the most widely distributed of the American Grebes. The Pied-billed Grebe is common along lake shores and shallow ponds in most of North America, breeding from British Columbia to Nova Scotia and south to Florida and Mexico.

Approximately 13 inches (33 cm) in length, the Pied-billed Grebe is colored brownish black above and lighter brown and white below. Its bill is short and thick, gray-toned, with a black band. The young and the adults in winter lack this band around the beak. Its wings are very short. It has no tail; therefore its end seems bluntly rounded. Greenish feet, placed far back near its rear, have broadly lobed webs.

Grebes belong to an order of birds whose scientific name, Pygopodes, means rump foot. The rump-footed ones have their legs positioned close to the rear ends of their bodies which causes them, when sitting, to appear perpendicular like Penguins. This posterior leg placement is great for swim-

ming and diving, but extremely inefficient for walking. On land, Grebes move only with the greatest difficulty, and sometimes propel themselves on their bellies in seal-like fashion. Most at home in water, the Grebe will more readily dive beneath the surface in time of danger than take to the air.

Sometimes called a Devil-diver or a Water-witch, the Pied-billed Grebe's streamlined, boat-shaped body with elongated neck exhibit design qualities necessary for aquatic speed and agility. While swimming or remaining still in water, it can submerge its body partially or completely to suit its purposes. This primitive water bird has many enemies, including minks, fish, frogs, snakes, muskrats and birds of prey. To hide from predators and still survey the scene, the Pied-billed Grebe will remain hanging hidden under water with only its bill and eyes breaking through the surface.

The feathers of the Grebe are compact and smooth, almost fur-like. From an oil gland at the base of its tail part, the bird spreads with its bill the waterproofing chemical throughout its plumage. The dressing of the feathers keeps the bird's body dry even though it spends much time in water.

The secretive ways of the Pied-billed Grebe are extended to its nesting behavior. The nest is built of dead grass, reeds and mud, atop a platform of floating plant stems that are sufficiently buoyant to bear the weight of the nest. Approximately six whitish, dirty-looking eggs are laid and are incubated by both sexes. If a parent leaves the nest, he or she covers it with decaying water-logged plant material, so the egg cluster is hidden and merely appears as a floating mass of weeds. Because the nest is almost always wet, the young hatch out into the watery conditions in which they spend their lives. Down covered, the hatchlings take immediately to their aquatic environment.

Above Left: A Pied-billed Grebe.
Left: A Horned Grebe (*Podiceps auritus*).
Right: The Eared Grebe's (*Podiceps caspicus*) neck is thinner than that of the Horned.

For protection, young Grebes hitch a ride on the mother's or father's back, tucked safely underwing with only the fuzzy heads protruding. A slight disturbance will cause the old bird to raise its feathers and cover the chicks completely, or even to dive quietly beneath the surface of the water with babes still securely placed.

Diving and pursuing food underwater, Grebes eat aquatic insects, crawfish, small fish, snails, tadpoles, worms and leeches. Scientists have also found quantities of Grebe feathers matted in the bird's stomach. The feathers lack nutritional value and do not serve as food. One explanation for this puzzling appetite is that the feathers act as a screen or filter, keeping sharp bones and shells from piercing the intestines until they have been softened by digestive juices.

GREENLET:
see Vireo, Red-eyed

GROSBEAK:
see Grosbeak, Evening

GROSBEAK, EVENING
(Hesperiphona vespertina)

The Evening Grosbeak breeds in western Canada and in unpredictable and irregular fashion moves south in winter to Kansas and Ohio and eastward to Ontario, New York and New England.

The Evening Grosbeak is a heavy bodied bird, 8 inches (20.32 cm) in length, with a short forked tail and a stout, cone-shaped yellow bill. The male Evening Grosbeak is richly colored in white, yellow and olive-brown with a conspicuous yellow band across the forehead and bright white patches on the black wings. Less bold in appearance, the female's tones are gray-olive with a faint wash of yellow on the underparts, but she shares with the male the contrasting pattern of the black and white wings.

As it meanders through the tops of trees, the Evening Grosbeak's feeding habit is to devour all the seed food that can possibly be garnered from one spot, then to hop on a little way and pick clean that location, too. Occasionally, when tree heights yield little nourishment, the bird feeds closer to the ground, foraging among tall stalks of weeds that bare abundant seeds. With its strong, thick, seed-cracking bill, the Evening Grosbeak is able to crush the hard kernel and disregard the pulpy portion of fruits such as wild cherries and chokeberries. Other

birds, without the Grosbeak's powerful beak, devour the soft pulpy covering, while the unyielding center passes through the digestive tract and drops intact where the bird alights.

Over the years, the Evening Grosbeak has gradually increased its winter range southward and steadily expanded its breeding range to the south and to the east. It is now nesting as far south as the highlands of New Jersey. An impetus to the extension of its range has been the planting in towns and cities of the ash-leaved maple tree, the buds and seeds of which are the Evening Grosbeak's favorite food. The increase in the number of winter feeding stations maintained by bird lovers has also contributed to the Evening Grosbeak's enlarged territory.

Migration to northern breeding grounds usually occurs in late March, but if food is abundant, flocks often remain in more southern localities until late April or early May. Gregarious in nature, several pairs of Grosbeaks often nest near each other, but not in the same tree. Preferably in conifers, but in other trees as well, the nest is built hidden in the dense foliage of a branch tip 15-60 feet (4.5-18 m)

high. A shallow construction, it is a loose twig structure lined with soft, fine grass to hold the three to four blue-green eggs with brown markings that comprise the clutch. Although the Evening Grosbeak is primarily a seed eater, the little ones are fattened on beetles and caterpillars.

Toward summer's end Grosbeaks form small foraging groups that gradually wander from their nesting grounds and migrate southward in undulating flight to congenial feeding grounds.

A Grosbeak that breeds in northeastern North America and visits in winter in southern New England and west to eastern Kansas and Minnesota is the Pine Grosbeak, *Pinicola enucleator*. The Rose-breasted Grosbeak, *Zamelodia ludoviciana*, breeds in eastern North America and winters in South America's warm climate.

GROSBEAK, PINE:
see Grosbeak, Evening

GROSBEAK, RED-BREASTED:
see Grosbeak, Evening

GROUSE, FRANKLIN'S:
see Grouse, Ruffed

GROUSE, RUFFED
(*Bonasa umbellus*)

An upland gamebird, the Ruffed Grouse is a permanent resident throughout its range. Its wide distribution extends from wooded Alaska to Nova Scotia and south to Georgia and northern California.

The Ruffed Grouse is 18 inches (45.72 cm) in length. Its color above is spotted reddish-brown, while below it is yellowish barred with black, its concealing coloration matching woodland haunts. A conspicuous ruff of feathers adorns the side of the neck, the feathered collar much larger in the male than in the female, and a pert crest of little plumes sits up on top of the head. Its species name, *umbellus*, refers to the umbrella-like tufts that fluff out from the neck.

Partial to rocky hilly country with thickly timbered stands and streams in silent woods away from man, the Ruffed Grouse roams widely to satisfy its varied diet, which consists of crickets, grasshoppers, berries, fruits, leaf buds and the stubble of cultivated fields. In its strong muscled gizzard, the Ruffed Grouse crushes hard-shelled seeds like beechnuts and

Left: **Ruffed Grouse have finely barred tails.**
Above: **The large Sage Grouse (*Centrocercus urophasianus*) feeds on sagebrush.**
Right: **The Sharp-tailed Grouse (*Pedioecetes phasianellus*) is common on prairies.**

acorns, and before the chestnut blight, chestnuts, too. The particular variety of its bill of fare accounts for the delicious favour of its flesh and makes it a sought-after gamebird.

The male Ruffed Grouse enacts a most dandified performance and produces an exceptional call in the execution of courtship behavior. Taking up his place on a fallen log or a broad stump, a stage used for many years and familiar to the nearby females as a meeting place, the cock fluffs out his feathers to appear twice his normal size. He raises his neck frills, erects his crest, fans out and lifts his tail, trails his wings beside him and with head held high, struts around his showplace with a jerking, cock-sure gait. Suddenly, he stops his gaudy stepping, stretches out his head and neck, and slowly at first, then with increasing speed, beats the air with his wings until there is just a blur where wings should be. The flapping wings moving faster than the eye can follow produce a sonorous thumping, a rolling boom sound, like the

BIRDS

deep muffled beating of a drum. The resounding love song carries for a mile and attracts the females of this species which are within hearing range to the vicinity. The drumming also discourages other male Ruffed Grouse from interfering in the reproductive scenario – let them attract their own mates – as the drumming dandy, a flagrant polygamist, fertilizes the eggs of all his admiring hens.

The female alone is in charge of nesting duties and of rearing the little brood. She scratches a slight depression hidden in the woods usually at the foot of a stump or log, and lines the hollow with wisps of dried plant material. Ten to fifteen eggs are deposited and for almost four weeks she patiently warms them, relying on the mimicry of her plumage to blend her into her woody surroundings, so she can remain unnoticed by her many enemies, including foxes, squirrels, hawks, owls and shotguns.

When the chicks hatch out, they wander around by day in search of food and gather under mother's sheltering wings at night. As they mature, they learn to roost in trees and shrubs. To prepare for winter, they store needed fat, grow a feathery

Below: A Ruffed Grouse camouflaged in its summer home, the open woods in Canada.

covering for their legs and develop little comb-like snowshoes from the sides of their toes to keep their bodies from sinking into the snow.

As a widely hunted gamebird, the Ruffed Grouse has developed wary ways. It sneaks off swiftly through the underbrush or flushes from cover with a sudden burst of velocity that confounds an attacker. Strong chest muscles allow for concentrated but limited flight as the bird hurls itself into the air and places a series of trees between itself and the hunter's gun. So that its scent cannot be followed by a dog, the Ruffed Grouse flies low, then drops to run again, which serves to confuse a pursuer. To escape pursuit, a grouse will often dive into the snow, which it also buries itself under as an insulating blanket in the extreme cold of winter.

The Ruffed Grouse is the state bird of Pennsylvania. Some close relatives of the Ruffed Grouse found within North America are the Hudsonian Spruce Partridge, *Canachites canadensis*; Franklin's Grouse, *Canachites franklini*; Willow Ptarmigan, *Lagopus lagopus*; Rock Ptarmigan, *Lagopus rupestris*; Greater Prairie Chicken, *Tympanuchus cupido*; and the Lesser Prairie Chicken, *Tympanuchus pallidicinctus*. The latter is a diminishing species protected by hunt regulations.

GUILLEMOT, BLACK
(*Cepphus grylle*)

A diving bird of cold, northern coastal waters, the Black Guillemot breeds from southern Greenland to Maine. In winter it can be found as far south as Cape Cod, and occasionally along the coasts of New York and New Jersey. The Pigeon Guillemot (*Cepphus columba*), which resembles its relative in appearance and behavior, is common on the west coast of North America.

Thirteen inches (33.02 cm) in length, the Black Guillemot is sooty black in summer with a large white patch on each wing. Coral red bill and feet accent its breeding coloration. Its winter plumage changes from black to gray, the bird appearing as if dusted all over with flour.

The Black Guillemot is also known as the Sea Pigeon, and in an even more confusing common name, it is sometimes called the White Guillemot when in winter coloration.

Because of the placement of the legs, which are positioned far to the rear of its body, the Black Guillemot sits in an upright stance and walks with an awkward shambling gait. Underwater, in pursuit of fish, it is a strong swimmer, using its wings for propulsion and its feet for steering. In the air,

Above: This Pigeon Guillemot is similar to the Black Guillemot, except for its black wing bars, and is more common.

flight is rapid and direct with fast wing beats, although Guillemots fly only a few feet above the water surface.

On the water, the Guillemot looks much like a duck, but its neck is shorter than a duck's and its bill is more pointed. When frightened it dives beneath the water with swift agility and reappears a considerable distance from the disturbance.

Black Guillemots nest in crevices among accumulations of rocky boulders on uninhabited islands in northern coastal waters. A related species, the Pigeon Guillemot, can be found in waters of the North Pacific south to Santa Catalina Island off California. Guillemots construct no nests. The two spotted eggs are deposited well hidden in deep concealments created by the rocky jumble among which they breed. The birds are silent, except during the nesting season, when with sibilant noises they defend their territories. The young are covered with black down on hatching. They remain in the nest for about 40 days with both parents participating in their care and feeding. When the chicks are fully feathered they leave the security of their crevice to find their food at sea.

The Black Guillemot makes no long journey south for its winter quarters. Hardly migrating at all, it can be found scarcely 200 miles below its southernmost nesting range, always swimming within sight of the coastline, never going inland or far out to sea.

GUILLEMOT, PIGEON:
see Guillemot, Black

GUILLEMOT, WHITE:
see Guillemot, Black

GULL, CALIFORNIA:
see Gull, Ring-billed

GULL, GREAT BLACK-BACKED
(Larus marinus)

One of the largest Gulls, the Great Black-backed Gull breeds on islands along the coast of the northeastern United States and from central Greenland to Nova Scotia. In late August, the Great Black-backed Gull begins to migrate south and can be found from Greenland to the Great Lakes and Delaware Bay. This species is greatly expanding its range, and in recent years has wintered as far south as Florida and as far west as Nebraska.

The Great Black-backed Gull is 30 inches (76.2 cm) in length. The color of its back and wings is a deep, slate gray with a purplish tinge. The remainder of its plumage is pure white. Its bill is chrome yellow and has a bright orange-red spot near the lower tip. Legs are a pale flesh color. The large size of this bird and the dark tone of its mantle give it a well deserved common name.

The Great Black-backed Gull, like other Gulls, eats food that is dead or alive. If live fish are unavailable, it will willingly turn to cleaning the beach of decaying crabs or shellfish. The scavenging propensity of Gulls makes them the garbage collectors of the shore, as they serve the valuable natural role of ridding their area of decomposing matter. Inland, various Gull species can often be seen in great flocks, picking over dumps and refuse piles in search of tasty morsels of rotten food. The increased population of Great Black-backed Gulls and the expansion of their range can probably be traced to the increased population of humans and the expansion of their garbage.

These Gulls, like others, are stout and broad around the breast. Because Great Black-backed Gulls are so chunky, they are not good divers. They alight upon the water to feed and, paddling with webbed feet, bob bouyantly along like corks. With ridged, hooked bills, they catch fish such as herring that swim close to the surface.

In June, small coastal islands are sought out for nesting by large colonies of Great Black-backed Gulls, often sharing breeding areas with Herring Gulls. Adult Great Black-backed Gulls prey upon unguarded eggs and young of the Herring Gulls. Great Black-backed Gull nests are deeply rounded and are constructed of dry grasses. The female lays two or three pale olive-gray eggs, blotched with black and purple. One or two days pass between the laying of each egg. Parents take turns brooding, maintaining the proper temperature for the developing embryos. Adult Gulls develop warm areas on their breasts by means of which eggs are kept a constant 103°F (39°C). These areas are called brood patches where feathers have fallen out and blood vessels near the surface of the skin have enlarged. The parents position themselves on the eggs so the warmth of these blood vessels is absorbed by the growing life within the shells.

After hatching, the young are cared for by both parents for five or six weeks. The plumage of juvenile birds is dull white with mottled brown, and not until a full four years does the Gull acquire mature coloration. Only then is it old enough to breed.

While in the nest, the young are fed by the adults who regurgitate the meal. Partially digested food is delivered to the babies carried in the adults' gullets, but the contents are not disgorged until the chick pecks on the red spot on the adult birds' lower beak.

GULL, HERRING:
(Larus argentatus)

The Herring Gull is the most common and the most widely distributed

BIRDS

Left and above: **A Herring Gull adult (*above*) and juvenile. These birds are found near salt and fresh water, in harbors and dumps.**

Gull in the United States. It breeds from south central Alaska, south to British Columbia and across to New York and Massachusetts. In winter, it can be found from southern Alaska to lower California, and from the Great Lakes south to Texas.

The Herring Gull's length is 24 inches (60.96 cm). The adult bird has a pure white head, neck, tail and underparts. Its back and wings are grayish blue in color. The tips of the wings are black. The webbed feet are a pale flesh tone and the chrome yellow bill has a bright red spot near the lower tip.

This familiar and abundant bird is often called by the general term of Sea Gull, a name which lumps together all species of Gulls, making no differentiation among the various kinds.

The preferred food of the Herring Gull is fish which the bird sometimes captures while paddling on the surface of the water like a buoyant float. Too broad and stout around the breast to be a good diver, it eats fish that swim close to the top, grabbing its prey with a strong, hooked beak. Lacking a fresh-caught meal, the Herring Gull dines on any decaying marine life, and by this habit helps keep the beaches cleared of decomposing matter.

To eat the soft morsels housed inside the tightly closed clam and mussel shells, the Herring Gull picks up mollusks with its feet and drops them from the air onto rocks. Landing on the stony surface, the shells crack open, and the Gull swoops down and snatches its tid-bit. Sometimes the bird lets go its missile over sand where, landing on the yielding ground, the shell remains intact. Again the Gull picks up the mussel and again drops it over sand or mud, persistently repeating the fruitless action until its attention is attracted to a more productive source of food.

The Herring Gull's wings are wide, long and pointed, enabling it to fly by flapping, soaring or gliding with equal agility. The Gull is a good swimmer and walks easily on land. Few birds are as adept at walking, swimming and flying as Gulls. At home in the air, on the sea or on dry land, eating food that is fresh or fetid, not shy or fearful of man, the Herring Gull can survive in many different circumstances. This ease of adaptation contributes to its greatly increased population. In addition it is now illegal to hunt these birds. Formerly, hundreds of thousands of this species were killed for the millinery trade, but now breeding colonies are protected, resulting in a proliferation of Herring Gulls.

Great gatherings of Herring Gulls take over the shores of rocky islands of the northern Atlantic coastline. Scanty ground nests are built using dried plant material, with three to five spotted eggs deposited within. In 24-28 days, the downy feathered young hatch out, cryptically colored dull cream, speckled with brown to match the background of grainy sand and mottled stones.

The chicks signal their parents to disgorge food from their gullets by pecking on the red spot on the adult bills. Sometimes the eager young peck on a neighboring adult beak, but this mistake proves fatal to the little bird, as the wrongly approached oldster bat-

ters the baby to death. What seems like callous viciousness is perhaps nature's way of preventing overpopulation of these adaptive birds.

GULL, LAUGHING
(Larus atricilla)

Laughing Gulls breed from Maine and Massachusetts, south along the Atlantic and Gulf of Mexico coasts to Texas. Moving south for the winter, they can be found from North Carolina throughout the Gulf of Mexico, the Carribean Sea and as far south as the Amazon Delta. Infrequent appearances are made in Colorado, Nebraska, Wisconsin and Iowa.

The Laughing Gull is 17 inches (43.18 cm) in length. The female is smaller than the male, and both sexes are similarly colored. The wings are dark gray, but the wing tips are solid black. In winter the head and throat are white and the legs and bill are black.

During the summer breeding season a radical change of coloration occurs, as old feathers are molted and nuptial plumage grows. The black legs and bill take on a deep shade of red, and the normally white head and neck become a dark charcoal black. In breeding plumage the bird looks as if it has donned a hood.

Many Laughing Gulls together can be seen spread over sand bars, as they comb the mud for marine worms,

Above: **Laughing Gulls are coastal birds.**

small crustaceans or dead fish cast up by the tide. Like other Gulls, the Laughing Gulls have developed hunting techniques that easily yield them food. They follow schools of porpoises and eat the small fish driven to the surface by the swimming mammals. The Laughing Gulls often try to steal the catch of Brown Pelicans. The Gulls wait for the Pelicans to surface after a dive, then they land quickly upon the brown bird's head and try to pluck the fish from its enlarged bill, sometimes successful in their treachery, sometimes not.

On islands off the Atlantic Coast of the United States, Laughing Gulls gradually gather during mating season in large colonies to breed. Gulls normally mate for life, but if one of the pair dies, the survivor finds another partner. Choosing the area they claimed the previous year, the Laughing Gull couple performs an elaborate courtship ritual involving calling, bobbing, grass tugging, rubbing, begging and feeding. After copulation, nests are woven on the ground from seaweed, sedges and eelgrass, molded by the bird's body into rounded form. Although great numbers of these Gulls nest in crowded rookeries, each couple defends its established territory against any intruders.

Two to five dull grayish eggs are laid, heavily blotched with brown,

BIRDS

GULL, RING-BILLED
(*Larus delawarenis*)

The Ring-billed Gull is essentially a bird of the inland waterways. It breeds from southern Alaska to the north shore of the Gulf of St Lawrence, south to southern Oregon, southern Colorado and northern New York. In winter it can be found from the northern United States southward to the Gulf Coast, often collecting in large flocks along the southern coasts.

The length of the Ring-billed Gull is 20 inches (50.8 cm) with a 50 inch (127 cm) wingspread. The back and shoulders are pale bluish-gray in color; the head and underparts are almost pure white. Wing tips are black with conspicuous white spots. Its legs and feet are yellow-green and it has a similarly colored bill encircled with a broad black band. This dark circle around its beak gives the bird its common name. The black ring and the bird's smaller size distinguish it from the Herring Gull, which it resembles.

The Ring-billed Gull is primarily a scavenger, eating dead fish, rodents, small aquatic animals and sometimes the contents of the nests of other birds. Gathering where food is easily attainable, flocks of Gulls haunt garbage dumps, awaiting the delivery of edible refuse. Accompanying ships, they eat the litter that is dumped overboard, often snapping up the morsels in mid-

black and lavender. For 20 days, both parents share the job of incubating the eggs, leaving them unattended only when the sun can temporarily substitute for the heat delivered by the body of the brooding bird. In cool or cloudy weather one or the other parent sits on the eggs. If the weather is hot and sunny, the parent shades the eggs instead of incubating them and ruffles its feathers to move the air and cool the eggs.

The first egg laid is the first to open, hatching occurring in one or two day intervals. Covered with wet down, the hatched chicks dry in a few hours and look like spotted ping-pong balls of fluff. Decorated with dark blotches against an off-white background, they blend into the grainy sand surroundings, camouflaged from predators. The babies beg for food by pecking at the parents' beaks and grabbing the meal as it is regurgitated.

In five or six weeks, the well-fed chicks are larger than their parents. In their brown, mottled juvenile plumage, the young gradually leave the colony to feed and fly on their own.

Top: The Ring-billed Gull, known for the black ring on its bill, prefers inland areas.

Above: Heermann's Gull, with its black feet and red bill, is a West Coast dweller.

Top and above: These California Gulls (*Larus californicus*), a juvenile (top) and adult, are smaller than the Herring Gull but similar in coloring.

air without so much as wetting a feather. If the ships the Gulls are following travel far out to sea, the birds return to shore. Gulls are not creatures of mid-ocean.

Ring-billed Gulls are frequently seen in the company of the somewhat larger California Gulls. Both nest together in large colonies on inland lakes throughout the western United States. These birds are of great help to farmers, as one of their preferred foods is insects, the constant scourge of growing crops. When farmers plow their fields, a flock of Gulls will follow along behind, eating the insects turned up by the plow.

The Mormon settlers in the West in 1848 were beseiged by thousands of grasshoppers, which were consuming whole fields of crops in minutes. To the Mormon farmers' rescue came a large flock of Ring-billed and California Gulls. Satisfying their natural appetite by devouring the grasshoppers, the birds put a thorough and hasty end to the plague. A statue stands today in Salt Lake City in commemorative devotion to the helpful birds.

When fields are irrigated and the rushing water in the ditches drives mice from their burrows, the Gulls swoop down and gorge on rodents. Gulls and humans live in accommodation of each other's needs. Man's activities of growing crops and disposing of leftovers creates and attracts food for Gulls, who move in to eat the garbage and keep down the number of insect and rodent pests.

Formerly, there were so many Ring-billed Gulls that John James Audubon called them the 'common American Gull.' Today, they are no longer so abundant. Many Gull breeding areas have been destroyed or developed for man's purposes, and now these Gulls nest only in a few areas of the interior of North America.

GULL, SEA: see Gull, Herring

HALCYON:
see Kingfisher, Belted

HARRIER: see Hawk, Marsh

BIRDS

HAWK, BROAD-WINGED:
see Hawk, Red-tailed

HAWK, BULLET:
see Hawk, Sharp-shinned

HAWK, CHICKEN:
see Hawk, Red-tailed;
Hawk, Sharp-shinned

HAWK, COOPER'S:
see Hawk, Sharp-shinned

HAWK, DUCK:
see Hawk, Sparrow

HAWK, HEN:
see Hawk, Red-tailed

HAWK, MARSH
(Circus cyaneus hudsonius)

Above: A young Marsh Hawk.

The Marsh Hawk, a hunting bird, is widely distributed throughout North America, breeding from northwestern Alaska and northern Quebec south to the southern border of the United States. It winters occasionally from southern British Columbia to New York, but during the cold season it is found mostly in the warmer southern states, south to the Bahamas, Cuba and Colombia.

The male Marsh Hawk has a length of 19 inches (48.26 cm), the female a longer 22 inches (55.88 cm). The male's upper and fore parts are colored ashy-gray, while the abdomen is white; the female's upper parts are dark amber and she is colored rusty-buff below.

With its sharply angled pointed bill and its deeply curved talons, the Marsh Hawk is well adapted as a raptor, or bird of prey. The food preferences of this hunter are decidedly of benefit to man, as the favorite target of the Marsh Hawk is mice. Nature's mousetraps, an average pair of these birds while rearing young destroys approximately 1000 mice during the nesting season. Other birds, rabbits, tree squirrels, ground squirrels, lizards, snakes and frogs also comprise portions of the Marsh Hawk's diet.

Its haunts not limited to marshes, the Marsh Hawk also hunts on prairies, meadows, and brush covered hills. Areas that are not thickly wooded are the bird's desired territories, as the Marsh Hawk is a low flyer, and trees and shrubs would impede its progress.

Its slow and steady, back and forth, sailing flight, skimming every inch of marsh or meadow, may appear a relaxed and graceful recreation, but for the Marsh Hawk the low and thorough searching is really the serious business of hunting food. Like the hunting dog bred to search out small mammals, this hawk's method of pursuit gives it the name of Harrier. When its keen eyes spot its quarry, its flight comes to an abrupt halt and the bird descends upon its prey, grabbing it with sharp talons and tearing the flesh with hooked beak. Usually the victim is devoured on the spot, but sometimes it is carried off to feed a mate or young.

When at rest, Marsh Hawks normally perch on stumps, fence posts or telegraph poles. At night, they sometimes roost on the ground, occasionally forming a loose roosting group consisting of from two to thirty birds. Both sexes assist in nest construction, the male delivering some sticks and dropping them off to be arranged by the female, which does the greater part of the collecting and arranging. Both members of the pair also incubate the four to six dull white eggs, alternating duties for the necessary 18-20 days. Incubation commences as soon as the first egg is laid, and as an egg a day is deposited, a chick a day hatches when the required warming period has passed.

At the appearance of the first ball of fluffy down and thereafter, one parent or the other hurries off to hunt for food for the little ones while one adult remains to guard the nest. The food is delivered to the waiting parent who holds it tightly in its beak while the nestlings tear off pieces by themselves. As the youngsters grow, both adults together are on the wing to fill the demanding little stomachs, so captured food is simply dropped in the nest and the nestlings rip it apart. Even after the young are able to fly, they are fed by the parents, but now while aloft. Above the nest, the old bird drops a mouse, and the young ones fly up to grab the furry morsel in their beaks and talons, the most adept youngster winning the prize.

The family group stays together hunting over familiar territory, the young always learning from their elders, until the autumn migratory flight separates the offspring from their parent-teachers.

HAWK, PIGEON:
see Hawk, Sharp-shinned; Kestrel, American

HAWK, RED-SHOULDERED:
see Hawk, Red-tailed

HAWK, RED-TAILED
(Buteo borealis)

The Red-tailed Hawk, with its various relatives, has a wide distribution and is the best known of all our hawks. It lives and breeds from southeastern Canada through United States to Mexico, the Gulf coast, Florida and the Greater Antilles.

The male Red-tailed Hawk is 22 inches (55.88 cm) in length, while the female measures a larger 24 inches (60.96 cm). The sexes are similarly colored dark brown above and whitish washed with buff below. The wide-spreading tail of medium length is a bright rust-red hue above with a distinct black bar near the end. In flight, a conspicuous white area shows on the breast, and the tail is unbanded.

Unfortunately for the Red-tailed Hawk, it is also known as Chicken Hawk or Hen Hawk. These descriptive but misplaced names give this bird of prey an undeserved bad reputation as a destroyer of barnyard fowl. Many scientific examinations of the contents of the Red-tailed Hawk's stomach reveal that a large proportion of rodents are eaten, as compared to a small number of birds the hawk consumes. The preferred diet of the Red-tailed Hawk consists of small mammals, including squirrels, rabbits, mice and voles. Grasshoppers, crickets, beetles and reptiles are also relished. Only when its favored, furry menu is unavailable will the Red-tailed Hawk resort to foraging in the farmyard, and then it usually captures only weakened and

diseased poultry specimens. For this limited and sometimes beneficial plundering, the Red-tailed Hawk has often been shot by hunters who make little distinction between bird-eating and mammal-eating hawks, ascribing to all birds of prey hunting habits that interfere with man's best interests. Certainly, the killing of a few sick chickens is small enough payment for the service the Red-tailed Hawk performs as a natural mousetrap, and the helpful habits of this hunting bird deserve wider recognition and acclaim.

Other hawks that also have diets consisting primarily of small mammals, but have been slaughtered for

Above: **The Red-tailed Hawk is a soaring bird.**

their supposed rapacious tendencies toward consuming man's domestic feathered properties, are the Red-shouldered Hawk, *Buteo lineatus*; Swainson's Hawk, *Buteo swainsoni*; Broad-winged Hawk, *Buteo platypterus*; and Rough-legged Hawk, *Archibuteo lagopus*.

Sailing overhead with a wingspread of about 50 inches (127 cm), the Red-tailed Hawk is a conspicuous object in the sky. In slow-moving leisurely ascents it mounts higher and higher until it appears as a tiny speck in the blue, then it floats in sailing descent with no perceptible flapping of the

BIRDS

Above: Rough-legged Hawk (*Buteo lagopus*).

wings. Rising currents of warm air maintain this broad-winged and broad-tailed bird aloft for often an entire day. When its keen eyes detect food far below, an arrow-straight nose dive delivers the hunter swiftly to its prey.

When not performing its relaxed aerial glides, the Red-tailed Hawk perches on a stump or limb near the edge of a patch of woods or above open fields or swamps. There it sits, sometimes for hours, patiently examining the ground, waiting for warm-blooded quarry to approach so with lightning speed it can pounce upon the little victim. Sharp-curved talons capture the prey, and a strong hooked beak rips it into gulp-sized pieces.

Red-tailed Hawks, like many other hawk species, remain mated for life, but if one of the couple is killed, the other soon finds another mate. It arrives in pairs at breeding grounds, and large nests are built high in the tallest trees of wooded areas. Typically 30 inches (76.2 cm) in outside diameter, of sticks and twigs and neatly lined with finer plant material, nests are constructed new each year or repaired and reused from a previous incubation. Sometimes a former nest of another hawk, an owl, a crow, or even a squirrel is appropriated.

Two to four dull white eggs are laid, sometimes marked with irregular sepia patterns, the female hawk alone incubating them for 28 days, while the male brings her food. After the young have hatched, the male continues to deliver mice and rabbits, pieces of which the female tears off and feeds to the little ones. By fall, the plumage of the young hawks, which were hatched well covered with long, soft, silky down, is indistinguishable from that of the parents.

Early in September, Red-tailed Hawks join mixed flights containing a variety of hawk species and hundreds of individuals, and embark upon their southward drifting migration.

HAWK, ROUGH-LEGGED: see Hawk, Red-tailed

HAWK, SHARP-SHINNED (*Accipiter velox*)

A terrorizer of small birds, the Sharp-shinned Hawk is a permanent resident within its broad range, except in the northern parts. It breeds nearly throughout United States and Canada and winters from British Columbia, Colorado, Iowa and Massachusetts south to Panama.

The Sharp-shinned Hawk has a length of 12 inches (30.48 cm), the female slightly larger than the male and measuring 14 inches (35.56 cm) in length. Its tail is long, slender and square tipped. Its color above is dark bluish-slate, while below it is white with broad transverse bars of rufous red.

The Sharp-shinned Hawk is a member of a genus of birds known as Accipiters. Accipiters represent the most populous genus of birds of prey, worldwide in distribution, species inhabiting pine forests of the cold far north to luxuriant tropical rainforests. All are broad-winged, long-tailed hawks, with rather long, thin legs, and the Sharp-shinned Hawk, little larger than a robin, is among the smaller individuals.

The menu of the Sharp-shinned Hawk is composed primarily of small birds, such as swifts, flycatchers, sandpipers or orioles. The rapacious little hunter is greatly feared by its victims, and they have learned to remain hidden and silent when this fierce marauder is near. The Sharp-shinned Hawk is especially fond of barnyard fowl, and it is strong enough to carry off, grasped in its talons, a half grown chicken or a domestic pigeon. This hawk even attacks birds larger than itself. Mice, rabbits, shrews, bats, frogs, lizards and various insects also contribute to its bill of fare.

Many species of hawks are shot by persons who see all these birds of prey as destructive to domestic fowl. Most raptors, though, nourish themselves primarily on rodents that are the abundant pests of farmlands and barnyards. The few poultry that are consumed by hawks are small payment for the efficient mouse-trapping service that hawks perform. The Sharp-shinned Hawk, its larger relative, Cooper's Hawk, *Accipiter cooperi*, and the Goshawk, *Astur atricapillus*, though, are no such beneficial exterminators, as their food preference over mice is indeed the flocks of barnyard chickens. With little discriminating sorting out by irate farmers, both helpful and destructive species are shot.

Not a bird of the forest, the Sharp-shinned Hawk is seldom seen in thickly timbered locations, but rather in more open, brushy fields. Its hunting method is a system of surprise attack after the hawk watches for a feathered quarry from an inconspicuous perch, then pounces swiftly and unexpectedly on the hapless victim. In approaching the poultry yard, the crafty raptor flies low and remains unseen behind a fence or building, until the time is right to swoop down and pick up a small chicken. In brushy fields or meadows, it often performs short low glides beneath the branches in search of a luckless robin or a thrush. From this habit of beating the bushes, it has been called Bushwacker. It is also known as

Right: An immature Sharp-shinned Hawk in its usual territory of open woods, where it preys on small-sized birds.

BIRDS

Above: A Sparrow Hawk with a rat.

Pigeon Hawk, Sparrow Hawk, Bird Hawk, Chicken Hawk, and Bullet Hawk.

In late summer, Sharp-shinned Hawks convene in large assemblages and proceed on southward migrations through New England, along the shores of Long Island Sound and down the coast of New Jersey to their winter quarters.

HAWK, SPARROW; KESTREL, AMERICAN (Falco sparverius)

The Kestrel, or Sparrow Hawk, is the smallest hawk in North America. Found in eastern North America from Great Slave Lake to northern South America, it nests from the northern limits of its territory to Florida, and winters from New Jersey southward.

The little Kestrel has a length to 12 inches (30.48 cm), the female slightly larger than the male. Its color above is a rufous-cinnamon, while its underparts are pale rust interwoven with white.

A member of a family of birds of prey or raptors called *Falconidae*, the Kestrel is swift of flight and keen of vision. Its bill is sharply hooked, toothed and notched, and projecting bony eyeshields give the bird a visage of an angry frown. Muscular legs and sharp curved talons enable the little hunter to grasp its prey, while its long, strong, pointed wings and short, rigid tail maneuver the bird through the air with quick and certain movements.

Although the Kestrel consumes very few sparrows, it was given the name Sparrow Hawk by English settlers of this country when they saw its resemblance to the British bird of that name.

When falconry was in fashion in England, the rank of an individual could be told by the species of falcon perched on his wrist. The Sparrow Hawk was carried by a priest and the Kestrel by a servant.

Perched on a vantage point offering a broad view of the fields below, the Kestrel surveys the panorama in search of insects, mice, small birds, reptiles and amphibians, which comprise its bill of fare. To scan the ground more closely, the hawk springs out and, in a gravity defying accomplishment, hovers in mid-air, its wings beating lazily. Then its wing beats cease entirely, and there it seems to hang as if suspended, before dropping like a heavy weight, seizing quarry with its sharp talons and flying back to its perch to enjoy the catch. For this aerial achievement, the Kestrel is sometimes known as the Windhover.

Unlike other birds of prey that build huge, bulky nests of sticks and plant stems, the Kestrel usually expends no energy in organizing a structure, but lays its eggs hidden in a tree cavity or in an abandoned woodpecker excavation. Holes in buildings and second-hand bird breeding boxes are also appropriated as incubation sites. For 30 days, the female warms the four or five creamy-white eggs that are spotted with various shades of brown.

The young hatch out helpless, eyes unopened and scantily covered with white down. The mother feeds them dainty morsels that she tears from captured small mammals, insects and birds. When the hawklets develop, she drops the prey entire into the nursery cavity where the young get practice ripping up their own food.

Kestrtels, undisturbed by man's proximity, increasingly are wintering in cities where roosting niches are available in buildings and flocks of Starlings and House Sparrows provide abundant food.

Other falcons distributed widely, although not necessarily commonly, throughout North America are the Duck Hawk or Peregrine Falcon, *Falco peregrinus*, which is an endangered species because of the large amounts of the insecticide DDT that was stored in its tissues, and the Pigeon Hawk or Merlin, *Falco columbarius*. The Pigeon Hawk does not appear in great numbers but is often seen flying low in the open country or near foothills, frightening other birds.

A male falcon is known as a tercel, given that name either because it is one-third smaller than a female or because of the mistaken belief that every third bird hatched is a male.

HAWK, SWAINSON'S: see Hawk, Red-tailed

HERON: see Heron, Black-crowned Night; Heron, Green

HERON, BLACK-CROWNED NIGHT (Nycticorax nycticorax)

The Black-crowned Night Heron is widely distributed throughout North and South America. It breeds from northern Oregon to Nova Scotia south to Patagonia, and winters from northern California to New York and south to Patagonia.

A medium sized heron, the Black-crowned Night Heron is 26 inches (66.04 cm) in length. As described in its common name, the head, back and shoulders of this bird are black, while the rest of its upper parts are ashy-gray in color and its underparts are white. In breeding season, a few long white filmy plumes appear, growing from the back of the crown.

Compared to other members of the heron family that are long and slender, the Black-crowned Night Heron is short legged, small necked, squat shaped, and has a shorter and heavier bill.

Although not a bird with entirely nocturnal habits as its name implies, the Black-crowned Night Heron feeds chiefly in the evening or at night. Its evening flight to its preferred hunting grounds in shallow tidal creeks, pond edges and swamp pools is often accompanied by a loud and raucous call, from which it received its popular names of Quawk and Squawk. The Night Heron moves briskly through shallow water with neck curved and head lowered and unerringly thrusts its dagger bill at a moving dinner target of fish or frog. In a still fishing method, the Night Heron stands as motionless as a statue, no movement warning off its prey, and patiently waits for food to deliver itself to its ready stroke.

Black-crowned Night Herons nest in colonies often of several hundred pairs in wooded areas that can be many miles from water. Feeding the young can require long and numerous flights by the parents from nesting grounds to hunting localities. Nests are sometimes crude and so loosely built that the eggs or young are shaken out during heavy storms. Other structures are of more solid bulk, built of sticks and twigs and lined with finer grasses, and are used year after year. Building materials and nest sites are determined by the availability of plants, with some nests placed in trees, some in bushes and some on the ground.

Three to six pale green eggs are laid, and for 24-26 days both sexes are actively involved in their incubation, sitting periods alternated several times a day. Although an egg is deposited about every other day, incubation starts immediately, each egg hatching separately after receiving its allotted warming time. There is then an inequality in the size of the babies, but all are helpless and all are fed by both parents on regurgitated food, a kind of fish chowder dropped into the little open mouths through the parent's bill.

A heronry is not known for the meticulous housekeeping of its occupants, as often the youngsters rain down the contents of their crops on the heads of

unwanted visitors, and uneaten fish in various stages of decomposition add to the general unpleasantness. Any disturbance causes uneasy scrabblings and flutterings of the young; shrill, high-pitched screeches and various croaks and squawkings of both young and old create an ear-splitting pandemonium.

The Yellow-crowned Night Heron, *Nyctanassa violacea*, is a southern species, rarely breeding north of Illinois and North Carolina. The Yellow-crowned Night Heron is a solitary bird, not well known, and, unlike the Black-crowned, it breeds only in small colonies of two or three pairs.

HERON, GREAT BLUE
(*Ardea herodias*)

A stately wading bird, the Great Blue Heron, or Blue Crane as it is sometimes called, breeds from Nova Scotia to southeastern British Columbia to Nebraska, South Carolina and Bermuda. In winter it can be found from Oregon and New York south to Florida, Venezuela, Colombia and Panama.

Above: **A Black-crowned Night Heron on a nest with its young.**

The Great Blue Heron is the largest of the American herons, measuring up to 50 inches (127 cm) in length, with bill and neck accounting for much of this dimension. The plumage is loose in texture and simple in its color pattern, slate-blue above and black below, with sexes colored alike. The head is crested with long plumes.

The Great Blue Heron's feet are particularly well adapted for wading through soft mud. With its four long and slender toes the bird's weight is distributed over the specialized toes, preventing it from sinking into the oozy bottom. The Great Blue Heron is found near water, usually rivers and lakes, but also quiet bays of the sea where the big bird satisfies an omnivorous appetite for fish, frogs, crawfish, snakes and salamanders, which it captures with seemingly little exertion. Standing motionless in shallow water, dignified in bearing, its long neck doubled into an S-shaped curve, its keen eyes alert to every movement, the big Heron does not stir from its

BIRDS

position. When a candidate for dinner approaches, the bird remains rigid until the prey comes within striking range, which the heron knows within a fraction of an inch. With a swift straightening of the neck and a rapid stroke of the rapier bill, the food is secured and quickly swallowed. If a captured fish is too large to be gulped down easily without a struggle, the heron may walk ashore and beat it to death on the ground.

Requiring slightly more energy than standing still, stalking is another method of food gathering employed by the Great Blue Heron. One foot and then the other is lifted from the water with great deliberation, the downward step so gentle that not a ripple stirs to warn off a tasty water creature.

Although most herons feed exclusively on fish and other forms of aquatic life, the Great Blue Heron sometimes visits fields and meadows to vary its diet, there consuming pocket gophers, ground squirrels, field mice and some grasshoppers, too. Even when eating insects, it stands very still and waits for the insects to come within reach of its unerring beak.

To become airborne, the Great Blue Heron leans forward with neck extended and takes a few steps, strokes its broad wings, and mounts gracefully. Its flight is strong, powered by long slow flaps, its neck is retracted, and its legs are extended backwards, acting as a rudder in place of its tail, which is too short for this purpose. This mode of flight with the neck re-

tracted distinguishes the true Heron from the Crane, which flies with its neck extended.

Although for most of the year Great Blue Herons lead solitary lives, their nests are built in congested communities, varying in size from a few pairs to several dozens. Nesting sites are chosen primarily for the availability of food for the young, and security for the eggs dictates a remote and inaccessible location. The most desired nesting spots are on topmost horizontal branches of tall, spreading trees, but sometimes nests are built in low trees or bushes, and sometimes even on the ground. Construction materials are big sticks and twigs, fashioned into a large flat bulky platform, slightly hollowed and lined with finer twigs.

Left: A Great Blue Heron among the reeds in the Chesapeake Bay area.
Above: The Little Blue Heron (*Florida caerulea*) is commonly seen but over a more limited range than the Great Blue.

Four to six eggs are laid, incubated for 28 days by both sexes. Several times a day there is a general commotion in the otherwise peaceful heronry as partners change incubation tours of duty.

With little to make them endearing except to their parents, little Great Blue Herons are at first feeble and helpless, then awkward, ungainly and feisty. The young are fed in the nest, both parents delivering a soft, soupy regurgitated food, which is passed from the adults' bill into the mouth of the youngsters. As the babies grow, whole fresh fish are deposited in the nest and picked up by the young bird. Feeding time in the heronry is heralded with continuous chatterings, squeals, grunts, screams and barks, the youngsters quieting down only after their stomachs are filled, often the loudest, most aggressive nestling getting more than its share.

The Great Blue Herons of the north mingle in winter with their near relatives of the southern Atlantic and Gulf States, including the Great White Heron, *Ardea occidentalis*, Louisiana Heron, *Hydranassa tricolor*, and Little Blue Heron, *Florida caerulea*.

HERON, GREAT WHITE: see Heron, Great Blue

HERON, GREEN (*Butorides virescens*)

The dark colored Green Heron lives near ponds, swamps and streams. It breeds from North Dakota to Nova Scotia, south to the West Indies and winters from West Indies southward. Rarely is it seen in winter in the southeastern United States.

With a length of 18 inches (45.72 cm), somewhat smaller than a crow, the Green Heron is dark green above and dark brown below. It has a cut-off tail, a dagger-shaped bill 2½ inches (6.35 cm) in length, and comparatively short orange-yellow legs. When excited, as a form of soundless communication it elevates a shaggy crest on top of its head.

BIRDS

Above: **Smaller than most herons, the Green Heron has orange or yellow legs.**

As a wading bird, the Green Heron has legs that seem pared down, compared to other wading species that are more long legged, like the Great Blue Heron, *Ardea herodias*, and the American Egret, *Casmerodias albus egretta*. To balance its shortened limbs, its neck can appear so stumpy as to seem nonexistent, but its length is greatly variable as determined by the necessity of the moment. The neck can be stretched out to equal the length of the body when needed for hunting or short flights, and for long flights it can be folded up and retracted.

With shortened limbs, the Green Heron is equipped to wade only in the shallow water, but it sometimes dives in after its food, which consists of fish, worms, crayfish, tadpoles, aquatic insects, grasshoppers and even small mammals. In an unusual method of fishing, the bird watches from a perch a few inches above the water, and from there jumps quickly down upon its prey.

To escape the notice of a potential enemy and as a method of catching live food, the bird can remain perfectly still. A common watching posture near the edge of a pond or salt marsh is with the back and neck held horizontally and the body flattened on the ground, looking like an innocuous log of wood. When a fish or frog approaches, the Green Heron pounces with an accurate thrust of its dagger-like bill. The bird also stalks its food, raising and lowering each leg in the water with slow deliberateness so as not to scare away the prey.

Frequently in the woods, but usually near the water, the Green Heron nests singly, unlike other members of its family which are more gregarious in their breeding practices. No crowded rookeries of Green Herons exist as, for instance, do the congregations of Black-crowned Night Herons, *Nycticorax nycticorax*. Not particular in its choice of these solitary nesting sites, the Green Heron will build high in treetops, low in bushes or even on the ground. The nest is a frail thin platform of sticks, not hollowed and not lined with any fine plant material. In this flimsy structure are deposited three to six pale greenish eggs, which are incubated for 17 days.

Long before the young can fly, they are expert climbers, transporting themselves among the branches of the nesting tree. To climb, they use their feet, wings and bill, hooking their beaks and chins over the twigs and pulling themselves up. If they fall into the water below while working out on their arboreal jungle gyms, they simply swim to shore. Green Herons have an ancestral trait of a distinct web between the middle and outer toes that enables the youngsters to feel at home while paddling about.

Young Green Herons, at a signal from the adult bird, employ a similar method of protection to the one used by the old bird – freezing into position at the approach of an intruder. Another ruse used by the little ones to discourage unwanted visitors is to regurgitate the contents of their crops, not especially aimed at but sometimes hitting a would-be enemy, and certainly creating an inhospitable aroma in the vicinity of the nest.

Green Herons are of no value as food to man, nor were their feathers especially desired as decoration at the time when millions of birds were slaughtered for their plumage. Still, some Green Herons are shot by amateur hunters because its slow flight makes it an easy target.

HERON, LITTLE BLUE:
see Heron, Great Blue

HERON, LOUISIANA:
see Heron, Great Blue

HERON, YELLOW-
CROWNED NIGHT:
see Heron, Black-crowned
Night

HIGH HOLDER: see Flicker

HIGH-HOLE: see Flicker

HONKER: see Goose, Canada

HUMMINGBIRD,
BLACK-CHINNED:
see Hummingbird,
Ruby-throated

HUMMINGBIRD,
BROAD-TAILED:
see Hummingbird,
Ruby-throated

HUMMINGBIRD,
RUBY-THROATED
(*Archilochus colubris*)

The range of the tiny Ruby-throated Hummingbird extends over a larger area than any other hummingbird in North America, the bird breeding from Alberta to Cape Breton Island and south to Texas, the Gulf coast and Florida. It winters in Mexico and Central America.

The diminutive Ruby-throated Hummingbird measures approximately 4 inches (10.16 cm) in length and weighs a mere ⅛ ounce (3.5 g), but in the fall before its long migration it adds half again its body weight in fat. The male and female are both colored in bronze-green jewel-like brilliance on the upper parts, and white and bronze-green below. The male is distinguished by its luminescent ruby throat, which in certain lights or from a

Above: A Ruby-throated Hummingbird.
Below: The Caliope Hummingbird (*Stellula calliope*), the smallest North American hummer, is a western-mountain dweller.

distance appears black. The forked tailfeathers of the male are rounded in the female.

This glistening mite of a bird resembles a lustrous bee as it zips around the garden or pauses above a nectar bearing flower, held aloft by what seems a whir where wings should be. The tiny winglets move too rapidly to

Above: The female Rufous Hummingbird (*Selasphorus rufus*) lacks the rufous back of the male.
Right: Anna's Hummingbird (*Calypte anna*) is found west of the Sierra Nevada. The male perches to sing.

be seen by human vision, but their blurred flutterings create a buzz which gives the bird its name of hummingbird and even allow it backward flight. Singularly adept in the air and capable of perching on a branch, its feet are so undeveloped that the hummingbird cannot progress on the ground by means of legs and feet alone.

While the Ruby-throat hovers, a long, needle-like beak probes deeply into tubular blossoms, and a double-tubed tongue capable of lengthy protrusion extracts the sweet juices from the flower. When small insects are drinking from the petaled cup, the hummingbird eats them also. The in-depth bill thrusts help to transfer pollen in elongated blooms, unreachable by other means.

Although the hummingbird is small in size, it is intolerant and pugnacious in temperament, and will readily drive off competitors for food, especially another hummingbird, or even birds larger than itself. A high metabolic rate requires frequent daytime feedings among the flowers, and its irascible nature together with its outstanding flight ability result in extraordinary vivacity and mobility. After dark, however, the little bird quietly perches on a twig in a somewhat torpid state, body temperature slightly reduced and activity, therefore, greatly diminished.

BIRDS

Above: A Costa's Hummingbird (*Calypte costae*) feeding her young. The more colorful male has violet plumage on the head and throat and long feathers on the side of its throat.

Above: A Rufous Hummingbird feeding from a foxglove. This male adult has the completely rufous-colored back that is lacking in the female.

After mating, the female alone gathers bud scales and lichens and fashions a walnut-sized cradle for her two tiny white eggs, the size of peas, 5000 of which would equal the volume of a single ostrich egg. The nest, 1 inch (2.54 cm) across and of equal depth, is threaded together with spider and caterpillar silk, lined with soft plant down, and fastened to a tree limb by the bird's own saliva. The little cup appears as a mere growth of the branch itself, a bump on a log.

The young hatch out so weak and helpless that they can scarcely raise their bills to receive the regurgitated insect food, pumped down their tiny gullets by the adult bird. In three weeks, though, the fledglings leave the nest and take up life on their own.

In the fall, the 500 mile (800 km) journey across the Gulf of Mexico on the way to winter grounds in Central America is made without a single stop for food or rest, and with only an infinitesimal measurement of fat used as fuel.

Other hummingbirds of North America are the Black-chinned Hummingbird, *Archilochus alexandri*, the Broad-tailed Hummingbird, *Selasphorus platycerus*, and the Rufous Hummingbird, *Selasphorus rufus*, all birds of the western states.

HUMMINGBIRD, RUFOUS: see Hummingbird, Ruby-throated

IBIS, GLOSSY: see Ibis, Wood

IBIS, WHITE: see Ibis, Wood

IBIS, WHITE-FACED GLOSSY: see Ibis, Wood

IBIS, WOOD (*Mycteria americana*)

The secretive Wood Ibis makes its home in the densely vegetated swamplands of the warm southern borders of the United States. As a permanent resident of the moist bayous, it lives in southern California, Texas, Louisiana, Florida and south to Argentina.

Above: Colonial Wood Ibises nest in trees.

The Wood Ibis reaches a length of 4 feet (1.2 m), the male larger than the female, although the sexes are colored alike. A white bird with wings and tail a glossy greenish-black color, the Wood Ibis has a bald head and neck. Its long, thin bill is thickened at the base and curved near its rather blunt tip. In flight, these great white birds can be easily recognized by their jet black flight feathers, long necks, heavy bills and long legs extended outward beyond the short tails.

Secretive and wary, living colonially only in the most inaccessible locations, Wood Ibises have sentinel birds that warn the roosting flock of approaching harm. The slightest sound or glimpse of man will cause these birds to take wing with a powerful bound. In the air in flocks, they rise and soar in wide circles; higher and higher they perform a spiralling ascent, then suddenly they plunge downward only to repeat the aerial spectacle or drift away.

The Wood Ibis is a wading bird that prefers to feed in shallow, muddy ponds and marshes, but occasionally nourishes itself by shuffling through salt water mud flats. In a peculiar manner of obtaining food, which consists of fish, frogs, young alligators, aquatic insects and water snakes, Wood Ibises proceed in a group, walking back and forth as in a dance, dragging their bills while opening and shutting them repeatedly, setting up a loud clattering. The water becomes so thick with mud stirred up by dancing feet and clacking bills that fish and other creatures are forced to rise to the surface, whereupon the Wood Ibis instantly delivers a fatal strike with its hammer beak. The forceful blow is reminiscent of the sudden clap of iron against flint in a flintlock musket and gives the bird the picturesque common names of Flinthead and Ironhead. The bare boniness of the bird's head accounts for another of its endearing names, Goardhead. The Wood Ibis is also known as Wood Stork.

The Wood Ibis nests in crowded colonies in cypress trees of steamy swamps. Placed 50-80 feet (15-24 m) high, nests are flat structures built on spreading horizontal limbs, often so close together that edges touch. A single tree can house as many as 30 platforms, more typically 12-20, made of coarse sticks and lined with moss and bay leaves. A single breeding area might contain 10,000 nests.

The natural enemy of the Wood Ibis is the crow which robs the Ibis nests of eggs. The Wood Ibis has evaded overt slaughter by man due to its wary ways, its tough flesh, and its general undesirability for plumage, but its numbers are reduced because its roosting and breeding territories are threatened by the effects of civilization.

Other Ibises which also live in temperate and tropical areas within the North American range are White Ibis, *Endocimus albus*, Glossy Ibis, *Plegadis falcinellus*, and White-faced Glossy Ibis, *Plegadis chihi*.

IRONHEAD: see Ibis, Wood

JAEGER, PARASITIC: ARCTIC SKUA (*Stercorarius parasiticus*)

The Parasitic Jaeger is an aggressive bird associated with the sea. It breeds on islands in the northern part of the northern hemisphere. A long distance migrant, it winters from the Aleutian Islands, south to California and from the New England coast, southward to Brazil.

A gull-like bird, the Parasitic Jaeger is 20 inches (50.8 cm) in length. Its color above is a sooty, brownish-black and it is white below. Its two middle tail feathers are narrow, long and pointed. A stocky bird, the Jaeger has sharp, curved claws, like talons, and a hooked, hawk-like beak. Young Jaegers are smaller than the adults and are streaked throughout with rust-colored feathers. The juvenile birds do not take on the adult coloration and dimensions for several years.

Jaeger is a German word for hunter. The name Parasitic Jaeger describes the hunting technique of this bird. Daring in behavior and powerful in flight, the forceful hunter can overtake a weaker species that is carrying a fresh caught fish in its bill. Through harassment, the robber forces the smaller bird to drop its meal, then in mid-air the Jaeger snaps the falling missile into its mouth. The feathered pirate frequently chases terns, colliding with them and buffeting them with its wings. Victory is often psychological, the tern dropping its fish before the aggressor strikes. Piracy is a preferred food-gathering style, but when no fresh fish is available the Jaeger will resort to eating dead marine life, scavenging like the gulls, its close relations.

Like gulls, Jaegers breed in colonies. On rocky islands in the north Atlantic, a slight depression in the ground is sparsely lined with grasses, moss and dead leaves, serving as a nest. Large spaces are left between neighbors. Two or three olive to greenish-gray eggs, marked with shades of brown and lavender, are deposited. The blotchings of the shells blends them into the background colors of the nest, hiding the eggs from predators.

The young are down-covered when hatched. They are helpless and are cared for by both parents in and out of the nest for some time. Any intruder

Top: The Blue Jay, often found in pine trees.
Above: The Steller's Jay is a western jay.

into the breeding area, whether man or animal, is attacked with the aggressive power of these dive-bombing birds.

When not breeding, Jaegers are pelagic birds, meaning they spend all their time at sea. There they are primarily loners. Young birds remain at sea until they are three or four years old and are ready to breed. Although Jaegers are related to gulls, they are rarely seen in gulls' company, and they lead somewhat different lives.

JAY, BLUE
(Cyanocitta cristata)

The boisterous Blue Jay, a very common bird, breeds from southern Alberta to Newfoundland, south to Colorado, central Texas and Virginia. During the winter, it ranges somewhat farther south, but it lives year-round throughout most of its habitat.

The Blue Jay is approximately 12 inches (30.48 cm) in length, a big bird, but not as large as a crow, to which it is related. The female Jay is somewhat smaller than the male. Both sexes are similarly colored a jewel-like grayish-violet blue with gray and white underparts. A black collar encircles the neck and black bars streak the rounded wings and long, round-tipped tail. A high pointed head crest can be used to express emotion, raised up straight to signify anger.

BIRDS

Not a fussy eater, the Blue Jay consumes almost anything edible, including mostly grains, seeds, acorns, fruit and berries. Animal foods that are also relished are insects, snails, fish, salamanders, frogs and mice. That portion of a Blue Jay's omnivorous diet that gives the bird an unsavory reputation is its taste for bird eggs, which the Jay steals from the nests of incubating birds. Frequently, the bully will torment a sitting mother until she abandons her treasures, at which time the Blue Jay flies off with a shelled dinner. Like a bird of prey, the Jay will also kill and eat the nestlings of birds that are not as large and not as strong.

In what could be viewed as a bid for acceptance as a not entirely unworthy avian citizen, the Blue Jay performs a valuable service for the woodland community by emitting loud and raucous shrieks at the intrusion of a stranger in the woods. Forest creatures are therefore warned in advance of approaching danger and have time to take protective cover.

Another example of the Blue Jay's beneficial behavior is the role it performs as an arborist. In those areas that Jays are year-round residents, they store away a winter cache of acorns and other nuts, similar to the provisionings of squirrels. Concealed under leaves in the grass or in tree hollows, the seeds of future trees sometimes germinate where they are hidden and grow into the next generation of oaks and other varieties of forest species.

The Blue Jay has a large vocabulary of various calls that sound like squawks, whistles and tinkles and are expressions of states of mind, such as anger, defiance, complaint and joy. The melody of this bird heard most infrequently is its song, delivered in an uncharacteristic retiring style in the solitude of a wooded thicket. The music of its song is a mixture of soft whistles and sweet notes, tunes which are all part of the bird's repertoire but changed in sound because the medley flows together and is performed in a sedate and subdued manner.

A naturally wild shy bird of the forest treetops, the Blue Jay's temperament has been altered by civilization. Adapting to man's encroachments on its unspoiled woodland territory, the bird now builds its nest in gardens and sometimes even close to houses. At nesting time the squawking bumptious bird of winter becomes a quiet parent-to-be, seeking out a well-hidden tree crotch 10-20 feet (3-6 m) above the ground. The task of nest construction is a shared venture, both partners bringing the twigs, bark, moss, lichens, leaves, dry grasses and assorted man-made materials such as paper, rags and string to weave a loose structure of approximately 8 inches (20.32 cm) in outer diameter. After 17 days of alternated incubation duties shared by both parents, the three to six limp, blind and naked infants hatch, totally dependent upon the frequent feedings of the adult birds. The young are fully fledged in about 21 days and are ready to leave the nest.

In autumn there is a general shift of population as companies of Blue Jays move southward in loosely ordered flocks. Flying during daylight hours, they skirt the treetops, remaining unnoticed as they quietly progress. Although the Blue Jay is found all year over most of its range, summer and winter residents may be different individuals.

Steller's Jay, *Cyanocitta stelleri*, lives in the coniferous forests of the northern Pacific coast; Woodhouse's Jay, *Aphelocoma woodhousei*, lives in the western United States; the California Jay, *Aphelocoma californica*, lives on the Pacific coast of the United States and the Canada Jay, *Perisoreus canadensis*, lives in the northern parts of the United States and in the British Provinces of North America.

JAY, CALIFORNIA:
see Jay, Blue

JAY, CANADA: see Jay, Blue

JAY, STELLER'S: see Jay, Blue

JAY, WOODHOUSE'S:
see Jay, Blue

JUNCO, OREGON:
see Junco, Slate-colored

JUNCO, SLATE-COLORED (Junco hyemalis)

The Slate-colored Junco breeds over most of Canada, northern and central Alaska, northern New England and in mountainous areas as far south as Georgia. It winters throughout much of the United States, but is rarely found along the Pacific coast and it is never seen in central and southern Florida.

The Slate-colored Junco, often called Snow Bird, is approximately 6 inches (15.24 cm) in length. It has a white belly and white outer tail feathers, while the rest of its plumage is colored a dark blue-gray. The somber gray of its upper parts resembles the color of a threatening winter sky, while its white underneath matches the snow in which it seems at home. The streaked breast of the young Junco shows its relationship to others in the sparrow family.

Tame, trusting and gregarious, the Junco during much of the year makes its living near human habitation. Because its food consists primarily of seeds, its name is derived from the Latin *juncus* meaning seed. It is a ground feeder requiring some uncovered land on which to find its little kernels, therefore heavy snows will force the bird to move farther south. The severity of a northern winter can be measured by the incidence of Juncos in the southern states.

Although Juncos travel in feeding flocks, the group fans out once on the ground, each member scouring its own selected area, picking up seeds directly from the earth or scratching for them amid the leaves and soil. Grass and ragweed seeds are high on its list of preferred food; seeds of crabgrass, pigweed, amaranth and sunflower are also relished. In summer its diet is evenly divided between plant and insect food.

In nesting season, the sociable Junco becomes a loner, the male

Above: An Oregon Junco.

guarding his chosen territory and his developing brood with musical warnings. From late March to late July, a song that is a simple trill or a rapid series of similarly pitched notes is performed from an elevated perch in a bush or low tree. At other times of year, its call note is a short *tsip*, a sound that resembles the striking together of two coins. Individuals in a flock keep in touch with one another by uttering this sharp, click sound.

Breeding in northern pine-spruce zones and high in mountains even above the tree line, the Slate-colored Junco is the only bird that nests on top of Mt Washington, the highest mountain in the northeast United States. Nesting on the ground, the preferred spots for the rather bulky construction are under the edge of an overhanging bank, entwined in a tangle of roots from an overturned tree, enveloped in brushy vegetation or amid a patch of moss. Sometimes two nests a year are built to house two broods, the nests made of grass, moss, rootlets and shredded bark, lined with finer soft materials. For 12 days, both male and female share the job of incubation and

both participate in the feeding of the young.

With breeding labors adequately performed, Slate-colored Juncos gather into flocks in which they spend the winter, groups averaging 16 birds in number with many members returning year after year to the same little foraging band. As well as Slate-colored Juncos, these flocks often are made up of Towhees, *Pipilo erythropthalmus*, Myrtle Warblers, *Dendroica coronata*, Fox Sparrows, *Passerella iliaca*, and White-throated Sparrows, *Zonotrichia albicollis*. In the western part of this Junco's range, they are usually seen in association with Oregon Juncos, *Junco oreganus*.

KESTREL, AMERICAN:
see Hawk, Sparrow

KILLDEER
(Oxyechus vociferus)

The most widely distributed of all our shore birds, the Killdeer breeds and winters throughout much of the United States. Nesting areas extend from British Columbia and Quebec south to the Gulf coast and central Mexico. In winter, the Killdeer can be found from California to New Jersey south to Venezuela and Peru.

A bird 10 inches (25.4 cm) in length, the Killdeer is olive-brown above and pure white below. The white of its breast is starkly interrupted by two horizontal black bands. It has long straw colored legs, a long rounded tail, and a white V that can be seen on its wings in flight. This dark and light banded coloration forms a disrupted pattern and creates an effective concealment by breaking up the outline of the bird.

Not of a retiring nature, the Killdeer runs speedily along the ground or swiftly flies and skims the earth, while announcing its presence with loud calls and cries; thus its scientific name, *vociferus*. Its cry of alarm, a strident two syllables that sound like its name, *kill-deer*, has remarkable carrying power. Warning every bird within hearing range, the raucous signals are

a bane to hunters, but an aid to other Killdeers in avoiding danger.

Although classed among the shore birds, the Killdeer's preferred localities are not confined solely to the edges of lakes and seas, but meadows and dry uplands many miles from water also provide it abundant sustenance. In its never-ending search for food, it runs quickly, then stops abruptly and stands motionless with head held high. Suddenly it bows forward and dabs at the ground for a worm or an insect. Large numbers of harmful insects are consumed, including grasshoppers, boll weevils, beetles, wireworms and caterpillars. To secure a juicy morsel, the Killdeer often follows the farmer's plow, gulping down the newly exposed earthworms.

Like others of its close relatives, which includes the Golden Plover, *Pluvialis dominica*; Piping Plover, *Charadrius melodus*; Snowy Plover, *Charadrius aleandrinus*; and Wilson's Plover, *Charadrius wilsonia*, the Killdeer has a comparatively short bill, which is hardened and somewhat swollen at the end. Ill-adapted for probing in the mud, the beak is better suited for picking food up from the surface of the ground.

The Killdeer is the first shore bird to come north in the spring and the last to go south in the fall. It may arrive at breeding grounds as early as mid-March and leave as late as the middle of November. Near water on the bare gravely ground, or often a mile away from water on roads or even roofs, the bird builds a simple nest, a saucer-shaped depression in the ground, lined scantily with bits of broken debris. Four cream colored eggs, irregularly blotched with blackish-brown, are deposited and incubated alternately by both male and female for 25 days.

Within two hours after hatching all traces of egg shell are carried away by the parents, leaving no clues for curious predators. As soon as their down has dried, the fluffy youngsters follow the parents to the nearest water, and like the adults, the youngsters perform bobbing motions and emit loud calls. Concealing coloration and the habit of

BIRDS

lying motionless on the ground when signaled by the parent offers the little ones so effective a camouflage that they cannot be seen in their surroundings.

Once an abundant species, the Killdeer was slaughtered for the table in such great numbers that it was thought to have been wiped out. Protective legislation has resulted in the gradual increase in the numbers of these birds.

KINGFISHER:
see Kingfisher, Belted

KINGFISHER, BELTED
(Megaceryle alcyon)

A skilled fisherman, the Belted Kingfisher is a common North American bird, found from Labrador to Florida, east and west. It winters chiefly from Virginia southward to South America.

With a length of 15 inches (38.1 cm), the Belted Kingfisher has upper parts

Below: **The Killdeer is found all across temperate North America.**

colored bluish-gray and underparts of white. The male has a band of the same gray color across the lower breast, and the female bird, which is more belted than the male, has this band plus an additional strip that is cinnamon-reddish in hue.

The Kingfisher is topheavy in appearance with a chunky head and a straight, pointed 2¼ inch (5.71 cm) bill that is longer than the head. A crest of erect feathers stands up like a fright wig on the stout crown. Short legs and tiny feet indicate that the bird spends little time in walking on the ground; it is more adept in flight or as a nose-diving fisherman.

Ranging over inland waterways, the solitary bird follows creek and river courses to their very beginnings. On aerial reconnaissance, the Kingfisher flies over a pond and with keenest eyesight spots a fish swimming beneath the surface of the water. Quarry sighted, the bird checks its flight in mid-air, hanging for a few seconds as if suspended, then plunges headlong into the water. A perched position on an overhanging branch also affords the

angler a view of its watery cafeteria, which is entered with a sudden swoop.

Sometimes the Kingfisher spears its catch with its rapier bill, but usually it snatches the fish and flies with it to a nearby perch where, if it is small enough, it is gulped down quickly. If the fish is large and bony, a few sharp knocks against a branch stop its squirming, but still requires from the bird great writhing and contortion to swallow it.

The menu of the Belted Kingfisher presents no competition to the human angler, as the bird eats mostly minnows, chubs and shallow-water species considered undesirable trashfish by man, but preferred dinner by the bird. When waters are rough or fished out, the Kingfisher satisfies its appetite with crawfish, frogs, beetles and grasshoppers.

When the breeding season approaches, the shrieking endearments of a mated Kingfisher pair sound like noisy strident rattles. Although their love song resembles a persistent quarrel, both work together in the tunnelling out of a nesting chamber. Like the

Right: The Belted Kingfisher lives near streams.

Right: The Belted Kingfisher lives near streams.

Bank Swallow, *Riparia riparia*, a Kingfisher's nest is excavated in the side of a high bank, a passageway from 4-15 feet (1.2-4.5 m) in depth, ending in an enlarged rounded hollow, spacious enough for the birds to turn around. The tunnel is wide enough to admit only one bird at a time, and while one scratches out the sand or clay with its feet and extends the depth with its bill, the other waits outside to spur its partner on. The breeding excavation may be reused time and time again.

Indigestible scales and fishbones are disgorged by the parents to line the bottom of the rounded nursery chamber, and on this prickly lining five to eight pure white eggs are deposited. For the necessary 16 days, each parent takes its turn as an egg warmer. The naked, helpless babies are fed inside the burrow by the parents, but when the young develop sufficiently, they sit on a branch overhanging the water and loudly squawk in opened mouth entreaty to be served entire fish.

Another name for this Kingfisher is Halcyon. In Greek mythology, Halcyone, the daughter of Aeolus, in grief for her drowned husband threw herself into the sea. The gods, out of compassion, changed her and her husband into Kingfishers. It is claimed that the Kingfisher or the Halcyon builds a floating nest at sea, and through a mysterious power calms the restless waves while the hatchlings are being reared. The term halcyon days describes fair and peaceful weather.

The Texas Kingfisher, *Ceryle americana*, is a smaller 8 inches (20.32 cm) in length, has no crest, and lives in southern Texas, Mexico and south to Panama.

KINGFISHER, TEXAS: see Kingfisher, Belted

KITE, EVERGLADES: see Kite, Swallow-tailed

KITE, MISSISSIPPI: see Kite, Swallow-tailed

KITE, SWALLOW-TAILED (*Elanoides forficatus*)

The swift flying Swallow-tailed Kite lives in North and South America. It can be found breeding from southern Saskatchewan, northern Minnesota, southern Wisconsin, southern Indiana and South Carolina, south through eastern Mexico and Central America. It winters chiefly south of the United States.

With a total length of 24 inches (60.96 cm), 8 inches (20.32 cm) of that measurement is the length of its tail. Its wings are very long and reach nearly to the tip of its deeply forked and lengthy tail. The Swallow-tailed Kite has a white head and white underparts; its upper parts are black.

The Swallow-tailed Kite is a member of a group of birds called *Raptores*, grouped together more for the similarity of their feeding habits than for the sameness of their physical characteristics. Each species in the order, though, has a strongly hooked beak with a soft area at the base, the bill more or less suitable for tearing food apart.

In the family known as *Buteonidae* to which the Swallow-tailed Kite belongs, all individuals are diurnal, hunting for food during the day. Their feet have three toes always pointed forward and one toe turned backward, unlike owls that can move the outer toe either to the front or to the back at will. The eyes of the Swallow-tailed Kite are placed on the sides of its head so each eye is looking in a separate direction, encompassing a broad range of vision.

The Swallow-tailed Kite has short, sharply curved talons, and feet that are stout and stumpy. Because the Kite uses its legs so seldom for walking, the legs are very short and almost invisible. The bird lives much of its life on the wing, gliding, soaring, swooping, spiralling, equally proficient at speedy flight and graceful movement. So little effort seems to be exerted in flight that it is said the bird even sleeps while gliding in the air.

With bony, hook-shaped claws designed for grasping, the Swallow-tailed Kite swoops down and, without pause, grabs its prey of snake, lizard, frog or grasshopper. Not bothering to stop to feed, the bird devours its catch while continuing to fly. This dining aloft is easily accomplished by thrusting forward the talons in which the food is held and bending the head to rip off a mouthful.

As it feeds on snakes and lizards, never on other birds, the Swallow-tailed Kite is considered a beneficial species and has not been persecuted by man.

When breeding season arrives, the wooing of these feathered aerialists is also accomplished in the air. Loosely

BIRDS

built nests of large twigs and hay, lined sometimes with moss, are placed on top of tall trees in inaccessible locations, but near water and a food supply. Nests are often built on the previous year's foundation. From two to four white eggs, blotched with rich amber markings, are laid from April to June, depending upon the latitude. Both sexes share the task of construction, incubation and the care of the young.

When leaving the nest, the sitting bird bolts upward as if released by a spring, but when returning, it descends so lightly on its eggs, it seems a feather has fallen from the sky.

Before migrating south in autumn, these kites convene in small assemblages and circle slowly in upward spirals until out of view.

Other kites in North America are the White-tailed Kite, *Elanus leucurus*, which eats small birds and mice, Mississippi Kite, *Ictinia mississippiensis*, with food preferences similar to the Swallow-tailed Kite, and the Everglades Kite, *Rostrhamus sociabillis*, with a bill designed to extract a fresh-water snail from its shell.

KITE, WHITE-TAILED:
see Kite, Swallow-tailed

KITTIWAKE
(Rissa tridactyla)

A Gull of the Arctic regions, the Kittiwake breeds from northern Greenland south to the Gulf of St Lawrence. It winters from this Gulf south to New Jersey. It is occasionally seen in Virginia and the Great Lakes region.

The Kittiwake measures approximately 18 inches (45.72 cm) in length. Its head, neck, underparts, and tail are pure white. Its back and wings are colored pale grayish-blue, with a definite triangular black patch on the wing tips. The Kittiwake's tail is slightly notched. It has a yellow bill and blackish feet bearing only three toes, the hind or fourth toe being absent. The species name of this bird, *tridactyla*, means three-toed.

Above: A rookery of Black-legged Kittiwakes on offshore breeding cliffs.

Most Gulls land freely on the water to feed, but the Kittiwake hovers and plunges vigorously into the water, similar to the manner of the Terns. Kittiwakes are often seen following the huge Right Whale, cleaning up its leftovers of fish, dead or alive.

Gulls can drink either fresh or salt water. Although other Gulls prefer their water fresh, Kittiwakes are partial to drinking from the ocean. To remove the excess salt from their blood after drinking, Gulls have a special gland in their heads. The salt is expelled from the body through the nares or nostrils, the holes in the Gull's upper bill.

Drinking water from the sea, eating fish that swim there and sleeping peacefully on the great waves with its head tucked under its wings, the Kittiwake is very much a water-going bird. Unlike most Gulls, which are mostly coastal dwellers, the Kittiwake is often seen in mid-ocean.

On small, rocky ledges of sea cliffs and off-shore islands, Kittiwakes gather to raise their young. The nests are untidy constructions of grass and seaweed, housing two or three brownish-gray eggs that are mottled with

Nova Scotia. In winter, however, they are mostly marine birds frequenting inshore waters from southern British Columbia, the Great Lakes and southern New England, south to Florida, the Gulf Coast and lower California.

A large bird, the Loon's length is from 28 to 36 inches (71.12-91.44 cm). In summer, the upper parts are glossy purplish-black, thickly marked with white spots; its underparts are white. A ring of white streaks encircles its lower throat and makes the bird appear to be wearing a necklace. In winter, the bird's upper parts are a somber gray and lack the spotted markings of the breeding coloration. Both sexes are similarly patterned.

A long, straight, narrow, sharp-pointed bill serves as an ideal spearing device for piercing and holding the slippery fish which comprise a major portion of the Loon's diet.

Scientists consider Loons to be among the most primitive birds as they resemble fossils of birds that lived 50 million years ago. Weighing 8-12 pounds (3.6-5.4 kg), the heavy bird has very short wings and rises into the air with great difficulty. The Loon can take off only from the water, powered up by running along the surface and lifted with the added impetus of wind. Once air-borne, its rapid wingbeats propel it speedily ahead.

The stumpy wings are useful to the Loon in other ways as well. Because its feet are positioned far back near the rear end of its body, progress on land becomes a clumsy, awkward tribulation. Its feet are used to flounder forward, but so are those shortened wings, which give leverage and support. Chasing a fish, the bird can swim underwater with speed and power by paddling with webbed feet and by flapping its wings, thus flying underneath the surface as swiftly as in the air.

Never venturing far from the water because of the difficulty of returning to it for protection, the Loon's nest is built near the water's edge on shore or on an island in a deserted lake or pond. The nest is usually so close to the lake that when disturbed, the bird can easily spring directly into the water by

shades of brown and lavender. Both parents incubate the eggs and care for the young. Newly hatched chicks are covered with thick, fluffy down feathers. They are fed at the nest until grown, the parents regurgitating the meal and the young grabbing at it eagerly.

Five to seven weeks after hatching, Kittiwake young have grown their complete juvenile plumage and are ready to fly. Immature birds are colored darker than the adults, mottled a patchy brown against a tannish background. Full adult dress is not attained for several years, and not until then are the birds ready to breed.

KOH-HO:
see Swan, Trumpeter

LOGCOCK:
see Woodpecker, Pileated

LOON
(Gavia immer)

An excellent diver and swimmer, the Loon is a bird of solitary places in the northern part of the Northern Hemisphere. In lakes, ponds and slow-moving rivers the Common Loon can be found in summer from Alaska to Greenland, south to northern California, across the United States to

BIRDS

plunging forward and sliding on its breast.

The nest is a shallow circular depression in the marshy ground, sometimes lined with grasses and bits of turf. The eggs, usually two in number, are oval-shaped, olive green in color and sparsely spotted with darker brown and black. Although no attempt is made to hide the nest, the mottled markings of the eggshells blend sufficiently with the colors of the sodden vegetation to hide the eggs from potential eaters.

Both parents share in the incubation of the eggs and in the care of the young. In about four weeks the babies hatch out, covered with nesting down. For a few days they are carried on the mother's back, but soon they take to the water on their own, still fed by the parents until they are fully grown.

The cry of the loon seems to evoke in humans the feeling of the wilderness. Once its distinctive call is heard it leaves a haunting impression, having been described as weird, unearthly, mournful, uncanny or sinister. Adding

Below: **A Loon, known for its wild call.**

to its mystery is the Loon's ability to submerge gradually with no apparent effort and with little rippling of the surface of the water. Its solitary ways, its outstanding swimming and diving ability, its quiet disappearances and its mournful wailings make the bird awesome and fascinating.

MALLARD
(Anas platyrhynchos)

The most abundant wild duck, the Mallard has a widespread distribution throughout the world. In North America, it breeds from the Arctic Circle south through United States to Virginia and is very common in the west. In winter, Mallards are found in the Southern Hemisphere, but they also remain in the north wherever open fresh water, in which they feed, can be found.

The Mallard grows to 24 inches (60.96 cm) in length. As is true of most ducks, there is a pronounced difference in the coloration of the sexes. The male has a head and upper neck of luminescent green. A white ring encircles the neck and the back is

a mellow grayish-brown. The gray underparts are fronted with a purplish-chestnut breast. An olive-colored bill and orange feet accessorize the male's richly hued feathered garb. Nowhere near as attractive as the drake, the dowdy female is colored a dusky-brown, streaked and speckled tawny. A lone adornment, a purple patch, brightens up her wings. Even her feet are dull in color, a faded yellow.

The colors of the sexes serve useful natural purposes. The male sports his splendor to attract the amorous attention of a female; therefore, flamboyancy works to his advantage, while the female uses her brown drabness to blend inconspicuously into the nesting environment as she alone incubates the eggs. Once she is ensconced on the nest, it is most helpful to the situation that the male departs; if he stayed nearby, his gorgeous coloration would reveal her hidden site.

Mallards are known as dabbling ducks, ducks that do not dive for food but tip their bodies forward into the water. When dabbling, the front part of the body disappears beneath the surface while the rear end is tilted

straight up in the air, posterior a-wiggle, the position maintained by paddling in place.

A duck's broad, flat bill is especially suited for probing in mud and for straining sand and water out of the mouth when feeding. Sieve-like, the bill is fitted along the edges with a series of flutings which have a membraneous coverings. Even with such a specifically designed food gathering apparatus, the Mallard has a wide-ranging appetite, consuming frogs, tadpoles, lizards, newts, fish, snails, mussels, earthworms, insects, mice, grass, seeds and aquatic plants. Grains nuts and fruits are also eaten. Because of the Mallard's omnivorous eating habits and its unfussy choice of nesting sites, it outnumbers all the world's waterfowl by taking advantage of every opportunity.

In breeding season, wearing full color dress, males display communally to interest a female partner. Many drakes often mate with a single duck, preceded by what appears to be rough water play, feather tuggings and underwater immersions.

Nests are constructed by the female near lakes, streams, ponds or even meager watering holes. On the ground, hidden in a tussock of vegetation, the female builds an incubator of fine reeds, grasses, or leaves, using whatever plant material is nearby. She lines the nest with soft down that she tugs from her body to provide a blanket of insulation. Six to ten greenish to gray-brown eggs are laid and kept warm for 28 days by her feathered body.

The female Mallard rarely leaves the eggs until they hatch, but during those short periods that the nest is unattended, she covers the eggs with down feathers. The young peck themselves out of their shells and emerge all feathered out in downy yellow. Immediately upon hatching, the ducklings are capable of walking, swimming and feeding, but not yet dabbling, nor can they fly until they have grown their flight feathers.

The first moving things the babies see when they hatch out is the item

Above: A male Mallard. *Below:* Green-headed males dabble with the mottled-brown females.

they will follow, and this initial sighting is usually a part of the rear end of the mother. Thus imprinted onto a portion of her body, the diminutive balls of fluff waddle in a line after the designated spot and are led by mother duck to the water. Her loud quacking warns the little ones of danger when on land or in water and they scatter for cover among the plants or disappear beneath the surface. Many ducklings fall prey to fish, turtles, frogs, snakes and hawks, but because the brood is large, many more manage to survive.

Mallards have supplied eggs, flesh, and feathers to humans in copious amounts for thousands of years. Because of the birds' pronounced ability to survive and reproduce and because of their ready domestication, the Mallard population has remained abundant, despite its age-old usefulness to man.

MALLARD, BLACK:
see Duck, Black

MARTIN, BANK:
see Swallow, Bank

MARTIN, PURPLE
(Progne subis)

Throughout temperate North America, except the Pacific coast area, the Purple Martin breeds from Nova Scotia to Ontario, Montana and Idaho, and southward to Florida and Texas. It winters from Florida and Mexico to Venezuela and Brazil.

Smaller than a robin and related to the swallows, the Purple Martin is 8 inches (20.32 cm) in length. The male is colored a rich glossy black with metallic reflections of blue and black, while the female is dressed in a mottled brownish hue and colored grayish below. The forked tail measures 3½ inches (8.89 cm) long, but despite its length, the wings when closed project out back beyond the tail.

The diet of the Purple Martin consists entirely of insects, and its lack of shyness in close proximity to human habitation makes this bird a decided friend of man. With streamlined grace

Above: **Martins use manmade nesting boxes.**

it sails overhead in typical swallow fashion, darting, swooping, circling, procuring insects on the wing. Extreme aerial agility allows the Martin to skim the surface of a pond to bathe and drink. Occasionally the Martin feeds on the ground, consuming ants and other earthbound insects.

During the month of April, the Purple Martin returns year after year to the same location in northern breeding grounds, the male arriving in advance of the female. A springtime cold snap, which eliminates the Martin's insect food, interrupts this pattern of regularity, and many years may pass before the birds return to that locality. An insectivorous bird, the Martin's metabolic rate is very rapid, therefore it must eat constantly to prevent starvation.

Originally, Martins nested in natural cavities, tree hollows or woodpecker holes, but they readily adopted facilities that man provided, moving into breeding residences supplied for their use. American Indians and people of the southern states set out hollowed gourds which were and still are used by Purple Martins. The Mohegan Indians, seeing the tireless insect hunter, called it 'the bird that never rests.' The southern farmer looks favorably upon the birds not only because they keep down the insect population, but because Purple Martins, in defense of their territory, gang together to chase off hawks or crows that may attack domestic poultry.

A model bird-box nester, the Purple Martin is not fussy about its hollow,

but will move into almost any fabricated opening. Human beings, concerned as much with design as with function, have set up elaborate miniature apartment houses on poles about 15 feet (4.5 m) high, containing as many as 20 or 30 rooms, often accommodating the colonially nesting Martins in all the vacancies. Accompanied by a bubbly twittering, a mated pair build inside the hollow their nest of grass and leaves, sometimes with feathers, mud, rags or paper.

Incubation of the four or five eggs is performed entirely by the female, but both parents cooperate in the care and feeding of the hatchlings. As each nestling is fed in turn about every 15 minutes, the busy parent birds deliver insect food to one of their youngsters every three minutes. The large food requirements of both the adults and their offspring make enormous inroads into the number of insects that infest a Martin territory. Nature's insecticides, these birds are viewed with special endearment because they consume large quantities of mosquitoes.

Its usefulness to man notwithstanding, the Purple Martin is being forced out of its breeding grounds, its birdbox nesting quarters usurped by more aggressive interlopers, Starlings and House Sparrows.

In late summer, congregations of Purple Martins and other species of swallows assemble in great flocks preparatory to and during a leisurely migration. Setting up a constant chattering, thousands of birds convene to roost at night and feed around the countryside by day.

MEADOWLARK, EASTERN:
see Meadowlark, Western

MEADOWLARK, WESTERN
(Sturnella neglecta)

The Western Meadowlark can be found in the western United States and the southwestern Canadian provinces, east to the prairie districts and south to northern Mexico.

About 10 inches (25.4 cm) in length, the Western Meadowlark's upper parts are brown, streaked with black, and its throat, breast, and abdomen are colored bright lemon yellow. A distinguishing feature of the Meadowlark is the rich black, broad crescent on its chest. The Western Meadowlark is similar in behavior and appearance to the Eastern Meadowlark, *Sturnella magna*, but the western species has slightly different proportions, its wings longer, its tail shorter and it is grayer in coloration.

Meadowlarks are really not larks at all, but are members of a family of birds called *Icteridae* that includes such species as Orioles, Red-winged Blackbirds and Starlings. True larks are classed in the *Alaudidae* family. Only one representative, the Horned Lark, *Otocoris alpestris*, and several subspecies of which are seen in North America.

Essentially terrestrial, the Meadowlark is often seen in the company of its feathered relatives, hunting on the ground for worms and insects. Adept on land, it neither hops nor runs, but places one foot in front of the other and walks in a form of travel uncharacteristic of birds. Its dark streaks and blotches against its light hued background color provide camouflage concealment in the grasses among which it often feeds, and the stripes and variegations of its feathers supply a form of protection known as disruptive coloration. The bold markings interrupt the bird's form and break up its outline so it is not seen as a meal by a potential enemy.

Primarily an insect eater, the Meadowlark consumes quantities of grasshoppers, beetles and caterpillars, even gorging on some hairy larvae that are avoided by fussier birds. Although most meadowlarks migrate to congenial southern feeding grounds during winter months, occasionally a hearty individual remains behind and changes its cold weather diet to seeds.

The Meadowlark is a ground nester, its cryptic coloration allowing it to remain well hidden in its brooding site. It takes the further concealing cautions of arching over its coarse grass nest with the construction material and of

building the structure in a protective tussock of grass or weeds. A short, winding path leads to the nursery location, and is used by the parent when coming to or going from the nest, so as not to lead a predator directly to the little family.

The female alone incubates the three to seven spotted eggs, by herself feeds the nestlings, and sometimes produces two broods a year, while the male provides a valuable service of territorial defense. In clear toned, slurred

Above: **Western Meadowlarks have a loud song.**

whistled warnings he keeps away other male Meadowlarks from as large an area as several acres.

Another member of the *Icteridae* family is the Bobolink, *Dolichonyx oryzivorus*, a bird found in spring and summer from the eastern coast of North America to the western prairies. Like the Meadowlark, it is a ground feeder and hides its nest in meadows.

MERGANSER
(Mergus merganser)

The Merganser is a fish-eating duck, widely distributed in ponds, lakes and rivers throughout North America. It breeds from Alaska across Canada to Newfoundland and south to central California, northern New Mexico and New York. It winters throughout the greater part of its range, south to lower California, Texas, Louisiana and Florida. In the coldest season, it will remain wherever fresh open water is available, and even in the dead of winter, pairs of these large wild ducks may be found swimming in rivers in New England where a bubbling course has kept a portion of the waterway from freezing. Early in the spring the Merganser follows the season north as the ice melts in the ponds and rivers.

The Merganser grows to a length of 25 inches (63.5 cm). The markings of the sexes are very different. The adult male has a dark green glossy head and its upper parts are also greenish-black in color. The female and the young have a head and neck of reddish brown with upper parts of gray. All Mergansers have white feathers underneath.

For a short time after the breeding season and before new flight feathers are grown, the male undergoes a molt which leaves him with coloration similar to the female. This short term loss of feathers, which renders him temporarily flightless, is called a nuptial molt, and the resulting dull and blotchy pattern is described as his eclipse plumage.

A distinctive feature of the Merganser is the slight fluff of feathers on the female's head, a decoration lacking in

Left: **A male Hooded Merganser (***Lophodytes cucullatus***) with black-rimmed white cockade.**

the male. A crested female and an uncrested male is an occurrence unique among American ducks.

The food of the Merganser is primarily fish. Its fishy diet imparts a pronounced rank flavor to its flesh, so the bird is not high on the list of favorite targets for the hunters of wild ducks. The taste of its meat has been compared to 'an old kerosene lamp-wick.'

The Merganser seldom utters any sounds; only when alarmed does it emit a subdued croak. Silently swimming, it dives and chases its prey while underwater. Like other fish-eating ducks to whom it is related, such as the Red-breasted Merganser, *Mergus serrator*, and the Hooded Merganser, *Lophodytes cucullatus*, its bill is long, narrow, and cylindrical in shape with saw-toothed edges. This well-designed hunting apparatus enables the Merganser to grasp and consume slippery fish of considerable size. Ducks that eat plants and worms have broad, flat bills, suited to probing through muddy water and straining out the excess liquid.

Male Mergansers conduct elaborate courtship displays to attract a mate, then continue courtship procedures to bond the pair together, albeit temporarily. The female alone constructs a nest in a hollow tree, a stump, a thicket or a crevice, on or off the ground. Built in woodlands near streams and lakes, nests are fabricated of grass, twigs and leaves and lined with a soft warm matting of gray down and straw. Six to ten pale brown, unspotted eggs are laid, and for 28 days the female alone sits patiently, keeping the eggs warm until they hatch. The male leaves the domestic scene and finds a quiet spot in which to molt his feathers. The young emerge fully covered with natal down and are able to swim immediately upon being delivered to the water. Mother Merganser transports her chicks from their nest site to the safety of the water by carrying them in her bill.

MERGANSER, HOODED:
see Merganser

MERGANSER,
RED-BREASTED:
see Merganser

MERLIN: see Hawk, Sparrow

MIRE DRUM: see Bittern

MOCKINGBIRD
(Mimus polyglottos)

The most brilliant vocalist of all North American birds, the Mockingbird is found most commonly in southern states to southern Mexico and the Gulf. In the East it is a permanent resident, while western Mockingbirds are somewhat migratory. Like the Cardinal and the Tufted Titmouse, the Mockingbird has gradually extended its range northward and is now seen sporadically as far north as Maine, Ontario, southern Wisconsin and southern Minnesota. Adapting to man's taming of the landscape, the Mockingbird has readily transferred its original habitat preferences of forest clearings and woodland edges to parks, ranches, orchards and roadsides, and is now more numerous than it was before the European settlement of North America.

The length of the Mockingbird is 11 inches (27.94 cm), the female somewhat smaller than the male. Its body is slender, its legs long and its wings short and rounded. Its long mobile tail acts as a support in short flights as the bird progresses from tree limb to tree limb. The upper parts of the Mockingbird are gray and the underneath is whitish, while white is the color of its outer tail feathers, wing bars and large wing patches. The female resembles the male in coloration, but her wings and tail bear less white.

The Mockingbird normally builds its nest and finds its food near the ground, but to perform its remarkable and wide-ranging repertoire of songs it assumes a higher stage and positions itself on a roadside wire, a chimney top or a television antenna. As a general rule, most species in the wild will not learn the vocalizations of other species. Yet several songbirds, among them Mockingbirds, Thrashers and Catbirds, members of the family *Mimidae* or mimics, imitate the calls and songs of many different kinds of birds they encounter or hear. The Mockingbird also mimics other environmental sounds as it peppers its recitals with imitations of a crowing rooster, cackling hen, a squeaking wheelbarrow, a postman's whistle or even sirens.

Well deserving of the name of *Mimus polyglottos* which means many-tongued mimic, a single Mockingbird has been credited with changing its tune 87 times in seven minutes, each tune repeated on the average of four times. It is no wonder that one author described the bird as Mimus the Matchless. The king of singers often holds forth at night, especially in the moonlight, is heard frequently in the fall and often vocalizes while on the wing.

Scientists attribute the Mockingbird's astounding song-learning abilities to an enlarged forebrain that corresponds roughly to the human cortex. The forebrain of the male expands further in size just before the arrival of the mating and nesting season when extensive singing and calling are necessary to establish territories and warn off possible dangers.

The Mockingbird is very energetic in defense of its chosen territory and exhibits a number of strategies to minimize feeding competition, especially during the breeding season when abundant food is required to nourish the young. To warn off other Mockingbirds, ritualized body movements are performed that serve as boundary-line demonstrations. Intruders of the same species are aggressively driven away, sometimes dogs and snakes are dive-bombed and a Mockingbird will even attack its own reflected image, thinking it an unwanted rival. But by far the most highly evolved and most powerful ploy to keep out other birds is the use of imitative birdsong to protect his territory.

Above: A Thin-billed Murre.

Usually a bird performs a song that is specific to its species, the melody warning off others of its kind. Trilling from a singing perch and sounding like many other birds, the Mockingbird's accomplished outpourings fool several different species, especially its chief competitors, Bluejays, Robins, Flickers and Wood Thrushes, all birds with similar diets.

Drawn to areas of human habitation in which to nest, the Mockingbird often constructs a nest at low elevations in porch-climbing vines or decorative plantings around houses. Both male and female labor with equal intensity to fashion the structure of small dead twigs, with grass, rootlets and sometimes cotton used as a soft lining. Although the female alone incubates the four or five blue-green eggs for approximately twelve days, both parents participate in feeding the young on crickets, grasshoppers and grubs. The diet of the adults is made up of primarily insects, wild fruits and berries, although they have been known to visit orchards and damage fruit crops. After breeding, Mockingbirds are very defensive of their territory.

MUD HEN: see Rail, Clapper

MURRE, CALIFORNIA
(Uria troille californica)

The California Murre is the most abundant sea bird of the offshore rocks and islands of the Pacific. It breeds from Norton Sound and the Pribilof Islands south to the Farallons in California. In winter it is found from the Aleutian Islands south to Santa Monica, California. The California Murre is closely related to the Common Murre whose natural habitat is the northern Atlantic Ocean and its coastal islands, wintering south to Maine.

The California Murre is about 18 inches (45.72 cm) in length. Its color is sooty brown above and bright white below. On the water this bird resembles a duck, but the Murre's neck is shorter than a duck's and its bill is longer. Its rear end sits higher in the water.

Walking with an awkward waddling gait, the Murre is designed primarily for swimming and diving. Even when it sits, it appears to be standing. When swimming, its feet are used as propellers and its wings as oars, moving the bird underwater so vigorously that it can easily catch a fish. Progress underneath propelled by wings is swifter than when swimming on the surface paddling with feet alone.

The Murre's limited talents for walking are exercized only in June and July during breeding season when huge colonies of birds leave the water and come together to nest. On cliff edges of rocky Pacific islands, a jumble of black and white Murres huddle together in such vast numbers that it seems they crowd each other out. Close inspection, though, will reveal that each bird has its own small territory, and when pushed or intruded upon will express extreme dissatisfaction in defense of its space. Ownership of a nesting area is indicated with body bobbings, beak sparrings, and utterances of hoarse, baritone, human-like sounds. Because too few rocky areas exist of the kind that appeal to the breeding instinct of Murres, available locations almost overflow with birds. The babble is continuous as everyone is warning off the other fellow while protecting the spot that was occupied the previous year.

No nest is built; the single egg is laid on bare ground. From bird to bird, the eggs show a wide variety of coloration, some white, some dark green, all with an assortment of spots, blotches or scratches in black, brown or lilac. For 30 days, the parents share the task of egg incubation, which they perform by holding the egg between their legs with the point outward. The egg is pointed at one end, somewhat top-shaped. The extreme tapering prevents the egg from rolling off the sloping ledge. Instead of rolling downward, it will circle around its point, then come to a standstill.

The young hatch out covered with downy, gray-brown feathers. By their first winter, they resemble the adults, although not yet as large.

The eggs of Murres have been prized by hungry sailors. Easily collected, the eggs provide fresh and colorful food, with red yolk and blue albumen. Eggshell fanciers, fascinated by the assorted markings, gathered Murre eggs to add to their collections, making further inroads into the numbers of these birds. Although the Murre populations have been enormously reduced, their nesting colonies remain a crowded mob scene.

MURRE, COMMON:
see Murre, California

NIGHTHAWK:
see Whip-poor-will

NUTHATCH:
see Nuthatch, White-breasted

NUTHATCH, RED-BREASTED:
see Nuthatch, White-breasted

NUTHATCH, WHITE-BREASTED
(Sitta carolinensis)

Throughout almost the entire United States and from southern Canada to southern Mexico, the White-breasted Nuthatch resides year-round. In the fall, a population shift occurs, as some birds change their breeding territories for more southern winter feeding grounds, although the move is of short distance. This Nuthatch is among the 25 most common birds seen in the winter.

The White-breasted Nuthatch is 6 inches (15.24 cm) in length and has a flat compact body and a slender pointed bill that is longer than its head. It has a blue-gray back, a black cap, a white breast, and brownish-black tail feathers with white bars that shade to reddish underneath.

About half the menu of the White-breasted Nuthatch is comprised of insects such as weevils, leaf hoppers, plant lice and wood-boring beetles, and the other half of its diet is made up of nuts, seeds and berries. In order to reach the nourishing meat contained within a brittle acorn shell, the Nuthatch implants the seed inside a bark cranny and strikes at it repeatedly with its sharp bill used as a hammer. The pounding action gave the bird its former common name of Nuthack from which the title Nuthatch is derived.

In mixed and deciduous woodlands, the Nuthatch minutely scrutinizes tree limbs and bark in search of insects and their eggs that may be secreted in the crevices and chinks. Clamped on with little sharpened talons, the agile bird seems to defy gravity as it walks along the underside of a branch or even proceeds head first down a tree trunk, a habit of locomotion that accounts for another common name of Devil Downhead.

Pairs of White-breasted Nuthatches are mated for life, but if one dies, an unmated bird quickly takes the place of the missing partner. To ready the female for mating, the male puts food directly in her bill, or tucks nuts into bark fissures for her to find. His low-toned whistled courtship song is a series of short notes delivered with repeated regularity, and is accompanied by bows that provide a varying display of his blue-gray, then black and white, then brownish colorations.

The White-breasted Nuthatch often builds its nest in or near its approximately 50 acre (20 ha) winter feeding area. In woods, orchards or tree-lined streets, the site of its brood chamber is a knothole in a dead branch or stump, or a nest excavation used formerly by a woodpecker, sometimes as high as 60 feet (18 m) and sometimes used by the Nuthatch couple for several breeding seasons. The nest chamber is lined with shreds of bark and softly matted with squirrel or rabbit fur on which are deposited five to eight eggs that are warmed by the female for 13 days.

The young Nuthatches leave the nest before they are able to fly, but they continue to be fed by the parents for about two weeks. The youngsters become adept climbers and sleep by clinging like flies to the underside of a branch.

The range of the White-breasted Nuthatch overlaps that of the Red-breasted Nuthatch, *Sitta canadensis*, but the latter occurs less commonly and, unlike the white-breasted bird, it nests in conifers.

Above: The curved-billed brown-backed Brown Creeper is less striking than the Nuthatch. Both probe tree bark for insects, the Creeper using its long, stiff tail feathers as a prop.

The most often heard autumn-winter call of the White-breasted Nuthatch is a harsh and nasal *yank-yank-yank*, sounded as a communicative signal to keep contact with the mate, as the birds feed among the leafless trees. Throughout the winter, Nuthatch pairs may be joined for a time by Chickadees, *Parus atricapillus*; Downy Woodpeckers, *Dendrocopus pubescens*; Titmice, *Parus bicolor*; Ruby-crowned Kinglets, *Regulus calendula*; or Brown Creepers, *Certhia familiarus*.

OLDSQUAW
(Clangula hyemalis)

The Oldsquaw is a diving duck that lives for part of the year at the top of the world. During breeding season, it can be found farther north than any other species, nesting from Alaska around Hudson Bay to Greenland and Iceland. Its southward migrations bring the Oldsquaw in winter to the Atlantic coast from Chesapeake Bay to Florida and along the Pacific coast to southern California.

The male Oldsquaw Duck measures 23 inches (58.42 cm) in length, the female a much smaller 16 inches (40.64 cm). Like the Pintail duck, *Anas acuta*, the male Oldsquaw has a long, pinlike tail which it points into the air while swimming. The female lacks these extended tailfeathers. The drake

in winter has a white head, neck and belly with a black breast, back and wings. In spring, he changes his colors to a much darker breeding plumage, his head and neck becoming a deep chocolate brown, the color change most unusual in the duck world. Females are a drab, grayish-brown above and whitish with dark shadings below.

As the Oldsquaws commune in great flocks along the coasts of the South Atlantic states in winter, they set up ceaseless chatterings. No wild duck in North America is so endlessly communicative to its fellows as is this species. This propensity for constant clacking is the reason for its name of Oldsquaw. Other names that describe its persistent banter are Old Wife, Old Injun, Old Granny, and Scolder, while its lengthened tailfeathers are commemorated in the names Long-tail and Swallow-tail Duck.

Although the Oldsquaw is considered a sea duck and lives on and near the ocean, it is sometimes found inland on large lakes and rivers. Its food is primarily shellfish, crustaceans and some small fish as well, which makes its flesh taste fishy and it is therefore spared the hunter's shotgun, being too rank in flavor for the table. Seeds, shoots, buds and fruits of water plants are also eaten, food gained by the execution of very deep dives from the water's surface. One diving depth was recorded

to be 180 feet (54 m), but dives are usually not so deep. Both feet and wings are used to propel the bird downward through the water.

Even though the bird is spared the gun, it often falls victim to the fishnet. While down beneath the surface, the Oldsquaw becomes ensnared in gill nets of commercial fishermen and drowns. In one area, 27,000 Oldsquaws were caught in a single spring.

Unlike most other diving ducks, the Oldsquaw does not run along the water to build up the momentum for a takeoff, but rather springs directly into the air in the same manner as ducks that dabble and surface feed. The Bufflehead, *Bucephala albeola*, too, is a diving duck which can execute a vaulting ascent. In flight, Oldsquaw flocks rise in great circles almost out of sight and descend in zigzag courses.

During courtship, males become aggressive and do ritual battle with one another. The fights do not result in injury, but serve to weed out the weaker individuals while the stronger winners take the female prizes. These courtship battles with robust victors insure that genetic strengths will be passed along to the coming generation.

In the Arctic north where daylight is plentiful in which to raise a brood, the

Below: An Oldsquaw male, with slender tail.

BIRDS

female builds a nest on the ground, placed under a bush or in grassy shelter, constructed of grasses and dry weed stems and lined with small, dark down feathers. Six to ten dull, gray-olive eggs are laid, which the female incubates for the necessary 25 days. The male Oldsquaw remains nearby throughout the brooding period, although he is of no assistance in egg-warming duties, but offers instead a guardianship service. Even this minimal cooperative function is unique, as most drakes of other duck species are nowhere around once incubation begins.

The male's color change in spring, the bird's remarkable diving ability, its bounding takeoffs, its continuous quackings, its northernmost nesting sites and the drake's remaining with the brooding female all are outstanding duck characteristics and make the Oldsquaw a special bird.

ORIOLE, BALTIMORE: see Oriole, Northern

ORIOLE, BULLOCK'S: see Oriole, Northern

ORIOLE, NORTHERN (Icterus galbula)

The flashy colored Northern Oriole, a bird of open terrain, can be found in spring and summer from Nova Scotia west to central Alberta and south to Georgia, Louisiana and Texas. Fall migrations bring flocks of Orioles south of the United States to southern Mexico and northern South America, but occasionally individuals remain during the winter in the northerly part of the range.

The Northern Oriole is 7½ inches (19.05 cm) in length and has a long, stout, sharply pointed bill. The male bird is decked out with a brilliant orange back and breast and a showy black and orange tail. Its all black head and two-toned tail distinguish it among the other North American orioles. More subdued in attire, the female Northern Oriole is mostly dull olive above with a light hued orange-yellow throat and breast and two white wing bars.

Until recently known as the Baltimore Oriole, the bird is neither a true

oriole, nor is its range confined geographically to the city of Baltimore. The Northern Oriole is a member of the family *Icteridae*, which includes such birds as Grackles and Cowbirds. It was named after Lord Baltimore, the original founder of the Maryland settlements whose personal colors were orange and black, the colors of the bird. In response to modern conditions that have contributed to this oriole's extended range, the Baltimore Oriole is now the Northern Oriole.

Unlike many bird populations that have been adversely effected by

Left: **A Northern Oriole, common in shade trees.**
Below: **The golden-crowned male Hooded Oriole (*Icterus cucullatus*) inhabits the southwest.**

human encroachment on their breeding grounds, the numbers of Northern Orioles have increased because of man's settlement and the resultant changes of the landscape. The Northern Oriole nests in tall trees that grow singly or in small groves, at least partially surrounded by open terrain. Thickly grown forests or wide open prairies, common environmental conditions before the taming of North America, were not as attractive to the bird for reproductive purposes as are locations in pastureland, in tall trees left standing as shade for livestock, or in high branches that line city streets and country roads.

Carefully examining various locations in a tree that has been taken over and defended by the male, the female

oriole chooses a tip of a high up overhanging branch on which to sling the swaying pouch that she will weave. The protection of the nest is derived more from its inaccessible placement than from its concealing construction. An outstanding example of bird architecture, the nest is a tightly interlaced hanging pocket with a rounded, padded bottom to cushion the nestlings and a narrow top to keep them tucked in when their cradle is rocked by high summer winds. Using plant fibers, milkweed stalks, strips of gray bark, horsehair and bits of string or cloth, she ties suspension strands firmly around a twig to form the warp and deftly entwines her materials in and out of the pendant fibers. Even though she works so quickly that her bill

moves faster than the eye can follow, it takes her five or six days to fashion the finely woven fabric that houses her four to six white spotted eggs on which she sits for 12 to 14 days.

The South American winters of the Northern Oriole are spent singly or in small groups, foraging through plantations, orchards and pastures, dining on fruits and insects.

A smaller, less common oriole with a more retiring manner and duller coloration than the Northern Oriole is the Orchard Oriole, *Icterus spurius*. It, too, ranges throughout the eastern United States, breeding from southern North Dakota east to southern New York and south to the Gulf coast. The Bullock's Oriole, *Icterus bullocki*, is a bird of the western United States and the western Canadian provinces. The male Bullock's Oriole has orange cheeks crossed by a dark line, while the male Northern Oriole has an all black head.

ORIOLE, ORCHARD:
see Oriole, Northern

OSPREY
(*Pandion haliaetus*)

The Osprey, a member of the hawk family, is also called a Fish Hawk or an Eagle Hawk. It lives near large bodies of fresh and salt water, along coasts, lakes and rivers of North America. The Osprey is found in small numbers in Florida and along the southern California and Mexican coasts throughout the year. The summer, or breeding, range extends from northwestern Alaska to the southernmost part of California, western Mexico and along the Gulf of Mexico. The Osprey winters in the southern states and down into northern Argentina and Paraguay.

The Osprey is a large bird of prey, measuring up to 24 inches (61 cm) in length, and has a wingspan that extends up to 6 feet (1.8 m). The plumage is dark brown above, with some white on the head. Underneath it is mainly white with brown streaks. Ospreys hold their wings in a charact-

Above: **Ospreys hover before plunging for fish.**

eristic arched position, and a black wrist patch on both adults and young easily distinguishes this bird from other similar ones.

Ospreys usually build their very large nests in the tops of tall trees, occasionally choosing telephone poles or ledges, out of twigs, branches and plant matter. Ospreys return to the same nest year after year, adding to it each year. They lay two to five white eggs with brown spots, which are incubated by both parents.

Often called Fish Hawks because they prey only on fish, Ospreys hover above the water before plunging feet first to grab the fish near the surface with their long sharp talons.

OUZEL, WATER; DIPPER
(*Cinclus mesicanus*)

The Water Ouzel, also known as the Dipper, is a small thrush-like bird that is commonly found along swiftly flowing streams with rapids in the mountainous regions of western North America, where it dwells year round.

This fearless little bird is about 6 inches (15 cm) long. It is slate gray or sooty in color all over. Water Ouzels carry their short tail upward, and they walk with a characteristic bobbing up and down of the entire body.

The Water Ouzel is a solitary bird. It builds a large, well-insulated nest out of moss, with a side entrance. It builds its nest near clear, fast-running streams, occasionally in the protected crevice of a rock behind waterfalls, in dead tree limbs, under projecting tree roots or along the bank of its home stream. The female lays a total of 3 to 6 white eggs.

The Water Ouzel is equipped with special oil glands which make it unusually adapted for flying through the water and 'dipping' into streams to pluck out insects, its only source of food. Where the water is deeper, this strong-legged bird walks under the water with its wings half open.

Below: **The Water Ouzel can walk under water.**

OWL, BARN
(Tyto alba)

The strange looking Barn Owl with the white, heart-shaped face has a wide distribution throughout the greater part of the United States and Mexico. It is a permanent resident from Washington to New York and south to southern Mexico, and seen occasionally in British Columbia, Ontario, Minnesota, Vermont and Massachusetts.

The Barn Owl has a length of 21 inches (53.34 cm), the female slightly larger than the male. Its plumage is whitish-buff, finely speckled with black. A radiating system of white feathers called facial discs surrounds the eyes in a heart-shaped pattern and gives the bird a comical masked appearance. The feathered facial arrangement accounts for the Barn Owl's descriptive name of Monkey-faced Owl. The discs act as sound collectors, augmenting the owl's acute hearing ability.

The Barn Owl, like other owls, is a nighttime hunter and specialized design features suit the bird for nocturnal foraging. Eyes that can expand dim moonlight into many times its brightness as compared to human eyesight capabilities allow the owl to see its prey of mice and rats, which also are active at night. Shrews, bats, frogs, grasshoppers and beetles enlarge its menu. As the Barn Owl moves out to catch its victim, soft and fluffy wing-feathers make no whirring sounds to frighten off the skittish mammal quarry.

A remarkably efficient natural mousetrap, a Barn Owl will catch as many mice a night as a dozen cats, its voracious rodent appetite, especially when feeding nestlings, making it a useful species to have around a farm. It does not eat poultry; nevertheless, the Barn Owl is killed in the mistaken notion that its food preferences make severe inroads into the barnyard chicken population.

It holds its prey down with long, sharp claws, then with its tearing beak rips off its favorite tid-bit, the mouse's

Above: The Barn Owl is a nocturnal bird.

head. The remainder of the animal is bolted whole if not too large, or torn apart into more manageable morsels, and swallowed meat, bones, skin, fur and all. These indigestible parts are coughed up later in pellets and are strewn on the ground below the owl's roost.

Not especially particular in its choice of nesting site as long as it is in some kind of cavity, a Barn Owl lays its eggs in tree hollows, cliff grottos, abandoned underground burrows, old mining shafts or barn holes. Natural excavations are often further enlarged, the owl using sharp claws to fashion the hole to suit its purposes. Both male and female birds occupy the cavity during the day, and often both together incubate the five to seven eggs, sitting side by side with a portion of the eggs under each of them.

The eggs are laid at intervals of two or three days, with incubation commencing soon after the first egg is deposited. After the necessary incubation period has been served, the young hatch out also in two or three day intervals, resulting in a great variety of sizes among the newly emerged occupants of the nesting chamber. The first to be fed are the largest and strongest owlets who beat out their smaller.weaker siblings in the grab for mice, which are delivered by the parents. When food is not plentiful enough to nourish the entire brood, the most recently hatched

babies are the last to eat and the first to die, thus linking the population level of owls for a particular year to the population level of available prey.

During the day, the Barn Owl shrinks from bright light, sleeping in a corner of an abandoned building, in a dark cave, a tree hollow or hidden among thick foliage disguised by the concealing coloration of its tawny plumage. In the fall and winter months, small colonies of roosting owls occasionally can be found, each bird sheltered in a separate cavity in the same tree.

OWL, BARRED:
see Owl, Great Horned

OWL, GREAT HORNED
(Bubo virginianus)

The Tiger of the Air, as the Great Horned Owl is sometimes called, lives in North America from Ontario, Quebec, New Brunswick and Newfoundland, south to the Gulf Coast and Florida, and west to Wisconsin and eastern Texas. It is a year-round resident, except in the most northerly locations of its range, which it leaves for more hospitable winter hunting territories.

The male Great Horned Owl measures 23 inches (58.42 cm) in length, the female somewhat larger. Both sexes are similarly colored grayish-brown with white mottlings, tones that blend the owl into its wooded background. Feathers cover the legs and even the toes are fully blanketed, suiting the bird to live in cold temperatures. Two conspicuous tufts of feathers stand pert on top of the head where ears might be, but these downy crests are neither ears nor horns, they are merely this bird's plume arrangement. The hearing of the Great Horned Owl is acute, and its ear openings are covered by feathers.

Soft, fluffy plumage expands the owl to twice its actual size, and the loose puffy feathers, especially on the margins of the wings, allow completely silent nighttime hunting flight, so as not to warn off prey with any sounds.

Left: A Great Horned Owl.
Above: A Great Horned Owl swoops down on a Kangaroo Rat, one of the many small rodents typical of its prey.

Great, round yellow eyes, adapted for use in darkness and in light, do not rotate in their sockets; instead, the head moves around to follow moving objects. Unusual in birds, the upper, not the lower, lid is used to close the eye, which can also be protected by a see-through covering called a nictitating membrane. The wide open, staring eyes give the owl an all-knowing look and account for its folkloric trait of wisdom.

The Great Horned Owl is a strong and well adapted nocturnal hunter with powerful tearing beak and sharply curved talons. A bird of prey of thickly wooded regions where the heavy forest yields an ample supply of small game, it sometimes leaves the thickets to raid the barnyard, adding domestic fowl to its varied menu of wild bird species, mice, rabbits, squirrels, muskrats, skunks, shrews, bats, snakes and even an occasional housecat. Not particular in choice of food, this ravenous owl will attack almost anything that runs, creeps, flies or swims, and when quarry is plentiful enough for it to indulge its tastes, the bird enjoys only the choicest parts of its victims, often only the brains. Between the Great Horned Owl and the Red-tailed Hawk, *Buteo borealis*, woodland creatures are subjected to thorough, round-the-clock surveillance, the hawk the daytime marauder and the owl covering the grounds at night.

The owl transports its quarry to its roost to be torn up and devoured. Hair, feathers and bones are all bolted, then coughed up as pellets, a compact mass composed of these indigestible materials.

The Great Horned Owl may nest in gorges or caves or on ledges, but more often it appropriates a former hawk, squirrel or crow nest, which it remodels with twigs, plant stems and feathers. Sometimes eggs are deposited on the bare ground in a haphazardly arranged bed of old bones, skulls, fur and feathers.

The two to five eggs are laid as early as January as far north as New England, and even after the approximately 28 day incubation period, parents have sufficient opportunity to feed the voracious nestlings before the trees leaf out and block off an easy view of the many little animals necessary to satisfy the young. When the fledglings have developed the power of flight and the ability to hunt and feed themselves, the adults drive their offspring away, thus eliminating the youngsters as a source of food competition.

Some other owls widely distributed throughout North America are the Long-eared Owl, *Asio wilsonianus*; Short-eared Owl, *Asio flammeus*; Barred Owl, *Strix varia*; Saw-whet Owl, *Aegolius acadicus*; and Snowy Owl, *Nyctea scandiaca*.

OWL, LITTLE HORNED:
see Owl, Screech

OWL, LONG-EARED:
see Owl, Great Horned

OWL, MONKEY-FACED:
see Owl, Barn

OWL, MOTTLED:
see Owl, Screech

OWL, SAW-WHET:
see Owl, Great Horned;
Owl, Screech

OWL, SCREECH
(Otus asio)

The little Screech Owl is common bird throughout wooded North America where it lives as a year-round resident. Eight variants or subspecies of this owl are recognized, ranging over most of the United States.

Measuring only 10 inches (25.4 cm) in length, the female is slightly larger than the male. Both sexes have prominent ear tufts, which are not ears but erect feather patches that stand up on top of the head. Eyes are large, yellow and round, and the loose downy feathers which cover the body fluff the bird up to almost twice its normal size.

An unusual feature of the Screech Owl, for which naturalists have no adequate explanation, is the bird's dichromatism, which means its two distinctly different color phases. Sometimes it is colored rusty-red, sometimes it appears in hues of mottled gray and black and sometimes it is in an intermediate stage. The color of its dress bears no relation to age, sex or season, but there is some evidence that its color changes are related to its diet. Its variety of chroma gives this owl the name of Mottled Owl.

Because of its tufts of head feathers, the Screech Owl is sometimes known as the Little Horned Owl, and because of the eerie tremolo of its love song, it is occasionally known as Shivering

Owl. Both titles are more descriptive of this bird than the name of Screech Owl, as the notes it warbles in the darkness of the woods bear no resemblance to a screech, but sound more like a plaintive whinny.

Most decidedly a nocturnal hunter, the Screech Owl moves at night on silent wings that emit no whir to warn off potential prey. Keen eyesight and sharp hearing ability help detect the whereabouts of varied quarry, consisting mostly of mice and insects, occasionally of small birds, rarely poultry. The habits of the Screech Owl of devouring mice and insects make this bird a beneficial species, an ally in man's constant battle against the gnawers and the nibblers.

During the day, the Screech Owl rests from its nighttime labors and remains concealed in dense woodland or in a favorite hollow in a tree. Sitting on a horizontal limb, wings and feathers held close to the body, its compact pose and its concealing colors make the bird appear a mere extension of the branch.

Mated for life, a faithful Screech Owl pair nests in a hollow tree or stump, rotting wood chips serving as a soft bottom layer. An abandoned woodpecker hole is also a favored

Left: **Young Screech Owls.**
Right: **The arctic Snowy Owl (*Nyctea scandiaca*) is large and has no ear tufts.**
Below: **The Burrowing Owl (*Speotyto cunicularia*), a small plains owl, is so-named because it nests in prairie dog burrows.**

nook, and bird boxes placed on trees or buildings are readily adopted by the owl. While the female incubates the three to six white eggs for about 25 days, the male attends her by delivering gifts of dead mice.

When first hatched, the young Screech Owls are covered with an insulating blanket of pure white down all the way to the tips of their toes. Almost nonstop feeders, the little ones' demanding appetites can require as many as 75 hunting forays each night by the diligent parents. When eight weeks old, the well-stuffed owlets are turned out to shift for themselves.

In winter, Screech Owls from northern areas often leave their woodland haunts for the more congenial hunting localities of farms and even towns and cities. There, mice, rats and English Sparrows nourish the little bird of prey.

The Screech Owl might be confused with the Saw-whet Owl, *Aegolius*

acadicos, which is also small, but the Saw-whet Owl lacks ear tufts and it is colored brown.

OWL, SHIVERING:
see Owl, Screech

OWL, SHORT-EARED:
see Owl, Great Horned

OWL, SNOWY:
see Owl, Great Horned

BIRDS

OYSTER CATCHER:
see Turnstone, Ruddy

PARTRIDGE, HUDSONIAN SPRUCE:
see Grouse, Ruffed

PEEP: see Sandpiper, Spotted

PELICAN, BROWN
(Pelecanus occidentalis)

An ungainly bird with an enormous pouch hanging from its lower bill, the Brown Pelican is found along the coast of Florida and the Gulf coast of the United States and the Atlantic coast of Central and South America. While most North American migrants fly north to breed, the Brown Pelican reverses the pattern and flies south to spring nesting grounds, which extend from North Carolina and California down to South America.

The length of the Brown Pelican is 4½ feet (1.35 m), with a wingspread of 6½ feet (1.95 m). It is smaller than the White Pelican, *Pelecanus erythrorhynchos*, which is found in the western part of the United States. The bird shows several shades of brown and tan, the general color of the Brown with the darker hue above, and a white head from which a dark brown stripe descends to the breast. Its most distinctive feature is the huge, 14 inch (35.56 cm) bill with an outsized sac as part of its lower mandible. During breeding season, further distorting the proportions of its beak, a horny prominence grows on the top of the bill of both male and female birds, dropping off during the nesting season.

The foot of the Brown Pelican has four toes joined by webbing, putting the bird in a group called totipalmate swimmers. This order includes birds such as Cormorants, Gannets and Anhingas, all of which also have throat pouches, called gular sacs, which can be extended.

The main food of the Brown Pelican is fish and its throat sac is used as an effective scoop. Snapping up its prey in its distorted pouch, it dribbles the large amount of collected water out of the sides of its bill before it swallows the fish.

Brown Pelicans are expert divers, plunging beak downward into the ocean water sometimes from as high as 70 feet (21.3 m), the impact sending up a whooshing fountain of spray. The bird emerges with the object of its dive held in its bill, as Laughing Gulls, hovering overhead, spot an easy mark. When the Pelican opens its huge mouth to swallow its prey, the Laughing Gull swoops down to grab the fish and fly away.

The Pelican does not use its pliant bag to store food for its later use, but immediately eats what it catches, if not outsmarted by another bird. At one time it was thought that the Pelicans delivered fresh, still swimming fish to its hungry nestlings by flying with pouch engorged with water and live food. As Audubon observed, it is questionable whether the Pelican could ever get off the ground or remain aloft so burdened with the liquid weight. The pouch is used to store and carry food to the babies, but the fish are served up dead and decomposing.

Brown Pelicans breed in large colonies, the nest construction varying with the locality. On some marshy islands bulky nests are constructed of sticks, grasses and weed stalks, lined with finer grasses and placed in low mangrove bushes. On low sandbars, the nest is a mere hollow in the sand, only sparsely lined. Eggs are two or three in number, large, coarse-shelled,

Above: A Brown Pelican in the Everglades.
Right: White Pelicans like to fly, not dive.

and white. Storms and floods often wash the ground nests away, the birds then producing another set of eggs.

In about one month, the young hatch out, naked at first, but soon developing a coat of down. The little Pelicans feed by dipping their beaks into the parents' serving dish, where partially digested food is regurgitated to the front of the pouch for easy access. As the youngsters grow, their fish stew is held farther back in the parents' gullet, causing the little ones almost to completely disappear into the gaping adult maw in order to reach the food.

Because of the former widespread use of the chemical insecticide, DDT, many fish-eating birds such as Pelicans are having difficulty reproducing. DDT is a persistent poison, requiring a long period of time before it loses its potency. It is stored in the fatty tissues of animals, accumulated in the bodies of the fish that eat the insects treated with the pesticide, then ingested and held in concentrated quantities in the tissues of birds that eat the insecticide-ridden fish. Although the stored DDT seems harmless to the Pelican as long as it has abundant food, the chemical affects the bird's calcium production, making its eggs too thin-shelled to be viable. After a build-up of abundant deadly evidence, the use of DDT was made illegal.

The Brown Pelican is the state bird of Louisiana.

PELICAN, WHITE
(Pelecanus erythrorhynchos)

White Pelicans are large, ill-proportioned birds with huge pouches hanging from the lower bills. They nest on islands and shores of inland lakes from southern Canada as far south as Texas. In winter, flocks move south into a range extending from California and Florida down to Guatemala. Formerly, the White Pelican was seen in the east as well as in the west, but it is now rarely found on the Atlantic coast. Its most eastern nesting site today in the United States is in North Dakota.

An ungainly bird, the White Pelican's length is 5 feet (1.5 m), with a wingspread of 9 feet (2.7 m). Its general color is white. The striking feature of this bird and indeed a feature outstanding in the bird world is the pouch, called a gular sac, that hangs from the underside of its 18 inch (45.72 cm) long beak. A further distortion of the beak is seen in both males and females during the breeding season when a horny protuberance grows on the top of the bill. This drops off during the nesting season. Immature White Pelicans are mostly brownish, and do not acquire adult coloration for several years.

As members of the order *Pelecaniformes*, Pelicans are related to Cormorants, Gannets, Anhingas, Frigatebirds and Tropicbirds, all of which have gular sacs and feet with all four toes joined by webbing (totipalmate).

When not being used, the pliant gular sac contracts and occupies very little space, but when distended, the bag can hold several quarts of water. By spreading the flexible bones of its lower mandible, the Pelican can expand its pouch into a large fish net. The bird scoops up many quarts of water when it catches its fish dinner, but the water drains out from the sides of its beak before the prey is swallowed.

White Pelicans move in large flocks of about 25 to 100 birds. When one bird flies, they all fly, moving in single file in close formation, often forming a V. Although rising from the water is laborious, their flight is strong and steady, a combination of flapping and sailing in nearly perfect unison. In breeding season, they often soar out of sight.

Hunting their prey from aloft over freshwater inland lakes, they glide to a feet-first landing on the water's surface, then scoop up the fish with a quick plunge of the beak, or they swim quietly about with pouch submerged, snatching a fish as it is encountered.

The nesting of the White Pelican is a colonial practice. The nest is built on the ground on small islands. The bird scrapes the sandy soil into a heap piled about 6 inches (15.24 cm) in height that acts as a base. A shallow platform of reeds and weeds surmounts the sandy foundation. In the nest is deposited two dull chalky-white eggs.

In 30 days the naked young hatch

out, in a few days acquiring a warming covering of down. The bill of the baby is small at first, but it develops quickly. The young move about the colony for some time until they are ready to fly. Both parents care for their offspring by delivering partially digested fish in their gullets, which the babies eat by thrusting their bills into the adults' capacious food bag.

Pelicans are usually silent, although croaking sounds are sometimes uttered by the adults and noisy chatter can be heard among the nestlings.

The numbers of White Pelicans have dwindled because of the former abundant use of the insecticide, DDT, which persists for many years as a poison in the environment and is stored in the fatty tissues of animals. Large amounts of this chlorinated hydrocarbon chemical were accumulated in the bodies of Pelicans, the poison causing the birds to produce thin-shelled eggs, which broke when being incubated. With the current banning of the use of DDT, it is hoped that the White Pelican population can return to its previous numbers.

PETER BIRD:
see Titmouse, Tufted

PEWEE, BRIDGE: see Phoebe

PEWEE, WOOD: see Phoebe

PHEASANT, RING-NECKED
(Phasianus torquatus)

The Chinese Ring-necked Pheasant was successfully introduced into North America by way of England after 1881. The word pheasant comes from Phasis, a river in the ancient Asiatic city of Colchis where these birds are historically very numerous. In the United States the Ring-necked Pheasant now ranges over the New England and Middle Atlantic States to the Dakotas and the Pacific Northwest. It is also abundant in Manitoba, Canada.

The male Ring-necked Pheasant is between 33 and 36 inches (84-91 cm) long, including its showy pointed tail, which advertises its membership in the peacock family. The average bird weighs between 3 and 4 pounds (1.3-1.8 kg). Its head and neck are an iridescent green, with a red patch around the eye and a white ring at the base of the neck. Its body and tail plumage are primarily brown, buff and black shot through with red, blue, purple, gold and green. The long, tapering tail is banded in black. The hen pheasant is smaller than the cock and less brilliantly colored. As the Ring-Necked Pheasant has interbred extensively with a similar introduced species, the English Pheasant, purebred specimens have become rare.

Ring-necked Pheasants nest on the ground in a hollow lined with leaves, grass or straw. Their preferred nesting sites are bushy pastures, moorlands and grass or grain fields. The female lays 8 to 14 buff-olive eggs with no markings and the young, like those of most ground-nesting birds, are fully fledged and capable of running only hours after hatching. These birds feed primarily on corn, wheat, barley, wild fruits and insects. Their grain-eating habits do not present a problem to farmers except where their populations are highly concentrated.

The Ring-Necked Pheasant has short, broads wings that give it a characteristic quick take-off and steep climbing ability. It is a popular game bird, widely considered a delicacy, and hunters are familiar with the 'rocketing' ascent of a Ring-necked Pheasant startled from cover.

PHOEBE
(Sayornis phoebe)

The Phoebe's wide range covers a large part of eastern North America from Newfoundland to the south Atlantic states and westward to the Rocky Mountains. It winters south of the Carolinas, into Mexico, Central America and the West Indies.

About an inch (2.54 cm) longer than an House Sparrow, the Phoebe measures 7 inches (17.78 cm) in length. Male and female birds are similarly colored a dull olive-brown above, the tone darkest on the slightly crested head. The underparts are also dingy, a hue of yellowish-white, and the outer edges of some tail feathers are whitish. Both bill and feet are black.

As is true of other members of the Flycatcher family to which the Phoebe belongs, the bird has small, weak feet, a short neck, broad shoulders and a large head. The sharply pointed bill with well developed bristles at the base can open widely, the stiff hairs and ample gape admirably designed for capturing insects, which comprise the Phoebe's exclusive food.

After spending the winter in the warm tropics where insect life abounds, the Phoebe is among the first spring arrivals at northern breeding grounds, its northward journey following closely the seasonal awakening of its food. With acrobatic grace while catching dinner on the wing, the Phoebe makes adept, sudden turns and tumbles before returning to its perch where its reconnoitering is accompanied by a wagging of its tail feathers.

The Phoebe performs no sweet and varied springtime arias, merely a two note, monotonous repetition of its name, the first syllable accented and ascending in pitch. A quiet song, it sounds like rough, whistled breathing.

The Phoebes' choices of nest construction sites are varied, but the birds return year after year to the same location. Naturally inclined to fashion a nest in a spot that provides an overhang, the Phoebe often builds in a rocky niche that affords firm support and some roof shelter. Artfully constructed of mud, grass and vegetable fibers and lined with soft hair and feathers, the nest is overlayed with green moss, which blends the little structure harmoniously into its background. Man-made constructions now greatly expand the Phoebe's mooring options, as the adaptable bird sets up housekeeping beneath barn eaves, ledges, roof overhangs, culverts and bridges, in fact almost any location that provides overhead protection from the elements. A common name for the Phoebe, which describes a favorite nesting place, is Bridge

Above: A Phoebe feeds its young.

PTARMIGAN, ROCK
(Lagopus mutus)

Pewee, although the Pewee is an entirely different species. While the nest is inconspicuous when placed among the rocky banks, it is not so well disguised attached to a rafter that is painted red or brown.

The female alone incubates the eggs, usually five in number. After the necessary fifteen days of warming, the young hatch out and are fed by both parents for about two weeks. A second brood is sometimes reared in a single nesting season, but for good housekeeping purposes another nest is built to house the other family. A Phoebe's nest and young are commonly infested with tiny parasites that arrived on the feathers collected as a lining for the nest.

A bird related to the Phoebe and very similar in demeanor is the Wood Pewee, *Myiochanes virens.* The Wood Pewee is also dull olive in color, it too says its name, and it too is a tireless hunter of insects. The Wood Pewee is much more retiring and timid than the Phoebe and is more at home in the deep woods.

Say's Phoebe, *Sayornis saya*, is the western representative of the eastern Phoebe, which it resembles in coloring and many of its habits.

PHOEBE, SAY'S: see Phoebe

PIGEON, BAND-TAILED:
see Dove, Morning

PIGEON, PASSENGER:
see Dove, Mourning

PIGEON, SEA:
see Guillemot, Black

PIGEON, WILD:
see Dove, Mourning

PINTAIL: see Duck, Black

The Rock Ptarmigan is a land bird that resembles a grouse. It is found in the Arctic region throughout the year, in a range from the Aleutian Islands to Greenland.

The heavy-bodied Rock Ptarmigan averages about 11 inches (28 cm) long and has short, round wings. Generally, this bird does not fly great distances. Summer plumage is reddish-brown and black for the male, and lighter and duller for the female. Except for a black-tipped tail, winter feathers are white for both sexes. The white feathers are composed of empty cells of air which provide insulation, and the color affords excellent protection for hiding in snowbanks. There is a transitional plumage in the fall and spring. The male is identifiable in winter by his black lores, and both sexes have caruncles of red skin over each eye. A strong runner, the Rock Ptarmigan has long legs, and its feet are covered with short feathers to facilitate walking on the snow.

BIRDS

Above: Rock Ptarmigans in summer.

Left: The Willow Ptarmigan feeds primarily on willow leaves.

Rock Ptarmigans remain in flocks in winter and in pairs in summer, when they build their nest on the ground, lining it with grass or leaves. Male Ptarmigans are known for their elaborate courtship displays, which include making noises by releasing air from the sacs in the neck. Females lay from three to 12 red or cream-colored eggs with brown or black speckles at intervals of every one or two days. Only the female incubates them and 10 days after hatching the young are able to fly.

The Rock Ptarmigan feeds on insects and seeds, and in winter special bacteria aid in digesting its diet of twigs and buds.

Above: **A White-tailed Ptarmigan in summer and winter (*right*) colors. Unlike the other Ptarmigans, its tail has no black markings.**

Related species include the Willow Ptarmigan (*Lagopus lagopus*), the state bird of Alaska, and the White-tailed Ptarmigan (*Lagopus leucurus*). The Willow Ptarmigan is the largest of the three and is common in the Arctic, where it eats willow leaves. The White-tailed Ptarmigan is the smallest of these species and is the only one that lacks the black tail marking. Like the Rock Ptarmigan, it is found above the tree line, but in the western part of North America. The Rock Ptarmigan prefers the highest, barren hills.

PTARMIGAN, WILLOW: see Ptarmigan, Rock

BIRDS

PUFFIN, COMMON
(Fratercula arctica)

The Puffin is a bird of the frigid coastal waters and islands of the North Atlantic. It breeds from Ungava in northern Quebec south to the Bay of Fundy and Maine. In winter, it can be found somewhat further south in Massachusetts and occasionally in Long Island and Delaware Bay.

Growing to a length of 13 inches (33 cm), the Puffin's coloration is a stark black on the upper parts and a snowy white on its breast and abdomen. Its face is a smoky gray. A remarkable feature of the Puffin is its bill, especially during mating time. The normal bill is large and parrot-like, not hooked, but deeply ridged. To announce his presence to the female and to activate her breeding chemistry, the male's beak becomes a gaudy appendage, brilliantly colored yellow, blue and predominantly vermillion, a flashy preliminary to mating. Brightly colored horny shields have formed covering the bill, giving it the appearance of a mask. In addition to these plates, horn-like structures grow above and below the eyes. After the breeding season, all these florid shields fall off, reducing the size of the bill and revealing the underlying plates which are a dingy brown. Except for its orange feet, the Puffin returns to a drab color until the next year.

The female, too, uses the beak to good advantage. In defense of her nest, she wields it as a powerful weapon, delivering crushing blows to any intruder.

A Puffin's legs are positioned near the rear end of its body. This leg arrangement helps to make it a skillful swimmer and an excellent diver, but an awkward walker. On land, the bird places its entire foot flat on the ground, moving with a waddling stride. When sitting, its feet stick out in front and the bird appears to be resting on its rump.

Its short wings beat laboriously to keep the bird aloft, but are very efficiently used as oars when the Puffin is swimming underwater. Plumage

Above: Common Puffins are the only Puffin species found in the North Atlantic.

that is remarkably thick and dense keeps the bird's body warm and dry as it spends almost all of its time at sea.

Only in breeding season does the Puffin come ashore where large colonies gather on stony, coastal cliffs. A single egg is laid in a rocky crevice, or a short burrow that twists and turns is dug, using the claw of the second toe as a digging tool. For 40 days, both parents alternate the chore of egg incubation, covering the egg with their bodies and keeping the developing chick warm. When the helpless downy young hatch out, again both parents share responsibility, shoving fish down the waiting open mouths. In about 50 days the young are fully feathered and they scramble down the cliffs and follow their parents to sea.

Formerly, large quantities of young Puffins were eaten during Lent. Because the major portion of the Puffin's diet consists of fish, its meat tasted fish-like enough to satisfy the devout.

Sailors view Puffins as land indicators. More than three birds together says land is within 150 miles; the greater the number of birds in a group, the closer the distance to shore.

Related species are the Horned Puffin (*Fratericula corniculata*) and Tufted Puffin (*Lunda cirrhata*).

QUAIL, CALIFORNIA:
(Lophortyx californicus)

The California Quail, State Bird of California, is commonly found in mixed woodland areas of the West

Right: The Gambel's Quail lives in dry areas.
Below right: A California Quail.

Coast and southwestern Canada. At the end of the breeding season, flocks can be seen in large city parks.

The California Quail is a small-sized bird ranging from 10½ to 11½ inches (27-29 cm) in length. The plumage of quails is generally slate-blue, olive-brown and black and white in color. The male of this species has a blue chest, gray flanks marked with white and a black face outlined in white. The belly feathers of both the male and female are scaled. Like the Gambel's Quail, the California species can be distinguished from all other quails by the teardrop top-knot on its head. The Mountain Quail has a long thin plume.

Like most quail, the California species is usually seen in a flock. But when threatened it scatters in thick ground cover. It feeds on insects and seeds on the ground but withdraws to the trees to roost or to seek protection. Because quail are sought after by hunters, many areas have established protective hunting laws.

Species related to the California Quail include the Scaled Quail (*Callipepla squamata*), Gambel's Quail (*Lophortyx gambelii*), Mountain Quail (*Oreoryx pictus*) and Harlequin Quail (*Cyrtonyx montezumae*). The Mountain Quail is the largest species and the Harlequin is the smallest.

QUAIL, GAMBEL'S:
see Quail, California

QUAIL, MOUNTAIN:
see Quail, California

BIRDS

QUAWK:
see Heron, Black-crowned Night

RAIL, CLAPPER
(Rallus crepitans)

In the salt water marshes of the Atlantic coast, the Clapper Rail breeds from Connecticut to North Carolina and winters south of New Jersey.

The Clapper Rail has a length of 16 inches (40.64 cm). Its upper parts are colored brownish-gray, its breast a pale brown with a grayish wash. The 2½ inch (6.35 cm) bill is long and slender.

Perfectly at home on the ground, the Clapper Rail, like other Rails such as King Rail, *Rallus elegans*, Virginia Rail, *Rallus virginianus*, and Sora Rail, *Porzana carolina*, takes to the air only under extreme duress. Its thin body – thin as a rail – fits easily between the slender reeds as it runs along, and long toes keep the bird from sinking in the mud. Well adapted for threading quickly through the reedy vegetation, the Clapper Rail has a long neck, small head, short rounded wings, short tail and long legs.

The Clapper Rail feeds on muddy shores during the night; otherwise it remains hidden in the dense cover of grass and rushes where it is more often heard than seen. With loud cries and strutting body movements similar to domestic fowl, the Clapper Rail, along with other members of its family, has received the name of Mud Hen. The Rail's food is insects, snails, young fish and crustaceans, all denizens of the marsh.

On the higher ground of the marsh that spring tides cover with just a few inches of water, Clapper Rails build nests on little clumps of Spartina grass, raised about 10 inches (24.5 cm) above the mud. Well-cupped and lined with fine dry grass, the nests are woven with the vegetation of the marsh. A green interlacing canopies the nine to 12 buff-yellow eggs that are blotched and spotted in camouflaging shades of browns and drab, matching the color

Above: The Clapper Rail has a flat belly.

of the dried plant material on which they are laid. The woven awning meant to conceal the eggs from predators instead calls attention to the nest and makes it easy for egg collectors to find the generous supplies.

In 14 days, after being incubated alternately by both sexes, the downy young emerge blanketed in jet black feathers, which are soon molted and replaced with plumage that is indistinguishable from that of the adult. The little rails hatch out capable of leaving the nest to follow the mother bird through the marshes and find their own food. They learn to swim, and most important, the youngsters learn to run and hide within the grassy jungle to escape from their numerous enemies such as hawks, minks, raccoons, turtles, fish and the hunter's gun. When an opportunity exists for self-defense or defense of the young, the parent rail strikes at the attacker with bill and claws, squawking loudly to increase fighting power.

With no means of protection against the game hunter's ammunition or the egg collector's basket, the Clapper Rail's ranks have been greatly thinned. Audubon himself in 1840 claimed to have collected 72 dozen eggs in one day, and in 1896 it was estimated that approximately 10,000 birds were killed near Atlantic City, New Jersey, easy to shoot because of their feeble, hesitating flight. Now Clapper Rails survive under enlightened game management practices.

RAIL, KING: see Rail, Clapper

RAIL, SORA:
see Rail, Clapper

RAIL, VIRGINIA:
see Rail, Clapper

RAVEN: see Crow, Common

RÉCOLLET:
see Waxwing, Cedar

REDHEAD: see Canvasback

REDPOLL:
see Goldfinch, American

RED-WING, TRI-COLORED:
see Blackbird, Red-winged

ROAD RUNNER:
see Cuckoo, Yellow-Billed

ROBIN
(Turdus migratorius)

A common bird of wide distribution, the Robin inhabits eastern and northern North America as far west as the Rocky Mountains and as far north as the limit of tree growth. Robins that breed in temperate zones migrate to southern Florida and to the Gulf Coast to Texas, but birds that have bred further north move south to fill in for those that have departed. Therefore, even in the dead of winter, Robins can be found in a northerly part of their range, seeking protection from the elements under the cover of swampy woodlands.

The 10 inch (25.4 cm) Robin has a black head and gray upper parts. Its length is a standard to which other birds are compared by ornithologists. Its well-known rusty red breast is deep-toned in the male and duller in color in the female. (American colonists pining for home named the Robin after a European member of the thrush family which had a much redder breast.)

On the wing and even at a distance a Robin can easily be recognized by its horizontal flight, straight back, puffed

out breast, and backward thrusted head. Robins are most commonly seen during the breeding season, as groups of these worm-hunting birds run over lawns with quick, tripping gaits, pausing to look or listen for prey. Examining the grass in a forward leaning position, the bird cocks its head to one side and brings an eye or ear close to the ground, presumably to hear or see a worm proceeding through the earth. With bill thrust deep in the soil, the Robin grabs the worm and carefully withdraws the wriggling morsel. Abundant nourishment is thus unearthed, especially to feed the hungry young. The easy availability of worms in certain locations accounts for the

Robin's presence in gardens, farms, parks and golf courses and for the bird's range expansion as pioneers settled the plains. Even in early spring and late autumn when worms are too deeply buried for pulling out, the Robin favors open field hunting, snapping up small insects among the grass and weeds.

Although the Robin vigorously defends a nesting territory of about ¾ acre (0.3 ha), feeding grounds are neutral territory shared by many of the same species, where large quantities of wild fruits and harmful insects are also consumed.

Northward springtime migration keeps pace with the advance of the

Above: A Robin, a sign of spring in the North.

season. Traveling at about 38 miles (60.8 km) per day, males arrive several days in advance of the females and establish a breeding area that is often in the region of their birthplace. So intent is the male Robin during the season of reproduction in keeping off unwanted intruders of the same species that he will even attack his own reflected image, thinking it a male rival on his breeding turf.

As a nesting site, the Robin chooses from a great variety of man-made structures, including crannies on porches, barns, sheds and outhouses. The bowl-shaped nest is fashioned on

Above: A juvenile Robin.

the outside of woven twigs and grasses, and inside it is roundly formed of mud by the female using her breast to smooth and shape the bowl. Both partners bring muddy pellets to be molded, but in dry weather dirt is dunked in water or water is brought to the building site to moisten the soil.

The three or four eggs are, of course, robin's-egg blue, take 13 days to hatch and are incubated mostly by the female. The young are hatched without feathers and in response to their bright orange gape, both parents feed them large quantities of earthworms while the demanding little ones remain in the nest for two weeks. Out of the nest for another two weeks, they are fed by the male, while the female incubates another brood.

In the fall, wandering Robins frequent woodland areas where their diet is changed to one of wild fruits and berries. Southward migrators often collect in huge assemblages of as many as 10,000 birds preparatory to flight. In southern winter grounds, Robins frequently gather in large nighttime roosting sites, often shared with other species such as Red-winged Blackbirds and Common Grackles.

ROBIN, BLUE: see Bluebird

**SAND MARTIN:
see Swallow, Bank**

**SANDERLING:
see Sandpiper, Spotted**

**SANDPIPER, LEAST:
see Sandpiper, Spotted**

**SANDPIPER, PECTORAL:
see Sandpiper, Spotted**

**SANDPIPER,
SEMIPALMATED:
see Sandpiper, Spotted**

**SANDPIPER, SOLITARY:
see Sandpiper, Spotted**

**SANDPIPER, SPOTTED
(*Actitis macularia*)**

A little shore bird of remarkably wide distribution, the Spotted Sandpiper breeds from the tree limit in northern Alaska, south to southern California, Louisiana and South Carolina. It winters from southern British Columbia, Louisiana and South Carolina southward to Brazil.

Above: A Spotted Sandpiper.

The Spotted Sandpiper is 7 inches (17.78 cm) in length and weighs a mere two ounces (56 g). Its color is ashy-olive above and in winter its underparts are pure white but in summer its breast becomes dotted with the round black spots that give it its name. The Spotted Sandpiper is the only Sandpiper that has large and distinct dots on its underside.

Popularly nicknamed Teeter-tail, Teeterer, Tip-up, Tilt-up and See-saw, the Spotted Sandpiper is constantly tilting its body. It runs along the shore of a pond or stream, stops, bobs its head and body up and down, then runs again. Its teetering tail is almost constantly in motion. To obtain its food of insects, including armyworms, grasshoppers, caterpillars, cutworms, cabbage worms and grubs, the little bird does not confine itself to the vicinity of water, but it also searches in meadows and in cultivated fields. It is often seen singly, bobbing for its food. In its habit of not gathering into flocks, the Spotted Sandpiper resembles the Solitary Sandpiper, *Tringa solitaria*. At the seacoast the Spotted Sandpiper hunts both on the beach and on the borders of creeks and inlets, although it wades into water less frequently than other Sandpipers.

Like others of its relatives, it easily captures flying insects even on the wing. When startled, the Spotted Sandpiper usually flies off in a circular course and lands again close to the original take-off point. Flying with a peculiar quivering motion, often swaying from side to side, the bird stays close to the surface of the water. It can dive from full flight, swim and propel itself underwater with the aid of its wings.

The Spotted Sandpiper shows a wide degree of adaptability regarding its choice of nesting site, but wherever its selection, the location must be near the water. The material used to construct the nest is also greatly varied, depending upon its availability. A typical nest is a saucer-shaped hollow excavation on the ground and thinly lined with fine plant material.

The four eggs, blotched with markings of various shades of brown, blend in with the brown spots on the underside of the bird. The male Spotted Sandpiper incubates the eggs.

Within one half hour after hatching, the puffy young are able to run and follow the parent, mimicking the teeters and the bobs. At a *peet-peet* danger signal from the adult, the chicks immediately flatten themselves down among the pebbles where their mottled brownish down feathers match the grainy ground. Another peeping note calls the chicks together under the shelter of the parent's half-spread wings.

Many relatives of the Spotted Sandpiper are only summer visitors or winter residents of southern shores. Often seen feeding and flying in little well coordinated flocks, and known collectively as Peeps, after their shrill piping sounds, they include the Pectoral Sandpiper, *Pisobia maculata*, Least Sandpiper, *Pisobia minutilla*, Semipalmated Sandpiper, *Ereunetes pusillus*, and Sanderling, *Calidris leucophaea*.

SAPSUCKER, YELLOW-BELLIED (Sphyrapicus varius)

The Yellow-bellied Sapsucker, sometimes known as the Yellow-bellied Woodpecker, breeds from central Mackenzie Territory to Cape Breton Island and south to Missouri and Massachusetts. In winter it can be found from Iowa to Massachusetts, south to Panama.

An 8 inch (20.32 cm) woodpecker, the Yellow-bellied Sapsucker is colored black, barred with brownish white above, and its lower parts are red, black, and yellow. The forehead, crown and throat of the adult male are a bright crimson hue, while the female's throat is white and she may have a small crown patch of red or none at all. In flight, a longitudinal white blotch can be seen on each black wing.

It is from the unique purpose of its drilling that the Sapsucker gets its name; the bird sucks sap. The most migratory of all woodpeckers, when the Sapsucker arrives at its breeding ground in spring, the season is right for the running of the sap in the leafing out trees. Braced to the tree trunk by stiff tail feathers and clamped there on feet that have two toes pointing forward and two toes pointing backward, the woodpecker bores a series of small, round or elliptical holes with its powerful drilling beak. Generally arranged in rings or partial rings around a tree limb, but sometimes in vertical rows, the regularly patterned borings are drilled deeply through the bark and cambium layer and often directly into the wood. As the flowing sap drips out through the punctures, the woodpecker dips its bill into the openings and thrusts out its brushy-tipped tongue to suck up the sweet liquid. The tongue tip is covered with fine hair-like projections, which draw up the sap by capillary suction. Sap consumed can amount to eight teaspoonfuls per bird during a 24 hour period.

When insects get stuck feeding on the sap, the woodpecker eats them, too. A large portion of its diet also consists of the jelly-like perishable material called cambium, growing beneath the bark, and it consumes the bast or delicate inner layer of wood, as well.

Occasionally, trees are weakened by the Sapsucker's numerous borings, rarely are they killed, but the most persistent damage is disfigurement of the wood. Blemishes and defects reducing the value of the wood have caused the lumber industry of the

BIRDS

Above: A Yellow-bellied Sapsucker.
Right: The Red-naped Sapsucker
(*Sphyrapicus varius*) eats insects from the
bark of trees.

southern states some financial losses.

In spring, the drumming of the woodpecker is a percussive communication, announcing land rights and mating desirability. Its ratatat song consists of five quick taps, followed by three short pauses, each pause interrupted by two taps.

Mated pairs begin nest excavation soon after spring arrival at breeding grounds, the two sharing the labor of hollowing out a nesting chamber high in a tree that is often dead. A week or more of work is required of the industrious couple to chisel out the 14 inch (35.56 cm) deep, gourd-shaped hole and to clean out the resulting wood chips. The entranceway is a tiny 1¼ inch (3.17 cm) in diameter, barely large enough to admit the bird, but small enough to bar entrance to larger predators. Both partners alternate incubation tours of duty, the bird that is not engaged in sitting on the five to six eggs, clings to the tree trunk outside the nest.

The newly hatched young are com-

pletely helpless and naked, and are fed by the devoted parents inside the nest. Sap, insects and berries nourish the little ones, which develop the strength to crawl up the length of their deep nesting cavity and poke their heads out of the entrance hole to get their food. After a while, they hop about the tree trunks, chasing one another, but still fed by the parents.

In the fall, the Yellow-bellied Sapsucker begins a solitary southward migratory journey, stopping off occasionally for a few days respite to peck at tree bark crevices for concealed food. Its few drill holes are unrewarding, as sap does not flow in autumn.

SCAUP, GREATER:
see Canvasback; Scaup, Lesser

SCAUP, LESSER
(Aythya affinis)

A diving duck often seen in huge flocks, the Lesser Scaup nests near ponds and marshy creeks in the north central United States and in the Canadian prairie provinces. In winter,

it can be found along the entire coastal rim of the United States, and during periods of migration, the bird can be found throughout the country.

The Lesser Scaup is 17 inches (43.18 cm) in length. It is similar in coloration to the Greater Scaup, *Aythya marila*, and varies principally in size, the Greater Scaup measuring 20 inches (50.8 cm) in length. The head, neck and foreparts of the male Lesser Scaup are an iridescent black, while the general appearance of the rest of the body is white. The female is a duskybrown above and a rufous-brown below. On both male and female in flight, a long white stripe can be seen.

Both sexes have a short wide bill, colored bluish-gray. The shape and color of the bill give the Scaup the common names of Broad-bill and Little Blue-bill.

Great flocks or rafts of Lesser Scaups congregate just off-shore in bays and harbors in winter and early spring all along the Atlantic coastline from Long Island Sound to Florida. Marine birds, they dive underwater to feed on mussels, which are tugged free of their moorings by the Scaup using its strong bill. Feeding on other sluggish

Above: The Lesser Scaup is common inland.

marine life as well, the Scaup's meat takes on a fishy flavor and is not considered a delicacy for the table.

In summer, the Lesser Scaup's food preference changes and it dines primarily on water vegetation, which imparts a more palatable taste to its flesh. It is then that it is hunted to be eaten. As a game bird, though, the Lesser Scaup is popular more for its numbers than for its flavor.

Most diving ducks take turns submerging and swimming underwater, so that others are on guard to warn against danger and intruders. The Lesser Scaup and Greater Scaup are less wary, and often an entire flock will be submerged at the same time in the hunt for food. The diving activity signals other flocks of Scaups that a meal is readily available and soon a passing group will join the others until a raft of these birds can number in the many thousands.

Next to the White-winged Scoter, *Oidemia deglandi*, the Lesser Scaup is the duck that breeds the latest in the season. Nesting in the prairie marshes of northwestern Canada, their egg layings are not complete until mid-June. Nests are built in the weeds or grass on a dry shore, somewhat away from the water's edge, although sometimes nests are constructed right on the margin of a boggy marsh, making it easy for the brooding female to slip into the water for a nibble or a drink.

Occasionally, a nest will be shared by two females, each laying her full complement of eggs, bringing the total to about 22. An especially large number of little ducklings will hatch out. Fortunately for the mother duck, a minimum of parental care is required as the young emerge covered with down and fully capable of walking, swimming, finding food while remaining in a tight cluster and heeding her warning quacks by hiding or disappearing underwater in case of danger.

In ten to twelve weeks, the ducklings lose their olive colored down and grow their flight feathers. Not until October, which is late for a duck, do the Scaup flocks converge for their trip to winter feeding grounds.

**SCISSORBILL:
see Skimmer, Black**

SCOLDER: see Oldsquaw

**SCOTER, WHITE-WINGED:
see Scaup, Lesser**

**SEE-SAW:
see Sandpiper, Spotted**

**SHAG:
see Cormorant,
Double-crested**

**SHEARWATER:
see Skimmer, Black**

**SHORT WHITE:
see Egret, Snowy**

SHOVELER: see Duck, Wood

**SISKIN, PINE:
see Goldfinch, American**

**SKIMMER:
see Skimmer, Black**

SKIMMER, BLACK
(Rynchops nigra)

A long-winged maritime bird, the Black Skimmer is distributed from Virginia to the Gulf Coast and Texas. It winters from the Gulf Coast south to Mexico and Costa Rica.

The Black Skimmer is 16-20 inches (40.64-50.8 cm) in length. Its upper parts are colored glossy black. Its forehead, sides of head and neck, and undersides are pure white, taking on a rosy tint in spring.

A unique structure of the Black Skimmer is its bill. Both upper and lower mandibles are very thin and flattened sideways, like a knife blade. These two parts come together edgewise, not like a duck's bill, which is flattened horizontally. The bill is straight with no hook at the tip. The lower beak is about an inch longer than the top one. The manner in which the Black Skimmer uses this long, flat appendage gives the bird its name. With its mouth agape, the Skimmer flies along just above the surface of the water. The lower bill cuts through the water, its thin shape offering little resistance to the water; therefore, the bird does not slow down. When the bottom beak strikes a fish or shrimp, the upper mandible snaps closed on its prey. Other common names of the Black Skimmer that are descriptive of its feeding technique are Cutwater, Scissorbill, and Shearwater.

Left: **Black Skimmers have large red bills.**

Skimmers feed together in groups, sharing the ocean's abundance. Not needing to see their food but to feel it with their bills, Black Skimmers often hunt at night. They follow narrow creeks and at times enter outer bays, but they never go inland, nor do they travel far out to sea.

When first appearing in the spring along the southern beaches, Skimmers arrive in huge flocks of sometimes thousands. Unsettled at this breeding season, they wheel overhead, continually moving from beach to beach and out to sandbars, their raucous calls competing with the sound of the waves. To capture food in shallow water, the Skimmer simply turns its bill on one side and achieves a greater gripping surface.

They nest colonially, and their breeding places are high sand flats, running out from shore, or small, isolated, shell beach islands. Exerting little effort in nest construction, the Black Skimmer hollows an unlined depression in the sand, which it fashions by using its body as a form. Three to five greenish, buff eggs are laid with brown, gray and lilac blotches, none matching exactly the mottlings of other eggs.

Young Skimmers have down feathers that are sand-colored, blending with the sandy beaches on which they spend their early lives. This form of protection is called cryptic coloration. The young birds can pick food up from ground more easily than can their parents, as the beaks of the babies are more equal in length than those of the adults.

As close relatives of Gulls, Black Skimmers and Gulls have some similarities in habits and appearance. Both Skimmers and Gulls have webbed feet, with the web connecting three toes. They all nest in large colonies, nests being built mostly on the ground, sometimes on cliffs, and occasionally in bushes. The eggs and young of all these birds are blotched and mottled with markings that hide them from predatory attacks. They all live near the water, fresh or salt, and much of their food consists of marine organisms.

Because the meat of the Black Skimmer is unpalatable to humans, the bird has not been hunted for food, but inroads in the Skimmer population have been made by egg collectors, fascinated with the variety of shell colorations.

SKUA, ARCTIC:
see Jaeger, Parasitic

SNAKE-BIRD:
see Turkey, Water

SNIPE, WILSON'S:
see Woodcock

SNOW BIRD:
see Junco, Slate-colored

SNOWY, LITTLE:
see Egret, Snowy

SPARROW, CHIPPING:
see Sparrow, Song

SPARROW, FIELD:
see Sparrow, Song

SPARROW, FOX:
see Junco, Slate-colored

SPARROW, HOUSE
(Passer domesticus)

Introduced throughout the temperate regions of the world, the House Sparrow or English Sparrow, as it is also known, is a permanent resident in North America from British Columbia, northern Manitoba and northern Quebec south to Baja, California, northern Mexico and Key West. Although widely distributed as a species, individuals and flocks of House Sparrows occupy a narrow range, a group foraging and nesting only within a particular area.

The length of the House Sparrow, a stout bird with a heavy, cone-shaped bill, is 6 inches (15.24 cm). The male is easily identified by its gray cap, ashy cheeks, black beak, chestnut-brown

Above: **Young House Sparrows.**

back, and especially by its large bib patch of sooty black. New spring plumage bears fresh reddish-brown tinges, but natural wear and city dirt dull its coloration. The female lacks the male's black bib; she is streaked brown above and washed in murky white below.

In 1850 the first House Sparrows in North America were brought from England to several locations between New York and Maine, and later additional introductions were made across the country as far west as Salt Lake City. By 1910 the prolific and resourceful House Sparrow became one of the most abundant birds in the United States, but since that time its numbers have steadily declined. The primary reason for the levelling off of the House Sparrow population is the disappearance of the horse as a mode of transportation and the resultant disappearance of the grain upon which both the horse and sparrow fed.

Still, the adaptability and boldness of the bird maintained its abundant numbers as it adeptly colonized all available city niches and many country ones as well. The House Sparrow and the Starling, too, have moved into our cities, firmly established themselves and effectively denied space to native species. Like the cockroach, the brown rat and the bedbug, the House Sparrow lives in close proximity to man and benefits greatly from the association.

The House Sparrow nourishes itself on garbage, seeds, fruits, young garden plants and insects, its bill of fare attesting to a great diversity of tastes. In rural areas, it consumes large quantities of seeds of wheat, oats and other grains. Marvelously adept at devising feeding methods most suited to the capture of particular prey, it hangs upside down to pick off aphids, clings to tree trunks to dine on insect eggs, hovers in mid-air to snap up hanging caterpillars and in flight pursues and snatches grasshoppers.

Its wide-ranging choices of nesting locations contribute to the bird's success; often three or more broods of no less than four hatchling are produced in a single year. A loosely woven, sloppy nest built of grasses and any easily available material, such as paper, rags and string, is placed in almost any spot that will hold it and afford it some degree of security. Nests are usually located about the eaves, rafters and drains of buildings, but

Above: The adult Song Sparrow has a characteristic spot on its streaked breast.

they are also built in electric light hoods, cornices, water spouts and air conditioners. Natural tree cavities, abandoned woodpecker holes, Bank Swallow burrows and bird boxes are eagerly snapped up as breeding quarters by the opportunistic bird, thus denying native, hole-nesting species a place in which to reproduce. As a year-round resident, the House Sparrow is an early nester, and it usually beats out other birds in the choice of available hollows, or evicts tenants that are already occupying desired nesting crannies.

The ten to 12 day incubation task is performed exclusively by the female, but both parents feed the little hatchlings. In response to their wide open chirping mouths, nestlings are fed lavish quantities of weevils and grasshoppers, initially by regurgitation, then with whole, raw food.

Not a migratory bird, the House Sparrow is able to withstand cold winter weather insulated by a thick coat of feathers, nourished by the seeds of weeds that have their heads above the snow and huddled together in small flocks sheltered in hedges, brush piles or buildings.

SPARROW, LINCOLN'S: see Sparrow, Song

SPARROW, SONG (*Melospiza melodia*)

A bird of the temperate and arctic regions of North America, the Song Sparrow breeds in southern Canada, southern Alaska and throughout the lower 48 states with the exception of the south Atlantic and the Gulf states. In winter it leaves the extreme northern portions of its range and is found southward to the Gulf coast and northern Florida, some remaining year-round from southern New England southward. Instead of wintering in their nesting area, a population shift occurs as birds move south replaced by birds from farther north.

Unassuming in appearance, as are most of our native sparrow species, the Song Sparrow is approximately 6 inches (15.24 cm) in length, and has dull brown and black streaked upper parts. Below it is somber whitish in tone, boldly streaked with marks that join to form a large, dark irregularly-shaped blotch on the upper center of the breast, a patch that serves as an

identifying feature. Both male and female bear similar streaks and hues.

As a result of adaptations to temperature, humidity and other localized geographic environmental conditions, approximately 25 different races or subspecies of the Song Sparrow have been recognized. Each subspecies is slightly different in size or color intensity, but all Song Sparrows possess the short, stout cone-shaped beak that is a feature of the largest family of birds, the Finch family, to which they belong. Primarily seed-eaters, as indicated by the structure of their beaks, they also eat large quantities of insects, especially when feeding youngsters in the springtime hatching of both birds and bugs.

Known for its clear, sweet springtime singing, the Song Sparrow, together with the Red-winged Blackbird and the Bluebird, is one of the first birds to be heard each mating season. Perched on top of a bush or fence post, head thrown backward, bill thrust upward, the male defends his established territory with brave recitals that sound to humans like pleasant musical twitterings, but to other male Song Sparrows these cadences are serious proclamations of area ownership and defense.

Many variations of the Song Sparrow's song are performed, but the commonest form begins with two notes of the same pitch, then a third four or five tones higher, followed by a rapid outpouring of notes and trills. Each bird performs from three to twenty modifications of the same general theme, all of which differ slightly from the songs of any other Song Sparrow, and differ also from the renditions of Song Sparrows from other regions.

Camouflaged by dull brown tones that harmonize with a vined or grassy background and protected by a streaked pattern that interrupts the form of the bird, the Song Sparrow can remain well concealed in a nest built on or near the ground. The cup shaped nest, built alone by the female, is woven of grasses, stems and leaves, lined with fine materials and hidden in a grassy tussock or a briar tangle. Streamside or swampy ground is preferred as a nesting location.

The incubation of the four or five pale green spotted eggs is performed for 10-12 days, sometimes entirely by the female, and sometimes by both sexes. Rapid development of the young is the general rule of ground-nesting species, the Song Sparrow no exception. Not remaining in place to become a snake's easy dinner, baby Song Sparrows leave the nest before they are able to fly and run about among the low plant growths with remarkable agility, also camouflaged by somber streaked protection.

By mid-November, migrating groups have drifted southward and winter populations have stabilized into little groups, the foraging flocks searching lawns and fields for seeds. In winter, Song Sparrows often join flocks which consist of many sparrow species, among them Chipping Sparrow, *Spizella passerina*; Field Sparrow, *Spizella pusilla*; White-crowned Sparrow, *Zonotrichia leucophrys*; Lincoln's Sparrow, *Melospiza lincolni*; Swamp Sparrow, *Melospiza georgiana*; and White-throated Sparrow, *Zonotrichia albicollis*.

SPARROW, SWAMP:
see Sparrow, Song

SPARROW, WHITE-CROWNED:
see Sparrow, Song

SPARROW, WHITE-THROATED:
see Junco, Slate-colored; Sparrow, Song

SPOONBILL, ROSEATE
(*Ajaia ajaja*)

The brilliantly plumed Roseate Spoonbill is a bird of both North and South America. It can be found from Texas, Louisiana, Florida and Georgia south to Patagonia and the Falkland Islands.

A large wading bird, the Roseate Spoonbill measures 32 inches (81.28

Above: The Roseate Spoonbill, a rare bird.

cm). The bird is outfitted in dazzling arrays of reddish colors, its general plumage pink, its wings and underparts a delicate rose, and parts of its wings and tail a rich vermillion. The legs and eyes are also scarlet. As befitting a wading bird, the neck and legs are long, and the neck can easily be bent into a strongly curved S-shape.

Spoonbills get their names from the curious shape of their beaks, which are spoon-shaped. This specially adapted bill is used by the bird in gathering its food, which consists of frogs, mollusks, small fish and aquatic insects. Wading in the water with opened mouth, the Spoonbill swings its long flattened beak from side to side through the mud while walking slowly forward. The bird does not pause to wait for food to approach, but simply moves on in uninterrupted probings, lilting its body in movements that match the semi-circles of the bill.

When a Spoonbill is resting either in a tree or on the ground, it can stand for as long as an hour on only one leg. When in flight, the head and neck are outstretched, and an easy flapping of the wings is alternated with some steady soaring. Spoonbills fly in long diagonal lines, with each bird behind and just to one side of the one in front, positioned near the beating wingtips of the bird ahead. This wedge-shaped flight formation makes flying easier, as the bird in front is cutting down on air turbulence for the one in back.

Nests are built in colonial rookeries in dense tropical marshes on the lower branches of cypress or mangrove trees. The nests are constructed of large sticks, deeply hollowed and lined with strips of inner bark and water moss. Three to four dull white eggs with various shades of tawny blotches are laid.

The young emerge all pink and downy, helpless, and unable to stand. They are flat and flabby babies with blown up abdomens and soft ducklike bills. They sleep quietly in the nest while parents are away, but when the adults return, the young birds pop up to attention and bob their heads, accompanying their activities with a chorus of trills and whistles. Thrusting little heads deep down the parents' gullet, the youngsters gobble up food regurgitated by their elders.

Unfortunately for the Roseate Spoonbill, also called the Pink Curlew, its gorgeous plumage caused its near extinction at a time before the 1900s when conservation of wildlife was of little importance compared to the market demand for decorative feathers. A woman of high fashion required a fluffy fan of red and pink Spoonbill plumes. Thousands of Roseate Spoonbills were shot by hunters in their communal nesting grounds between the years 1880 and 1890 until the bird became a rarity in the wild. Protected now, the birds are still an uncommon sight in their former tropical haunts.

SQUAWK:
see Heron, Black-crowned Night

STAKE DRIVER: see Bittern

STARLING
(*Sturnus vulgaris*)

The Starling, unloved and abundant, is a naturalized American citizen that has intruded itself in great numbers upon the landscape. In 1880 eighty Starlings were imported into New York and other American cities, and due to their fecundity and strength they now number in the several millions, spreading their range westward. Although highly migratory in its native

BIRDS

Europe, the Starling here has changed its habits and remains a year-round resident, even as individual flocks seek favorable feeding locations during the winter. New areas are exploited by these traveling bands, which remain in spring to raise a family or two, thereby increasing Starling numbers and territory.

A muscular and powerful bird, the Starling measures 8 inches (20.32 cm) in length. It is glossy metallic black in color with narrow, wedge-shaped, light colored spots that are more evident in winter. Its dusky-colored bill, which becomes a brighter yellow during the breeding season, is straight, long, tapering, and is as keen as a sharpened axe.

The Starling is an introduced species whose lifeways did not develop amidst the environmental factors of North America. The bird was imposed upon the existing natural scheme and it had to create an ecological niche for itself or perish for lack of one. Aggressive and adaptive, the Starling insinuated itself into the North American pattern by usurping some places already occupied by native birds. Its success was derived in part from its European experience of living for centuries near

Below: **Starlings can be a pest in cities.**

dense populations of people and in close proximity to cultivated lands. Accustomed to getting its living in and around human habitation, the Starling was well equipped for settling in North America, even better suited to farm and city life than many wild woodland species.

When breeding season arrives the Starling seeks out a nesting place, a function served by any one of an enormous variety of cavities, such as a church steeple, a house crevice, a ledge under eaves, a bird nesting box, a tree hollow or a woodpecker hole. Once the chamber is secured, it is lined with twigs, grasses, leaves and paper.

Sociable and gregarious at other times of year, the Starling become extremely pushy and pugnacious to beat out the native competition in the gaining of a nesting site. The Starling appropriates holes that normally would be used by Screech Owls, Sparrow Hawks, Nuthatches, Martins, Bluebirds, Tree Swallows, Wrens and especially Woodpeckers. The bird waits patiently at a respectful distance while a Flicker diligently chips out a breeding excavation, then occupies the hollow as soon as the Flicker completes its task. Driven by biological compulsion, the dispossessed Flicker persistently hacks out other burrows,

which are similarly unceremoniously confiscated by the Starlings, until the hounded woodpecker abandons the area for a friendlier neighborhood.

After 12 days of incubation, three to six voracious young emerge to be fed more than 100 times a day by both parents. In its feeding habits, and especially in the feeding of the nestlings, the Starling redeems itself and exhibits behavior that is of benefit to man by consuming quantities of destructive cutworms, caterpillars, beetles and grasshoppers.

In two to three weeks the well-nourished fledglings leave the nest and gather in flocks of young and adult birds, the assemblies growing larger in size as fall approaches. Often joined by groups of Red-winged Blackbirds, Grackles and Cowbirds, the huge gatherings comb the countryside to glean the ripening crops and fruits.

In winter, communal nocturnal roosts are established by the foraging multitudes in a wooded grove or on a large building to which the birds return each evening to rest from the day's feeding labors. In cities, these enormous aggregations are entirely unwelcome, as the birds deface the buildings with their droppings and remain unmoved by all man's assorted efforts to discourage their bedding down.

STORK, WOOD:
see Ibis, Wood

SWALLOW, BANK
(Riparia riparia)

A long distance migrator, the Bank Swallow breeds from arctic regions south to Georgia, Texas and Arizona and winters in Mexico, Central and South America.

The male Bank Swallow measures 5½ inches (13.97 cm) in overall length, its forked tail about one half of that measurement. The female is slightly smaller than the male. A brown-backed swallow, it has a conspicuous dark band across the breast.

A short, flat, triangular bill and a large mouth aid in the Bank Swallow's entrapment of its food, composed exclusively of insects. Extremely long, well developed wings transport the bird through the air with remarkable agility, as it snatches food while bird and insect are on the wing. Since most of its mobile time is spent in flight, its legs and feet are small and feeble, the toes useful only for perching.

During migration, the Bank Swallow, like others of its relatives, travels only during the daylight hours, proceeding slowly and pausing for rest stops that are used with such regularity that they are known as migration stations. Sometimes these roosting locations are in trees, but more often they are in marshes. Since they are in no particular hurry, rather than travel over water swallows will fly around it.

The arrival of the swallows in spring at northern breeding grounds is usually startling, since the birds migrate in vast numbers and perform in the air with extraordinary acrobatics. By the end of April Bank Swallows appear in large assemblies and concentrate their attentions on gorging near streams and lakes where flying insects provide abundant fare.

In late May earnest nest building begins, the birds digging tunnels in the bank of a lake or stream. The scientific name, *Riparia*, means bank of stream, and common names descriptive of this swallow's temporary homesite are

Above: Cliff Swallows (*Petrochelidon pyrrhonota*) often nest in crevices of cliffs.

Above, both: A nest of young Violet Green Swallows (*Tachycineta thalassina*) in a colony.

BIRDS

Above: **Adult Tree Swallows have green backs.**

Sand Swallow, Sand Martin, and Bank Martin. Because the Bank Swallow is specific in its environmental needs for a nesting site, large colonies are concentrated in an area where desirable materials are found. Where sand and gravel banks have been deposited by the retreating glacier, the birds honeycomb the substance with burrows, excavating a passageway ranging in depth from 14 inches (35.56 cm) to 65 inches (165 cm), depending upon the material in which they are dug.

Both male and female birds actively participate in enlarging the shaft. Bill and claws are used as pecking tools and the loosened dirt is ejected in little spurts by a rapid backward kicking action of the feet, as well as by a backward sweeping motion of the wings. One partner works while the other waits outside to relieve its mate.

The entranceway is just large enough to admit the bird, and small enough to deny access to a larger predator. At the end of the narrow gully, an enlarged rounded cavity holds the four or five pure white eggs, which are laid in a weaving of grass, rootlets and pine needles on a scanty feather lining. Both parents alternate egg incubation sessions and both collect insects to feed their nestlings. In constant comings and goings in and out of the little holes, the adults make about one trip every five minutes to poke their food laden bills down the tiny demanding gullets. On entering the tunnel, the birds swiftly, directly and unhaltingly fly into the openings as if sucked up by the tip of a vacuum cleaner hose.

Vacated burrows are often later appropriated by other hole nesting birds, such as House Sparrows and Starlings, and occasionally even a snake will move into the lengthy hollow.

Toward the middle to the end of summer, large concentrations of various species of swallows convene in huge roosts to settle down at night among the branches. Sunrise starts the birds' daytime feeding forays and sunset brings them back again from miles around to rest. As well as Bank Swallows, these huge assemblies are made up of Barn Swallows, *Hirundo eryth-rogastra*, which nest in barns or other buildings, Tree Swallows, *Iridoprocne bicolor*, which nest in abandoned woodpecker holes, and Purple Martins, *Progne subis*, which nest in boxes erected for their use. By mid September all the swallows have moved out, embarked upon their southward migratory flight.

SWALLOW, BARN: see Swallow, Barn

SWALLOW, SAND: see Swallow, Bank

SWALLOW, TREE: see Swallow, Bank

SWAN, TRUMPETER (Olor buccinator)

The world's largest migratory bird, the Trumpeter Swan once nested from northern United States to the Arctic Ocean, and wintered along the lower Mississippi River and the grassy marshes of the Gulf coasts of Texas and Louisiana. Like other migratory birds, Trumpeter Swans followed definite flight paths or flyways, as they journeyed north in the spring and south in the autumn. Today, the more than 1000 surviving Trumpeters in the lower 48 states no longer respond to the instinctive urge to migrate, but instead have learned to remain in the safety of the remote 40,000 acre (16,000 ha) Red Rock Lakes National Wildlife Refuge just west of Yellowstone National Park, protected by the federal government.

Mature male Trumpeter Swans or cobs weigh from 25-30 pounds (11.25-13.5 kilos), and the females or pens weigh slightly less. Their bodies measure nearly 5 feet (1.5 m) long, and their huge white wings are 8 feet (2.4 m) from tip to tip. Snowy white all over, the Trumpeter Swan is in the same family as ducks and geese, and is also a close relative of another North American all-white swan, the Whistling Swan, *Olor columbianus*.

The swan holds its long neck in a graceful S-shaped curve as it swims along. To feed on succulent aquatic plants, it dips its bill beneath the water's surface, and with its extensive neck, it is able to reach plants that grow at the bottom of the lake.

The Cree Indians called the Trumpeter Swan Ko-hoh, a name they thought sounded like the call the swan emits. Holding forth with the loudest voice of any North American bird, the Trumpeter's sound can be heard for up to two miles, the powerful vocalization coming from the swan's coiled windpipe. The coiled arrangement lengthens the trachea, thereby increasing the volume and carrying ability of the trumpeting. After dark, especially on moonlit nights in the early spring in breeding territory, the mated pairs serenade in amorous bellowings, performing for each other their noisy ritualized communication. During nesting season and in the autumn and winter, their voices are seldom heard.

In lakes nests are usually built in extremely selective sites on the exposed tops of muskrat lodges. Both partners alternate nest construction while perched atop the muskrat house surrounded by water, and reach out with long necks to gather reeds and sedges.

Six creamy-white eggs, nearly twice the size of chicken eggs, are laid in the saucer-shaped, plant-stem structure which covers the entire top of the muskrat lodge. For 35 days the pen alone incubates the eggs, while the faithful cob exhibits watchful guard around his developing family, the couple mated for life. The puffy yellow chicks, or cygnets, resembling baby geese, feed for several weeks on aquatic insects until their necks grow long enough to dip down like their parents to pull up water plants. The long hours of Arctic daylight at former breeding grounds allowed the young much time to feed and grow their feathers. By October, when the flocks converged in family groupings, the juvenile swans were strong enough to have flown to winter grounds.

In the past, Indians occasionally killed the swans for food, and made beads and sewing awls from their

Above: Trumpeter Swans nesting. They often use abandoned beaver lodges for breeding.

bones. The conservative taking of Trumpeter Swans by Indians in no way matched the eventual unrestrained slaughter of these majestic birds by hunters. Swans were shot in the sky and nests were raided on the ground for cygnets and eggs. Swan pelts were collected by the thousands, in demand for millinery, powder puffs and coverlets. The Hudson's Bay Company alone sold 17,671 swan skins from 1853 to 1877. By the turn of the century, the population of Trumpeter Swans was so decimated that fewer than 100 birds remained. Today, Trumpeter Swans are a protected species, their numbers somewhat on the increase. The bird's strong instinct for survival has overridden the ancient urge to migrate, and they live on the refuge provided them in 1935 by the federal government, and in other sanctuaries. Trumpeter Swans are still relatively numerous in Canada and Alaska.

SWAN, WHISTLING:
see Swan, Trumpeter

SWIFT, CHIMNEY
(Chaetura pelagica)

A most aerial bird, the Chimney Swift breeds in North America east of the Rocky Mountains from central Alberta to Newfoundland and south to Florida, the Gulf states and eastern Texas. It winters in western Brazil and eastern Peru.

Only 5½ inches (13.97 cm) in length, the Chimney Swift has extremely long wings, their spread measuring 12 inches (30.48 cm) in width. The tail, half the length of the wing, has stiff bristle-like tips. Both sexes are similarly colored, sooty-black above, lighter below.

Swifts do not rest on a perch because they cannot wrap their toes around a branch to grasp a fixed position. Instead of perching, they cling to a vertical surface such as the inside of a tree hollow, a rock or a chimney, holding on with short legs and sharp claws and supported by stiffened tail feathers.

The Chimney Swift could be mistaken for a bat as its dark little form searches out flying insects at night. Often using one wing and then the other in an alternating rowing stroke, the bird darts about for hours to capture and consume its flying food while both Swift and insect are on the wing. Pellets of indigestible insect parts are disgorged. Like the Swallow with which it is often confused, the Chimney Swift has small feet, a triangular bill and a large mouth that opens widely to entrap its prey.

The Chimney Swift is so adapted as a flying creature that it drinks and bathes from the air by skimming the water and regularly spends the night gliding on the wing. Although flights of 1000 miles (1600 km) per day have been reported during Swift migratory journeys, these distances remain unsubstantiated.

Even though inclined to build a nest in a tree hollow, the Chimney Swift often appropriates a man-made structure as a hospitable site for incubating and rearing young. Attached to the inside of a chimney, the Swift constructs a loosely woven nest of twigs that resembles a little basket, glued together with a sticky mucilage secreted in the bird's well-developed salivary glands. Related Asiatic species produce nests composed entirely of this mucus, which are considered great delicacies and are made into bird's nest soup.

The Chimney Swift obtains its nest material of small dry twigs from a dead tree by using its feet, not its beak, to yank off a stick and to carry it to the building site. The nest is built in a semicircular shape, criss-crossed, interwoven and spread with saliva around the edges to fasten it securely to the chimney. Sometimes the fragile structure cannot hold up under the weight of its occupants or sometimes it collapses during a heavy rain. Eggs and young are therefore sacrificed, but if the young accidentally fall out of their glued-on basket, they climb back in by means of their sharp claws.

As gathering places, the Chimney Swifts use selected chimneys, where during spring and fall migrations they convene in huge flocks to take refuge for the night. Before settling down inside the cavity, fluttering masses of

Above: **A Scarlet Tanager male.**

Swifts whirl and swarm above the opening, then disappear inside, only to be disgorged and seemingly sucked up again.

A close relative of a bed bug infests the feathers and the nest of the Chimney Swift, and for this association the bird is blamed as the bearer of those hated vermin. The Chimney Swift, though, is not to be blamed as the deliverer of the bed bug pest; the bug that shares quarters with the bird cannot live without its feathered host.

TANAGER, SCARLET: see Tanager, Western

TANAGER, SUMMER: see Tanager, Western

TANAGER, WESTERN (*Piranga ludoviciana*)

A bird of western zones, the Western Tanager breeds from British Columbia to Mexico and from the Black Hills to the Pacific Ocean. It winters in Central America.

The Western Tanager is 7 inches (17.78 cm) in length with a heavy, blunt bill and a notched tail. As colorful as a tropical bird, the brightly hued male has a red head and a black back, the remainder of its body yellow with some black on the wings and tail. The

female is olive toned above and yellow below, and she has a sharply pointed bill.

High in the leafy canopy of pine-fir forests and in mixed woodlands as well, the Western Tanager spends the day solitarily foraging for insects and for some fruits. With sluggish movements and great deliberation, it gleans the leaves of tallest trees, and with straight flight and rapid wingbeats, it catches insects in the air. During migratory journeys it swoops down from a fencepost to pick up insects from the ground.

In the evergreen forests of the California mountains, its songs and calls are among the most often heard animal sounds, but except for an occasional glimpse of gold, the bird itself is rarely seen. The Western Tanager often perches for long periods emitting short, musical phrases with ascending and descending accents that sound much like a robin's song, but are hoarser and lower in pitch.

The Western Tanager breeds in high altitudes throughout the open coniferous woodlands of western mountains. It builds its nest up to a 10,000 foot (3000 m) elevation in Utah and New Mexico and from 3000 feet (900 m) to the summits of the Sierra Nevadas. The flimsy saucer-shaped nest is usually placed on a horizontal evergreen branch and the three or four pale greenish-blue spotted eggs are incu-

Above: A male Western Tanager, a forest bird with a vigorous but harsh song.

bated exclusively by the female. She sits with such persistence that when egg collecting was legal, she would not be deterred from her warming duties until she was lifted off the clutch by ardent hobbyists.

As is true of most brightly colored species, the male remains a distance from the developing family so as not to lure enemies with his flamboyance, but he does help feed the young.

Breeding chores completed, the birds come down from the high terrain, wander among streamside willows and cottonwoods, then scatter widely near low ground during migration.

The Summer Tanager, *Piranga rubra*, is found in summer from coast to coast throughout the lowlands and foothills of the southern United States. The plumage of the male is all rose-red, while the female is a dull olive-green above and subdued brown-orange below. North America's other all red bird, the male Cardinal, *Richmondena cardinalis*, is bedecked in brilliant crimson and has a crested head, which the Summer Tanager lacks.

The Scarlet Tanager, *Piranga olivacea*, in summer inhabits the Eastern United States north to the southern Canadian provinces and south to Virginia and Missouri. The male Scarlet Tanager has a vivid flame-like chroma with shoulders, wings and tail a uniform deep black. Despite its intense coloration, the bird is seldom seen as it quietly searches for insects in the tree tops while hidden in the canopy of verdant foliage.

BIRDS

TEAL, CINNAMON:
see Teal, Green-winged

TEAL, BLUE-WINGED:
see Teal, Green-winged

TEAL, GREEN-WINGED
(*Anas carolinensis*)

The swift Green-winged Teal is a duck that is distributed throughout North America. It breeds in the Canadian prairies, south through central California, northern New Mexico, southern Minnesota, western New York and Quebec. The majority of Green-wings winter in the Gulf states and Mexico, but they can be found along the Atlantic coast as well.

The Green-winged Teal is the smallest of North American surface feeding puddle ducks, a diminutive 14 inches (35.56 cm) in length. In gorgeous feathered raiment, it is outdone only by the dazzling Wood Duck, *Aix sponsa*. The male Green-wing's general appearance is gray with a rich, chestnut colored head. A conspicuous white patch marks the front of its wing, and green patches adorn the side of the wing and the side of the head. The somber-hued female is brownish above and white below with a green patch on her wing. The young are colored like the female.

The male Teal employs his brilliant plumage in a display competition against other Green-wing drakes, all vying for the amorous attentions of a female. By being colorful, its mating purpose is thus served, while startling hues for the female would be a distinct disadvantage as she sits patiently on her eggs. In the vital task of continuation of the species, the female must remain concealed from predators, and her dull brown tones hide her effectively in her timbered nesting environment.

The Green-winged Teal and the Blue-winged Teal, *Anas discors*, are the two Teals of North America, both of which are widely distributed. They are similar in many ways, but the Green-wing is the hardier of the two, remaining in the northern states sometimes well into the winter as long as there is open water in which to dabble for aquatic plants to eat. The Blue-wing is less able to endure the cold, and before the heavy autumn frosts arrive it journeys southward to warmer winter feeding grounds.

For speed of flight, the Green-wing must take the prize; it often moves at speeds clocked at 100 miles (160 kph) per hour. In close formation, flocks of Green-wings pivot and wheel in unison, a coordinated aerial performance of great precision. Like other ducks that dabble, this bird vaults into the air from water with astounding swiftness in an almost vertical ascent.

In the water, the Green-winged Teal bobs about in the shallows, searching for sedges, pondweed and algae. Like most dabbling ducks, its menu is primarily plant matter and it has a special fondness for wild oats, wild rice and

Above left: The pale blue markings of the blue-winged Teal are well defined in flight. *Left:* Green-winged Teals are fast fliers but stay in small groups for safety.

grass seeds. Chestnuts and acorns are also eaten, crushed in its gizzard by powerful muscles. The grinding action of this organ replaces teeth, aided by bits of gravel which the duck swallows and retains for crushing purposes.

The flesh of the Green-winged Teal is considered excellent when its food is confined to plant material, but when the Teal occasionally dines on insects, mollusks or fish, its taste is rank and unpalatable.

In the brushy timbered regions of the west and north, the Green-winged Teal constructs her nest. Well hidden, the nest is built on the ground, a distance from the water, usually in a thick growth of grass. It is constructed of grasses shaped into a hollow, the bowl lined with fluffy down feathers, which the female plucks from her breast to insulate the eggs. Eight to twelve pale, buff eggs are deposited in among the down, and for the necessary 21-23 days the female alone sits patiently on her eggs, keeping them at an even, warm temperature by close contact with blood vessels near the surface of her skin. The hatched ducklings are gray-brown in color with a brown crown, eye line and back of neck, the fluffy babies covered with natal down.

The numbers of both the Green-winged and the Blue-winged Teals have greatly dwindled because of the elimination of their nesting sites. Drought, drainage and agriculture have destroyed a large percentage of their breeding grounds. Wildlife sanctuaries and big broods of as many as 15 eggs help keep the birds from entirely succumbing to the pressures of man's and nature's encroachment.

Another Teal that inhabits North America is the Cinnamon Teal, *Anas cyanoptera*. A popular game bird of the west, it was formerly slaughtered in great numbers by market hunters.

TEETERER:
see Sandpiper, Spotted

TEETER-TAIL:
see Sandpiper, Spotted

TERN, ARCTIC:
(Sterna paradisaea)

The Arctic Tern holds the world's championship record for long distance migratory flight. It summers in the Arctic and winters in the Antarctic, a round trip of 22,000 miles (35,200 km). It breeds from Massachusetts north to northern Greenland, across Arctic regions to northern Alaska. In winter it is found in the Antarctic Ocean.

The length of the Arctic Tern is 16 inches (40.64 cm), including an 8 inch (20.32 cm) pure white tail with a 5 inch (12.7 cm) fork. The upper surface of its wings is gray, darkening towards the tips. The throat and belly are white and its head is white with narrow black lines. Feet and bill are rich red in color. During breeding season, the Arctic Tern develops a shiny, greenish-black crown. Many sea birds are colored black and white with shades of gray, their gradations of color blending into the light and dark ripples of the moving water.

For 14 weeks from June to August, the Arctic Tern nests as far north as there is stable land on which to build a nest. On rocky or pebbly shores of sea islands, these birds congregate in colonies and establish nests that are mere hollows in the ground. In 21 days the downy young hatch out, bearing a dusky patch on their foreheads. Often the parents must scoop the snow out of the nest to keep the baby warm.

When the young are well fed and fully feathered, the entire family leaves the Arctic breeding territory and in a few months arrives at their winter grounds, the Antarctic Ocean. During the 11,000 miles (17,600 km) one way flight, food consisting of small fish and crustaceans is plucked from the ocean. During breeding season, the Arctic Tern rarely travels 100 miles (160 km) from shore, but at other times it may be seen any distance from land, over almost any sea.

Approximately 20 weeks of the Arctic Tern's year are spent in flight, covering its prodigious course. To travel the distance in that amount of time, the bird must fly at least 150

Above: **Arctic Terns nest in colonies.**

miles (240 km) per day, with some miles added to that number for twists and turns in the constant search for food.

The Arctic Tern's migration route is somewhat of a mystery. Scatterings of individuals have been noted along the Atlantic and Pacific coasts, but even though many thousands of these birds make this astounding journey twice each year, ornithologists have not yet made a proper study of the entire trip. Why the birds undertake a migration of such long distance is also not known.

One reason for these extreme travels might be to follow the sun for survival value. Abundant hours of daylight and sunshine are experienced by the Tern, as the time spent at the poles is when the sun there never sets; the winter in the South Pole is the local summer. The Arctic Tern has the longest day of any creature on earth, the non-stop sunshine giving it extended hours of light for finding ocean-going prey. Because it flies so far, it requires large amounts of food energy, and because it hunts so successfully, aided by the sun, it can power its long excursion.

Another reason for the Arctic Tern's pronounced nomadism is birds generally winter in a place that is similar to their breeding area, as regards food, vegetation and geography. Holding to this theory, a bird that breeds at the extreme North Pole is most likely to winter in the extreme

BIRDS

South Pole. These terminal points were developed during the evolutionary process and now are an instinctive part of the Arctic Tern's migratory pattern.

The compass direction of the flight is also inherited from ancestors. To follow its predestined course, it has been suggested that the bird is guided by the wind. In the spring in the eastern half of the United States, there is an almost continuous pattern of southerly winds.

Although studies continue to yield information about bird migration, many questions remain unanswered. The Arctic Tern is of great interest to ornithologists because it accomplishes the most remarkable athletic feat in the entire bird world.

TERN, BLACK:
see Common Tern

TERN, CABOT'S:
see Tern, Common

TERN, CASPIAN
(Hydroprogne caspia)

The Caspian Tern is the largest of the Terns of which there are over 50 species throughout the world. Ten kinds of Terns can be found in North America. Widespread in distribution, the Caspian Tern breeds from Great Slave Lake to the Gulf of St Lawrence and south to lower California, Texas, Louisiana and South Carolina. It winters from southern California to South Carolina and Mexico in the coastal waters.

The Caspian Tern measures 23 inches (58.42 cm) in length, with a wingspread of 55 inches (139.7 cm). Its color is white all over with the exception of its back and wings which are grayish-blue. The slightly forked tail has pointed outer feathers and its wings are long and slender. A bright vermillion bill is straight and slim. In summer, adult birds develop a glossy, greenish-black crown, which in winter is broken with white.

Closely related to the Gulls, the Caspian Tern is a fish-eating sea bird. It can be distinguished from the similarly appearing Herring Gull by its forked tail, black crown, large red bill, smaller size and manner of hunting for fish. The Tern hovers in the air then plunges into the water, diving bill down for prey which swim near the surface, while the Gull alights readily on the water to feed. Terns seldom land in the water and swim. They spend more time in the air than do Gulls. Some Terns eat insects caught on the wing.

Decidedly gregarious, Caspian Terns nest in vast colonies on off-shore islands, often shared with Gulls. A simple nest is a mere depression in the

Above: **The Caspian Tern is very noisy and steals fish from other sea birds.**

ground, scooped out of dry sand and lacking any nesting material. Two or three pale, olive-buff eggs are laid, sparingly marked with brown and gray.

Nesting sites are very close together, but each small territory is vigorously defended by the parents against any intrusion. Both sexes share the incubation duties, and in 20 days the young hatch out. The hatchlings are downy at first, then frowsy, then feathered. Adults are fierce in the protection of their young. Any fluffy wanderers from the safety of the nest are immediately pounced upon by the parents or by neighboring adults who, in their exaggerated zeal to keep the babies from straying and keep them out of strange turf, often peck and batter them to death.

Caspian Terns, and other Terns as well, were almost exterminated by plume hunters until hunting them became illegal. Unwittingly cooperating in their own extinction, a behavior characteristic made them simple targets. Numbers of Terns are attracted to a wounded companion who may be floating on the surface of the water. Solicitiously hovering overhead, the inquisitive flock made easily bagged decorations for women's hats.

TERN, COMMON
(Sterna hirundo)

A sea-bird widely distributed throughout the Northern Hemisphere, the Common Tern breeds from the Gulf of St Lawrence and northern Manitoba south to the Great Lakes and the Gulf of Mexico. It winters from Florida southward to Brazil.

Terns are related to Gulls, both members of an order of birds called *Laridae* or Long-winged Swimmers. Ten of the world's 50 Tern species can be found in North America, among them the Gull-billed Tern, *Gelochelidon nilotica*; Forster's Tern, *Sterna forsteri*; Royal Tern, *Thalasseus maximus*; Cabot's Tern, *Sterna sandvicensis*; Roseate Tern, *Sterna dougalli*; Black Tern, *Hydrochelidon niger* and Sooty Tern, *Sterna fuscata*.

The Common Tern achieves a length of 16 inches (40.64 cm), the female smaller than the male. In winter, its color is white with back and wings of pale pearl blue-gray. The white and gray coloration blends into the hues of rippling ocean water, played upon by light. The bill is orange-red with a black tip and the feet are also red.

During breeding season, the Common Tern's head coloration undergoes a startling change as the bird grows new feathers, called nuptial plumage, to replace the molted ones of winter's coat. The bill and feet become a brighter red, and a crown of lustrous greenish-black plumage develops on the top part of its head, just below the eyes. Other body parts remain gray and white.

The Common Tern feeds mostly on small fry, shrimps and small crustaceans found swimming just under the surface of the water. With its downward pointed tapering bill, it plunges from the air to catch the prey seen with its telescopic eyes, immersing its head but seldom disappearing underwater. Although the Tern has webbed feet well designed for swimming, it seldom alights upon the water, preferring to spend its time in the air. On the wing it devours insects such as flying ants, butterflies and cicadas.

Above: A Common Tern with its young.

Terns will often work together to help a wounded companion or to fight a common enemy. This habit of flocking made them ready targets when formerly thousands of these birds were shot by plume hunters for the millinery trade, a practice now illegal.

In spring or summer, depending upon the latitude, colonies of Terns convene to breed on islands in the sea or lake. Graceful aerial dartings in which a couple fly around in very close formation, and tender courtship feedings in which the female begs for food and the male obliges, often are performed as a ritualized mating display. Nest construction varies, determined by the availability of supplies. Sometimes nests are merely simple hollows in bare sand with minimal furnishings of a few stones or bits of seaweed. Where nesting material is abundant, the Common Tern will construct an elaborate structure of sticks, seaweed and grasses, placing it just above high tide mark along the beach. Occasionally, nests are built in dense grasslands on high islands, and sometimes this bird can be found breeding as much as 200 feet (60 m) above the level of the ocean.

Two to six eggs are laid, highly variable in shape and color even in the same nest, from white to buff, olive or green, with markings or without. Both sexes share the task of incubation for 21 days, until the downy chicks emerge. Sometimes the young will enter the water on their own accord, but always under the watchful guardianship of the nearby parents, upon whom the young are dependent until they develop the power of flight. Parents are bold in making threatening dives at any intruders into the nesting area, sometimes actually striking.

Common Terns are useful to fishermen as they plunge and dive in areas that abound with fish, thereby signaling the presence of a school.

TERN, FORSTER'S:
see Tern, Common

TERN, GULL-BILLED:
see Tern, Common

TERN, LEAST
(Sterna alibfrons)

The smallest of American sea birds, the Least Tern has a wide distribution. It breeds on the coast of southern California and on the Gulf coast from Texas eastward, also north to Missouri and Nebraska. On the east coast of the United States, it breeds from Massachusetts south through Florida. It winters from the Gulf coast south to Venezuela and Peru.

BIRDS

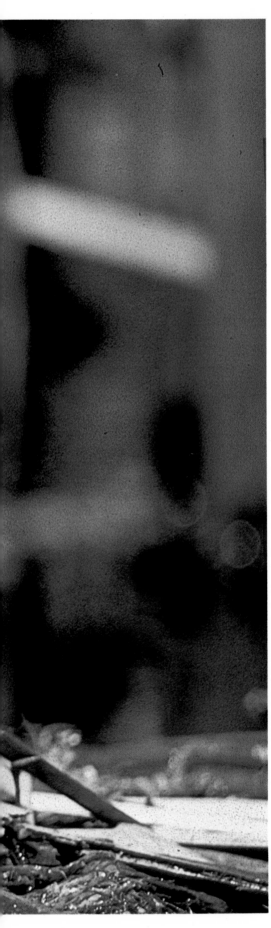

Left: **Insect-eating Black Terns rarely dive.**
Above: **Least Terns are coastal birds.**

A dainty bird, the Least Tern is only 9 inches (22.86 cm) in length. In its winter plumage, its upper parts are pale grayish blue below a snowy white. Its head is also white. The gray and white colorations of sea birds blend them into the ripples on the water as the sunlight plays upon the waves. The Least Tern's bill is yellow tipped with contrasting black, and its feet are a bright orange-yellow color. In breeding season, the adult birds change their feathered hats for a crown of glossy greenish-black plumage, their nuptial coloration.

Least Terns are usually seen in small flocks. Like other Terns, their food is mainly small fish and crustaceans, which they capture by a swift dive from the air, snatching the prey in long, tapered bills. Least Terns are also natural insect destroyers as they dart after insects that fly over the marsh.

With thin, pointed wings and long, forked tail, the little Least Tern is a graceful flyer and like other Terns, shows a remarkable endurance in flight. From its tropical winter home it travels thousands of miles up the coastlines of United States to California and Massachusetts, ceasing its wanderings long enough to breed.

On deserted beaches or on pebbly islands off the coasts, Least Terns congregate in numbers that were formerly in the many thousands and now have been enormously reduced. Little energy is exerted by the Terns in nest construction, as nests are simply slight depressions in the sand or pebbles, unrelieved by a soft lining of plant material. One to four pale, greenish to dull olive eggs are laid, spotted over the surface with spatterings of various shades of brown and lilac. Shells with these blotchy colorations match and blend into their grainy, pebbly backgrounds, thus making them less noticeable to predators who might find bird eggs tasty. Tern chicks, too, are marked with blotched protection, called cryptic coloration.

Tern partners are mated for life, and each returns to its place of origin to perform the rites that will continue the species. Each partner is attentive to the other as they alternate the job of incubation, the one not sitting delivering food to the one warming the eggs.

Traveling in small and scattered flocks, Least Terns, like others in their family, exhibit a surprising degree of caring for a wounded member of the group. If one of their number is hurt, the others rally around, flying anxiously about and uttering high-pitched sounds of solicitation and concern. This sympathetic behavior facilitated their near extinction, as the massed birds made an easy target for the guns of hunters.

At the turn of the century, fashion dictated that women's hats be adorned with entire birds and their fluffy plumage. Women wore various kinds of birds on their heads, but the most desired species to surmount the well-dressed female was the dainty Least Tern. Thousands and thousands of Least Terns were shot by plume

BIRDS

hunters to satisfy the needs of the millinery trade. Great numbers of birds were bagged while in the air or in nesting colonies, leaving the helpless, newly hatched chicks to perish, without the necessary parental care.

Early in the 1900s legislation was enacted making the hunting of wild birds for plumage illegal. Although Least Tern populations had a chance to recover from the extremes of slaughter, the birds live on only to be threatened by a different set of anti-survival conditions. Today, only isolated pockets of Least Terns nest off our coastlines, their habitats destroyed by man's encroachment. Rats, marsh hawks and nest site disturbances also contribute to keeping down their numbers. Audubon Society wardens attempt to protect many off-shore colonial nesting species by posting, fencing off, policing and studying the breeding areas.

**TERN, ROSEATE:
see Tern, Common**

**TERN, ROYAL:
see Tern, Common**

**TERN, SOOTY:
see Tern, Common**

**THUNDER PUMPER:
see Bittern**

**TILT-UP:
see Sandpiper, Spotted**

**TIP-UP: see Sandpiper,
Spotted**

**TITMOUSE, TUFTED
(Parus bicolor)**

The Tufted Titmouse lives as a year-round resident throughout all of its range, which extends from the Gulf of Mexico west to the plains and as far north as Minnesota and New York. It is gradually occurring in increasing numbers in the northern sections of its territory, as oak-beach-hickory woodlands replace abandoned farms. According to the Audubon Society bird count records, the Tufted Titmouse is among the 20 most abundant winter birds in eastern North America.

Not of showy coloration, the blue-gray bird with a blackish forehead measures 6 inches (15.24 cm) in length. The female is slightly smaller and duller than the male. The Tufted Titmouse has a short, thin, straight bill and black eyes that shine like glassy marbles. A cone-shaped feathered crest stands pert on top of the head, the peaked cap raised or lowered as a visible means of communicating emotional states from one Titmouse to another. When the crest is flattened, its long feathers project behind the crown.

More often heard than seen, the most familiar notes of the Tufted Titmouse sound very much like a call of the Cardinal, *Richmondena cardinalis*, or the Carolina Wren, *Thryothorus ludovicianus*, a loud, sharp *peto, peto, peto*, which both sexes whistle nearly all year round. Because of its clear two-syllable call, the Titmouse is sometimes known as Peter Bird. Like the conversational exchanges of the Black-capped Chickadee, *Parus atricapillus*, male and female Titmice are in almost constant vocal communication with each other and with others of their species. During the spring, summer and early fall when the birds are nesting and then molting their feathers, they are unusually silent as they retire to the deep woods for seclusion and protection.

During the springtime hatching of insect eggs the Tufted Titmouse gorges on the newly emerged caterpillars, as well as on great numbers of wasps. It searches out its insect food by minute examination of bark, buds, twigs and leaves, and by hanging from a branch in an upsidedown position; no surface of the tree remains unexplored. In winter, acorns comprise a major portion of the Titmouse diet. The nut having been pierced by the sharp, closed bill, the bird transports it to a tree limb, holds the seed between its feet, and hacks it open with strong hammerings of the beak to reach the soft edible interior.

The Tufted Titmouse incubates its eggs and raises its young inside tree cavities not of its own making. Instead, it finds holes that have been fashioned and abandoned by woodpeckers, openings that once housed squirrels, or slits that were caused by lightning. Preferred locations are in deep woods, but the birds will also use hollows found in orchards, parks and sometimes in trees close to human habitation, the nesting sites returned to year after year, if undisturbed. If the opening is too large, an abundance of nesting material is packed in to bring the chamber down to comfortable size, the building supplies consisting of moss and leaves, and for some unexplained reason, always a few pieces of snakeskin. The entire accumulation is lined with soft warm fur of mammals that is picked up from the ground, but often the Titmouse is bold enough to tug the fur from a living squirrel or a woodchuck, and even to alight upon a human head and yank out a hank of hair.

Five or six pure white eggs, spotted with burnt sienna markings, are deposited, and for twelve days the female sits closely until the flightless, naked, blind hatchlings emerge, completely dependent upon the parents to be fed. Young birds hatched in such a helpless state are called altricial birds, as opposed to the hatchlings of birds such as ducks and geese that emerge fully feathered, able to run, capable of feeding themselves and known as precocial birds.

In about two weeks after being fed abundantly on caterpillars, the fledgling Titmice leave the nest. Offspring and parents remain loosely together in family assemblies until they join in other groups of Titmice and sometimes other species, as well. In fall and winter these little flocks forage throughout areas of limited range in search of insect eggs and seeds.

**TOWHEE, RUFOUS-SIDED
(Pipilo erythropthalmus)**

The Towhee and various subspecies breed from coast to coast from southern British Columbia, southern Ontario and southern Maine to Louisiana, Florida and Guatemala. They winter south to the Gulf coast and Guatemala, but a few linger in northern portions of the winter range, particularly near the coast. In the west, those that breed high in the mountains simply move to the warmer valleys for the winter.

Of a total measurement of 8 inches (20.32 cm), the length of the rounded tail accounts for 4 inches (10.16 cm). The male's head and upper parts are dressed in sooty black, while its belly is white and its sides are chestnut-brown, a coloration that accounts for the descriptive title, Rufous-sided Towhee. A female Towhee has breast tones similar to the male, but her distinction is in having brown plumage where his is black.

Slight variations in appearance among the Towhee subspecies are white spots on the back and shoulders of some western males, the red eyes of northeastern birds, and the white eyes of southern individuals. Western races are larger and darker in humid areas, and smaller and lighter in arid zones.

The Towhee is partial to open, brushy, dry conditions, living in the east in hedgerows, thickets, overgrown pastures, parks and gardens, while in the west it prefers chaparral and canyons. It favors burned over and blown down situations which result from fires and hurricanes, and it also benefits from wood cutting and lumbering, occurrences which cause shrubby openings in the forest. Because of man's marks upon the woodlands, the Towhee's numbers are increasing.

The diet of the Towhee consists of both animal and vegetable food, the plant material outweighing insects. Ants, bees, wasps and caterpillars augment the primary menu of weed seeds, fruit and berries, all of which are searched out on the ground. If food is not in ready evidence, the Towhee uncovers it by scratching like a chicken with it sturdy legs. Amidst bushy undergrowth, the Towhee whips up any loose ground covering with alter-

Above: A Rufous-sided Towhee.

nate backward thrusts, sending little spurts of leaves flying up behind, causing a crackling commotion that would befit a larger animal such as a woodchuck or a squirrel.

The Towhee is a solitary bird, and although thousands are scattered over miles of bushy woodlands, the average feeding territory for a pair is only about one acre (0.4 ha).

In spring and summer, even during midday when almost all other birds except the Red-eyed Virio, *Vireosylva olivacea*, are silent, the vocal Towhee's brisk and energetic song is easily recognized. Above the sound of rustling leaves, the Towhee trills an invitation to *drink-your-tea-e-e-e-, drink-your-tea-e-e-e*, the song consisting of three notes, the first two strongly accented and the second lower in tone, these followed by several rapid notes of the same pitch. To Thoreau, the Towhee's performance sounded like *hip-you-he-he-he-he*.

The names Towhee and Chewink, by which the bird is also known, are meant to resemble a characteristic call note of the bird. The great difference in the sound of these two names illustrates the usual inaccurate results of rendering a bird call in a human word.

Towhee nests are well concealed on the ground under the protection of a grassy clump in open woods. Sometimes the nest is sunk to the level of the ground surface and partially arched over. To raise another brood in the same season, a second nest is placed

higher up in a shrub or vine where it is concealed by growing vegetation. Four white eggs, strongly spotted with chestnut sprinkles, are deposited in the well-cupped structure made of twigs and leaves and lined with grass and rootlets.

The Cowbird, *Molothrus ater*, a parasitic bird that lays its eggs in the nests of others rather than trouble itself to build its own, often chooses the Towhee's nest in which to deposit its treasures. A close sitter, mother Towhee incubates the Cowbird eggs often at the expense of her own legitimate heirs, but when the interloper leaves off too many charges, the normally agreeable hostess simply deserts the entire domestic operation.

TURKEY, EASTERN WILD: see Turkey, Wild

TURKEY, FLORIDA WILD: see Turkey, Wild

TURKEY, GOULD'S WILD: see Turkey, Wild

TURKEY, MERRIAM'S WILD: see Turkey, Wild

TURKEY, MEXICAN WILD: see Turkey, Wild

TURKEY, RIO GRANDE WILD: see Turkey, Wild

TURKEY, WATER (Anhinga anhiga)

Birds with snake-like necks, Water Turkeys live in dense, fresh water swamps in southern Illinois and North Carolina south to Texas and Florida.

A measurement of about 36 inches (91.44 cm) includes the Water Turkey's neck and yellow bill, which are one-third its total length, and its tail, which measures nearly another one-third. The color of the adult male is generally a glossy greenish-black, with grayish flecks on its head, neck, wings and back and a white tip on it tail. The female shows more chestnut brown coloration throughout.

BIRDS

The Water Turkey bears no resemblance to a turkey, but that is what it was commonly called by the people of the southern states in which the bird is found. Ornithologists have now adopted the popular name, instead of calling it Anhinga, as it was formerly referred to. Another of this bird's common titles is Snake-bird, a more descriptive term than Water Turkey. With its elongated body, very long, thin neck, small head, and slender, unhooked, sharply pointed bill nearly twice the length of its head, the streamlined narrowness of its structure gives the appearance of an undulating serpent.

The Water Turkey often swims with its body submerged, with only its neck and head showing, and moving to and fro, strongly suggestive of a water snake. Underwater in speedy pursuit of fish, its favorite food, this bird swims with its neck in the shape of a Z. A powerful muscle enables the Water Turkey to thrust its neck swiftly forward and spear its prey on its needle-like bill. Like a spring uncoiled, this neck lunge gives the bird yet another name, American Darter.

Although the Water Turkey takes off from the water clumsily, it is a skilled flyer and dives with precision and grace. The feathers are coarse and, like the Cormorant's, the plumage is not waterproof. The long bird with the crooked neck perches on a limb overhanging the water with wings outstretched to dry them in the sun. Living in silent places in the wilderness, the bird is timid and watchful. If disturbed, it drops from its perch above the water and disappears beneath the surface without a noise and with barely a ripple.

The Water Turkey builds its nest in communal rookeries, often in the company of Herons or Ibises. Poorly constructed of sticks and grasses, the clumsy mass is placed in bushes or small trees overhanging swamps and bayous. Three or four pale bluish-

Top: **A Water Turkey in the Everglades.**
Left: **A Water Turkey airs its wings to dry since its feathers are not water repellent.**

white eggs are laid. The young are naked on hatching, but later they acquire down. Both parents incubate the eggs and tend the babies, which are reared for a time in the nest.

TURKEY, WILD
(Meleagris gallopavo)

When the early settlers arrived in this country, Wild Turkeys lived and raised their young from southern Ontario, Iowa and Colorado into southern Mexico, and from the Rockies east to the Atlantic Coast. Notwithstanding Benjamin Franklin's view of these big North American birds as beautiful, clever and courageous and his favoring them over the Bald Eagle as the national symbol of the United States, Wild Turkeys have been almost totally eliminated from their original range.

There are six surviving subspecies or races of Wild Turkeys: the Eastern, Florida, Rio Grande, Merriam's, Mexican and Gould's. With only slight variations among them, they are not different enough to be considered as separate species.

The largest game bird in North America, a full grown two year old Wild Turkey has an average weight of 25 pounds (11.25 kg). The Wild Turkey resembles its domestic cousin, which was bred from the Mexican subspecies, but it is more streamlined with long neck, tail and legs, and a slender body. The feathers of the neck, chest and back are colored in black and browns, and the tail is a deep chestnut brown. The female is smaller, trimmer, and duller in color than the male. The naked, scaly head of the male or gobbler is adorned with fleshy growths hanging from the throat, called wattles, from the neck, called caruncles, and from above the bill, called a snood. Filling with blood when the bird is excited, these fatty hangings change color depending upon the bird's emotional state and upon the season. When the gobbler is in full courtship strut, his wattles and his caruncles become bright red. They are also red when the gobbler warns off another male.

The male turkey also has a growth of feathers, called a beard, about 8 inches (20.32 cm) in length, sprouting from the middle of the breast and textured like a horse's tail. On each leg, a few inches above the foot, the gobbler has a sharp, pointed spur, which he uses as a fighting implement.

Separate flocks of sibling hens and toms, consisting of from 10-40 birds in a group, feed on forest mast of seeds and on berries, grasses, insects and snails. When the prescribed amount of daylight triggers breeding hormones in the male, he emits his deep bass gobbling sound. With tail feathers erect and fanned, wings dragging behind, body feathers fluffed so he appears twice his normal size, head growths reddened and expanded, he performs his courting strut, accompanying his exhibition with sonorous gobbling. Only the largest, healthiest males win mates, thus assuring that genetic strengths will enhance future generations.

The Wild Turkey nests in many places including cultivated fields, forest brush and near trails or roads, but hidden by low-growing plants. A slight depression in the ground, made by the weight of the hen's body and haphazardly lined with debris, serves as a nest for the 10-12 eggs. The female alone incubates the eggs for the necessary 28 days, turning them over to prevent the embryo from sticking to one side of the inner wall.

Above: Wild Turkeys are more colorful than the cultivated turkey and they are slimmer.

A ground nest being an extremely unsafe place to rear a brood of young, the female leads her downy poults away only one day after hatching. Among plants that provide concealment, the fluffy babies roost beneath the mother's body. They peck at all small, bright objects on the ground, learning from experience what is edible. In about six weeks, the poults can fly and, like the adults, they roost at night in trees where the little ones have a greater chance of avoiding hungry predators.

Fast runners, Wild Turkeys can cover 18 miles (28.8 km) in an hour, and will often run from danger rather than exert the effort to become airborne. The Turkey is a strong, swift flyer, though not a long-distance one, and despite its size is capable of extremely rapid takeoffs, with powerful wings lifting it at a sharp angle to clear tree branches.

With keen eyesight, acute hearing, and quick departure, the Wild Turkey is not an easy target for the hunter. Before the settlement of North America, Wild Turkeys were abundant and they had no fear of man, but they became a favorite target of pioneer hunters. As the pressures of hunting grew, so did the wariness of the bird. Although market hunting and trapping contributed greatly to the

BIRDS

big bird's decline in numbers, habitat destruction caused their near-total extinction. Today Wild Turkeys occupy only a small fraction of their original territories, and attempts are being made to reintroduce them in many states.

TURNSTONE, RUDDY
(*Arenaria interpres*)

A wide-ranging shorebird, the Ruddy Turnstone inhabits both North and South America. It breeds on the Arctic shores and winters from central California, Texas, Louisiana and South Carolina south to Brazil.

The Turnstone achieves a length of 9 inches (22.86 cm). Its upper parts are chestnut, black and white in color, while its lower parts are black and white. A low, compact bird with orange legs, both sexes have a similar color pattern, but the female is duller than the male.

Many shorebirds are among the earth's most traveled creatures, and foremost among them is the Ruddy Turnstone. It breeds in the Arctic tundra and often winters on the farthest end of South America. Its wings are long and sharply pointed, their quick flaps alternating with frequent glidings, the shape and manner of their use making possible the extended uninterrupted flights. During the prolonged journey south in the fall and northward in the spring, migrating Turnstones fly very high in large flocks, usually by themselves or with Black-bellied Plovers, *Squatarola squatarola*. While travelling over water, the Turnstones alight to swim and rest, then rise up easily to continue their extensive flight.

The Turnstones' favorite feeding grounds are stony beaches of coasts and inlets on which they stop to feed along the migratory route. Flying low while feeding, they can be seen in small numbers, sometimes singly, and sometimes in mixed flocks with Semi-palmated Plovers, *Charadrius semipalmatus*, Sanderlings, *Calidris leucophaea* and other small wading birds.

The Ruddy Turnstone has a wedge-shaped bill, flattened like a knife, that is turned slightly upward at the tip. The manner in which the bird wields this specialized appendage is the reason for its name of Turnstone. Inserting the beak-tool under a stone, a pebble or a shell, the bird tosses back its head and pries up the obstacle, causing rocky missiles to fly this way and that in its diligent hunt for food. Larger impediments are pushed aside with surprising force by the Turnstone's breast. It also roots like a pig in insect-infested piles of seaweed or in the open sand, devouring in its feeding activities small crustaceans, sand fleas, worms, horseshoe crabs and eggs of many kinds. In nature's system, all niches are exploited to sustain the earth's inhabitants, and in its constant search for nourishment the Turnstone leaves no stone unturned.

Ruddy Turnstones do not always have to exert such efforts to uncover food. Fast runners, they chase small fiddler crabs on the muddy banks of tidal creeks, or resort to eating berries from thick bushes growing near the shore. In bold marauding tactics, they raid the nesting colonies of gentle terns and devour the contents of the eggs, cracking open the shells with sharp chisel beaks.

In breeding plumage, the Turnstone's coat shows a variegated patchwork of colors in rufous, black, brown and white, causing hunters to name this bird Calico-jacket. The Turnstone is most daring in its showy coloration, as most shore birds are colored in tones of buff and brown to match the grains and pebbles of the sand. Even its nest is not concealed, being simply a shallow circular depression in the ground, lined haphazardly with bits of plant material. The Turnstone depends for concealment of its eggs upon the similarity of shell markings to their surroundings, strong brownish blotchings well covering the olive colored eggs.

Both sexes take turns at egg incubation duties, one sitting while the other guards the brooding partner. They also both participate in the protection of the fluffy young with violent squawkings and driving off an enemy with stabbing bills.

Another bird that uses its beak as a prying instrument is a close relative of the Turnstone, the Oyster Catcher, *Haematopus palliatus*. The Oyster Catcher inserts its hard flat bill between the slightly opened shells of bivalves, severs the muscle that hold the shells together, and savors the soft-bodied animal enclosed within.

VIREO, BELL'S:
see Vireo, Red-eyed

VIREO, BLUE-HEADED:
see Vireo, Red-eyed

VIREO, PHILADELPHIA:
see Vireo, Red-eyed

VIREO, RED-EYED
(*Vireo olivaceus*)

The most common of all Vireos, the Red-eyed Vireo is found in summer throughout temperate North America, except in arid districts, north to southern Canada, west to British Columbia, south to Texas and southern Florida. It winters in Central and South America.

Slightly smaller than an English Sparrow, the Red-eyed Vireo is 6½ inches (16.51 cm) in length. Its upper parts are a plain grayish-olive green and the underparts are white. Sometimes also known as Greenlet, the bird's Latin name Vireo translates 'I am green.' The iris of the eye of this Vireo is ruby-red in adults, but only from a close-up view can the color be discerned, so it does not serve well as an identifying feature.

A small, active, tree-gleaning bird, the Red-eyed Vireo's favorite haunts are woodland clearings with an undergrowth of slender saplings. Burned-over areas become appealing habitats, as do places in a forest where the canopy is open. Although primarily a woodland-loving species, summer months are sometimes spent in parks, orchards, gardens or tree-bordered city streets.

Above: **The Red-eyed Vireo is a vigorous and persistent singer.**

Hidden amidst dense foliage, moving constantly about among the leaves, the little green bird is well concealed as its coloration blends harmoniously with its sylvan background. Behind its covering of green, the Red-eyed Vireo is a voracious consumer of insects, an appetite that makes the bird a natural insecticide. This Vireo destroys more span worms and leaf rollers than any other bird, and if large numbers of other insect species occur within its feeding territory, the Vireo greedily devours them, also.

The Red-eyed Vireo's assiduous snapping up of insects does not interrupt its constant vocalizations. Almost incessantly, hour after hour, day after day, undaunted recitations of short hurried phrases emit from the syrinx of the busy bird. The persistence of its utterances has earned for the locquacious performer the name of Preacher Bird.

The song of the Red-eyed Vireo sounds like short declarative sentences that end with a rising inflection and have a short pause between them as if awaiting a reply. The oration has a choppy cadence and a colorless quality that make it seem more like talking than like singing. The pronouncements of the bird have been rendered as *You see it – You know it – Do you hear me? – Do you believe it?* The feathered orator sometimes assumes a position of delivery from a low perch where, first facing one way then another, it effects the manner of a trained public speaker addressing a large outdoor crowd.

Just below eye level, suspended from a horizontal branch of a shrub or a low limb of a tree, the Red-eyed Vireo fashions a hanging fabric nest to house its eggs and envelop its little ones. The nest is a skillfully woven example of avian artistry, constructed of fine grasses, rootlets, bits of birch bark and wasp nest paper, tied to the supporting branch with spider silk or caterpillar webbing. Pieces of lichen decorate the outside of the rounded pendant and disguise it to appear as a natural extension of the tree.

The pensile nest of the Red-eyed Vireo is frequently the container for Cowbird eggs, the parasitic Cowbird leaving the incubation and rearing of its young to the normally unsuspecting Vireo. Occasionally this Vireo builds a new nest floor to cover over the intruding eggs, but more often the accommodating host and hostess incubate and feed the three or four Cowbird eggs and babies at the expense of their own rightful offspring.

In autumn, after its lengthy season of exuberant song is finished, the Red-eyed Vireo journeys to its part-time home in Central America where it is a winter visitor.

Other Vireos found throughout eastern North America are Yellow-throated Vireo, *Vireo flavifrons*, Philadelphia Vireo, *Vireo philadelphica*, and the Blue-headed Vireo, *Vireo solitarius*. The White-eyed Vireo, *Vireo griseus*, inhabits the eastern United States as far west as Texas and Bell's Vireo, *Vireo bellii*, lives in the prairie districts of the Mississippi valley.

VIREO, WHITE-EYED: see Vireo, Red-eyed

VIREO, YELLOW-THROATED: see Vireo, Red-eyed

VULTURE, BLACK: see Vulture, Turkey

TURKEY VULTURE (Cathartes aura)

A scavenging bird of prey, the Turkey Vulture or Turkey Buzzard is

BIRDS

Above: **Turkey Vultures scavenge in fields.**

found in temperate North America from the Atlantic to the Pacific Ocean, and occasionally as far north as British Columbia. It is a permanent resident except at the extreme northern limit of its range.

A big bird, the Turkey Vulture measures 30 inches (81.28 cm) in length, with a 72 inch (182.88 cm) wingspread. Male and female are of equal size. Its general appearance is black, but when in flight, the tail and rear margins of the wings show a pale brown. Lacking feathers on the head and neck, the Turkey Vulture's head is a scaly, often livid, crimson color.

Primarily carrion-feeders, Turkey Vultures lack the specialized feet of other birds of prey necessary for killing living quarry. Vultures are members of a family of birds called *Cathartidae*, from a Greek word meaning cleanser or scavenger. They feed on dead and dying animals, and their ghoulish appetite serves the invaluable purpose in the natural scheme of acting as a garbage disposal, helping to rid the world of decomposing matter.

The Turkey Vulture has a stout, blunt, hooked bill suitably constructed to tackle its meal, and dull talons, only slightly curved. It need not pounce upon its food to capture it, as dead prey cannot escape. Because a Vulture's beak cannot tear a tough hide, the avian scavenger must wait until decay makes a carcass soft and ripe. As it feeds, its naked head provides no feathery hiding place for small organisms that also dine on carrion.

Although the Turkey Vulture some-times eats live snakes, toads and rats, it does not attack poultry or gamebirds. The sight of a Vulture is calmly received by the domestic flock, whereas spotting a hawk will cause chaos in the barnyard. Wherever it earns its living, the Vulture is protected and is respected as a beneficial species.

While on the ground, the Turkey Vulture's walk is slow and awkward, but in the air the bird is a picture of majestic grace and ease. On broad wings that act like kites, the Vulture glides for hours on air currents that hold it aloft without a single wing flap. Not an idle sailor, the big dark bird, using eyesight many times more powerful than human vision, is on the keen look-out for a fallen animal. Plummetting from a height of thousands of feet, the Turkey Vulture swoops down at the sight of a dead dinner, and is quickly followed by other buzzards that were also circling with eyes on both the ground and on their soaring neighbors.

At night, buzzards fly toward their favorite perches in dead trees in which they roost in good-sized flocks. Often they will huddle like dark bundles on the chimneys of houses, especially in winter, in order to warm their bodies by the rising heat. After a rain, they spread their wings over the flues to dry their water-soaked feathers. When the sun comes out after a shower, the vulture hangs its wings out to dry wherever it may be.

The Turkey Vulture prefers warm latitudes, never nesting farther north than New Jersey on the Atlantic coast, although a few are seen on the west coast as far north as British Columbia.

Two dull yellowish eggs, blotched with brown, are deposited in a cavity of a rotting tree stump, or even directly on the ground in a secluded swamp or on a sunny hillside. The female incubates the eggs for 30 days, while the male feeds her regurgitated carrion. The young hatch out naked, but very soon they develop a whitish down and black face feathers.

The little ones are fed by both parents, thrusting their bills well into the adult's gullet to reach their meal. The food of the young was decomposed before it was eaten by the old birds and predigested by them before being fed to the babies. When frightened or angry, the little vultures, like the adult birds, have an unappetizing habit of vomiting a liquid of such offensive odor as to discourage any prolonged study of their nesting behavior.

Overlapping the range of the Turkey Vulture, is the Black Vulture, *Coragyps atratus*. Compared to the Turkey Buzzard, the Black Vulture's tail is shorter, its wing strokes more frequent, it is chunkier and its naked head is black, not red.

WARBLER, BLACK AND WHITE:
see Warbler Myrtle

WARBLER, BLACK-THROATED GREEN:
see Warbler, Myrtle

WARBLER, BLUE-WINGED:
see Warbler, Myrtle

WARBLER, CERULEAN:
see Warbler, Myrtle

WARBLER, MAGNOLIA:
see Warbler, Myrtle

WARBLER, MYRTLE
(*Dendroica coronata*)

Of the 150 species of Warblers that inhabit North America, the Myrtle Warbler is the most common. It spends the summer in woodlands extending along the northern portion of

Above: **Blackburnian Warblers (*Dendroica fusca*) live in the East in spruce or pine trees.**

the United States from Massachusetts to Minnesota, north and west to the tree limit in Canada and Alaska. It winters from the middle United States southward into Central America, but a few Myrtle Warblers remain as winter residents in the northern United States.

About 5 inches (12.7 cm) in length, the Myrtle Warbler is active and spritely, although it moves in a more leisurely fashion than the other more bustling members of its large family. It has a thin, sharply pointed bill and a fan-shaped tail. The four bright yellow spots on the crown, lower back and sides are the male's distinguishing marks, while the rest of his plumage is colored slate-blue above and white with dark streaks below. It is the only

Warbler plainly displaying yellow tones that has a white throat. The yellow patch just above the tail accounts for one of its common names, Yellow-rumped Warbler. The female is similar in appearance to the male, but her yellow patches are smaller and dimmer and dull gray-brown tones replace his of slate blue. In his winter plumage, the male is colored like the female.

The first of the Warblers to arrive in spring at northern breeding grounds and the last to leave in autumn, the Myrtle Warbler appears in late April and departs in late November. In summer, its most commonly heard musical offering is described as a 'sleigh-bell trill,' a quavering little twitter of four or five repetitions of the same note, followed by two or three

somewhat higher or lower in tone.

In late May the Myrtle Warbler builds a bulky nest of dried grasses, weeds and small evergreen twigs, lines it with hair or plant down and binds it with spider webbing. Usually placed in a coniferous tree a few feet off the ground, the nest is woven in about a week by the female, although the male sometimes brings her bits of construction materials. The female alone incubates the three to five creamy speckled eggs, while the male remains nearby emitting warning warbling tinkles to keep unmated rivals away from the nesting territory.

For two weeks after hatching, the

BIRDS

Above: The uncommon Cape May Warbler (*Dendroica tigrina*) in Canada.

young remain in the nest, fed by the adults large quantities of the same insect food eaten by the parent birds. No leaf or twig or outer branches remains uninspected, as the Myrtle Warbler gleans the trees for aphids, plant lice and an assortment of small flying insects.

When the task of rearing little ones is completed, the family disperses throughout the forest. Quietly and secretively, the male adults and offspring gradually transform their coats, the young changing their juvenile plumage to colors that resemble the female and the male shedding his summer blue-grays to dull brown winter hues.

All across central and eastern United States between September and November, Myrtle Warblers stream southward in enormous numbers, pausing in their migratory journeys to visit woodlands, parks and gardens. The coastline offers the most congenial stopping over places, where as many as an estimated 10,000 birds have been seen in one location in a single morning. Throughout the winter, the Myrtle Warbler remains one of the most common birds in areas along the Atlantic, Gulf and Caribbean coasts, and is the only Warbler that winters in any appreciable numbers in the northern United States.

Primarily insect eaters, those Myrtle Warblers that winter in the tropics continue their normal diet, but those that winter in the north change their menus from insects to seeds and berries. The big food attractions of the coastal areas are the waxy-coated nutlets of the bayberry or wax myrtle, *Myrica cerifera*, the plant that gives the Myrtle Warbler its name. A plentitude of bayberry seeds in a locality attracts a large concentration of these birds, but when the bayberry crop is low, the birds, though fewer in number, still gorge on seeds of seashore plants such as poison ivy, sumac, juniper and goldenrod, and on insects that live amid beached and drying seaweeds.

Some other Warblers of wide distribution in North America are Black and White Warbler, *Mniotilta varia*; Blue-winged Warbler, *Vermivora pinus*; Yellow Warbler, *Dendroica aestiva*; Magnolia Warbler, *Dendroica magnolia*; Cerulean Warbler, *Dendroica cerulea*; and Black-throated Green Warbler, *Dendroica virens*.

WARBLER, YELLOW:
see Warbler, Myrtle

WARBLER, YELLOW-HEADED:
see Warbler, Myrtle

WATER-WITCH:
see Grebe, Pied-billed

WAXWING, BOHEMIAN:
see Waxwing, Cedar

WAXWING, CEDAR:
(Bombycilla cedrorum)

A roving resident without fixed seasons for migrating, the Cedar Waxwing inhabits temperate North America in general, wintering in the wooded districts of the United States, south to the West Indies and Central America.

The Cedar Waxwing is approximately 7 inches (17.78 cm) in length colored in a perfect blending of rich grayish-brown with delicate plum tints appearing on the crest, throat, breast, wings and tail. The lighter toned breast shades into yellow underneath. A velvety black line crosses the eye to the back of the head, and the chin is also black. Brilliant vermillion wing tips, like drops of sealing wax, give the elegantly hued bird the name of Waxwing. The female is similar in coloration to the male, but duller in tone.

A pointed cap of crested plumage adorns the head and is used to convey the feelings of the bird. Loosely lying feathers signify contentment, a tightly compressed flattened arrangement shows fear, and great excitement or surprise causes the crest to become immediately erect. Among the French Canadians, the Cedar Waxwing is called Récollet, from the color of the crest which resembles the hood of the religious order of that name.

Cedar Waxwings travel throughout most of the year in social groupings of from 30 to 60 individuals. In harmonious companionship the birds comb the countryside for their favorite food of ripened wild fruits, occasionally consuming insects also. Because the bird

Above: **The Cedar Waxwing loves berries.**

assemblage quickly exhausts its special food supply in a particular area, the gentle gathering moves quietly away, resulting in a decided nomadic existence. Flying in close order, they suddenly circle in unison and swoop downward, alighting together in tree tops.

While sitting lined up on a branch, the members of the close-knit group dress one another's feathers and have been seen to pass an uneaten cherry or worm from bill to bill down the row, no bird consuming the morsel. Ornithologists have ascribed this unusual performance to playful antics, polite demeanor or full stomachs.

The nesting season finds Cedar Waxwings coupled off in devoted pairs where berry passing and mutual rubbing and billing are expressions of courtship feeding and behavior. The nest of the Cedar Waxwing in the north is generally a bulky structure, but in the southern states, the nest is smaller and more compact. Often built in an orchard and about 20 feet (6 m) from the ground, the nest is made of twigs, leaves, grass and strips of bark. Usnea moss is used where available and when wool, string, cloth or paper are found, those materials also are incorporated into the woven quarters. Both birds work diligently in bringing the materials and building the nest.

One egg a day is laid until the total number of three to five is reached. Waxwings breed in July or early August, later in the season than most other birds, when their infant food of fruits and berries is ripened. Nests are constructed in one-half acre areas that abut territories of other Waxwings. So gregarious is their nature that when procuring food for nestlings, a task normally performed by other birds as a solitary activity, Waxwings travel in small companies. Group gathering of food implies an abundant fruit supply, especially at a time when large quantities of edibles are required to nourish hungry, growing broods.

The Bohemian Waxwing, *Bombycilla garrula*, is a beautifully colored, close relative of the Cedar Waxwing and has similar behavior and disposition. A rare bird, it is found only in the upper Mississippi Valley and in some of the mountain states.

WHIP-POOR-WILL (*Caprimulgus vociferus*)

Often heard but seldom seen, the Whip-poor-will is a bird of the eastern United States and southern Canada, its range extending west to eastern Kansas and Nebraska. It winters in the Gulf states and southward through Mexico and Central America.

Approximately 10 inches (25.4 cm) in length, the Whip-poor-will is a bird of such remarkably inconspicuous appearance that it can almost make itself disappear. Its plumage is a patchwork pattern of black, brown, gray and buff coloration, a combination of dull colors that renders the bird almost invisible in its woodsy surroundings. If flushed from the ground where it perches, the cryptically colored bird flies quickly and silently away, only to land again nearby in a vanishing act, swallowed up by its uncanny ability to blend.

A nocturnal hunter, the Whip-poor-will remains well hidden during the day as it rests on a low branch or on the forest floor. Its time in motion is spent in darkness on long pointed wings, hunting insects; therefore, its seldom-used feet are small and weak, totally unfit for perching on a branch. The bill of the Whip-poor-will is small and insignificant, but the mouth is deeply clefted, enabling the bird to open wide to entrap flying insects. Strong bristles encircling the beak increase the efficiency of its gaping mouth as a bug collector and force the wings of insects to close before being swallowed.

For several hours after sunset and again before dawn, the Whip-poor-will pronounces its name hundreds of times without pause in loud, high-pitched repetitions, as if to validate its existence and counteract the obscurity of its daytime demeanor. The season of its singing lasts from early spring arrival on breeding grounds to late July or early August, both male and female birds indulging in spirited voices.

No nest is built as protection for the two Whip-poor-will eggs; they are deposited on the ground in deep woods among the fallen leaves, the concealing patterns of both eggs and bird providing sufficient camouflage in the shaded light of the forest floor. In 20 days the downy, buff color chicks hatch out, they, too, blending magically into their backgrounds and relying for their survival upon not being seen. The infant birds are fed partially digested insects by the parents and in about two weeks whole food is delivered to the young. The offspring continue to receive their morsels for a short time after they can fly, and are often fed even while in the air.

Owing to its obscurity in both daylight hours and under the cover of darkness, the Whip-poor-will has been able to survive despite its loss of woodland habitat. The adaptable bird still finds sufficiently undisturbed territory secluded enough for its breeding purposes, and because of the abundant nature of its food, eating heartily presents no problem.

A close but larger relative of the Whip-poor-will is the Chuck-will's Widow, *Antrostomus carolensis*, ranging from Virginia to Illinois, southward, and a smaller member of the family is the Poor-will, *Phalaenoptilus*

BIRDS

Top: The Nighthawk has long, pointed wings and can be seen at dusk in cities.
Above: The Poor-will, a small native of the West, blends in well with its woodland surroundings.

nuttalli, a native of the western United States. The Nighthawk, *Chordeiles virginianus*, another member of this family, called Goatsuckers, is distributed throughout North and South America.

WIDGEON, AMERICAN: see Baldpate

WINDHOVER: see Kestrel

WOODCOCK (Philohela minor)

The Woodcock is a secretive, solitary bird of brushy fields and moist temperate woodlands. With a wide range, it breeds from southern Manitoba to southern New Brunswick and south to Colorado, northern Missouri to New Jersey and south to Texas and Florida, wintering within its breeding range.

The Woodcock has a compact body, blunt wings, short legs, and almost no neck, and measures 12 inches (30.48 cm) in length. Its finely blended colors of black, warm browns, gray, and chestnut match perfectly its background on the forest floor.

In sharp contrast to the squat body is the Woodcock's thin straight beak, which is 3 inches (7.62 cm) long. The slender bill is inserted into the ground in search of earthworms, the bird's preferred food. The tip of this probing instrument is very flexible and the poking end of the bill can be opened below ground to grasp any prey it locates. Because the Woodcock's head is so often stuck into the ground, its eyes are placed far back to enable the bird to see behind him, on the lookout for would-be marauders even while it spears for food. The Woodcock literally has eyes on the back of its head. The disadvantage of having eyes positioned so far to the rear is swift short forward flight is sometimes impaired when the bird bangs into unseen branches.

For a bird of normally retiring demeanor, the Woodcock exhibits a remarkably conspicuous mating performance. Soon after sunset, the exuberant evening song-flight begins and continues until darkness, but in moonlight, it is often kept up through much of the night. Uttering rasping and guttural notes, the male Woodcock suddenly rises in the air, circling higher and higher in increasingly larger spirals until it almost disappears from sight, whistling all the while. The downward zigzag is accompanied by a loud, musical, three-syllable note. Starting again with rasping notes and rising spirals, each entire courtship maneuver lasts about one minute.

The nesting sites of the Woodcock are widely varied and include locations such as stream bank thickets, rich bottom lands, scrubby hollows – any place with moist, well-drained soil, well supplied with earthworms. The bird sometimes even settles down in city parks, yards, orchards and lawns.

The nest is a mere hollow in the ground lined with dead leaves, often placed out in the open, which could be deadly to a more brightly colored bird. For 21 days, both sexes alternate sitting on the eggs, usually four in number, each bird blending so thoroughly with its surroundings that it appears simply as a rock. The eggs, too, are spotted and streaked with concealing shades of cinnamon and drab that render them inconspicuous. An incubating Woodcock takes its job so seriously that it will not budge from the nest; often it can be touched or lifted from the eggs.

By feigning a broken wing, a mother Woodcock, like many other birds, will lure away an attacker that threatens harm to the young, thus offering herself as a sacrificial target to spare the little ones. The devoted mother will also transport her young to safety by carrying them one at a time grasped between her thighs.

In 1840, the abundance of Woodcocks caused Audubon to remark that although the birds whizzed overhead singly in their migratory flights, they followed each other with such rapidity it seemed they flew in flocks. Due to excessive hunting, no such population density exists today. As a gamebird,

the Woodcock was an epicure's delight, and enormous numbers of these easily killed birds were shot to satisfy hearty Victorian appetites.

The Woodcock is closely related to Wilson's Snipe, *Gallinago delicata*, also a delicious gamebird. Both are considered shore birds, but their habits bring them more often to meadows and marshes than to the edge of water.

WOODPECKER, DOWNY
(Dendrocopus pubescens)

The sparrow-sized Downy Woodpecker is a common bird, widely distributed as a permanent resident throughout the northern and central parts of eastern North America. Five other varieties or subspecies of the Downy inhabit nearly the entire wooded areas of North America.

The little Downy Woodpecker is only about 7 inches (17.78 cm) in length and weighs a mere 1½ ounces (28 g). The male and female, almost identical in appearance, are streaked with black and white, and white outer tail feathers are marked with black spots. The outstanding identifying feature of the male is the red spot on the back of its head, this patch of crimson lacking in the female bird.

The many highly specialized food gathering adaptations of the Downy Woodpecker, and other woodpeckers

as well, make the bird seem a well engineered feathered feeding machine, designed for eating insects that tunnel into trees. Two toes pointing forward and two toes pointing backward serve as a clamp by which the woodpecker attaches securely to a branch. Its stiff, sharply pointed tail feathers brace the bird and prop it while heavy hammer blows are delivered with its strong drilling beak. A long tongue darts out, extending well beyond the length of the beak and equipped with rigid bristles on its tip to spear the insects that meander under bark. An acute sense of hearing helps the woodpecker locate the active grubs by the sound of their chewing of the wood.

The normally silent Downy comes alive as spring advances, spurred on by the instinctive need to reproduce its kind. Using its small, but powerful 1 inch (2.54 cm) long beak, the male performs a long, unbroken rolling tattoo as a form of love song, drumming on hollow wood to announce his availability to a female Downy Woodpecker. Once the male secures a partner, he ceases his drumming and replaces it with a loud *wick, wick, wick* note, while chasing her from tree to tree.

Both partners work for about one week in the excavation of a nesting hole which they drill 8-50 feet (2.4-15 m) above the ground, generally in

Below: **The Woodcock is endowed with a perfect camouflage for its woodland habitat.**

BIRDS

Above: The common Downy Woodpecker.

dead or dying wood. These chipped out hollows aid in weakening a still standing trunk and promote the decomposition of the wood, which contributes to the richness of the soil. The entrance to the cavity is a perfectly round hole, 1¼ inches (3.17 cm) in diameter, the exact size that allows the little bird entrance and egress with no superfluous space. Inside the tree, the nest turns downward and measures 8-12 inches (20.32-30.48 cm) in depth.

For 12 days both partners share the task of incubating the four or five pure white eggs. When the helpless young develop sufficiently to climb up the height of their interior cradle, they stick their heads out of the door to receive the insect food delivered to them by diligent parents. The strongest babies reaching the entranceway and thrusting their heads completely out, get the most to eat, while the weaker siblings depend upon the parents to come down the hole to feed them. When food is not sufficient to be apportioned among the entire brood, the weakest are the first to die of undernourishment, nature's way of assuring that only the fittest survive.

Instead of retreating in the face of man's encroachment on its forest habitat, the Downy Woodpecker, a persistent and adaptable species, makes use of orchards and shade trees in which to raise a brood. The smallest of our woodpeckers is a welcome winter addition to home bird feeding stations, where it enjoys suet meals.

In appearance and habits, the Downy Woodpecker greatly resembles the Hairy Woodpecker, *Dendrocopus villosus*, but the Hairy Woodpecker is larger, 10 inches (25.4 cm) in length, has a longer bill, and is more restless in behavior.

WOODPECKER, GILA:
see Flicker

WOODPECKER, HAIRY:
see Woodpecker, Pileated

WOODPECKER, LEWIS'S:
see Flicker

WOODPECKER, PILEATED
(Dryocopus pileatus)

The largest North American Woodpecker, the Pileated Woodpecker, lives as a year-round resident in densely wooded regions of North America, mainly east of the Rocky Mountains.

The 19 inch (48.26 cm) long Pileated Woodpecker, about the size of a crow, is colored brownish-black with a conspicuous crest of bright red plumage crowning its head. Flashes of white appear in flight. Both sexes have similar coloration, but the slightly smaller female has a slate gray cheek area. From the feathered covering of its pileus or cap, it gets the name of Pileated Woodpecker, but less pretentiously and aptly descriptive, it is sometimes known as Logcock.

The Pileated Woodpecker's choicest residences are in heavily forested regions of first growth trees, but because so many original woodlands have been cut down, the favored habitat of the bird has been largely eliminated, thereby reducing the population of these woodpeckers. Where dense thickets still exist, the big dark bird will come surprisingly close to man, providing it has the shelter of large old trees.

The bony hardness of the Pileated Woodpecker's bill suits it for food acquisition, for home and nursery excavations, and for beating out its Morse Code love song. The beak, longer than the head, has a wedge-like tip, and is a formidable tool to chisel through bark and wood to reach the ant-infested inside of a tree. In only a few hours, the driving beak can chip out of a tree trunk a large, uneven hole, some as large in size as 6 inches (15.24 cm) square and just as deep,

Above: The Gila Woodpecker (*Centurus uropygialis*) is commonly found near large cacti.

and some excavations even more spacious. The favorite cold weather repast of the Pileated Woodpecker is thus reached, and the winter-quieted, big, black carpenter ants that tunnel deep in tree boles are speared by the rigid bristled tongue tip of the woodpecker. The mobile tongue darts out in a long protrusion, owing to the great length of the tongue's supporting bone which is anchored in the right nostril, curves around the back of the skull and ends near the base of the bill. Unerringly, the bird targets the ant colony, having detected its presence by the particular odor emitted by the ants and by the sound of their chewing of the wood.

Numerous, large sloppy borings of the Pileated Woodpecker can appear in a single tree, the big holes serving to weaken a dead, standing tree trunk, furthering decomposition and contributing the wood's locked up nutrients to the soil.

Often the same tree serves as a cafeteria for the Pileated Woodpecker, Hairy Woodpecker, *Dendrocopus villosus*, and Downy Woodpecker, *Dendrocopus pubescens*, as well. Although all these birds are insect eaters, they do not compete for food because each has a bill and tongue of different length and can eat only those beetles or ants that inhabit a tree depth that can be reached by its bill and tongue.

In summer, when food is easily available without laborious hammering, the Pileated Woodpecker dines on wild fruit, berries and nuts. Except for the Flicker, *Colaptes auratus*, the Pileated Woodpecker is the only woodpecker that feeds on the ground, where it sometimes tears apart ant hills and feasts on the insects and their larvae.

Like other male woodpeckers, the Pileated Woodpecker performs a springtime percussive serenade to proclaim his territorial wardenship and to broadcast his availability as a mate. The sound of his heavy, rolling 12 stroke tattoo, resonated against a hollow tree limb, carries for as long a distance as 1½ miles (2.4 km).

Above: The uncommon Pileated Woodpecker.

Pileated Woodpeckers are creatures of habit, returning year after year to the same nesting sites, often in the same tree. Never will a nursery cavity be drilled in a tree that the bird has already riddled and pock-marked in the search for food. In dense woodlands, in the still standing barren trunk of a dead tree, an average of 45 feet (13.5 m) above the ground, a large nesting hole is excavated. The female alone works in chiseling out the cavity, which turns downward inside the tree, the hole measuring 15-19 inches (38.1-48.26 cm) deep, with an entranceway approximately 4 inches (10.16 cm) in diameter, somewhat triangular in shape. The cavity walls are all neatly and evenly sculpted and the floor bedded with wood chips, the careful work taking about a month or more to complete.

The three or four featherless young are fed regurgitated food that is probed well into the little gullets by the parent's beak. The overall size of the nursery chamber is the perfect accommodation for both the parent and the offspring in the feeding operation, as the adult, perched at the entranceway, can lean down and forward and reach the little open mouths to pump in the soupy insect food. When the hungry young are stronger, they stick their heads out of the doorway and scream for nourishment.

The Pileated Woodpecker sometimes uses its nesting holes and roosting quarters at other times of year. If not used by the woodpecker, these ready made apartments may be appropriated for raising a family by Wood Ducks, *Aix sponsa*, Screech Owls, *Otus asio*, or Kestrels *Falco sparverius*, all of which are cavity nesting birds unable to fashion hollows of their own.

WOODPECKER, RED-COCKADED: see Flicker

WOODPECKER, RED-HEADED: see Flicker

WOODPECKER, YELLOW-BELLIED: see Sapsucker, Yellow-bellied

WREN, CACTUS: see Wren, House

WREN, HOUSE (Troglodytes aedon)

The House Wren, with its various subspecies, is found throughout most of North America. The eastern race lives from Manitoba to the Gulf of Mexico, and is most common in the United States from the Mississippi River eastward. It winters in southern and Gulf states and through eastern Texas and eastern Mexico.

The length of the House Wren measures only 5 inches (12.7 cm), half of that length the size of its diminutive body and the other half the measurement of its rounded tail. Its bill, slightly shorter than its head, is slender and tapered. Dull in color, its upper parts are brown and its underparts are whitish with a grayish-brown wash.

The food habits of the House Wren help humans, as the little bird consumes enormous quantities of insects, such as grasshoppers, crickets, locusts, beetles, cabbage worms and gypsy moths. The demanding appetites of the nestling House Wrens make marked inroads into the insect populations; an all day feeding observation revealed an adult bird making 1217 visits to the nest with food. The somachs of the young are larger than

BIRDS

those of the older birds and therefore have a greater carrying capacity.

Despite the desirable insect devouring habits of the House Wren, its virtue is somewhat offset by its aggressive behavior toward other birds that may be nesting within its environment. In the continuing struggle for survival of the fittest and in the age-old interest of self preservation, when Wren populations are high, the male House Wren may destroys the nests, eggs and young of species that may be its direct competitors. This is especially true in areas where humans have erected many nesting boxes and too many hole-nesting birds have moved into too small a territory.

One of the most outstanding characteristics of the House Wren is the male's capacity for singing. As soon as he arrives on his breeding grounds in spring he announces his territorial ownership in song, he lures a mate with his bubbling musical intensity, and he even vocalizes while feeding his little ones. With tail upcocked, his energetic outpourings are delivered in loud, hurried, shrill cascades, always performed with tireless repetition.

The Chippewa Indians, keen and knowledgable observers of plant and animal life, called the little recitalist by a name that means a big noise for its size. Singing continues until after the nesting season, the rapid notes heard until the last week of July.

The House Wren formerly nested in natural cavities of a tree or stump, but this bird has readily adapted to facilities provided by humans. If a nesting box is not available for its use, the resourceful bird will build a nest in an imaginative variety of nursery sites, including hollows of other hole-breeding species, in rusty tin cans, teapots, old shoes and even inside abandoned paper nests of the bald-faced hornet. Whatever the capacity of the cavity, the energetic House Wren labors mightily to bring the opening down to size by filling it – except for a narrow doorway that leads to the eggs and young – with dried twigs and grass and lining it with soft feathers, hair, wool or spider cocoons. Partners work together, stuffing material into their chosen grotto. Although sometimes nests are prepared by the male prior to the female's spring arrival, the female

has the choice of accepting the location or finding a more suitable one.

The House Wren often lays two clutches of eggs each breeding season, a brood usually consisting of six youngsters that remain in the nest for 12 to 18 days. A tireless provider, the polygamous male brings food to more than one incubating mate and assists in feeding his several families. His excess energy is devoted to the construction of other nests that may or may not be occupied.

Most House Wrens have departed their summer range by early October. In changed plumage that is grayer and darker than their breeding garb, they have flown to the congenial southern states where insect food remains abundant.

The Winter Wren, *Nannus hiemalis*, resembles the House Wren and occupies a similar range that extends farther north. When the Winter Wren holds its tail up over its back in Wren-like fashion, the tail feathers can be seen to be about one inch (2.54 cm) shorter than those of the House Wren.

The Long-billed Marsh Wren, *Telmatodytes palustris*, and the Short-billed Marsh Wren, *Cistothorus stellaris*, are both birds of Eastern North America and both construct their nests among the plants of the marsh, the former in salt water areas and the later in fresh water locations. The Cactus Wren, *Heleodytes brunneicapillus*, a bird of the southwest desert regions, fashions a gourd-shaped nesting hole in thorny cactus.

WREN, LONG-BILLED MARSH: see Wren, House

WREN, SHORT-BILLED MARSH: see Wren, House

WREN, WINTER: see Wren, House

YARRUP: see Flicker

REPTILES

A reptile is a cold-blooded, air-breathing animal which has scales and a backbone. All reptiles lay their eggs on land, as opposed to amphibian animals such as frogs and salamanders, which lay their eggs in water. Some reptiles give birth to live young which hatch from eggs inside the mother's body.

Today, reptiles represent just a small fraction of the dominant class of animals that for approximately 100 million years reigned over the prehistoric earth. About 70 millions years ago, major changes in topography and climate began to erode the former habitats and food supplies of many reptiles. The rise of the mammals may also have been a factor in their decline. The reptiles of our world today are the turtles, snakes, lizards, alligators and crocodiles.

Reptiles still occupy a diversity of habitats, including woods, parks, meadows, streams, ponds, oceans, deserts and mountains. On the ground and underneath it, in trees and in water, reptiles burrow, climb, crawl, run, slither, waddle and swim. Only the flying reptiles have disappeared completely.

The ability of the reptilian egg to survive the effects of being deposited on dry land instead of in water is a step up the evolutionary ladder. Even turtles that spend all their lives in water come ashore to lay their eggs. Reptile eggs are protected by a porous, parchment-like or leathery shell which absorbs oxygen and discharges carbon dioxide. The shell keeps the developing embryo from drying out. Not dependent upon the water for any part of their reproductive cycle, reptiles range far more widely throughout North America, and the world, than do the amphibians.

Reptiles lack an internal heating mechanism, therefore their blood must absorb heat from the surrounding air. The temperature inside their bodies then becomes the same as the temperature outside their bodies. When a reptile gets cold, it cannot eat because it lacks the heat energy necessary to operate its metabolic processes. The common reptilian behavior of basking in the sun is not just an idle pastime, but is an essential activity in maintaining life. Most reptiles spend more time raising and lowering their temperatures by seeking or avoiding the sun than they do in searching for food.

In colder latitudes of the temperate zone, reptiles hibernate for the winter. Buried underground below the frostline in rocky crevices, in hollows of their own making or in abandoned burrows of other animals, many reptiles hole up to prevent their blood from freezing in the frigid air. During this time their body temperatures may hover close to 32° (0°C), their oxygen requirements are minimal and their hearts beat so slowly that it seems all body functions have stopped. Only the returning warming rays of the springtime sun can activate these animals again.

Objects of fear and fascination, reptiles are of

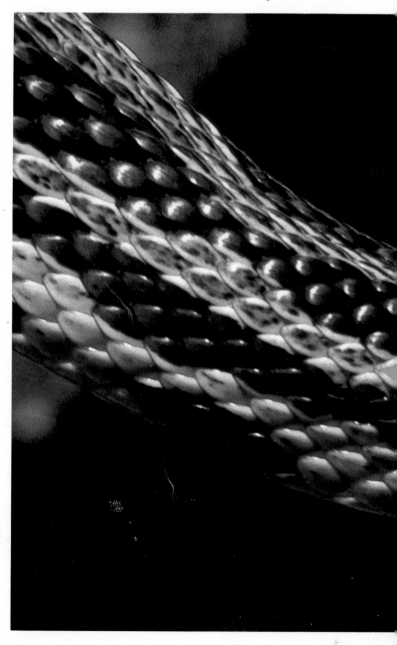

economic service to mankind, and as a result the numbers of many are threatened. The meat of many species of turtles, snakes and even lizards is relished as a delicacy. The skins of snakes, lizards, alligators and crocodiles are fashioned into expensive articles of personal adornment, while the shell of the Hawksbill Turtle is the source of the decorative tortoiseshell.

Oddly enough, the reptile that some people find the most repulsive is also the most useful: the snake. With their penchant for consuming small rodents, many snakes are better 'mousers' than either cats or dogs. In addition, as if to compensate for their venomous ways, the toxins injected by the bites of poisonous snakes also provide the medicine to cure those snake-bites. In north America only a very small proportion of snakes are actually poisonous.

Above: Hunters have been the most serious threat to the Alligator.
Below: The Fox Snake often vibrates its tail when aroused and sounds like a Rattlesnake.

SNAKES

Snakes are scaly, legless reptiles with elongated, flexible bodies. The approximately 3000 different kinds of snakes are found in all continents except Antarctica. They live in a wide assortment of environments from water to desert, from forest to meadow, from the tropics to Alaska, in trees and on and under the ground.

Considering their limitations, snakes have amazing capabilities. The absence of legs seems no handicap as they can crawl rapidly, swim, and some even climb trees. The absence of ears is compensated for by the snake's ability to 'hear' through the ground by sensing vibrations. Having no moveable eyelids results in an inblinking stare, but a thin, transparent layer of skin protects a snake's eyes.

Snakes are covered with scales, as are all reptiles. The color and arrangement of these scales gives snakes a wide assortment of patterns which can be striped, banded, blotched or spotted. Not slimy, they are smooth and dry to the touch.

In the remote and distant past, perhaps more than 100 million years ago, snakes had legs. They were then more like lizards. Somewhere in their development, for reasons not clearly understood, snakes lost their legs, developing other means of locomotion. Snakes move by using broad scaly plates which are arranged along the length of their bellies. These plates overlap like shingles on a roof. The edges of these plates catch on rough surfaces and help move the snake's body forward. On smooth surfaces, they crawl only with great difficulty.

The outside of a snake's skin is made up of thin, transparent, dead cells which are shed as the living, inner layer of the skin grows. When a snake sheds, the skin comes off in one piece, something like an unrolled stocking. Even the thin skin covering of the eyes is shed. Skin is molted throughout the life of the animal, the frequency determined by how fast the snake is growing.

Snakes feed on a large variety of animal food, swallowing it whole by slowly encompassing it with stretched-out head and body muscles. Although snakes have teeth, the teeth are not constructed for chewing but for holding the food in place while it is swallowed. Elastic muscles in its head and specially-hinged jaws allow a snake to open its mouth very wide to accommodate food that is larger around in size than the snake's own body. A small garter snake can swallow a sizeable frog.

Snakes eat irregularly, and some may go for several months to a year without food. Digestion takes place in the snake's stomach as strong stomach acids slowly dissolve the food and release the nutrients in small doses which sustain the creature for long periods.

Snakes that eat food that can escape, like mice and rats, have evolved a means of suffocating their prey. Killing their dinner by throwing several coils around the victim and squeezing it, these snakes are the constrictors. Venomous snakes do not need to constrict, but instead use their poison to subdue their prey.

Like other reptiles, snakes hatch out of eggs as miniature replicas of the adults. The female lays her eggs in a warm, damp, but well-drained spot under a stone or log. Parental guarding of the eggs is unusual; sunshine and rain provide the proper conditions for incubation. Some snakes bear live young, the female retaining the eggs in her body until they hatch.

To avoid freezing, these cold-blooded animals must hibernate in winter. In the warmer regions of the temperate zone a snake will find a root hole or a rotted stump and curl up alone for the brief cold period. In colder climates of the temperate zone, hibernation is a group practice. As the weather chills, snakes from about a one mile radius congregate. Rock crevices or southward-facing slopes are sought-out wintering quarters where dozens of snakes from a variety of species den up together. The body temperature of a hibernating snake is between 32° and 40°F (0°-4.5°C).

The darting tongue of a snake is not a stinging device. As the forked tongue is flicked in and out, it detects the odors of something to eat. The forked arrangement of the tongue provides an increased sensing surface when exposed to the air. The tongue picks up the smell of chemical particles from the ground or air, enabling it to follow the trail of a prey animal.

Although snakes are often greatly feared, most snakes are not harmful to man. Many snakes serve useful purposes ecologically and commercially. Most snakes eat animals which are considered nuisances and which are major competitors of man for his farm products. Many farmers recognize that snakes catch more mice than cats and dogs.

Snake skins provide leather for such products as handbags, shoes and belts. Most of these skins come from Asian species. The small amount of rattlesnake skins produced in the United States makes little inroad into the large international snake skin market. The rattlesnake is most appreciated for its succulent meat, which is eaten fresh in the United States or canned and shipped worldwide as a gourmet delicacy.

Snake venom is an object of horror as a potential poison to man and an object of value as a cure for snakebite. The venom is milked by hand from the hypodermic needle-like fangs of poisonous species. It is then injected into horses in progressively increasing doses until the horse builds an immunity to the venom. The immune horse blood becomes an antivenom medication, injected into victims of bites from poisonous snakes. Snake venom is also used in experimental work on nervous diseases.

In many religions, snakes are viewed as beings with mystical powers. The Hopi Indians of the southwestern United States had a Snake Dance to call down rain to water the corn crop. In this religious ceremony, rattlesnakes were captured, washed, danced with, sprinkled with corn meal and released back to the four directions. The rattlesnakes, according to Hopi belief, acted as messengers to the gods, telling the gods of the people's need for rain.

ANACONDA: see Boa, Rubber

BLACK SNAKE: see Racer

BLACK SNAKE, PILOT: see Corn Snake, Rat Snake

BLACK RACER: see Racer

BOA: see Boa, Rubber

BOA, ROSY: see Boa, Rubber

BOA, RUBBER
(Charina bottae)

The Rubber Boa is one of only two kinds of boas that live in North America. From British Columbia to southern California and eastward to Montana, Wyoming and Utah, the Rubber Boa is found in damp woodlands, grassy areas and stream beds.

The Rubber Boa is a small representative of a family of snakes that includes giants such as the Anaconda of South America which has been reported to grow to a length of 25 feet (7.5 m). The little Rubber Boa grows only to about 33 inches (83.8 cm). This Boa is a stout snake with its tail almost as blunt as its head, giving it a two-headed appearance. Dull in color, it is an unpatterned brown, gray or olive. It has rather small scales above and a row of enlarged plates on its abdomen.

Rubber Boas, like other Boas and Pythons, are primitive snakes which exhibit evidence that at a time in the greatly distant past – over 100 million years ago – snakes possessed limbs. Toward the rear end of their bodies are

Below: **The Rubber Boa is nocturnal.**

slight protrusions which represent the remains of hind legs.

Not lacking in means of locomotion or escape, the Rubber Boa is an accomplished burrower, a strong swimmer, and an adept climber. Non-poisonous, it eats small mammals, birds and lizards, killing its prey by constriction or squeezing. The numerous backward-pointing, needle-like teeth of this constrictor aid it in securing a firm grip on food that could escape. While the prey is speared by teeth, the snake wraps several coils tightly around its victim's body. When the pressure suffocates the captive, the serpent engulfs its food with a wide open mouth. Elastic muscles in the snake's jaws and body and an extra jaw hinge are stretched to encompass food that is larger around than the snake itself. Slowly, the reptile swallows its dinner.

In late summer, the Rubber Boa bears two to eight live young. The eggs hatch within the female and the 7 inch (17.8 cm) long young come crawling out.

When threatened the Rubber Boa always seeks retreat. If a hiding place is not immediately available, it will curl itself into a ball as a method of defense.

The only other boa in North America, the Rosy Boa, *Lichanura trivirgata*, can be found in dry desert brushlands of California and Arizona. The Rosy Boa, colored tannish or rosy-red, has three brown stripes down its body.

BROWN SNAKE, DeKAYE'S SNAKE
(Storeria dekayi)

Ranging throughout most of the United States, the DeKaye's Snake is found from Maine to Minnesota, south

REPTILES

Above: DeKaye's Snakes live near water.

through Florida and west through Texas. It can be found living in a wide assortment of situations, such as woodlands, marshlands, bogs, ponds, vacant lots, gardens and golf courses.

The DeKaye's Snake is small; a large specimen is only 14 inches (35.56 cm) long. Its color above is brown. A pale streak on the back is bordered with a row of black dots. Its belly is pink.

In August, about 10-20 young are born alive. The eggs are housed inside the female until the 4 inch (10.16 cm) long babies are hatched. The hatchlings are black with a white collar, altogether different in appearance from their parents.

DeKaye's Snakes hide under flat rocks, logs or trash. They eat slugs, snails, insect larvae and earthworms.

A common inhabitant of vacant lots, the DeKaye's Snake is often captured by young snake fanciers. The little snake makes an ideal pet, as it is extremely gentle and rarely bites, even when abused.

Another small brown snake, measuring 8-16 inch (20.3-40.6 cm), is the wide-ranging Red-bellied Snake, *Storeria occipitomaculata*. It has a red, orange, or yellow belly and three light spots on the nape of its neck which sometimes fuse to form a collar.

BULL SNAKE
(Pituophis melanocleucus sayi)

One of the largest North American snakes, the Bull Snake grows to almost 108 inches (274.32 cm). Bull Snakes and six other subspecies of the Pine-Gopher Snake range from Wisconsin and Indiana west to the Pacific Coast.

The Bull Snake is yellow-brown above with a row of large, rectangular dark blotches down its back and its sides.

The eggs of this snake are larger than hens' eggs. In about eight weeks at summer temperatures the 16 inch (40 cm) young hatch out of the 10-24 leathery-shelled, creamy-white eggs.

A Bull Snake's food is mostly gophers, rats, mice and rabbits, which it kills by constriction. It also eats birds' eggs, swallowing them whole and crushing them with muscles in its stomach. Able to climb and burrow, this powerful constrictor has no trouble in tracking down its food.

When a Bull Snake is approached, it will not slip quietly away, but instead will emit a loud and threatening hiss which can be heard for 50 yards (45 m). It will vibrate its tail rapidly and lunge at the intruder. Despite its intimidating behavior, it is commonly kept as a pet, as it quiets down in captivity.

Because Bull Snakes are a farmer's friend, they are rightfully protected by the food growers. A pair of these serpents can rid a barn of rats and mice. In addition, the Bull Snake's burrowing ability makes it a formidable foe of pesty gophers which pattern farmland with disruptive mounds and tunnels.

CHAINKING:
see Kingsnake, Common

COACHWHIP SNAKE
(Masticophis flagellum)

Coachwhip Snakes live in the southern United States from North Carolina west to central California. North America's fastest moving snakes, they inhabit dry open terrains like grassland prairies and desert scrub.

Growing to a length of 102 inches (259 cm), the Coachwhip is a large, quick, and high-strung snake. Its long, slender, tapering tail is covered with rather large scales that give the impression of a braided whip. Its popular name, Coachwhip, because of the appearance of its scales, is most descriptive. The typical Coachwhip has a blackish head and neck, gradually fading to brown toward the rear.

Snakes move by thrusting their bodies into patterns of wavy S-curves. A series of muscle contractions and relaxations bends the spine, and the snake gets a forward push against a rough surface. Long, thin snakes, like Coachwhips, move their bodies into longer curves than short, fat snakes; therefore, they are able to crawl faster using these graceful, undulating wiggles. Traveling at a remarkable speed for a snake, the Coachwhip moves so quickly that to catch it one must reach in front of it. Even though it is our fastest moving snake, it moves only about four miles per hour, about the speed a man walks.

Lunging swiftly forward, the Coachwhip has no trouble catching its food of rodents, insects, birds and smaller snakes. It also has an appetite for birds' eggs. If it is cornered, it will coil, vibrate its tail and strike repeatedly. When pursued, it escapes speedily by going up or down; it either climbs a tree or disappears into an animal burrow.

Many outlandish snake stories are told. One serpent species is said to arrange itself into a big circle and roll like a hoop. Some snakes are reputed to harbor their young in their mouths in time of danger. Snakes are believed by some people to sting or bite with their tongues. Ascribed to the Coachwhip is an unusual ability – a fantastic tale says the snake uses its speed to chase down victims and whip them to death with its tail.

COBRA:
see Coral Snake, Eastern

COPPERHEAD
(Agkistrodon contortex)

The Copperhead snake is one of a family of dangerously poisonous snakes called pit vipers because of their characteristic facial pits between eyes and nostrils. Copperheads are mainly found east of the Mississippi River from southern Massachusetts to northern Florida and in Texas to the Rio Grande River. They find a variety of condition inhabitable, including rocky outcroppings, edges of swamps, and cane stands along the Rio Grande.

A Copperhead can grow to a length of 53 inches (134.62 cm). It has a stout, coppery-colored body. Its back is crossed with bold chestnut or reddish-brown blotches, somewhat hourglass in shape. Its head is a uniform coppery tinge. Coiled on a northern forest floor, the Copperhead's rich chestnut pattern makes the snake resemble a small heap of brightly colored leaves.

Close observation of this viper will show that its eyes have vertical pupils, as do the eyes of other members of this venomous family. Between the Copperhead's eyes and its nostrils are two heat sensitive pits, used to locate warm-blooded prey.

Live-bearing, only about 1-14 young are born each year between August and October. Copperhead babies are born enclosed in a transparent membrane sac. The young have bright sulphur yellow tails which they twitch to lure their prey.

Copperheads feed on small rodents,

Below: **The Bullsnake is a powerful snake.**

REPTILES

lizards, frogs and large caterpillars. Poisonous snakes use their venom to kill their prey before they eat it. Injecting poison is an efficient feeding technique which eliminates the need for the snake to kill its prey by squeezing or constriction.

Copperheads have curved-back retractable hollow fangs that act as hypodermic needles and deliver the poisonous injection. When not needed, the fangs are folded back, but when the snake must strike, the lethal instruments are swung forward.

The Copperhead is inoffensive if undisturbed. Its bite is painful, although rarely fatal to adults. It is more dangerous to children, whose bodyweight is less. The venom keeps blood from clotting and aggravates internal bleeding.

CORAL SNAKE, ARIZONA:
see Coral Snake, Eastern

CORAL SNAKE, EASTERN
(Micrurus fulvius)

Coral Snakes are members of a family which includes the highly venomous Cobras, Kraits, Mambas, Tai-pans, and Sea Snakes. Only two members of this deadly family are found in the United States, the Eastern Coral Snake and the Arizona Coral Snake (*Micruroides euryxanthus*).

The Eastern Coral Snake lives in the southern United States from North Carolina to Florida and west to Texas in moist hummocks near ponds and streams and in rocky hillsides and canyons. The Arizona Coral Snake has a much smaller range confined to Arizona and New Mexico.

The Eastern Coral Snake grows to a length of 47 inches (119.38 cm). It is brilliantly colored with broad alternating bands of red and black, separated by narrow yellow rings. The rings go entirely around the body. The red rings have black spots. The snout is black and blunt with a yellow ring behind each eye.

One of the deadliest snakes in North America, Coral Snakes are gentle and secretive. Their burrowing habits permit them to live in residential neighborhoods where their docile natures usually cause no trouble. But one should not be deceived by their retiring ways, as a bite from this venomous serpent can mean a painful death. Its neurotoxin dissolves cell tissue, para-lyzes nerves, damages blood cells, and ruptures walls of capillaries.

Coral Snakes are different than other poisonous snakes. Unlike the venomous pit vipers, like rattlesnakes whose fangs retract, the enlarged fangs of the Coral Snake are fixed in position on the front part of the upper jaw and cannot be folded back.

Several harmless snakes have colors which mimic the poisonous Coral Snake – the Scarlet Snake and the Scarlet Kingsnake. In nature, when a species looks like another species which has more highly developed defense mechanisms such as poison, the less protected animal benefits from the resemblance. Confused with the more offensive individual, it is left alone.

CORN SNAKE
(Elaphe guttata)

One of the most beautifully colored and patterned snakes in the United States, the Corn Snake lives from New Jersey to Florida and west to Texas and eastern New Mexico.

Below: **A Copperhead has just delivered her young, born live and encased in membrane sacs. They will mature in 2 to 3 years.**

Above: A juvenile Corn Snake, a tree climber.   *Below:* The colorfully striped Coral Snake often hides under dead leaves.

REPTILES

Corn Snakes can grow to a length of 72 inches (182.88 cm). This richly colored species is reddish-yellow with a series of large coppery-crimson blotches outlined with black arranged down its length. The abdomen is marked with large squarish black patterns which become stripes under the tail.

The color of the crimson blotches on the back of the Corn Snake resembles the color of the differently shaped patterns of the poisonous Copperhead snake. Where their ranges overlap, the harmless Corn Snake is sometimes mistaken for the poisonous Copperhead. When this mistake in identity occurs, the corn snake is often killed.

Corn snakes are found in wooded groves and meadowlands, but their most productive hunting grounds are woodlots, barnyards, and abandoned houses. There, especially in barns and corncribs, the Corn Snake easily can find the mice, rats and birds which make up its diet. Its penchant for exploring corn piles in search of food gives one explanation for its common name.

Another reason for the Corn Snake's popular name is the similarity of its colors and pattern to certain species of Indian corn. For whatever reason it received its name, the Corn Snake's appetite for rodents, which

are among man's chief competitors for food, clearly illustrates how snakes are often beneficial to man.

The Corn Snake is closely related to snakes known as rat snakes, names appropriately bestowed because of their penchant for consuming rodents. The Rat Snake or Pilot Black Snake, *Elaphe obsoleta*, often colored black, ranges widely from Ontario south to Florida, west to Texas and north to Minnesota and Michigan. The Fox Snake, *Elaphe vulpina*, lives in the Great Lakes region, west to Nebraska and South Dakota. Because of its bold chocolate-brown patches, the Fox Snake, like the Corn Snake, is often mistaken for the poisonous Copperhead, *Agkistrodon contortrix*, and killed.

COTTONMOUTH; WATER MOCCASIN
(Agkistrodon piscivorus)

The Cottonmouth is a poisonous aquatic snake, closely related to the Copperhead and a member of the same pit viper snake family. The Cottonmouth infests the lagoons and waterways of the southeastern United States where it feeds extensively on fish.

One of the deadliest of North American vipers, the average Water Moccasin is about 48 inches (121.92 cm) long, although some grow to 74

inches (187.96 cm). Its body is stout and heavy with a flat-topped chunky head that is noticeably wider than its neck. Decidedly unattractive in color, the Cottonmouth is dull olive with indistinct, wide, blackish blotches on its back, but boldly defined on its sides.

Live bearing, female Moccasins give birth every other year in August or September to 1-15 young. Young Cottonmouths resemble the richly colored Copperheads in pattern, but they darken as they age.

People are rightly fearful and cautious near the Water Moccasin. Its bite is far more serious than that of the Copperhead and can be fatal. Bites by this viper are often followed by the death of tissue around the bitten area. This is caused by digestive enzymes in the snake's venom and by damage to the local blood supply. A Cottonmouth attack often results in nothing more than a scar, but sometimes the entire affected digit or limb must be amputated.

When a Cottonmouth feels threatened, it rears up and repeatedly opens its wide mouth, displaying the conspicuous white 'cotton' lining. It is from this that the Cottonmouth gets its common name.

DeKAYE'S SNAKE: see Brown Snake

FOX SNAKE: see Corn Snake

GARTER SNAKE, BUTLER'S: see Garter Snake, Common

GARTER SNAKE, COMMON (Thamnophis sirtalis)

The Common Garter Snake can rightly be described as the most abundant snake in North America. Its range is from the Atlantic to the Pacific Coast and all regions in between, except the deserts of the southwest. Favoring wet conditions, the Common Garter Snake can be found in meadows, marshes, irrigation and drainage ditches, woodlands, farms and parks. Several species of Garter Snakes are recognized.

Below: **A threatened Cottonmouth is deadly.**

Garter Snakes can grow to be 51 inches (129.54 cm) long. The Common Garter Snake shows a high degree of variation in pattern and color. Typically, it is dark brown above with three yellowish stripes down its length. Between the stripes are two rows of alternating black spots. The color of the snake underneath is greenish or yellow.

The continued survival and prevalence of the Common Garter Snake seems to be secure, even when other species are in danger of extinction. Their tenacity for endurance is due to several reasons. This common reptile brings forth extremely large broods of young. Live-bearing, it gives birth to 7-85 hatchlings during June through August. The young feed readily on easily available food such as earthworms, as well as on frogs and salamanders. The babies grow rapidly and are very secretive. They do not need to prowl in dangerous zones to hunt out their food, as do rodent-eating serpents.

Garter Snakes can tolerate colder temperatures than can other snakes. In the south, they may be active all year round while in the north, they hibernate in huge congregations to insure their winter survival.

When a Garter Snake is first captured, it will bite and give off a foul-smelling, musky odor, but it tames quickly and soon becomes a docile pet.

Other species of garter snakes in North America include Butler's Garter Snake, *Thamnophis butleri*, which lives in Ontario, Michigan, Indiana, Ohio and Wisconsin; Western Aquatic Garter Snake, *Thamnophis couchi*, found in coastal California and southwestern Oregon; Western Terrestrial Garter Snake, *Thamnophis elegans*, inhabiting southwest Manitoba and southern British Columbia, southward into Mexico; and Plains Garter Snake, *Thamnophis radix*, a resident of the Great Plains to the Rocky Mountains.

The Eastern Ribbon Snake, *Thamnophis sauritus*, found east of the Mississippi River, is a slender streamlined garter snake with three well-defined stripes down the length of its body. Feeding on frogs, salamanders, and small fish, the Ribbon Snake is semi-aquatic and glides smoothly across the water's surface.

GARTER SNAKE, PLAINS:
see Garter Snake, Common

GARTER SNAKE, WESTERN AQUATIC:
see Garter Snake, Common

GARTER SNAKE, WESTERN TERRESTRIAL:
see Garter Snake, Common

GOPHER SNAKE:
see Indigo Snake

HOGNOSE SNAKE, COMMON
(Heterodon platyrhinos)

Of the three kinds of Hognose Snakes in the United States, the Eastern or Common Hognose has the widest range. The Common Hognose occurs from southern New England to the Missouri River, south through Florida, and west into Texas.

The Common Hognose Snake reaches a maximum length of 46 inches (116.84 cm). Its coloration varies widely from individual to individual. It may be pale brownish, yellow, or gray, with irregular, darker blotches on the back. The sides and the abdomen are thickly adorned with black dots.

Hognose Snakes get their names from the shape of their sharply-upturned, shovel-like snouts. This useful adaptation enables the snake to burrow into the ground to escape hot or cold conditions. These shovel-nosed snakes live entirely on the ground where with a sharpened sense of smell they can find their food even if it is buried. Not a constrictor, the Hognose eats toads, snakes, and reptile eggs which are captured in the snake's jaw.

The Hognose Snake is sometimes erroneously called a 'Puff Adder,' which is a deadly poisonous African species. This mistaken name is given due to the Hognose's defensive display. When disturbed, it flattens, inflates, and hoods the front part of its

Below: **A Common Garter Snake.**

Above: Two views of a Hognose emphasize its distinctly pale-colored belly.
Right: The Indigo is an egg-laying snake.

body, raising up in Cobra fashion. The Hognose then emits a hissing sound which resembles the sound of the venomous Puff Adder, the hiss designed to discourage an intruder.

If the Hognose finds that its accomplished imitation of a poisonous snake fails to ward off a possible enemy, it resorts to an even more dramatic ploy. Like an opposum, it plays dead. With mouth agape and tongue hanging out, it rolls over and feigns death. It persists in this lifeless attitude even if it is handled. If the 'corpse' is replaced right side up, it will roll over and resume its imitation of death, a convincing actor but not a very bright one.

Armed with so many highly developed protective tricks, the Hognose Snake does not need to use biting as a means of defense. It rarely bites people.

The Southern Hognose Snake, *Heterodon simus*, smaller than the Common Hognose, lives in open dry sandy areas of North Carolina, Florida and Mississippi. It, too, displays the protective behavior of feigning death so as not to appear an enticing meal to a hungry predator.

HOGNOSE SNAKE, EASTERN:
see **Hognose Snake, Common**

HOGNOSE SNAKE, SOUTHERN:
see **Hognose Snake, Common**

INDIGO SNAKE
(Drymarchon corais)

The Indigo Snake lives in tropical hummocks and dry grasslands adjacent to water from the Carolinas to Florida and west to Texas. In the west, it favors sandy flats where gopher burrows are abundant.

One of the largest North American snakes, the Indigo Snake may reach a length of 103 inches (263 cm). Heavy-bodied, it is a shiny blue-black above and below, with its chin and the sides of its head colored cream or red.

Indigo Snakes eat small mammals, birds, frogs, turtles and other snakes. Not a constrictor, this reptile immobilizes its prey with its jaws. While the food is being swallowed, it is held firmly to the ground under the weight of a portion of the snake's body.

Another name for the Indigo Snake is Gopher Snake. The name 'Gopher Snake' comes from the reptile's habit of disappearing into the burrow of a Gopher Tortoise when pursued. The practice of gassing tortoise burrows to rid the terrain of Gopher Tortoises kills not only the turtles but also the Indigo Snake who retreats to the burrows for protection. Because of this practice, the Indigo Snake is decreasing in numbers.

KINGSNAKE, CHAIN:
see **Kingsnake, Common**

KINGSNAKE, COMMON; CHAIN KINGSNAKE
(Lampropeltis getalus)

The best known Kingsnake in the United States is the Common Kingsnake or the Chain Kingsnake. The Chain King occurs in greatly diverse habitats, covering a wide range. The Common Kingsnake lives in swamps, marshes, woodlands, prairies and deserts from southern New Jersey through Florida and west to the Mississippi River. Other varieties extend westward to the Pacific Coast.

Highly variable in pattern, the Common Kingsnake is often a lustrous, pitch black with narrow white or yellow crossbands on the back, forming a chain-like pattern. It is this pattern which gives this snake one of its popular names, Chain King. Sometimes on the back there are stripes, blotches, or speckles. The abdomens of Common Kingsnakes range from plain white to plain black, or can be heavily blotched. These snakes can grow to 82 inches (91.4 cm) in length.

The Kingsnake usually travels in early morning or late afternoon, but in warm summer, it travels at night. This snake is a strong constrictor. It eats mice, lizards, birds and eggs, but its favorite food is other snakes. It is from this penchant for devouring other snake species that the Kingsnake gets its name. Even poisonous snakes like Rattlesnakes, Copperheads, and

Coral Snakes do not escape the Kingsnake's voracious appetite, although the Kingsnake is immune to their venoms.

By stretching out muscles down its entire length, a Kingsnake can eat a snake its own size. After such a hearty dinner, the well-fed reptile can go for many months without another meal.

The Kingsnake serves man in several ways. As well as eating rodents, as do many other species, the Kingsnake devours other snakes that may be dangerous. Despite its pugnacious nature toward other serpents, it is entirely harmless to man. It rarely bites in captivity, but does emit an unpleasant, musky odor and an angry hiss when disturbed.

The Prairie Kingsnake, *Lampropeltis calligaster*, lives in open fields and farmlands from Maryland south to northern Florida and west to Nebraska and Texas. A secretive species, the Prairie Kingsnake often burrows under several inches of loose soil or curls up in an abandoned animal excavation.

**KINGSNAKE, PRAIRIE:
see Kingsnake, Common**

**KINGSNAKE, SCARLET:
see Coral Snake, Eastern**

**KRAIT:
see Coral Snake, Eastern**

**MAMBA:
see Coral Snake, Eastern**

**MILK SNAKE
(Lampropeltis triangulum)**

Milk Snakes range widely from Maine west to Wisconsin and Minnesota, and south through most of the United States east of the Rocky Mountains. As is expected for such a wide range, Milk Snakes are found in varied habitats from bottomland to mountains, from pine forests to deciduous woodlands, from farmlands to suburban areas.

Richly colored, Milk Snakes are gray or tan with brown to reddish-brown black-bordered blotches down

Above: **The large, terrestrial Kingsnake eats venomous snakes, its favorite food.**

their backs and sides. Often mistaken for the poisonous Copperhead snake because of its coppery-chestnut blotches, the Milk Snake is killed as a harmful reptile.

The Milk Snake can grow to a length of 78 inches (198.12 cm).

The explanation of how the Milk Snake got its common name is an illustration of one of the many preposterous beliefs held about snakes. A Milk Snake's food is chiefly rats and mice, which it kills by constriction. Often the snake will follow its prey into barns. Not giving this useful reptile its earned credit, it was commonly and mistakenly thought that the snake was entering the barn to milk the cows, taking enormous amounts of milk in the process. Actually, a snake cannot possibly milk a cow, nor can it retain even a small quantity of milk.

Another myth that exists about the Milk Snake is that if one is killed, its mate will return to avenge it.

REPTILES

PIT VIPER:
see Copperhead; Rattlesnake,
Eastern Diamondback

'PUFF ADDER':
see Hognose Snake, Common

PYTHON: see Boa, Rubber

RACER; BLACK RACER; BLACK SNAKE
(Coluber constrictor)

Racers are among the most common snakes living in the United States. In every state but Alaska, Racers inhabit fields, grasslands and rocky hillsides.

Sometimes known as the Black Snake, sometimes as the Black Racer, its names describe its appearance and speed. A Racer is shiny black, its satiny scales giving off a gun-barrel luster. On the chin is a patch of white. Its underparts are uniformly dark or medium gray. A large Black Racer will grow to 72 inches (182.88 cm) long.

The Black Racer travels with surprising rapidity over ground or through bush in search of prey. It eats a wide assortment of food, dining on other snakes, rats, mice, rabbits, moles, frogs, birds, birds' eggs and insects. In spite of its scientific name, *Coluber constrictor*, the Racer does not kill its food by constriction. Instead it traps its food under the weight of its body while holding it firmly by its needle-like teeth.

Racers lay 5-28 leathery eggs that appear rough as if covered with salt. Its favorite nesting sites are moist, decaying wood, under rocks or in small tunnels dug by another animal. Females may, at times, deposit their eggs in a common nest.

In cold temperatures, Racers often congregate in large numbers, joining other species to hibernate in hollows in rocky hillsides. There they spend the winter coiled in a mass, reducing the amount of body surface exposed to the frigid air.

When threatened, the Racer can make a buzzing noise with the tip of its tail by vibrating it in dry leaves. Tail vibration is a warning technique not confined exclusively to rattlesnakes. Many snakes vibrate their tails to warn off potential enemies.

RAT SNAKE
(Elaphe obsoleta)

Rat Snakes are snakes which live in a diversity of habitats from forest to farmland, from old field to barnyard, and from wet to arid conditions. They range from Ontario south through Florida, west to Texas, and north to Minnesota and Michigan. They are powerful constrictors and can grow to 101 inches (256.5 cm) in length.

There are several subspecies of Rat Snakes, all quite sensationally patterned and all seemingly unrelated. Related kinds can be plain or striped or blotched. Although the adults appear so different, the pattern of the young Rat Snakes are similar. All the young are vividly blotched.

The most widely distributed Rat Snake is the Black Rat Snake or Pilot Black Snake. Adults are usually glossy black with traces of white between the scales. The adults occasionally retain traces of the juvenile blotches.

Rat Snakes hunt at night during the summer and during the day in spring and fall, probably choosing their hunting hours based on a comfortable temperature range. They are adept

Below: **Rarely seen in the open during the day, Milk Snakes hide under logs or debris.**

climbers, searching in trees and abandoned buildings for birds' eggs, birds and mice. A strong constrictor, the Rat Snake subdues its prey by coiling part of its long, muscular body around its victim, and squeezing. The pressure finally suffocates the prey animal. Once the food is dead, the snake maneuvers its body so that its mouth can encompass its dinner. Opening its mouth very wide by using elastic hinged jaws, the Rat Snake slowly swallows its food whole.

The Rat Snake got the name of Pilot Black Snake because of an erroneous understanding of its wintering behavior. In northern areas, Rat Snakes often share their hibernating quarters with other species, including Copperheads and Timber Rattlesnakes. It was thought that the Pilot Black Snake warned the slower rattlesnake of danger, and led it to a safe retreat.

RAT SNAKE, BLACK:
see Rat Snake

RATTLESNAKE, DIAMONDBACK:
see Rattlesnake, Eastern Diamondback

RATTLESNAKE, EASTERN DIAMONDBACK
(Crotalus adamanteus)

The Eastern Diamondback Rattlesnake is the largest rattlesnake in the United States and one of the largest poisonous snakes in the world. It ranges from the coastal region of North Carolina south through Florida and westward into Southern Mississippi and Louisiana.

A similar western species, the Western Diamondback Rattlesnake (Crotalus atrox) ranges from southeastern California eastward to central Arkansas and south into New Mexico.

The Eastern Diamondback lives in dry pine woods and abandoned farmlands where it hunts rodents and sometimes lizards. Growing to a length of 96 inches (243.84 cm), this venomous reptile is heavy bodied with a large head much wider than its neck. Its back is patterned with light-bordered dark diamond-shaped blotches. There are two light lines on the sides of its face.

Rattlesnakes have vertical pupils in their eyes and a small pit on the sides of their faces, between the eyes and the nostrils. These pits are heat sensing devices and those snakes which have them are called pit vipers.

When disturbed, the Rattlesnake stands its ground, lifts its head high and rattles its coils as a warning to an intruder to stay away. The rattles, a series of horny joints at the end of the snake's tail, make a hissing or buzzing sound. Tail vibrating is a common nervous habit of many snakes, not just rattlesnakes. This audible defensive technique was developed to avoid being accidently trampled.

It is erroneously believed that counting the number of rattles in a rattlesnake's tail will tell the snake's age. Rattlesnakes do not add a rattle for every year of their lives, but rather add one for every time they shed their skins. Skin-shedding may occur several times a year, depending upon how fast the snake is growing.

Through retractable fangs that move forward when needed, Diamondbacks are capable of inflicting a fatal bite. Rattlesnakes account for most of the snakebites in the United

Below: **Western Yellow-bellied Racers (***Coluber constrictor***) are agile climbers.**

Above: Eastern Diamondback Rattlesnakes, the most poisonous in North America, entwined in a combat dance.

States, and for 90 percent of the fatalities. These snakes do not always rattle before striking, which makes them especially dangerous.

Because of man's destruction of Diamondback retreats in stumpholes and tortoise burrows, and because of the collection of this snake for its venom, its meat and its leather, the numbers of this poisonous viper have been greatly reduced.

The common Prairie Rattlesnake, *Crotalus confluentus*, may be identified by a series of rounded and well separated blotches on its back, while the Pacific Rattlesnake, *Crotalus*

oregonus, has a similar pattern. Both of these rattlesnakes range from Utah northward, extending slightly over the boundary of the United States.

The Pigmy Rattlesnake, *Sistrurus miliaruis*, also called the Ground Rattlesnake, is common in the southeast portion of the United States. Its total length is about 20 inches (50.8 cm) and its rattle is so tiny it can be heard over only a few feet. Prompt treatment of a Pigmy Rattlesnake bite can render the bite harmless.

RATTLESNAKE, GROUND: see Rattlesnake, Eastern Diamondback

RATTLESNAKE, HORNED: see Sidewinder

RATTLESNAKE, PACIFIC: see Rattlesnake, Eastern Diamondback

RATTLESNAKE, PIGMY: see Rattlesnake, Eastern Diamondback

RATTLESNAKE, PRAIRIE: see Rattlesnake, Eastern Diamondback

RATTLESNAKE, TIMBER (Crotalus horridus)

The Timber Rattlesnake is one of the most beautiful rattlesnakes in the United States and the only rattlesnake that occurs in the Northeast. It and the Copperhead are the only two poisonous snakes of the northeastern area. Timber Rattlers can be found from southwestern Maine to north Florida, west to southeastern Minnesota and central Texas.

Growing to a length of 74 inches (187.95 cm), the Timber Rattlesnake shows a difference in coloration between the sexes. The males are often a rich, velvety black, lacking the banded pattern of the females. The females are sulphur yellow, adorned with irregular brownish transverse bands.

In remote, wooded, rocky hillsides in the North, and in uninhabited, swampy areas in the South, the Timber Rattlesnake is most at home. Every other year, females give birth to 5-17 young which are about 12 inches long (30.48 cm). Young are born with only one segment of their rattles. More sections are added as the snakes grow. Each time the rattlesnake sheds its skin another horny segment develops at the tip of its tail. Rattlesnakes vibrate their tails and produce a buzzing sound as a means of warning. The noise keeps the snake from being trampled and discourages a would-be assailant from grappling with the snake.

The Timber Rattlesnake spends much of its time coiled up in wait for prey. Poised for action, it strikes swiftly and its poison-laden fangs inject their contents into the snake's dinner of a squirrel, mouse, chipmunk or small bird.

Where temperatures are coldest, Timber Rattlesnakes congregate in large numbers near their rocky den sites. Winter hibernating quarters are shared with several other species, like Rat Snakes and Copperheads.

Due to man's encroachment into the habitats of a snake which prefers uninhabited areas, the Timber Rattler's numbers are decreasing.

RATTLESNAKE, WESTERN DIAMONDBACK: see Rattlesnake, Eastern Diamondback

RED-BELLIED SNAKE: see Brown Snake

Top: **An Eastern Diamondback Rattler.**

Above: **A Timber Rattler, typically coiled.**

RIBBON SNAKE: see Garter Snake, Common

RIBBON SNAKE, EASTERN: see Garter Snake, Common

RINGNECK SNAKE (Diadophis punctatus)

Ringneck Snakes are secretive little reptiles, seldom growing to a length of 24 inches (60.96 cm). These snakes can be found in widely varied habitats from Nova Scotia to the Florida Keys and west to the Pacific coast.

Ringneck Snakes have uniform gray, olive or brownish backs. They are dull in color and slender in appearance. The distinctive markings of this thin snake is its yellow or orange neck ring and its bright yellow or red belly.

Ringneck Snakes like to hide under flat stones or under the loose bark of fallen trees. They eat the young of other small snakes. Young lizards, salamanders and earthworms are also on their menu.

REPTILES

When threatened, Ringneck Snakes exhibit unusual defensive behavior. In an attempt to intimidate an enemy, they curl their tails upward to display their bright red abdominal hue. If that display is ineffective, they can also emit a foul-smelling substance from an opening at the base of their tails.

Two other species of Ringneck Snakes inhabit North America: *Diadophis regulis* occurs from Illinois to Arizona and southward to Vera Cruz, while *Diadophis amabilis*, a western reptile, may be found from Texas to the Pacific coast. The number of scale rows and the number of plates on the abdomen are used as distinguishing characteristics to separate the species.

SCARLET SNAKE
(Cemophora coccinea)

The Scarlet Snake is a rather small, brightly colored snake whose range is from southern New Jersey to Florida and west to south Texas. It grows to about 30 inches (76.2 cm).

The non-poisonous Scarlet Snake is often confused with a venomous species of the southeastern United States, the Coral Snake (*Elaps fulvius*). Both of these snakes are brilliantly colored with the same hues, but the arrangement of their banded patterns differs. The Scarlet Snake has a pattern of broad scarlet rings, separated by narrower yellow rings that are bordered on each side with even narrower bands of black. The top of the head of the Scarlet Snake and the tip of its snout are red. It has a glistening, unpatterned white or yellow belly.

The deadly Coral Snake has alternate, wide, black and red rings, each ring bordered by a narrow band of yellow. Unlike the Scarlet Snake, these rings encircle the Coral Snake's body. The Coral Snake's snout is black, whereas the snout of the Scarlet Snake is red.

A bite from the fangs of the Coral Snake is deadly, while a bite from the Scarlet Snake is harmless. When the

Left: **A Pacific Ringneck in defensive posture.**

Coral Snake delivers its venom, the puncture appears as two pinpoints where its fangs broke the skin. A bite from the non-poisonous Scarlet Snake appears as a series of tiny pinpricks, imitating the pattern of the snake's teeth.

The Scarlet Snake is secretive in its behavior. It burrows under wood piles or stones and is rarely seen during the day. In June, it lays 3-8 eggs. The 6 inch (15 cm) long young hatch in late summer.

A constrictor, the Scarlet Snake eats lizards, small snakes and young mice which it kills by wrapping a few coils of its body around its victim and squeezing. It prefers to eat the eggs of reptiles and has been known to devour even its own eggs.

SEA SNAKE:
see Coral Snake, Eastern

SIDEWINDER, HORNED RATTLESNAKE
(Crotalus cerastes)

One of the smallest rattlesnakes in the United States, the Sidewinder lives in sandy desert flatlands in southern Nevada, adjacent California, and southwestern Utah.

The poisonous Sidewinder can grow to a length of 32 inches (81.28 cm). It is superbly adapted to its desert surroundings, and its color blends in perfectly with its habitat. It is pale-shaded cream, gray, or pink without a conspicuous pattern. The Sidewinder is sometimes called the Horned Rattler because of the hornlike projection over each eye.

Like all desert vipers, the Sidewinder burrows into the loose sand during the day to escape the heat of the sun. It may also shelter in animal burrows or underbrush. By a remarkable series of wave-like motions traveling the length of the body, the snake sinks into the sand or works the sand over its back. It travels quickly, about two miles an hour, over the loosely packed surface by 'sidewinding,' a crawling process which uses friction and keeps the snake from slipping.

The Sidewinder feeds on pocket mice, kangaroo rats and lizards which it kills with a venomous injection. The poison is delivered through hollow fangs which retract when not in use and fold forward when the lethal work needs to be done.

To escape an enemy, the Sidewinder takes maximum advantage of its protective coloration. It merely 'freezes' if an assailant is in pursuit. When the snake stops moving, it can no longer be seen because its hues blend in so well with the desert sands.

TAIPAN:
see Coral Snake, Eastern

VIPER:
see Copperhead; Cottonmouth; Rattlesnake, Eastern Diamondback; Sidewinder

WATER MOCCASIN:
see Cottonmouth; Water Snake, Northern

WATER SNAKE, NORTHERN
(Natrix sipedon)

Water Snakes and their close relatives can be found in lakes, streams and freshwater marshes. They live in northern and eastern United States down to Florida and west to Texas.

Water Snakes grow to about 53 inches (134.6 cm) in length. They are light brown with dark brown, dingy blotches on the back and sides. As the snake ages, the pattern darkens to black; the young are most vividly colored.

In late summer 16 to 44 young are born alive, hatching from eggs that were carried inside the female. The family separates immediately, the young shifting for themselves.

Water Snakes bask on rocks or bushes near ponds and streams, and drop into the water at the slightest provocation. Strong swimmers, active day and night, they feed on aquatic animals and vegetation. Fish, frogs, tadpoles, salamanders, turtles and insects are captured by pursuit and killed by being swallowed whole.

If a Water Snake is cornered, it will flatten its body, give off an unpleasant odor, lunge repeatedly at the intruder and bite readily. Bites from a Water Snake bleed freely because of the anticoagulant in the snake's saliva.

Water Snakes are non-poisonous, but they are often mistaken for the venomous Water Moccasin. The Water Moccasin's range is confined to the southern United States, but because it is a serpent of freshwater haunts like the Water Snake, the two are often confused even where their ranges do not overlap. The mistake is usually fatal to the Water Snake; it is killed by people who think it is a Moccasin.

Below: A Northern Brown Water Snake, often seen basking near shores where it finds its food.

CROCODILIANS

Crocodilians are the largest animals among the reptiles, heirs of the giant reptiles that inhabited the earth 70 to 140 million years ago, and descended from even more primitive creatures, called thecodonts, which live 230 million years ago.

Alligators, crocodiles, caimans and gavials comprise the zoological order of crocodilians. Of these, only alligators and crocodiles are found in North America, alligators in swamps and bogs of the southeastern United States and crocodiles in coastal waters of southern Florida.

Nearly all crocodilians live in the tropics or in warm temperate areas. The balmy climate maintains their body heat, since crocodilians, like all reptiles, are cold-blooded, and lack the internal mechanism for warming themselves. Temperatures that are either too high or too low cannot be tolerated by these animals, so to avoid the heat of the noonday sun, they retire to the comfort of the shade, and if it is still too warm, they wallow in the cooler water.

Crocodilians, with a body plan well suited for a watery habitat, live in wetter areas than do most other reptiles, never venturing far from their swamp or river home. Five-clawed front feet and four-clawed, longer back feet are webbed and are used for slow paddling and balance when swimming. For speed in chasing prey in water, an alligator or crocodile mobilizes its huge tail in vigorous undulations that move the reptile swiftly forward.

Appearing as a felled tree trunk, well hidden in the murky water among the thick plant growth, a croco-dilian waits quietly for its prey of duck, fish or other unsuspecting animal to happen by. Crocodilians have voracious appetites, snapping up their meal with a sudden plunge of powerful jaws, and often holding the victim underwater to drown it. A special air passage from the nostrils, located on the tip of the snout, leads to the throat, allowing the crocodilian to breathe with only its nose sticking out of water. A valve closes off a portion of the throat, enabling the reptile to open its mouth underwater without flooding its respiratory passages, and similar valves keep water out of ear openings.

The crocodilian's dagger-shaped teeth are designed for grabbing and holding, but not for chewing. Large prey is swallowed in the reptile's big throat, but if the meal is too large to be consumed in one piece, the food is twisted apart into more manageable, gulp-sized portions.

With eyes bulging from their head for a panoramic view, crocodilians have a third eyelid, a see-through membrane that acts as a cover and protects the eye underwater.

Alligators and crocodiles are often confused with one another, as they are similar in appearance, although their habitat preference differs and some of their physical characteristics are dissimilar. Crocodiles live in coastal areas and salt marshes, while alligators are found in freshwater rivers, lakes and

Below: **Motionless as it awaits its prey, the American Alligator is well camouflaged in swampy waters.**

swamps. Crocodiles are thinner and more agile than alligators and they have narrower heads and snouts. The crocodile has a fourth tooth on each side of the lower jaw that overlaps the upper jaw and is visible when the mouth is closed. These same teeth of the alligator are also enlarged, but they are not exposed when the mouth is shut. Crocodile young are gray with black crossbars; alligator young are black with yellow crossbars.

All crocodilians lay eggs, the nests constructed by the female and guarded until the young emerge. Heat from the sun and the warmth of the decomposing plant material covering the eggs promotes the development of the young within. Immediately upon hatching, the babies can care for themselves, although at this vulnerable new-born period, the little crocodilians may become food for other animals.

Crocodilians are covered with scaly skin, the scales not overlapping like those on snakes. Small bony plates are imbedded in some of the scales, especially those on the back, which accounts for the armored appearance of these reptiles. The belly lacks these bony fortifiers, therefore making it excellent leather for shoes, handbags, belts, and wallets. Overhunting for their quality hides, destruction of their habitats and killing them when they are viewed as a menace to other animals and man have reduced crocodilian numbers. Conservation laws now protect alligators and crocodiles, the alligator protected in every state where it occurs except Texas.

ALLIGATOR, AMERICAN
(Alligator mississippiensis)

The American Alligator, one of the seven species of the family Alligator-idae, is found in the lowlands and swamps of the southeastern United States. A cold-blooded animal, its habitat is partly determined by temperature, which limits its northern range to about 35° north latitude.

The male Alligator can grow to a length of 12 feet (3.6 m) and weigh up to 550 pounds (250 kg). Females are typically smaller and rarely measure

Below: **Alligators dig deep holes which furnish water for other animals during droughts.**

more than 9 feet (2.7 m) or weigh more than 160 pounds (73 kg).

The American Alligator has a broader, shorter head than the true crocodiles found on other continents. The skin of the alligator is tough, thick and rough and is colored a dark gray or olive. Its jaw is set with sharp teeth, 19-20 on each side. Its eyes and nostrils sit high on its snout so that alligators can see and breathe while their bodies are submerged. Their short, stocky legs are used for walking. In the water, alligators swim by sweeping their powerful tails from side to side.

Alligators spend much of their time lying on the banks of streams in the sun or swimming underwater with only the tops of their heads showing. They feed on various kinds of aquatic and terrestrial animals, including fish, snakes, frogs, turtles and small mammals. Some large males have been known to attack dogs or cattle. Alligators frequently drag their victims into the water and drown them before they either tear them apart or swallow them whole.

During the summer mating season, the male utters loud calls to attract the females. There are frequent clashes between males and many are injured. Females build nests near the water's edge using branches and decaying vegetation. The nest is almost 3 feet (1.1 m) high and more than 6 feet

(2.2 m) in length. After laying about 30-40 eggs the female remains nearby to guard them throughout the incubation period. The heat from the decaying vegetation contributes to the incubation. The eggs are white and slightly larger than hen's eggs. The shells are hard. When first hatched, the young alligators are about 9 inches (22.5 cm) long. Many remain with the mother until the following spring.

In winter, alligators frequently bury themselves in mud, go into deep holes or remain resting with most of their bodies submerged.

Even the largest Alligators rarely attack human beings. They are less active and aggressive than the crocodiles. Their jaws can easily be held shut by a grown man, and they have occasionally been hunted and captured this way without weapons. The great jaw power of all the Crocodilians works toward closing the jaws, not opening them.

CROCODILE, AMERICAN (Crocodylus acutus)

The American Crocodile lives in the brakish bogs and mangrove swamps of the extreme coastal areas of southern Florida and the Florida Keys.

Crocodiles and alligators are often confused with one another, as they belong to the same family and look somewhat alike. The long, slender, narrow snout of the crocodile distinguishes it from the American Alligator, which has a short, blunt snout. Crocodiles have four large teeth on each side of their bottom jaws which are visible when their mouths are closed. In alligators, these teeth cannot be seen when the reptile's mouth is unopened.

Below: **The yellowish cross bands on this young Alligator will obscure with age.**

The American Crocodile grows from 7-15 feet (2.1-4.6 m), not as large as the alligator. The crocodile is gray-green, or gray-brown with dark cross-bands on its back and tail. The cross-bars grow more obscure as the reptile ages. Its scaly covering is like thick-plated armor.

In early May, the female crocodile constructs a mounded nest of soil, sand and rotting debris. In it she lays 35-50 eggs. The warmth of the decaying vegetation with which the nest is covered incubates the eggs, while the mother remains nearby, keeping a careful vigil. The young hatch out in early August, about 9 inches (22.9 cm) long.

The Crocodile is a vicious adversary and strong fighter, but the female exhibits surprising tenderness toward her newborn babies. Drawn to the nest by their peeping sounds, she carefully digs them out. She gently carries them to the water in her mouth, three or four at a time. However, the male Crocodile is likely to eat his young if the chance presents itself.

Nostrils and eyes are on the top of a crocodile's head, enabling the giant reptile to see and breathe while swimming or floating on the water. While underwater, a large flap of skin at the back of its tongue closes to seal off the air passage to its lungs, as a crocodile cannot shut its lips to make its mouth airtight. Ear and nostril openings also close when crocodiles submerge.

To maintain its body heat, the cold-blooded crocodile spends the night in the water, which does not lose warmth as quickly as the air. When the sun rises, it hauls its bulk on to land and soaks up the solar power, thus providing the energy needed to catch and digest its food. To prevent overheating, it gapes. The blood coursing through thin capillaries in its mouth lining is quickly cooled by air.

The peg-like teeth of a Crocodile are used to hold its food in place while it tears its prey apart and gulps it down. Its diet includes crabs, fish, raccoons, water birds and the occasional young crocodile. Instead of being chewed, food is ground up in one part of its two-sectioned stomach. In this organ, called a gizzard, are pebbles which the crocodile swallows and which act like teeth.

Countless numbers of crocodiles have been killed for their beautiful and durable hides which are made into shoes, belts and handbags. The de-struction of many of their swampy habitats has also contributed to their decreased population. In 1975, when they were fewer than 500 in number, the crocodile was declared an endangered species.

Below: Crocodiles gape to cool themselves.

LIZARDS

Lizards are scaly, cold-blooded animals which today represent the largest living reptile group. Approximately 3000 species live worldwide, 115 kinds in North America, mostly in warmer regions, with only a small number in the temperate zone. Occupying a wide diversity of habitats, lizards may be found on the ground, underneath the soil, in trees, on buildings or in the water.

Lizards appear in a dizzying array of colors, sizes and forms, but the typical scaly-coated reptile with four legs and tapering tail is the most familiar. Surprisingly, there are also legless lizards. These strange creatures can easily be confused with snakes, but unlike snakes which cannot close their eyes or cannot hear, limbless lizards have moveable eyelids and external ear openings.

Keen vision enables lizards to pinpoint their prey with accuracy. Many are insect eaters. Oil droplets inside lizards' eyes act as sunglasses and filter out excess light. In some species, a light-sensing organ on the top of the head helps tell the lizards how much sunlight or heat their bodies are receiving. Lizards can hear, but with the exception of geckos, they are voiceless.

A lizard, like a snake, uses its tongue to both smell and taste. To smell with its tongue, the lizard licks the air which carries microscopic particles of odor. Inside its mouth, a sense organ detects these odor particles accumulated on the tongue. Using its tongue, the lizard can follow the fresh scent of prey.

As the body of a lizard grows, the outside layer of its scales does not. This outer covering becomes too small and the animals must shed its outgrown skin. Some lizards molt in large flakes, while some species shed their skins in one piece. Some lizards take a day or two to complete the shedding process, while others require several weeks. Almost all shed upon emerging from hibernation, some shed every two or three weeks, others once or twice a year. A few kinds eat their old skin as it comes off.

Most lizards in the United States find the climate of the hot, dry desert areas satisfactory to meet their physical needs. Many are daytime hunters, but because they are cold-blooded, they require an external source of heat to get them going. The heat of the sun provides the thermal energy necessary to activate their systems, enabling them to pursue their prey. Lizards soak up the sun to engage their metabolic mechanisms, but in warmer climates, they must also escape the sun's heat in the middle of the day. To keep from being cooked, many burrow underground or hide in shaded rocky crevices. Lizards that are active

Above: An Island Night Lizard (*Xantusia riversiana*), an endangered species, on San Clemente Island.

during the day have eyes with rounded pupils, while nocturnal hunters have pupils shaped like slits.

Male lizards, like many other male animals, are territorial, which simply means that lizards exert a kind of guardianship over a certain portion of their habitats. The protected areas might be their nesting sites or their hunting grounds. Territories are defended against male trespassers of the same species who might become competitors for food or space. In territorial display to establish dominance, the owner lizard exposes to the would-be rival his brilliant coloration. To warn off the intruder, often a male bobs up and down in what seems a comic imitation of push-ups. If the visitor bobs in return, it is a male; otherwise, it is female.

Many lizards have tails of extraordinary length: four or five times the length of their bodies. Others possess small, stumpy tails. These appendages are often employed in a unique method of defense. If certain types of lizards are attacked, they can readily discard a portion of the tail. The cast-off section continues to writhe and wriggle, occupying the attacker's full attention while that part of the lizard bearing its vital body organs scampers off to safety.

Most lizard species can regenerate their tails, although the new tail section is never as long as the old one and does not have vertebrae. Instead, a rod of gristle regrows, covered with scales of color and pattern slightly different from the original appendage.

Only one species of lizard in the United States is poisonous, the Gila Monster of the southwest. The severity of the effects of a Gila Monster bite varies greatly. It can cause severe local pain and swelling, but seldom is this venomous lizard's bite fatal to humans.

Most species lay eggs, and sometimes the egg clutch is guarded by the female. In some species the young are born alive. Young lizards often differ markedly from their parents in color and pattern.

ALLIGATOR LIZARD, ARIZONA:
see Alligator Lizard, Northern

ALLIGATOR LIZARD, NORTHERN
(Gerrhonotus coeruleus)

The Northern Alligator Lizard is one of five kinds of Alligator Lizards in North America. These lizards can be found where temperatures are cool, in moist woodlands of high elevation under rotten logs, rocks, or loose bark. They live along the Pacific coast and in the Sierra Nevada Mountains from southern British Columbia to northern California into northern Idaho and western Montana.

Alligator Lizards get their name because of their resemblance to alligators. They have short, stiff bodies, stubby legs, and a long tail. The Northern Alligator Lizard grows to an overall length of 13 inches (33.0). Its back is olive to bluish in color, usually with brownish spots or blotches. It has dark eyes.

Because of an abundance of bony armor in its scaly skin, the Northern Alligator Lizard's body lacks flexibility. A lengthwise, grooved fold of soft, granular scales runs along the sides of its body. This groove permits expansion of the stiff body so the lizard can breathe. The groove also enlarges when the stomach is gorged with food or when the female is packed with eggs.

Staying close to the ground, the Northern Alligator Lizard is solitary, secretive, slow-moving and quiet. Throughout the day, it hunts its food of insects, spiders and snails. Females bear their 2-15 young alive, which have hatched out of eggs incubated for 7-10 weeks inside the mother's body.

Sometimes the alligator lizard will go into the water to escape from enemies. Its most commonly used protection is flight, but if that line of defense is closed off, it will smear an interloper with excrement. It can also resort to the often used lizard ploy of disengaging part of its tail. The detached tail section thrashes about,

occupying the attacker's attention, while the remainder of the lizard speeds away to safety.

The Arizona Alligator Lizard, *Gerrhonotus kingi*, has spots and bars on its belly but no stripes as in the Northern Alligator Lizard; the Texas Alligator Lizard, *Gerrhonotus liocephalus*, has a gray belly mottled with white; and the Southern Alligator Lizard, *Gerrhonotus multicarinatus*, of the western United States coast, has distinct crossbands on its back and tail.

ALLIGATOR LIZARD, SOUTHERN:
see Alligator Lizard, Northern

ALLIGATOR LIZARD, TEXAS:
see Spiny Lizard, Desert

ANOLE, BARK:
see Anole, Green

ANOLE, BROWN:
see Anole, Green

ANOLE, CAROLINA:
see Anole, Green

ANOLE, CRESTED:
see Anole, Green

ANOLE, GREEN
(Anolis carolinensis)

Often called the American 'chameleons,' Green or Carolina Anoles are found in southeastern United States from southern Virginia through Florida, west to central Texas and

Above: **A Northern Alligator Lizard.**

Oklahoma.

Green Anoles are slender lizards, growing to a length of 8 inches (20.3 cm). The males have fan-like flaps of skin, called dewlaps, under their chins which expose an unexpected, bright patch of color as a signal to another lizard. To another male anole, the colorful warning means stay away, while to a female, the brilliant skin-flap says come closer.

As its name describes, the Green Anole is usually bright green, but in seconds it can change to brown or colors somewhere in between. It is this ability to change color which gives it the name 'chameleon.' True chameleons do not live in the United States, but are lizards of India, Ceylon, Africa and southern Spain. True chameleons do quickly change color at will, but so do many other species of lizards, such as Green Anoles. Anoles are therefore incorrectly called chameleons. They are often sold here in carnivals and circuses.

Changes of hue are brought about by light, by temperature and by the mental condition of the lizard. Basking in the sun, a Green Anole is usually a somber brown tone. Fighting males distend their throat fans and flash a brilliant, pink warning to each other while turning an excited green. When climbing in the greenery of shrubs and grasses, the anole matches its background and uses its green as a protective coloration.

Anoles are good climbers and are

REPTILES

often seen in vertical ascent on walls, shrubs, and vines. Large toe pads enable the lizard to grasp the upright surfaces. Like a stalking cat, the anole moves slowly towards its food of flies, beetles, moths and spiders. The lizard spears its prey with a speedy thrust of its tongue.

Male Anoles court the females with extensive head bobbing and dewlap flashing. Single eggs are laid every 14 days from April to September. The young take between five to seven weeks to hatch.

Captive Green Anoles should be fed live insects. Water should be sprinkled on leaves in the lizard's cage. As the anole laps water from green plants in the wild, so should it do so in captivity. It will not drink from a dish.

Because these lizards are superior insect destroyers, they are worthy of protection.

Other Anoles inhabiting North America are Crested Anole, *Anolis cristatellus*; Large-headed Anole, *Anolis cybotes*; Bark Anole, *Anolis distichus*; Knight Anole, *Anolis equestres*; and Brown Anole, *Anolis sagrei*. All are introduced species from their native Cuba, Caribbean Islands or the Bahamas and now can be found in the state of Florida.

ANOLE, KNIGHT:
see Anole, Green

ANOLE, LARGE-HEADED:
see Anole, Green

BLUE BELLY:
see Swift

'CHAMELEON':
see Anole, Green

CHUCKWALLA
(*Sauramalus obesus*)

With a name of American Indian origin, the Chuckwalla is a lizard of the southwestern United States found in the deserts of Arizona, New Mexico and Utah.

A large, potbellied lizard, the Chuckwalla grows to approximately 16 inches (40.64 cm). It has loose folds of skin around its neck and shoulders. Its thick, stumpy tail is devoid of spines. The color of the male is black on its forward parts, red, gray, or yellow toward the tail. The female and young are banded or marbled with gray and yellow.

The Chuckwalla moves over the hot desert ground at hardly more than a rapid waddle. No necessity exists for a speedy chase to get its dinner; the Chuckwalla eats only flowers and tender leaves. To escape its many desert enemies such as coyotes, foxes, hawks and owls, this lizard takes refuge in a rock crevice. So that it will not be dragged out of its hiding place by a hungry predator, it will inflate its body with air, becoming big enough to be wedged firmly in among the rocks. There it stays until danger passes. Because it does not require large supplies of oxygen, the Chuckwalla holds its breath until it is safe to deflate and warily move out.

The flesh of the Chuckwalla is firm and palatable and was eaten by the Indians of the Southwest. To capture the edible lizard, the Indians removed it from its stuck position by deflating its body with a sharp object.

Upon emerging each morning from its nighttime sleeping crevice, the Chuckwalla raises its body temperature by basking in the heat of the sun. Not until its slow-moving body reaches a temperature of 100°F (38°C) can this cold-blooded creature begin its search for food.

Below: A Chuckawalla, a large but harmless lizard, can inflate or flatten itself as a defense. It can also change colors.

Above: The large-headed Collared Lizard.

Captive Chuckwalla specimens will not eat unless the heat of their native desert is reproduced. If they are too cold, their metabolism slows down, they become sluggish and they slowly starve to death.

COLLARED LIZARD
(Crotaphytus collaris)

The Collared Lizard lives in rocky, hilly, arid regions of the western United States from Utah and Colorado to southwestern Illinois, south through Texas and west into central Arizona.

The Collared Lizard can grow to a length of 14 inches (35.6 cm), with its tail measuring twice as long as its body. It has a large head with a conspicuous black and white collar across the back of its neck, which accounts for the lizard's name. Its body is stout. The background color of this reptile is extremely variable, but it is usually some shade of green with bluish highlights.

During the breeding season, the Collared Lizard exhibits startling coloration. The male becomes a rich green, spotted yellow. His throat turns a deep orange hue and rusty spots appear scattered over his hind legs. This striking display is meant to attract a female. Triggered by his brilliance, hormones in her body are produced which make her ready and receptive to mating. Before she lays her eggs, her sides assume a brick redness and similarly colored dots appear on her limbs and tail.

The hind legs of the Collared Lizard are strong and powerful, befitting a reptile which runs and hops swiftly over rocky terrain. These long, rear appendages enable it to jump like a frog as it hunts down its insect food or escapes an enemy. Living where there are rocks and open spaces for running, it is usually found perched atop a stony outlook appraising the surroundings for its next meal.

Pugnacious, the Collared Lizard will bite hard if cornered, but more readily it will flee a possible attacker. It lifts body and tail and dashes swiftly on its strong hind legs, appearing strangely as a vicious diminutive dinosaur.

The Desert Collared Lizard, *Crotaphytus insularis*, inhabits areas of Oregon, Idaho and California. Unlike the Collared Lizard, the tail of the Desert Collared Lizard is flattened from side to side. The Reticulate Collared Lizard, *Crotaphytus reticulatus*, an inhabitant of the Rio Grande valley of Texas and Mexico, has an open net-like pattern of thread-like lines.

COLLARED LIZARD, DESERT: see Collared Lizard

COLLARED LIZARD, RETICULATE: see Collared Lizard

FENCE LIZARD, WESTERN: see Swift

GECKO, BANDED
(Coleonyx variegatus)

The Banded Gecko is one of five species of geckos that live in the United States. In sand dunes and desert areas, it inhabits southern California, Nevada, Utah and Arizona.

The Banded Gecko grows to a length of 6 inches (15 cm). Its tail is one-half the length of its body. This gecko has protruding eyelids. It is light tan in color with dark brown crossbands. With age, these crossbands break up into blotches and variegations.

The Banded Gecko feeds at night on insects and spiders, which it captures with a speedy thrust of its long, sticky, swollen-tipped tongue. When stalking prey, it waves its tail in the air. To avoid the heat of the day, it hides in rock crevices or under fallen logs. Because lizards lack internal temperature regulating systems, they keep cool by getting out of the sun.

Most species of geckos have flattened pads on their toes. Each toe pad is covered with thousands of microscopic hairlike bristles, enabling the lizard to run over smooth, vertical surfaces such as windows, or to run on the underside of flat, horizontal surfaces such as ceilings. For those species of geckos which live in the fine sands of the open desert, this sticky-pad toe adaptation would be a decided hindrance. Instead, the sand-running creatures like the Banded Geckos have slender toes, fringed on each side with scales. The fringe of scales acts as a support and keeps the lizards' feet from sinking into the soft and yielding sand.

When handled, the Banded Gecko emits a cricket-like chirp. A constriction at the base of its slender tail marks the point where the gecko loses its tail which it does as a measure of defense. The discarded tail keeps wiggling energetically, occupying a confounded attacker's attention while the lizard exercize a hasty retreat. A new tail grows, although it is not as beautiful as the original. Because these appendages break so readily, many individuals have tails in some stages of regeneration.

Like the Banded Gecko, the Yellow-headed Gecko, *Gonatodes albogularis*, lacks expanded toe pads. Native to Central and South America, the Yellow-headed Gecko was introduced into Florida. Other introduced Geckos are the Indo-Pacific Gecko, *Hemidactylus garnoti*, also found in Florida, and the Mediterranean Gecko, *Hemidactylus turcicus*, inhabiting Florida, Louisiana and Texas, both of which can be seen at night darting after insects on walls and ceilings.

GECKO, INDO-PACIFIC: see Gecko, Banded

GECKO, MEDITERRANEAN: see Gecko, Banded

REPTILES

GECKO, YELLOW-HEADED:
see Gecko, Banded

GILA MONSTER
(*Heloderma suspectum*)

The Gila Monster is the only poisonous lizard in the United States. It lives in dry and semi-arid regions with sandy soils in southwest Utah, southern Nevada and south through Arizona and southwest New Mexico.

The Gila Monster can grow to a length of 24 inches (61 cm). It is a heavy bodied lizard with short, thick legs, and a stout, stumpy tail about one-quarter the size of its body. The small, beadlike scales on its back are marbled with pink or orange and black, the pale hue predominating.

In August, the female Gila Monster lays about one dozen soft-shelled eggs, burying them in the loose soil where the sun's heat will incubate them. In about one month, the 4 inch (10.16 cm) young hatch out, each more brilliantly colored than the adults.

With apparent sluggishness, the Gila Monster crawls at night over the desert ground and climbs in shrubs in search of small birds, eggs, small rodents and other lizards. It stalks its prey by tasting the ground with a long, thick, forked, purple tongue. Most of its prey is small enough to be taken without venom. The Gila Monster uses its poison more as a means of self protection than as a means of capturing food.

Extra food is stored as fat in the Gila Monster's tail. During periods of scarcity, the tail may lose almost one-quarter of its size, as the accumulated fat is used to nourish the lizard.

A Gila Monster's bite is vicious and painful, although seldom fatal. With the speed and strength of a Snapping Turtle, the poisonous lizard clamps its jaws on its enemy. For a good ten minutes, the reptile persists in hanging on while it works its venom into its victim with grinding motions of its jaw. The poison is delivered through grooved teeth. A wide range of symptoms can result from a Gila Monster bite, including sweating, nausea, thirst, sore throat, ringing of the ears, weakness, rapid breathing, faintness and collapse.

In defense of this pugnacious lizard, it should be said that it is not aggressive; most bites are caused by careless handling. In Arizona it is protected by law as an endangered species.

Left: **The Banded Gecko appears at night.**
Below: **The Gila Monster, North America's largest lizard, has a bone-like armor.**

GLASS LIZARD, ISLAND:
see Glass Lizard, Slender

REPTILES

Left: **The legless Slender Glass Lizard.**

GLASS LIZARD, SLENDER; GLASS SNAKE; JOINTED SNAKE
(Ophisaurus attenuatus)

A legless reptile, the Slender Glass Lizard can easily be mistaken for a snake. In dry grasslands and open woodlands from Virginia to Florida, west to Texas, Oklahoma and Nebraska, and north to southern Wisconsin and Illinois, this snake-like lizard lives by hunting insects.

The Glass Lizard has a long, slim body, often growing to a length of 42 inches (106.7 cm). It has a prominent dark stripe down the middle of its back and a long groove along its sides. Its tail is very long and brittle; the scales of the body and tail have a highly polished appearance, like glass.

Because this lizard lacks legs, it is often called a Glass Snake or Jointed Snake. Close observation will show that this elongated reptile has movable eyelids enabling it to shut its eyes, and it has external ear openings. Snakes have neither eyelids nor ears.

Because the Glass Lizard spends its day burrowing two or three inches (5.06 or 7.62 cm) below the surface in pursuit of slow moving insects, it is suitably adapted for underground life. It digs with a shovel-shaped snout. So that dirt and grit will not enter its mouth while digging, its lower jaw fits tightly into the upper one. Its smooth, slippery scales allow the lizard to move easily through loose soil. When it smells with its tongue, the little, forked appendage can protrude through a slit at the tip of its snout, enabling the lizard to keep its mouth closed. Occasionally, this lizard emerges at night to continue the hunt for insects.

Fantastic stories try to explain the strange behavior of the Glass Lizard. According to a 'jointed snake' myth, this reptile can break its body into several pieces when it is attacked. Later these pieces will reassemble to form a complete snake. The creature is reputed to be deadly poisonous and only burying its various pieces will kill it.

Actually, the body of the Slender Glass Lizard does not break into pieces, but the long, fragile tail may be broken with a light blow. When threatened, the lizard, in lizard-like fashion, simply disengages that organ with a slight twist. More than one piece may break off. No blood is shed as tail is cast off, but the pieces wiggle violently about. While the attacker is occupied subduing the fiercely writhing tail, the lizard escapes to the safety of a bush or burrow. The pieces of the tail never reunite. Having lost its tail, the lizard grows a new one, but it is shorter than the original.

The Island Glass Lizard, *Ophisaurus compressus*, is also a legless lizard, and like other lizards it has eyelids and external ear openings. It can be found among the scrubby coastal vegetation of South Carolina, Georgia and Florida. The tail of this lizard does not break as readily as do the tails of other Glass Lizards.

The Worm Lizard, *Rhineura floridana*, found in Florida, is a legless lizard that resembles an earthworm. Specialized for burrowing, external ear openings are lacking and eyes are set under the skin.

GLASS SNAKE:
see Glass Lizard, Slender

HORNED LIZARD:
see Horned Toad

HORNED LIZARD, COAST:
see Horned Toad

HORNED LIZARD, DESERT:
see Horned Toad

HORNED TOAD, TEXAS; HORNED LIZARD
(Phrynosoma cornutum)

The Horned Toad is not a toad at all, but is a true lizard inhabiting the southwest part of the United States. It lives in dry, hot, open country from Kansas to Texas and west to southeast Arizona. There are seven different species of horned lizards in the southwest.

The Horned Toad is mistakenly referred to as a toad because of its extremely warty appearance. Its wide, flat, scaly body has a row of spines along the sides. The head of this lizard is topped with a large crown of spines, the two center spines being the longest. Appearing as horns, these elongated spikes give the lizard its descriptive though incorrect common name.

Growing to a length of 7 inches (17.78 cm), the Horned Lizard is gray, spotted with brown, with a yellow band down the middle of its back. The iridescent colors on its spines and scales are the same colors as the coarse terrain on which it lives.

The food of the Horned Lizard is large live ants which it captures with great rapidity. This lizard spends most of its time on the ground where the ants are, eating as many as 300-400 a day of several varieties.

The Horned Lizard is capable of living in hot, dry, sandy wastes where the heat would be prohibitive to many other animals. The increased body surface with all its scaly warts and spines acts as a kind of air conditioning system, soaking up and releasing heat as needed. To conserve body fluids, the Horned Toad, as is true of other lizards, does not excrete water in its urine. Instead, its urine is pastelike and its bladder is quite small.

The Horned Lizard has an impressive variety of protective devices. When threatened, it inflates with air, appearing ferocious and much too large to swallow. Its camouflage coloration on its ashy background hides it from view of possible predators. Its flattened body casts only a small shadow to signal its presence as it re-

Below: A Texas Horned Lizard.

mains perfectly still, suitably matching its surroundings. When all else fails, it quickly burrows under the loose soil, hiding completely and escaping the noonday heat.

The most unusual technique the Horned Lizard uses in its own defense is to squirt blood. When disturbed, it sprays a stream of blood from the corner of its eyes. This occurrence is the result of a rise in blood pressure which may take place during fright or anger. The blood pressure rise causes the capillaries near the corners of the eye sockets to rupture.

The Coast Horned Lizard, *Phrynosoma coranatum*, inhabits sandy open areas of most of western California. The Short-horned Lizard, *Phrynosoma douglassi*, can be found from southern British Columbia to northern California, Idaho and Utah, and from Saskatchewan south to Kansas and

Mexico. The Desert Horned Lizard, *Phrynosoma platyrhinos*, has a head crown of relatively short spines, and lives in Oregon and Idaho south through eastern California and western Arizona.

IGUANA, DESERT
(*Dipsosaurus dorsalis*)

The Desert Iguana is the only iguana native to the United States. It is found in the desert regions of southern California, Nevada and western Arizona and south into Mexico.

The Desert Iguana grows to a length of 16 inches (40.6 cm) overall, with its tail nearly twice the length of its head and body. It has a low crest of enlarged, keeled scales down its back. This iguana is grayish-brown in color with an irregular pattern of reddish-brown and gray markings. The tail is

Above: **A Desert Iguana will retreat at any sign of danger.**

JOINTED SNAKE:
see Glass Lizard, Slender

RACERUNNER; SIX-LINED LIZARD; SAND LIZARD
(Cnemidophorus sexlineatus)

Racerunners are slender lizards with whiplike tails. They can be found from Delaware south through Florida and west to Texas, New Mexico and Colorado in dry, sunny locations such as grasslands and open woodlands. Twelve kinds of Racerunners or Whiptails are found in the United States.

Of its 10 inch (25.4 cm) length, 7 inches (17.78 cm) may be the Racerunner's Tail. The long, thin streamlined shape of its body, legs and tail and even of its hind toes all serve as designs for running with lightning speed. Using its quick movements both to escape an attacker and to hunt down food, this sleek lizard eats mostly insects. It also laps up the contents of bird eggs after crushing the shells with its jaws.

Racerunners are dark brown in color with six narrow, yellow stripes running from head to tail. The underparts of males are a striking blue. The scales on this lizard are so small that in some places they are indistinct.

The male racerunner exhibits dazzling color displays which can change seasonally. During breeding time, his flashy hues attract the female and cause chemical changes in her body, making her receptive to his attentions. During territorial disputes, the male's brilliant coloration warns off other males who might compete for food or space.

Some species of Racerunners are unisex, made up only of females. No mating takes place. A mature female lays fertile, but unfertilized eggs, which hatch into more females. This system of reproduction is known as parthenogenesis.

Racerunners spend their lives strictly on the ground where often they bask on sandy roads. When approached, they dart rapidly ahead always staying on the road, appearing to be inviting a race.

gray or white banded with dark spots. During the breeding season, mature adults develop reddish lines on the sides of their abdomens.

Primarily a vegetarian, the Desert Iguana runs along the ground during the day, nibbling on desert plants. The Iguana must be warmed by the sun before it has the energy to scamper after its food. Occasionally it eats insects. When disturbed, this wary lizard flees to the nearest rodent burrow.

The females find the underground a hospitable place for egg laying. From June to August three to eight eggs are laid in the protection of a hollow beneath the surface. Hatchlings appear in about two months.

The Desert Iguana is tolerant of the arid daytime heat, and is active even at 115°F (46°C). When ground temperature gets too hot for this lizard, instead of retreating to the coolness of a familiar burrow, it climbs higher into desert shrubs where air layers are cooler than the air on the surface. The Desert Iguana, like all reptiles, has no perspiration glands through which to lose water. To keep from drying out its scaly skin seals in body moisture and no water is excreted in its urine. Instead, its urine is pastelike and its bladder is very small.

The Western Whiptail, *Cnemido-phorus tigris*, inhabits California, eastern Oregon and southern Idaho, and south to Texas. Like most whiptails or racerunners, the Western Whiptail stalks any small moving object, usually insects, but sometimes the objects of the chase are fluttering leaves.

RED-HEADED LIZARD:
see Skink, Five-lined

SAGEBRUSH LIZARD:
see Spiny Lizard, Desert

SAND LIZARD:
see Racerunner

SHORT-HORNED LIZARD:
see Horned Toad

SIX-LINED LIZARD:
see Racerunner

SKINK, COAL:
see Skink, Five-lined

SKINK, FIVE-LINED
(Eumeces fasciatus)

The Five-lined Skink is a lizard that spends most of its life on the ground in humid woodlands among decaying leaf litter and rotting logs. Found from southern New England to northern Florida, west to eastern Texas and north to Kansas, Wisconsin and southern Ontario, the skink may be encountered in gardens and trash piles close to houses. The skink is rarely seen in the northern states, but swarms of them inhabit the pine regions of the southeast. There are 15 kinds of skinks in North America.

A wary lizard, the Five-line Skink grows to only about 8 inches long (20.32 cm). The head and body measure 3 inches (7.62 cm), the remainder is tail.

As the Five-lined Skink matures, its coloration alters markedly from that of its youth. Young and old appear so different in color it was thought that they were separate species. Immature specimens are a glossy black with five bright yellow stripes running down the body. The tails of youngsters are a brilliant blue, a startling contrast to the black and yellow of the rest of the body. As the lizard ages, the stripes fade and adults may become a uniform brown.

Not always dingy brown, the heads of adult males take on a brilliant hue during breeding season. At this phase, the skink is known as the Red-headed Lizard. Fearing that the flaming head colors announce a poisonous quality, uninformed persons called the skink a 'scorpion.'

Above: A bright, young Five-lined Skink.

In colder regions, the Five-lined Skinks hibernate by burying themselves under the ground to prevent their bodies from freezing. Soon after they emerge from hibernation, the males enact their startling courtship rituals. With bright red head flashing, the male rushes open-mouthed at the female, performing this bizarre performance over and over for about seven minutes. His seemingly peculiar behavior triggers hormones in her body which ready her for mating.

Six to seven weeks later, 2-18 eggs are laid in soil or in rotting logs. Displaying unusual reptile behavior, the female skink coils around the eggs and guards the nest, poised to attack an intruder.

Daytime hunters and ground-loving, Five-lined Skinks climb only to sun themselves on stumps or tree trunks. When basking, skinks are never far away from a snug retreat in which to dart if frightened. Insects, spiders, earthworms, lizards and small mice make up the skink's diet.

The Coal Skink, *Eumeces anthracenus*, lives in scattered populations, from New York through the Appalachian Mountains to the Gulf Coast, west to Kansas, Oklahoma and Texas. To avoid capture, it dives into water

REPTILES

and hides under rocks. Both the Coal Skink and the Mole Skink, *Eumeces egreguis*, of the coastal plains of Georgia, Alabama and Florida, have four light stripes on the head and body. The Mole Skink and the Ground Skink, *Scincella lateralis*, which lives from New Jersey south through Florida, west to Texas and north to Nebraska and Missouri, have see-through patches on the lower movable eyelid that enables them to see when burrowing even when the eyelid is closed to keep out the dirt.

SKINK, GROUND:
see Skink, Five-lined

SKINK, MOLE:
see Skink, Five-lined

SPINY LIZARD, CLARK'S:
see Spiny Lizard, Desert

SPINY LIZARD, CREVICE:
see Spiny Lizard, Desert

SPINY LIZARD, DESERT
(*Sceloporus magister*)

The Desert Spiny Lizard is a lizard of arid and semi-arid regions. It is found from southern Nevada into Baja California and southwest through Arizona, New Mexico and western Texas, where vegetation and rocks provide protective cover.

The Desert Spiny Lizard is a large lizard compared to other of its close relatives. It grows to about 12 inches (30.5 cm) in overall length. The scales on its back are large, keeled, overlapping and sharply pointed, giving this lizard a decidedly bristly appearance. Yellow to light brown in color, this reptile has a black patch on each shoulder. Males have blue throats and belly marks which are lacking in the females and in the young.

Desert Spiny Lizards can be seen during the day sunning on rocks, warming up their body temperatures to power their chase after insect food. Very wary, these lizards dash into the safety of rocky niches, rodent holes, or plant cover when alarmed. To run

swiftly, lizards use their claws to grab the dirt or sand, and dash forward in a combination pull-push movement.

The Desert Spiny Lizard can withstand colder temperatures than many other lizards, but when the air gets too cold to fuel their metabolic requirements, they hibernate. In crevices of rocky boulders, they go into a resting period where heartbeat and breathing are so slow that it seems all body functions have ceased. Older lizards crawl far into the hibernating hole until spring, while younger and hungrier individuals bed down closer to the crevice opening. A warm day will entice the youngsters out to hunt.

Some other Spiny Lizards are the Sagebrush Lizard, *Sceloporus graciousus*, found in the gravelly areas of Montana, New Mexico, Washington and Oregon; Clark's Spiny Lizard, *Sceloporus clarki*, living in semi-arid regions of Arizona and New Mexico; Texas Spiny Lizard, *Sceloporus olivaceus*, a tree-loving species of Oklahoma and Texas; and Crevice Spiny Lizard, *Sceloporus poinsetti*, inhabiting rocky outcroppings in New Mexico and Texas.

SPINY LIZARD, TEXAS:
see Spiny Lizard, Desert

Above: The Western Skink (*Eumeces skiltonianus*) has four light stripes down to its tail.
Below: The Yarrow's Spiny Lizard (*Sceloporus jarrovi*) has light blue or pink back scales. It is less wary than other lizards.

Fence Lizard has a black blotch under its chin and two blue abdominal areas. Because of this coloring, sometimes these lizards are called Blue Bellies.

A daytime hunter, the Fence Lizard eats almost any insect, spider, centipede or snail, but beetles are its predominant food.

As their name implies, these fast-moving little lizards spend much of their time perched on old fences, or clinging to the protection of trees or walls. To avoid capture, they will quickly flee. In the western states, the Fence Lizard stays closer to the ground, hiding under brush, or in burrows.

As well as protecting itself by speedy escape, the Fence Lizard's inconspicuous colors camouflage it, hiding it from enemies. If caught, like many other lizards, it can shed its tail. To defend its home area, a male will perform a series of 'push-ups' as a territorial display.

When the female Fence Lizard is only one year old, she lays a clutch of from 3-13 eggs. Older females lay two to four clutches. The young hatch out in six to eight weeks as miniature replicas of the adults and are able to care for themselves immediately.

The Western Fence Lizard, *Sceloporus occidentalis*, of Idaho and Nevada and west to the Pacific coast, inhabits a wide variety of conditions in rocky, mixed forest areas from sea level to above 9000 feet (2700 m).

SWIFT, COMMON:
see Swift

SWIFT, FENCE:
see Swift

WHIPTAIL: see Racerunner

WHIPTAIL, WESTERN:
see Racerunner

WORM LIZARD:
see Glass Lizard, Slender

SWIFT; EASTERN FENCE LIZARD; FENCE SWIFT; COMMON SWIFT
(Sceloporus undulatus)

From Delaware to Florida and west to New Mexico and Arizona in open, sunny woodlands, dunes and prairies, the Swift or Eastern Fence Lizard and its many close relatives can be found.

Of all the Fence Lizards in the United States, the Eastern Fence Lizard's range is the widest.

The Fence Lizard grows to about 7 inches (17.78 cm); approximately one half of its length is tail. The color of the lizard varies geographically. Generally, it is grayish in hue, with wavy, black crossbars which are often broken into two series of irregular Vs. A male

TURTLES

Turtles are cold-blooded, scaly-skinned reptiles that have shells. More than 225 species of turtles exist in the world today; 48 kinds can be found in the United States and Canada. Land dwellers are sometimes known as tortoises, while aquatic species are sometimes called terrapins.

Although a turtle's shell appears cumbersome, it is actually a marvel of mechanics and construction. Ancestors of turtles from the remote and distant past were covered with scaly skin like other reptiles. Some of the scales grew larger and thicker until eventually they became horny plates that fused together into upper shells, or carapaces, and lower shells called plastrons. These two shells are joined at the sides enveloping the animal in bony armor into which can be withdrawn the soft and vulnerable head, neck and limbs. The top shell is fused to the spinal column and is actually a part of it, made up of enlarged and flattened ribs, resulting in the turtle's wearing part of its skeleton on the outside. A turtle can no more crawl out of its shell than a person can walk out of his skin.

The shell is made of two layers laminated together, an inside layer of bone and an outside of horny scales. Both the shell and the scales increase in size as the turtle grows. To accommodate the growth, the scales flake off, peel or are worn away as new and larger shields are formed under the old ones. It is these outer, horny, flexible shields of the Hawksbill Turtle that supplies the tortoiseshell material from which decorative articles are made.

Turtles lack teeth. Instead, they have developed horned, pointed beaks on the upper and lower jaws that enable them to rip their food into bite-sized pieces. The nails on the forelimbs are also used as food-tearing devices as insects, grubs, worms, shellfish, fish or plants are devoured. Senses of sight, touch, smell and hearing are rather well developed. A turtle can detect odors while submerged by taking in a small amount of water through its nostrils. Internal ears with small openings just behind the eyes can pick up low-pitched sounds.

All turtles lay their eggs on land, and even those that spend their entire lives in water must come ashore to nest. In most species, the female excavates a nesting cavity, using her hind legs as digging tools. She deposits her eggs in the hole, covers the nest with earth, with sand or with decaying vegetation, then lumbers off, leaving the incubation to the warmth of the sun. Some turtles lay as few as two or three eggs per laying, and some deposit several clutches of a hundred or more eggs.

Turtle eggs are fertilized within the female's body, with one mating fertilizing eggs for several years. The egg shells have a rubbery consistency and act as water-conserving coverings, preventing the developing embryos from drying out. This moisture-saving shell enables reptiles to lay their eggs on land, while amphibians with their jelly-covered eggs are still dependent upon watery conditions to reproduce.

The turtle egg serves as a cozy nursery, a warming shelter, and a complete food supply, enclosed in the waterproof but porous coat. The egg is made up of about one-half albumen, that part of a chicken's egg we call the white. The other half consists of yellow yolk, composed chiefly of fat and protein. The turtle embryo lies on top of the nutritious material inside the shell and develops as it digests the chemicals. In 60-90 days the hatchlings peck their way out of their leathery coverings and appear as miniature replicas of the adults. For a short time, the newborns have a piece of yolk sac attached to their bottom shells from which they continue to draw nourishment. Soon absorbed, this little feed bag allows the vulnerable baby to remain in hiding and still be fed.

In winter in northern climates, the cold-blooded turtle must keep from freezing. Because a turtle's body takes on the temperature of the surrounding environment, the reptile must seek out temperatures which remain above the freezing mark. To solve this problem, the turtle hibernates. Burrowed underground below the frost line in mud or soil, the turtle's temperature remains high enough to prevent death and its metabolic demands low enough to require no food and little oxygen. With body processes so greatly slowed, what oxygen is required is taken in by means of muscles at the base of the tail. Richly supplied with blood vessels in gill-like fashion, these muscles can separate out the oxygen from the mud in which the turtle is buried.

As cold temperatures benumb them and prevent their bodies from functioning, so warm conditions rev up their metabolisms and activate the hunt. In early springtime, basking colonies of gregarious species can be seen lined up on logs or clustered on each others' backs, as the blood-warming rays of the energizing sunshine are absorbed to power their limbs.

Once the darlings of the pet trade, thousands of Map, Painted and Red-eared Turtles were sold in dime stores and pet shops. After it was discovered that many of these turtles carried bacteria that cause salmonella poisoning, the US Food and Drug Administration banned the sale of most turtles as pets.

Because of their desirability and usefulness to man, many species of turtles have been greatly reduced in numbers, some near extinction. Turtle flesh is eaten or simmered into soup. Turtle eggs are robbed for the table. Turtle fats are rendered into valuable oils. The

Diamondback Terrapin was an often-hunted delicacy at the turn of the century; now it is rarely found in the tidal flats and marshes of the east and southern coasts that once were its home. Wood and Box Turtles are suffering similar fates. The Green Sea Turtle is also captured for food and other giant swimmers provide leather and tortoiseshell.

Man's constructions have interfered with turtles's habitats and ways of life. Where once a turtle nested on a beach, now stands a development of homes, and while newborn sea turtles scamper naturally from their eggs toward the reflected light of water, they now are sometimes attracted to the bright lights of the highway and are accidently killed.

COOTER: see Pond Slider

POND SLIDER
(Chrysemys scripta)

The Pond Slider makes its home in sluggish rivers, shallow streams, swamps and ponds with soft bottoms and abundant plant growth. The natural range of the Pond Slider is southeast Virginia to northern Florida, west to New Mexico and south to Brazil. Because these turtles have been so widely distributed as pets, they have been introduced in many parts of the country outside of their original territory.

In the wild, a fully grown Pond Slider can attain a length of about 12 inches (30.48 cm), although specimens in captivity rarely reach that size. Young Sliders have a conspicuous red or yellow patch behind each eye that becomes masked as the turtle ages and is better able to protect itself. These patches, located near the position of the ears, give Pond Sliders the name of Red-eared Sliders.

The colored markings on the head of the young turtle help break up its silhouette, thereby preventing a would-be predator from viewing the turtle in full outline. This broken pattern, called disruptive coloration, matches the pond vegetation among which the turtle lives, and the little reptile can blend into its surroundings. The protective colorings enable some of the young to survive the ravages of their many enemies.

The upper shell of the Pond Slider is oval shaped. It is olive to brown in color and patterned with yellow marblings. With age, the shell pattern and the bright head markings become masked by a black pigment.

Top: The Western Box Turtle (*Terrapene ornata*) has a high-domed carapace.
Above: The highly aquatic Common Snapping Turtle is usually found in warm shallow water.

Pond Sliders are strong swimmers, using hind legs that are longer than front ones. When they swim, they are powered by these long rear legs, kicking them alternately up and down. The front legs are held against their body, since they are no help at all in propelling the turtle through the water.

From March to June, depending upon the latitude, Pond Sliders conduct elaborate, aquatic courtship rituals. While swimming backward in front of his mate, the male strokes her face with the long nails of his forelimbs. Fertilization of the eggs is internal.

REPTILES

Top: **Cooters, Slider relatives, love to bask.**
Above: **A Plymouth Red-bellied Turtle.**

In a flask-shaped nest cavity, which may be located some distance from the water, 4-23 oval-shaped, leathery-shelled eggs are deposited. Turtle eggs are usually white. Because they are buried, they do not need the concealing protective colors, blotches and patterns of bird or snake eggs. In about two months, the Slider hatchlings emerge from their shelled incubators as fully developed replicas of the adults. Often the young overwinter in the nest.

The Pond Slider is the familiar dime store turtle. Young Sliders were often seen swimming in tanks in pet shops and five and ten cent stores. To satisfy the pet trade, millions of these turtles have been raised on farms and sold, although few have survived to adulthood. Because many of these pet turtles have been found to carry the salmonella bacteria, the Food and Drug Administration in 1957 banned the sale of most turtles as pets.

A close relative of the Pond Slider, the River Cooter, *Chrysemys concinna*, of the southeastern United States, is a large turtle having an olive-colored yellow-barred top shell and orange and red stripes on its head. Another Cooter, *Chrysemys floridana*, ranges from Virginia to Texas, north in the Mississippi Valley to Illinois and Oklahoma. It has a very high dome-like shell, a small head, and can attain a weight of 14 pounds (6.3 kg). *Chrysemys rubriventris*, the Plymouth Red-bellied Turtle, can be found from southern New Jersey to northeastern North Carolina.

RED-EARED SLIDER: see Pond Slider

RIVER COOTER: see Pond Slider

SNAPPING TURTLE: see Snapping Turtle, Alligator; Snapping Turtle, Common

SNAPPING TURTLE, ALLIGATOR (*Macroclemys temmincki*)

The Alligator Snapping Turtle is the largest freshwater turtle in the world. It lives in streams and rivers that empty into the Gulf of Mexico from Florida to western Texas and north to Missouri.

Reaching a length of more than 26 inches (66+ cm), the Alligator Snapper's record weight is 219 pounds (99.5 kg). The head of a large specimen can measure 25 inches (63.5 cm) around. Its massive head ends in a strongly hooked beak. For a turtle, it has a very long tail. Its top shell is rough and keeled in texture, colored a drab yellowish-brown, the rear end deeply serrated. Its wrinkled skin matches the dingy hue of the carapace. Compared to the size of its enormous top shell, its plastron is small and gray.

The Alligator Snapping Turtle can be distinguished from the Common Snapping Turtle by its enormous head, prominent tearing beak, and the yellowish tone of the upper shell and head.

What the Alligator Snapper lacks in protection because of the small size of its bottom shell, it makes up for in hidden and tricky behavior. Its drabness blends in perfectly with the coffee-colored waters of the lower Mississippi River where this turtle is commonly found. Except when speed and strength are required to clamp shut its powerful jaws, it is a slow-moving goliath. Its movements are so languid that green algae grows on its rough carapace like aquatic plants growing on a rock. The thin, green plant layer covering its subdued shell disguises the turtle so it resembles a submerged stone.

Hidden in the oozy river bottom, the Alligator Snapper lies motionless while it practices its passive and deceptive hunting technique. On its tongue is a pink wormlike filament that resembles bait. With mouth agape, the turtle wiggles its 'worm,' attracting its misguided food into its waiting maw.

Only nesting females ever leave the water. To bask in the sun, the Alligator Snapper finds a rock or log sticking out of the stream. If the number of these sunny locations is limited and if positions are already taken up by others of the same species, the Alligator Snapper merely climbs upon the back of the occupant or occupants. This towering of turtles uses all available space exposed to the warming sun, but still keeps the baskers in close proximity to the water's security.

SNAPPING TURTLE, COMMON
(Chelydra serpentina)

The Common Snapping Turtle is one of the largest freshwater turtles in North America. It ranges from southern Canada to Nova Scotia and south to Florida.

These large, feisty turtles are best known for their tendency to eat everything, including young ducklings, game fish and human fingers. Wild specimens can reach a weight of 45 pounds (20.5 kg). Primitive and unpleasant looking, Snappers have big heads, chin barbels, hooked upper jaws, and long tails. The top shell is unrelieved by any bright pattern; it is round and rough, a somber dark gray with strong saw-toothed shapes at the rear end. The bottom shell or plastron is surprisingly small and shaped like a cross. Decidedly aquatic, Snapping Turtles have broadly webbed feet.

Mating occurs from early summer to

Above: **A Common Snapping Turtle.**

late fall with 8-30 eggs hatching in about three months, if they survive the predations of skunks, snakes, raccoons and other egg-eating species. The soft-shelled hatchlings are most vulnerable for several weeks.

The Common Snapping Turtle is seldom found basking in the sun as are other aquatic species. Usually it rests quietly in murky water with just the tip of its snout protruding. Appearing as a muddy rock, it darts its huge head forward and clamps its powerful jaws around any fish or fowl unlucky enough to cross its path. During the cold months it hibernates in overhanging mud banks or abandoned muskrat lodges.

Because the plastron of the Snapping Turtle is so small, it offers no protection to the turtle's soft and fleshy parts. To compensate for lack of shell protection, the jaws of a full grown individual could easily bite off a man's finger or chop off his hand. This predator moves slowly, but attacks with lightning speed.

Strong and vicious, Snapping Turtles are more feared than loved by man. Although they are disliked in the wild, they are considered excellent for the table, for soups and stews.

STINKING JIM:
see Turtle, Musk

STINKPOT: see Turtle, Musk

TERRAPIN:
see Terrapin, Diamondback

TERRAPIN, DIAMONDBACK
(Malaclemys terrapin)

The Diamondback Terrapin was once a common turtle in salt marsh estuaries, tidal flats and lagoons from Cape Cod to Texas, along the Atlantic and Gulf coasts.

The female Diamondback reaches a size of almost 10 inches (25.4 cm), while the smaller male grows to about 6 inches (15.24 cm). The head and neck of the terrapin are gray, flecked with black. Its eyes are black and prominent.

The top shell or carapace of the Diamondback Terrapin has a rough, sculptured appearance; this bumpiness is due to deep growth rings on the large shields of the shell. The rings are not reliable indicators of the age of the turtle, as sometimes two or three grooves can be added in one year. The rate of the turtle's growth is determined by the availability of its food.

Terrapin is a word that originated in the Algonkian Indian language, and refers generally to any species of salt or freshwater turtle. A more specific usage now refers to the Diamondback Terrapin, the saltmarsh dweller of coastal zones.

REPTILES

The Diamondback Terrapin is at home on land or in water. However, it is usually found in a brackish aquatic environment. A strong swimmer, it hunts a wide assortment of seafood, including shrimps, snails, clams and worms. It swims using all four legs, its webbed feet performing as paddles. Its legs move alternately, left front and right hind paddle together, then right front and left hind push the water to the side. Some other turtles swim using only their hind legs, while holding their front ones against their body.

From April to May in the south, later in the north, the female lays about nine pinkish-white, thin-shelled, leathery eggs. The 4-8 inch (10-20 cm) deep nest cavities are dug in sandy open edges of marshes and dunes. The warmth of the sun incubates the eggs. In 9 to 15 weeks the young emerge as tiny copies of their parents, who in true turtle fashion are nowhere near their hatchlings.

The Diamondback Terrapin was considerd an epicure's costly delight, and was simmered into a delectable turtle soup. The heavy market demand for its tasty flesh, the development of the coastal marshes which destroyed much of its habitat, and the Diamondback Terrapin's unfortunate habit of following automobile lights and being run down are all reasons for its greatly reduced numbers. Experimental farms where these turtles are being raised in captivity have not rescued them from near extinction, although recent protective legislation has restored some populations.

Above: **The Gopher Tortoise has light-centered scutes on its long carapace. Webless toes make it an exceptional burrower.**

Other highly aquatic species of the family Emydidae, of which the Diamondback Terrapin is a member, are Map Turtles, all of the genus *Graptemys*. The Map Turtle, *Graptemys geographica*, of the Great Lakes drainage area south to Tennessee and Alabama, has a greenish-brown carapace decorated with a net-like pattern of thin yellowish lines, which are obscured in adult females. The False Map Turtle, *Graptemys pseudogeographica*, once common in the drainage areas of the Mississippi, Missouri and Ohio Rivers, has been greatly reduced in numbers because of water pollution.

TORTOISE, GOPHER (*Gopherus polyphemus*)

The Gopher Tortoise, one of the most terrestrial of all turtles, is an accomplished burrower in the southeastern United States. This land-loving tortoise ranges from the dry, scrubby coastal plain of southern South Carolina to Florida and west to eastern Louisiana.

Gopher Tortoises have a body structure which is admirably adapted for life on land and underneath it. Their feet are completely unwebbed. Their hind legs are round and blunt like an elephant's foot and there is an armor of bony plates covering their much-flattened front legs. These hardened plates aid the turtles in digging their straight, unbranched burrows. It is this burrowing behavior which gives this tortoise the name of 'Gopher.'

When the midday temperatures of the Gopher Tortoise's range get very high, it retires to the coolness and protection of an underground, hollowed-out home among rocks or bushes. In the cooler temperatures of the early morning and evening, they lumber from their hollows to forage for food of grass and leaves.

Gopher Tortoise burrows can be as short as 3 feet (0.9 m) or as long as 47 feet (14.1 m). The longer tunnels may hold one turtle or more than ten, or may offer shelter to small mammals, snakes, frogs, toads and insects. Shorter tunnels are dug for temporary shelter while the extended ones are used for hibernation or estivation. Estivation is a resting state like hibernation, but it is entered into in response to extreme heat rather than to cold. Much of the lives of these tortoises is spent attempting to regulate their body temperatures to keep from cooking or freezing.

Even if the Gopher Tortoise cannot be seen, signs of its occupation are evident throughout its habitat. Numerous tracks in the sand lead to their burrows and mounds of loose soil are piled up at the entrances.

Other turtles closely related to the Gopher Tortoise living in North America are the Desert Tortoise, *Gopherus agassizii*, of the arid, gravelly areas of California and Nevada and the Berlandier's Tortoise, *Gopherus berlandieri*, which inhabits southern Texas into Mexico.

TURTLE, ATLANTIC RIDLEY: see Turtle, Green

TURTLE, EASTERN BOX (*Terrapene carolina*)

The Eastern Box Turtle, a land dweller, inhabits forested areas and wet meadows of most of the eastern United States from Maine to Florida and west to Michigan and eastern Kansas, Oklahoma and Texas.

Growing to a length of 4-8½ inches (10-21.6 cm), the Box Turtle has a high-domed, keeled top shell. Its markings are extremely variable, tan to dark brown with yellow, orange, or olive blotches. Males have red eyes and a concave shell; females have yellowish-brown eyes with a flat bottom shell. Most turtles have five short claws on each foot, but the Box Turtle has only three on each hind foot.

A distinctive feature of the Box Turtle is the cartilaginous hinge which divides its plastron or bottom shell. This hinge enables the turtle to close its bottom lobes tightly against the the lower margins of the top shell. Once so encased, it appears the turtle is enclosed in a box, thus its common name. With its shells firmly clamped and its head, legs and tail tucked safely within the armor, the bony fortress is impenetrable to enemies.

The blotched brownish-yellow patterns of the upper shell or carapace mimic the color of the dead leaves lying on the forest floor, offering protective coloration to the turtle as it conducts its daily lumbering hunt for food. Box Turtles eat berries, earthworms, insects and even mushrooms poisonous to man. A western species searches cattle dung for beetles.

Formerly, Indians found this turtle's meat edible and desirable, and their shells useful for ceremonial rattles and utilitarian containers. As a result of overhunting, the Box Turtle has been almost eliminated from the area between Ohio and New England.

From May to July, depending upon the latitude, the female Box Turtle

Below: **An Ornate Box Turtle.**

Above: **Green Sea Turtles mating.**

lays three to eight eggs that have very thin but tough shells. Incubation takes nine to ten weeks, the hatchlings sometimes overwintering in the nest. Capable of storing sperm, the female can produce fertilized eggs for several years after a single mating.

With its clublike legs and feet, the Box Turtle is well equipped for life on land, better suited for digging than for swimming. If it is thrown into the water, it floats like a cork and moves awkwardly toward the shore. Clawed forefeet enable this terrestrial turtle to dig down swiftly into loose soil to prepare its place of winter hibernation. In the northern part of its range, Box Turtles have been found four feet and more below the ground, beneath the frost line.

For its entire life span of sometimes more than 100 years, the Box Turtle can inhabit an area only the size of a football field. If taken away from its home range, it can find its way back by a navigational strategy using the sun. Its homing technique will not work on a cloudy day.

The Western Box Turtle, *Terrapene ornata*, lives in open prairies and dry, sandy grasslands of South Dakota and Iowa, south to Louisiana and Texas and west to Arizona.

TURTLE, FALSE MAP:
see Terrapin, Diamondback

TURTLE, GREEN
(Chelonia mydas)

Of all the giant Sea Turtles, the Green Turtle seems to travel the greatest distance from tropical seas. Much of the year, the Green Turtle feeds on aquatic vegetation in the shallow, warm waters of the Atlantic and Pacific Oceans. In summer, following the Gulf Stream northward, it migrates along the Atlantic coast and is frequently seen in New York Harbor. A Pacific Green Turtle reaches the coast of southern California. The approach of fall and the cooling of the water benumbs them. Green Turtles are then easily caught by fishermen.

The Green Turtle gets its name not from the color of its shell, but from the color of its fat. Its shell is olive or brown, liberally marbled with yellow. A large Green Turtle has a shell 3½ feet long (1.05 m) and can weigh about 400 pounds (180 kg). Its flat, flipper-like feet move and steer the turtle quickly through its watery element.

Until recently, Green Turtles could be found lying helpless on their backs in fishmarkets, waiting to be made into soup. If they were placed in an upright position while out of water, their great weight would crush them to death. While swimming, the water supports their weight.

A few Green Turtles now nest along the southeast coast of Florida. Every two to four years, females laboriously

REPTILES

Above: A Green Turtle with paddle-like feet.
Right: An Olive Ridley Turtle.

waddle ashore one to eight times a season. Under the protection of darkness, they dig an urn-shaped nest with their hind flippers. They deposit about 100 round, golfball-sized eggs in the nest, cover the hole with sand and return to their watery ease, while the sun's warmth incubates the eggs. The young hatch out in about two months, but do not reach sexual maturity for 20 to 30 years. Over that period of time, very few hatchlings survive. Those that outlive the depredations of man and animal return with pinpoint accuracy to the beaches where they hatched to lay more eggs to perpetuate their kind.

The products of the Green Turtle are in high demand. Its meat is considered a gourmet delicacy, its flippers are made into leather goods, and its fat is used for cosmetics and cooking oil. Because the nesting habits of the Green Turtle are so well known, this species is extremely vulnerable to man's destruction, resulting in the

Below: A Hawksbill hatchling crawls to sea.

rapid disappearance of this reptile.

The Atlantic Ridley Turtle, *Lepidochelys kempi*, a giant sea turtle, is also in danger of extinction. Egg robbing, slaughter of nesting females for food and drownings in shrimp boat nets have resulted in its near demise. The Olive Ridley (*Lepidochelys olivacea*) is also a threatened species.

TURTLE, HAWKSBILL (*Eretmochelys imbicata*)

The Hawksbill Turtle is a Sea Turtle which inhabits the warm, shallow, coastal waters of the Atlantic and Pacific Oceans. Sometimes they reach New England or southern California.

The smallest of the giant marine turtles, the Hawksbill grows to 36 inches (91 cm). This turtle gets its name from the shape of its upper jaw which resembles the beak of a hawk. The limbs of this sea-going turtle have developed into flat, seal-like flippers or paddles which serve as powerful swimming organs.

Hawksbill Turtles mate in shallow water near beaches in which they dig their nests. The females leave the

water only to lay their eggs. Two or more times a season, these lumbering giants labor over the sand to dig a deep nesting cavity with their hind legs and in it deposit 50-200 or more leather-shelled eggs. Once the eggs are deposited, they cover the hole with sand and waddle awkwardly back to the sea. The nest is built at an angle that causes it to cave in after the young have hatched, making it easy for the babies to crawl out.

In about two months, the young emerge from their leathery shells and make their way to shallow inlets until they become strong enough to lead a strictly sea-going existence. Upon hatching, they crawl towards the sea, attracted by the light it reflects, but sometimes the little ones mistakenly move toward artificial highway lights and are accidently killed. Many of the young are preyed upon by fish and birds. Although the female lays an impressive number of eggs, only a small portion of the abundant hatchlings ever reach maturity.

Hawksbill Turtles are the turtles from whose shell comes the tortoise-shell once so commonly used in combs, brushes, buttons and decorative articles. The tortoiseshell is made of the thin, clear, horny shields covering the bony portion of the carapace. Smooth and translucent, these shields are richly marbled in black or brown and yellow. The shields are removed by heat from the live turtle, then polished to a fine sheen. The Hawksbill then grows a new layer of shields, but nowhere near as desirable as the originals. With the modern, widespread use of plastic materials which replace the tortoiseshell, the economic value of the Hawksbill Turtle has declined.

Although the demand for tortoiseshell has lessened, the Hawksbill Turtle is still hunted for its meat and eggs. Many of its nesting sites have been destroyed as beaches and coastal islands are developed. Many turtles drown in shrimp nets and many more never reach adulthood. The Hawksbill Turtle is now an endangered species.

TURTLE, LOGGERHEAD
(Caretta caretta)

The Loggerhead Turtle is a huge ocean-going species that inhabits the warm waters of the Atlantic and Pacific Oceans. In summer, Atlantic Loggerheads swim as far north as New England, occasionally further, and Pacific dwellers sometimes range to southern California. These large, swimming reptiles live in coastal bays, lagoons, estuaries and the open seas.

A giant of the turtle world, the Loggerhead can grow to 48 inches (122 cm) in length. Past reports tell of these turtles weighing 1000 pounds (455 kg) or more. The Loggerhead's upper shell is thick and heavy, a heart-shaped, dull colored brown. Its limbs are like paddles and move the reptile through the water with powerful thrusts. Swimming tools of fine design, the flippers are ill-suited to transport the turtle while ashore.

Poorly equipped for life on land, the sea-dwelling Loggerhead comes to shore only to lay eggs. In May and June, the female labors over the sand to a point above the high tide line. Under protection of darkness, the nest is excavated on a wide, sloping beach along the Atlantic or Gulf Coasts from New Jersey to Texas. She scoops a hollow with her front flippers, then shoves the sand out of the burrow behind her with her rear paddles.

As so many of the young become food for other animals, to assure the continuation of the species, an enormous number of eggs are laid. From 50 to 1000 are deposited, depending upon the size and age of the female. She covers the eggs with sand and returns to the security of the ocean. Floundering up the beach and back again to the water, the female traces an erratic course so it is impossible to discover by the tracks the exact spot of egg deposition. Persons determined to find the eggs take soundings with the aid of a sharp stick along the zig-zag path until they locate the nest.

If undisturbed, the young hatch out in about two months. Their journey to the water over the open and unpro-

Above: **A young Loggerhead Sea Turtle.**

tected beach is a perilous migration, and many hatchlings become food for waiting birds. Attracted to the light reflected off the ocean, the little ones scamper toward the brightness, but some become confused by the artificial highway lights and never reach their aquatic destination.

In summer months, Loggerheads follow the warm currents of the Gulf Stream and formerly were harpooned off the northern coasts of the United States. Although their flesh is considered inferior to that of the Green Turtle, many Loggerheads were sent to market. Their meat is dark and red; it looks and tastes like beef.

The numbers of Loggerhead Turtles have been greatly reduced. Overhunting, nest robbing, nesting site destruction, drownings in shrimp nets and the increased death rate of the young all have contributed to their threatened survival.

TURTLE, LOGGERHEAD MUSK: see Turtle, Musk

TURTLE, MAP:
see Terrapin, Diamondback

TURTLE, MUD
(Kinosternon subrubrum)

The Mud Turtle lives in soft-bottomed, slow-moving water with abundant plant growth. It ranges throughout the eastern United States from southwest Connecticut, south to southern Florida, west to central Texas and north to southern Illinois and southwest Indiana.

Reaching barely 5 inches (12.7 cm) in length, the Mud Turtle has the smooth, patternless, olive to dark brown upper shell that is characteristic of its family. Many other kinds of turtles have top shells or carapaces with serrated edges or with upturned margins, but the Mud Turtle's carapace is smooth. The bottom shell or plastron is double hinged. These hinges make the shell more flexible so it can be closed more tightly to protect the soft body parts drawn within it.

Female Mud Turtles have very short tails. The tails of the male are much longer and end in a well developed, blunt, spiny growth.

Although Mud Turtles are largely aquatic, they spend more time on land than others of their family. They can often be found prowling the bottoms of sluggish fresh or brackish water, searching amidst the lush vegetation for insects, snails, dead fish and algae. If their stream or pond should dry up, Mud Turtles will search for a more permanent watering hole. If another aquatic habitat cannot be found, these turtles will burrow into mud to conserve their vital body fluids.

In the north, Mud Turtles hibernate in oozy pond bottoms or in rotten wood. From November to early April they disappear into their winter retreats. In the warmer south, this species does not hibernate. The hibernating turtle prevents its cold blood from freezing, as its body takes on the same temperature as the above 32°F (0°C) mud in which it is buried. What oxygen is required during this period of greatly slowed down metabolic processes is extracted from the moisture in the earth through blood vessels at the base of its tail.

The female Mud Turtle matures sexually at from five to seven years of age. In June she lays 1-6 oval-shaped, hard-shelled eggs. The 1 inch (2.54 cm) pinkish or bluish-white eggs are deposited in an excavation dug in decaying vegetation or in loamy soil. Occasionally a lazy mother will use the already prepared muskrat or beaver

REPTILES

lodge or alligator nest as a repository for her eggs.

Of no economic importance to man, Mud Turtles are probably best known to fishermen who catch turtles instead of fish.

The Yellow Mud Turtle, *Kinosternon flavescens*, ranging from Arkansas and Texas to Arizona, has a bright lemon-yellow color on the side of the neck. The Striped Mud Turtle, *Kinosternon bauri*, is unique in having three yellow bands on the upper shell.

TURTLE, MUSK; STINKPOT
(Sternotherus odoratus)

The Musk Turtle lives in slow-moving, shallow muddy-bottomed water. Its range is widespread, from central Maine, south to Florida, west to central Texas, and north to southern Wisconsin.

The Musk Turtle grows to approximately 5 inches (12.7 cm) in length. It can be distinguished from other species of Musk Turtles by the two bright yellow lines, one on each side of the head, and by the barbels on its chin and throat. The top shell or carapace is smooth, highly domed, oval-shaped and olive-brown to dark gray. Its subdued coloration lets the turtle blend perfectly into the muddy bottoms along which it forages. The bottom shell of this turtle is small and it has a single hinge.

Although the hinge on the under shell or plastron of the Musk Turtle is

Above and below: **The Painted Turtle is the most widespread turtle in North America.**

designed to make the shell more flexible, enabling the fleshy legs to be enclosed within it, the small size of the plastron offers little protection. Instead, this turtle has developed other methods of defense. Highly aquatic bottom-crawlers, the males are especially aggressive and bite readily. The jaws are wide and strong. The long neck of the Musk Turtle can bring its jaws as far back as its hind limbs. The long distance forward thrust of its head brings speed and power to its attack. Once a fisherman has snared a Musk Turtle on the hook meant for a fish, the tenacious turtle can be forced to let go only with the greatest difficulty.

If pugnacious behavior fails to repel a would-be attacker, a back-up measure can be used. From musk glands located in front of their hind legs, Musk Turtles can discharge a foul-smelling, yellowish secretion. This offensive habit has earned for this turtle the endearing names of Stinkpot and Stinking Jim.

Mating takes place under water. In spring or late summer, depending upon the latitude, 1-9 eggs are deposited in a shallow cavity in a rotting stump or in a muskrat lodge. The thick-shelled eggs are off-white with a stark white band around them. In approximately 9-12 weeks, the young hatch, having been kept warm by the decaying vegetation in which they were buried and kept moist by the thick, watertight shells with which they were covered.

Musk Turtles rarely leave the water, but they occasionally sun themselves on floating vegetation in order to raise their normally cold body temperatures. Using their sharp claws, these turtles perform a feat most unusual in the turtle world; they climb trees. Musk Turtles can sometimes be seen basking on low branches overhanging a stream. When alarmed, they plop directly into the protection of the water, sometimes falling into boats or on to fishermen.

The Razor-backed Musk Turtle, *Sternotherus carinatus*, is fairly common from Georgia to the Gulf states and westward to Arizona. It has a spotted head differentiating it from northern species. The Loggerhead Musk Turtle, *Sternotherus minor*, also lives in the southeastern portion of the United States. It has a keeled top shell that may be patterned with dark spots or radiating streaks.

TURTLE, PAINTED
(Chrysemys picta)

The Painted Turtle lives in slow-moving, shallow streams, rivers and lakes. It can be found from British Columbia to Nova Scotia, south to Georgia, west to Louisiana, north to Oklahoma and northwest to Oregon. Its range is the most widespread of turtle in North America.

The Painted Turtle averages 5 inches (12.7 cm) in length, the male much smaller than the female. It has an olive or black, oval, smooth, somewhat flattened carapace. The brilliant colors of the upper shell margins make this little turtle distinctive. Appearing as the product of an artist's brush, both the top and bottom of the carapace borders are alive with striking red and yellow bars and crescents. Matching the upper shell, as a suit jacket matches the pants, the Painted Turtle has red and yellow stripes on its neck, legs, and tail. Its bottom shell or plastron is an unpatterned yellow.

The brightly colored designs that border the Painted Turtle's top shell break up its outline, so to a would-be predator it does not appear to be a turtle. Unrecognized and unmolested, the turtle survives thanks to its deceptive coloration.

As befits a turtle that spends almost its entire life in water, the Painted Turtle's hind feet are flattened, elongated and webbed. It is a very strong swimmer, and when occasionally it comes on land, it is a fast walker as well. Paddling through the water fast enough to catch small fish to satisfy its voracious appetite, the Painted Turtle also dines on tadpoles, frogs, insect larvae and on the tender shoots of aquatic plants. Turtles can smell food when they are under water. By taking a small amount of water

through their noses, odors can be detected by a sensory device called the Jacobson's organ.

Most turtles do not have lips, nor do they have teeth. Their beak-shaped jaws are covered with a horny material. The Painted Turtle, like other turtles, uses this pointed beak to rip pieces of food into bite-size chunks. It also uses the long nails on its forelimbs to tear apart its food. Its tongue helps it to swallow.

After an involved aquatic courtship ritual, the smaller male swimming backward in front of a female and carressing her face tenderly with the long nails of his forelimbs, eggs are fertilized internally. In the north, the female lays one or two clutches of eggs; in the south, two to four. Two to twenty eggs are deposited in a flask-shaped nest cavity, 4 inches (10 cm) deep. In ten to eleven weeks, the young force a hole through the rubbery egg shell, using a sharp, horny knob which has developed for that purpose on the upper jaw. This growth is called a shell caruncle or an egg tooth. Its purpose served, the special knob disappears. Newly hatched, the baby turtles are most vulnerable to predation. With their unique protective coloration, the young Painted Turtles are soon lost in their surroundings.

Above: **The Florida Softshell Turtle has dark-edged eye bands extending to the jaw.**

The Painted Turtle spends much of its time in the early spring basking in the sun. Often dozens of these turtles can be seen perched in a neat row on a single log, taking a communal sunbath. The line of turtles soaks up the warmth to rev up their cold-blooded metabolisms in preparation for the pursuit of prey.

TURTLE, PLYMOUTH RED-BELLIED: see Pond Slider

TURTLE, RAZOR-BACKED MUSK: see Turtle, Musk

TURTLE, SMOOTH SOFTSHELL
(Trionyx muticus)

The Smooth Softshell Turtle is one of four kinds of Softshell Turtles that live in the United States. The Smooth Softshell is seldom found away from the water and lives in rivers and large streams which drain into the Ohio, Mississippi, Missouri, Arkansas and Alabama Rivers.

Unlike other Softshell Turtles, the Smooth Softshell has no bumps or spines on its back. Its upper shell is soft and pliable and appears to be

REPTILES

covered with soft and leathery skin rather than with hard and bony plates as are other turtles. The top shell is flat and almost circular in shape. In keeping with its aquatic habits, the Smooth Softshell has paddlelike, broadly webbed feet which move the turtle quickly through the water.

Softshell Turtles dig down and bury themselves in the mud or sand on the bottom of the waterways. Their drab, olive-gray color blends in perfectly with the muddy surroundings. Hidden by camouflage with only their heads protruding, the turtles wait for shrimp, frogs or fish. When prey approach, the turtle darts forth its long neck and grabs the food in its jaws. The turtle breathes through its snorkel-like snout while submerged.

The Softshell turtle has a sharp beak which is enclosed in loose, skin-like fleshy lips. When the turtle is burrowed, the skin keeps grains of sand out of its mouth.

The flesh of the Smooth Softshell Turtle is good to eat, but caution must be exercized when catching it. With its strong jaws and sudden, accurate striking ability, this turtle could inflict a nasty bite on a careless captor. Holding it by the tail prevents the turtle from biting.

The Spiny Softshell Turtle, *Trionyx spiniferus*, ranging throughout the United States as far west as the Continental Divide, gets its name from an unusual structural development jutting from the front margin of the top shell, consisting of a fringe of pointed, projecting tubercles. The Florida Softshell Turtle, *Tryonix ferox*, can be found in Florida, South Carolina, Georgia and Alabama.

TURTLE, SOFTSHELL:
see Turtle, Smooth Softshell

TURTLE, SPINY SOFTSHELL:
see Turtle, Smooth Softshell

TURTLE, SPOTTED
(Clemmys guttata)

The Spotted Turtle is a common turtle of the north and eastern part of North America, ranging from southern Canada to South Carolina and westward to Ohio. This populous species can be found in marshy meadows and shallow, muddy-bottomed streams.

The Spotted Turtle grows to about 5 inches (12.7 cm) in length. This small, attractive turtle is decorated in very simple, uncluttered design. Its black, smooth, unridged, untoothed upper shell is flecked with little, round, yellow spots, forming a polka-dot pattern. The yellow spotting on its dark-colored head, neck and limbs matches that of its carapace. Along the border of its cream-colored bottom shell or plastron are large, black blotches. Its spots and blotches, which contrast in hue to that of the shell they adorn, offer a disruption to the overall shape of the turtle, and to its enemies make it difficult to see as an article of food. This protective device is called disruptive coloration.

In June in an open, sunny location, the female Spotted Turtle digs a shallow, flask-shaped cavity and in it deposits up to eight rubbery-shelled, oval-shaped eggs. The egg serves as a compact nursery, a warming shelter and a complete food supply to the developing embryo enclosed in a waterproof but porous covering. The turtle egg is comprised of about one-half albumen, that portion of an egg we sometimes call the white. The other half consists of yellow yolk, composed chiefly of fat and protein. The turtle embryo lies on top of the nutritious material inside the shell and digests the yolk chemicals. In 60-90 days, the little Spotted Turtles emerge from their shelled enclosures, having developed into tiny replicas of the adults. The hatchlings have a piece of yolk sac attached to a spot on their bottom shells from which they continue to receive nourishment. Soon dissolving, this little feed bag allows the vulnerable baby to stay hidden from enemies and at the same time to be fed.

Sometimes young Spotted Turtles and other species as well, nourished by their yolk sacs, do not leave the nest immediately upon hatching, but over-winter in its protection until the following spring.

Decidedly aquatic, the Spotted Turtle cannot eat unless its head is under water. It captures insects, insect larvae and tadpoles. Never venturing away from water, it hibernates under the soft mud or in a muskrat burrow.

In the cool months of spring, these cold-blooded reptiles must warm up their bodies. All cold-blooded animals receive their heat from the external source, the sun. Only when turtles have raised their body temperatures sufficiently can their systems be powered to move and hunt for food. They expose themselves to the warming rays and soak up the heat and energy.

When basking in the sun, the Spotted Turtle exhibits gregarious behavior. Clusters of sunbathers share a floating log or a miniature, grassy island in the middle of a pond. If favorite spots are occupied, the turtles simply form a second tier by roosting on the shells of the bottom row. The slightest disturbance swiftly unscrambles the warming crowd, and with multiple plops the frightened turtles disappear into the protection of the water.

TURTLE, STRIPED MUD:
see Turtle, Mud

TURTLE, WESTERN BOX:
see Turtle, Eastern Box

TURTLE, WOOD
(Clemmys insculpta)

The Wood Turtle lives near cool streams and swampy woodlands from Nova Scotia south to Virginia and west through the Great Lakes region.

The Wood Turtle can grow to a length of 9 inches (23 cm). The color of its carapace or upper shell is dark, dull brown; its texture rough and sculptured. A covering of shields, called scutes, adorns the shell. Inside each shield is a series of rings like the grooves on a phonograph record. These incisings are growth rings, but they give an unreliable count regard-

ing the age of the turtle. Two or three ridges may be formed in a single year, depending upon the availability of food and upon how fast the turtle is growing. Although the exact age of a turtle is difficult to determine, they do live as long, if not longer than humans.

Because these concentric growth channels resemble the annual rings of a tree, the Wood Turtle's top shell looks woody and gives the turtle its common name. The resemblance to wood also camouflages the turtle as it shuffles among the dead leaves on the forest floor in search of earthworms, slugs, insects, wild fruits and berries.

The back end of the Wood Turtle's sculptured carapace is deeply indented with tooth-like shapes that flare up-

ward. Its plastron or bottom shell is yellow with dark blotches around the outer edges. The male's plastron is concave in shape, the slight indentation to accommodate mating. In marked contrast to the dingy brownish coloration of the turtle's top shell, its neck and limbs are a brilliant brick red.

Although the Wood Turtle is an admirable swimmer, it leaves the water for the greater part of the summer in search of food. Like all other turtles, the female leaves the water to lay her eggs. In May or June, she deposits one batch of six to eight oval-shaped, rubbery-shelled eggs. The eggs are laid in a moist depression excavated by the female and covered with decaying plant material which

Above: **A Wood Turtle, an excellent climber.**

keeps the developing embryos warm. In September or October, the young hatch out, having developed without motherly attention. In the north, the hatchlings may spend the winter in the nest, buried against the fatal frost.

The Wood Turtle has a placid temperament and seldom bites. Capable of begging food, it is an intelligent animal. Once taken for food in large quantities, it is threatened by over-collection. In some states, the Wood Turtle is currently protected.

TURTLE, YELLOW MUD: see Turtle, Mud

AMPHIBIANS

An amphibian is a cold-blooded, wet-skinned animal that leads a double life. 'Amphi' means double and 'bios' means life. Salamanders, frogs, and toads are amphibians. Most of them spend part of their existences in the water and part of their time on land, although some salamanders have never given up their water habitat and some of them completely bypass an aquatic stage. Another group of amphibians is known as caecilians – primitive, earthworm-like creatures, most leading secretive, subterranean existences and none known to be living in North America.

The ancestors of today's amphibians lived 350 million years ago, having crawled out of the water onto land by means of muscular fins that later developed into legs. Swim bladders evolved into air-breathing lungs. Although these earliest amphibians developed a method of moving about on dry land and a system of breathing the air, they were never able to overcome their need for water.

Amphibians have thin, usually smooth skin. Even that time spent as terrestrial beings must be lived in moist conditions or they will quickly dry out. Water is absorbed through their fine, permeable body coverings, and in this way their need for fluids is met. The wet amphibian skins are richly supplied with blood vessels, so oxygen can be extracted from the moisture which surrounds the animal. When on land, many amphibians breathe through their skins, as well as through their lungs.

It is in the reproductive phase of their life cycle that the amphibian need for moisture is most evident. Drawn to breeding pools by cyclic, internal chemical activity, amphibians usually lay their eggs in fresh water. Some species lay their eggs on land in wet conditions. The eggs are covered with one, two or three transparent, permeable, jelly-like envelopes which allow moisture, oxygen and warmth to be supplied to the embryos developing within. Amphibian eggs, so in danger of drying out if not in fluid surroundings, lack the waterproof shells of reptiles. Because reptiles can lay their eggs in dry conditions, they have been able to roam far afield and to populate the land, while amphibians are still tied to the water to reproduce.

Once hatched, most amphibians spend the immature larval stage of their development swimming in water and breathing through gills like a fish. As the young mature, they lose their gills, develop lungs and legs and crawl out of the water to live a land-based existence, returning to the water again only to breed.

Despite their essential moisture requirements, amphibians live in a wide variety of conditions with the exception of the completely waterless desert, regions of permanent freezing cold and the salty ocean. If their chosen habitats become too dry, they hide away in the dampness of an underground burrow, and when the temperature drops in winter, most of these cold-blooded animals hibernate. Buried deep

in mud or soil to keep from freezing, their greatly reduced need for air is met by absorbing oxygen through their skins. During hibernation, their body processes have almost ceased, and their food needs are at a minimum. What little nourishment is required is supplied by stored body fat.

Because most amphibians are secretive animals, hidden away in their moisture-conserving crevices and lairs, commonly seen and heard only during breeding season, little is popularly known of their natural ways. Our acquaintanceships with frogs have usually been confined to a bullfrog's hind legs on a restaurant plate, or with the cut-up insides of a leopard frog in a school biology laboratory. As animals in service to mankind, frogs and toads are suberb natural insect destroyers, and even the lowly salamander is used as fisherman's bait.

Above: The Woodhouse's Toad (*Bufo woodhousei*) is active at night catching insects.
Below: The diurnal, masked Wood Frog is widespread.

FROGS AND TOADS

Noisier and less secretive, frogs are much more familiar to us than are their relatives, the salamanders. Frog voices often signal springtime and their vaulting leaps give them higher visibility.

Although the terms frog and toad are used interchangeably, each has distinguishing characteristics. Frogs generally have very moist, smooth, thin skin. They have powerful hind legs which enable them to jump astonishing distances for creatures their size and which make tasty edibles for a person's dinner. Semi-aquatic, the webs between their toes suit them admirably for swimming.

Toads, in less danger than frogs of drying out, spend more time on land and range further away from water. Toads' thicker, wartier skins keep their bodies more watertight and moisture is lost at a slower rate through their less permeable body coverings. They have squat, chunky bodies without the long, strong, hind legs of frogs, so they move in short, jerky hops.

As a defensive strategy, toads secrete a noxious chemical through their skins and through special glands, called paretoids, located behind their eyes. They are equipped with hardened tubercles on their hind feet that act as digging tools, enabling toads to burrow underground quickly to escape an enemy or to keep from freezing or drying out.

Even though their basic body form was fixed early in their evolution, differences have developed among the various frog species which adapt each specifically to its environment. Frogs cannot aim their eyes, but their bulging eyes give them a wide field of vision. Frogs that live in trees have their eyes positioned to give them an extra-wide range of view in all directions, especially down.

Those species that spend much time in water have their protruding eyes positioned on the tops of their heads, allowing them to float on the surface, to survey the surrounding scene and, at the same time, to keep their heads beneath the water. The kinds of frogs that burrow have short legs, which give them good leverage for digging, and horny spades on their heels, which serve as shovels.

Upon emergence from hibernation, their muddy winter subterranean burial, the cold-blooded amphibians are drawn to their breeding ponds to mate. The length of daylight and to some extent the temperature of the air triggers chemical changes in their bodies that propel the reproductive instinct to water and while approaching it, males hold forth with noisy trills, quacks, croaks and bellowings which advertise their presence to the egg-laden females. The

Above: **The American Toad has poison glands behind cranial crests.**

male hops on the slippery back of a female of his species and with forearms swollen for that purpose, clasps her tightly. Thus encoupled, the female deposits in the water her numerous jelly-covered eggs, while the male fertilizes the eggs by ejecting a milky, seminal substance over them. Eggs are laid in clusters, mats, strings or singly, depending upon the species.

Only the males perform the mating serenades. Females are usually silent, but may cry out when they are injured or disturbed. The male's sound is produced by air moving back and forth between the lung and the mouth, while the mouth and nostrils are closed. Most species have one or two vocal sacs that amplify the sound, giving it greater carrying power. When these voice pouches are inflated, the frog appears to be blowing bubbles.

When the tadpoles hatch out of their eggs, they breathe the oxygen in the water through external gills. Their tails serve as rudders as the tadpoles lead an aquatic life feeding on tiny water plants and animals. In a few weeks they begin to breathe through internal gills; soon they grow hind legs, then front legs. Lungs develop, tails are absorbed into their bodies and the froglets are ready to leave the water. The transformation usually takes from two to three months, but varies with the species, the temperature of the water, and the availability of food.

Once on land, frogs and toads occupy a variety of habitats that include treetops, subterranean burrows and numerous niches in between, but when their internal chemistry signals the season for procreation, the amphibians must return again to the water to fulfill the roles that have successfully and unchangeably maintained their populations for approximately 350 million years.

BULLFROG
(Rana catesbeiana)

The Bullfrog is the largest frog in North America. It lives in ponds, lakes and slow-moving streams with muddy bottoms and sufficient vegetation to provide easy cover. The Bullfrog can be found in eastern and central United States, also in New Brunswick and parts of Nova Scotia. Because of the use of its plump legs as a gourmet delicacy, it has been extensively introduced west of the Rocky Mountains, outside of its natural range.

A giant of the frog world, the Bullfrog in sitting position can attain a length of 8 inches (20.3 cm). When its hind feet are extended, they alone can be 10 inches (25.4 cm) long. This big amphibian can leap about 26 inches (66 cm). The Bullfrog is less aquatic than some of its relatives and is frequently observed on pond or stream banks.

The back of the Bullfrog is green to yellow with scattered mottlings of darker gray; its belly is white or yellow. During the breeding season, the male has a yellow throat. The rear hind

Above: A Bullfrog, in Lake Bison, Connecticut, will hide in vegetation when in danger.

feet of this frog are fully webbed. It has a ridge of skin running behind each eye, but this ridge does not run completely down its back as it does in many other species. Its eardrums, called timpani, appear as large round circles behind each eye and are very evident. The Bullfrog emerges from hibernation later than other species. Bullfrogs in the northern part of the range breed in July and in the southern part in February. With the familiar, deep-

AMPHIBIANS

pitched *jug-O-rum* bellow, the male can sound like a gutteral foghorn that can be heard for half a mile. The low-toned vocalizations are limited to the males who perform their bass arias to attract the amorous attentions of the females. Female frogs are usually mute, but they occasionally emit a cry when they are injured or bothered.

To sing the mating song, the male bullfrog closes its mouth and nostrils, and forces the air back and forth between its mouth and its lungs. Sound is produced by the action of the air passing over the vocal cords and causing them to vibrate. Not only is the Bullfrog the biggest frog in the United States, but it is also the loudest.

The female Bullfrog is a prodigious egg layer. She deposits approximately 20,000 eggs which form 3-5 inch (0.9-1.5 m) surface mats, floating on the water. The entire mass is enclosed in one thick coat of loose jelly. The tadpoles are large. They grow to 4-6 inches (10.2-15.2 cm) in length and may take almost two years to develop into adult frogs. The natural enemies include herons and other wading birds, snakes, fish and raccoons.

Because of their huge size, adult Bullfrogs can swallow large prey and are not satisfied with the more usual frog diet of insects. They will eat almost anything smaller than themselves, including other frogs, water birds, fish and young turtles. Turtle shell can be dissolved by strong digestive juices. Having no teeth for biting and chewing, the frogs food must swallow its food whole. To aid in the swallowing process, the frog can retract its eyes into the roof of its mouth and push the food down its throat. As the frog gulps, its normally bulging eyeballs appear flush against its face.

The Pig Frog, *Rana grylio*, found from South Carolina through Florida and west to Texas, is similar in appearance to the Bullfrog. Decidedly aquatic, the Pig Frog has fully webbed hind feet and is known as a Bullfrog throughout much of the South.

FROG, CHORUS:
see Treefrog, Common Gray

FROG, CRAWFISH
(*Rana areolata*)

The Crawfish Frog can be found near water in coastal plains and drainage systems from North Carolina to Florida and along the Gulf coast to eastern Louisiana.

The Crawfish Frog can measure from 2¼-4½ inches (5.7-11.4 cm). It has a stout body and short legs, making its appearance more toad-like than frog-like. Like other frogs, the Crawfish Frog has smooth skin, but the skin is somewhat warty. On its cream to brown or black colored back are large, round, light-bordered spots. These spots are frequently fused into horizontal blotches. Extending down each side of its back is a ridge of skin called the dorsolateral fold. Its hind feet are webbed, with the web extending about half the length of its longest rear toe.

Year-round breeders in their southern range, Crawfish Frogs travel great distances to reach the ponds in which they mate and deposit their eggs. The males project a deep, resounding, gutteral snore to advertise their presence and to attract the attention of the females. The chorus is said to sound like a group of hogs at feeding time. The male hops on the female's back, and with swollen forearms and thumbs, he grasps the female behind her forelegs. They remain coupled in that fashion for several days until her eggs are deposited.

Eggs are laid in masses in shallow water, attached to vegetation. After the eggs emerge from the female's body, the male sheds millions of sperm over them in a milky whitish substance called milt. Ejected into the water in such prodigious numbers, the microscopic sperm wiggle-swim to their targets, their sheer abundance guaranteeing that most of the eggs will be fertilized and thus will be able to develop.

Breeding males clasp any passing female and then seize other males. A special pig-like grunt emitted by the wrongly accosted male signals a letting-go. Females who have already spawned utter a similar note and they, too, are released.

The popular name of the Crawfish Frog comes from their habit of hiding in abandoned crawfish burrows, but these frogs also occupy holes in banks or sewers, the hollows of small rodents and the active tunnels of Gopher Tortoises. Crawfish Frogs spend the day in their retreats and at night when they emerge to hunt for insects, worms and other frogs, they seldom range far from the entrances to their hidden homes.

FROG, GREEN
(*Rana clamitans*)

The Green Frog spends its entire life either in or within jumping distance of a permanent pond or lake. Living in a widespread area, it can be found throughout eastern North America from Canada to Florida.

The Green Frog grows to about 4 inches (10.2 cm) in length. The color of this frog is often green, but in spite of its common name, it may be brown or bronze in hue. Its white belly has a darker pattern of lines and spots. During breeding season, males have yellow throats and swollen thumbs, the swellings an aid to grasping the slippery female. Its eardrums, which look like flattened discs on each side of the head, are larger than its eyes.

In both sexes of Green Frog, there is a wrinkle of skin running down each side of the back, known among zoologists as dorsolateral folds. The Green Frog resembles its larger relative, the Bullfrog, but the Bullfrog lacks this skin ridge down its back.

In early summer, the repeated, resonant, banjo-like twang of the male Green Frog lures the female to the breeding ponds. Jumping on her back and clutching her under her forearms, the male hangs on until all her eggs are laid. In a thin layer afloat on the surface of shallow water, 1000 to 4000 eggs are deposited. The eggs are fertilized by the sperm which the male ejects into the water and which find their wiggly way to the spawn. The flattened egg mass soaks up the sun's rays and the tadpoles develop in the warmth.

Above: A pair of Northern Leopard Frogs.

The eggs are dark in tone and are surrounded by a bubble of clear jelly. The deep-colored eggs attract the heat of the sun and the transparent coating allows it to enter. Because the jelly does not conduct the heat, as in a greenhouse, the warmth does not escape. This thermal trap keeps the eggs even warmer than the water in which they float. The jelly also acts as a protection for the eggs. It is made up of 98 percent water, giving it little food value, and its nasty taste makes it unpalatable to hungry predators.

In about three to five days, the surrounding jelly becomes almost liquid and the Green Frog larvae free themselves. For a short time, the tadpoles breathe through feathery gills which stick out of the sides of their heads. Their food is microscopic aquatic plants and animals called plankton. As they grow, they first develop their back legs, then their front ones. The tail is gradually absorbed into the body and the mouth increases in size to eat the larger adult food of insects, minnows and other frogs. In about one year, the Green Frog changes from a gill breathing to a lung breathing amphibian, and moves out onto land.

In winter, to keep from freezing, Green Frogs, like other frogs, hibernate in the mud at the bottom of ponds. Although they normally breathe air through lungs, enough oxygen is absorbed through their skins for their reduced needs during hibernation.

**FROG, LITTLE GRASS:
see Treefrog, Common Gray**

**FROG, MEADOW:
see Frog, Northern Leopard**

**FROG, NORTHERN CRICKET
(Acris crepitans)**

The Northern Cricket Frog is a member of the Treefrog family, but it spends most of its time on the ground,

AMPHIBIANS

instead of in trees. In a widespread range, the Northern Cricket Frog can be found from southern New York to Florida, west to Texas, north to South Dakota, Wisconsin and Michigan. It lives in and near sunny ponds of shallow, thickly vegetated water.

A tiny frog, the Northern Cricket Frog grows to only 1½ inches (3.8 cm). Its variably-colored, rough skin is often greenish-brown. Two consistent elements of its pattern are a dark triangle between its eyes and one or more dark stripes going down the back of its thighs. Although this frog is an active leaper, its legs are relatively short. It has extensive webbing on its hind feet.

Other members of the Treefrog family have large, adhesive toe pads which enable them to hang on while climbing, but the Cricket Frog lacks these sticky discs. The Cricket Frog has descended from the trees and has returned to a down-to-earth existence, mostly close to water. When alarmed, it retreats to the security of a pond, as does a true aquatic frog. Hunting insects during the day, great numbers of them hop amidst the protection of the plants at the water's edge.

For many people, spring is proclaimed by the shrill voices of the little Cricket Frogs. While perched on plants in or near the water, his vocal sac distended, the male serenades the female with a measured clicking tick. The sound can be imitated by striking together two pebbles, beginning slowly, then more rapidly for 30 or 40 strokes. The Cricket Frog gets its name from its song which sounds like the chirping of a cricket. Individual voices can be discerned only with great difficulty, as the vocalizations are performed in noisy ensemble which often includes Spring Peepers and Chorus Frogs, as well.

Like other frogs, the mating Cricket Frog couples are clasped together, the male grasping the female just behind her forelimbs. From April to July, eggs are deposited in the water, either separately or in small groups, attached to blades of grass or to underwater leaves. Young cricket frogs, as well as older ones, seek shelter from the cold under stones or leaves around the edge of their brooks or marshes.

The Southern Cricket Frog, *Acris gryllus*, with a pointed snout and longer legs than its northern relative, *Acris crepitans*, can be found in swamps, marshes, and streams of Virginia to Mississippi and Louisiana.

FROG, NORTHERN LEOPARD; MEADOW FROG (*Rana pipiens*)

The most wide ranging amphibian in North America, the Leopard Frog is found from southern Canada south through most of the United States. It is commonly found in marshes and ponds in springtime, but in summer it wanders away from water to the moist vegetation of meadows and grassy woodlands in search of insects on which to dine.

The Leopard Frog grows to about 4 inches (10.15 cm) in length, the female slightly larger than the male. Its moist smooth skin is green with whitish-edged, dark, irregularly shaped blotches on its back. Its underparts are white. A light-colored ridge of skin runs down each side of its back.

Even though during summer the Leopard Frog ventures away from water, it must continue to live in moist conditions, or it will dry out. It lacks the scaly, watertight covering of reptiles, and has only thin, permeable skin through which gases can be exchanged. Evaporation of body fluids through the thin skin is so rapid that the frog must continuously replace these fluids by soaking itself in moisture. Frogs breathe air through lungs, but they also extract oxygen from the moisture that covers them.

The Leopard Frog has developed impressive methods of defense. When pursued, it hops in zig-zag leaps to the security of the water. Its powerful hind legs allow it to cover a whopping 36 inches (81 cm) in a single jump. Attracted by the light reflected by the water, it senses the correct direction to aim its escape gymnastics. Continuing its confusing motions while submerged, the elusive amphibian surfaces amid plants that conceal it at the water's edge, while the pursuing raccoon or water bird keeps searching in the area of the original dive. The patchy blotches on the Leopard Frog's back harmonize with the irregular patterns of the water weeds.

In April, male Leopard Frogs mass in ponds and swamps and sing their mating chorus of long, low, gutteral notes, three seconds in duration, followed by three to six short clucks, each a second in length. The sounds are made in vocal sacs located on each side of its head which fill with air. The inflated sacs make the frog appear to be blowing balloons out of each cheek. Individuals snort in moderated tones, but a full complement of choristers cannot go unnoticed.

The egg mass is a flattened sphere measuring 3-6 inches (7.62-15.24 cm) attached to submerged plants or sticks, or resting unattached on the bottom of the pond. Because Leopard Frogs congregate in such large numbers, often 40 or more egg bunches can be found within a small area. In a few days, the eggs hatch into tadpoles and in eight to twelve weeks, depending upon the temperature of the water, the young develop into froglets, approximately 1 inch (2.54 cm) long.

The Southern Leopard Frog, *Rana sphenocephala*, like its northern cousin, *Rana pipiens*, has large dark spots appearing between two light colored ridges which line the side of the back. A light spot in the center of the eardrum distinguishes the Southern Frog, which is the most common and widespread frog of the eastern United States.

FROG, PICKEREL (*Rana palustris*)

The Pickerel Frog is commonly found throughout the eastern United States with the exception of the extreme Southeast section. It lives in slow-moving streams, in swamps and in damp meadows with low, dense plant growth. Occasionally during the summer months it comes out of the water to hunt in weed patches for the insects found there.

Smooth skinned and tan in color, the Pickerel Frog grows to 2-3 inches (5.08-7.62 cm) long. It is easily identified by the two regular rows of dark squarish blotches running down its back. Its undersurfaces are bright yellow or orange. A yellow fold of skin like a raised ridge lines each side of its upper portion.

The Pickerel Frog's pattern serves as a valuable camouflage, both as a strategy for attack and as a method of defense. Sitting very still, it is not seen by either the predator or the prey. The big blotches of interrupted pattern arranged down its back blend the frog perfectly into its background. Instead of seeing one color in the shape of a frog, an enemy or an insect sees only random blotches. This blending-in technique is called disruptive coloration.

When the frog is leaping, the bright orange colors of its undersides flash a teasing lure to a would-be attacker. When the frog sits quietly with legs folded up, the brilliant chroma disappears and, magically, so does the target, thus totally confusing a pursuing predator.

Indeed, the Pickerel Frog's enemies are well advised to stay away. This amphibian secretes a noxious chemical in its skin which makes it an extremely unappetizing meal. The toxic substance severely irritates the membranes in the mouths of animals which try to eat the Pickerel Frog, and the secretion will even kill other frogs closely confined with this species.

Pickerel Frogs hibernate from October to March or April. Upon emergence from their winter-long retreat, they converge en masse in shallow ponds. In early spring, from breeding pools, the male Pickerel Frog serenades the female Pickerels with a steady, low croak. Because frogs normally sing with their mouths and nostrils closed, they are able to vocalize even under water. Although the water somewhat deadens the sound, the Pickerel Frog holds forth, while submerged, with a heavy snore.

Above: **The skin of the Pickerel Frog supplies camouflage and a toxic secretion.**

About 3000 Pickerel Frogs are laid in a firm, round mass, attached underwater to aquatic plants. Frog eggs must be laid in the water as they lack the waterproof shell protection of reptiles and birds. The liquid environment in which the eggs float keeps the spawn of frogs from drying out. The Pickerel tadpoles hatch in 6-19 days, depending upon the temperature of the water.

FROG, PIG: see Bullfrog

FROG, SOUTHERN CRICKET: see Frog, Northern Cricket

FROG, SOUTHERN LEOPARD: see Frog, Northern Leopard

FROG, TAILED (*Ascaphus truei*)

The Tailed Frog is the only one of its kind that lives in North America. In cold, swift-flowing mountain streams in northwestern United States and southwestern Canada, Tailed Frogs make their home.

The Tailed Frog is a small, flat bodied, rough-skinned amphibian which grows from 1-2 inches (2.5-5.1 cm) in length. Varying considerably in color from individual to individual, its upper parts are usually a mottled cinnamon brown with many dark spots and its undersides are pink to gray or almost black. Its toes are long and slender, with the outer toes of its hind feet thicker than its other toes. It lacks an external eardrum, a prominent feature in other frogs.

This little amphibian is called a Tailed Frog, but its name belies its structure. No frog has a tail. One of the scientific names for frogs is 'anurans' which means tailless ones. Although the Tailed Frog lacks that body part after which it was named, it does have muscles capable of wagging that missing appendage. What sets this frog apart from all others is the unique, pear-shaped extension of the rear of its body which could be mistaken for a tail, but is actually a copulatory organ. In a mating procedure confined to this species, the male uses this organ to internally fertilize the female's eggs, while other frogs fertilize their eggs externally.

The Tailed Frog cannot hear, and unlike the many noisier jumping amphibians, it is voiceless. Living as it does in among the rocks of turbulent mountain streams, even if it had ears, a voice would not be heard above the loudness of the cascading water. To find himself a mate, instead of employing vocalizations as do other kinds of frogs, this inconspicuous creature must search among the rocks.

The female attaches her eggs to the downstream side of a rock where the eggs adhere firmly in the foaming currents. Sucking discs around the tadpoles' mouths enable them to cling firmly to rocks in the fast-flowing water in which they live. The hatched-out larvae will attach themselves to anything solid, including human flesh. They feed on algae and insects, scraping the nourishment from the stones. It takes from one to three years for the tadpoles of Tailed Frogs to transform into adults and emerge from their water habitat to live their lives on land.

FROG, WOOD
(Rana sylvatica)

The Wood Frog is the only North American frog found north of the Arctic Circle. In moist woodlands in the east, open grasslands in the west, and tundra in the north, the Wood Frog is widespread throughout northern North America. Its southernmost range reaches South Carolina and west to Arkansas.

The Wood Frog grows to about 3 inches (7.62 cm) in length. Showing considerable color variation, its back may be pink, coppery-brown or nearly black. It is white below, sometimes darkly speckled. The lower surfaces of its thighs may be awash with yellow. A distinctive feature of the Wood Frog is the prominent dark, mask-like patch extending backward from each eye. On each side of its smooth-skinned back are light ridges running lengthwise.

The coppery tannish colors of the Wood Frog provide excellent concealment as it hunts in daylight for insects among the dead leaves of the forest floor. It catches prey with a lightning-like thrust of its tongue which is attached to the front of its mouth. This forward tongue hinge makes frogs the masters of the quick flick.

The Wood Frog, like many other species, uses its coloration as a heat regulator. In ten minutes to a half hour, the Wood Frog can lighten or darken the color of its skin, depending upon the intensity of daylight or upon the temperature of the air. Brightness or heat causes dark skin cells containing melanin to contract and light skin cells to expand, thus making the frog lighter in color. Lack of light or cold conditions cause expansion of the melanin, resulting in deeper skin tones. The frog's body temperature is thus regulated, the darker color absorbing heat, the lighter color reflecting it.

Because it lives in cold climates, the Wood Frog spends much of its cold-blooded life trying to stay alive. It burrows under woodland litter or beneath the surface of the ground to survive the winter in hibernation, a condition of drastically reduced metabolic activity. Normally breathing through lungs, during hibernation the Wood Frog breathes through its moist skin which is richly supplied with blood vessels. The instinct to hibernate is signaled by the temperature of the air which effects the frog's response to light. At lower temperatures, the frog proceeds away from light and goes toward the darkness of the underground place in which it will hibernate.

Wood Frogs, able to function in colder conditions than other frogs, are the last to hibernate, the first to emerge. In the early spring, sometimes even before the ice has melted from the water, they appear in crowds at their breeding pools as if by magic. Their pleasant, low-pitched, clacking calls make a chorus of male Wood Frogs sound like the collective quackings of male Mallards. The female Wood Frog lays an egg mass of about 5 inches (12.7 cm) in diameter, containing from 1000 to 3000 eggs. After a week, the mass flattens and rests on the surface of the pond. The jelly coated egg pancake turns green like pond scum, due to the growth of microscopic plants which thrive on it. The tiny green plants feed on the carbon dioxide breathed out by the developing tadpoles, and the tadpoles use the oxygen given off by the plants. By this mutually beneficial arrangement, the tadpoles breathe pure air in spite of the crowded conditions inside their jelly nursery.

SPRING PEEPER
(Hyla crucifer)

The Spring Peeper's shrill, high-pitched trillings herald springtime in the eastern part of North America. This tiny frog lives in wooded areas near ponds and swamps, ranging from Manitoba to the Maritime Provinces, south through Florida, west to eastern Texas, and north into Wisconsin.

The Spring Peeper grows to little over 1 inch (2.54 cm) in length. It is tan to brown to gray in color, with a dark mark on its back which resembles an irregularly-shaped cross. This mark gives the Peeper its scientific species name of crucifer, which means 'bearing a cross'. The ragged outline gives the frog a disrupted form of coloration, breaking up its appearance as an article of food and making it appear rather as a bit of bark or a dead leaf.

The Spring Peeper has expanded, sticky toe pads, characteristic of most of the Treefrog family of which the Spring Peeper is a member. Despite its admirable adaptation for climbing and clinging to smooth surfaces, this amphibian spends more time lower down than many other Treefrog species, which live high in trees. The Spring Peeper can be found on low bushes or on the ground.

In southern areas from November to March and in northern areas from March to June, the Peeper trills its shrill serenade. The males sing from the edges of the breeding pond, from vegetation which overhangs the pool or from the water itself. The high ascending whistle can be heard for about one mile, and a chorus of these noisy pipers sounds like the bells of a sleigh. For frogs so small, the volume of their singing is astonishing. Any unexpected sound in the vicinity of their performances will quiet down the concert immediately, but only briefly. One resumed peep is soon answered by dozens of voices. The songs usually begin late in the afternoon and continue until the morning.

The male's vocal sac lies in loose folds under its chin. Inside its mouth, two slits open into the sac and provide the air which inflates the bag. The blown-up voice pouch becomes a thin-skinned balloon and resembles a bubble-gum bubble which the frog has blown from its mouth. The vocal sac stores the air for many peeps and acts as a resonator to increase the volume of the sound.

On one day the female lays her 800-1000 eggs. The eggs are deposited singly, attached to submerged, matted vegetation near the bottom of the pond. They are creamy and brownish in color and are each surrounded by a firm jelly covering.

While the female is disgorging her little transparent spheres, she is surmounted by the darker colored male who, with the aid of thickened pads on the insides of his thumbs, clasps her tightly under her forelimbs. Thus coupled, she lays her eggs, one at a time, and he squirts his sperm to fertil-

ize the eggs. The young hatch out in 5-15 days, and in about three or four months the tadpoles transform into froglet Peepers. The developing frog leaves the water, but not until it has attained sufficient maturity in three or four years does it return to breed. Its survival for that length of time is questionable, as the tiny Spring Peeper is sought by many predators, including fish, salamanders, snakes, birds, squirrels, raccoons and other frogs.

TOAD, AMERICAN
(Bufo americanus)

The American Toad is common in gardens and lawns where the soil is damp and the plant growth concealing. This toad can be found throughout the eastern part of North America, in Canada from Manitoba to Labrador, south to Georgia, east to Oklahoma and Kansas, and north through Wis-

Above: **The Spring Peeper has toepads for climbing.**

consin into Canada. There are 18 other toad species within that range.

Squat and short bodied, the rough-skinned American Toad can reach a length of 5½ inches (13.97 cm), the female larger than the male which rarely exceeds 3½ inches (8.89 cm). Varying greatly in color, it may be brown, brick-red, olive, or gray, marked with dark spots and sometimes with light blotches. The undersides are usually dark-spotted.

Toads have a pair of raised, smooth, light brown lumps called paratoid glands behind their eyes. These oblong-shaped discs secrete a thick, whitish poisonous fluid when the toad is attacked. The toxic substance is very caustic to the mucous membranes of

Below: **The American Toad is an insect eater.**

AMPHIBIANS

most other animals. A dog or a fox that has once seized a toad in its mouth will seldom do it again. Additional poison glands are scattered over the toad's body, giving the amphibian its bumpy appearance. Although handling a toad will not cause warts, its roughened skin can exude an ooze which can be irritating to a person's eyes or mouth, and can be strong enough to paralyze a smaller attacker.

Used in China for medicinal purposes, toad secretion, a digitalis-like chemical, is administered in the treatment of heart disease. German violinists use toad poisons to prevent their hands from perspiring greatly during a performance.

The warty skin of *Bufo americanus* allows it to inhabit less moist areas than most other amphibians. Its dry, heavy body covering prevents the rapid evaporation of water from its system.

The toad has a voracious appetite, eating mostly insects, and an admirable technique for hunting. Both toads and insects are attracted to light, so the dinner and the diner often converge. The toad's 2 inch (5 cm) long tongue is attached to the front of its mouth, enabling it to be flicked out and back in a fraction of a second. With a speedy, well-aimed flick, the toad captures an insect with the tongue's sticky tip. Having snared its prey, the toad then retracts its eyeballs into the roof of its mouth, squashing the food and pushing the food down its throat.

To escape an enemy, the American Toad simply disappears by slipping into a crevice, hiding under fallen leaves or burrowing into the soft earth. With the aid of hardened tubercles on its hind feet that act as shovels, the toad can dig itself into the ground. Cold weather or summer drought will trigger the digging reflex, as toads tend to move toward darkness at lower or higher temperatures. Three feet down, below the frost line, the toad will spend the winter in hibernation.

In spring, males proceed to shallow breeding ponds and call to the females with an ear-piercing, high-pitched, sustained trill, lasting for about 30

seconds. The eggs, 4000-8000 in number, are laid in long, paired strings like beads, enclosed in two spiral tubes of jelly. In three to twelve days, the tiny black tadpoles hatch, and after about two months they change into miniature toadlets that leave the water in vast numbers, especially after a summer rain. Seeing such a migration might prompt one to believe in a rain of toads.

As effective destroyers of insects, toads are welcomed residents in any garden.

Among other members within the range of the genus Bufo, the only genus of toad occurring in North America, are Western toad, *Bufo boreas*; Great Plains Toad, *Bufo canorus*; Green Toad, *Bufo debilis*; Canadian Toad, *Bufo hemiophyrs*; Southern Toad, *Bufo terrestris*; Woodhouse's Toad, *Bufo woodhousei* and Black Toad, *Bufo exsul*.

TOAD, BLACK:
see Toad, American

TOAD, CANADIAN:
see Toad, American

TOAD, EASTERN SPADEFOOT
(Scaphiopus holbrooki)

The Eastern Spadefoot Toad is one of five species of Spadefoots that live in North America. In forested, brushy, or cultivated areas of loose soil, this little amphibian can be found from Massachusetts to Florida and west to Texas, Arkansas and Indiana.

The terms frog and toad are often used interchangeably, but the Spadefoot Toad is more a true frog than a true toad. Toads have rough, warty skin, while the Spadefoot's skin is relatively smooth with only scattered tiny tubercles. Toads lack teeth in the upper jaw, while Spadefoot Toads have them. Spadefoots lack the poison glands on each side of their heads possessed by true toads.

Spadefoot Toads are so named because of the 'spades' or horny dark structures on the inner sides of the

soles of their hind feet. The spade is a useful tool which these frogs use to dig themselves quickly into loose or sandy soil. The soil is kicked to one side so that the amphibian's body sinks down into the excavation in an instant. The Eastern Spadefoot Toad remains buried during the day and emerges at night, especially after rain, to hunt insects and earthworms. Food is captured with a speedy dart of the tongue.

Male Spadefoot Toads lure the females with a coarse, low-pitched repeated *wonk*. When many sing in chorus, their harsh sounds are so loud they can be heard for half a mile. From March to September, after heavy rains fill temporary pools, the seldom-seen frogs come together to call and mate and lay their eggs. Eggs are deposited in jelly-like strings, interwoven among the stems of underwater plants.

The eggs hatch very quickly; within two days the wriggling larvae emerge from their transparent envelopes. In two to eight weeks, depending upon the level of the water, the immature forms grow the necessary equipment of lungs and legs which suits them for life on land. A dwindling water supply in their breeding pool causes the tadpoles to speed up the time of their development into frogs. As the liquid nursery evaporates, allowing the young less space in which to swim, bumping neighbors and warmer water temperatures spell impending doom. In a competition over who dries up first, the tadpoles or the water, still bearing the stubs of tails, they leave the pool before the pool leaves them. Soon the tissues of the tail are reabsorbed into the bloodstream of the nearly developed froglets, giving them extra internal nourishment.

Some other members of the Spadefoot Toad family, of which only one genus is represented in North America, are Plains Spadefoot, *Scaphiopus bombifrons*; Western Spadefoot, *Scaphiopus hammondi* and Great Basin Spadefoot, *Scaphiopus intermontanus*.

TOAD, GREAT PLAINS:
see Toad, American

TOAD, GREEN:
see Toad, American

TOAD, PLAINS SPADEFOOT:
see Toad, Eastern Spadefoot

TOAD, SOUTHERN:
see Toad, American

TOAD, WESTERN:
see Toad, American

TOAD, WESTERN SPADEFOOT:
see Toad, Eastern Spadefoot

TOAD, WOODHOUSE'S:
see Toad, American

TREEFROG, COMMON GRAY
(Hyla versicolor)

A tiny frog that spends almost all of its life in tree tops, the Common Gray Treefrog lives from Maine to the Gulf states and west to Texas, Oklahoma and into Minnesota.

Only about 2 inches (5.08 cm) in length, this seldom seen but clearly heard amphibian can be found in other colors besides the gray of its name. It may be green, brown, or almost white, with a dark, irregular star-shaped pattern on its upper side. It is often orange under its hind parts. The throat of the male is loose and dark, that of the female, whitish. The granular texture of its skin and the blotchy designs on its back make this frog resemble a little piece of bark.

The skin texture and design and the numerous color variations of the Gray Treefrog enable it to harmonize with its surroundings, thus hiding it from view of possible predators. Its normal pattern mimics the appearance of lichens – flat, crusty-scaly plants which grow on the barks of the trees in the diminutive frog's habitat. If the Gray Treefrog lands on another surface, it can change its hues to solid green or brown or to a patched arrangement, as the situation demands. Because this frog can remain perfectly still for long periods of time, its color camouflage

Above: A tree-dwelling Common Gray Treefrog rests serenely on a branch.

works effectively in protecting it from the ravages of its many enemies.

Living high in trees, these arboreal amphibians are walkers and climbers. As climbing aids, the tips of the Gray Treefrog's toes, like the toes of most other species of Treefrogs, are expanded into adhesive pads. These sticky discs act like suction cups, enabling the frogs to cling even to smooth, slippery leaf surfaces. The long, slender legs of the Treefrogs give them power for leaping from twig to twig, while their enlarged toe surfaces gain them firm footholds upon completion of their aerial vaults.

Anytime from April to August, depending upon where it lives, the Gray Treefrog comes down from its leafy heights, drawn to its breeding pool by its overwhelming instinct for repro-

Above: A rare Pine Barrens Treefrog.

duction. During the breeding season, every evening and sometimes during the day after rain, the males are heard as they slowly proceed to their annual procreative reunions. Their call is a loud, resonant trill, ending abruptly, repeated about twenty times a minute. When they sing in chorus, the sound of their collective resonances can be deafening.

The brown and yellow colored eggs are laid in small scattered packets, each containing about thirty or forty eggs. On the surface of quiet pools, the egg masses can be loosely attached to vegetation. In four to five days, the eggs hatch. The tadpoles transform into froglets in 45-65 days, move out of the water, and hop their way back up to the treetops until their cyclic chemistry draws them back again to mate.

Other treefrogs of wide distribution in North America are Northern Cricket Frog, *Acris crepitans*; Southern Cricket Frog, *Acris gryllus*; Green Treefrog, *Hyla cinerea*; Spring Peeper, *Hyla crucifer*; Pine Woods Treefrog, *Hyla femoralis*; Little Grass Frog, *Limnaoedus ocularis*; Chorus Frog, *Pseudacris triseriata* and Pine Barrens Treefrog, *Hyla andersoni*.

SALAMANDERS

Salamanders are lizard-like amphibians, most of them living part of their lives in water and part of their lives on land. The biological order in which salamanders have been grouped includes many families represented in the North American range, such as Sirens, Hellbenders, Mudpuppies and Newts.

Salamanders got their name from an ancient myth. The term salamander comes from a Greek word meaning fire animal. In medieval times, when men brought in wood and burned it in their hearths, salamanders were often driven from their hiding places in the logs by the heat of the flames. This gave rise to the belief that the mysterious little animals arose from fire and were even impervious to it.

The cool moist conditions in which salamanders must live are quite the opposite of their rising from flames. Although salamanders resemble lizards with their well-developed legs, lizards have thick, scaly, water-conserving skin coverings that salamanders lack. Like all amphibians, salamanders have thin, moist, permeable skins through which the animals are supplied with moisture and oxygen. Unable to drink, all of its body fluids are absorbed through the skin, the moisture in constant need of replenishment as fluid is quickly evaporated through the thin skin layer. Similar to the way gills function, the skin is amply supplied with blood vessels which extract oxygen from the wetness covering the water-dependent amphibian. Most salamanders breathe air with lungs as well as through their skins, although some species, the Lungless Salamanders, breathe entirely through their skins and through the linings of their mouths and throats.

In northern climates, some salamanders hibernate in winter, while others that live in water survive the cold by moving around under ice or on pond bottoms.

During breeding season, usually springtime, appearing as if out of nowhere, huge numbers of salamanders migrate towards their ponds and pools, propelled by the powerful, annual instinct for reproduction. Lacking the vocal abilities of frogs and toads, which are noisily resonated to attract the amorous attentions of females, salamanders have developed other attention-getting behaviors. The water boils with their rituals as they perform vigorous nuptial dances like primitive aquatic ballets, involving much wriggling, bumping and snout rubbing. Many individuals participate in this chemically inspired procreative activity. During the frenzied courtship, the male deposits a cone-shaped, jelly-like mass, topped with a cap of sperm, called a spermatophore. The female picks up this seminal bundle and takes it into her body

Above: A Red-spotted Newt (Notophthalmus viridescens viridescens).

through an opening at the base of her tail, called a cloaca. Thus her eggs are internally fertilized. With the exception of the Hellbender that squirts its sperm over the eggs once they are laid, salamander eggs are fertilized inside the female's body.

Like frog eggs, salamander eggs are covered with one or more jelly coverings which absorb water after the eggs are deposited. The females of many species, especially those which lay their eggs on land, remain with their eggs protecting them and keeping them moist. In differing lengths of time, depending upon the species and upon environmental conditions, the salamander larvae hatch. The young salamanders have a greater resemblance to the adults than do the tadpoles of frogs.

Most salamanders begin their lives in water, move on to land when they mature, and return again to their place of origin to breed. A few live on land throughout their lives, and some never leave their liquid spawning place. In the immature aquatic stage, salamanders breathe through feathery gills that stick out of their heads on either side. When swimming, they move with snake-like undulations of the body, their tiny legs of little use. As they mature, these amphibians lose their external gills, most develop lungs, their legs become stronger, and they leave the water to lead terrestrial lives.

Salamanders are seldom seen on land. They are secretive creatures that hide in crevices, curl up under logs, and burrow into underground recesses in constant search of moisture and food. Insects comprise the greatest portion of their diets. The infrequency of their appearance causes these animals to be little understood and even ascribes to them properties of mystery and magic.

ALLEGHENY ALLIGATOR:
see Hellbender

AXOLOTL:
see Salamander, Tiger

DEVIL DOG: see Hellbender

HELLBENDER
(Cryptobranchus
alleganiensis)

A Hellbender is a squat, ungainly salamander that spends it entire life in the water. Hellbenders can be found in fast-moving, rocky-bottomed streams and rivers from southeast New York to northern Alabama.

A giant among salamanders, the Hellbender can grow to from 12-29 inches (30.5-73.66 cm) in length. Its body and head are flattened and a loose flap of skin along the lower sides of its body makes its skin appear to fit too loosely. These wrinkled folds work as respiration aids as they are kept in motion while the animal reposes on pond bottoms where oxygen supplies are low.

This big salamander has four legs, but its legs are of little use. The Hellbender is strictly aquatic and swims by flexing its body and tail. Its gray or olive-brown coloration, sometimes mottled, camouflages the salamander among the rocks and debris of river beds. Prowling over watery bottoms, it eats mostly crayfish, snails and worms.

Hellbenders mate in late August in the North, and September to early November in the South. Under water, the male digs a saucer-shaped nest hollow beneath a flat stone or a submerged log. He induces gravid females to lay their eggs in it. Several females often use the same nest, each depositing about 450 yellowish eggs in long, tangled, beadlike strings. The nest may ultimately contain as many as 2000 eggs. The male discharges a white, cloudy seminal fluid called milt over the mass of eggs, which fertilizes them. Like a dutiful father, the male remains at the nest opening guarding the developing embryos until in about two to three months, they hatch.

About 1 inch (2.54 cm) long at hatching, the larvae are light with dark spots. Young Hellbenders are born with external gills and no legs, but at one year, their gills are reduced in size and small legs develop. Unlike most other salamanders which emerge from the water and spend their adult live on moist land, Hellbenders remain in the water throughout their existences.

The Hellbender is known to fishermen as a stealer of bait, and has the popular names of Allegheny Alligator or Devil Dog. Folklore claims that this salamander can inflict a poisonous bite or smear fishing lines with slime. Peculiar in appearance though it may be, this amphibian is completely harmless.

MUDPUPPY; WATERDOG
(Necturus maculosus)

A Mudpuppy is a large aquatic salamander. It lives in rivers and quiet streams of fresh water at depths of four to eight feet (1.2-2.4 m) usually among water weeds. One was found at a record depth of 90 feet in Lake Michigan. The natural range of the Mudpuppy is from southeast Manitoba to southern Quebec, and south to Georgia and Louisiana. It has been introduced into the large rivers of New England.

Growing to a length of from 8-17 inches (20.3-43.2 cm), the Mudpuppy has four short legs and weak, four-toed feet. Its tail is flattened and acts as a rudder. Behind its head are three pairs of feathery, bright red gills and two pairs of open gill slits that act as respiratory organs. Its dark brown or gray brown color, usually with mottlings, harmonizes with the river bottom on which it lives.

The size of a Mudpuppy's gills is an indication of the temperature and oxygen content of the water in which it is found. Where the water is warm, sluggish, and low in oxygen, the gills are larger. The plumy breathing organs are kept in constant motion to extract what oxygen there is from the water. Where the water is cool, fast moving and higher in oxygen supply, the gills are smaller and contracted.

In autumn the male Mudpuppy deposits in the water jelly-like little cones of sperm which are called spermatophores. The female takes a sperm mass into her body through an opening at the base of her tail, and retains it until the following spring. Thus her eggs are fertilized. She lays over 140 eggs singly and attaches them to the lower surfaces of submerged stones or logs. The

Below: **The Mudpuppy has external gills similar to the Siren.**

AMPHIBIANS

Above: **Eastern Newts forage in shallow water.**

eggs are ¼ inches (.63 cm) jelly-like spheres, light yellow in color. They hatch in about six to nine weeks, the female guarding them during the incubation period.

The Mudpuppy forages at night for worms, crayfish, insects and small fish. The popular but mistaken belief that this aquatic salamander barks like a dog accounts for its common name of Waterdog. Feared poisonous, there is no basis for this belief. The Mudpuppy's value to man lies in its use in classes in animal anatomy; some biological supply houses can sell as many as 2000 in one year.

The Alabama Waterdog, *Necturus alabamensis*, lives in Mississippi and Georgia, south to the Gulf of Mexico. The Dwarf Waterdog, *Necturus punctatus*, is the smallest of the waterdogs and inhabits the coastal plain of Virginia and Georgia.

NEWT, CALIFORNIA: see Newt, Eastern

NEWT, EASTERN (Notophthalmus viridescens)

Spending a large part of their lives in water, Eastern Newts live in damp woodlands and in ponds and lakes with dense submerged vegetation. From Nova Scotia to Florida and west to southwest Ontario and Texas, Newts cover a wide range.

The two stages of the life cycle of the Newt are different enough for this salamander to appear as two separate species. When the Newt is an adult, it is dark green or brown with red dots, surrounded by black rings. At this time, the Newt's skin is smooth and its

tail is compressed like a rudder to act as a swimming device. During the adult portion of its life span, the Newt is completely aquatic. It is about 5 inches (12.7 cm) in length.

Adult Newts are often seen foraging in shallow water, always in search of food. Their wide-ranging tastes include worms, insects, small crustaceans and mollusks. They snap up tadpoles and destroy a great number of mosquito larvae. Because Newts secrete a toxic substance in their skins they are avoided by fish and other predators.

In an immature stage of its existence, the Eastern Newt can be found on land. During its terrestrial period, the salamander is brick red or coral in color, meriting the popular name of Red Eft. Its bright coloration is a warning device, signaling an attacker to ignore the Eft as food because of its peppery taste and, moreover, because of its poisonous secretions. The youthful Eft has thick, roughened skin and a rounded tail.

Haunting the forest floor, the Red Eft has a voracious appetite for insects. It goes about its hunting activities quite boldly, armed as it is with poisonous protection. To avoid the freezing effects of winter on its cold blood, the Eft hibernates under the forest debris.

The Red Eft remains on land in moist conditions for one to three years, the duration of the Eft stage varying regionally. It then returns to the water as a mature adult and enters the aquatic period of its life as a fully developed Newt. The terms eft and newt are old Anglo-Saxon words meaning 'lizardlike.'

As breeding season approaches in early spring, the male Newt develops

enlarged hind legs with black, horny structures on the inner surfaces of his thighs. He deposits in the water a cone-shaped, jelly-like mass of seminal material called a spermatophore. Through an opening at the base of her tail, the female collects the spermatophore which fertilizes her eggs inside her body. She lays 200-400 jelly-covered eggs singly on submerged plants. In about 3-8 weeks, gilled larvae emerge and spend the summer in the water. In early fall, the young absorb their gills, develop legs and move out on to the land to begin their lives as Efts.

Along the west coast, the genus *Taricha* is represented by three species of newts: Rough-skinned Newt, *Taricha granulosa*; Red-bellied Newt, *Taricha rivularis*; and California Newt, *Taricha torosa*. In contrast to eastern newts, these western newts do not undergo an eft stage. Primarily terrestrial species, they hatch as aquatic larvae, then transform as land-dwelling adults, returning to the water only at breeding time.

NEWT, RED-BELLIED: see Newt, Eastern

NEWT, ROUGH-SKINNED: see Newt, Eastern

RED EFT: see Newt, Eastern

SALAMANDER, DUSKY (Desmognathus fuscus)

A member of the largest family of salamanders, the Dusky Salamander lives in rock-strewn, leafy accumulations near woodland creeks and springs. This species has a wide range and can be found from New Brunswick south to Florida, west to Texas, Oklahoma, southern Illinois and central Ohio.

Growing to approximately 5 inches (12.7 cm), the Dusky Salamander has a short body and a long, triangular-shaped tail. Highly variable in color and pattern, the adults usually have a brownish, uniformly colored back, sometimes with black-edged blotches

fused to form a stripe. With age, the patterns become obscured with dark pigment.

Dusky Salamanders are members of a huge family, called Lungless Salamanders, 80 of which occur in North America. As the name of their family indicates, Dusky Salamanders do not have lungs with which to breathe. Instead, they take in oxygen through their thin skins, which are richly supplied with blood vessels, and through the linings of their mouths and throats. Their permeable skin covering must always remain moist to provide the salamanders a constant source of body fluid and a supply of oxygen which passes through the cells in their respiratory coating.

The tongue of the Dusky Salamander is attached to the front of its mouth, free at the sides and the back. Its lower jaw is immovable, which means it must open its mouth by lifting its upper jaw and head.

Largely nocturnal, the food of the Dusky Salamander is earthworms, snails, slugs, spiders, insects and some vegetable material. A land-dwelling amphibian, it is often found in dried stream beds with little water remaining.

Dusky Salamanders, as do many other species, engage in elaborate courtship performances. Males may court females in the spring or in the fall. In amorous behavior, males may rub and prod females by applying their

snouts and cheeks to females' snouts. The female may straddle his tail while he drops a sperm case, or spermatophore, into the water which she retrieves by taking it up into her body to fertilize her eggs.

From June to September, the female Dusky Salamander lays a compact mass of from 12-26 yellow-white eggs in wet areas near water but not in it. The eggs are attached to the underside of rocks or rotting logs and are enclosed in three layers of jelly. The little cluster of round, transparent balls appears as a bunch of grapes. In motherly fashion, the female protects her eggs until they hatch.

Hatching on the ground and not in water as do most other salamander young, the larvae must make their perilous way, wiggling through minute trickles, to a pond or stream to continue their development. They live in water for eight to ten months, then transform into 1 inch (2.54 cm) long adults that walk out on to land to continue living with terrestrial habits.

The range of the Dusky Salamander has been widened unintentionally by fishermen who use them for bait.

The Southern Dusky Salamander, *Desmognathus auriculatus*, having a row or two of round, reddish spots on its side, ranges from Virginia to Florida and west to Texas. Like its northern relative, the Southern Dusky Salamander can lighten or darken its color to camouflage itself. It is often

Above: The dusky Salamander has a distinctive triangular tail.

found with the Mud Salamander, *Pseudotriton montanus*. The Long-tailed Salamander, *Eurycea longicauda*, another member of the lungless salamander family, has a wide distribution from New York to Florida and west to the Mississippi River. The bright red-orange colors and the black spots of the northern form of this species often make it quite easily seen.

The Spring Salamander, *Gyrinophilus porphyriticus*, one of the largest lungless salamanders, can achieve a length of approximately 8 inches (20.32 cm). It ranges from Quebec south to Georgia, Alabama and Mississippi. Brownish-pink in color with varied patterns, it has a keeled tail and a light bar that runs from eye to nostril.

SALAMANDER, FOUR-TOED: see Salamander, Red-backed

SALAMANDER, JEFFERSON (*Ambystoma jeffersonianum*)

Jefferson Salamanders are members of the Mole Salamander family, a group in which the adult specimens are confirmed burrowers. In deciduous forests under moist debris near swamps and ponds from western New England and southern New York to Virginia and Indiana, the Jefferson Salamander leads its secret life.

AMPHIBIANS

Most Mole Salamanders have robust bodies and limbs, and short, blunt heads, but the Jefferson Salamander is moderately slim with long digits. It has the characteristic wide snout. Growing to a length of 8 inches (60 cm), it is a brownish-gray color, often with bluish flecks on its limbs and the lower sides of its belly.

In late March or early April, Jefferson Salamanders in great numbers make their way to their breeding ponds, as if drawn by an unseen magnet. Responding to the primordial call to perpetuate their kind, the salamanders churn the water with their mating activity. When their reproductive rites are completed, these amphibians leave the water just as suddenly as they appeared. For another year, they burrow into their moist and secret hiding places in temperate woods, only to emerge at night to feed on earthworms and insects.

A single female Jefferson Salamander lays over 200 jelly-covered eggs, placed in 10-20 cylindrical masses of about 15 eggs each. These egg strings are attached to submerged plant stems or twigs. The larvae hatch in 30-45 days, just ½ inch (.12 cm) long. The gilled and legless young spend from 8-18 weeks in the water until they loose their external gills and develop lungs and legs, enabling them to crawl out on to land. The following spring, they return to the ponds in which they were spawned to perform again the rituals that ensure their continuation.

SALAMANDER, LONG-TAILED:
see Salamander, Dusky

SALAMANDER, MARBLED
(Ambystoma opacum)

The Marbled Salamander is an amphibian that can be found in low, swampy areas or in almost dry hillsides from southern New Hampshire to northern Florida, west to eastern Texas, and north to Lakes Michigan and Erie.

A chunky salamander, the Marbled Salamander can grow to a length of 5 inches (12.7 cm). Dark, shiny black above, this species has bold silvery crossbars. There are four to seven of these bands which are wider on the salamander's sides than on its back. Males have brighter coloration than females.

Unlike most other salamanders which lay their eggs in water, the Marbled Salamander lays its eggs on land. Also, the Marbled Salamander lays its eggs in the fall instead of the spring, as do most other species. In September to October in the North and in October to December in the South, the female lays 50-200 eggs singly in a shallow hole under debris. She remains with the eggs, curling her body around them, until rain floods the depression. The eggs hatch in varying lengths of time depending upon the amount of moisture and the temperature of the air. If there is little autumn rain, the eggs will not hatch until the following spring. With sufficient moisture, the hatched-out larvae wriggle or float to the water. In the pond or stream, they live as gilled, swimming immature salamanders until they lose their gills, develop lungs and legs, and move out on to land.

As with all amphibians, the eggs are covered with a jelly-like, watery envelope. Unprotected by a hardened shell which seals in moisture as in reptile eggs, amphibian eggs would dry out where it not for their liquid coating and fluid surroundings. Even though the Marbled Salamander lays its eggs on land, the eggs still require watery conditions in order to develop.

The Marbled Salamander can withstand dryer conditions than many other salamanders. It is often found in dry, hilly regions, although it may also live in damp gravel near streams. Even conditions which are relatively dry for a salamander must have sufficient moisture to prevent the thin-skinned amphibian from drying out. Salamanders do not drink. Their skins are not scaly and watertight as are the skins of reptiles, therefore body fluids, quickly lost, need constant replenishment.

The larvae of the Marbled Salamander often share ponds with the larvae of the Spotted Salamander, *Ambystoma maculatum*. The Spotted Salamander spends most of its time underground, so adults are rarely seen.

SALAMANDER, MOLE:
see Salamander, Spotted; Salamander, Tiger

SALAMANDER, MUD:
see Salamander, Dusky

SALAMANDER, RED:
see Salamander, Red-backed

SALAMANDER, RED-BACKED
(Plethodon cinereus)

The Red-backed Salamander lives in cool, moist woodlands from western Ontario to southern Quebec and Newfoundland, south to North Carolina and southern Indiana.

Long and slender, the Red-backed Salamander can grow to 5 inches (12.7 cm) in length. Highly variable in hue, this salamander has two color phases. In its red-backed phase, a wide stripe covers almost its entire back. This stripe may be any shade of pink or red, even yellow or gray, with tiny black dots within it. The other color phase is called the lead-backed. In this phase, the broad dorsal stripe is missing, so that the amphibian's back is uniformly black. To make identification even more confusing, individuals may be intermediate between these two color stages, and the dorsal stripe may be greatly mottled.

The Red-backed Salamander is a lungless amphibian which extracts oxygen from the air through abundant blood vessels in its moist skin and its mouth lining. This salamander is completely terrestrial, having no aquatic stage and living its entire life on land. Because of its ability to tolerate low temperatures, it can live in extremely cold climates and has even survived in glaciated areas of northeast United States and Canada.

Found under stumps, leaves, bark or moss in moist forests, the Red-

Above: **The terrestrial Red-backed Salamander.**

backed Salamander hunts at night for insects. Food is captured by a swift, forward dart of the tongue which can be accurately directed. To protect itself from becoming food for other animals, this salamander secretes a toxic slime. In lizard fashion, it can snap off a portion of its tail if grabbed by an attacker. The discarded tail section thrashes about, engaging the enemy's attention, while the salamander quickly dashes for cover.

The animals mate in fall, the male depositing his sperm package on land under rotting logs and rocks where it is picked up by the female. The female harbors the sperm until the following spring when she deposits her fertilized eggs. A small group of 6-12 eggs in a whitish, grape-like cluster is attached by a stalk to the roof of a cavity under a rock or a log. She coils around her eggs, protecting them until, in about two months, they hatch. The young pass through the larval stage while still within the egg. Once hatched, the baby Red-backed Salamander have gills for only a short time and then become land-living amphibians. Although they live a completely land-based existence, as befits true amphibians, they live in moist conditions to keep from drying out.

The Four-toed Salamander, *Hemidactylium scutatum*, is a lungless salamander found chiefly east of the Mississippi River and, like the Red-

backed Salamander, can discard its tail if grabbed by a predator. A new tail is soon regenerated.

The Red-backed Salamander is not to be confused with the Red Salamander, *Pseudotriton ruber*, which is also a member of the lungless salamander family. The Red Salamander is coral-red when young and orange-brown in adulthood and is covered with many irregularly shaped black spots. Often found in leaf litter some distance from water, it inhabits most of the eastern portion of the United States.

SALAMANDER, SLIMY
(*Plethodon glutinosus*)

The Slimy Salamander is an amphibian of shaded slopes and wooded flood plains from central New York south to Florida, and west to southern Missouri, northwest Arkansas and eastern Oklahoma.

The Slimy Salamander can attain a length of approximately 8 inches (20.32 cm). It is smooth, slender, and shining in appearance. Its back is colored dark violet-black, while its undersides are gray. It is usually well sprinkled with silvery white flecks and spots, but the amount of spotting varies enormously from individual to individual.

The Slimy Salamander needs very moist conditions and lives under

Above: **The terrestrial Red-backed Salamander.**

stones or logs in wooded areas. A member of the family of lungless salamanders, it takes in oxygen through its wet skin and through the lining of its mouth and throat, all of which are richly supplied with blood vessels. Salamanders are unable to drink, therefore their moisture requirements are absorbed through their smooth, scaleless body covering which must remain wet to maintain a constant supply of body fluids.

After a rain, this moisture-greedy amphibian emerges from its damp hiding place to prowl the forest floor in search of food. Insects, sow bugs, worms and millipedes comprise its diet.

The Slimy Salamander courts and mates in spring and fall in the north, summer in the south. The white eggs are laid in clusters of 6-36 in underground crevices or under rotting logs. The female stays coiled around the nest, guarding the eggs until, in about two months, the well-developed ½ inch (1.27 cm) long young hatch out. The larvae do not enter the water, having bypassed their aquatic stage inside the egg. They spend all their lives on land, leading a damp, terrestrial existence.

Many species of salamanders secrete toxic substances through their skins, which are poisonous to small

prey. The Slimy Salamander secretes a substance whose appearance gives the animal the descriptive name of slimy, but the ooze is not slimy at all. When touched, the Slimy Salamander's skin glands produce a sticky chemical that is so gluey it is almost impossible to remove from one's fingers.

SALAMANDER, SOUTHERN DUSKY:
see Salamander, Dusky

SALAMANDER, SPOTTED
(*Ambystoma maculatum*)

The Spotted Salamander is a rather large salamander which can be found in moist woodland conditions within a wide range from Ontario to Nova Scotia and south to Georgia and Texas.

Stoutly built, the Spotted Salamander can attain a length of 6-10 inches (15.2-25.4 cm) of which its tail is about half. The rows of bright yellow, golden or orange spots down each side of its smooth, glossy, brownish-black back give this salamander a striking appearance. Its sides are dark gray, its belly slate gray and unspotted. Its shiny moist skin becomes mucous-covered when the salamander is disturbed.

Very secretive, the Spotted Sala-

mander spends most of its time underground, hiding under earth or debris. Its burrowing ways are like the Mole Salamanders, of which zoological family the Spotted Salamander is a member. Under the cover of darkness, it emerges to hunt for worms, snails and insects. In cold climates, this salamander hibernates underground in piles of leaves or in rotting logs. Some may occasionally be found in cellars or in window wells.

In late March or early April, full grown Spotted Salamanders descend in great numbers on woodland ponds to enact their primordial ritual of reproduction. The females are distended with eggs, while the spots on the males have become brighter. Swimming around in a courtship dance, they rub each other's noses. For three or four nights, the water is achurn with their activity, until the female takes up, through an opening at the base of her tail called a vent or cloaca, the male sperm package. He has deposited a cone-shaped mass of seminal material which fertilizes her eggs inside her body.

The female Spotted Salamander lays one or more compact egg masses of from twelve to over one hundred eggs on submerged vegetation. Each

Above: The adult Spotted Salamander is rarely seen because it lives underground.

egg is surrounded by a little ball of jelly and the entire mass, which measures about 3 inches (7.62 cm) in diameter is enclosed in a clear, jelly-like envelope. Soon the egg cluster acquires a greenish hue, the color from a beneficial algae that grows on the jelly. Resembling pond scum, the microscopic green plants absorb the carbon dioxide breathed out by the developing tadpoles within the eggs. The embryonic salamanders breath in the oxygen given off by the plants. Through this mutually agreeable arrangement, the growing larvae receive an ample supply of pure air even in the crowded conditions inside the egg mass.

In four to seven weeks, depending upon the temperature of the water, the eggs hatch. The larvae are about ½ inch (0.12 cm) long. They are greenish-yellow with dark spots on their backs. The young have fringed gills and small bud-like structures which will become forelegs, but the hind legs do not develop until the salamanders are ready to crawl out on to land. The larvae of salamanders resemble the adults more closely than do the tadpoles of frogs and toads.

Near the end of the summer, the gills of the young are absorbed into the body, the legs grow and straighten and the adult form emerges from the water to lead a terrestrial life. The following spring, the adult Spotted Salamanders return to the ponds to fulfill again their reproductive destiny.

SALAMANDER, SPRING:
see Salamander, Dusky

SALAMANDER, TIGER
(Ambystoma tigrinuam)

Tiger Salamanders are the largest land-dwelling salamanders in the world. They can be found in varied habitats, such as arid sagebrush plains, mountains, forests and damp meadows. The range of this species is widespread from Alberta and Saskatchewan south to Florida and Mexico. They are not found in New England.

With a stout body, broad head, distinct neck and small eyes, the Tiger Salamander can grow to a length of 13 inches (33.02 cm). Although the color and pattern are highly variable in such a widely distributed species, usually its color is deep brown to black, marked with pale, irregular, yellow-brown blotches which form bands.

Tiger Salamanders live where the ground is easily burrowed. During the day they hide beneath debris or in crayfish or mammal burrows, awaiting the protective cover of darkness. Nocturnal, they consume prodigious amounts of earthworms, insects, small mice and other amphibians.

From January to March, depending upon the level of warmth and the amount of daylight, prompted by the rain, Tiger Salamanders emerge from their places beneath the ground to make their inexorable trek to shallow breeding ponds. The water they seek may be temporary pools, fishless ponds, streams, backwaters or lakes. There they perform their age-old courtship rituals in perpetuation of their species. The male deposits his spermataphore, a sperm package, in the water, and the female takes this little seminal bundle into her body through a ventral opening called a cloaca. Her eggs are thus internally fertilized. She lays 100 or more eggs, enclosed in a three envelope jelly mass. The mass is kidney-shaped and is attached to submerged vegetation or debris.

In three to four weeks, the larvae hatch and live a swimming existence. In about four months, most Tiger Salamanders lose their gills and develop lungs and legs. Once changed into adult forms, they spend their lives on land as secretive, burrowing animals.

Some types of Tiger Salamanders, especially those found in the western United States, remain in the water as gilled larvae all their lives, never developing into the adult stage. These permanent larvae become very large, often nearly 13 inches (33.02 cm) and are referred to by biologists as 'axolotls.'

The Mole Salamander, *Ambystoma talpoideum*, as its name implies, is a burrower, its underground habits similar to those of the Tiger Salamander. The Mole Salamander's breeding sites are often shared with the Tiger Salamander, the Marbled Salamander, *Ambystoma opacum*, or with the Spotted Salamander, *Ambystoma maculatum*.

SIREN, DWARF:
see Siren, Greater

SIREN, GREATER
(Siren lacertina)

The Greater Siren is a long, thin, snake-like amphibian which spends its entire life in water. It lives in shallow, muddy-bottomed, weed-choked water in the coastal plain from the District of Columbia through Florida and southern Alabama.

The Greater Siren can easily be mistaken for an eel, as it has a long body, external gills, gill slits, no hind legs and two tiny front legs which are completely useless. It is gray or olive above, sometimes spotted. Its sides are lighter in color, with many faint greenish-yellow blotches. The Siren may attain a length of over 36 inches (91.44 cm), although few exceed 30 inches (76.2 cm). The external gills appear as feathery growths on the sides of the neck. It has minute eyes, and jaws that are covered with horn. A primitive amphibian, the Siren seems to have gotten stuck in the larval stage and never developed the legs or lungs necessary to move it out of water onto land as have many other salamanders.

The Greater Siren has a smooth, moist, permeable skin, unprotected by scaly covering. Body water is easily lost through the skin, so the Siren must stay in moist conditions to prevent drying out. When lack of rainfall dries up its habitat, the Siren estivates in muddy burrows. As in hibernation, the body processes of an animal in estivation slow down markedly, making the individual appear near death. While buried in the mud, the Siren's skin secretes a cocoon which covers its body and seals in the moisture. When the ground becomes wet again, it emerges from its burrow, none the worse for its experience.

Awake at night, the Siren eats snails, insect larvae, small fish and aquatic plants. It spendss it day secretively burrowed in the mud or hidden in the thick water vegetation of its swampy home. When caught, Sirens make yelping noises while squirming about vigorously.

The Lesser Siren, *Siren intermedia*, is a smaller, slimmer version of the Greater Siren. These two Sirens share a similar range, although the Lesser Siren can be found further north into Michigan. The Dwarf Siren, *Pseudobranchus striatus*, is the smallest siren and lives in the coastal plain of South Carolina, Georgia and Florida.

SIREN, LESSER:
see Siren, Greater

WATERDOG: see Mudpuppy

WATERDOG, ALABAMA:
see Mudpuppy

WATERDOG, DWARF:
see Mudpuppy

FISH

Fish are cold-blooded animals that live in water. They respire by means of gills, structures that support capillaries – tiny blood vessels – so that water can flow over them and oxygen dissolved in the water can diffuse directly into the blood of the animal.

Although we may think of any animal that spends its life submerged in water as a 'fish,' all water animals are not fish, and not all fish are closely related. For example, animals commonly called 'shellfish' are not fish at all, but crustaceans or mollusks.

Today, all the fish in the world belong to the three groups: Agnatha, Chondrichthyes, and Osteichthyes. Although there are many differences between these groups of fish, they have some characteristics in common: they breathe by means of gills, they are cold-blooded and they have a two-chambered heart (mammals have a four-chambered heart).

The Agnatha is a very small group. The best known examples are the sea lamprey and the hagfish. These fish have no jaws, no scales, and do not have paired fins. They have exposed gill slits and a poorly developed cartilaginous skeleton. Both the hagfish and the sea lamprey are parasitic fish that destroy large numbers of valuable food fish. They latch on to the fish with their mouths that act like sucker discs, and suck blood, body fluids and flesh out of their victims.

The Chondrichthyes or cartilaginous fish include sharks, rays, skates, and chimaeràs. Almost all fish in the group are marine, although some may occasionally wander into brackish or freshwater parts of rivers and estuaries, and there is a species of shark in a lake in Nicaragua. They have well-developed cartilaginous skeletons, true jaws, paired appendages or fins, exposed gill slits, and the beginnings of scales.

Most cartilaginous fish have placoid scales. These are very hard scales that are built like the teeth of higher vertebrates. The scale is made mostly of a substance called dentin (our teeth contain the same material) and is covered with a hard enamel. The scales point backward on the shark and give its skin a rough, 'sandpaper' texture. The teeth of the shark have the same basic construction as the scales. They are easily lost but are also easily replaced. Cartilaginous fish do not have swim bladders. Consequently, they must keep moving to maintain position in the water. It was once thought that cartilaginous fish had to keep moving in order to breathe and stay alive. However, it is now known that some sharks common-ly rest on the bottom and actually sleep.

The Osteichthyes, or bony fish, are often referred to as the 'true' fish, although the cartilaginous fish are no less fish than are the bony fish. As the name implies, the bony fish have a bony skeleton. They are the most numerous of the vertebrates in numbers of species; more than 20,000 species are believed to exist. Bony fish live in both fresh and salt water. They are found in all climates, at all ocean depths, and in every kind of body of fresh water at all altitudes. They are, by far, the most successful of the fish.

In addition to the bony skeleton, bony fish are characterized by having an air bladder and paired fins, and most have scales. Like all fish, they have a two-chambered heart, and the gills are covered.

Although bony fish occur in a wide variety of shapes, most can be described as 'streamlined' with the head, trunk and tail merged into a shape that allows for the most efficient flow of water over the body. The scales overlap toward the rear, and are covered with a slimy substance secreted by many mucus glands just under the scales. The slime protects the fish against infection and helps it to move through the water more easily. The fin pattern is similar in most bony fish. The dorsal fins are on the back; the pectoral fins are just behind the gill cover on the side of the body; the pelvic fins are on the underside toward the back and the caudal fin is at the back or tail. Most bony fish have well-developed eyes and a well-developed sense of vision. They have nostrils or nares, which are organs of smell, not breathing.

The gills are supported by curved gill arches. A double row of gill filaments on each arch is richly supplied with blood vessels. Dissolved oxygen diffuses directly from the water into the blood.

Most fish reproduce by shedding eggs and sperm directly into the water. Many fish migrate to shallow parts of lakes, rivers and streams for spawning, an action that increases the chances that sperm and eggs of a particular species will come into contact. Some saltwater fish, notably the salmon, swim miles up rivers to shallow streams for mating. Although most fish do not care for their young, a few guard the newly hatched fish.

Some sharks give birth to live young. However, these young develop inside an egg and are not nourished by a placenta as is the case with most mammals. The young shark hatches inside and emerges through the genital opening of the female. Some skates deposit their eggs in cases or purses.

The bony fish are extremely important to mankind, supplying food and many other needs. Pollution is already having an adverse effect on the populations of some food fish, and it is feared that unless management of worldwide stocks is improved, many important food fish may become extinct.

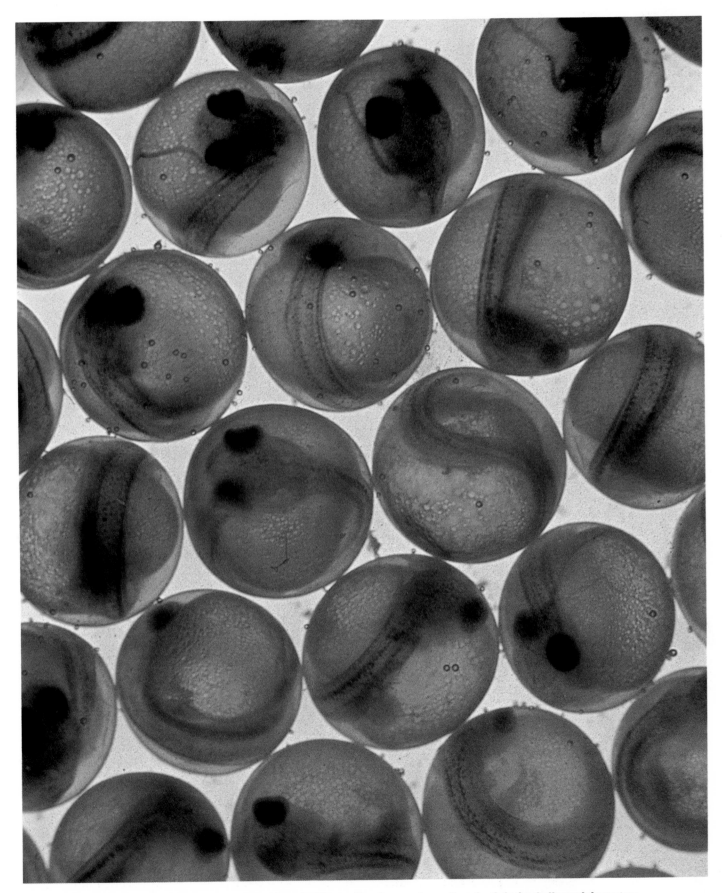

Above: Eyed Lake Trout eggs. As many as 18,000 are deposited by one female on rocky reefs or shoals in the shallower lake waters.

ALEWIFE: see Menhaden

BARRACUDA; GREAT BARRACUDA
(Sphyraena barracuda)

A familiar fish of warm waters in the Atlantic Ocean and Caribbean Sea coastal areas, the Barracuda also ranges northward to New England as well as southward to Brazil. The Barracuda thrives in a variety of marine habitats, including heads and edges of coral reefs, deep oceans, sandy shores and weedy bottoms. The Barracuda found closer in to shore are more likely to be younger specimens than those in the reefs and deeper parts of the ocean. A solitary fish, Barracuda do not school and are found together only at spawning time. Not much is known about their breeding habits. However, they are believed to deposit their eggs in the open sea.

Capable of growing to 10 feet (3 m), and to weights in excess of 200 pounds (91 kg), most adults rarely exceed 5 feet (1.5 m) and achieve a maximum weight from around 100 to 110 pounds (45 to 50 kg). Most Barracuda that are caught are considerably smaller. Bearing a resemblance to fresh water pike and muskellunge, the Barracuda has a slender body with anal and dorsal fins set well back. The body is silvery in color with flecks of black on the sides that increase in density toward the tail, and the anal and caudal fins are almost all black.

A fierce hunter, often called the 'Tiger of the Sea,' the Barracuda commonly hides in cover such as a reef or in vegetation, and strikes with great speed and force at a passing prey. The Barracuda eats practically any other fish including 'grunts,' jack, sea bass, and other Barracuda. It also occasionally takes sea birds. The Barracuda is potentially dangerous to swimmers and waders. Although attacks are rare, a Barracuda bite can be a serious wound. Wounds from Barracuda bites are, indeed, large, but they are straight and clean. Most attacks on humans stem from the fish being attracted to bright, shiny objects such as

Above: **Largemouth Bass, abundant in lakes.**

belt buckles and jewelry on the victim which the Barracuda perceives as potential prey. A wise scuba diver diving in waters where Barracuda are found does not use bright, shiny metal hardware on his diving gear.

A popular game fish, the Barracuda is often taken with a bright metal lure on a rod and reel. Although it is a commonly consumed fish in some areas of Central and South America, eating Barracuda can be dangerous. Many of the fish that the Barracuda eats are toxic, and the toxins are sometimes concentrated in the Barracuda's flesh. The meat also spoils quickly.

The Pacific Barracuda, ranging from Alaska to Baja California, is quite similar to the Atlantic Barracuda, but is smaller, generally reaching a length of 3¾ feet (1.1 m) and a weight of 15 to 20 pounds (6 to 9 kg). In contrast to its Atlantic cousin, the Pacific Barracuda is an excellent food fish that is standard fare in West Coast fish markets. The roe of the Pacific Barracuda is also consumed as caviar. The Atlantic Mackerel is in the same classification order as the Barracuda and has similar coloration. It has a more ovoid body than the Barracuda and is much smaller, seldom exceeding 2 feet (.6 m) and 7 or 8 pounds (3.1 to 3.6 kg).

BASS, LARGEMOUTH; LARGEMOUTH BLACK BASS; BLACK BASS
(Micropterus salmoides)

The Largemouth Bass is native to eastern North America in lakes and rivers from the Great Lakes southward to Florida, Texas and Mexico, and westward through the Mississippi River Valley to Nebraska and Kansas. It has been successfully introduced to lakes and rivers in the western United States, Europe and South Africa.

The average weight of the Largemouth Bass is 5 to 15 pounds (2.2 to 6.8 kg), although specimens of 25 pounds (11 kg) and larger have been taken. Lengths of 12 to 15 inches (30 to 38 cm) are common, and lengths of 3 feet (.9 m) and more are on record. The well-scaled Largemouth Bass is black to green and has a horizontal band running along the side from the gills to the tail. The dorsal fin, almost but not quite split, has a short spiny forward part, and a softer, higher, backwards-raked rear part. The name of the Largemouth Bass stems from the size of the mouth, the angle of which is well below and behind the eye when the mouth is only partially opened.

A voracious feeder, the Largemouth Bass prefers to hunt in shallow waters of lakes and rivers, where it feeds on insects, small crustaceans, frogs and fish, including young Largemouth Bass.

Spawning occurs in late spring or early summer when the temperature reaches at least 50°F (10°C). The male digs a nest some 12 inches (.3 m) in diameter in sand or gravel in water about 6 feet (1.8 m) deep. The female deposits her eggs in the nest and then leaves. The male stands guard over the eggs and the newly hatched young. The young Largemouth Bass grow faster in warm water than in cold. In warm water they may reach a length of 14 inches (.35 m) in three years.

The Largemouth Bass is one of the most avidly sought of sport fish among anglers in North America. It fights vigorously when hooked, but does not leap out of the water as does the Smallmouth Bass. The Largemouth Bass is often stocked in farm ponds.

Similar species include the Smallmouth Bass (*Micropterus dolomieui*), Rock Bass (*Ambloplites rupestris*), Sunfish and Crappie (*Pomoxis annularis*).

BASS, SMALLMOUTH; SMALLMOUTH BLACK BASS
(Micropterus dolomieui)

A native of North America, the Smallmouth Bass is found in cool lakes and streams from Quebec, southward to South Carolina, Alabama and Oklahoma. The Smallmouth Bass has been introduced into many new areas in North America, Europe – particularly France – and in South Africa.

A bit smaller than the related largemouth bass, the Smallmouth Bass seldom exceeds 7 pounds (3.2 kg); catches of 2 to 3 pounds (.9 to 1.3 kg) are considered to be good. An ovoid, slightly chunky fish, the Smallmouth is brownish to bronze and has several olive-colored vertical bars. The forward part of the dorsal fin is short and spiny, while the rear part is softer and raked backwards.

A predaceous fish, it eats insects, crustaceans, insect larvae and whatever fish are small enough for it to take.

The Smallmouth Bass breeds in shallow waters when the temperature exceeds 50°F (10°C). The male digs a nest close to a boulder or fallen log in gravel or fine sand on the lake or stream bottom. The female deposits her eggs in the nest, the male fertilizes them and stands guard over them and the young fry when they hatch.

The Smallmouth Bass is considered to be the most exciting freshwater game fish in North America, if not the world. When hooked, it leaps out of the water, then fights tenaciously until it is completely exhausted. The flesh is considered to be quite tasty.

Similar species include the Largemouth Bass (*Micropterus salmoides*), the Rock Bass (*Ambloplites rupestris*), Sunfish and Crappies.

BLUE SUNFISH: see Bluegill

BLUEGILL; BREAM; BLUE SUNFISH
(Lepomis macrochirus)

The Bluegill is found in quiet freshwater habitats throughout most of North America east of the Rocky Mountains.

The Bluegill has the typical rounded shape characteristic of the sunfish. Although it may grow to a length of 15 inches (38 cm) or more and weigh as much as 4½ pounds (2 kg), few ever reach that size. Most Bluegills taken with rod and reel are ½ to 1 pound (.2 to .45 kg) and about 7 to 9 inches (18 to 23 cm) in length. Covered with moderately large blue scales in the upper part of the body, the sides are blue and the underside is white. The gill covers and cheeks are a dark blue, and there are dark vertical bars of color on the sides.

The Bluegill spends a great deal of time hiding in quiet, weedy water. Larger Bluegills may spend most of the day in deep water and move to shore in the morning and evening. Bluegills feed mostly on insects, but may also eat small crustaceans and aquatic plants.

Breeding takes place from May to July. Males build a saucer-shaped nest on or near bottom in a depth of 1 to 4 feet (.3 to 1.2 m). The eggs deposited by the female are covered with a sticky substance and stick to stones and other bottom debris. The male guards the eggs and the young fry.

The Bluegill is one of the more popular panfishes, those fish that are small enough to fry whole in a pan. For its size it is a scrappy fish that takes the bait with an audible smack and fights vigorously to shake the hook. Fairly easy to catch with worms and live bait, they are ideal for the novice angler. The meat has a fine texture and a good flavor.

Similar species include the Sunfish and the Pumpkinseed.

BREAM: see Bluegill

BUNKER FISH: see Menhaden

CADE: see Carp

CARP
(Cyprinus carpio)

One of the most widely distributed fish in the world, the Carp is found in pools, lakes, rivers and ponds in most of the world, including all of North America. The Carp may have originated in rivers that flow into the Black Sea and Aegean, particularly the Danube River. However, there is also evidence that it originated in China. It was important as a food fish in antiquity, and, as people migrated to all parts of the world, the Carp was introduced into new areas.

One of the few fish to have been selectively bred by man, the Carp occurs in many variations. This deep-bodied fish is fully scaled in the wild, but selectively bred varieties such as the Mirror Carp have only a few large scales, and the Leather Carp has no scales at all. The back and upper sides are dark, generally brown to black, while the sides have a golden color. The large mouth can be protruded for bottom feeding, and is surrounded by barbels. A hulky, deep fish that has a massive appearance, the Carp can grow to be fairly large both in the wild and in Carp farms. Rod and reel catches of 8 to 10 pounds (3.6-4.5 kg) Carp around a foot (30 cm) long are not unusual, but there are occasional catches of specimens close to or exceeding 60 pounds (27 kg). In farms, they are allowed to grow to whatever size is best for market conditions.

Carp do best in quiet lakes, pools and lowland rivers where the water is warm and the conditions weedy. They can survive in waters where the oxygen level is so low that many other fish would die. Bottom feeders when young, they eat crustaceans, insect larvae, and other bottom creatures. As they get bigger, they look through the water at all levels for larger crustaceans, mollusks, insect larvae, small fish and, in the summer, aquatic vegetation.

Breeding takes place in the late spring or summer when the temperature reaches 73° to 75°F (23° to 24°C). Small yellowish eggs, deposited in shallows or on vegetation, hatch in five to twelve days, depending on the temperature. Fast growers, Carp reach maturity in two to three years. One of the most long-lived of the fishes, Carp

Above: Channel Catfish prefer swift streams.

Above: A freshwater *Gila cypha* a member of the carp and minnow family (*Cyprinidae*).

are thought to live as long as 20 years in the wild and have lived 40 to 50 years in captivity.

Many sport fishermen consider the Carp to be a rough fish, that is, one that destroys game fish. Although the Carp does not eat large numbers of fish, when it bottom feeds it rolls in the mud, stirring up sediment and often destroying the eggs of game fish or disrupting the protective cover of the eggs. The Carp is, nonetheless, a popular quarry for many sport fishermen, and, in addition to rod and reel fishing, many are taken with bow and arrow, particularly in shallow waters where they are large and abundant. A valuable commercial food fish and a major source of food in many parts of the world, hundreds of millions of pounds are harvested annually. It is considered to be basic cheap food rather than a delicacy. As a food fish, it is much more popular in eastern Europe than in western Europe and North America.

The carp is taxonomically related to a number of smaller fishes including the Goldfish (*Carassius auratus*), Common Shiner, and Cade (Chub).

CATFISH, CHANNEL
(*Ictalurus punctatus*)

The Channel Catfish ranges widely over much of North America from the central plains provinces of Canada and Hudson Bay, southward to the Great Lakes region, the Mississippi River to Florida and Mexico. In contrast to most other catfish, the Channel Catfish is found in clear fast streams rather than mud-bottomed lakes and the streams preferred by most other cat-

fish species. It has been introduced to many areas outside of its original range.

In appearance, the Channel Catfish is more typically a catfish with a long, smooth, unscaled body, a flattened head, and many long barbels around the mouth. The Channel Catfish is deep brown on the back and silvery on the sides. When it is young it has dark spots on the side. The Channel Catfish is capable of growing to weights of around 60 pounds (27 kg). Most catches, however, are in the 5 pound (2.26 kg) range, and weights above 10 (.45 kg) pounds are exceptional.

Like all catfish, the Channel Catfish is omnivorous and nocturnal. It finds its prey by smell, sight and by feeling out the bottom with its barbels.

The Channel Catfish spawns in shallow depressions scooped out in mud. The male guards the eggs, and after hatching, one or both parents stand watch over the dense schools of young catfish, driving away potential predators.

The Channel Catfish is an excellent food and sport fish, and commands a high price in the southern states. Young fish are sometimes sent to England for ornamental garden ponds.

CHAR:
see Trout, Brook; Trout, Lake

CHUB, BERMUDA
(*Kyphosus secatrix*)

The range of the Bermuda Chub extends from Massachusetts south to

the Caribbean, the Gulf of Mexico and the waters of the Atlantic Ocean off Brazil, eastward to the coast of Africa. It is likely to be found in rocky areas and reefs in shallow water, although young Bermuda Chubs are often found among the thick sargassum weed of the Sargasso Sea. Adults are often found around driftwood and frequently follow the wake of ships, a habit that has earned them the name Rudderfish in some areas.

The Bermuda Chub is a deep-bodied fish with a small rounded head and small jaws and a bulge on the back. The color is variable, but a prevalent color pattern is gray with horizontal darker stripes and wide yellowish marks on the head.

Young Bermuda Chub feed on algae and the adult fish expand their diet to include other plants and small invertebrates. In the open ocean they frequently swim in schools. A good game fish, it fights well when hooked. The common name Chub also applies to unrelated freshwater species, which includes the minnow and carp family.

CHUM: see Salmon

CISCO: see Whitefish

COHO: see Salmon

CRAPPIE:
see Bass, Largemouth; Bass, Smallmouth

CUTTHROAT, BROWN:
see Trout, Cutthroat; Trout,
Rainbow

CUTTHROAT, COLORADO:
see Trout, Cutthroat

CUTTHROAT, RIO GRANDE:
see Cutthroat Trout

**CUTTHROAT, SNAKE
RIVER:**
see Trout, Cutthroat

CUTTHROAT, TAHOE:
see Trout, Cutthroat

**EEL, AMERICAN;
COMMON EEL
(Anguilla rostrata)**

The American Eel spends most of its life in rivers and streams all along the Atlantic Coast of North America from Greenland and Newfoundland southward to the Gulf Coast of the United States and Mexico.

The female of the slender-bodied, snake-like American Eel can grow to a length of 5 feet (1.5 m), while the male seldom exceeds 3 feet (.9 m) in length. A long feathery dorsal fin begins well back on the body and appears to be continuous with the equally feathery tail and anal fins. The body is covered with tiny scales and varies in color from greenish-brown to a yellowish-brown, gradually shading to a light yellow to white below.

American Eels, living in rivers and estuaries, begin to migrate downstream to the sea when they are eight to nine years old. They swim to waters southeast of Bermuda where each female lays approximately 100,000 eggs. Soon after spawning, the adults die. Flat, transparent larvae, called leptocephali, hatch and grow to a length of about 4 inches (10 cm). After a year in Bermuda waters, the leptocephali migrate to inshore water, arriving in spring and early summer, and change into elvers which look somewhat like adult eels but are, of course, much smaller. The elvers move farther upstream, and slowly mature into adult

Above: **The Flounder is a saltwater flatfish.**

eels. When they reach the age of eight to nine, the cycle is repeated. They migrate upstream to elevations of 8000 feet (2438 m). Occasionally they move up into reservoirs and come out of water spigots.

Adults do not feed during the mating migration, nor when they are spawning. Elvers feed on crustaceans, fish and insect larvae while the adults tend to be scavengers. While the European Eel is an important commercial food fish, the American Eel is not widely consumed. Its use as a food fish is mostly among ethnic groups that used the fish as food in Europe and continue the tradition of eating this nutritious and, to many, delicious fish.

The European eel is similar in appearance and habits to the American Eel. The European Eel spawns in the South Atlantic just to the east of the American Eel spawning area. They remain in the Atlantic three years before returning to fresh water in Europe and Africa.

**FLOUNDER; WINTER
FLOUNDER; FLATFISH
(Pseudopleuronectes
americanus)**

The Flounder occurs in shallow seas and brackish water along the Atlantic Coast from Labrador to Georgia.

The Flounder is from 16 to 20 inches (40 to 50 cm) long and can weigh up to 16 pounds (7.6 kg). As an adult, the Flounder has a flat body. Both eyes are on one side of the body and the fish lies on the bottom with the eyes facing upward. The overall body shape is somewhat roundish. The Flounder is red-

dish brown, gray-green or dark gray to black on one side and light yellow to buff white on the other. The pigment is usually on the top or right side – the side that has the eyes. A fish with this distribution of pigment is called a 'right-handed' fish. Occasionally, the pigment is on the bottom or left side of the fish. Fins extend around the edge of the body almost encircling it, except for the head region.

The adult Flounder is primarily a bottom feeder. A small-mouthed fish, it is limited in the size of the food it eats, including crustaceans, worms and other invertebrates.

Spawning takes place in winter and early spring at depths from 10 to 20 feet (3 to 6 m), usually at night. Young hatch from the heavy, sticky eggs in about two weeks. The young have bodies that are typically fish-shaped with eyes on both sides of the head. Gradually, the body flattens, the left eye moves toward the right eye and the fish assumes the shape of an adult Flounder.

An excellent food fish, the Flounder has a firm textured meat and a delicate flavor. Reasonably easy to catch, Flounders are favorites with amateur saltwater anglers. Similar fish include the halibut or Atlantic Halibut *(Hippoglossus hippoglossus)*, the Plaice, the Sole, and the Turbot.

GOLDFISH: see Carp

HALIBUT: see Flounder

**HALIBUT, ATLANTIC:
see Flounder**

**HERRING, AMERICAN:
see Shad**

**HERRING, ATLANTIC:
see Menhaden**

**LAMPREY; SEA LAMPREY
(Petromyzon mariunus)**

The Lamprey is found in coastal waters on both sides of the Atlantic Ocean and the Mediterranean Sea. In Europe and North America it is also

Above: A Sea Lamprey, once a menace.

found in fresh water. It found its way into the Great Lakes after the building of the Welland Ship Canal that by-passes Niagara Falls. The Lamprey came in holding on to the hulls of ships with their sucker disc mouths.

The Lamprey is a slender eel-like jawless fish that can reach a length of 3 feet (.9 m). The round mouth is filled with circular rows of toothlike projections. The scaleless body is covered with mucous glands, and there are rows of gill slits behind the head. Not a vertebrate, the Lamprey has a noto-chord rather than a backbone.

As an adult, the Lamprey is a parasitic feeder on other fishes. It latches on to the side of a fish with its mouth and rasps away at the flesh, skin and scales, secreting a substance that prevents the host's blood from clotting. The Lamprey sucks body fluids, blood and digested meat from its victim. Lampreys attack many species of fresh water and salt water fishes, and may also attempt to attack whales, although they cannot pierce the skin of the animal.

Lampreys in the sea swim far up river to spawn, while those in lakes move up tributary streams for spawning. The adults dig nests in rocky bottoms for deposition of eggs. The worm-like, blind, toothless larvae remain buried in silt downstream from the spawning site for four to six years before they change into an adult and move downstream into the sea or a lake.

The Lamprey had a devastating effect on sport and commercial fishing in the Great Lakes, causing a sharp reduction in the populations of lake trout and Great Lakes whitefish and many other species. In recent years, as the result of massive research efforts, the Lamprey has been controlled. Weirs and dams have kept them from migrating upriver to spawn, and a number of chemical controls have been successful in controlling the larvae.

LEAST CISCO: see Whitefish

MACKEREL, ATLANTIC: see Barracuda

MARLIN, BLUE (Makaira nigricans)

The Blue Marlin has a wide distribution in tropical and warmer temperate ocean waters. It is particularly prevalent in the water around the Bahamas and the Atlantic coastal waters of Florida and the Gulf of Mexico coastal waters from Florida to Texas and Mexico. Those found around Hawaii, Japan and the Mexican Pacific Coast are considered to be a separate species by some biologists.

A large fish, the Blue Marlin can grow to impressive sizes. The average size of Blue Marlin caught with rod and reel is around 400 pounds (182 kg). Specimens weighing 600 to 1000 pounds (270 to 455 kg) and more than 17 feet (5 m) long are not uncommon. The Blue Marlin is a dark metallic blue on the upper parts of the body, which shades gradually to a silvery white on the underside. The dorsal fin is peaked in front and continues in a sloping downward profile almost to the tail fin. The tail fin is split, extending in a steep arc above and below. A bill-fish, the Blue Marlin has a long sword-like upper jaw.

Primarily a fish eater, the Blue Marlin will also take squid and other mollusks. Swimming fairly close to the surface, it commonly goes after tuna. A migratory fish, it is more common in off-shore waters in the winter months, particularly in the cooler parts of its range. Very little is known about its reproductive habits. It probably deposits its eggs in the ocean. Larval Marlin are commonly picked up in fishing and shrimp nets.

Both the Atlantic and Pacific varieties are highly prized big-game sport fish. In the Orient, particularly in Taiwan, it is widely exploited as a commercial food fish. Charter boats to Blue Marlin and other big game fishing areas are an important industry in the resort areas of the Caribbean and Gulf of Mexico, as well as in Hawaii and other Pacific Coastal areas. The Blue Marlin is a strong fighter, capable of giving the most experienced sport fisherman a demanding challenge and a spectacular show, with its high leaps out of the water.

The Atlantic and Pacific Blue Marlin are similar in most respects, but the Pacific Marlin tends to be larger than its Atlantic counterpart. Those biologists designating the Pacific Blue Marlin as a separate species refer to it as *Makaira mazara*.

The White Marlin (*Makaira albida*) ranges from Venezuela northward along the Atlantic Coast to Massachusetts. A smaller species than the Blue Marlin, it draws hopeful fishermen to the resort of Ocean City, Maryland, where boat chartering is concentrated. The Striped Marlin (*Makaira mitsukurii*) is a Pacific species found in North American waters from Panama north to southern California. The Black Marlin (*Makaira indica*) is another Pacific species that tends to be quite large; the record catch is 1560 pounds (707 kg).

MENHADEN; BUNKER FISH (Brevoortia tyrannus)

A salt water fish, the Menhaden is found in large numbers in coastal waters from Nova Scotia to Brazil.

This large-headed fish ranges in color from dark blue to green to gray mixed with brown highlights in the upper parts of the body. When caught, the lower parts of the body, the sides and fins appear as a metallic, almost brassy yellow-orange. The Menhaden has a distinctive black spot just behind the gills and several smaller black spots on the sides. The Menhaden is usually

Above: The lower half of the cheeks and gill cover of the Muskellunge lacks scales.

from 12 to 18 inches (30 to 46 cm) long and weighs from about ¾ to 1 pound (.3 to .45 kg).

Swimming in large schools, the Menhaden feeds on plankton which it strains out of the water with its long, thin gill rakers. When it is feeding, its mouth seems to be filled with food. In addition to plankton, Menhaden eat small worms, shrimp and other crustaceans, and plants that have grown beyond the stage of being plankton. When frightened by predators, they may jump out of the water. Often the entire school jumps out in perfect unison as though it is one body.

Not anadromous, Menhaden lay their eggs in salt water. The eggs float just beneath the surface and hatch in about two days. Menhaden usually reach a length of 6 inches (15 cm) and a weight of 1½ ounces (42 gm) in the first year, 10 inches (25 cm) and 7 ounces (200 gm) in the second year, and are sexually mature at age three years.

Although Menhaden are not a popular food fish, they are, in terms of the value of the catch, the most important commercial fish in the United States. More than 600 million pounds (272.4 million kg) are taken annually in New England waters alone. Menhaden are needed for their rich oil content, the quality that makes them undesirable as food fish. The oil is used in the preparation of poultry food, and the residue left after the oil is extracted is used as fertilizer. Cut-up Menhaden is considered to be a good bait for larger fish such as striped bass.

Similar species include the Atlantic Herring, the Alewife (*Pomolobus pseudoharengus*), and the American Shad (*Alosa sapidissima*).

MINNOW:
see Chub, Bermuda

MUSKELLUNGE, MUSKIE
(*Esox masquinongy*)

The Muskellunge is found in lakes and rivers of the Great Lakes region, and is occasionally caught in the Ohio River and Tennessee River systems. From time to time, there are reports of Muskellunge in lakes and rivers as far south as North Carolina.

The largest of the pikes, Muskellunge as long as 8 feet (2.4 m) and weighing 80 pounds (36 kg) are not unknown. Twelve foot (3.6 m) specimens weighing 150 pounds (68.1 kg) or more were taken 100 years ago. The color of the Muskellunge varies from olive to dark gray, and the scales are limited to the upper half of the rather elongated body. The belly and undersides are cream colored. The face is flat, somewhat like a duck's bill, and has a baleful, evil-looking cast that probably inspired many of the wild stories about this fish. The dorsal and anal fins are set far back on the body, very close to the tail fin. The fish may live up to 20 years.

A predaceous fish, the Muskellunge feeds on smaller fish, particularly perch and shiners, water birds such as young ducklings, crayfish, frogs, insects and an occasional small mammal such as a young muskrat. Requiring a great deal of food daily, the Muskellunge hunts almost constantly. The Muskellunge lurks in a hiding place and strikes at unsuspecting prey that happen to pass.

Spawning takes place from April to June, usually in shallow streams at night when temperatures are between 50° to 60°F (10° to 15.5°C). A 35 to 40 pound (16 to 18 kg) female deposits as many as 270,000 individual nonsticky eggs which hatch in a two to three week period.

It is considered to be an excellent sporting fish, more perhaps for its size potential than for its fighting qualities. Accounts of 100 to 150 pounds (45 to 68 kg), 12 foot (3.6 m) specimens that attack boats as they get away are nothing more than fish stories. The Muskellunge is generally considered to be a fair to good food fish.

Similar species include the smaller Pickerel and Northern Pike (*Esox lucius*). The Pickerel is a good gamefish that is often fished through holes in the ice on frozen lakes. Its flesh is fair to good but is rather bony.

PERCH, YELLOW
(Perca flavescens)

The Yellow Perch ranges from Nova Scotia to Florida and westward to Montana and Great Slave Lake. It is readily recognized by the yellow background color on its sides, which is interrupted by broad vertical olive-green bands. The Yellow Perch has two separate dorsal fins, the anterior being spiny and the posterior soft. Its teeth are all uniform in size, that is, it has no canine teeth. Its average length is between 10 and 11 inches (25-28 cm).

The Yellow Perch spawns at night in early spring when the water has warmed up to at least 44 degrees Farenheit. Each female may carry from 3,000 to 100,000 eggs, depending on her size; the average is between 20- and 30,000. A single female leads a long double line of males around a circuitous course and finally extrudes a long gelatinous string of eggs, which they then fertilize. The eggs are contained in a gelatinous tube which is folded like an accordion. This semibuoyant tube not only protects the eggs from shock and desiccation, but aerates them by means of its pumping action in the water.

The young hatch in a week to 10 days and remain close to the bottom and relatively inactive until the yolk sac is absorbed. Their first food is zooplankton, followed by small insects. As adults, they continue to eat insects, but also feed on crayfish and small fish. Perch are shallow-water fish and move in large, loosely organized groups. They are inactive at night and can be seen resting on the bottom by shining a powerful light into the water on a summer evening. They do not become inactive in the winter, but continue to move and feed under the ice.

The Yellow Perch is popular with fishermen not because it is a good fighting fish (it is easily caught), but because it is very good eating. It is most often taken on live bait fished just off the bottom. If its population becomes too large for the food supply, the Perch has a tendency to become stunted.

PICKEREL:
see Muskellunge; Pike, Northern

PIKE, NORTHERN
(Esox lucius)

Found in shallow lakes and rivers in most of the northern areas of the world, the range of the Northern Pike in North America extends from northern Alaska and Canada southward to the Hudson and Missouri Rivers. Usually found close to shore, it is a frequent inhabitant of quiet backwaters, including oxbow lakes – crescent shaped lakes formed when meandering rivers change course.

Northern Pike more than 8 feet (2.4 m) long and 65 pounds (29.5 kg) are not uncommon. However, 3 to 4 feet (.9 to 1.2 m) and 30 to 45 pounds (13.6 to 20.4 kg) are considered to be spectacular catches. Specimens in excess of 75 pounds (34 kg) are occasionally found, while stories of pike weighing in at more than 100 pounds (45 kg) are probably just that – stories.

The slender body of the Pike gives it an elongated appearance. Covered with small scales, the color of the Northern Pike ranges from blue to greenish gray. As is the case with all fish in the Pike family, the dorsal and anal fins are set far back on the body very close to the tail fin. The overall appearance is barred and mottled and provides camouflage.

A predaceous fish, the Northern Pike feeds on other fish such as perch and sucker, frogs, crayfish, insects, small birds such as ducklings and small mammals such as young muskrats. It

Below: **The Pike has partly scaled gill covers.**

hunts by lurking in vegetation, springing out swiftly at most passing things that might be prey. Hunting by sight rather than smell, it is almost always found swimming in clear water that is unsilted.

The Pike spawns in the early spring when snow melt has caused some overflow in the lower reaches of rivers. Spawning usually takes place along the riverbanks and sometimes on grassy floodplain that has a shallow covering of water. The female, usually accompanied by two or more males, deposits 100,000 or more nonsticky eggs among vegetation. Young Pike hatch some two to three weeks after the eggs are deposited, depending on the temperature. Fending for themselves as soon as they hatch, the young are five to seven inches (13 to 18 cm) when they are five months old, about 8 to 12 inches (20 to 30 cm) at age one year, and they finally reach a length of 14 to 18 inches (35 to 46 cm) when they are two years old.

Highly prized as a game fish, the Northern Pike usually fights when hooked, and provides excellent eating. Although it is raised in hatcheries for stocking streams, it is not a commercial food fish in North America as it is in eastern Europe.

Similar species include the smaller Pickerel and the larger Muskellunge (*Esox masquinongy*). Both are considered good game fish particularly the Muskellunge because of its size.

PLAICE: see Flounder

PUMPKINSEED: see Bluegill

RUDDERFISH:
see Chub, Bermuda

SALMON (Oncorhynchus)

Five species of salmon are found in North American waters. All are anadromous, hatching in freshwater and migrating to the sea where they spend most of their lives, returning to freshwater and swimming upstream to spawn. Some swim up rivers that flow into the Arctic Ocean.

Some species of Pacific salmon swim thousands of miles upstream against currents that are strong enough in some areas to be described as torrents or small waterfalls. Dams also impede their progress, although some dams have been designed to include 'fish ladders' which provide a graded access for the salmon to get upstream. Many die on the way, are eaten by predators, and millions are netted by commercial fishermen. In danger of becoming seriously depleted, limits are set on the number that can be taken commercially each year.

CHINOOK SALMON; KING SALMON; SPRING SALMON (Oncorhynchus tschawytscha)

A widely distributed Salmon in the northern Pacific, the Chinook ranges from Alaska to southern California in North American waters and is also found in Asia from Hokkaido to the Soviet Union.

The largest of the salmons, specimens of Chinook weighing more than 100 pounds (45 kg) have been caught. However, most migrating Chinook weigh around 20 pounds (9 kg) and those caught at sea are generally around 10 pounds (4.5 kg). The Chinook has dark spots on its back, dorsal and tail fins. During the spawning run, the jaws of the male become hooked and the teeth enlarge, but less so than other species of Salmon.

Spawning runs begin late May and reach a peak in June. Chinook swim long distances up large rivers. They have been found in Alaska's Yukon River, more than 1250 miles (2000 km) from the mouth. The Chinook generally reaches the spawning grounds around late July and early August. The female digs a redd into which she deposits her eggs. Often a particular male in an area establishes dominance and is the one that fertilizes the eggs, or at least fertilizes most of them. Males with less dominance but who manage to get close enough to the eggs also fertilize some of them.

The eggs hatch in seven to nine weeks. The fry remain hidden in the gravelly bottom for some two to three weeks before emerging and forming

Above: A Coho or Silver Salmon.

temporary schools. They later become territorial and spread themselves out along the river. After living in the river for about two to three years, most of them begin to migrate downstream, usually at night, often swimming tail first. Some males become sexually mature when they are only about 4 inches (10 cm) long and do not migrate.

At sea Chinook Salmon feed on fish, mainly herring and anchovies, crustaceans and squid. Growing rapidly, the males mature in two to three years, and females in four to five, at which time they return to the rivers to spawn. While most Chinook die soon after spawning, some live long enough after spawning to be caught at the mouth of rivers as they return to the sea. However, none is known to have lived long enough to spawn a second time.

A valuable commercial food fish, the Chinook is second only to the Sockeye Salmon in the value of the catch. Most Chinook are caught in nets at the mouths of rivers as they swim upstream to spawn. However, they are also caught on rod and reel. They are

consumed fresh, canned, and dried. Large numbers are taken as they swim upstream by animals such as bears.

CHUM SALMON; KETA SALMON; DOG SALMON; FALL SALMON (Oncorhynchus keta)

More widely distributed than other salmon, the Chum ranges on the North American Pacific coast from California to the Bering Sea and on the Asian Pacific Coast from Korea to the Arctic Ocean. It is also found in the Arctic Ocean, both on the Canadian coast and the coast of the USSR.

Averaging about 6 pounds (2.7 kg), the Chum Salmon is distinguished by not having dark spots on the back and fins. Spawning males are strikingly colored. The upper regions have a dusky background with red blotches scattered over the undersides and greenish bars on the sides. The females have similar but less vivid coloration. Spawning males also have the characteristic hooked jaws and large teeth.

Chum Salmon begin their spawning run in July, and swim far upstream to the headwaters of rivers. The eggs are deposited in riffles, and the hatching young remain hidden in the gravel for several weeks after hatching. The adults die soon after spawning. After emerging from the gravel, the young Chum Salmon begin to make their way downstream. They spend very little time in fresh water, usually reaching the sea when they are about a year old.

Chum Salmon are a valuable commercial food fishery in northern Canada.

COHO SALMON; SILVER SALMON (*Oncorhynchus kisutch*)

The Coho Salmon is found in coastal Pacific waters of North America from Baja California to Alaska, and in Asia from northern Japan to the northern Soviet Union. Unlike other species of salmon, it does not swim very far out to sea. It is, rather, found close in shore. However, when it makes its spawning run, it swims great distances upstream. Coho have been found almost 1200 miles up the Yukon River in Alaska.

A deep-bodied fish, the Coho has scattered black spots on its back and tail fin. At spawning time, the body darkens, the head turns a bluish-green, and a red line develops along the side. Hooked jaws develop on the males and the teeth become larger.

The spawning run begins in June and continues through August. They work their way upstream slowly, and spawn around November in small streams that feed directly into large rivers. The female lays her eggs in a redd in a gravelly area. The eggs are fertilized usually by one male, although occasionally two may deposit milt in one redd. The adults die soon after spawning. The eggs hatch in six to eight weeks, after which the fry remain hidden in the gravel for some two to three weeks and then form small schools that hover near the shore. Eventually, the young Coho spread out and swim in their own territories. Some migrate to the sea at age two years, while others do not go to the sea until they are three years old. They remain at sea until about age four

Above: **A Chinook Salmon jumping upstream in Alaska.**

years, when they start the spawning run.

The Coho is less important as a commercial food fish than other species of salmon. It is, however, a good sport fish and is taken by trolling or fly fishing.

PINK SALMON; HUMPBACK SALMON (*Oncorhynchus gorbuscha*)

The original range of the Pink Salmon is the Pacific coast of North America from California to the Bering Strait and the Mackenzie River. The Pink Salmon has been introduced to the Atlantic Ocean in Newfoundland, and to the White Sea and other waters off the coast of the Soviet Union. These fish have ranged as far as Iceland and the British Isles.

A small fish in comparison to other salmons, the Pink Salmon ranges from about 2 to 6 pounds (.9 to 2.7 kg). Oval black spots on the back and tail fin help to distinguish the Pink from other salmon. At spawning time, the males develop, in addition to the usual hooked jaws and large teeth, a markedly humped back. The males also change in color; the back becomes black and the sides become red.

The spawning run of the Pink begins in the autumn, from September to November. The Pink Salmon's upstream swim is limited to about 100 miles (160 km) maximum in large rivers. The eggs, laid in a redd dug in rough gravel, hatch from December to February. The fry stay hidden in the bottom gravel for a few weeks and remain in fresh water for only a few days before migrating down river to the sea. They go back upstream on their spawning run when they are two years old.

The Pink Salmon is an important food fish, although the total catch is far less than that of the Chinook. It is much more popular as a food fish in Asia than in North America.

SOCKEYE SALMON; RED SALMON; BLUEBACK SALMON; KOKANEE SALMON (*Oncorhynchus nerka*)

The Sockeye is found in the northern Pacific, and rivers flowing into the north Pacific from Alaska to northern California and from Hokkaido to the

Right: The Dwarf Seahorse, an unlikely looking fish, is covered with a thin bony plate.

northern Soviet Union. Like other salmon, most Sockeyes are anadromous, being found at sea, in coastal areas, and at the mouths of rivers. In addition, they are often found in lakes, and many Sockeye are not anadromous, spending their entire lives in fresh water lakes.

The lake dwelling, nonmigratory fish known as Kokanee, were once thought to be separate species from the Sockeye.

The Sockeye is distinguished from other salmon by not having black spots on the back and sides. At spawning time, the backs and sides become red; males usually have a deeper red color than the females and also develop the characteristic hooked lower jaw of the spawning male. The average weight of netted Sockeye is about 7 pounds (3.2 kg). The hump of the back, however, is less prominent in the spawning Sockeye than in the humpback or chum salmon.

The spawning migration of the Sockeye begins in June and continues through the summer months. It often goes up rivers into lakes, spawning in feeder brooks and streams, as well as along the shores of the lakes. The female digs a redd into which the eggs are deposited. After the eggs are fertilized, the redds are covered by the female. Both males and female die soon after spawning.

The young Sockeyes hatch in six to nine weeks and those hatching in feeder streams almost immediately move down to lakes where they remain for one to two years, feeding on planctonic crustaceans, before migrating to the sea. Sockeye return to rivers and lakes from the sea for spawning when they are four to eight years old.

The Sockeye Salmon is one of the most valuable commercial food fishes in North America. Millions of pounds of Sockeye are netted every year as they migrate upstream. The Kokanee, on the other hand, is not important commercially. It does, however, provide sport fishing.

SEAHORSE, DWARF
(Hippocampus zosterae)

Seahorses are distributed in warm, shallow ocean waters throughout the world. The smallest of the seahorses, the Dwarf Seahorse is found from Bermuda to Florida throughout the Gulf of Mexico and the northern Caribbean.

Only about 1½ inches (3.8 cm) long, the Dwarf Seahorse swims upright, as do all seahorses, propelling itself forward mainly with its dorsal fin, and, to a lesser extent, with its pectoral fins. The body has a somewhat armor-plated appearance, accentuated by rings that circle the body. The name seahorse stems from the angle at which the head joins the body, which gives the head and neck a definite equine appearance. The long snout and position of the eyes also contribute to the horse-like appearance. The body tapers down to a prehensile tail which is used for holding onto vegetation and for holding onto other seahorses. It feeds on tiny crustaceans which it sucks in through its snout.

The Dwarf Seahorse and other seahorses exhibit some interesting reproductive behavior. The female deposits eggs in a brood pouch located on the ventral surface of the male. The eggs are fertilized in the pouch and the male carries the developing young for about a month. The Dwarf Seahorse male carries about 50 eggs, while other species carry as many as 200. The young, about ¼ inch (.6 cm) long are expelled through a genital pore, one or a few at a time. At first, the young swim in a horizontal position, gradually assuming the upright swimming position of adult seahorses. They reach maturity in about a year. The breeding season of the Dwarf Seahorse extends from February to October.

The ability to survive in a wide range of salinity and temperature is a quality that makes this and other seahorses popular with marine aquarium hobbyists. Dried bodies are kept as ornaments, and, in some parts of the world, ground up dried seahorse is believed to have various medicinal properties.

Similar North American species include the Offshore Seahorse (*Hippocampus obtusus*) which ranges from Florida to Nova Scotia, the Lined Seahorse (*Hippocampus erectus*), found in coastal water from Florida to New Jersey, and the Pacific Seahorse (*Hippocampus ingens*), which is found in coastal waters along the Pacific Coast. All of these are considerably larger than the Dwarf Seahorse. *Hippocampus obtusus* can reach a length of some 6 inches (15 cm).

SHAD; AMERICAN SHAD
(Alosa sapidissima)

The American Shad is found in the Atlantic Coast of North America from the southern coast of Newfoundland and the St Lawrence River, southward to the St James and Apalachicola Rivers in Florida. There were successful attempts to introduce the Shad to the West Coast in the 1870s and 1880s, and it is now also found in western rivers such as the Sacramento, Columbia, Logue and Feather.

A herring-like fish, the Shad attains a usual maximum length of about 2½ feet (.76 m) and a weight of some 13 pounds (4 kg). Typical catches are 1 foot (.3 m) long and about a pound (.45 kg) in weight. Covered with large, loosely attached scales, the Shad is dark blue to greenish above, white and silvery on the sides and belly, and has a dusky, blotchy spot just behind the head at the top of the gill cover.

An anadromous fish, the Shad spends most of its life at sea and migrates up rivers to spawn. In the oceans it often swims in schools, swarming to the surface to feed on plankton, mostly copepods, near the surface. It also feeds on other fish.

The spawning runs begin in the spring and extend through the early summer months, the males preceding the females. Migrating up large rivers as far as 200 to 300 miles (320 to 480 km) inland, some go into tiny feeder streams. The female lays about 160,000 individual, nonsticky eggs that sink to the bottom. At a temperature of about 60°F (15°C), the eggs hatch in about a week to ½ inch (1.25 cm) larvae that reach some 4½ inches (11.4 cm) in about two weeks. The adults return to the ocean in late autumn and the young Shad go down river to the ocean during their first summer. They mature in three to eight years.

Often called the 'poor man's salmon,' the Shad was enormously abundant in Colonial days and rapidly became one of the most frequently consumed food fish. They were caught by the hundreds of thousands in weirs and nets as they swam upstream to spawn, a practice that soon drastically reduced their numbers. Although by no means rare, and still a commercial food fish, Shad is caught in only a small fraction of the earlier numbers. Shad roe is a less expensive alternative to sturgeon roe for caviar.

Similar species include the Hickory Shad (*Pomolobus mediocris*) and the Atlantic Herring. While the Atlantic Herring is still a widely consumed food fish, the Hickory Shad has been almost depleted.

SHARK, BLUE; WHALER
(Prionace glauca)

The Blue Shark is found in ocean waters throughout the world. However, it becomes particularly abundant in New England waters during the summer months. It is more likely to be found in open waters, although it oc-

casionally comes in close to shore. A graceful shark of striking appearance, the Blue Shark is slim-bodied and has rather long pointed pectoral fins. The upper regions of the body are brilliant indigo blue, fading to a pure white on the undersides. A medium-sized shark, the Blue Shark is commonly 10 to 13 feet (3 to 4 m) long.

Blue Sharks can sometimes be seen swimming slowly near the surface. They are, however, powerful swimmers, capable of great speed and endurance. A varied diet includes many schooling fish and species of squid found near the surface. It is also a scavenger. The name 'whaler' comes from their being attracted to whales tied alongside whaling vessels for flensing. Among shark fishermen, it is considered to be one of the more desirable sharks, and is actively sought.

Although verified attacks on humans are rare, these fish are unpredictable and should be treated with extreme caution if encountered.

SHARK, LEMON
(Negaprion brevirostris)

The Lemon Shark is found in the western Atlantic Ocean from New Jersey to Brazil. It is one of the most commonly seen sharks in the waters around Florida and the Bahamas. It is a shallow water shark, often found close in to shore in brackish creeks, inlets, and even in freshwater.

Above: Sharks are a primitive fish, with a cartilagenous skeleton.

A small to medium-sized shark, the Lemon Shark seldom exceeds 11 feet (3.3 m). It is yellowish-brown on the back, shading to a pale yellow on the underside.

Its inshore feeding habits bring it into contact with bathers and swimmers, and there have been reports of attacks on humans. Although, like all sharks, its behavior is unpredictable, most attacks seem to be the result of provocation. Compared to most other sharks, Lemon Sharks are easy to keep in captivity, and have been widely studied.

Similar species are found throughout the world and include *Negaprion acutides* in the Red Sea and Indian Ocean and *Negaprion queenlandicus* in Australian waters, both are called Lemon Sharks.

SHINER, COMMON: see Carp

SKATE, LITTLE; HEDGEHOG SKATE
(Raja erinaces)

The most common skate along the Northwest Atlantic Coast, the range of the Little Skate extends along the Atlantic coast of North America from North Carolina to Nova Scotia to the southern parts of the Gulf of St Lawrence. It is found more often on gravelly and sandy bottoms, and less in mud, as is the case with other skates. The Little Skate has the flat, winglike shape and long tail common to all skates and rays. The ventrally located mouth has slatelike teeth similar to those in other skates and rays. The Little Skate is grayish to light brown on the back and a pale gray or white on the underside. It has round, dark spots on the back. Like all skates, it swims by moving its pectoral fins or 'wings' up and down.

The Little Skate feeds on a variety of organisms, including crustaceans, worms, clams, oysters and other bivalves, squid and fish.

Breeding takes place throughout the year, but there are two peak egg-laying periods, one from October to January, and another in June and July. The eggs are laid in gold-amber egg cases or purses that have long slender horns at each corner. The young develop for six to nine months in the cases, emerging at a size of about 4 inches (10 cm).

Although it is occasionally caught and used for food, the Little Skate does not have great value as a food fish. One of the more common ways skates and rays are used for food is cutting or punching meat in the 'wings' or pectoral fins for use as 'sea scallops.'

Although the size differences are great, the Little Skate is similar in many ways to the Big Skate, *Raja bionoculata*, which is found in the eastern Pacific from southern California to the Gulf of Alaska. It is widely used as food fish.

SOLE: see Flounder

STICKLEBACK, BROOK (Eucalia inconstans)

The Brook Stickleback is a common fish in small brooks and streams from Maine to Kansas and northwest to Saskatchewan. It is most likely to be found in clear cold, relatively unpolluted mountain snow-fed streams. Its presence in a brook is an index of a low level or lack of pollution.

A small fish, the Brook Stickleback seldom exceeds 2½ inches (6.2 cm) in

Above: The Skate is a saltwater fish.

length. The body is without scales and topped with five stiff, sharp dorsal spines. The color varies from green to olive green on the top and sides, fading to white or cream below.

The Stickleback male exhibits some unusual reproductive behavior. It builds a hollow dome-shaped nest of plant material held together with mucus from its body. After the nest is built, the male searches for a female. He forces the female into the nest, chasing after her and nipping at her fins to make sure she goes into the nest. Once inside the nest, the female deposits about 300 eggs and then leaves. The male immediately enters the nest and fertilizes the eggs. The male stands guard over the eggs for the ten-day incubation period, often fanning with its fins to keep water circulating over the eggs. He continues to watch over the newly hatched fry, often taking strays into his mouth and bringing them back into the nest. The guarding continues until they can take care of themselves.

The Stickleback is neither a food nor a sport fish. It is an interesting aquarium fish, although it must be kept away from other fish because of its aggressive disposition.

Other Sticklebacks include the Three-spine Stickleback (*Gastroestus aculeatus*) and the Nine-spine Stickleback (*Pengitius pengitius*), both of which are found in North America and exhibit reproductive behavior similar to that of the Brook Stickleback.

STICKLEBACK, NINE-SPINE: see Stickleback, Brook

STURGEON; ATLANTIC STURGEON; AMERICAN STURGEON (Acipenser sturio)

The Sturgeon's range extends from the Gulf of Mexico north to the St Lawrence River. The Sturgeon's range once included the Great Lakes and the Mississippi Valley. However, largely because of pollution, it has disappeared from that area and is generally rare in the range it still inhabits.

A large fish, Sturgeon as long as 12 feet (3.7 m) and weighing as much as 500 pounds (227 kg) have been caught. Larger specimens were once fairly common, but they are extremely rare today. One of the more primitive of the bony fishes, the Atlantic Sturgeon is partly covered with bony plates, and has five rows of bony scales on its body. There are four short barbels just forward of the mouth, and the mouth can be retracted for bottom feeding.

Sturgeon are bottom feeders, eating a variety of aquatic invertebrates and possibly small fish. An anadromous species, the Atlantic Sturgeon goes up river from the sea in the spring to breed. The female deposits from 800,000 to 3,000,000 eggs in a heavy sticky mass on pebbly bottoms in moderate current. The eggs, which constitute up to 30 percent of the female's body weight, are covered by milt by the male after they are deposited. Three to seven days after the eggs are deposited, ½ inch (1.25 cm) young sturgeon hatch. Growing rapidly, those young that survive reach a length of about 5½ (14 cm) in a month. The adult Sturgeons return to the ocean; the young remain in the river for one to three years, or until they reach a length of about 5 feet (1.5 m).

The Atlantic Sturgeon is considered to be an excellent game fish, but catching one is getting to be more and more of a rare event. Some are occasionally taken by spearing. Sturgeon, smoked or canned, is an expensive delicacy, and the roe is consumed as caviar.

The Lake Sturgeon (*Acipenser fulvescens*) is a similar species. Rang-

312

FISH

Top: The American Sturgeon has a primitive tail and feels for food with chin barbels.
Above: The Razorback Sucker has a prominent and distinguishing hump behind its head.

ing from the Saskatchewan River in Alberta to the lower St Lawrence River and south to Alabama, the Lake Sturgeon is considered by many to be a more desirable food fish than the Atlantic Sturgeon. The species is also becoming quite rare because of pollution and overfishing.

SUCKER, RAZORBACK; HUMPBACK SUCKER
(Xyrauche texanus)

The range of the Razorback Sucker is limited to the Colorado River and Gila River Basins of North America. Although it is most frequently seen in swift running waters of large rivers, it is also found in lakes.

A longish, slender fish, the Razorback Sucker has the ventrally located fleshy mouth and sucking lips common to all Suckers. The body is covered with small scales, while the flattened head is scaleless. The snout of the Razorback Sucker is somewhat blunt, and the lips are less enlarged than

those of other Suckers. Its back is much higher and sharper than those of other Suckers, characteristics that give this fish its name. The high sharp back and the flattened head are adaptations for life in swift running water. Razorback Suckers as large as 10 pounds (4.5 kg) have been taken, but 2 and 3 pound (.9 to 1.4 kg) are more typical.

The Razorback Sucker is a bottom feeder, a feeding method for which its mouth is well adapted. The mouth 'sucks up' vegetation, algae and assorted bottom debris.

The Razorback Sucker breeds in swift water, pushing its body down into the bottom gravel as it spawns.

Although it is not highly regarded as a game fish, it is popular in some parts of the country as a food fish. The soft and bony flesh is thought to be better in the winter when cold temperatures make it firmer. They were important food fish for the Indians who lived along the Colorado River. Able to survive in a wide variety of conditions, they can live in rivers in which pollution has reduced the oxygen content to levels many other fish could not tolerate.

It is similar to the Common Sucker (Catostomus commersoni).

SUNFISH:
see Bluegill; Bass, Largemouth; Bass, Smallmouth

TARPON
(Tarpon atlanticus)

The Tarpon is a fish of the warmer waters of the Atlantic and Caribbean coasts of North America from Panama to the Carolinas.

Adult Tarpon taken by anglers vary widely in weight from 2 to 3 pounds (.9 to 1.4 kg) specimens to around 350 pounds (159 kg). A sturdily built fish, the Tarpon's elongated body is compressed from side to side and is covered with large scales. The color varies from dark blue to greenish-black along the back, gradually shading to a bright silver on the sides and belly. The dorsal fin has a backwards-projecting narrow appendage.

Young Tarpon start out as plankton feeders, gradually adding larger organisms such as insects, crustaceans and, ultimately, fish to their diet. The Tarpon swims close to shore along beaches and reefs, frequently following the tide into brackish rivers and bays to feed on crabs, pinfish and mullet.

During the mating season from March to May, males form schools over shoals about a mile from shore in blue water where spawning takes place. A 100 pound (45 kg) female lays millions of eggs, some of which float, while others sink. Ribbon-like transparent larvae hatch from the eggs and quickly develop into forms that look more like fish.

The Tarpon is considered to be the supreme big game fish by many anglers, providing a challenge for the most experienced fisherman. When it takes the hook, it makes spectacular leaps of 15 to 30 feet (4.6 to 9.1 m) and more. Opinions on the quality of the Tarpon as food fish are mixed. It is, however, consumed in fairly large numbers in Latin America.

Distantly related to Herring and Alewife (Pomolobus pseudo-harengus), the only other species of Tarpon is found off India.

TROUT, BROOK; CHAR
(Salvelinus fortinalis)

The original range of the Brook Trout extended from Hudson Bay, Labrador and Newfoundland southward to the upper Mississippi River system and streams in the Appalachians. It has been introduced into fresh waters, particularly rivers, in many temperate areas, including Europe and South Africa.

A sturdily built fish, the Brook Trout can grow to weights of 15 to 20 pounds (7-9 kg). However, catches of 5 pounds (2.3 kg) are considered to be good. The color of the Brook Trout varies with the food it eats and a number of other factors. There are usually red spots on the body and wiggly markings on the back. The lower fins have white, black and orange markings.

Brook Trout, when they are young, feed on insects and take small fish as they get older. They also feed on bottom organisms.

Spawning takes place in autumn in small streams and rivers. The female digs a shallow excavation called a redd. About 5000 eggs are deposited in the redd. After spawning, the eggs are covered and they hatch the following spring. Along the Pacific Coast, some Brook Trout swim down river into the Pacific Ocean.

Considered to be one of the finest sport fish in North America, it is a good fighter and a challenge for the most experienced angler.

The Brook Trout is similar to the Dolly Varden (*Salvelinus malma spectabilis*) and the Lake Trout (*Salvelinus namaycush*). All of them are Char rather than true Trout.

TROUT, CUTTHROAT
(Salmo clarki)

The Cutthroat Trout is found in Pacific Coast rivers of North America from California north to Prince William Sound in Alaska. Some Cutthroat Trout migrate to spawning areas, while others feed and spawn in the same area. Migratory Cutthroat Trout are more likely to be found in the northern part of the range. It is also found in the headwaters of large rivers such as the Missouri, Columbia, Fraser and Saskatchewan.

A slender fish with a typical trout shape, the Cutthroat Trout weighs from about 6 to 40 pounds (2.7 to 18 kg), although most that are caught are in the 3 to 5 pound (1.4 to 2.25 kg) range. Color is variable but it is generally silvery with round black spots on the head, back and fins. Under the head in the throat area there is a group of conspicuous red to orange parallel blotches, a flash of color that gives the Cutthroat Trout its name.

The Cutthroat feeds on aquatic insects, terrestrial insects, crayfish, and small fish. Migratory forms tend to

Above: **Brook Trout live in cold, clear waters.**

stay near estuaries feeding on the rich abundance of insects, plankton, small crabs and minnows in these habitats.

Spawning takes place in spring and early summer. Cutthroat Trout living in rivers migrate to smaller streams to spawn while those in lakes move to feeder streams. Eggs are buried in gravelly redds dug by the female. Usually, one male fertilizes the eggs in a particular redd. The eggs hatch about seven weeks after they are laid.

The Cutthroat is one of the better sport fish of the western United States. However, some fishermen accuse it of being a harmful fish because it destroys salmon and Rainbow Trout eggs and young Rainbow Trout.

The Cutthroat has been hybridized extensively with the Rainbow Trout, particularly in Wyoming and Montana. Many varieties exist in different parts of the country, and there is disagreement among biologists over the classification of these varieties. Some of the local names given to varieties of Cutthroat Trout are Snake River Cutthroat, Rio Grande Cutthroat, Colorado Cutthroat, and Tahoe Cutthroat. Populations of Cutthroat Trout have been reduced in many areas of its range, primarily due to overfishing.

The Cutthroat Trout is similar to the Lake (*Salvelinus namaycush*), Brown (*Salmo eriox*) and Rainbow Trout (*Salmo gairdneri*).

FISH

Top: The Golden Trout (*Salmo agua-bonita*) is the most beautifully colored of all trout. Rainbow Trout (*second from top*) are the most widely distributed trout and most popular. The Cutthroat Trout (*second from bottom*) is a native of the West. The Rio Grande Cutthroat Trout (*above*) is recognizable by its posterior spots.

TROUT, LAKE; CHAR
(*Salvelinus namaycush*)

The Lake Trout has a wide distribution in fresh waters throughout much of North America from Alaska and Canada southward to the Great Lakes Basin, New England and the northern areas of the Mississippi River system. It has been introduced into many other areas.

A slender-bodied fish, the Lake Trout is the largest of the fish referred to as trouts. Catches between 20 to 30 pounds (9 to 13 kg) are not unusual, and 10 pounders (4.5 kg) are fairly common. The Lake Trout is dark green or gray along the back shading gradually to a pale white or yellowish underside. Irregularly sized pale spots are heavily distributed over the back, sides and head. The fins on the underside are orange with white on the leading edge.

In the southern part of the range, the Lake Trout is most likely to be found in deep, cold lakes, while in the north it is found in shallow lakes and rivers of the tundra. It feeds mainly on fishes and rounds out its fare with insects, crustaceans and plankton.

Spawning takes place in late summer and autumn in gravelly bottoms of lake shallows. The male, arriving at the spawning site before the females, clears the area of silt and leaves, but does not dig a nest as do many other trout. The ¼ inch (4 to 5 mm) eggs are scattered loosely over the gravel and hatch in the early spring. Lake Trout grow much faster in the warmer, southern waters than in the north, where it may take as long as nine years to reach a weight of 40 pounds (18 kg).

The Lake Trout is both a commercial food fish and a sport fish. The flesh has a fine texture and an excellent flavor, and it is considered to be a gourmet fare in many areas. The Great Lakes provide most commercially fished Lake Trout.

The Lake Trout is similar to the Dolly Varden Trout (*Salvelinus malma spectabilis*) and Brook Trout (*Salvelinus fortinalis*), which are actually chars rather than true trout.

TROUT, RAINBOW; STEELHEAD TROUT; SHASTA TROUT; KAMLOOP'S TROUT (*Salmo gairdneri*)

The range of the Rainbow Trout is in the streams and lakes of the Rocky Mountains and the Pacific slopes of North America from Alaska south to California and northwest Mexico. The name Steelhead stems from a name given to a phase of the Rainbow Trout once thought to be a separate species. However, it is now known that the coloration of the Steelhead represents a form of the Rainbow Trout that migrates to salt water. The Rainbow Trout has been raised in hatcheries and stocked in streams, lakes, and ponds throughout the United States and in Europe. The Rainbow Trout does best in clean, well-oxygenated water.

The name Rainbow Trout stems from the multihued band of color on the sides. Also distinctive are dense, small, dark spots on the sides, back, and on the dorsal and tail fins. The color of the Rainbow Trout, however, is highly variable. The average weight is about 3 pounds (1.4 kg) and the record weight is 37 pounds (17 kg). The migratory Steelhead form is dark blue with silvery sides and belly. The Steelhead phase is generally larger than the rainbow phase. The body neither slender nor deep, is about 4.5 times as long as it is deep.

Rainbow Trout of average size feed on insect larvae, snails and other mollusks, crustaceans and, occasionally, eggs and fry of other fish, particularly Pacific salmon. Larger Trout may eat other fish, including other trout.

In North America, spawning takes place in early spring. The female digs a cavity, called a redd, usually in a gravelly area. The fairly large ⅛-⅕ inch (3 to 5 mm) eggs are deposited in the redd and fertilized there by the male. The redd is then covered over, and the female digs another redd upstream. Nonmigratory Rainbow Trout lay about 2000 eggs while the migratory Steelhead lays about 7000 eggs.

The eggs hatch about three weeks after they are deposited. For the first month, the young Trout remain in the riffle. As they grow, they move downstream to deeper lakes and pounds, generally getting to them in the winter.

The Rainbow Trout is considered to be an excellent, challenging game fish to take with a rod and reel. It grows well in practically all areas it has been introduced, although in some places along the east coast fish of legal size are usually taken almost as soon as they are put into the water. Rainbow Trout is becoming an increasingly important commercial food fish. Similar species include other trout such as Brown Trout (*Salmo eriox*), Lake Trout (*Salvelinus namaycush*), and Brook Trout (*Salvelinus fortinalis*).

WHITEFISH; LAKE WHITEFISH; GREAT LAKES WHITEFISH; HUMPBACK (*Coregonus clupeaformis*)

An inhabitant of lakes in northern North America from the Great Lakes north to the Arctic Circle, and of northern Europe and Asia, the Whitefish is most likely to be found in cold waters. Because of its value as a food fish, it has been introduced elsewhere.

A large fish, the Whitefish can attain weights in excess of 40 pounds (18 kg), and a length of more than 2 feet (.6 m). However, most that are caught weigh in between 10 and 20 pounds (4.5 to 9 kg). Specimens between 20 and 30 pounds (9 to 14 kg) are infrequent. The back of the Whitefish is olive green and the sides and underside are white. The sturdy body is a bit

Above: **The Rocky Mountain Whitefish (*Prosopium williamsoni*) has trout-like habits.**

compressed laterally, and the back is somewhat humped. The face has a distinctive thick, projecting upper lip.

The Whitefish has a varied diet that changes as it gets older. Young Whitefish eat plankton by straining it through their gill rakers. Older Whitefish tend to become bottom feeders but still feed on mollusks, insect larvae and shrimp-like organisms.

Spawning takes place in the autumn. The small eggs of the Whitefish are scattered on gravel beds in lake shallows and in the mouths of tributary rivers and hatch the following spring. A female Whitefish lays approximately 10,000 eggs per pound of body weight. The rate of growth varies with the prevailing temperature of the region, being slower in the north than it is in the southern parts of the range.

The most valuable food fish of the Great Lakes, 4 to 5 million pounds (2-2.3 million kg) are taken yearly, although there is fear that stocks are being overfished and that the populations may be adversely affected by pollution. Whitefish are taken with gill nets in the Great Lakes and are marketed in both fresh and smoked forms. The roe has assumed increased importance as a source of caviar since imports of caviar from Iran stopped, and those from the Soviet Union were sharply reduced. It is also a sport fish. both in open water and in ice fishing.

Similar species include the Eurasian Whitefish, which many biologists consider to be the same species, the Cisco and the Least Cisco.

Selected Group of National Organizations for the Conservation and Protection of Wildlife

American Cetacean Society
PO Box 4416
San Pedro, CA 90731

American Committee for
International Conservation
1601 Connecticut Avenue N.W.
Washington, DC 20009

American Conservation Assoc
30 Rockefeller Plaza
New York, NY 10020

American Wilderness Alliance
4260 East Evans
Denver, CO 80222

Audubon Society
Washington, DC 20015

Center for
Environmental Education
1925 K Street
Washington, DC 20006

Cousteau Society
777 Third Avenue
New York, NY 10017

Defenders of Wildlife
1244 19th Street N.W.
Washington, DC 20036

Ducks Unlimited
PO Box 66300
Chicago, IL 60666

Friends of Animals
11 West 60th Street
New York, NY 10023

Fund for Animals
140 West 57th Street
New York, NY 10019

Humane Society
of the United States
2100 L Street N.W.
Washington, DC 20037

International Association of
Fish and Wildlife Agencies
1412 16th Street N.W.
Washington, DC 20036

International Ecological
Society
1471 Barclay Street
St. Paul, MN 55106

International Society for
the Protection of Animals
29 Perkins Street
Boston, MA 02130

National Coalition
for Marine Conservation
PO Box 23298
Savannah, GA 31403

National Parks and
Conservation Association
1701 18th Street N.W.
Washington, DC 20009

National Wildlife
Federation
1412 16th Street N.W.
Washington, DC 20036

Nature Conservancy
1800 No. Kent Street
Arlington, VA 22209

North American
Wildlife Foundation
709 Wire Building
Washington, DC 20005

Oceanic Society
Magee Avenue
Stamford, CT 06902

Sea Shepherd International
PO Box 48446
Vancouver, British
Columbia

Sierra Club
530 Bush Street
San Francisco, CA 94108

Wetlands for Wildlife
39710 Mary Lane
Oconomowoc, WI 53066

Whale Center
3929 Piedmont Avenue
Oakland, CA 94617

Wilderness Society
1901 Pennsylvania Avenue N.W.
Washington, DC

Wildlife Preservation Trust
International
34th Street and Girard Avenue
Philadelphia, PA 19104

Wildlife Society
7101 Wisconsin Avenue N.W.
Washington, DC 20014

World Wildlife Fund
1601 Connecticut Avenue N.W.
Washington, DC 20009

BIBLIOGRAPHY

GENERAL WORKS

Fisher, James, Noel Simon, and Jack Vincent. *Wildlife in Danger.* N.Y. Viking Press, 1969

Grzimek, Bernhard, ed. *Grzimek's Animal Life Encyclopedia*, 13v. N.Y. Van Nostrand-Reinhold, 1972-75.

Handbooks of American Natural History. Ithaca, N.Y. Comstock, 1942 –.
especially the following titles:
Carr, A.F. *Handbook of Turtles.* 1952.
Comstock, A. *Handbook of Nature Study.* 1939.
Hamilton, W. J. *The Mammals of Eastern United States.* 1943.
Johnsgard, P. A. *Handbook of Water-fowl Behavior.* 1965.
Smith, H. B. *Handbook of Lizards.* 1946.
Wright, A. and A. H. *Handbook of Frogs and Toads.* 1949.

Wright, A. H. *Handbook of Snakes of the United States and Canada.* 2v. 1957.

Jarman, Cathy. *Atlas of Animal Migration.* John Day, 1972.

Larousse Encyclopedia of Animal Life. N.Y. McGraw-Hill, 1967.

Leftwick, A. W. *Dictionary of Zoology.* 3d ed. London, Constable, 1973.

The Naturalists' Directory International. South Orange, N.J., Naturalists' Directory, 1876 –. Irregular. (43rd. ed. 1977)

Palmer, E. Laurence. *Fieldbook of Natural History.* 2d ed. Revised by H. Seymour Fowler. N.Y.: McGraw-Hill, 1975.

Peterson, Roger Tory. *The Peterson Field Guide Series.* Sponsored by the National Audubon Society and the National Wildlife Federation. Boston. Houghton, 1947 –
especially the following titles:
Field Guide to the Birds. 1947.
Field Guide to Western Birds. 1972.
Field Guide to the Mammals: Field Marks of all North American Species Found North of the Mexican Boundary. 3rd ed. 1976.
Field Guide to Animal Tracks. 2nd ed. 1975.
Field Guide to Reptiles and Amphibians of Eastern and Central North America. 1975.
Field Guide to the Birds of Texas and Adjacent States. 1963.
Field Guide to Western Reptiles and Amphibians. 1975.
Field Guide to Birds' Nests Found East of the Mississippi River. 1975.
Field Guide to Western Birds' Nests of 520 Species Found Breeding in the United States West of the Mississippi River. 1979.

Rand McNally Atlas of World Wildlife. Rand McNally, 1973.

Thompson, John W. *Index to Illustrations of the Natural World: Where to Find Pictures of the Living Things of North America.* Syracuse, N.Y.: Gaylord, 1977.

MAMMALS
Desmond, Morris. *The Mammals: A Guide to the Living Species.* N.Y.: Harper, 1965.

Hall, Eugene Raymond and Keith R. Kelson. *Mammals of North America.* 2v. New York, Ronald, 1959.

Walker, Ernest P. *Mammals of the World.* 3rd ed. Baltimore: Johns Hopkins University Press, 1975. 3v.

BIRDS
Campbell, Bruce. *The Dictionary of Birds in Color.* Viking, 1974.

Milne, Lorus and Margery Milne. *North American Birds.* Englewood Cliffs, N.J.: Prentice-Hall, 1969.

Palmer, Ralph S., ed. *Handbook of North American Birds.* New Haven, CT.: Yale University Press, 1962-76. 3v.

Terres, John K. *The Audubon Society Encyclopedia of North American Birds.* Knopf, 1980.
Choice 4-81: 1078

REPTILES AND AMPHIBIANS

Coleman, Doris M. and J. Goin Coleman. *The New Field Book of Reptiles and Amphibians.* New York: Putnam, 1970.

Ditmars, Raymond Lee. *The Reptiles of North America: A Review of the Crocodilians, Lizards, Snakes, Turtles and Tortoises Inhabiting the United States and Northern Mexico.* N.Y.: Doubleday, 1936.

Ernst, Carl H. and Roger W. Barbour. *Turtles of the United States.* Lexington, KY: University Press of Kentucky, 1973.

FISH
Herald, Earl Stannard. *Fishes of North America.* Garden City, N.Y.: Doubleday, 1972.

Hoedeman, J. J. *Naturalists' Guide to Fresh-Water Aquarium Fish.* New York: Sterling, 1974.

Sterba, Gunther. *Freshwater Fishes of the World.* Translated and revised by Denys W. Tucker. London: Vista Books, 1962.

Wheeler, Alwyne C. *Fishes of the World: An Illustrated Dictionary.* N.Y.: Macmillan, 1975.

LIST OF ENDANGERED SPECIES* (NORTH AMERICA)

*US Dept of the Interior January 1982

MAMMALS

Bat, gray (Central and Southeastern US)
Bat, Indiana (East and Midwestern US)
Bat, Ozark big-eared (MO, OK, AR)
Bat, Virginia big-eared (KY, WV, VA, IN, IL, OH)
Bison, wood (Can., Northwest, USA)
Cougar, eastern (Eastern US)
Deer, Columbian white-tailed (OR, WA)
Deer, key (FL)
Ferret, black-footed (Western US)
Fox, Northern swift (USA, Can.)
Fox, San Joaquin kit (CA)
Jaguar (TX, NM, AZ)
Jaguarundi (TX, AX)
Manatee, West Indian (Florida) (Southeastern US)
Margay (NM, AZ)
Mouse, salt marsh harvest (CA)
Ocelot (USA (SW))
Panther, Florida (LA and AR east to SC and FL)
Prairie Dog, Utah (UT)
Pronghorn, Sonoran (AZ)
Rat, Morro Bay kangaroo (CA)
Seal, Carribbean monk (Gulf of Mexico)
Squirrel, Delmarva Peninsula fox (MD, VA, DE)
Whale, blue (Oceanic)
Whale, bowhead (Oceanic)
Whale, finback (Oceanic)
Whale, gray (Oceanic)
Whale, humpback (Oceanic)
Whale, right (Oceanic)
Whale, Sei (Oceanic)
Whale, sperm (Oceanic)
Wolf, gray (48 conterminous States, other than MN)
Wolf, red (Southeast US west to TX)

BIRDS

Bobwhite, masked (quail) (AZ)
Condor, California (CA, OR)
Crane, Mississippi sandhill (MS)
Crane, whooping (Great Plains and Rocky Mt. States)
Curlew, Eskimo (AK and Northern Canada through Southern US)
Eagle, bald (48 conterminous States except WA, OR, MN, WI, MI)
Falcon, American peregrine (All States)
Falcon, Arctic peregrine (All States except HI)
Goose, Aleutian Canada (AK, CA, OR, WA)
Kite, Everglade (snail kite) (FL)
Pelican, brown (Carolinas to TX, CA)
Prairie chicken, Attwater's greater (TX)
Rail, California clapper (CA)
Rail, light-footed clapper (CA)
Rail, Yuma clapper (AZ, CA)
Shrike, San Clemente loggerhead (CA)
Sparrow, Cape Sable seaside (FL)
Sparrow, dusky seaside (FL)
Sparrow, Santa Barbara song (CA)
Tern, California least (CA)
Warbler (wood), Bachman's (Southeastern US)
Warbler (wood), Kirtland's (MI)
Woodpecker, ivory-billed (Southcentral and Southeastern US)
Woodpecker, red-cockaded (Southcentral and Southeastern US)

REPTILES

Alligator, American (Southeastern US except FL, GA, LA, SC, TX)
Anole, Culebra giant (USA)
Boa, Mona (USA)
Crocodile, American (FL)
Lizard, blunt-nosed leopard (CA)
Snake, San Francisco garter (CA)
Turtle, green sea (FL)
Turtle, hawksbill sea (=carey) (Tropic seas)
Turtle, Kemp's Ridley sea (Tropic and temperate seas)
Turtle, leatherback sea (Tropic, temperate, and subpolar seas)
Turtle, Plymouth red-bellied (MA)

AMPHIBIANS

Salamander, desert slender (CA)
Salamander, Santa Cruz long-toed (CA)
Salamander, Texas blind (TX)
Toad, Houston (TX)
Treefrog, pine barrens (FL)

FISH

Bonytail, Pahranagat (NV)

Chub, bonytail (AZ, CA, CO, NV, UT, WY)

Chub, Borax Lake (OR)

Chub, humpback (AZ, CO, UT, WY)

Chub, Mohave (CA)

Cisco, longjaw (Lakes Michigan, Huron, Erie)

Cui-ui (NV)

Dace, Kendall Warm Springs (WY)

Dace, Moapa (NV)

Darter, fountain (TX)

Darter, Maryland (MD)

Darter, Okaloosa (FL)

Darter, snail (TN)

Darter, watercress (AL)

Gambusia, Big Bend (TX)

Gambusia, Clear Creek (TX)

Gambusia, Goodenough (TX)

Gambusia, Pecos (NM, TX)

Gambusia, San Marcos (TX)

Killifish, Pahrump (NV)

Madtom, Sciotom (OH)

Pike, blue (Lakes Erie, Ontario)

Pupfish, Comanche Springs (TX)

Pupfish, Devil's Hole (NV)

Pupfish, Leon Springs (TX)

Pupfish, Owens River (CA)

Pupfish, Tecopa (CA)

Pupfish, Warm Springs (NV)

Squawfish, Colorado River (AZ, CA, CO, NM, NV, UT, WY)

Stickleback, unarmored threespine (CA)

Sturgeon, shortnose (Atlantic coast of US)

Topminnow, Gila (AZ, NM)

Trout, Gila (NM)

Woundfin (AZ, NV, UT)

INDEX OF LATIN NAMES

MAMMALS

Alces americana
(Moose)

Alopex lagopus
(Arctic Fox)

Antilocarpa americanus
(Pronghorn Antelope)

Arvicola richardsoni
(Water Vole, Richardson Vole)

Bassariscus astutus
(Ringtail, Civet Cat, Miner's Cat, Cacomistle)

Bison bison
(Bison, American Buffalo)

Blarina brevicauda
(Short-tailed Shrew)

Canis latrans
(Coyote)

Canis lupus
(Gray Wolf, Wolf, Timber Wolf)

Callorhinus ursinus
(Northern Fur Seal, Alaska Fur Seal)

Castor canadensis
(Beaver)

Cervus canadensis
(Elk)

Cevis dama
(Fallow Deer)

Condylura cristata
(Starnosed Mole)

Cynomys leucurus
(White-tailed Prairie Dog)

Cynomys ludovicianus
(Black-tailed Prairie Dog)

Dasypus novemcinctus
(Nine-banded Armadillo)

Didelphis marsupialis
(Virginia Opposum)

Diphylla ecaudata
(Hairy-legged Vampire Bat, Vampire Bat)

Dipodomys ingens
(Giant Kangaroo Rat)

Dipodomys ordii
(Ord's Kangaroo Rat)

Enhydra lutra
(Sea Otter)

Eptesicus fuscus
(Big Brown Bat)

Erethizon dorsatus
(Porcupine)

Eschrichtius gibbosus
(Gray Whale)

Eutamais minimus
(Least Chipmunk)

Felis concolor
(Mountain Lion, Catamount, Cougar, Puma)

Felis lynx
(Lynx)

Felis onca
(Jaguar)

Felis pardalis
(Ocelot)

Felis rufus
(Bobcat)

Geomys bursarius
(Plains Pocket Gopher)

Glaucomys volans
(Southern Flying Squirrel)

Gulo luscus
(Wolverine, Glutton)

Lasiurus borealis
(Red Bat)

Lemmus sibiricus
(Brown Lemming, Common Lemming, Blackfooted Lemming)

Lepus americanus
(Snowshoe Hare, Varying Hare)

Lepus californicus
(Black-tailed Jack Rabbit)

Lepus townsendii
(White-tailed Jack Rabbit)

Lutra canadensis
(River Otter)

Macrotus californicus
(California Leaf-nosed Bat, Leaf-nosed Bat)

Marmota monax
(Woodchuck, Groundhog, Marmot)

Marmota flaviventris
(Yellow-bellied Marmot, Mountain Marmot, Rock-chuck, Yellow-footed Marmot)

Martes americana
(Marten, Pine Marten, American Sable)

Martes pennanti
(Fisher)

Mephitis mephitis
(Striped Skunk, Common Skunk)

Microtus pennsylvanicus
(Meadow Vole, Field Mouse)

Microtus pinetorum
(Woodland Vole, Pine Vole)

Mirounga angustirostris
(Northern Elephant Seal)

Mus musculus
(House Mouse)

Mustela erminea
(Ermine, short-tailed Weasel)

Mustela frenata
(Long-tailed Weasel)

Mustela hivalis
(Least Weasel)

Mustela vison
(Mink)

Myocaster coypus
(Nutria, Coypu)

Myotis lucifugus
(Little Brown Myotis, Little Brown Bat)

Myotis sodalis
(Indiana Myotis, Social Myotis)

Nasua nasua
(Caoti)

Neotoma cinerea
(Bushy-tailed Woodrat, Pack Rat, Mountain Pack Rat)

Ochotona princeps
(Pika, Cony, Whistling Hare, Piping Hare)

Odobenus rosmarus
(Walrus)

Odocoileus hemionus
(Mule Deer)

Odocoileus virginianus
(White-tailed Deer, Virginia Deer)

Ondatra zibethicus
(Muskrat)

Orcinus orca
(Killer Whale, Sea Wolf)

Oreamnos americanus
(Mountain Goat)

Oryctolagus cuniculus
(European Rabbit, Domestic Rabbit)

Oryzomys palustris
(Marsh Rice Rat, Rice Rat)

Ovibus moschatus
(Muskox)

Ovis canadensis
(Bighorn Sheep, Mountain Sheep, Rocky Mountain Bighorn Sheep)

Perognathus flavescens
(Plains Pocket Mouse)

Peromyscus gossypinus
(Cotton Mouse)

Peromyscus leucopus
(White-footed Mouse, Wood Mouse)

Peromyscus maniculatus
(Deer Mouse)

Phoca vitulina
(Harbor Seal, Leopard Seal, Hair Seal)

Procyon lotor
(Raccoon)

Rattus norvegicus
(Norway Rat, Brown Rat, Water Rat, Sewer Rat)

Rattus rattus
(Black Rat, Ship Rat, Roof Rat, Wharf Rat)

Scalopus aquaticus
(Eastern Mole, Common Mole)

Sciurus carolinensis
(Eastern Gray Squirrel, Gray Squirrel)

Sciurus niger
(Fox Squirrel, Eastern Fox Squirrel)

Sorex cinereus
(Masked Shrew, Common Shrew, Cinerous Shrew)

Sorex palustris
(Water Shrew, Northern Water Shrew)

Sorex vagrans
(Vagrant Shrew, Wandering Shrew)

Spermophilus tridecemlineatus
(Thirteen-lined Ground Squirrel, Striped Gopher)

Spilogale putorius
(Eastern Spotted Skunk, Spotted Skunk)

Sus scrofa
(Wild Boar)

Sylvilagus floridanus
(Eastern Cottontail)

Sylvilagus palustris
(Marsh Rabbit)

Synaptomys cooperi
(Southern Bog Lemming)

Tadarida brasiliensis
(Brazilian Free-tailed Bat, Mexican Free-tailed Bat)

Tamias striatus
(Eastern Chipmunk, Tamais)

Tamiasciurus hudsonicus
(Red Squirrel, Pine Squirrel, Spruce Squirrel, Chickaree)

Taxidea taxus
(Badger)

Thomomys talpoides
(Northern Pocket Gopher)

Triechechus manatus
(Manatee)

Tursiops truncatus
(Atlantic Bottle-nosed Dolphin, Porpoise, Dolphin)

Urocyon cinereoargenteus
(Gray Fox)

Ursus americanus
(Black Bear)

Ursus arctos
((Grizzly Bear, Kodiak Bear, Brown Bear)

Ursus maritimus
(Polar Bear)

Vulpes vulpes
(Red Fox)

Zalophus californianus
(California Sea Lion)

Zapus hudsonius
(Meadow Jumping Mouse)

BIRDS

Accipiter velox
  (Sharp-shinned Hawk)
Actitis macularia
  (Spotted Sandpiper)
Agelaius phoeniceus
  (Red-winged Blackbird)
Aix sponsa
  (Wood Duck)
Ajaia ajaia
  (Roseate Spoonbill)
Alle alle
  (Dovekie)
Anas carolinensis
  (Green-winged Teal)
Anas platyrhynchos
  (Mallard)
Anas rubripes
  (Black Duck)
Anhinga anhinga
  (Water Turkey)
Aquila chrysaetos
  (Golden Eagle)
Archilochus colubris
  (Ruby-throated Hummingbird)
Ardea herodias
  (Great Blue Heron)
Arenaria interpres
  (Ruddy turnstone)
Aythya affinis
  (Lesser Scaup)
Aythya valisineria
  (Canvasback)
Bombycilla cedrorum
  (Cedar Waxwing)
Bonasa umbellus
  (Ruffed Grouse)
Botaurus lentiginosus
  (Bittern)
Brnta bernicla
  (Brant)
Branta canadensis
  (Canada Goose)
Bubo virginianus
  (Great Horned owl)
Buteo borealis
  (Red-tailed Hawk)
Butorides virescens
  (Green Heron)
Caprimulgus vociferus
  (Whip-poor-will)
Carpodacus purpureus
  (Purple Finch)
Casmerodias albus egretta
  (American Egret)
Cathartes aura
  ((Turkey Vulture)
Cepphus grylle
  (Black Guillemot)
Chaetura pelagica
  (Chimney Swift)
Chen hyperborea
  (Snow Goose)
Cinclus mexicanus
  (Water Ouzel, Dipper)
Circus cyaneus hudsonius
  (Marsh Hawk)
Clangula hyemalis
  (Oldsquaw)
Coccyzus americanus
  (Yellow-billed Cuckoo)
Colaptes auratus
  (Flicker)
Colinus virginianus
  (Bob-white)
Corvus brachyrhynchos
  (Common Crow)
Cyanocitta cristata
  (Blue Jay)
Dendrocopus pubescens
  (Downy Woodpecker)
Dendroica coronata
  (Myrtle Warbler)
Dryocopus pileatus
  (Pileated Woodpecker)
Egretta candidissima
  (Snowy Egret)
Elanoides forficatus
  (Swallow-tailed Kite)
Falco sparverius
  (Sparrow Hawk, American Kestrel)
Fratercula arctica
  (Puffin)
Gavia immer
  (Loon)
Gymnogyps californianus
  (California Condor)
Haliaetus leucocephalus
  (Bald Eagle)
Hesperiphona vespertina
  (Evening Grosbeak)
Hydroprogne caspia
  (Caspian Tern)
Icterus galbula
  (Northern Oriole)
Junco hyemalis
  (Slate-colored Junco)
Lagopus mutus
  (Rock Ptarmigan)
Larus argentatus
  (Herring Gull)
Laurus atricilla
  (Laughing Gull)
Larus delawarensis
  (Ring-billed Gull)
Larus marinus
  (Great Black-backed Gull)
Lophortyx californicus
  (California Quail)
Mareca americana
  (Baldpate)
Megaceryle alcyon
  (Belted Kingfisher)
Meleagris gallopavo
  (Wild Turkey)
Melospiza melodia
  (Song Sparrow)
Mergus merganser
  (Merganser)
Mimus polyglottos
  (Mockingbird)
Molothrus ater
  (Cowbird)
Morus bassanus
  (Gannet)
Muscivora forficata
  (Scissor-tailed Flycatcher)
Mycteria americana
  (Wood Ibis)
Nycticorax nycticorax
  (Black-crowned Night Heron)
Olor buccinator
  (Trumpeter Swan)
Otus asio
  (Screech Owl)
Oxyechus vociferus
  (Killdeer)
Pandion haliaetus
  (Osprey, Fish Hawk)
Parus atricapillus
  (Black-capped Chickadee)
Parus bicolor
  (Tufted Titmouse)
Passer domesticus
  (House Sparrow)
Passerina cyanea
  (Indigo Bunting)
Pelecanus erythrorhynchos
  (White Pelican)
Pelecanus occidentalis
  (Brown Pelican)
Phalacrocorax auritus
  (Double-crested Cormorant)
Phasianus torquatus
  (Ring-necked Pheasant)
Philohela minor
  (Woodcock)
Phoenicopterus ruber
  (Flamingo)
Pipilo erythropthalmus
  (Towhee)
Piranga ludoviciana
  (Western Tanager)
Podilymbus podiceps
  (Pied-billed Grebe)
Progne subis
  (Purple Martin)
Quiscalis quiscula
  (Common Grackle)
Rallus crepitans
  (Clapper Rail)
Richmondena cardinalis
  (Cardinal)
Riparia riparia
  (Bank Swallow)
Rissa tridactyla
  (Kittiwake)
Rynchops nigra
  (Black Skimmer)
Sayornis phoebe
  (Phoebe)
Sialia sialis
  (Bluebird)
Sitta carolinensis
  (White-breasted Nuthatch)
Somateria millissima
  (Common Eider)
Sphyrapicus varius
  (Yellow-bellied Sapsucker)
Spinus tristis
  (American Goldfinch)
Stercorarius parasiticus
  (Parasitic Jaeger, Arctic Skua)
Sterna albifrons
  (Least Tern)
Sterna hirundo
  (Common Tern)
Sterna paradisaea
  (Arctic Tern)
Sturnella neglecta
  (Western Meadowlark)
Sturnus vulgaris
  (Starling)
Troglodytes aedon
  (House Wren)
Turdus migratorius
  (Robin)
Tuto alba
  (Barn Owl)
Uria troille californica
  (California Murre)
Vireo olivaceus
  (Red-eyed Vireo)
Zendaidura macroura
  (Mourning Dove)

REPTILES
Crocodilians

Alligator mississippiensis
  (American Alligator)
Crocodylus acutus
  (American Crocodile)

Snakes

Agkistrodon contortex
  (Copperhead)
Agkistrodon piscivorus
  (Cottonmouth, Water Moccasin)
Cemophora coccinea
  (Scarlet Snake)
Charina bottae
  (Rubber Boa)
Coluber constrictor
  (Racer, Black Racer, Black Snake)
Crotalus adamanteus
  (Eastern Diamondback Rattlesnake)
Crotalus cerastes
  (Sidewinder, Horned Rattlesnake)
Crotalus horridus
  (Timber Rattlesnake)
Diadophis punctatus
  (Ringneck Snake)
Drymarchon corais
  (Indigo Snake)
Elaphe guttata
  (Corn Snake)
Elaphe obsoleta
  (Rat Snake)
Heterodon platyrhinos
  (Common Hognose Snake)
Lampropeltis getalus
  (Common Kingsnake,
   Chain Kingsnake)
Lampropeltis triangulum
  (Milk Snake)
Masticophis flagellum
  (Coachwhip Snake)
Micrurus fulvius
  (Eastern Coral Snake)
Natrix sipedon
  (Water Snake)
Pituophis melanocleucus
  (Bull Snake)
Storeria dekayi
  (Brown Snake, DeKaye's Snake)
Thamnophis sirtalis
  (Common Garter Snake)

Lizards

Anolis carolinensis
  (Green Anole)
Cnemidophorus sexlineatus
  (Racerunner, Six-lined Lizard,
   Sand Lizard)
Coleonyx variegatus
  (Banded Gecko)
Crotaphytus collaris
  (Collared Lizard)
Dipsosaurus dorsalis
  (Desert Iguana)
Eumeces fasciatus
  (Five-lined Skink)
Gerrhonotus coeruleus
  (Northern Alligator Lizard)
Heloderma suspectum
  (Gila Monster)
Ophisaurus ventralis
  (Slender Glass Lizard, Glass Snake,
   Jointed Snake)
Phrynosoma coranatum
  (Coast Horned Lizard)
Sauramalus obesus
  (Chuckwalla)
Sceloporus magister
  (Desert Spiny Lizard)
Sceloporus undulatus
  (Eastern Fence Lizard, Fence Swift,
   Common Swift)

Turtles

Caretta caretta
(Loggerhead Turtle)
Chelonia mydas
(Green Turtle)
Chelydra serpentina
(Common Snapping Turtle)
Chrysemys picta
(Painted Turtle)
Chrysemys scripta
(Pond Slider)
Clemmys guttata
(Spotted Turtle)
Clemmys insculpta
(Wood Turtle)
Eretmochelys imbicata
(Hawksbill Turtle)
Gopherus polyphemus
(Gopher Tortoise
Kinosternon subrubrum
(Mud Turtle)
Macroclemys temmincki
(Alligator Snapping Turtle)
Malaclemys terrapin
(Diamondback Terrapin)
Sternotheraerus odoratus
(Musk Turtle, Stinkpot)
Terrapene carolina
(Eastern Box Turtle)
Trionyx muticus
(Smooth Softshell Turtle)

AMPHIBIANS
Frogs and Toads

Acris crepitans
(Northern Cricket Frog)
Ascaphus truei
(Tailed Frog)
Bufo americanus
(American Toad)

Hyla crucifer
(Spring Peeper)
Hyla versicolor
(Common Gray Treefrog)
Rana areolata
(Crawfish Frog)
Rana catesbeiana
(Bullfrog)
Rana clamitans
(Green Frog)
Rana palustris
(Pickerel Frog)
Rana pipiens
(Leopard Frog, Meadow Frog)
Rana sylvatica
(Wood Frog)
Scaphiopus holbrooki
(Eastern Spadefoot Toad)

Salamanders

Ambystoma jeffersonianum
(Jefferson Salamander)
Ambystoma maculatum
(Spotted Salamander)
Ambystoma opacum
(Marbled Salamander)
Ambystoma tigrinum
(Tiger Salamander)
Cryptobranchus alleganiensis
(Hellbender)
Desmognathus fuscus
(Dusky Salamander)
Necturus maculosus
(Mudpuppy, Waterdog)
Notophthalmus viridescens
(Eastern Newt)
Plethodon cinereus
(Red-backed Salamander)
Plethodon glutinosus
(Slimy Salamander)
Siren lacertina
(Greater Siren)

FISH

Acipenser sturio
(Sturgeon, Atlantic Sturgeon.
American Sturgeon)
Alosa sapidissima
(American Shad, Shad)
Anguilla rostrata
(American Eel, Common Eel)
Brevoortia tyrannus
(Menhaden, Bunker Fish)
Coregonus clupeaformis
(Whitefish, Lake Whitefish,
Great Lakes Whitefish, Humpback)
Cyprinus carpio
(Carp)
Esox lucius
(Northern Pike)
Esox masquinongy
(Muskellunge, Muskie)
Eucalia inconstans
(Brook Stickleback)
Hippocampus zosterae
(Dwarf Seahorse)
Ictalurus punctatus
(Channel Catfish)
Kyphosus secatrix
(Bermuda Chub)
Lepomis macrochrius
(Bluegill, Bream, Blue Sunfish)
Makaira nigricans
(Blue Marlin)
Micropterus dolomieui
(Smallmouth Bass,
Smallmouth Black Bass)
Micropterus salmoides
(Largemouth Bass, Black Bass,
Largemouth Black Bass)
Negaprion brevirostris
(Lemon Shark)
Oncorhynchus gorbuscha
(Pink Salmon, Humpback Salmon)

Oncorhynchus keta
(Chum Salmon, Keta Salmon,
Dog Salmon, Fall Salmon)
Oncorhynchus kisutch
(Coho Salmon, Silver Salmon)
Oncorhynchus nerka
(Sockeye Salmon, Red Salmon.
Blueback Salmon, Kokanee Salmon)
Oncorhynchus tschawytscha
(Chinook Salmon, King Salmon,
Spring Salmon)
Perca flavescens
(Yellow Perch)
Petromyzon mariunus
(Lamprey, Sea Lamprey)
Prionace glauca
(Blue Shark, Whaler)
Pseudopleuronectes americanus
(Flounder, Flatfish, Winter Flounder)
Raja erinaces
(Little Skate, Hedgehog Skate)
Salmo clarki
(Cutthroat Trout)
Salmo gairdneri
(Rainbow Trout, Steelhead Trout,
Shasta Trout, Kamloop's Trout)
Salvelinus fortinalis
(Brook Trout, Char)
Salvelinus namaycush
(Lake Trout, Char)
Sphyraena barracuda
(Barracuda, Great Barracuda)
Tarpon atlanticus
(Tarpon)
Xyrauche texanus
(Razorback Sucker, Humpback Sucker)